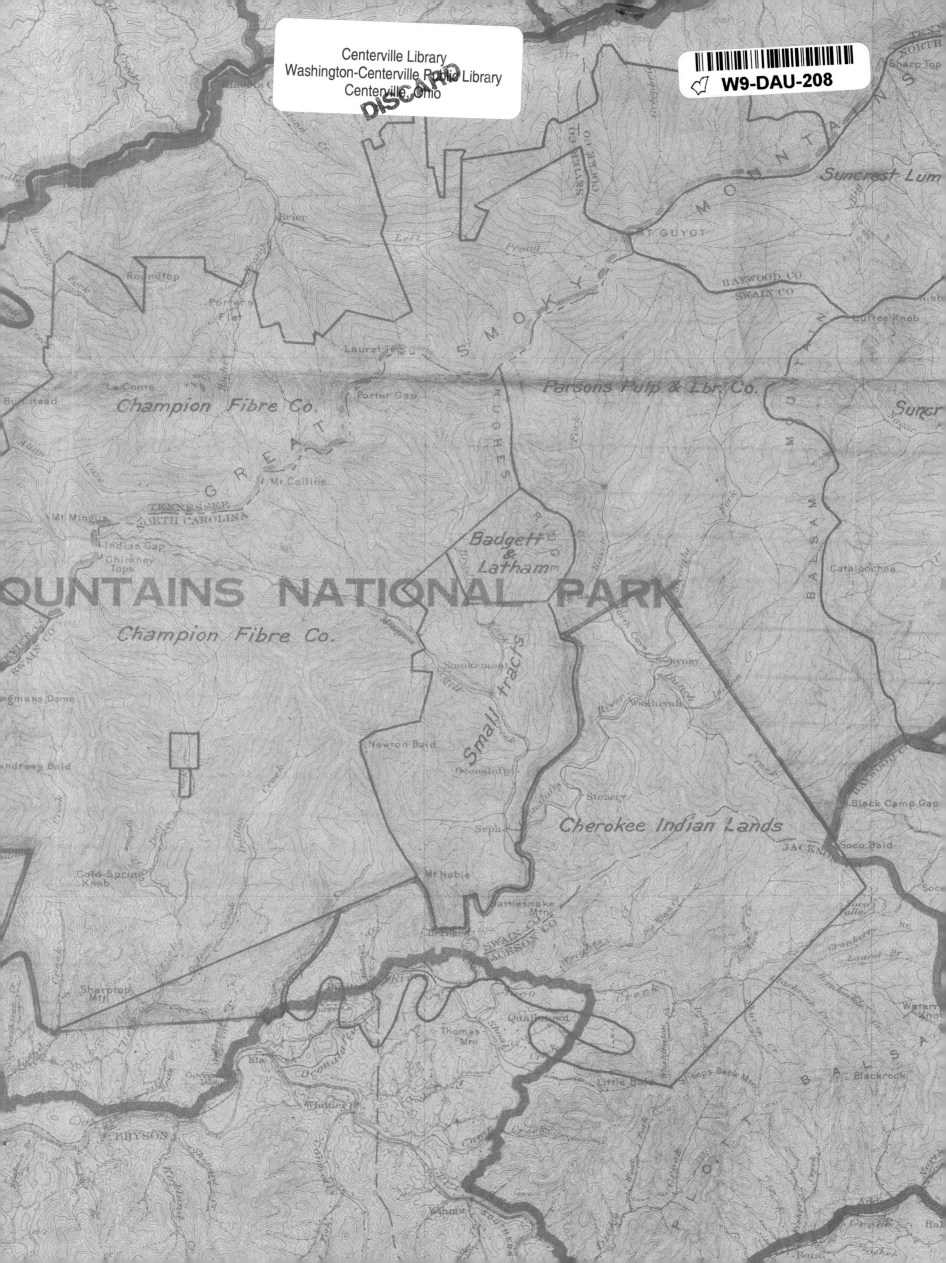

ALSO BY THE AUTHOR

*Chasing Denali: The Sourdoughs, Cheechakos, and Frauds Behind
the Most Unbelievable Feat in Mountaineering*

Northern Exposures: An Adventuring Career in Stories and Images

The Colorado River: Flowing Through Conflict

Running Dry: A Journey From Source to Sea Down the Colorado River

*Where Mountains Are Nameless: Passion and Politics in the
Arctic National Wildlife Refuge*

*Arctic Crossing: A Journey Through the Northwest Passage
and Inuit Culture*

*The Quotable Climber: Literary, Humorous, Inspirational,
and Fearful Moments of Climbing*

*A Most Hostile Mountain: Re-Creating the Duke of Abruzzi's
Historic Expedition on Alaska's Mount St. Elias*

Kayaking the Vermilion Sea: Eight Hundred Miles Down the Baja

In the Shadow of Denali: Life and Death on Alaska's Mt. McKinley

Cloud Dancers: Portraits of North American Mountaineers

*High Alaska: A Historical Guide to Denali, Mount Foraker
and Mount Hunter*

Surviving Denali: A Study of Accidents on Mount McKinley

Hoodoos, spires, and fins are revealed through the fog at Bryce Canyon National Park in Utah.

NATIONAL GEOGRAPHIC

ATLAS OF THE NATIONAL PARKS

JON WATERMAN

Foreword by Gary Knell
Chairman, National Geographic Partners

NATIONAL GEOGRAPHIC
WASHINGTON, DC

CONTENTS

A **signature blue haze** hangs over the mountains in Shenandoah National Park, as seen from Skyline Drive, one of the country's most popular scenic drives through a national park.

FOREWORD

Gary Knell
Chairman, National Geographic Partners

Having grown up as a city kid, I will never forget the night I emerged from my pup tent in Zion National Park to see an ocean of stars spanning the sky. That image, framed by the spectacular cliffs of Zion Canyon, was breathtaking and left an indelible impression on me. At that moment, which still feels like yesterday, I fully realized the magic of our world and the need to share that experience with everyone.

Little did I know then that, many years later, I would be in a position to promote the enduring, mutually supportive relationship between the National Park Service and National Geographic. This partnership dates back to the beginning of both storied organizations and has stood the test of time. What better way to capture the magic of these sacred lands and to honor that relationship than with this glorious new atlas, the first ever to collect authoritative maps of every national park into one volume?

The connections between these two legendary organizations indeed go back more than a century. In 1912, four years before a National Park Service even existed, *National Geographic* magazine introduced its readers to the 11 parks then under federal protection. "Within these great reserves may be found scenery and natural phenomena that are unequaled in their majesty and grandeur," the article began. Some are accessible "by coach, on horseback, or on foot," but others are accessible by horseback and pack train only—"and after all, this is the best way to enjoy thoroughly the beauties of the mountain and the forest."

Four years later, an entire issue of the magazine was dedicated to "The Land of the Best—A Tribute to the Scenic Grandeur and Unsurpassed Natural Resources of Our Own Country." Addressing a readership more likely to embark on a Grand Tour of Europe than travel to the American West, editor Gilbert H. Grosvenor used words and photos to lure them home. "Any of our readers could spend an entire

lifetime seeing nature's masterpieces within our boundaries and not reach the end of the catalogue," he wrote. At the time Franklin K. Lane, Secretary of the Interior, sat on the board of managers of the National Geographic Society. Every member of Congress received a copy of that issue of *National Geographic*. Grosvenor helped to draft the legislation that was soon signed into law by Woodrow Wilson on August 25, 1916, establishing the National Park Service.

National Geographic has gone on to publish the most popular line of National Park trail maps. Our guidebooks to the parks are repeatedly updated and continue to be best sellers. National Geographic leads thousands of adventurers into the parks each year, whether on a family trip to the Grand Canyon, a cruise through Glacier Bay, or a private expedition to Yellowstone and the Grand Tetons. We post the best photographs digitally and on social media. And our award-winning television networks tell stories of our parks through narrative documentaries and live events each year.

Some 200 articles about national parks have appeared in *National Geographic* magazine. Many have involved scientific and exploratory endeavors, such as the December 2012 article about "The World's Largest Trees," reporting new research on sequoia and redwood growth patterns, part of a long-term study supported by the National Park Service. As part of that article we published Michael Nichols's massive composite photograph of the President, the second tallest tree in the world, which stands 247 feet tall in Sequoia National Park. The photograph took two weeks and a professional climbing crew to accomplish and was published as a removable fold-out poster.

In 2016, we shared in the celebration of the National Park Service's centennial in several ways. Once again, as we had 100 years before, we devoted an entire issue of *National Geographic* magazine to the parks, photographed by a number of our top photographers and written in full by acclaimed natural historian David Quammen: a set of stories both celebratory and unflinching about the challenges facing the parks in the 21st century. We also published a milestone illustrated history of the National Park Service, Kim Heacox's

The National Parks: An Illustrated History, created (as was this book) with the advice of a board of experts knowledgeable on and dedicated to the national parks.

And now National Geographic takes pride in publishing this first complete illustrated atlas of the national parks, written by former park ranger and lifelong adventurer Jon Waterman. These pages, full of grand photographs, exquisite maps, and illustrative graphics, confirm the magnificence of our country's wild places, from the stony coastline of Maine to the red-rock deserts of Arizona, from Florida's subtropical Everglades to the glacial reaches of Alaska. The stories that accompany these visuals evoke both delight and concern, as we learn of the threats of urban encroachment, changing climate, and political missteps impinging on these beloved pieces of wilderness.

WHAT BETTER WAY TO CAPTURE THE MAGIC OF THESE SACRED LANDS THAN WITH THIS GLORIOUS NEW ATLAS?

This land is our land, as the famous folk song says, and it is a land that stretches out in all its grandeur, many of its precious wild places under the protection of the National Park Service. This land, and these parks, continue to evoke awe and instill pride—and they deserve unswerving protection, not only from our government but also from every one of us as individuals dedicated to preserving the health and balance of the planet.

"Seeing our national parks through books will never replace the real experience," wrote former National Park Service director Jonathan B. Jarvis in his foreword to our 2016 illustrated history, but a book can "inform and encourage the American people to visit and support their parks." As we at National Geographic share this new atlas with you, it is our hope that it will inspire not only years of travel—whether by camper van or on horseback, as you relax in a favorite armchair or emerge from a pup tent—but also an understanding of how precious the wild places of our planet are, and how deserving they are of our care in the coming decades. ∎

In winter bison graze on grass in the northern and lower, less snow-filled elevations of Yellowstone National Park. This American icon was almost wiped out in the 19th century, but protection on parklands has helped bring their numbers back up.

ABOUT THIS ATLAS

"A map is the greatest of all epic poems," said Gilbert H. Grosvenor, legendary editor of *National Geographic* magazine. "Its lines and colors show the realization of great dreams."

So this book of more than 200 maps, graphics, and illustrations—alongside an equal topography of photos—is a dream-come-true opus of national park geography. There are historical maps—see Great Smoky Mountains (page 87), Grand Canyon (page 219), or Mount Rainier (page 285), among others, showing how explorers, cartographers, scientists, and artists perceived the land in earlier times. These are striking for their meticulous—and often precise—detail, as well as their artistry.

And then there are the contemporary maps, created in a modern style with the most up-to-date information available. National Geographic's researchers consulted with scientists, National Park Service staff, and local experts whenever possible to obtain the latest data, often using official data sets from the National Park Service. The atlas was created in close collaboration with cartographers at

Alaska cotton grass edges a pond that reflects Denali—the highest peak in North America, with more vertical land relief than any mountain in the world.

ATLAS LEGEND

National Park Service land	--- Ferry
National Grassland	--- Passenger ferry
National Forest Service land	---- Hiking trail
National Preserve	—— Railroad
National Wildlife Refuge	♠ Ranger Station
Indian Reserve	♠ Wilderness Patrol cabin
State Park or Provincial Park	✈ Scheduled Service Airport
Urban area	✛ Airstrip
Wilderness	← Directional arrow
⋯⋯ Continental Divide	● Geothermal site
⋯⋯ International border	▪ Historic structure
⋯⋯ State border	⊤ Lighthouse
—— Highlighted (Park loop) road	ⵊ Observation tower
—— Limited access highway	+ Peak
—— Primary road	▪ Point of interest
—— Secondary road	⁜ Shipwreck
—— Unpaved road	▪ Trailhead
⋯⋯ Carriage road	⸽ Waterfall
⋯⋯ Primitive road	

Most national parks are found west of the Mississippi. The Bureau of Land Management (BLM) manages the bulk of these federal lands as grazing areas; the U.S. Forest Service (USFS) manages the timber in national forests, and the U.S. Fish and Wildlife Service (USFWS) manages wildlife in refuges.

the Park Service's Harpers Ferry Center for Interpretive Media, and it includes works from the Harpers Ferry Center Commissioned Art Collection.

The reference maps that open each entry are adapted from official National Park Service maps and highlight major points of interest in each park. Other federally managed lands (shown on the map above) are not always delineated on the reference maps, keeping the focus on the national park lands. Six national parks in Alaska and one in Colorado include preserves managed by the National Park System, and those are shown on the reference maps.

Each national park is represented by a reference map. In addition, myriad supporting maps and graphics explore the parks from different perspectives, marking trails, revealing stratigraphy and geological processes, charting weather patterns, tracking animal migrations, showcasing the astonishing web of ecosystems that parklands encompass, and so much more. These collections

are by no means exhaustive for each park; rather, they are a sampling of the richness of these wild places, created with the resources available.

To begin this book, we have created a section titled "Inside the National Park System," using maps and graphics to explore the wider context of the National Park System and its more than 400 units, from national seashores to memorials, through thematic lenses such as history, geology, culture, visitor experience, and more, offering new ways of understanding the National Park System and all it contains.

We have chosen and created maps and graphics that are as current as possible, but new studies are always under way and new data are continually being published. Official National Park Service map updates are ongoing, and the parks are dynamic. Information often changes, and so these maps should not be used for activities such as backcountry hiking or water navigation. Contact the National Park Service for the latest details on trails and facilities inside each park. ■

INSIDE THE NATIONAL PARK SYSTEM

CONTENTS

Double Arch is one of more than 2,000 such formations in Arches National Park, Utah.

NATIONAL PARK SYSTEM

Many visitors to the 61 national parks are surprised to learn that these land and water sanctuaries are part of a system of more than 400 units that the Park Service administers. These federal properties—from battlefields to national seashores—are chosen for the protection of their natural, historic, and cultural values and are specially designated by an act of Congress (or in some cases, an executive order). Over 131,875 square miles in locations spanning from Maine to Guam are maintained for the enjoyment and education of the public and future generations.

These units vary in size from a single home—the smallest site in the park system is Thaddeus Kosciuszko National Memorial in Pennsylvania—to larger than the size of Switzerland, as is Wrangell–St. Elias National Park and Preserve in Alaska.

The system includes more than 400 units; 85,000 miles of rivers and streams; 7,035 square miles of reservoirs, lakes, or ocean; more than 43,000 miles of shoreline; 21,000 buildings; 27,000 historic structures; over 18,000 miles of trails; and nearly 9,000 miles of roads. ◾

NORTH DAKOTA

MINN.

SOUTH DAKOTA

Voyageurs N.P.

Lake Superior

Isle Royale N.P.

MAINE

Acadia
N.P.

VERMONT

NEW HAMPSHIRE

MICHIGAN

WISCONSIN

Lake Huron

Lake Ontario

MASSACHUSETTS

Boston

NEW YORK

RHODE
ISLAND

CONNECTICUT

Mississippi

Lake Erie

New York

NEBRASKA

IOWA

Lake Michigan

Cuyahoga
Valley N.P.

PENNSYLVANIA

NEW
JERSEY

Philadelphia

Indiana
Dunes N.P.

OHIO

MARYLAND

DELAWARE

ILLINOIS

INDIANA

Ohio

Washington, D.C.

KANSAS

Missouri

Gateway Arch
N.P.

MISSOURI

KENTUCKY

Shenandoah
N.P.

WEST
VIRGINIA

VIRGINIA

Mammoth Cave
N.P.

NORTH
CAROLINA

OKLAHOMA

ARKANSAS

TENN.

Great Smoky Mts. N.P.

SOUTH
CAROLINA

Congaree N.P.

Hot Springs
N.P.

Mississippi

GEORGIA

ALABAMA

MISSISSIPPI

TEXAS

LOUISIANA

FLORIDA

National park

National lakeshore
or seashore

National monument

National preserve
or reserve

National recreation
area

National river
or national wild and
scenic river and
riverways

Parkway

National scenic trail
held by the NPS

National battlefield,
battlefield park,
battlefield site,
or military park

National historical park

National historic site

National memorial

Other National Park
Service property

Albers Conic Equal-Area Projection

200 mi

200 km

Everglades N.P.

Biscayne
N.P.

Dry Tortugas N.P.

Virgin Islands
N.P.

PUERTO RICO
(U.S.)

U.S.

U.K.

Virgin Islands

40 mi

40 km

Alaska

U.S.

Puerto
Rico

GUAM

Hawai'i

PACIFIC
OCEAN

EQUATOR

AMERICAN
SAMOA

HISTORY OF THE PARKS

From the 22nd Congress enacting Hot Springs Reservation in 1832 to the 115th Congress creating Gateway Arch National Park in 2018, the *Congressional Record* is rich with park additions and refinements. This national park movement would define and protect natural beauty and historic treasures, with access for all and relief from burgeoning cities and the bulwarks of industry. Even from its beginnings—with the support of landscape architects like Frederick Law Olmsted and son, Frederick Jr., who wrote the

preamble to the 1916 NPS Organic Act—the concept of setting aside parcels of nature proved adaptable enough to create urban NPS units (today there are two dozen national parks in U.S. cities).

Parks are embedded in the fabric of our democracy, dreamed of, shaped, and designed by the icons of American history—from President Lincoln, who in 1864 signed the act that gave Yosemite to California for protection, to President Obama, who added 22 new parks to the system during his tenure from 2009 to 2017.

President Grant signed the first act to mention the word "park" in 1872. This large tract of land in the territories of Montana and Wyoming would be "a public park and pleasuring-ground for the benefit and enjoyment of the people." Two months later, in the Secretary of the Interior Columbus Delano's letter appointing Nathaniel Langford as the first superintendent, he named this wildlife-rich landscape of rivers and geysers Yellowstone National Park—officially the first park anywhere.

After Yellowstone, Congress identified and set aside more areas to be administered by the Department of the Interior, as well as wildlands, battlegrounds, and historic sites to be administered by other government agencies. In 1906, the American Antiquities Act allowed presidents to proclaim monuments on federal lands to protect historic Native American culture, with ruin sites or archaeological value. As written in the *Congressional Record,* monuments could also be "historic landmarks, historic and prehistoric structures, and other objects of historic or scientific interest." These national monuments (many later to become national parks) included names as descriptive and varied as nature itself: Devils Tower, Grand Canyon, Petrified Forest, Dinosaur, Mukuntuweap (later named Zion), and Great Sand Dunes.

In the early years, the U.S. Army managed many of the western parks. But with the addition of monuments, historical sites, and various military parks, the care of these landscapes became a juggling act. By 1916, there were 35 different federally preserved units that would later fall under Park Service jurisdiction. Many were created before the states had been carved from territories.

To protect these and future parks, President Wilson signed the Organic Act in 1916, creating the National Park Service (NPS) within the Department of the Interior. Throughout these set-aside land and waterscapes, the Organic Act declared that the National Park Service would "conserve the scenery and the natural and historic objects and the wild life therein and to provide for the enjoyment of the same in such manner and by such means as will leave them unimpaired for the enjoyment of future generations." Although not initially considered a balancing "act," the dual mandate of preservation and enjoyment would eventually provide the Department of the Interior one of its greatest challenges.

In a broadening 1933 moment, President Franklin D. Roosevelt transferred scores of national monuments and military sites from the Forest Service and the War Department to the National Park Service. Along with the principal national park designation, the system would eventually include over 20 different classifications—from national battlefields to national wild and scenic rivers. The General Authorities Act of 1970 established that the parks would henceforth be managed as part of a system rather than as isolated, individual parks.

Today the National Park Service performs environmental advocacy in a time of climate change; acts as a guardian of diverse

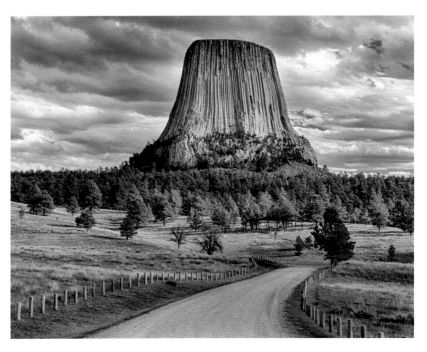

Efforts to protect the 867-foot-high rock formation of Wyoming's Devils Tower began in the 1890s, amid westward expansion. It became the country's first national monument in 1906.

NATIONAL PARK SYSTEM GROWTH

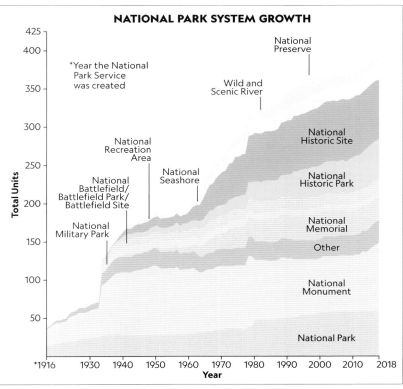

*Year the National Park Service was created

National Recreation Area

National Battlefield/ Battlefield Park/ Battlefield Site

National Military Park

National Seashore

National Preserve

Wild and Scenic River

National Historic Site

National Historic Park

National Memorial

Other

National Monument

National Park

Total Units

425
400
350
300
250
200
150
100
50

*1916 1930 1940 1950 1960 1970 1980 1990 2000 2010 2018

Year

ABOVE: **Conservationist John Muir** (fourth from right) showed Teddy Roosevelt (center) places out west that he hoped could gain federal protection, which had a profound impact. In a 1903 speech at this coastal redwood grove in Santa Cruz, Roosevelt urged the protection of the giant trees.

LEFT: **Alongside** nearly two centuries of legislation that has shaped the nation, lawmakers have also created National Park Service–administered units totaling over 84 million acres.

recreational, cultural, and historical resources; and serves as an ambassador to park preservation around the world—inspiring more than 100 countries to follow suit. Since 1916, the mission— to preserve these natural crown jewels for the education, enjoyment and inspiration of this and future generations—has not changed.

As the Milky Way burns across the dark skies of Death Valley and the northern lights finish shimmering above Denali, the first sunbeams hit the continent at Acadia. Bats wing their way back into Mammoth Cave, the bison herds stir at Yellowstone, and the Colima warbler trills its first song at Big Bend. Priceless national treasures, parks were created for these creatures, the land and its waters, and a rekindling of the human spirit. ■

TECTONICS

Like a cracked, hard-boiled eggshell, the Earth's outermost, rocky layer is broken into nearly 20 tectonic plates that influence all geology. The movement of these plates has continuously shaped the planet. When plates collide, they push rock layers up into mountains; as plates pulled apart, oceans formed; when plates skim past one another earthquakes will rattle the land; and if one plate slides beneath another, volcanoes erupt. The national parks have intentionally protected some of the most stunning exhibitions

of this tectonic activity. Most parks are underlain by the North American plate, which spans 29 million square miles. The plate covers most of the continent and stretches to mid–Atlantic Ocean. The North American plate creeps west at nearly an inch a year, while the adjoining Pacific plate—the largest of them all—moves northwest, horizontally, from two to four inches a year.

The boundary of the Pacific and North American plates, the seismically active San Andreas Fault, runs alongside Joshua Tree National Park, Pinnacles National Park, and Point Reyes National Seashore. Joshua Tree is crisscrossed with smaller faults, and shows how earthquakes have repeatedly broken the landscape into jigsaw pieces.

Farther north, Mount Rainier, Crater Lake, and Lassen Volcanic National Parks exhibit both active seismic and eruption activity. Volcanic eruptions emanate from miles below the plates in the Earth's molten mantle (or white of the egg), which is explosively

forced up and out by gasses and the heat-producing friction of moving plates. Often prefaced by earthquakes, these volcanoes have erupted repeatedly since prehistoric times. Rainier, in particular, is one of the most dangerous volcanoes on the planet because of potential lahars (or mudflows) that have historically been triggered by relatively small eruptions and earthquakes.

The most frequent and visible tectonic activity—caused by the Pacific plate's slide over magma hot spots—can be found in Hawai'i Volcanoes National Park. Visitors can drive to the Kīlauea caldera, which has erupted and spewed spectacular rivers of lava for decades. The park's Mauna Loa is the largest active volcano in the world. Whether bearing witness to ongoing eruptions, seismic activity, the ancient supervolcano calderas of Yellowstone, or the volcanic bedrock of the continent at Voyageurs, these national parks were created to showcase the dynamic and staggering forces at work on our tectonic Earth. ■

Crater Lake and Wizard Island in Oregon's Crater Lake National Park are the results of volcanic eruptions.

Yellowstone's Castle Geyser showcases the power of underlying tectonic shifting that shapes the planet anew.

Time and natural forces warped the nearly 100-mile Waterpocket Fold out of the Earth's crust in Capitol Reef National Park, Utah.

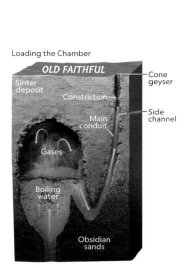

Loading the Chamber

OLD FAITHFUL

Sinter deposit — Cone geyser
Constriction
Main conduit — Side channel
Gases
Boiling water
Obsidian sands

Explosive Release

OLD FAITHFUL

Cone
40 ft.
Constriction
Chamber
66 ft
Boiling water

HOT SPOTS There are fewer than 1,000 geysers worldwide, and half of them are in Yellowstone National Park, which protects the world's most famous geyser, Old Faithful. As rain and snow collect underground in chambers, it interacts with hot underlying rock. As with water warming in a lidded teapot, the pressure builds until it releases steam and hot water out of tubelike holes in Earth's surface. Once geysers form, they're self-perpetuating: As the chamber drains after the first eruption, pressure drops and the cycle begins anew.

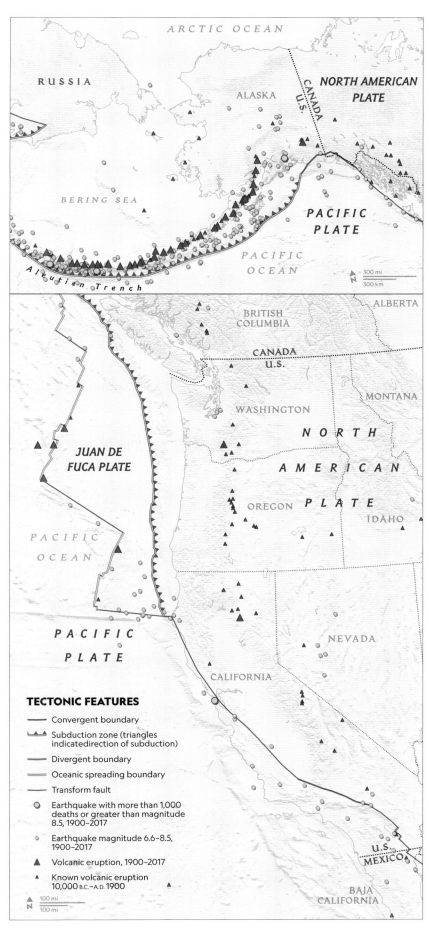

TECTONIC FEATURES

— Convergent boundary
⊾⊾ Subduction zone (triangles indicate direction of subduction)
— Divergent boundary
═ Oceanic spreading boundary
— Transform fault
◯ Earthquake with more than 1,000 deaths or greater than magnitude 8.5, 1900–2017
○ Earthquake magnitude 6.6–8.5, 1900–2017
▲ Volcanic eruption, 1900–2017
▴ Known volcanic eruption 10,000 B.C.–A.D. 1900

100 mi
100 mi

WEST COAST TECTONICS Earth's outermost layer is split into tectonic plates that shift and collide over time. The Aleutian Trench formed where the Pacific plate descends below the North American plate between Alaska and Russia, creating a string of volcanic islands. On the West Coast of the United States, the interactions between three plates—the North American, Pacific, and Juan de Fuca—make it prone to earthquakes.

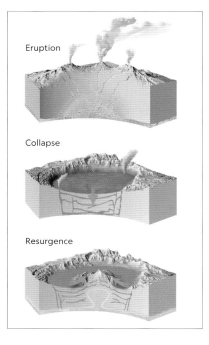

Eruption

Collapse

Resurgence

VOLCANISM A colossal eruption 1.25 million years ago created the volcanic caldera at Valles Caldera National Preserve. As magma exploded rapidly, the chamber emptied, causing the land above it to collapse and form a bowl-like caldera. After the collapse, more magma filled the chamber, lifting the floor upward and creating a central dome.

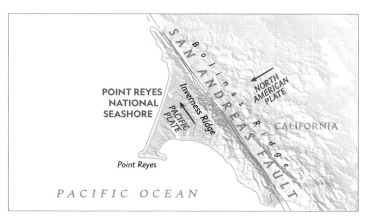

FAULTS Point Reyes National Seashore is one of many National Park Service units located along the San Andreas Fault. In this fault zone, which separates the Pacific plate from the slow-moving North American plate, the Pacific plate shifts northwest an estimated two to four inches a year in transform movement.

GEOLOGY

Among many wonders within the national parks, geologic history and ongoing movement are seen most everywhere you look. There are the Badlands' eroded sedimentary forms, appearing like alien hills and gullies; the ancient seabed now more than 20,000 feet above sea level atop Denali, North America's highest mountain; the glacial-striated granite slabs of Yosemite; the prehistoric bones held in Mesozoic rocks in Dinosaur National Monument; caverns in Mammoth Cave National Park;

and Death Valley's dried lake beds—called playas—and stark salt pans sprawling for miles. These distinct formations chronicle Earth's evolution.

To conceptualize the mind-boggling sweep of geologic time, imagine a person's arms outstretched wide. One set of fingertips represents the Earth's formation 4.6 billion years ago. On the opposite outspread hand, the wrist represents the Cambrian period's emergence of shelled animals (530 million years ago). The base of the fingers shows the Permian extinction that killed off many insects (252 million years ago). A fingertip displays the beginning of mammals in the Cenozoic era (65.5 million years ago)—and human life is represented in the matter from "a single stroke of a medium-grained nail file," as John McPhee wrote in *Annals of the Former World*.

Yet park visitors can reach farther back in time than they can fathom to palm the Earth's beginnings. From the Precambrian gneiss foun-

dations of our continent—up to 4 billion years old in Grand Teton National Park to 2.7-billion-year-old schist in the Grand Canyon—the national parks hold some of the oldest rocks on the planet.

Devils Postpile National Monument in California has continuous basalt columns—almost perfectly hexagonal—over 60 feet high, created from ancient lava flows that were later carved by glaciers 10,000 years ago. Along the seashore in Washington's Olympic National Park, 40-million-year-old sea creatures embedded in huge mélange outcrops reek of petroleum. Texas' rugged Guadalupe Mountains are a jaw-dropping example of reefs from Permian period seas. Wyoming's seldom visited prehistoric lake in Fossil Butte National Monument showcases some of the most perfectly preserved early plant and animal organisms in the world. One could spend a lifetime studying colorful layers deposited in ancient seas, crawling through caves, hunting for fossils, or photographing these wonders. ∎

In Theodore Roosevelt National Park in North Dakota, badlands formed from sediments laid down as long as 65 million years ago.

Breccia—cemented fragments of minerals or rock—give clues to the forces that shaped what is now Death Valley's Mosaic Canyon.

KARST LANDSCAPES

Karst landscapes are characterized by caves, sinkholes, and underground drainage systems. This map simplifies karst into major categories: karst (carbonate rock, evaporite rock) and pseudokarst (volcanic, erosional, and permafrost). Caves and karst can be found across the park system, from Mammoth Cave National Park to Lava Beds National Monument.

KARST OR PSEUDOKARST

- Carbonate
- Erosional
- Gypsum and salt
- Permafrost (continuous and discontinuous)
- Volcanic
- National Park Service unit

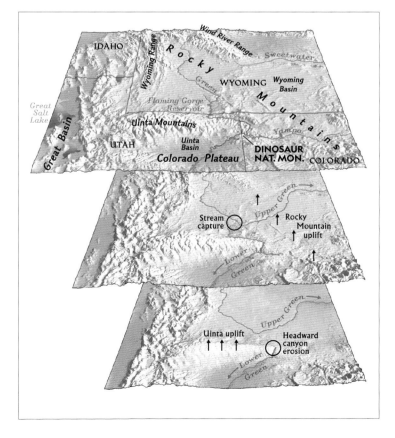

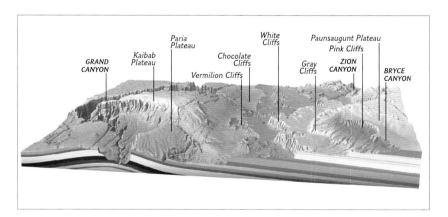

SEDIMENTARY ROCKS Stretching from Bryce Canyon to the Grand Canyon, the Grand Staircase forms one of the world's most complete sequences of sedimentary rocks. In the 1870s, geologist Clarence Dutton envisioned the area as a giant stairway, giving each step a colorful name to differentiate the type of rock, some of which date back approximately 270 million years. In studying it, modern geologists have divided it even further.

PHYSIOGRAPHY At Dinosaur National Monument, a record of 23 rock layers expose evidence of extinct ecosystems spanning 1.2 billion years. As the Rocky Mountains rose during the Laramide orogeny some 40 to 70 million years ago, the rest of the area rose with it. The earth was pushed upward while it was also squeezed from the sides, then warped and lifted along fault lines.

CLIMATE CHANGE

From Dry Tortugas in the Straits of Florida to Gates of the Arctic in northern Alaska, our national park land and seascapes are undergoing dramatic changes. Despite the political debate on whether to call it variations in the weather, global "weirding," or climate change, these alterations in temperature and precipitation were unforeseen when the National Park System began in the 19th century. The 1990 Global Change Research Act mandated that a "National Climate Assessment" be released to Congress and the

president every four years. The U.S. Global Change Research Program released its most recent assessment in November 2018, and the 300 researchers and expert authors (including Park Service scientists) reported some startling findings: Without more significant mitigation, there will be "substantial damages on the U.S. economy, human health, and the environment." The authors also repeated their conclusion from the 2013 report: "It is extremely likely that human influence has been the dominant cause of the observed warming since the mid-20th century."

Today, the effects are seen in the drying of western parks, as forest fires intensify, and become harder to contain. Rapid glacial retreat and thawing permafrost is regularly being documented in northern parks; animal migrations have been disrupted and hibernations shortened. In the Midwest, severe storms and catastrophic floods are the new normal. Along national seashores, rising sea levels are inundating coasts, while ocean warming and acidification are killing coral reefs in several parks. Because national parks have long documented climate, changes to park ecosystems are repeatedly covered in the "National Climate Assessment."

In 2007, the Park Service director proactively established the Climate Change Response Program. Regional science centers and cooperatives were created around the country to study and react through more energy-efficient park operations aimed at reduction of carbon dioxide in the atmosphere. Today, more than 120 parks participate in the Climate Friendly Park Program. Its goals include measuring greenhouse gas emissions in each park, educational programs, and the development of actions to minimize the effect of climate change on park resources. Hopefully, continued federal protection for these sanctuaries will inspire the public and community leaders to tackle climate change and join a clean energy future. ■

Clam shells lie above water level during a dry period in Llewellyn Gulch in the Glen Canyon National Recreation Area, Utah.

This drought-ruined Joshua tree shows how plants are affected by climate change that scientists are documenting in the region.

Wildfire smoke shrouds the peaks of the northern Rockies in Glacier National Park, Montana, where dead trees and past suppression of forest fires add fuel.

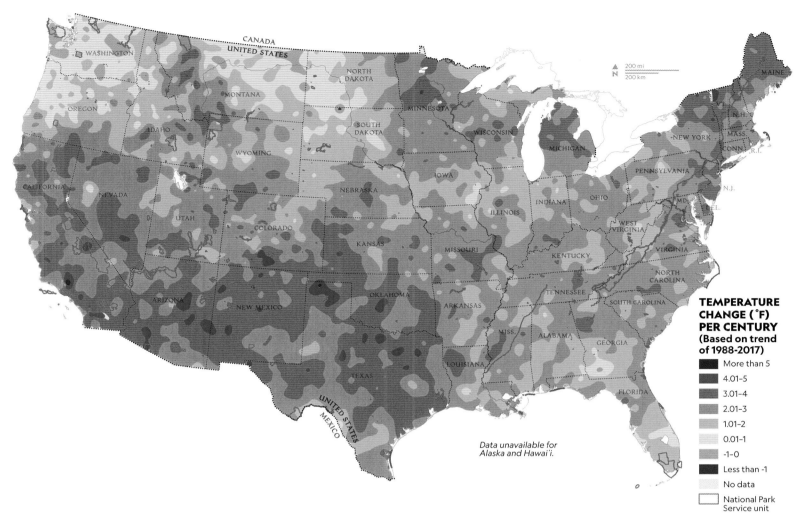

TEMPERATURE CHANGE (°F) PER CENTURY (Based on trend of 1988-2017)

- More than 5
- 4.01–5
- 3.01–4
- 2.01–3
- 1.01–2
- 0.01–1
- -1–0
- Less than -1
- No data
- National Park Service unit

Data unavailable for Alaska and Hawai'i.

AVERAGE TEMPERATURE TRENDS This map shows what temperature change may occur in the next century if the average trends from the past 30 years continue. Even a few degrees can impact park ecosystems, shifting growing seasons and putting stress on plants and animals.

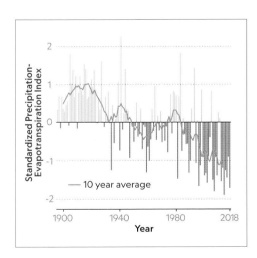

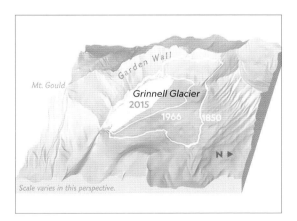

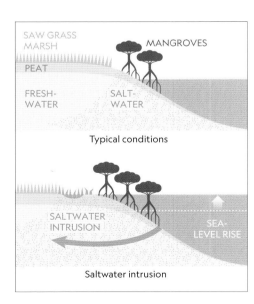

EXTREME DROUGHT Dry spells in Joshua Tree National Park have become more frequent and longer lasting. The index in the above graph examines water supply and demand: The green line shows a significant drying trend over the past 30 years. Scientists predict that by 2100, only isolated pockets of the now widespread Joshua tree will be found within park boundaries, as their seedlings need rain to endure the summer heat—and that, too, has been increasing.

GLACIAL RETREAT Glaciers are a stunning sight in many national parks, but changing temperatures are speeding up the rate at which they melt. In 1850, what is now Glacier National Park had about 150 glaciers; today, only 26 glaciers larger than 25 acres remain. In measuring glacial melt in the park over a 50-year period, the U.S. Geological Survey estimated the average glacier grew smaller by 39 percent. The area of Grinnell Glacier, shown above, has decreased in area by more than 75 percent. Projections suggest it won't be long before the park's glaciers are gone entirely.

SEA-LEVEL RISE With 84 percent of Everglades National Park already at an altitude of less than a meter (3.3 ft), sea-level rise is increasing saltwater intrusion into inland freshwater marshes during storms and high tides. Too much encroaching saltwater degrades peat, causes marshes to recede and collapse, and lets mangroves advance inland.

ECO-REGIONS & FLORA

Across our National Park System, from the mainland to offshore islands, are a score of broad-based eco-regions defined by their distinct geography and systems of life. These vary from northern tundra to eastern temperate forests; from the Great Plains to the Desert Southwest; from the more moderate Sierras to the tropical rainforests of Hawai'i. Within these eco-regions, Washington's Olympic National Park protects the most varied ecosystems in one unit. Created partly to save its old-growth, temperate rainforest,

Olympic also encompasses sandy coastal beaches, lakes, and streams, and culminates in glaciated, high-alpine peaks. On the opposite coast, Florida's Everglades spans an even wider mosaic of habitats, including marine and estuarine, mangrove, cypress, freshwater marsh, pine rockland, and tropical hardwood hammocks.

These ecosystems shelter microorganisms, plants, and animals that give each park its unique signature—from massive, thousands-of-years-old sequoia and bristlecone trees to vast numbers of brilliant wildflowers with fleeting spring blooms. But caring for these complex ecosystems involves a big-picture approach that recognizes the connectedness of life and land. The National Park Service will often collectively manage grazing wildlife and water drainage, as well as wildfire or invasive species just to preserve one rare native plant.

Take the sentry milk vetch: a delicate, lavender-flowered plant growing along the Grand Canyon cliff edges. Park visitors nearly trampled the endangered plant, found nowhere else in the world, to extinction. So in 2008, the Park Service removed a parking lot next to the last surviving milk vetch, began restoring the soil and planting a variety of other supportive native plants, and cultivated the milk vetch in nurseries. A decade into the ambitious replanting program, several thousand of the fragile plants exist in the wild.

The vetch is unique, but not alone; the parks harbor hundreds of threatened or endangered plant species—ranging from spherical silverswords that brighten the volcanic soils of Haleakalā to green, antler-shaped rock gnome lichen of the Great Smoky Mountains. Tasked with identifying these species, the U.S. Fish and Wildlife Service lists 900 flowering plants and 44 ferns, trees, and lichens as endangered or threatened—many of which are found in the national parks. These sanctuaries often offer the last habitats to prevent plant species—and their essential ecosystems—from being lost forever. ▪

Introduced to control erosion, reed grass is an aggressive non-native plant that threatens to outcompete native marsh plants.

This dwarf mangrove in Florida's Everglades is part of an ecosystem of salt-tolerant trees that can survive the coastal conditions including high winds and surges.

Plants like mosses, ferns, and lichens growing on other plants are hallmarks of the temperate rainforest in Washington's Olympic National Park.

WILDERNESS AND FEDERAL LAND

- Designated wilderness
- Proposed wilderness (awaiting approval)
- Land managed by the National Park Service, U.S. Forest Service, U.S. Fish and Wildlife Service, or Bureau of Land Managment
- Urban area

WILDERNESS AREAS The Wilderness Act of 1964 defined wilderness as "an area where the earth and its community of life are untrammeled by man, where man himself is a visitor who does not remain." More than 109 million acres of public lands have been protected as legal wilderness—5 percent of the United States. Alaska contains over half of the nation's wilderness.

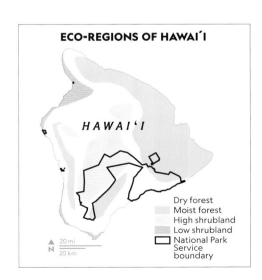

ECO-REGIONS OF HAWAI'I

- Dry forest
- Moist forest
- High shrubland
- Low shrubland
- National Park Service boundary

ECO-REGIONS National parks encompass a wealth of eco-regions, each of which supports different plants and animals. Located 2,400 miles from the nearest continent, Hawai'i boasts a spectacular mosaic of habitats. Visitors to Hawai'i Volcanoes National Park can cross three eco-regions—dry forest, moist forest, and high shrubland—within park bounds. A high number of endemic species live within the Hawai'i Volcanoes National Park's tropical moist forests.

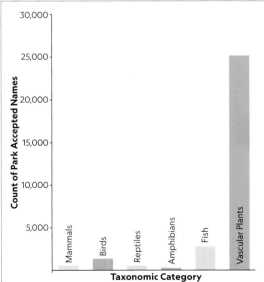

SPECIES RICHNESS The park system is rich in biodiversity, protecting a vast array of plants and animals in their wild habitat. Of the six taxonomic categories shown on the graph above, the number of vascular plants the Park Service protects far surpasses all other taxa. Vascular plants, such as trees, shrubs, grasses, and ferns, have systems of veins that conduct water and nutrients.

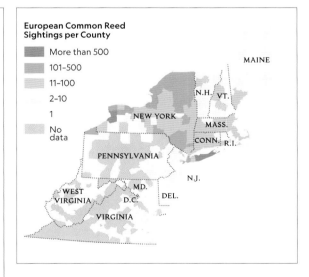

European Common Reed Sightings per County

- More than 500
- 101–500
- 11–100
- 2–10
- 1
- No data

NON-NATIVE SPECIES Invasive plant life—species that are alien and potentially harmful to the ecosystem—threatens the survival of native plants in national parks and beyond. The European common reed was probably introduced to North America in the 1880s, and the invasive species now impacts vegetation across parks in the Northeast.

WILDLIFE

The incredible diversity of ecosystems in the national parks protects 5,399 species of vertebrates. Found as residents or migrants in parklands and waters are more than 1,100 fish species, 900-plus bird species, over 400 mammal species, nearly 600 reptile species, and more than 300 amphibian species. And the tally of invertebrate species—over 100,000 spineless flying and crawling buglike creatures—far surpasses all other park animals. The Organic Act that created the National Park Service in 1916 identified wildlife

preservation as one of its primary missions. As the parks—and the planet—have evolved over the last century, the goal of saving endangered or vanishing species has elevated the protected areas to sacred places where irreplaceable animals like the Mission blue butterfly, green sea turtle, and California condor can endure.

Each park is uniquely equipped for the biological needs and patterns of a remarkable assemblage of life. Yellowstone, for example, holds the finest habitat in the lower 48 for large animals called megafauna—mainly because of its vast acreage. It is the only place in the country where 2,200-pound bison have lived continuously since prehistoric times. Elsewhere in the plains, mountains, and lakes of western parks, coyotes can be heard howling, snakes and lizards tolerate harsh conditions, mule deer are ubiquitous and preyed upon by cougars or black bears (found in most national parks).

Forested eastern parks are known for common white-tailed deer, along with gray and red foxes, scarcely seen bobcats, nocturnal opossums and lordly skunks, and playful river otters. In Florida's Everglades, American alligators prey on fish, turtles, birds, and are in turn eaten by introduced Burmese pythons in freshwater marshes, swamps, and rivers.

The desert parks of the Southwest shelter reptiles such as the native Gila monster—the only venomous lizard in the U.S.—and a dozen rattlesnake species. The biodiverse Grand Canyon has more than 1,400 insect species supporting its ecosystem, from flower-pollinating bees to ants that aid decomposition.

Pacific Northwest and Alaskan waters hold sea lions, harbor seals, and whales. Incredible caribou and bird migrations evoke the storied animal populations found throughout the continent before European settlement. ∎

Pinnacles National Park, California, has become a safe haven for newly released and endangered California condors.

Seen nowhere else on Earth, the Channel Island fox is a third smaller than its mainland ancestor, the gray fox.

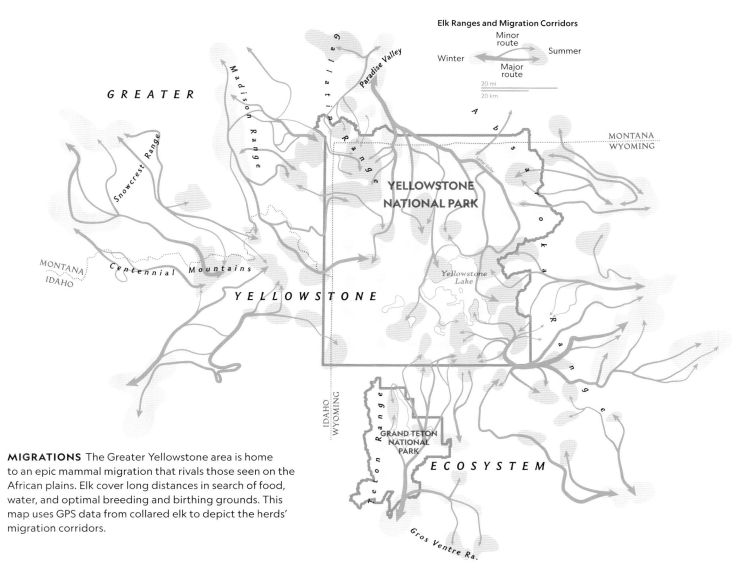

Elk Ranges and Migration Corridors

Minor route
Winter — Summer
Major route

20 mi
20 km

GREATER

YELLOWSTONE

ECOSYSTEM

YELLOWSTONE NATIONAL PARK

GRAND TETON NATIONAL PARK

Yellowstone Lake

MONTANA / WYOMING

MONTANA / IDAHO

IDAHO / WYOMING

Gallatin Range

Madison Range

Snowcrest Range

Centennial Mountains

Paradise Valley

Absaroka Range

Teton Range

Gros Ventre Ra.

MIGRATIONS The Greater Yellowstone area is home to an epic mammal migration that rivals those seen on the African plains. Elk cover long distances in search of food, water, and optimal breeding and birthing grounds. This map uses GPS data from collared elk to depict the herds' migration corridors.

Humpback Chub Habitat
— Critical
— Current
— Historic
National Park Service unit

WYOMING
NEVADA
UTAH
COLORADO
NEW MEXICO
ARIZONA

Yampa
Green
Colorado

DINOSAUR N.M.
COLORADO N.M.
CANYONLANDS N.P.
GLEN CANYON N.R.A.
GRAND CANYON N.P.
LAKE MEAD N.R.A.

100 mi
100 km

ENDEMIC SPECIES The endangered humpback chub is endemic to the Colorado River Basin, but the species' habitat has been severely reduced compared to its historical range due to threats from dam construction, changes in water flow and temperature, and introduced species. Many Park Service units protect critical populations of humpback chub: Grand Canyon National Park contains the world's largest remaining population. In 2009, the National Park Service began translocating chubs in an effort to help the species survive.

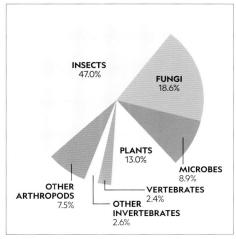

INSECTS 47.0%
FUNGI 18.6%
PLANTS 13.0%
MICROBES 8.9%
OTHER ARTHROPODS 7.5%
VERTEBRATES 2.4%
OTHER INVERTEBRATES 2.6%

BIODIVERSITY Great Smoky Mountains National Park is the most biodiverse park in the system: Some 19,000 species have been identified there, but scientists think there could be up to 100,000 more and continue to monitor the area. The rich mix of insects, plants, vertebrates, and other organisms comes from the park's combination of mountains, climate, and weather. Elevations range from 850 to 6,643 feet, allowing for a range of microclimates, while an approximate average of 55 to 85-plus inches of annual rainfall and fairly humid summers make for a long and prosperous growing season.

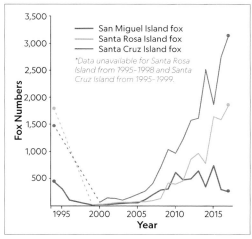

San Miguel Island fox
Santa Rosa Island fox
Santa Cruz Island fox

Data unavailable for Santa Rosa Island from 1995–1998 and Santa Cruz Island from 1995–1999.

Fox Numbers
Year

ENDANGERED SPECIES Island fox populations in Channel Islands National Park plummeted in the 1990s due to predation from golden eagles. The foxes were listed as "endangered" under the Endangered Species Act of 2004, and attempts to rehabilitate their populations began. Through captive breeding, predator relocation, and species reintroduction, fox numbers rebounded. The successful recoveries of the San Miguel Island fox, Santa Rosa Island fox, and Santa Cruz Island fox illustrate the Endangered Species Act's power to prevent extinction.

ARCHAEOLOGY & PALEONTOLOGY

Before the national parks were established, many paleontological or archaeological sites had already stirred curiosity about the continent's prehistoric and cultural beginnings. By the late 19th century—as artifact collectors began exploiting these places—philanthropists and scientists tried to preserve fossil-rich sites and Native American

ruins throughout the West. In southern Colorado in particular, ancestral Puebloan artifacts were being looted, sold, or shipped outside of the country. So in 1906, President Theodore Roosevelt created Mesa Verde National Park in conjunction with that year's federal Antiquities Act passed to protect archaeological sites. It was the first national park to protect a location of cultural significance and respectfully "preserve the works of man." Over the next three years, utilizing the Antiquities Act, Roosevelt created 18 archaeologically imbued national monuments, including the southwestern ruin sites of early Native Americans at El Morro, Montezuma Castle, Chaco Culture Gila Cliff Dwellings, Tonto, and Tumacácori.

After the creation of the National Park Service in 1916, eastern parks were included with a broadened thematic and geographic scope. For instance, Chickamauga & Chattanooga National Military Park was created in 1890 for its historic and archaeological values,

and Biscayne National Park protects 200- to 300-year-old shipwrecks. The National Historic Preservation Act of 1966, which established the National Register of Historic Places and National Historic Landmarks Program, and the Archaeological Resources Protection Act of 1979, strengthened the preservation of ruin and fossil sites.

As for paleontology, more than 260 National Park Service areas, from Agate Fossil Beds National Monument to Waco Mammoth National Monument, preserve evidence of prehistoric life (sometimes with a cultural context). These fossil-infused parks safeguard billion-year-old stromatolites in Utah's Capitol Reef National Park, or the 12,400-year-old, partially intact, elephant-size woolly mammoth remains recently found in Alaska's remote Bering Land Bridge National Preserve.

One of the most celebrated sites, Dinosaur National Monument in Colorado and Utah, houses the most well-preserved and plentiful collection of prehistoric fossils in the world. ∎

Visitors explore the many dinosaur fossils on display at the Quarry in Dinosaur National Monument, Utah.

The Hopewell burial mounds in Ohio shed light on a Native American culture that may have reached as far as the Gulf of Mexico.

Small remains like this stone projectile point in Petrified Forest National Park, Arizona, speak volumes about past peoples and their cultures.

TOP ARCHAEOLOGY AND PALEONTOLOGY SITES This map depicts the top parks for archaeology and paleontology curated by the National Park Service. Not every site of value is shown here: The park system has more than 88,000 archaeological sites and more than 260 units with paleontological sites.

NPS UNITS WITH MAJOR ARCHAEOLOGY AND PALEONTOLOGY SITES

- Archaeology site
- Paleontology site
- Both

CENOZOIC ERA FOSSILS The Cenozoic era or the "age of mammals" is the fourth time period on the geologic timescale, which organizes Earth's 4.5-billion-year history into four distinct eras. Starting 65.5 million years ago, birds and mammals rose in this period to fill the vacuum left by the extinction of the dinosaurs: big cats, horses, and woolly mammoths ruled the day. The western parks shown above preserve some of the highest concentrations of Cenozoic fossils.

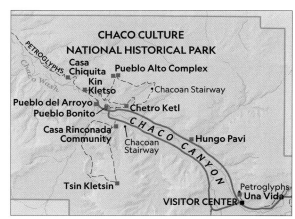

ANCESTRAL PUEBLOAN Chaco Culture National Historical Park in New Mexico preserves the cultural past of the ancestral Pueblo people (formerly called Anasazi). Designated as a UNESCO World Heritage site in 1987, the park has 4,000 archaeological sites—from Chaco "great houses" to petroglyphs—and more than 1.5 million artifacts, from shell ornaments to bone tools, that represent thousands of years of human history in Chaco Canyon. Protecting these sites means striking a delicate balance between public access and preservation.

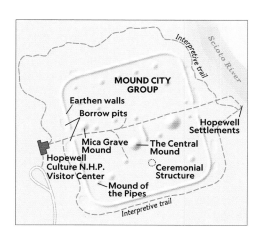

MOUND BUILDERS Almost 2,000 years ago in the Ohio Valley, Native Americans built earthen mounds and embankments where they gathered for feasts, funerals, and ceremonies. Hopewell Culture National Historical Park protects six earthwork complexes, including the only fully restored Hopewell earthwork complex, Mound City Group (shown above).

CULTURAL LANDSCAPES

Over 800 cultural landscapes found among the more than 400 national park units tell the story of America and our relationship with the natural world. Found in the wilderness and in cities alike, a cultural landscape is a geographic area that has been influenced or shaped by human activity. From natural landmarks imbued with spiritual significance—such as Wyoming's Devils Tower, a monolithic rock feature that Northern Plains Indians and indigenous people consider sacred—to specially designed structures like Gateway Arch

(recently made a park), cultural landscapes show us how we find and make meaning in the world. Whether natural or human-created, decades or millennia old, these places are evaluated and designated based on their historical weight and authenticity to a specific time period.

John Muir National Historic Site preserves a 14-room mansion in California, where America's great conservationist raised a family and wrote treatises that inspired the government to set aside the nation's earliest parks and create the National Park Service. His preserved "scribbling den" study holds the desk that Muir used for all of these writings.

Other cultural sites cast light on a humbler existence. Cades Cove, in Great Smoky Mountains National Park, has an 11-mile-loop road that illustrates how early settlers lived in an intact forest of pine, hemlock and poplar, and built their cemeteries, churches and mills,

and went about their days husking corn, making molasses, gathering chestnuts, and living off the abundant herds of bison and elk.

The cultural landscapes concept was enlarged in the 1930s, when the Park Service took over battlefields, forts, and monuments from the War Department. Many sites showcase ethnic diversity, women's history, and labor—remembering tragic and painful moments as well as celebratory ones. South Dakota's Wounded Knee National Historic Landmark, for example, pays tribute to the hundreds of lives lost in an 1890 massacre of Lakota Indians.

Fruit orchards that sustained frontier communities, roads planned for their panoramic views, precontact ruins: These and more cultural parks illuminate what the World Heritage Committee calls "the combined works of nature and man" so that visitors might reflect again and again on the sites that belong to all of us. ▪

Ghost teepees evoke the tragic slaughter that took place at Big Hole National Battlefield at Nez Perce National Historical Park in Montana.

The parks celebrate the lives of influential figures, like famed Underground Railroad conductor Harriet Tubman.

Immigrants await questioning in 1900 in the Registry Room of Ellis Island, which is restored and now part of the park system.

CLIFF DWELLINGS Long before Europeans explored the American West, a group of people settled at Mesa Verde. They lived there for over 700 years, coming to be known as ancestral Pueblo or "village dwellers" (formerly called Anasazi). Classic Pueblo period (1150–1300) cliff dwellings are protected in the national park.

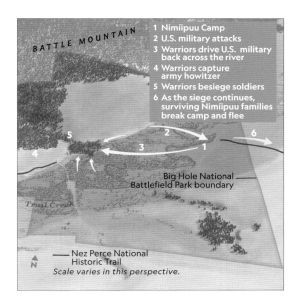

NATIVE AMERICANS The Park Service protects battlefields like Montana's Big Hole National Battlefield, where about 800 Nez Perce Indians (Nimíipuu, or "walking people") made camp on August 7, 1877, after being evicted from their reservation. They hoped the U.S. military would not pursue them, but on August 9, gunshots rang out at dawn. The warriors drove the military back across the river, but fighting continued: In all, 60 to 90 Nez Perce, including women and children, and 31 soldiers and volunteers perished.

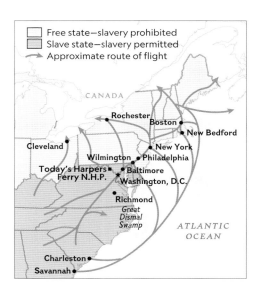

UNDERGROUND RAILROAD Many parks along the eastern seaboard preserve remnants and stories of the Underground Railroad—a network of safe houses and places that enslaved people used to escape to freedom, often led by guides or "conductors" who helped them find their way. These historical routes tell tales of pain, resistance, and courage as those in bondage fled for freedom in the North. For many freedom seekers, Harpers Ferry National Historic Park was a crucial stop along their dangerous journey.

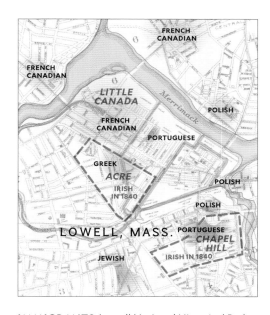

IMMIGRANTS Lowell National Historical Park protects the dynamic history of the industrial revolution. The water-powered textile mills at Lowell, Massachusetts, launched the nation—including immigrant families and some of the country's first female factory workers—into a new industrial era. The above map shows the locations of five major immigrant communities, as groups lived away from the mills in their own neighborhoods.

VISITOR EXPERIENCE

The experiences that draw increasing crowds to our national parks are as diverse as the parks themselves. Most visitors come for the stellar hiking, sightseeing, and wildlife-watching, but the parks also offer many other unexpected adventures. Isle Royale is renowned among the diving community for its many shipwrecks. Denali is the only park in the country that patrols with dogsleds, and although summer dog demonstrations are given at the park, interested mushers have to wait until winter to bring their own

sled dogs. Channel Islands—with its waters hosting nearly one-third of Earth's cetacean species—is famous for whale-watching. Big Bend is not so well known for the natural hot spring on the north bank of its Rio Grande River, but given its wild beauty, the spring is considered a jewel of the Chihuahuan Desert. Although many parks offer boating opportunities, Everglades features unique, winding water trails that allow paddlers to explore the mangroves and observe wading birds, as well as both the resident alligators and crocodiles. Petrified Forest National Park is a destination for the high-tech, hide-and-go-seek pastime of geocaching, in which clues received on a GPS device or cell phone lead to the Park Service's caches hidden among the ancient fossilized trees.

Pursuing these and other experiences, more than 330 million visitors frequent the national parks each year—an onslaught that suggests that the parks are being loved to death. Under this traffic,

maintaining the trails, campgrounds, bridges, and buildings is an enormous task. Enhancing the visitor experience, let alone protecting the parks, would be impossible without the highly trained and dedicated rangers, interpreters, resource managers, maintenance personnel, and administrators. The invaluable visitor centers—gateways to the parks—are replete with interpretive exhibits, bookstores, and expert advice. Still, the backlog of needed repairs—repaving roads, removing trail blowdowns, fixing older or damaged visitor centers—has become an increasing challenge.

While waiting for the congressional funds that would resolve deferred maintenance and overcrowding—let alone environmental issues caused by climate change—it's helpful to remember: "National parks are the best idea we ever had," as the author Wallace Stegner said. "Absolutely American, absolutely democratic, they reflect us at our best rather than our worst." Therein will be our solution. ■

A ranger gives visitors a tour along the one-mile Carver Trail in George Washington Carver National Monument in Missouri.

One of some 150 wild horses descended from domestic stock at Maryland's Assateague Island National Seashore

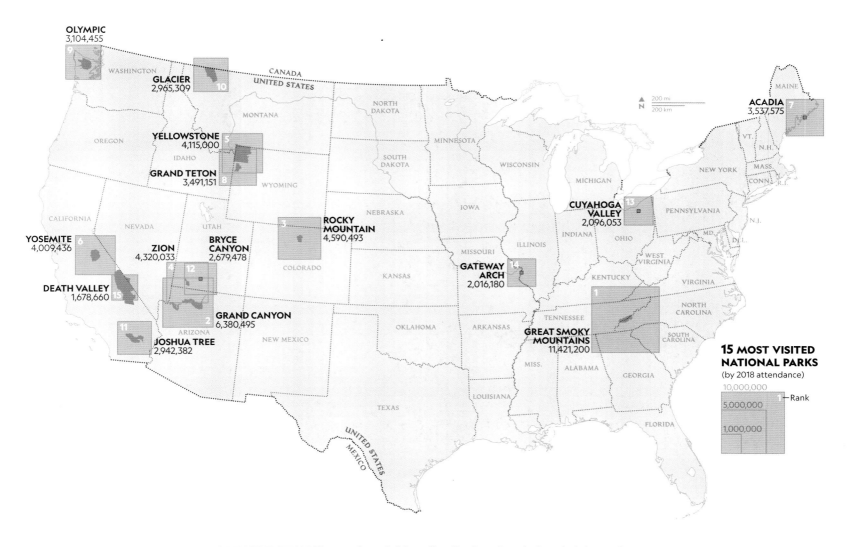

PARK VISITATION The number of visitors flooding into America's parks is increasing, which is both cause for celebration and a signal to take caution. High visitor numbers can increase stress on the parks, but it also means that people are excited to explore America's natural wonders—and that helps to keep them alive.

15 MOST VISITED NATIONAL PARKS
(by 2018 attendance)

Yellowstone N.P. Visitors, 2016

By Age	Millennials		Baby Boomers
30%	14%	24%	32%
Others	Generation X		

By Race		
15%		White 82%
Asian Black 1%		Other* 2%

Share of U.S. Population, 2016

By Age	Millennials		Baby Boomers
31%	25%	20%	24%
Others	Generation X		

By Race		
13%		White 77%
Asian Black 6%		Other* 4%

*In totals by race in the U.S. population, "Other" includes two or more races, which was not a category surveyed at Yellowstone N.P.

DIVERSITY Yellowstone National Park has some of the park system's highest tourist numbers, but there's a considerable diversity gap among visitors. A 2016 visitor use study at Yellowstone shows why park officials are targeting millennials and blacks. They have visited Yellowstone in numbers well below their share of the U.S. population.

ACCESSIBILITY The park system has something for everyone, be it a well-paved, flat walkway or a backcountry hike far off the beaten path. The 1.5-mile-long, eight-foot-wide Pa'rus Trail in Zion National Park provides wheelchair access, with parking and restrooms nearby. Zion's shuttle buses and visitor centers are also accessible.

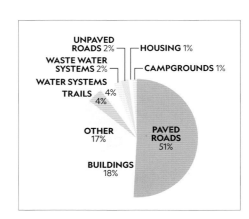

Category	Percent
PAVED ROADS	51%
BUILDINGS	18%
OTHER	17%
TRAILS	4%
WATER SYSTEMS	4%
WASTE WATER SYSTEMS	2%
UNPAVED ROADS	2%
HOUSING	1%
CAMPGROUNDS	1%

DEFERRED MAINTENANCE America's parks require constant maintenance, but budget constraints mean that work often needs to be deferred until a later date. In 2017, some $275 million was deferred during the fiscal year, bringing the total deferred maintenance tally to nearly $12 billion. Roads—including bridges, tunnels, paved parking areas, and roadways—require the most upkeep, which is no surprise; they see some of the heaviest visitor traffic. Addressing deferred maintenance issues—from managing campgrounds to water systems—means better preserving parks for the future.

HUMAN IMPACTS

As the National Park Service celebrated its 2016 centennial, the popularity of the parks soared. But this public endearment comes at a price: Several hundred million visitors to the parks annually have had an inevitable impact—litter or left-behind food, trampled vegetation, traffic and tailpipe emissions, and the rumble of sightseeing aircraft. These effects and others not only detract from the human experience, but can also disrupt the natural behaviors of wildlife, potentially driving away animals.

Yosemite—with over four million visitors in 2018—exemplifies the paradox of popular parks: They are created for preservation and public enjoyment, yet too much enjoyment can jeopardize the pristine qualities.

Adding to visitation impacts on these fragile places are challenges originating far beyond park boundaries. Air pollution is one of the most significant threats. Forest fires surround Yosemite and produce airborne particulates that reduce visibility. In 2018, a fire shut down the park for nearly three weeks. (The 2019 government shutdown left most parks open, but without staff on duty, the impacts—overflowing trash, sanitation, off-road driving, and plant poaching—will be long lasting.) Although Yosemite's night skies experience only minor light pollution, city lights often compromise the wilderness character of parks closer to urban areas in the lower 48, such as Saguaro National Park, which straddles Tucson. Unaltered land-scapes are essential to wildlife, the natural cycles of plants, and visitors who come to search for stars and constellations best viewed in dark skies—now a vanishing resource in much of the world.

In Arizona's Grand Canyon or Alaska's Lake Clark, old and newly proposed mining operations in adjacent lands threaten water quality. In Florida's Everglades, urban growth and sugar producers have disrupted and polluted park waters. And throughout the Southwest, 10 different parks alongside the Colorado River or its tributaries are losing water due to agricultural demands or thirsty cities.

Yet there are manifold examples of restoring the landscape and waterways. Completing the largest river restoral in U.S. history in 2014, Olympic National Park removed two dams so the Elwha River could flow freely to the sea—allowing salmon to spawn in the headwaters and supporting the Park Service mission to protect the pristine for future generations. ◼

Light pollution in Arizona's Santa Catalina Mountains, amid burgeoning population north of Tucson, suggests that pristine dark skies are increasingly rare.

Yet another grizzly bear sighting along the Brooks River draws a flood of tourists to the viewing platform in Katmai National Park and Preserve, Alaska.

Smoke from a forest fire hangs over the Yosemite Valley. In recent years, fires have caused closures there and in other western parks.

PARK PROXIMITY TO CITIES In the lower 48 states, very few parks are truly remote. Most lie within just a few hours' drive of a major city. And although that makes them more accessible, it also threatens the pristine qualities of their wildness—air pollution, light pollution, and human traffic all impact the land's natural rhythms.

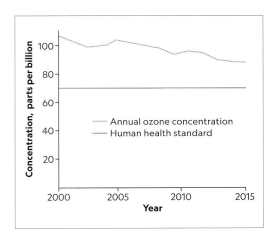

AIR QUALITY In 2017, Sequoia and Kings Canyon National Parks experienced 80 days with unsafe ozone levels—more than two and a half months. In summer, it isn't uncommon for concentrations to exceed the federal ozone health standards, which can have a particularly adverse effect on people with heart or lung disease, children, and the elderly. It can also impact the park's ecosystem, potentially altering how well plants grow, photosynthesize, and store food.

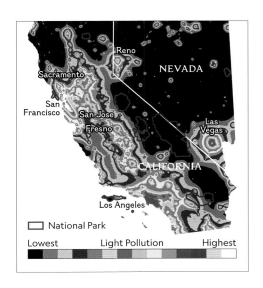

NIGHT SKY LIGHT POLLUTION The darkest skies are farthest from artificial light sources. That makes Death Valley National Park all the more impressive in highly populated California: The park harbors some of the country's darkest night skies—crucial for stargazers as well as animals that rely on darkness for refuge from the heat of the day. Efforts to maintain the park's pristine skies, like minimizing artificial lighting, led to its certification as the world's third International Dark Sky Park in 2008.

WATER QUALITY Extensive cleanup efforts in the late 1900s transformed the polluted Delaware River into a healthy waterway. Water quality indicators are closely monitored to maintain established standards. The waters upstream and downstream from Delaware Water Gap National Recreation Area are protected under Special Protection Waters regulations, designed to prevent river degradation. Keeping the upper headwaters clean has a flow-on effect for the rest of the river.

EXTREMES

The Department of the Interior manages a system of extreme wonders, distinguished by diverse and record-setting physical attributes—from the world's largest gypsum dune field to the highest peak in North America.

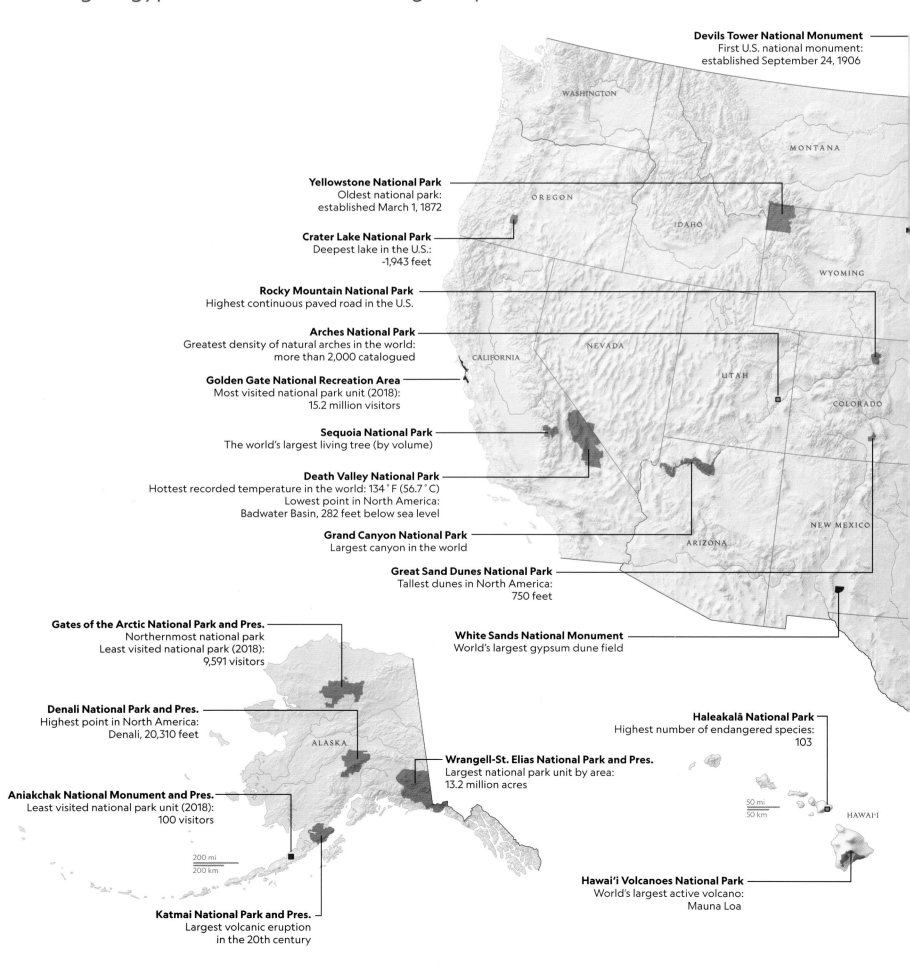

Devils Tower National Monument
First U.S. national monument:
established September 24, 1906

Yellowstone National Park
Oldest national park:
established March 1, 1872

Crater Lake National Park
Deepest lake in the U.S.:
-1,943 feet

Rocky Mountain National Park
Highest continuous paved road in the U.S.

Arches National Park
Greatest density of natural arches in the world:
more than 2,000 catalogued

Golden Gate National Recreation Area
Most visited national park unit (2018):
15.2 million visitors

Sequoia National Park
The world's largest living tree (by volume)

Death Valley National Park
Hottest recorded temperature in the world: 134˚F (56.7˚C)
Lowest point in North America:
Badwater Basin, 282 feet below sea level

Grand Canyon National Park
Largest canyon in the world

Great Sand Dunes National Park
Tallest dunes in North America:
750 feet

White Sands National Monument
World's largest gypsum dune field

Gates of the Arctic National Park and Pres.
Northernmost national park
Least visited national park (2018):
9,591 visitors

Denali National Park and Pres.
Highest point in North America:
Denali, 20,310 feet

Aniakchak National Monument and Pres.
Least visited national park unit (2018):
100 visitors

Wrangell-St. Elias National Park and Pres.
Largest national park unit by area:
13.2 million acres

Haleakalā National Park
Highest number of endangered species:
103

Katmai National Park and Pres.
Largest volcanic eruption
in the 20th century

Hawai'i Volcanoes National Park
World's largest active volcano:
Mauna Loa

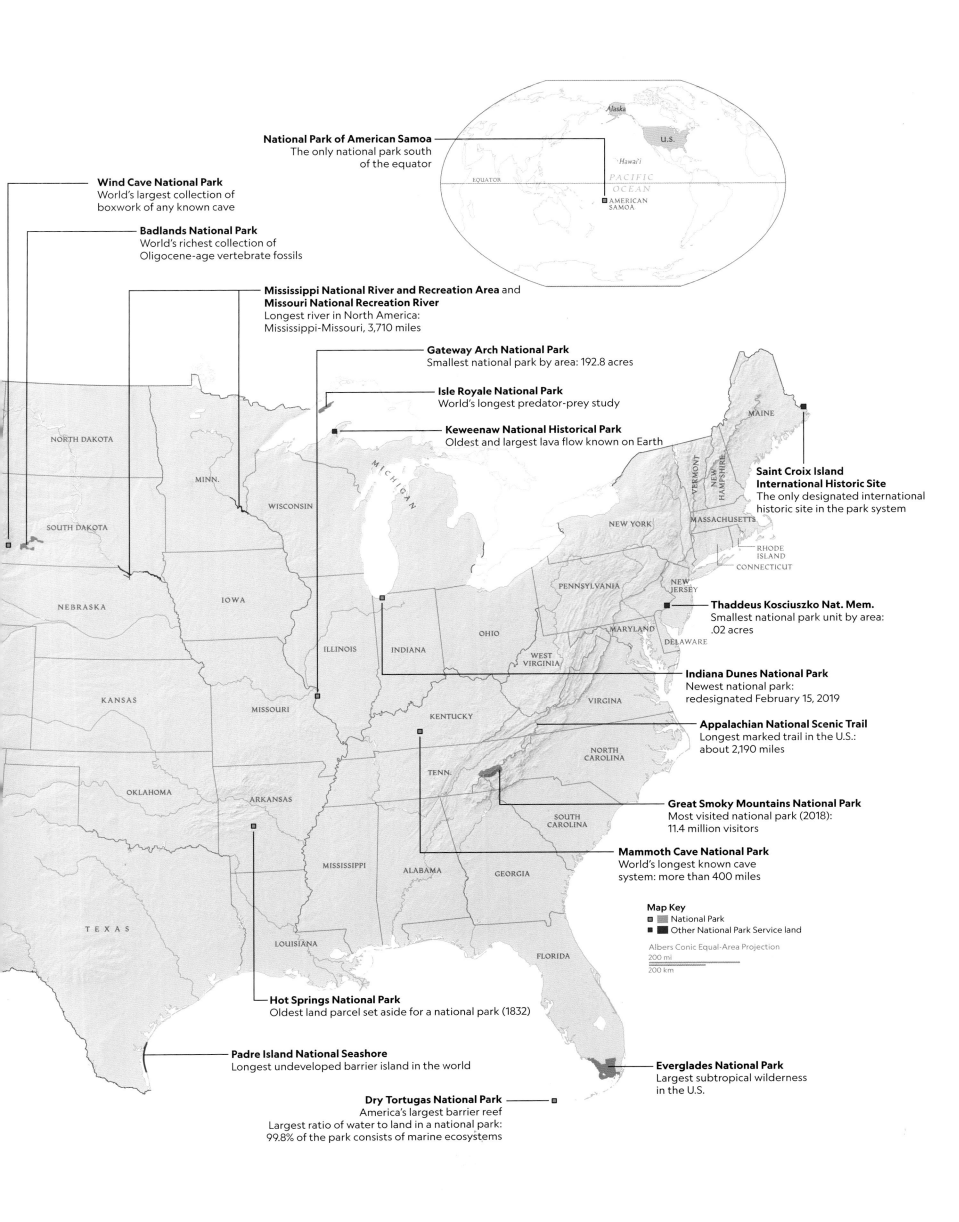

National Park of American Samoa
The only national park south of the equator

Alaska

U.S.

Hawai'i

PACIFIC
OCEAN

EQUATOR

AMERICAN
SAMOA

Wind Cave National Park
World's largest collection of
boxwork of any known cave

Badlands National Park
World's richest collection of
Oligocene-age vertebrate fossils

Mississippi National River and Recreation Area and
Missouri National Recreation River
Longest river in North America:
Mississippi-Missouri, 3,710 miles

Gateway Arch National Park
Smallest national park by area: 192.8 acres

Isle Royale National Park
World's longest predator-prey study

Keweenaw National Historical Park
Oldest and largest lava flow known on Earth

**Saint Croix Island
International Historic Site**
The only designated international
historic site in the park system

Thaddeus Kosciuszko Nat. Mem.
Smallest national park unit by area:
.02 acres

Indiana Dunes National Park
Newest national park:
redesignated February 15, 2019

Appalachian National Scenic Trail
Longest marked trail in the U.S.:
about 2,190 miles

Great Smoky Mountains National Park
Most visited national park (2018):
11.4 million visitors

Mammoth Cave National Park
World's longest known cave
system: more than 400 miles

Hot Springs National Park
Oldest land parcel set aside for a national park (1832)

Padre Island National Seashore
Longest undeveloped barrier island in the world

Everglades National Park
Largest subtropical wilderness
in the U.S.

Dry Tortugas National Park
America's largest barrier reef
Largest ratio of water to land in a national park:
99.8% of the park consists of marine ecosystems

Map Key
◻ ▨ National Park
◼ ▰ Other National Park Service land

Albers Conic Equal-Area Projection
200 mi
200 km

NORTH DAKOTA

SOUTH DAKOTA

NEBRASKA

KANSAS

OKLAHOMA

TEXAS

MINN.

WISCONSIN

IOWA

MISSOURI

ARKANSAS

LOUISIANA

ILLINOIS

INDIANA

MICHIGAN

OHIO

KENTUCKY

TENN.

MISSISSIPPI

ALABAMA

GEORGIA

FLORIDA

SOUTH
CAROLINA

NORTH
CAROLINA

VIRGINIA

WEST
VIRGINIA

PENNSYLVANIA

NEW YORK

MAINE

VERMONT

NEW
HAMPSHIRE

MASSACHUSETTS

RHODE
ISLAND

CONNECTICUT

NEW
JERSEY

MARYLAND

DELAWARE

THE GLORY OF THE NATIONAL PARKS

CONTENTS

St. Mary Lake in Glacier National Park, Montana, with its mountains rising a vertical mile above, is one of the most photographed vistas in the park.

From Florida's vibrant coral reefs to Washington State's temperate rainforest, from Arizona's dry desert to Alaska's mammoth ice fields—the national parks of the United States defy simple definition. The National Park Service portrays them as "large natural places having a wide variety of attributes, at times including significant historic assets," and yet they are so much more. The landscapes, the wildlife, the history, and the natural wonders that these parklands protect are vast and varied, reflecting the magnitude of our shared backyard.

This atlas, designed and written to reveal the glory of the 61 national parks, is organized by region, following an east-to-west progression through the book and within each section. For every park, we have developed an authoritative map in collaboration with cartographers in the National Park Service. Thirty-three parks are explored in depth; the other 28 are contained in the book's last section.

The selection of parks to be featured in greater depth was a difficult one. Decisions were made in the spirit of the 1918 directive from Franklin K. Lane, secretary of the interior, to Stephen T. Mather, the first director of the National Park Service. At this point 18 national parks had already been established, and Mather had been charged with initiating "new park projects." Lane told Mather to seek out scenery or features so extraordinary as to be of national importance, "exemplifying the highest accomplishment of stream erosion . . . the oldest rock forms . . . and the luxuriance of deciduous forests."

Thus, in a similar spirit, the 33 featured parks were selected to represent a wide and wondrous spread of the following criteria, listed here in no specific order:

- biodiversity
- spectacular scenery
- extraordinary national features
- distinguished natural architecture or geology
- abundance of recreational opportunities
- threat of endangerment
- unique wildlife
- modern newsworthiness
- uniqueness of the region or qualities within
- superb historical aspects
- pristine character
- cultural story

With these prerequisites as a guide, the featured parks leapt into the appropriate pages. Most of them fit at least eight of the criteria; all of them are sanctuaries that deserve to be preserved for posterity. ∎

A bald eagle perches on a rock in Katmai National Park and Preserve in Alaska. Once endangered, this American emblem is now thriving thanks to restrictions on pesticides and reintroduction programs, among other measures.

PARK LOCATIONS

The 61 national parks are located in 28 different states. California has nine parks, including some of the oldest, followed by Alaska's eight massive parks, and Utah's increasingly popular "Grand Circle" of five. Most of the states in the Eastern Coast & Forest section—along with Michigan, Minnesota, Montana, Nevada, New Mexico, North Dakota, Ohio, Oregon, Missouri, Indiana, and Arkansas—have only one park (with the exception of Florida, which has three). Each of the territories of American Samoa and the U.S. Virgin Islands has a national park.

Six of the featured national parks adjoin international borders with Canada, and one Texas park, Big Bend, adjoins Mexico. Although international designations are not shown on most of the maps, many are recognized by the United Nations Educational, Scientific, and Cultural Organization: 14 are UNESCO World Heritage sites, 21 are designated UNESCO biosphere reserves, and 8 of these parks have been designated with both UNESCO programs. The value of these protected areas transcends not just states and regions, but also countries, connecting us around the globe. ■

Olympic N.P.
North Cascades N.P.
WASHINGTON
Glacier N.P.
Mt. Rainier N.P.
MONTANA
Theodore Roosevelt N.P.
OREGON
IDAHO
Crater Lake N.P.
Yellowstone N.P.
Redwood National and State Parks
Grand Teton N.P.
WYOMING
Wind Cave N.P.
Lassen Volcanic N.P.
NEVADA
CALIFORNIA
Rocky Mountain N.P.
Great Basin N.P.
UTAH
COLORADO
Yosemite N.P.
Capitol Reef N.P.
Arches N.P.
Black Canyon of the Gunnison N.P.
Bryce Canyon N.P.
Canyonlands N.P.
Pinnacles N.P.
Sequoia and Kings Canyon N.P.
Zion N.P.
Mesa Verde N.P.
Great Sand Dunes N.P. & Pres.
Death Valley N.P.
Grand Canyon N.P.
Channel Islands N.P.
ARIZONA
Petrified Forest N.P.
NEW MEXICO
Joshua Tree N.P.
Saguaro N.P.
Carlsbad Caverns N.P.
Guadalupe Mts. N.P.

Kobuk Valley N.P.
Gates of the Arctic N.P. & Preserve
ALASKA
Denali N.P. & Pres.
Wrangell-St.Elias N.P. & Preserve
Lake Clark N.P. & Pres.
Katmai N.P. & Pres.
Kenai Fjords N.P.
Glacier Bay N.P. & Pres.

Big Bend N.P.
50 mi
50 km
Haleakalā N.P.
HAWAI'I
Hawai'i Volcanoes N.P.

200 mi
200 km

Voyageurs N.P.

Isle Royale N.P.

NORTH DAKOTA

MINN.

WISCONSIN

MICHIGAN

MAINE

VERMONT

NEW HAMPSHIRE

Acadia N.P.

SOUTH DAKOTA

Badlands N.P.

NEBRASKA

IOWA

ILLINOIS

INDIANA

Indiana Dunes N.P.

Cuyahoga Valley N.P.

OHIO

NEW YORK

MASSACHUSETTS

RHODE ISLAND

CONNECTICUT

PENNSYLVANIA

NEW JERSEY

MARYLAND

DELAWARE

KANSAS

MISSOURI

Gateway Arch N.P.

KENTUCKY

Mammoth Cave N.P.

WEST VIRGINIA

Shenandoah N.P.

VIRGINA

NORTH CAROLINA

Great Smoky Mts. N.P.

OKLAHOMA

ARKANSAS

TENN.

SOUTH CAROLINA

Congaree N.P.

Hot Springs N.P.

MISSISSIPPI

ALABAMA

GEORGIA

TEXAS

LOUISIANA

FLORIDA

Everglades N.P.

Biscayne N.P.

Dry Tortugas N.P.

Alaska

U.S.

Hawai'i

U.S. VIRGIN IS.

PACIFIC OCEAN

EQUATOR

AMERICAN SAMOA

Map Key
National Park

Albers Conic Equal-Area Projection
200 mi
200 km

EASTERN COAST & FOREST PARKS

The map shows the following locations:

CANADA
U.S.

Lake Michigan
Lake Huron
Lake Ontario
Lake Erie
Ohio

MICHIGAN
MAINE
VERMONT
NEW HAMPSHIRE
NEW YORK
MASSACHUSETTS
RHODE ISLAND
CONNECTICUT

ACADIA NATIONAL PARK

INDIANA
OHIO
PENNSYLVANIA
NEW JERSEY
MARYLAND
DELAWARE

WEST VIRGINIA
SHENANDOAH NATIONAL PARK

KENTUCKY
VIRGINIA

MAMMOTH CAVE NATIONAL PARK

TENNESSEE
NORTH CAROLINA

GREAT SMOKY MOUNTAINS NATIONAL PARK

SOUTH CAROLINA

ATLANTIC OCEAN

ALABAMA
GEORGIA

FLORIDA

Gulf of Mexico

200 mi
200 km
N

EVERGLADES NATIONAL PARK
DRY TORTUGAS NATIONAL PARK

BAHAMAS

The sun rises over grass not far from the Anhinga Trail in Everglades National Park, Florida.

▶ LOCATION **50 MILES SE OF BANGOR, MAINE**

▶ SIZE **75 SQUARE MILES**

▶ HIGHEST POINT **CADILLAC MOUNTAIN, 1,530 FEET**

▶ VISITORS **3,537,575 IN 2018**

▶ ESTABLISHED **1919**

ACADIA NATIONAL PARK

With its glacier-polished granite mountains and quartz-streaked schist on ocean shores surrounded by volcanic extrusions, Acadia showcases the continent's birth. Located in northern Maine, due west of Nova Scotia, the park boundaries enclose 60 percent of the lobster claw–shaped Mount Desert Island, alongside a patchwork of small towns. Separate park parcels lie to the east and south, on the mainland's Schoodic Peninsula and on the small Isle au Haut.

The 75-square-mile Acadia is ringed by sea cliffs and scenic drives, gouged out by glacial lakes and ocean bays, and covered by dense forests. On Cadillac Mountain, the continent's first sunrise can be seen from October through March. At sunrise or sunset, some visitors can bear witness to the fabled green flash, caused by light waves bending through the atmosphere.

As daylight illuminates Acadia National Park, its creation story can be read in the two most ancient rocks found along the shores of Mount Desert Island: green or gray schist and sandstone or siltstones. Over 500 million years ago during the Paleozoic era, the Iapetus Ocean—predecessor of the Atlantic—covered the

Built in the 1850s to guide wayward sailors to shore, Bass Harbor Lighthouse remains as the only lighthouse on Mount Desert Island.

region. After vast amounts of silt and earthen debris ran off from rivers and collected on the sea bottom, it was compressed, throughout the millennia, into sedimentary rock. Tectonic plate activity shifted, pushed, and superheated the rock, eventually transforming it into the metamorphic Ellsworth schist. Further river runoff and sedimentation atop that ocean floor layer created the Bar Harbor formation.

Four hundred million years ago, centuries of volcanic ash spewed over the Bar Harbor formation, ultimately hardening to create the Cranberry Isle series: lighter-colored and textured volcanic rocks. Along with the Ellsworth schist and Bar Harbor formation, the volcanic buildup formed the elongated, mini continent of Avalonia, which was then forced up against Laurentia (the early North American continent) by the continued movement of tectonic plates. This friction of moving landmasses created magma that then cooled into pink or gray granites.

Over the millennia, continued tectonic action shoved Laurentia into Africa and Eurasia, creating the supercontinent Pangaea. The region of Maine, centered amid Pangaea, was pushed toward the Equator and into a tropical climate. The forceful earth-building impacts of these continental shifts created and lifted the Appalachian Mountains as high as the Himalaya.

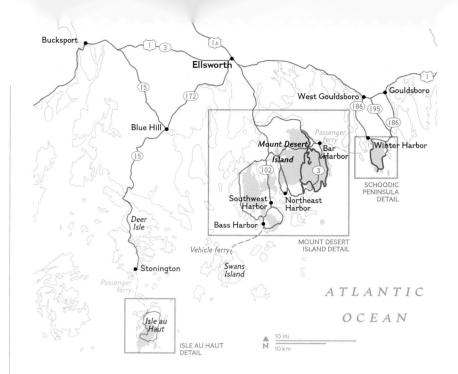

Two hundred million years ago—during the Mesozoic era and the age of dinosaurs—Pangaea moved north and broke in two. Europe drifted away from the nascent continent of North America, separated by the newly formed Atlantic Ocean. Half of the former Avalonia clung to the eastern seaboard, while the other half pulled apart

Every autumn in Acadia, seen from this aerial vantage point, foliage transforms the mixed hardwood forest, with its richest colors emerging in September and peaking in October.

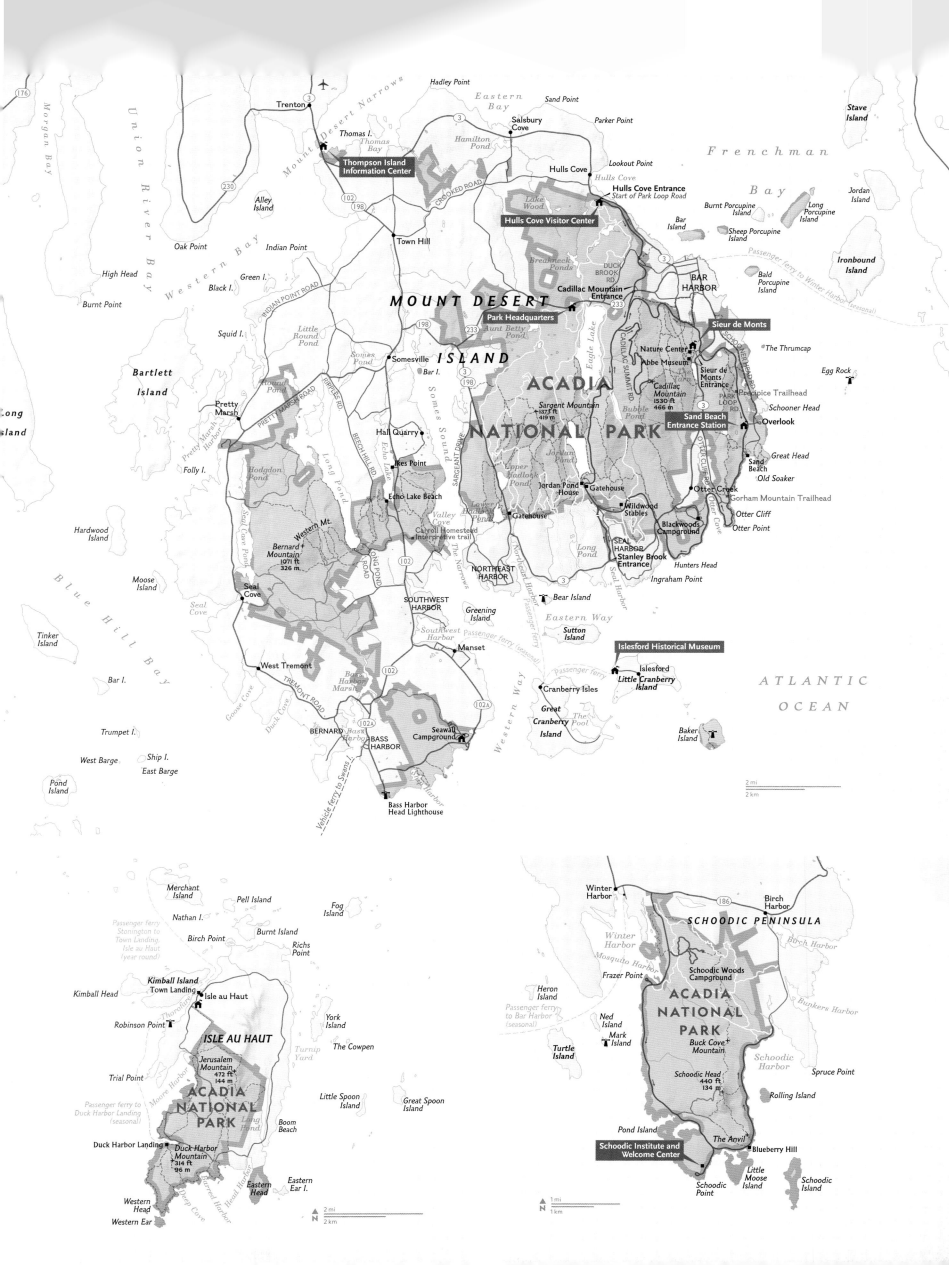

with Europe. Today, Acadia shares the same Avalonian rocks found in Scotland, while the Atlantic continues to widen an inch a year.

During the ensuing period of unconformity and time missing from the rock record, erosion wore away the mountaintops to expose the strata of Acadia several miles below. Then, during the Cenozoic era 65.5 million years ago, uplift created streams and valleys amid the high mountains of the yet-to-be-born island.

The final sculpting of this mainland ridge along the sea began over the last three million years as a succession of ice sheets moved south, flowing under the pressure of their own weight and covering the region under a mile of ice. Sea level dropped 330 feet. Soil and surface rocks were carried away and deposited elsewhere as till, while the ice shaped the land as if it were putty. The ice compressed and rounded off the park's mountaintops, scooped out lake beds, polished the bedrock granite, scratched striations, and gouged in crescent-shaped "chatter" marks.

During the final Wisconsin glaciation 18,000 years ago, the ice slowly began melting throughout Maine. As it receded several thousand years later, the land rose, relieved of the ice fields' crushing, unfathomable weight. Temperatures rose and the sea invaded,

LEFT: **Frenchman Bay** and the Porcupine Islands are part of the view from the top of Cadillac Mountain. At 1,530 feet, Cadillac is the tallest mountain both in the park and along the East Coast.

BELOW: **Tremendous geologic forces** formed Acadia's striking landscape more than 500 million years ago. The park's rich geologic history is recorded in the bedrock—from wavy, light and dark gray layers of Ellsworth schist, the oldest known rock in the Mount Desert region, to Cadillac Mountain, which boasts the largest body of granite on the island.

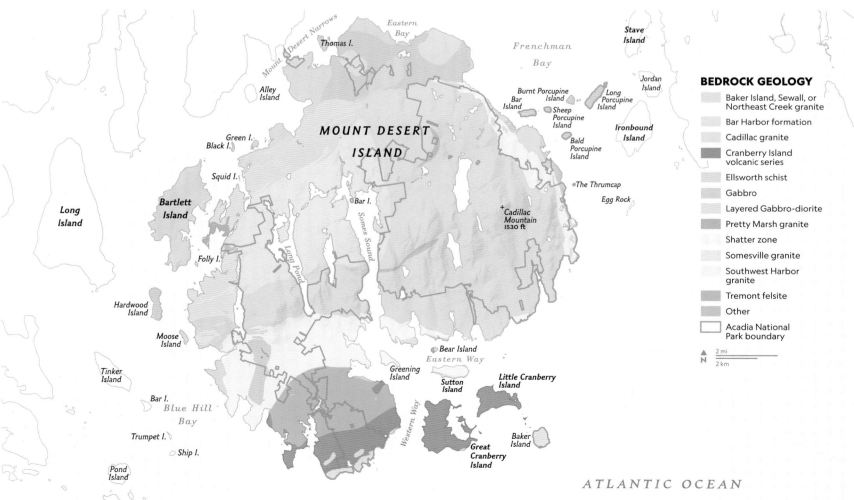

BEDROCK GEOLOGY

- Baker Island, Sewall, or Northeast Creek granite
- Bar Harbor formation
- Cadillac granite
- Cranberry Island volcanic series
- Ellsworth schist
- Gabbro
- Layered Gabbro-diorite
- Pretty Marsh granite
- Shatter zone
- Somesville granite
- Southwest Harbor granite
- Tremont felsite
- Other
- Acadia National Park boundary

covering the lowlands and rendering mountains into islands. Mount Desert Island itself would then be separated from the mainland.

Plants and animals colonized the bare landscape, while rivers carved new drainage paths. As the land rebounded, greened, and weathered, 5,000 years ago the first humans—known as Red Paint People—began to inhabit the Maine coast, leaving behind piles of shells.

Meanwhile, the slough and polish of erosion continued to shape the land. Evidence of thousands of years of storm-driven ocean forces can be seen today along the shore in cliff fissures, sea caves, and sea stacks. Farther inland, the bulldozing power of the glaciers can be viewed in left-behind "erratic" boulders, moraine piles, and U-shaped valleys. The many signposts marking this geologic wonder world helped inspire the creation of Acadia National Park.

In the legislation leading to the original Sieur de Monts National Monument in July 1916, Congress cited the great scientific interest in its geology, topography, fauna, and flora. The proclamation establishing the monument advised unauthorized people "not to appropriate, injure, destroy, or remove any of the features or objects included within the boundaries."

The monument was also created for its historical significance. In 1604, French explorers Sieur de Monts and Samuel de Champlain landed here and claimed most of Maine and the Canadian Maritimes as a French colony. They called it Acadia, meaning "heaven on earth."

"It is very high and cleft in places," Champlain wrote in his journal, "giving it the appearance from the sea of seven or eight mountains one alongside the other. The tops of them are bare of trees, because

there is nothing there but rocks." He named it Isles des Monts Déserts. French maps showed their Acadia colony in the country of "New France"—16 years before the pilgrims landed at nearby Plymouth Rock. Jesuits arrived on the island and established the first French mission in America, baptizing the local Wabanaki people, until a British warship promptly destroyed their fort.

At the time of French settlement, four different tribes—Passamaquoddy, Penobscot, Micmac, and Maliseet people, collectively known as the Wabanaki or "People of the Dawn Land"—lived in conical shelters and paddled birchbark canoes. They called Mount Desert Island's steep topography *Pemetic,* the "sloping land." Archaeological remains show that the Wabanaki wintered on the island, took advantage of shellfish and spring salmon runs, and then moved inland for the summers.

Private ownership began in the latter 17th century as Antoine de la Mothe Cadillac (who later founded the city of Detroit) claimed Mount Desert Island, which was eventually lost to the English and then sold to American settlers after the Revolutionary War. As homesteaders and farmers arrived, the island also prospered with lumbering, fishing, and shipbuilding.

By the mid-19th century, artists and journalists attracted the island's tourism industry. Mount Desert Island became known as a wealthy summer retreat for prominent millionaires who would define preservation of the island's natural ecosystem. Most notably, to leave behind the noisy clamor of the city, they banned cars for half a dozen years and mapped out a system of elegant roads

With its famously clear water, Jordan Pond is hemmed in by mountains, including two rounded peaks called the Bubbles, and the forested, granite ridgelines of Penobscot Mountain to the west and Pemetic Mountain to the east. Acadia's tallest peak, Cadillac Mountain looms just beyond, providing views of the evergreen- and rock-ringed lake below.

PARK BOUNDARY EVOLUTION

- 1916
- 1929
- 1986
- Present

5 mi
5 km

ABOVE: **Built by** Acadia's first superintendent, George B. Dorr, the Spring House at Sieur de Monts Spring captures the spirit of early park proponents.

LEFT: **The first national park** created from private lands gifted to the public, Acadia originated as Sieur de Monts National Monument in 1916. Three years later, President Wilson signed the act establishing Lafayette National Park, and in 1929, the park was renamed Acadia. An act of Congress in 1986 formally established the park boundary.

designed for horse-driven carriages and a slower way of life.

By 1913, George Dorr—who had worked with several influential islanders to conceptualize, advocate, and save land for a public park—offered 6,000 acres to the government. President Wilson proclaimed it a monument a month before the Organic Act created the National Park Service in August 1916. Three years later, on the same February 26 that Grand Canyon became a national park, President Wilson proclaimed the land Lafayette National Park, renaming it after the Frenchman who advocated American independence. Dorr became its first superintendent.

Meanwhile John D. Rockefeller, Jr., whose generosity infused many early parks, had already donated thousands of acres to the park and begun building 57 miles of carriage stone roads, quarried from the ancient granite foundations of the island. Designed to preserve the sanctity of this landscape, these 16-foot-wide auto-free roads were engineered with three layers of rock, undercut by stone culverts, and run alongside wide drainage ditches. Retaining walls were built to protect hillsides and trees, and rather than flattening hillsides, Rockefeller graded the roads with gradual inclines, taking advantage of natural contours and scenic views. Laborers installed huge granite blocks—later called Rockefeller's Teeth—as guardrails. Stonemasons spent years building 17 large granite bridges to span rivers, streams, and gullies. Finally, Rockefeller landscaped the roads with native ferns and blueberry bushes.

It took Rockefeller's laborers 27 years to finish the sinuous road network—now used by horseback riders, bicyclists, and hikers. As legend has it, Rockefeller told Superintendent Dorr that, for what it cost him, the roads could have been constructed of diamonds. Nonetheless, these carriage and later motor roads came to exemplify the National Park Service ideal of public access through aesthetic passages that minimize impact to the landscape and encourage drivers to appreciate surrounding native flora and fauna. As Acadia grew more popular, a set of approved motor roads would eventually cut down vehicle traffic through the use of free Park Service buses— yet another model implemented in parks throughout the country.

Dorr continued to acquire land; Rockefeller continued to donate. In 1929, the national park was renamed Acadia and expanded with the inclusion of Schoodic Peninsula, north of Mount Desert Island. Two years later, the Cadillac Mountain Summit Road was completed.

To keep the inevitable automobile off his sculpted carriage roads, Rockefeller spent 19 years building the Park Loop Road. Designed by the famed landscape architect Frederick Law Olmsted, Jr., the road winds around the outside of the island and takes in some of its most spectacular views.

Disaster struck in the parched October of 1947, when a month-long fire swept through Maine, consuming 10,000 acres of the park and hundreds of the island's private mansions and cottages. Conifers in the eastern park were devastated, but the natural regrowth of

THE PARK'S TALLEST MOUNTAIN, CADILLAC, IS THE HIGHEST PEAK ON THE ATLANTIC COAST, AND FROM OCTOBER TO MARCH IS THE FIRST PLACE IN AMERICA TO SEE THE SUN RISE.

deciduous trees allowed Dorr to successfully reintroduce trapped-out beavers that subsist on birch and aspen.

Thirty-seven mammal species—including black bears, bobcats, coyotes, raccoons, foxes, minks, muskrats, and white-tailed deer—are found in Acadia. Whales and porpoises can be seen blowing offshore, while otters and seals play in the waves. Along 40 miles of seashore are colorful beaches of rounded rocks, broken shells, or pink sand.

Relative to its size, the park supports a huge diversity of plant life. Alongside the natural spring, called Sieur de Monts, the Wild Gardens of Acadia showcases over 400 indigenous plant species found throughout the park, while the Abbe Museum delves into past and present-day Wabanaki culture.

Below these plants along cobbled-rock shores that hum with surf, or above the tree line on windswept mountaintops plastered with granite, Mount Desert Island mirrors the expanse of time. Whether through colliding continents, volcanic eruptions, or the inundation of massive ice sheets, the ages have been at work on Acadia National Park, molding the island and humbling its visitors. ■

George B. Dorr stops on the Beachcroft Path on Huguenot Head. Dorr and friends like John D. Rockefeller, Jr., campaigned for and then expanded New England's only national park.

▶ LOCATION **30 MILES W OF MIAMI, FLORIDA**

▶ SIZE **2,410 SQUARE MILES**

▶ HIGHEST POINT **GROSSMAN HAMMOCK, 8 FEET**

▶ VISITORS **597,124 IN 2018**

▶ ESTABLISHED **1947**

EVERGLADES NATIONAL PARK

t's not commonly known that the Everglades is the third largest national park in the contiguous United States, within a Delaware-size wilderness 80 miles long and 50 miles wide. Draining Lake Okeechobee to its north and covered by ocean on the southern tip of Florida, the Everglades is a limitless-looking expanse of brackish mangroves, cypress swamps, grass marshes, pinelands, and hardwood hammocks; it's the first national park created solely for its biodiverse (rather than scenic) wonders. In recognition of its distinctiveness, Everglades was designated as a World Heritage site and an international biosphere reserve.

The early Pay-Hai-o-Kee (Grass Water) name for the region came from the Seminoles in the 1700s and was shown on a 1773 British map above its newly given "River Glades" name. In 1823, a surveyor first used "Everglades" on a military map and the name stuck, although many local naturalists now refer to the park and its surrounding ecosystem as the river of grass.

The park is also known for its alligators and the largest concentration of wading birds in North America. But human-related pressures including water diversions, rising sea level, and invasive

Life in the Everglades has long been defined by its water. When Lake Okeechobee would overflow in the wet season, it made a river that flowed through the park's saw grass marshes, forming what locals call the river of grass.

species have shrunken and irrevocably changed the region. Repeatedly smashed by hurricanes and a lack of restorative funding, the Everglades is one of the most endangered sanctuaries in the National Park System, making its expanse of living treasures more striking and precious than ever.

The Everglades was built upon its ancient, limestone foundation. Two hundred million years ago, Florida was pulled off of Africa as the supercontinent Pangaea separated and opened up the Atlantic Ocean. During the ensuing Cretaceous period, Florida existed below a shallow ocean, while fluctuating sea levels compressed calcium carbonate, sand, and shells into ancient limestone formations later covered by impermeable sedimentary rock and now found deep underground.

As limestone accrued over millennia, the Florida peninsula emerged from the Atlantic. A massive river began to flow south out of what is now Lake Okeechobee in central Florida, running above and below the tilted and permeable limestone floor of the Everglades.

As the continental ice fields melted during the Pleistocene, the sea rose and the resulting back pressure of ocean against aquifer

Still water catches sunrise at Sweet Bay Pond, home to an abundance of fish and wading birds such as ibises, roseate spoonbills, egrets, and herons.

GULF OF

MEXICO

FLORIDA KEYS NATIONAL MARINE SANCTUARY

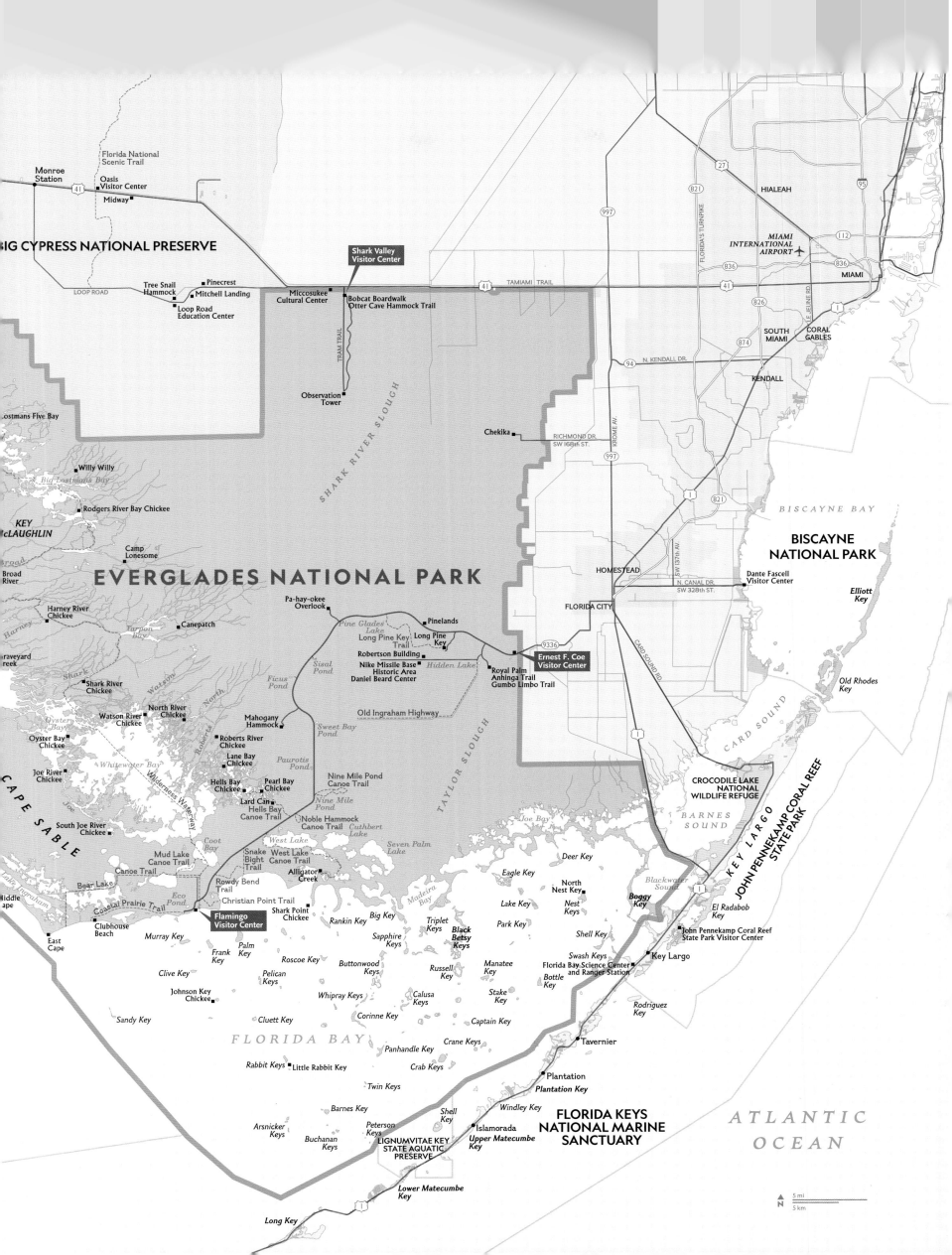

discharges slowed the big river. This changing hydrology, along with a buildup of peat atop the limestone 5,000 years ago, caused the shallow, 60-mile-wide, 100-mile-long river to crawl through the Everglades at a quarter mile a day. The water that drained or held in the deeper porous limestone layers became south Florida's freshwater supply: the Biscayne aquifer. Elsewhere the invisible river ran through its vast limestone basement into Florida Bay and the Gulf of Mexico.

Depending on the ebb and flow of rain through wet and dry seasons, the mineral-rich Okeechobee water—fed by rivers—can take years to reach the sea. This porous, outsize limestone artery channels the lifeblood for the myriad plant life and animals that thrive in Everglades National Park.

In early April 1513, the conquistador Juan Ponce de León arrived and named La Florida for Easter (Pascua Florida in Spanish). A month

Taken circa 1910, this photo of Seminoles in their dugout canoe hints at life's dependence on water. Seminoles who were not forced from the area in the 19th century lived subsistence lifestyles.

later, he met the resident Calusa ("fierce people"), descendants of Paleo-Indians who had inhabited the Everglades region for 12,000 years. Their shell middens—built from waste dumps into functional dry ridges reaching a dozen feet above the highest damp ground—are still found throughout the park. The other residents, the Tequesta people, built still passable canoe trails in the park, one of them 20 feet wide and several miles long. By the 1700s, European diseases had wiped out both cultures—yet not before a Calusa arrow killed Ponce de León.

Three hundred years later, the American military waged a ruthless, protracted war against the Seminole descendants of the Creek people, who fled other southern states and came to Florida to raise cattle. By 1859, nearly 6,000 Native Americans were either killed or forcibly moved to Oklahoma reservations, while several hundred survivors refused to surrender and retreated deep into the Everglades.

In the early 1900s, the remaining Seminoles—peaceably living subsistence lifestyles—watched in shock as developers began diverting Lake Okeechobee with massive dredge and fill projects. They dug canals and then changed the vital flow of water into the Everglades by filling in the wetlands with canal or ocean dredging. Hunters decimated animal populations, while agriculture, lumber, and oil development further desiccated or polluted the region.

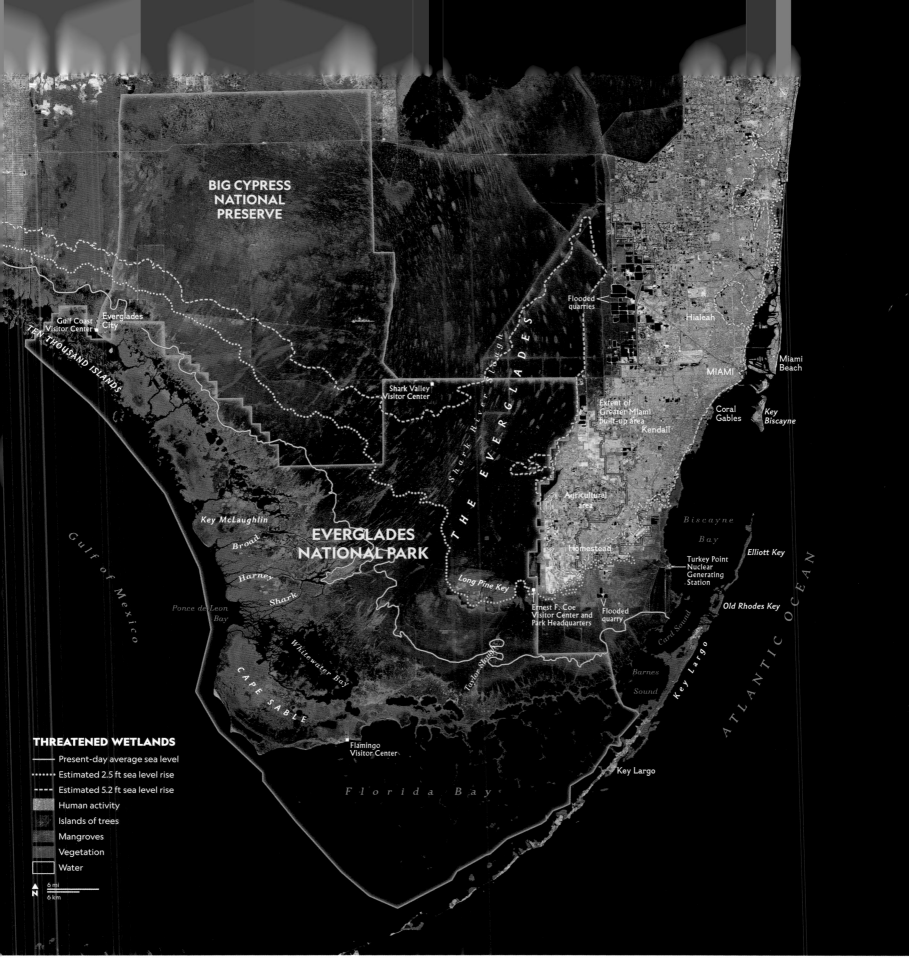

BIG CYPRESS
NATIONAL
PRESERVE

Gulf Coast
Visitor Center
Everglades
City

TEN THOUSAND ISLANDS

Flooded
quarries

Hialeah

MIAMI

Miami
Beach

Shark Valley
Visitor Center

THE EVERGLADES

Shark River Slough

Extent of
Greater Miami
built-up area
Kendall

Coral
Gables

Key
Biscayne

Key McLaughlin

Broad

EVERGLADES
NATIONAL PARK

Agricultural
area

Biscayne
Bay

Gulf of Mexico

Harney

Shark

Long Pine Key

Homestead

Turkey Point
Nuclear
Generating
Station

Elliott Key

Old Rhodes Key

Ponce de Leon
Bay

Ernest F. Coe
Visitor Center and
Park Headquarters

Flooded
quarry

Whitewater Bay

Card Sound

Key Largo

ATLANTIC OCEAN

CAPE SABLE

Taylor Slough

Barnes

Sound

THREATENED WETLANDS

—— Present-day average sea level
······ Estimated 2.5 ft sea level rise
------ Estimated 5.2 ft sea level rise
▨ Human activity
▨ Islands of trees
▨ Mangroves
▨ Vegetation
▢ Water

Flamingo
Visitor Center

Key Largo

Florida Bay

N
6 mi
6 km

In 1934, after more than a decade of preservation advocacy by journalists, biologically astute conservationists, and Park Service scientists, the 73rd Congress passed an act to establish Everglades National Park. As with other parks legislated after the Great Depression, public money could not be spent on the land purchase, so "approximately two thousand square miles" had to be donated, and the park would not be accepted until the state gave up the land "in a form satisfactory to the Secretary of the Interior." Congressional lawmakers, partially atoning for past injustices, wrote that the act could not "lessen any existing rights of the Seminole Indians which

Using false-color infrared satellite imagery, this map highlights parts of Florida's famed wetlands that could be dramatically altered by 2100. The Everglades are pinched between a burgeoning Miami to the east and encroaching saltwater to the west. Agricultural pollution from as far as 50 miles north harms the wetlands. Scientists say sea levels could rise 2.5 to 5.2 feet by the end of the century, causing much of the freshwater marsh to be inundated by saltwater.

are not in conflict with the purposes for which the Everglades National Park is created."

It took 14 years over the bureaucratic hiatus of World War II for the park to finally be funded and dedicated in 1947. Caught in the

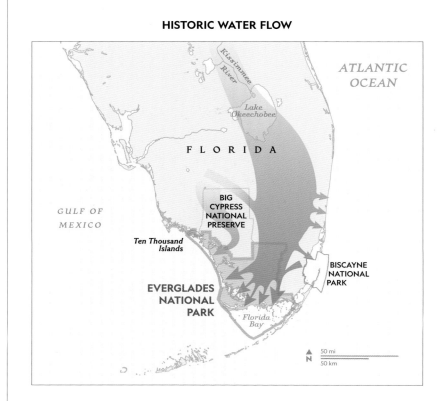

HISTORIC WATER FLOW

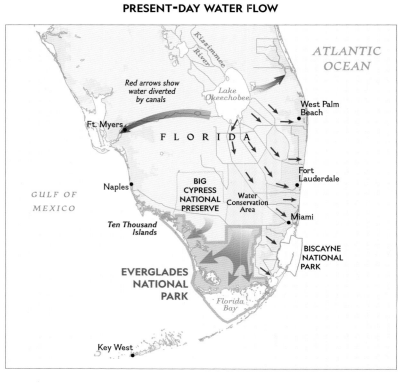

PRESENT-DAY WATER FLOW

ABOVE: **Dredged, dammed, and drained** for over 100 years, the Everglades ecosystem is imperiled. Man-made systems divert water from natural wetlands, reducing freshwater flow in the greater ecosystem, which extends south from the Kissimmee River to Florida Bay. A restoration plan aims to bring life back to the Everglades by mimicking the historic natural flow of the water.

OPPOSITE: **Walter Weber's painting** of snowy egrets flaunting their plumage among the mangroves—one of the many mating displays of the park's 300-plus bird species

postwar whirl of nation building rather than conservation, Congress mandated that same year that 1,400 miles of canals be built to stop flooding and divert Okeechobee water to cities booming on the Florida coasts. In 1948, 750 square miles utilizing Everglades water south of Lake Okeechobee became sugar plantations, and since then, the agricultural region has continued to expand.

An unprecedented population spike in 20th-century Florida showed how continuing development could strain resources and threaten the park habitats. Finally, counterefforts were initiated.

In 1962, construction of a canal was authorized to deliver water to the park. A half dozen years later, it was modified, but it wasn't enough. By 1971, with half the original Everglades region ditched or dried up, ecosystems were failing. The Florida panther and the iconic alligator—both listed as endangered in a 1967 law that predated the Endangered Species Act—almost disappeared due to loss of habitat and hunting. Also called the mountain lion or cougar, the Florida panther is the only known breeding panther in the eastern United States. Since listing the species, the U.S. Fish and Wildlife Service (USFWS) began working with the park, the state, and other private partners to establish a sustainable population of the Florida panther.

Meanwhile, Congress guaranteed that a minimum amount of water had to be returned to the park each month. In 1974, the 1,139 square miles of Big Cypress National Preserve was created adjacent to the northwest corner of Everglades; in 1979, 168 square miles were added to the park. Alligator populations rebounded, but panthers remain on the list created by the 1973 Endangered Species Act. Under the most recent recovery plan, the USFWS will consider "delisting" the panther when three separate populations of at least 240 mature animals are established, along with sufficient habitat to support the panthers. In an attempt to improve water in the Ever-

glades, a 1994 bill—the Everglades Forever Act—succeeded in significantly dropping phosphorus levels in the water. And as for the Seminoles, after decades of legal battle, the United States awarded $10 million to the tribe in land and water claims, for what the Seminoles called "unconscionable acts."

Yet even as protective efforts continue, the subtropical wilderness—that environmental activist Marjory Stoneman Douglas famously called *The Everglades: River of Grass* in her 1947 book—remains at risk. The million-plus people who visit the park each year know that this tranquil haven is a delicate, singular world. The plants and animals within—from the dainty yellow- and black-striped zebra longwing butterfly to the sea grass–munching manatees—rely on a pristine habitat just as patrons of the park seek refuge in its undisturbed beauty.

More than any national park, people associate the Everglades with its colorful birds—more than 300 species' worth. Seldom seen birds such as flamingos, purple gallinules, storks, snail kites, roseate spoonbills, and American bitterns are regularly observed and easily photographed from January through March. The Anhinga Trail, in particular, has world-renowned bird-watching vantage points.

A **Burmese python** coils around a man's arm. Rarely seen, the lurking predators squeeze their prey—whether small deer or rodents—to death.

As for water trails, the Everglades offers a tropical version of Voyageurs National Park for canoeists and kayakers (only low-powered motorboats are allowed in the Everglades). The 99-mile Wilderness Waterway, part of the 1,515-mile Florida Circumnavigational Saltwater Paddling Trail—a marine version of the Appalachian Trail—is the most stellar getaway among dozens of paddling routes and remote campsites. Connecting Flamingo and Everglades City, the waterway navigates twisting creeks, rivers, and bays, and takes about eight to 10 days to complete. Secluded sand beaches and *chickees*—elevated wooden platforms along the water—provide primitive campsites.

Boaters and anglers throughout the park commonly observe manatees, crocodiles, snapping turtles, alligators, sharks, and snakes. Swimming, of course, is discouraged.

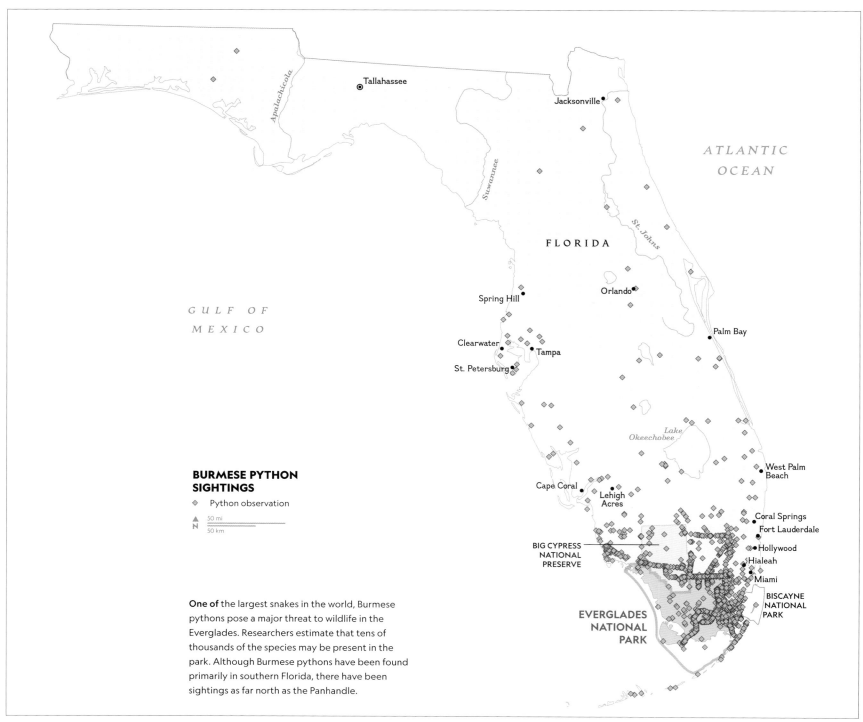

BURMESE PYTHON SIGHTINGS

◇ Python observation

50 mi
50 km

One of the largest snakes in the world, Burmese pythons pose a major threat to wildlife in the Everglades. Researchers estimate that tens of thousands of the species may be present in the park. Although Burmese pythons have been found primarily in southern Florida, there have been sightings as far north as the Panhandle.

Cutting through saw grass marshes and tangled mangroves, the Anhinga Trail is a popular place to observe alligators, turtles, wood storks, and many other avian species.

On foot, hikers ready to meet mosquitoes can follow trails through a wealth of habitats, accessible from the eastern entrance in Homestead, Florida, and the northern entrance near the Shark Valley Visitor Center. Boardwalks meander by sweeping vistas of grasses; into shaded hardwood hammock stands, found at slightly higher elevations; through coastal prairie strewn with buttonwoods; and past dense tangles of mangrove trees.

All dynamically linked to one another, the park's distinct ecosystems include marine and estuarine, mangrove, cypress, freshwater marsh, pine rockland, and tropical hardwood hammocks. From domes of cypress trees rising from standing water filled with saw grass to sea grass and algae along the marine bottom, this biodiversity is a world-renowned marvel.

And yet up to a quarter of the total native plant species within the park have been listed by the state of Florida as threatened, endangered, or commercially exploited. Chief among the threats are aliens—invasive or non-native plant and animal species. Unfortunately, aliens—such as the 22 species of exotic fish that devour or compete with native

fish species—cannot be easily subdued. Relatively safe within the confines of a park closed to hunting and filled with protected wildlife to prey upon, many of these animals or plants have a competitive advantage. The Burmese python, for example, has become an apex predator, known to kill white-tailed deer and alligators.

Studies have shown that great numbers of nocturnal mammals native to the park could be regularly observed at night before the year 2000, while surveys between 2003 and 2011 showed that the number of rabbits, raccoons, opossums, and bobcats dropped 90 percent or more after the pythons arrived in the Everglades. The species may have been liberated in 1992, when Hurricane Andrew devastated zoos, pet shops, and exotic animal refuges—allowing the snakes to slither and swim back into the wild.

Invasive plants—arriving by way of experimental agriculture, storms, or passing vehicles, among other chance circumstances—are

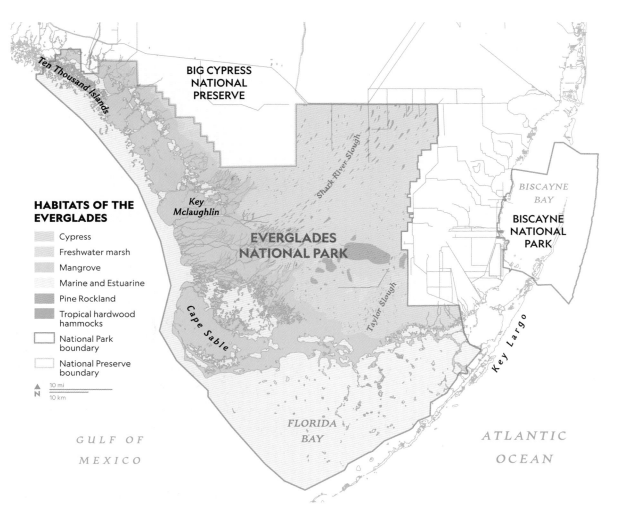

HABITATS OF THE EVERGLADES

- Cypress
- Freshwater marsh
- Mangrove
- Marine and Estuarine
- Pine Rockland
- Tropical hardwood hammocks
- National Park boundary
- National Preserve boundary

10 mi
10 km

BIG CYPRESS NATIONAL PRESERVE

Ten Thousand Islands

Shark-River Slough

Key Mclaughlin

EVERGLADES NATIONAL PARK

BISCAYNE BAY

BISCAYNE NATIONAL PARK

Taylor Slough

Cape Sable

Key Largo

FLORIDA BAY

GULF OF MEXICO

ATLANTIC OCEAN

LEFT: **Slight variations** in elevation, underlying rock, and water flow make the Everglades a spectacular mosaic of ecosystems: Cypress trees and wetland plants thrive in flooded conditions; broad, low-lying marsh channels freshwater slowly through grass; mangroves grow in coastal channels and rivers where saltwater and freshwater intermix; and marine and estuarine waters span from the Ten Thousand Islands to Florida Bay. Higher, drier areas accommodate dense forest islands with tropical and temperate trees, and—along an eastern limestone ridge—more open pine rockland blanketed with saw palmetto.

BELOW: **A stunning array** of life flourishes in the park, from tiny pink shrimp to elegant great egrets and yellow rat snakes. Native animals rely on the natural communities that the Everglades' unique hydrology creates: The green sea turtle, an endangered species, feeds on sea grasses and algae and warms itself near the surface of shallow waters. Majestic roseate spoonbills nest during winter in mangroves, trees, or shrubs—usually five to 15 feet above ground or water. A well-adapted swimmer and apex predator, the American alligator thrives in freshwater rivers, lakes, swamps, and marshes. The elusive Florida panther prefers hardwood hammocks and pinelands for resting, denning, and hunting white-tailed deer, raccoon, and other small mammals. But development outside the park, a changing climate, and invasive species put this delicate web of life at risk.

an even more epic challenge. Since Florida rose from the sea and the wetlands formed 5,000 years ago, 1,301 native plant species—both tropical and subtropical—have thrived in the Everglades. Of all the parks in the continental United States, Everglades has the highest diversity of orchids. Whitewater lilies, purple thistle, and coral beans are among the hundreds of species of wildflowers. Cacti and succulents can also be spotted low to the ground in sandy soils. Lichens tinge forested areas with patches of green, yellow, and even red or white. Reaching upward are tree species as varied as the iconic royal palm, soldierwoods (named for the gunfire-like sound of their exploding fruits), and slash pines.

The invasive flora of greatest concern is the Brazilian peppertree, aka the Florida holly, regrettably introduced by landscapers outside of the park as an ornamental. The Brazilian peppertree has now spread to tens of thousands of acres within the park, crowding out native plant life and spreading rapidly as birds eat from the trees and defecate the seed berries as they fly throughout South Florida.

In most cases, native flora depend on the land's dynamic hydrology, as well as restorative forest fires and seed-spreading hurricanes. Restoration is difficult in this lush jungle of wetlands, but one former agricultural site in the park is being carefully replanted with only native species that might thrive over the invaders.

SOUTHERN FLORIDA IS THE LARGEST MANGROVE ECOSYSTEM IN THE WESTERN HEMISPHERE AND ONE OF ONLY SEVERAL PLACES WHERE AMERICA'S NATIVE ALLIGATORS AND CROCODILES COEXIST.

Climate change has also begun to alter the lowland park, surrounded on three sides by a warming and rising ocean. The freshwater marshes of Cape Sable, in the southwest Everglades, have been inundated with brackish water as ocean waters have risen over beaches and up man-made canals—now plugged up in an attempt to slow the sea. On the north and eastern edges of the park, other canals have been reengineered to keep freshwater in the Everglades, rather than to divert it.

Over the last half century in other park locations, as ocean levels have risen, park researchers have observed a consistent rise in freshwater sites inland. The surging ocean is now pushing into the ancient limestone foundations of South Florida, slowly supplanting the Biscayne aquifer with saltwater. Short of stopping climate change, running more freshwater into the Everglades could theoretically create a back pressure to repel the ocean.

In the year 2000, Congress authorized the multibillion-dollar Comprehensive Everglades Restoration Plan (CERP) as a strategy to replumb the Everglades as the effects of climate change mount. The catch is that funding has slowed and rising saltwater could outpace the decades-long plan. But CERP has already begun to increase freshwater storage, improve water quality, and reestablish the natural water flow through the greater Everglades ecosystem. If successful, these efforts will help protect subterranean aquifers from saltwater intrusion and delay the impacts of sea-level rise. Still, additional measures will be needed to protect this remarkable nexus of land and water, where pink roseate spoonbills soar above frolicking manatees. The Everglades shelters that rare park collision of temperate and tropical: alligators sunning alongside crocodiles, or Virginia live oaks growing in concert with red-barked gumbo limbo trees. ■

Tropical Hardwood Hammocks

Rat snake

Snail kite

Freshwater Marsh

White-tailed deer

Wood stork

Tricolored heron

Purple gallinule

Florida panther

Cooter

Florida gar

Largemouth bass

▷ LOCATION **75 MILES SW OF WASHINGTON, D.C.**

▷ SIZE **310 SQUARE MILES**

▷ HIGHEST POINT **HAWKSBILL MOUNTAIN, 4,051 FEET**

▷ VISITORS **1,264,880 IN 2018**

▷ ESTABLISHED **1935**

SHENANDOAH NATIONAL PARK

Enveloping a section of the Blue Ridge Mountains in western Virginia, Shenandoah is a narrow, 70-mile-long, fish-bone-shaped park. More than 60 of its misty blue peaks exceed 3,000 feet, rising more than a half mile above sloping ground to the east and Shenandoah Valley to the west. The renowned Skyline Drive winds 105 miles along the ancient granite crest of the automobile-friendly park. With 75 scenic pullouts, it's popular during the spectacular fall foliage.

The more moderately trafficked Appalachian Trail runs 105 miles through the park, along with another 400 miles of hiking and horseback trails. Lush with plant and animal life, including hundreds of black bears and thousands of white-tailed deer, Shenandoah's restored, stream-cut wilderness is also famous for its trout fishing.

Nearly half of the park is legislated wilderness, protected in its natural state, without motor vehicle use. Unlike western parks, Shenandoah was created entirely from private, nongovernment land, resulting in an uncommon habitat island of restored wilderness, surrounded by increasing urbanization. Private lands border most of its 345-mile boundary.

As if wrapped in a haze, the Blue Ridge Mountains emit their namesake hue as the trees release a hydrocarbon called isoprene to fight heat stress.

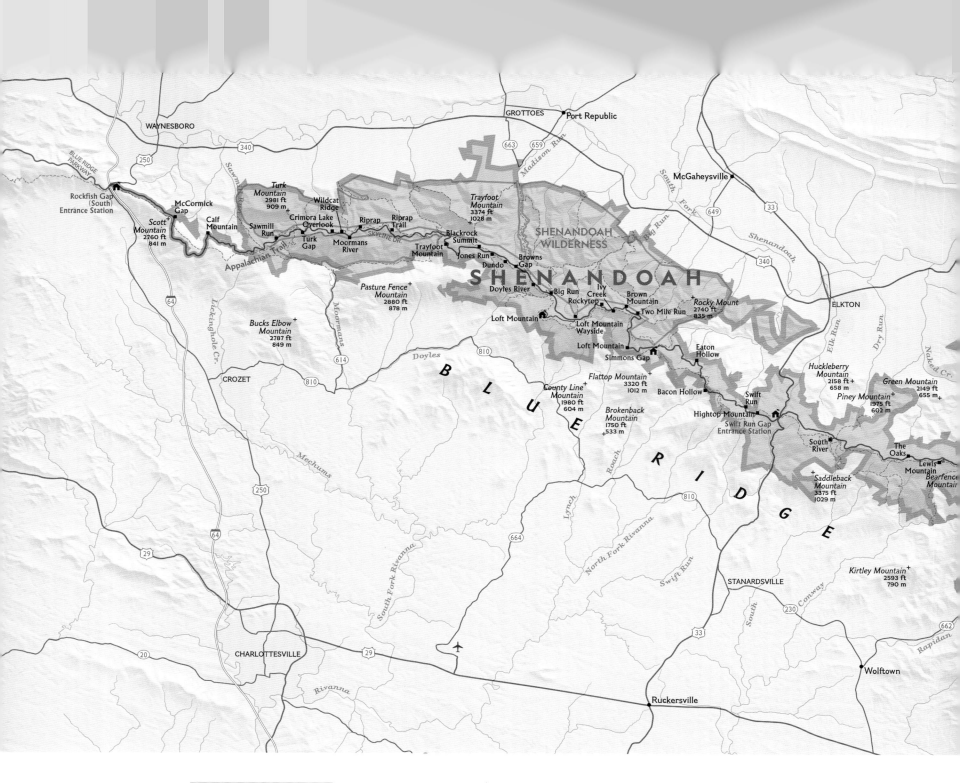

Although President Theodore Roosevelt created many parks on government lands in the American West, his support for an early Appalachian region park failed just after the turn of the 20th century. Once Lafayette (later named Acadia) National Park was carved out of Maine's private lands in 1919, a template arose for establishing parks on nongovernment lands. So, in 1926, President Calvin Coolidge authorized Shenandoah National Park. The challenge was that more than 5,000 parcels of private land existed in the proposed park and many owners were reluctant to leave.

Acquisition efforts crept along over the years, with the state of Virginia using the law of eminent domain to acquire property and then donate it to the park. For these property purchases, more than 24,000 Virginians pledged—through minimum six-dollar donations—in a "Buy an Acre" campaign that raised over one million dollars. The state legislature allocated another one million dollars. Even the newly elected President Herbert Hoover bought and developed a piece of property that he would eventually donate to the park. (During his tenure from 1929 to 1933, the land designated for other

new national parks and monuments increased by 40 percent.)

By 1929, the National Park Service director under Hoover, Horace M. Albright, began forcing residents—many without electricity and running water—to leave the proposed park boundaries. The controversy intensified as cabins were burned down to prevent squatters from returning. Two thousand residents left, mostly without protest and in fear of the government. Of the 197 owners who received money, only 34 were paid more than $2,000. Many homesteaders couldn't sell their land.

The state of Virginia, however, purchased two dozen farms outside the park and gave them to the needy. One hundred and seventy-two families were placed in new homes on land, but these relocated descendants of British and German immigrants were unaccustomed to paying mortgages and other bills that came with the luxuries of running water and electricity. Within two decades, none of these original mountain families were still occupying a resettlement house.

By 1933, hobbled by a lack of funds to buy land, the prospective new park had to shrink its proposed boundaries by two-thirds. Finally, the day after Christmas 1935, Shenandoah National Park was established—but it was not opened to visitors for another half year.

Once the land was acquired, Congress appropriated over one million dollars to finish the construction of the curving Skyline Drive, with the aid of low-cost Civilian Conservation Corps workers.

An 85-year-old, local mountaineer—who sat on the platform with President Franklin D. Roosevelt during the 1936 park dedication ceremony—said, "I ain't so crazy about leavin' these hills but I never believed in bein' ag'in the Government. I signed everythin' they asked me."

The National Park Service listed 43 families as "aged and especially meritorious" people who could live out their lives inside the park after selling their land. The last resident, Annie Shenk, had lived alone in her park cabin since her husband died in 1943. In 1976, nearly 90 years old, she left Shenandoah for a nursing home. Park rangers had looked after her for 33 years, hauling in her firewood during the winters.

"Removal of the mountain people," the first park employee and historian Darwin Lambert wrote, "to return the land to nature's way after more than 300 years of heavy exploitation by white people was an episode rare in history. Rare, too, is the half-century regeneration of wilderness. Where else has the supposedly inevitable trend toward

The postmaster for Old Rag village, settled before the park was established, rests on a wood fence along what would become a popular mountain hike.

civility, toward more consumption of earth's resources, been so completely reversed?"

From the early 1700s settlement to the creation of the park two centuries later, hunting, grazing, logging, and farming denuded the Blue Ridge Mountains of trees and undergrowth. Chestnut trees, stricken by blight, lay fallen or horizontally propped and strewn throughout the thinning forests that remained. By 1940, 85 percent of the park was forested, with new-growth chestnut oak and red hickory surrounding open ground; by the 1980s the park was almost completely forested. Today, oak and red hickory dominate the forest, along with poplar, spruce, and fir.

These forests also shelter over 1,400 species of vascular plants, found in varying habitats with over 3,500 feet in elevation gain. This includes abundant mosses, the occasional prickly pear cactus, innumerable herbs, shrubs, ferns, trillium flowers, blueberries, jack-in-the-pulpit, azaleas, and lady slipper orchids.

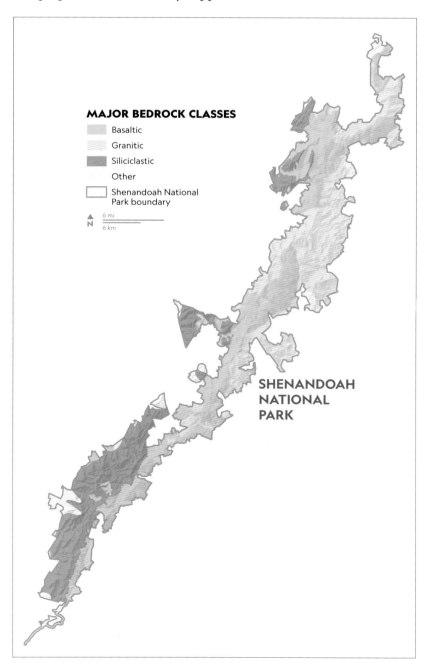

MAJOR BEDROCK CLASSES
- Basaltic
- Granitic
- Siliciclastic
- Other
- Shenandoah National Park boundary

6 mi
6 km
N

SHENANDOAH
NATIONAL
PARK

SKYLINE DRIVE PROVIDES ACCESS TO OVER 500 MILES OF HIKING TRAILS, INCLUDING THE APPALACHIAN TRAIL, WHICH ROUGHLY PARALLELS THE ROAD THROUGH THE PARK.

Fall's waning daylight and cooler weather transform the green canopy and forest floor into a riot of red, orange, and yellow leaves that typically peak in October. The views in Shenandoah are so popular, with the mountain slopes displaying the full sweep of hues, that the Park Service runs a weekly Fall Color Report during the season.

Yet amid all this beauty, plant poachers, invasive plant species, insects, excessive deer browsing, air pollution, and climate change plague Shenandoah. Between these threats and past settler activities, 5 percent of the park's forests remain "catastrophically disturbed"— according to a survey conducted by the park in 2009. The once abundant American chestnut tree, for example, can still be found in the park, but because of the blight, the trees die off before reaching maturity, without reproducing.

After 80 years closed to hunting, animal populations also recovered. This includes coyotes, skunks, raccoons, beavers, otters, woodchucks, foxes, and rabbits. Cougar sightings have been reported, but the once abundant elk, American bison, and eastern timber wolves are now gone.

As the wilds are restored and visitors continue to enjoy flora, fauna, and scenery, other threats are less visible. Of all national parks monitored for acid rain, Shenandoah receives among the highest

LEFT: **Three major bedrock classes** underlying Shenandoah National Park are exposed to some of the highest acidic deposition levels in the country. The geologic classes are arranged from the least sensitive to acidification (basaltic) to the most sensitive (siliciclastic).

OPPOSITE: **After years** of farming in the Shenandoah, the park is returning to its wild, natural state, home to a variety of trees and more than 1,000 species of vascular plants.

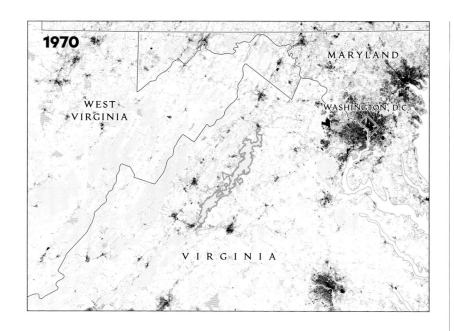

1970

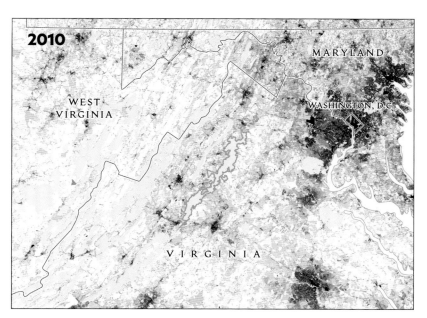

2010

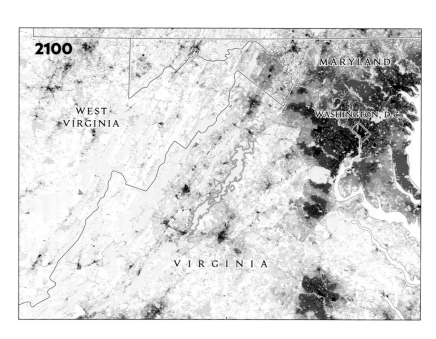

2100

HOUSING DENSITY OF THE MID-ATLANTIC

Low   High

☐ Shenandoah N.P. boundary

■ Commercial or industrial land

▨ Urban or regional park

░ Other land

▲N   25 mi / 25 km

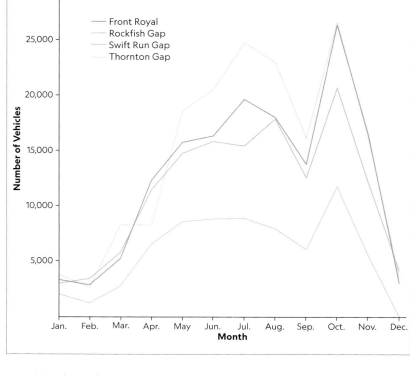

AVERAGE TRAFFIC COUNT BY ENTRANCE, 2018

— Front Royal
— Rockfish Gap
— Swift Run Gap
— Thornton Gap

Number of Vehicles

Month — Jan. Feb. Mar. Apr. May Jun. Jul. Aug. Sep. Oct. Nov. Dec.

ABOVE: **Meandering along** the crest of the Blue Ridge Mountains, Skyline Drive spans 105 miles between the northern entrance, Front Royal, and the southern entrance, Rockfish Gap. Weather permitting, traveling the length of the park takes roughly three hours—but that can vary depending on the amount of time spent along its 75 vistas. Year after year, the traffic along this national scenic byway peaks during the fall foliage.

LEFT: **A mere 75 miles** from the nation's capital, Shenandoah National Park is a nature sanctuary amid burgeoning development in the mid-Atlantic. Housing growth in the region is projected to swell by 2100, affirming the importance of protecting the park's pristine character.

measured sulfur dioxide and nitrogen oxide pollution. Research into the effects on soil, vegetation, and certain wildlife is ongoing.

Acid rain is caused by fossil fuel emissions—mostly from power plants—that are blown into park streams as sulfate precipitation, and occasionally, as dry particles. Since 1990 amendments to the Clean Air Act, total U.S. emissions have significantly reduced—from a high of 32 million tons in 1973, to less than 9 million tons by 2010. According to the Environmental Protection Agency, the eastern United States has decreased airborne sulfate concentrations 71 to 75 percent between 1989 and 1991 and 2014 and 2016.

Yet the problem remains: Years of acid accumulation prior to the Clean Air Act have left many already sensitive Shenandoah streams in a fragile state of recovery. Specifically, many park streams suffer from a loss of acid-neutralizing capacity that adversely affects fish and aquatic life. Although acid rain falls in the same concentrations across the park, researchers have found that the underlying bedrock partly determines the streams' danger to fish. Many other national parks are relatively unaffected by acid rain because of the presence of neutralizing limestone—but it's scant in Shenandoah's streams.

Basaltic, granitic, and siliciclastic are Shenandoah's three main bedrock types, each underlying roughly a third of the park. The basaltic rocks are best for neutralizing acid rain inputs; granitic rocks are intermediate; and siliciclastic rocks poor. Slopes also play a role:

Still popular in the park today, fly-fishing helped inspire politicians like President Herbert Hoover to preserve Shenandoah's waterways for future generations.

Steeper slopes generally prevent acid rain from being neutralized in streams. Of 231 park streams, 86 have limited acid-neutralizing capacity with values that could impact aquatic life.

And much is at stake: Shenandoah's clear, cold streams support 220 taxa of aquatic insects—from midges to mayflies. These in turn support 39 species of fish, including the native eastern brook trout; the rosyside, blacknose, and longnose dace; the mottled sculpin; the bluehead chub; and the fantail darter. For fishermen, just the names of these fish can summon a sense of delight and wonder.

It's fitting that an essential part of the park's stewardship mission is to protect water quality, partly so that visitors can enjoy it. Waterfall viewing is popular in Shenandoah. Forested trails lead hikers along gently cascading streams and past dozens of cascades—some feed cool, clear swimming holes—scattered throughout the park. Overall Run Falls' 93-foot drop is the longest, best seen after a heavy rainfall.

Another draw is hiking to the many exposed outcroppings of bedrock to take in park panoramas. At Old Rag Mountain, a nine-mile loop includes the huge granite boulders and spectacular views from the summit, while the climb several miles up the second highest mountain in the park, Little Stony Man, passes a rock climber's cliff and offers a spectacular view of the Shenandoah River.

More than 500 miles of trails hug Shenandoah's terrain, but perhaps the biggest pull remains at water's edge. Fishing has been the heritage of Shenandoah National Park since President Hoover built his Rapidan Camp there in 1929. He called his cabin the Brown House and used it as an essential retreat from the frenetic politics of the White House.

"Fishing is an excuse and a valid reason of the widest range of usefulness for temporary retreat from our busy world," Hoover said in a speech about Shenandoah. He would eventually donate all 164 acres to the park (Trout Unlimited rates Rapidan River as one of America's 100 best fishing streams). A lifelong conservationist, Hoover finished his speech:

In this case it is the excuse for return to the woods and streams with their retouch of the simpler life of the frontier from which every American springs . . . [to] find relief from the pneumatic hammer of constant personal contacts, and refreshment of mind in the babble of rippling brooks. Moreover, it is a constant reminder of the democracy of life, of humility, and of human frailty—for all men are equal before fishes. ▪

▷ LOCATION **68 MILES W OF KEY WEST, FLORIDA**

▷ SIZE **100 SQUARE MILES**

▷ HIGHEST POINT **LOGGERHEAD KEY, 10 FEET**

▷ VISITORS **56,810 IN 2018**

▷ ESTABLISHED **1992**

DRY TORTUGAS NATIONAL PARK

Seen from the stratosphere, Dry Tortugas' white-sand beaches and greenish hued shoals resemble a broken-off barb on the fishhook of Florida and its Keys. The park is centered in turquoise waters between Miami and Havana. Here, in the Straits of Florida, the narrow passage from the Caribbean into the Gulf of Mexico, boats or seaplanes are the only access.

One percent of this park—comprising seven islets of 143 acres—lies above sea level, on the edge of the continental shelf. So 99 percent of Dry Tortugas National Park must be explored underwater. A wonder world of coral lies below.

Cohabiting with clusters of coral reef are anemones, sponges, sea stars, turtles, nurse sharks, and colorful fish galore—a snorkeling and diving paradise. Coral is formed as a several-millimeter-wide polyp attaches to hard surfaces and begins cloning more polyps. These attach to one another with calcium-carbonate skeletons. As polyps die, their hard limestone shells become foundations for more living polyps. Over thousands of years, these polyp colonies became vast reefs. Dry Tortugas forms the southern end of the 358-mile-long, four-mile-wide Florida Reef System: the third largest coral

The largest masonry fort in the Western Hemisphere, Fort Jefferson endures despite the ongoing assault of tidal surges and tumultuous weather.

barrier reef in the world and the only tropical reef in the continental United States.

The greater reef system—outside the more pristine and protected coral of the Tortugas—is imperiled. Shrunken and battered by years of fishing, anchor dragging, bacteria-laden microplastics, and polluted runoff, the Florida Reef System now faces a test of survival above and beyond the protection given by national park boundaries. As sections of this reef die, breaking down protective offshore barriers, coastal storm erosion begins. Beaches wash away. And as a home or feeding ground for species large and small—25 percent of the world's ocean life depends upon reefs—fisheries feel the impact.

The recent dilemma of ocean acidification is one of the more serious concerns likely to affect the Dry Tortugas. Although the ocean has become more acidic due to the absorption of excess carbon dioxide—emitted since the industrial revolution began more than 200 years ago—the future of its coral is both uncertain and ominous.

Meanwhile, ocean temperatures are increasing. As algae are forced out of coral by this warming, reefs are whitened by "bleaching events" that weaken or destroy them. The last severe bleaching in Florida started in 2014 and lasted for two years; it was the third such major, worldwide ocean warming, after 1998 and 2010 El Niño weather shifts. Bleached coral can, in fact, recover when the water cools and allows algae to return and reinvigorate the paled reef. Still, after using a supercomputer to analyze weather data, scientists from the National Oceanic and Atmospheric Administration (NOAA) believe that by mid-century, bleaching will be much more widespread—even into Dry Tortugas' waters.

Brilliant yellow smallmouth grunts swim around coral protected in the park's clear waters, adding to the montage of underwater life that attracts divers.

GULF OF MEXICO

NORTHWEST

PARK BOUNDARY

Y "G"

Y "F"

Y "E"
Fl Y 6s

Loggerhead Key
Fl W 20s 167ft 24M

Windjammer wreck

Loggerhead Reef

□"3"

DRY
TORTUG

G "1"

Y "D"

RESEARCH NATURAL AREA BOUNDARY

W "C"

SOUTHWEST CHANNEL

Y "C"
Fl Y 4s

Y "B"

▲ Red daymark   ■ White daymark   Buoy

□ Green daymark   △ Daybeacon   Lighted buoy

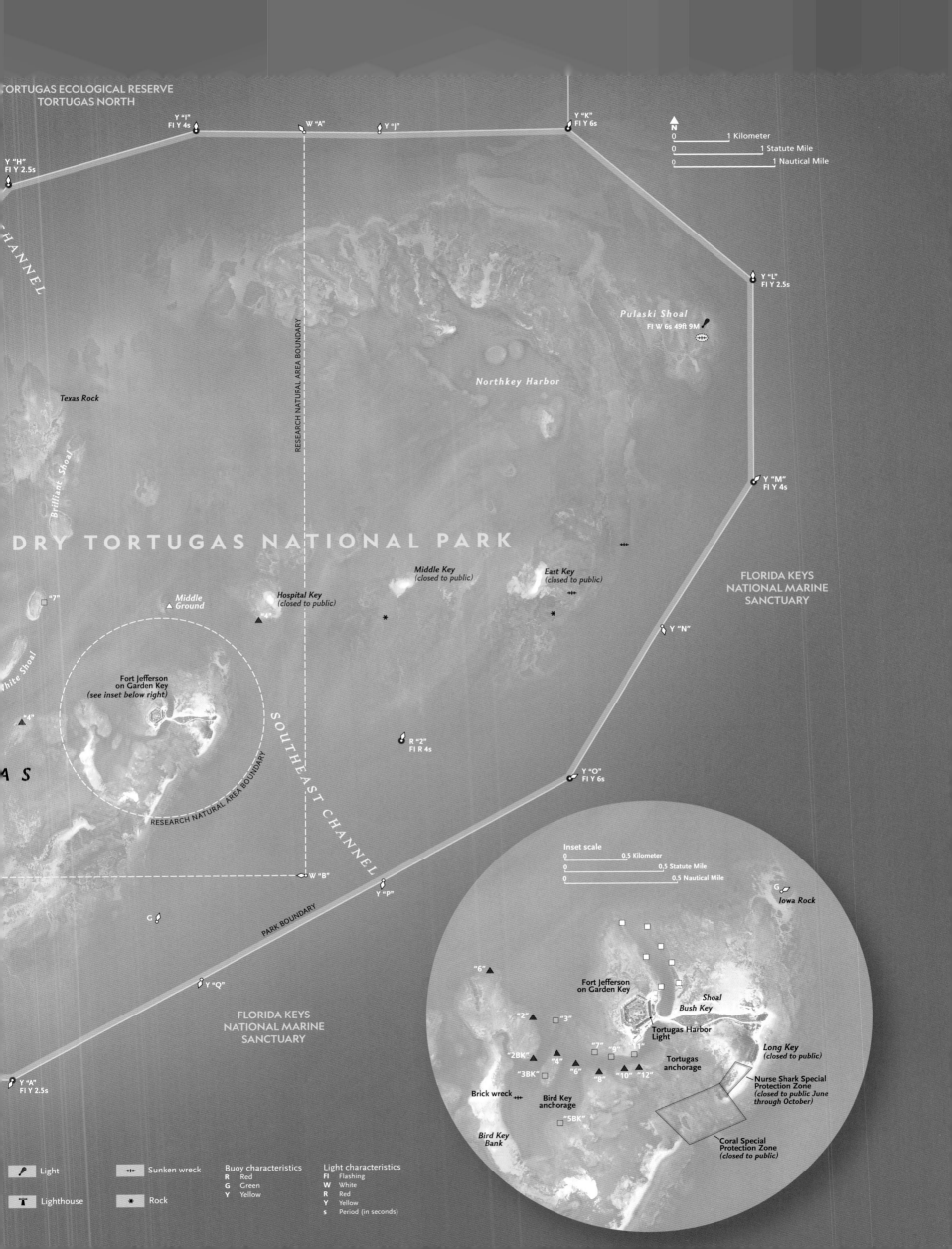

TORTUGAS ECOLOGICAL RESERVE
TORTUGAS NORTH

Y "I"
Fl Y 4s

W "A"   Y "J"

Y "K"
Fl Y 6s

Y "H"
Fl Y 2.5s

CHANNEL

N

0   1 Kilometer
0   1 Statute Mile
0   1 Nautical Mile

Y "L"
Fl Y 2.5s

RESEARCH NATURAL AREA BOUNDARY

Pulaski Shoal
Fl W 6s 49ft 9M

Texas Rock

Northkey Harbor

Brilliant Shoal

Y "M"
Fl Y 4s

DRY TORTUGAS NATIONAL PARK

FLORIDA KEYS
NATIONAL MARINE
SANCTUARY

Middle Key
(closed to public)

East Key
(closed to public)

"7"

Middle
Ground

Hospital Key
(closed to public)

"4"

White Shoal

Y "N"

"4"

Fort Jefferson
on Garden Key
(see inset below right)

R "2"
Fl R 4s

A S

RESEARCH NATURAL AREA BOUNDARY

SOUTHEAST CHANNEL

Y "O"
Fl Y 6s

Inset scale

0   0.5 Kilometer
0   0.5 Statute Mile
0   0.5 Nautical Mile

W "B"

Y "P"

G
Iowa Rock

PARK BOUNDARY

G

"6"

Fort Jefferson
on Garden Key

Shoal
Bush Key

Y "Q"

"2"   "3"

Tortugas Harbor
Light

Long Key
(closed to public)

FLORIDA KEYS
NATIONAL MARINE
SANCTUARY

"7"   "9"   "1"

"2BK"   "4"
"3BK"   "6"   "8"

Tortugas
anchorage

Nurse Shark Special
Protection Zone
(closed to public June
through October)

"10" "12"

Y "A"
Fl Y 2.5s

Brick wreck

Bird Key
anchorage

"5BK"

Coral Special
Protection Zone
(closed to public)

Bird Key
Bank

Light   Sunken wreck   Buoy characteristics   Light characteristics
                                           R   Red   Fl   Flashing
                                           G   Green   W   White
Lighthouse   Rock   Y   Yellow   R   Red
                                                                         Y   Yellow
                                                                         s   Period (in seconds)

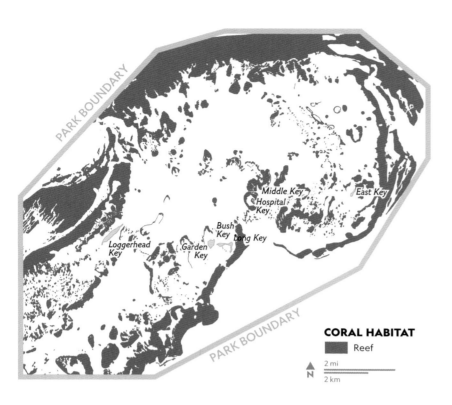

CORAL HABITAT
■ Reef

2 mi
N
2 km

Teeming with aquatic life, Dry Tortugas' clear blue waters offer some of the best snorkeling opportunities in the United States. Thirty species of coral—including two threatened species, elkhorn and staghorn—live in the park. These reefs support a host of colorful marine species, from parrot fish and angelfish to moray eels.

As a climate change event, bleaching is part and parcel of the specter of rising sea levels. A sea-level gauge at Key West, 70 miles from Dry Tortugas, shows that the ocean there has risen nine inches since 1913. Since 1850, it has risen a foot. For the continued protection of coral, plants, animals, and historical resources in Dry Tortugas, the Park Service recently installed a similar gauge to monitor these changes more closely and plan for the future.

Rising sea levels here have already caused higher turbidity, lower salinity, and more varied water temperatures—all detrimental to reefs. By 2045, according to an Army Corps of Engineers projection, the sea will rise another 15 inches in Key West. Compounding this change is the devastating rise of much larger storm surges that now flood low-lying sections of Miami, Key West, and the Dry Tortugas.

Fortunately, due to commercial fishing closures and the protective sanctity of Dry Tortugas National Park, 28 of 30 species of coral here are intact. Still, elkhorn and staghorn coral—two species that may be more susceptible to recent ocean changes—have diminished here and in the Florida Reef at a rate not experienced in thousands of years, as evidenced by core samples taken from the ancient reefs. Scientists have begun proactively working closely with the Park Service above and underwater in Dry Tortugas. Divers in the park have started replanting staghorn coral—engineered and grown in laboratories to better survive disease, warming, and acidification—in addition to tens of thousands more coral plantings throughout the state.

In 2007, a 46-square-mile section of the park waters was closed and designated as a Research Natural Area (RNA). In the most recent 2012 progress report, comparing the effectiveness between the RNA and nearby areas open to fishing, scientists learned that the population and sizes of park reef fish—including red grouper, mutton snapper, yellowtail snapper, and hogfish—have increased: a sign that efforts at improving the health of these protected waters are succeeding.

Conversely, turtle populations have suffered. Although hundreds of millions of green turtles had occupied the Caribbean until 19th-century depredations, today only a fraction of those numbers is left. Dry Tortugas National Park remains the most active nesting sanctuary in the state for the 300-pound species, now endangered in Florida. Along with the more common loggerhead turtles, hundreds of green turtles nest and lay eggs in the park each year; statistics show that these nestings on protected park islands are on the rise.

The national park ideal of preservation and sanctuary, along with coral reengineering, may offer at least one parcel of the Florida Reef System genuine hope. Only time will show how well the coral and its inhabitants, let alone the historical resources of the park, will survive changes that have occurred since humankind first wandered into the Dry Tortugas.

In 1513, the Spanish explorer Juan Ponce de León discovered this archipelago. At first he called the islands *cayos* ("tiny islands" in Spanish led to the English *cay* or *key*). Then, after his crew harvested 170 large turtles, he named the islands *Tortugas* ("turtles"). Later the islands received the appellation "Dry" because freshwater is nonexistent amid the thick coral sand, sparse mangroves, and grass.

Winter is also dry here with less than two inches of rainfall a month; temperatures range from 64° to 75°F (18° to 24°C). Summer—averaging up to 90°F (32°C)—is twice as rainy, becoming even wetter from August through November, during hurricane season.

ABOVE: **Sailors and pirates** hunted green sea turtles for decades, but since the creation of Dry Tortugas National Park, the turtle population is recovering.

OPPOSITE: **The waters** surrounding Loggerhead Key and its lighthouse, built in 1858, hold hundreds of shipwrecks that have long lured divers and treasure hunters.

The Gulf of Mexico is one of the most active hurricane areas of the United States, and four Tortugas islets disappeared between the mid-19th century and 1935 as a result of rising sea levels and storm surges. Otherwise, the region is nearly tideless. In 1989 Hurricane Hugo destroyed a weather station and shallow water navigational light; in 2017, Irma knocked down 60 feet of historic, bricked wall.

Stormy seas amid these low-lying islands and shallow reefed waters have caused nearly 200 storied shipwrecks and require careful navigation (today, two lighthouses in the park act as directional aids). In 1742, a British crew of castaways ran aground here, and after hauling their cannons out of their sinking ship, they lived on the islands for two months, skirmishing with pirates and Spanish sailors. The British survivors then spent 56 days sailing their lifeboats 600 miles south around Cuba to reach Jamaica (today Cuban refugees seeking U.S. asylum often arrive on the islands).

Amid a well-used shipping route into the Gulf of Mexico, the islands served as a base camp for pirates who scuttled and destroyed ships laden with riches. (In 1985, treasure hunters salvaged $450 million in silver and gold from a ship driven by hurricane into reefs east of the Tortugas in 1622.) Robert Louis Stevenson described "dreadful stories" in *Treasure Island,* "about hanging, and walking the plank, and storms at sea, and the Dry Tortugas."

Five years after Spain sold Florida to America, manning these islands proved a key defense for the American heartland and the shipping riches of the Mississippi River. In 1846, slave laborers and masons began building a stupendous, hexagonal fort named after President Thomas Jefferson. Laying 16 million bricks and eventually dominating the more than 14-acre Garden Key, the archipelago's second biggest island, Fort Jefferson would become the largest masonry fort in the Western Hemisphere.

Nesting colonies of sooty terns and brown noddies fly over Bush Key at sunrise. During the nesting season, this area sees about 80,000 sooty terns at once.

JOHN JAMES AUDUBON SAILED IN MAY 1832 FROM KEY WEST TO THE DRY TORTUGAS DURING THE HEIGHT OF THE BUSY NESTING SEASON TO OBSERVE THE REMARKABLE BIRDLIFE.

More than a dozen years into construction, the fort rose 45 feet high and eight feet thick and sagged with iron frameworks to house 420 cannons as heavy as 25 tons. Then the Civil War broke out. In the midst of preparing the fort for cannons, a Confederate ship arrived and sent ashore a messenger who demanded Fort Jefferson's Union troops to surrender. "Tell your captain," the Union Army's Major Arnold bluffed to the rebel messenger standing in front of the massive fort walls, "I will blow his ship out of the water if he's not gone in 10 minutes." The Confederates fled.

Even after Union cannons arrived and were installed on the massive gun platform, shots were never fired. As enemy ships developed more efficient guns that could pierce the fort's walls, the reef-protected harbor instead moored warships to chase mostly nonexistent enemy boats.

Isolated from the Confederates, Fort Jefferson became the country's largest military prison. President Abraham Lincoln commuted Union deserters' executions in exchange for grueling construction labor at the fort. Prisoners reduced by subhuman conditions and appalling storms called it "Devil's Island."

Ironically, the most famous prisoner, Dr. Samuel Mudd, had been life-sentenced to Fort Jefferson for sheltering and splinting the broken leg of John Wilkes Booth, who had just assassinated President Lincoln. In 1865, Mudd arrived bound in chains, but he was pardoned several years later after saving his captors' lives during one of many yellow fever outbreaks.

Construction halted as the Army abandoned the fort amid bruising hurricanes and concerns that the colossal weight of the structure would collapse and sink Garden Key underwater. Used for brief periods as a quarantine or coaling station, or for military ships during the Spanish-American War, President Theodore

North Coaling Dock *ruins*

East Swim Beach

Bush Key

North Swim Beach

Tortugas
Harbor Light

Seaplane Beach

Garden Key Harbor

Fort Jefferson

Visitor Center

Dock

Headquarters

Dinghy Beach

South Coaling
Dock *ruins*

moat

▼N

Garden Key

South Swim Beach

Roosevelt designated the islands a federal bird reservation in 1908.

Bush Key is closed half the year to protect a rookery of up to 80,000 nesting sooty terns—the tropical species' only significant nesting ground in the continental United States. The birds arrive in winter and the island becomes a cacophony of terns–incessantly screeching *wide-awake, wide awake!*—until mid-August. Then the large-winged birds depart for West Africa to spend five years at sea, without touching land, before returning to Dry Tortugas.

The islands are also frequented by brown noddies (who nest alongside the terns), frigate birds, pelicans, and brown boobies (that James Audubon painted here in 1832). With nearly 300 species passing through each year, the park is subsumed by a blizzard of birdlife in the spring.

In 1935, to honor its military history along with the birdlife, President Franklin D. Roosevelt created Fort Jefferson National Monument through presidential proclamation (legislatively affirmed by Congress in 1980). Its borders expanded in 1983. On October 26, 1992, an act of Congress abolished the national monument and established Dry Tortugas National Park "to preserve and protect for the education, inspiration and enjoyment of present and future generations nationally significant natural, historic, scenic, marine, and scientific values in South Florida." ■

ABOVE: **During the Civil War,** Fort Jefferson became one of the country's most isolated military prisons, where difficult conditions led prisoners to call it "Devil's Island."

TOP: **Sixteen million red bricks** make up Fort Jefferson, one of the largest 1800s forts in the United States. Now the nucleus of Dry Tortugas National Park, the hexagonal fort sits atop Garden Key, the second largest island in Dry Tortugas, and holds the park headquarters and visitor center within its storied walls.

- LOCATION **25 MILES S OF KNOXVILLE, TENNESSEE**
- SIZE **816 SQUARE MILES**
- HIGHEST POINT **CLINGMANS DOME, 6,643 FEET**
- VISITORS **11,421,200 IN 2018**
- ESTABLISHED **1934**

GREAT SMOKY MOUNTAINS NATIONAL PARK

Named after the mountain range it encompasses, Great Smoky is the only national park evenly shared by two states. The 54-mile-long, 19-mile-wide park lies between Tennessee and North Carolina, split by 16 rocky-ledged peaks over 6,000 feet, bulging above dense forests. Its mountaintop state boundary includes a section of the famed Appalachian Trail, amid another 850 miles of park trails.

Whereas other archetypal parks are widely celebrated for their geysers, glaciers, or peaks, it is not commonly known that Great Smoky Mountains National Park is a veritable conservatory of plants. Its 1,500 flowering species make for a mind-boggling palette of color and fragrance, often growing in impenetrable thickets called heath *balds* or shiny laurel slicks. Much of this green fertility comes from 55 to 85 inches of rainfall a year, depending upon the elevation. The humidity is twice that of most mountain regions in the West. Still, unlike most of the South's broiling summers, temperatures at the higher elevations in the Smoky Mountains seldom exceed 80 degrees.

In this cool garden of a national park, another several hundred species of nonflowering plants include 50 species of lush swaying ferns, fields of fungi, elongated carpets of mosses, and more than a

Amid the cool woods and ridgelines of the Great Smoky Mountains, places like Newfound Gap offer prime views as leaves from the park's many tree species burst into color.

hundred species of trees. The park has the greatest old-growth hardwood forest remaining on the East Coast—blanketing 292 square miles, or more than a third of Great Smoky.

The park's signature blue haze comes from plants and trees emitting oxygen, water vapor, and volatile organic compounds (VOCs). Released mostly from trees responding to heat, the airborne VOC particles (different from highly toxic indoor chemicals) interact with and reflect a blue light.

Dwelling below the haze in this lush jungle—from clear streams to wind-raked summits—is a staggering variety of animal species: more than 80 reptiles and amphibians, over 200 varieties of birds, 67 native fish, and 65 species of mammals. With its additional plants, fungi, and other organisms, Great Smoky Mountains is one of the most biodiverse regions on Earth.

As Congress mandated on June 15, 1934, the park was created "to preserve exceptionally diverse resources and to provide for public benefit from and enjoyment of those resources in ways which will leave them basically unaltered by human influences." But there is a mounting paradox within Great Smoky's mission statement: Given its proximity to many large population centers, free admission, and 384 miles of scenic roads, it is easily the most popular park in the nation as measured by visitor numbers. Since 1995, over nine million people visit annually; the second most visited national park, Grand Canyon, had five million fewer visitors than Great Smoky in 2018.

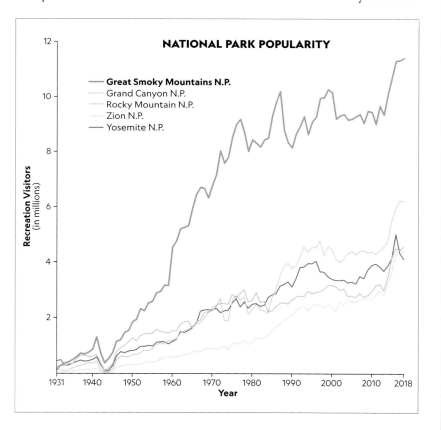

NATIONAL PARK POPULARITY

— Great Smoky Mountains N.P.
— Grand Canyon N.P.
— Rocky Mountain N.P.
— Zion N.P.
— Yosemite N.P.

Since 1933, Great Smoky Mountains has drawn more visitors than any other national park. The park hit one million visitors in 1941 and, after a drop during World War II, visitation continued to soar, climbing to six million in 1966. More than 11.4 million visitors came to the park in 2018, nearly double the crowds seen at Grand Canyon National Park.

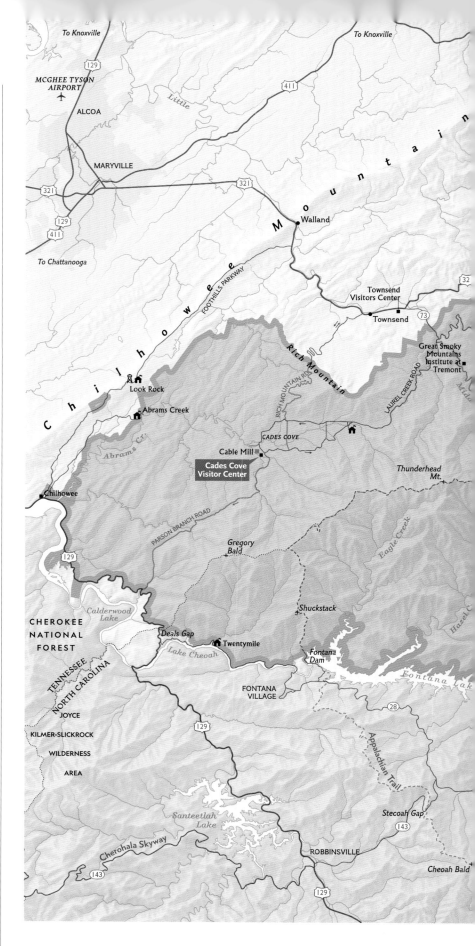

Because of this traffic, the Great Smoky Mountains superintendent has received complaints that one popular, 11-mile roadway can take five hours to drive. In response, the park began temporary closures to vehicles and provided bikes. Rangers patrol for poachers who hunt bears (for gallbladders, claws, and teeth to be sold in Asian markets), or who uproot orchids, trillium, or ginseng (roots of the last are worth hundreds of dollars a pound on the black market). Researchers have found that more than 30 native plants are now being damaged by ground-level ozone pollution—produced when

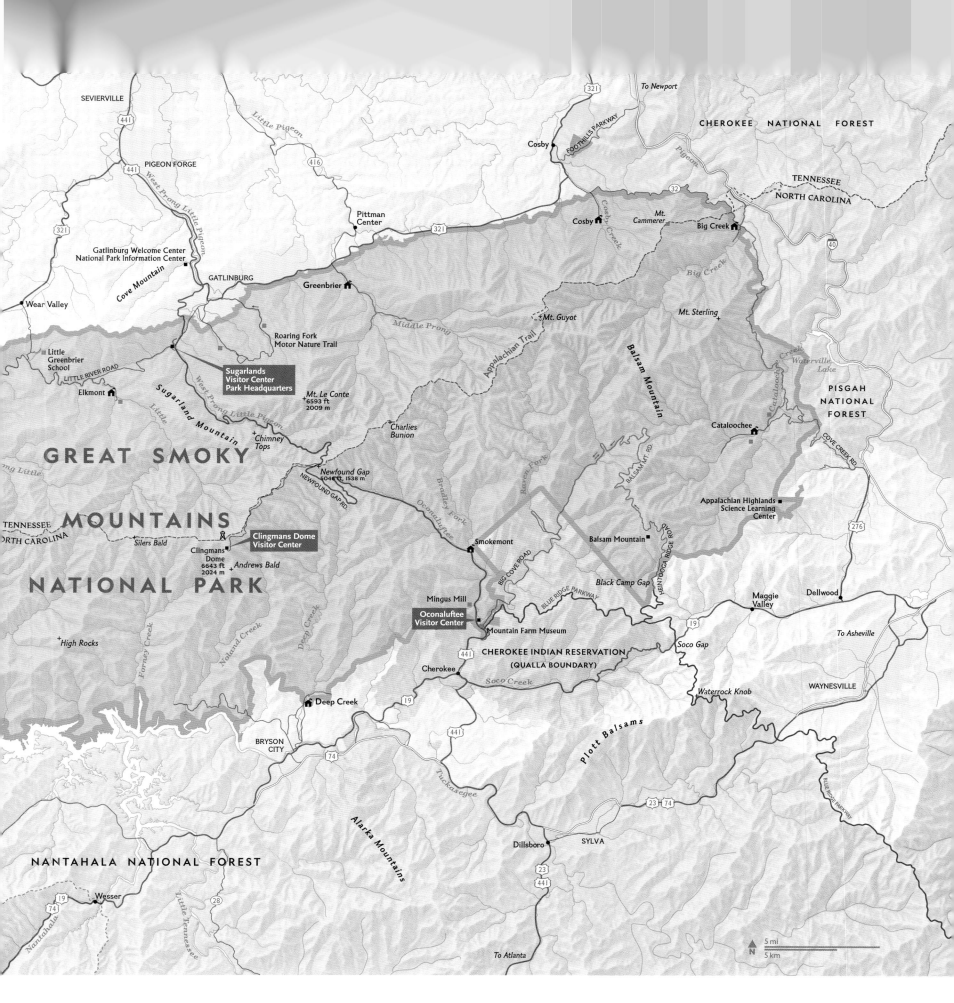

naturally emitted VOCs interact with industrial pollution from outside the park. In the 20th century, industrial pollution reduced visibility from scenic park vistas by 40 percent in winter and 80 percent in summer, often limiting views to less than 20 miles. Mandates for clean air protection in national parks, including the Clean Air Act of 1970 and its amendments in 1977 and 1990 have helped because ozone and visibility conditions improved after 2005.

To help protect other popular natural refuges, the diverse Great Smoky Mountains could serve as a laboratory for measuring how much impact flora and fauna can withstand. Can the "exceptionally diverse resources" identified by Congress remain "unaltered by human influences"? To safeguard the park, managers are now trying to quantify Great Smoky's human-carrying capacity.

The Cherokee—who had inhabited the region since around A.D. 1000—referred to these mountains as *Shaconage* ("land of blue

THE SMOKY HAZE THAT INSPIRED THE PARK'S NAME COMES FROM PLANTS EMITTING VOLATILE ORGANIC COMPOUNDS INTO THE AIR AND FOG CREATED BY RAINY CONDITIONS.

smoke"). But by 1838, most of the Cherokee Nation had been marched to western reservations as English and Scottish settlers arrived. The lifestyle of these impoverished mountaineers, isolated from the outside world and often stereotyped by their banjo picking and moonshine stills, morphed into America's unique Appalachian culture. They built homes and communities throughout the Smoky Mountains and subsisted by farming, hunting, trapping, and logging.

Logging companies—similarly drawn to the vast forests of elm, oak, chestnut, and conifers—arrived in the late 19th century, even as the park was first proposed in 1899. But by the early 20th century, following the fate of hardwood stands throughout the eastern seaboard, most of the region and its forests were reduced to stumps.

Congress provided authorization for the park in 1926, but without funding it fell to North Carolina and Tennessee to raise the capital. John D. Rockefeller, Jr., the country's national park philanthropist, upped the states' ante with a five-million-dollar donation as logging companies held out for as much money as they could get for selling their land. The state governments began forcing out local mountaineers and vacation homeowners by "condemning" properties for what was termed "the higher use" of the future park; 5,665 people were displaced from numerous communities within the park. Still, it would take until 1939 and $12 million to finish buying more than 6,000 pieces of property. Several dozen holdouts—and those too old or sick to move—remained in their homes with lifetime leases (the last expired in 2001). Among these locals, resentment against the authorities would linger for years.

In 1932, North Carolina and Tennessee finished building a steep, switchbacked road through a 5,046-foot mountain pass called Newfound Gap. Remarkable for its time, the road climbed 3,000 feet, from moist hardwoods into evergreens normally found much farther north.

TOP: **A vast network** of trails weaves through the park past rock formations, creeks, and scenic waterfalls like this one along the Little River.

ABOVE: **The park** maintains more than 90 historic structures—including the John Oliver cabin above—that once sheltered the land's inhabitants. Built in the 1820s, the cabin is the park's oldest surviving building.

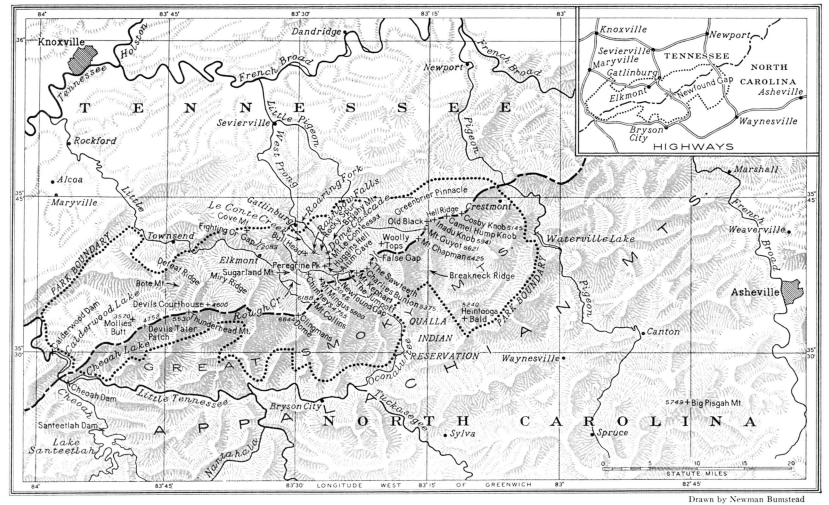

ABOUT EVENLY DIVIDED BETWEEN TENNESSEE AND NORTH CAROLINA, THE GREAT SMOKY MOUNTAINS NATIONAL PARK EMBRACES
427,000 ACRES OF RUGGED HEIGHTS AND DEEP VALLEYS

In 1933 Civilian Conservation Corps (CCC) laborers arrived as part of a federal work project to ease unemployment during the Great Depression. The CCC set up 22 camps and began assembling the infrastructure of trails and roads and bridges endemic to the national park ideal of public access.

Unlike in other parks, the mountain people added a historic context and culture to this landscape. They gave America a distinctive strain of music and preserved a language not spoken since colonial times. Often overlooked as hillbillies, they created frontier heroes who provided the country with a sense of identity (the television show *Davy Crockett* would be shot around the park's old cabins). So until 1942, the CCC also rebuilt and shored up old farmhouses, barns, log cabins, mills, schools, and churches so that visitors could access and view scores of intact and rehabilitated buildings dating back to mid-19th century. Interpretive sites into the culture of Appalachia were created, and restoration continues to this day.

Thanks in large part to the CCC, which helped improve early Cherokee paths and settler routes, as well as hack through dense thickets, more than 150 trails run 850 miles through the park. Whether traversing coves, circling gaps, or climbing to the Chimney Tops,

This 1936 National Geographic map of Great Smoky Mountains National Park illustrates why it has been called the "Rooftop of Eastern America," with a score of peaks that rise over a mile above sea level. The inset map shows the park's main roads, now heavily trafficked, and nearby cities.

Great Smoky serves day hikers, trail runners, peak baggers, bird-watchers, anglers, cross-country skiers, horseback riders, or overnight backpackers.

An estimated 1,500 wild black bears, or two bears per square mile, subsist on backcountry plants, berries, and insects. The prolific species has come to symbolize the park. Despite the dense population, bear attacks are rare. Nonetheless, for the safety of both humans and bears, the park recommends hiking in groups of three or four, carrying bear spray, and keeping food or garbage in bear-proof containers.

Of the thousands of hikers who attempt to walk the length of the Appalachian Trail (AT) each year, about one in four complete the 2,190-mile trail—ever alert to bears, and spending a week to cross the 70 miles of trail through the park. Most "thru-hikers" take up to seven months to walk the length of the trail, but in summer 2018, a Belgian ultrarunner set a record time of 41 days, 7 hours, and 39 minutes. Beginning in 1921, it took 15 years to acquire land and build the famous trail spanning 14 states from Georgia to Maine.

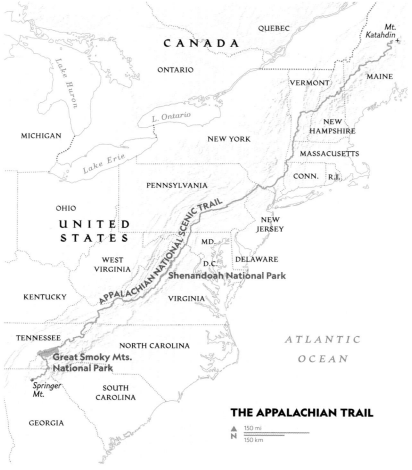

From the first trek completed in 1936 until 2018, 20,115 hikers have hiked the entire trail. The AT's highest point is in Great Smoky Mountains National Park, where the trail traverses beneath Clingmans Dome behind the modular concrete observation tower on the summit. Beginning on this peak, leaving the Appalachian Trail, more than half of a 1,200-mile Mountains to Sea Trail has been completed toward the Outer Banks.

The most remote Great Smoky hike skirts Fontana Lake on the southern edge of the park and passes cemeteries and old homesteads along the 33-mile-long Lakeshore Trail. It remains the largest tract of roadless land on the East Coast. The Fontana Dam, built to create electricity during World War II, flooded several communities and Highway 288, forcing residents—who gave private lands to the park—to move. The federal government offered, in turn, to build a 34-mile road access to the north shore of the lake. But beyond a tunnel, construction halted

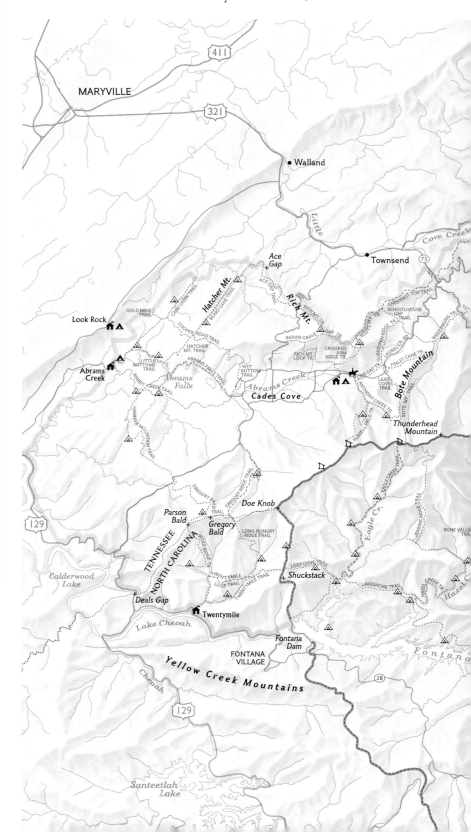

RIGHT: **More than 400,000 hikers** traverse the park's 850 miles of trails annually, with the Rainbow Falls Trail and the Chimney Tops Trail among the most popular hikes. Stretching roughly 2,190 miles across 14 states, the renowned Appalachian Trail (above) crosses through the heart of the park for 70 miles.

TOP: **This Jordan's salamander,** glimpsed near Chimney Tops Trail, is one of the 30 species of salamanders that populate the forest floor and make the region the world's salamander capital.

after only six miles. The expensive "Road to Nowhere" project was abandoned, adding to the region's troubled history of evictions.

THE PARK'S MOUNTAINS ARE AMONG THE TALLEST IN THE APPALACHIAN CHAIN THAT BEGAN TO FORM ABOUT 200 TO 300 MILLION YEARS AGO.

Hidden quietly from the hubbub amid moist forest litter, alongside streams and under rocks, is an amphibian that showcases the park's incredible biodiversity. Herpetologists know Great Smoky Mountains as the salamander capitol of the world.

Among 30 different species, the untold millions of resident salamanders easily outnumbered the park's record 47,000 human visitors during the August 21, 2017, total solar eclipse. If weighed, the salamander biomass would also bypass that of all other vertebrate park resident species combined, from two-gram shrews to 700-pound elk—reintroduced here in 2001.

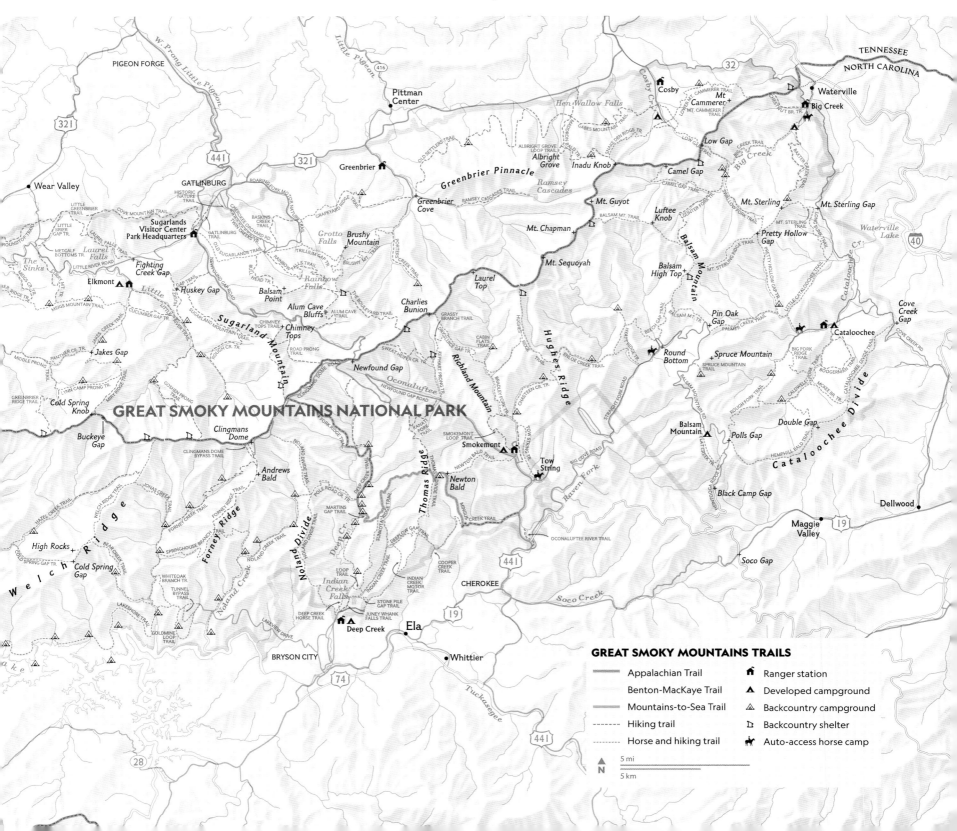

GREAT SMOKY MOUNTAINS TRAILS

Appalachian Trail	Ranger station
Benton-MacKaye Trail	Developed campground
Mountains-to-Sea Trail	Backcountry campground
Hiking trail	Backcountry shelter
Horse and hiking trail	Auto-access horse camp

5 mi
5 km

MAJOR FOREST HABITATS

Cove hardwood forest
Hemlock forest
Northern hardwood forest
Pine-and-oak forest
Spruce-fir forest
Other
Great Smoky Mountains
National Park boundary

5 mi
5 km

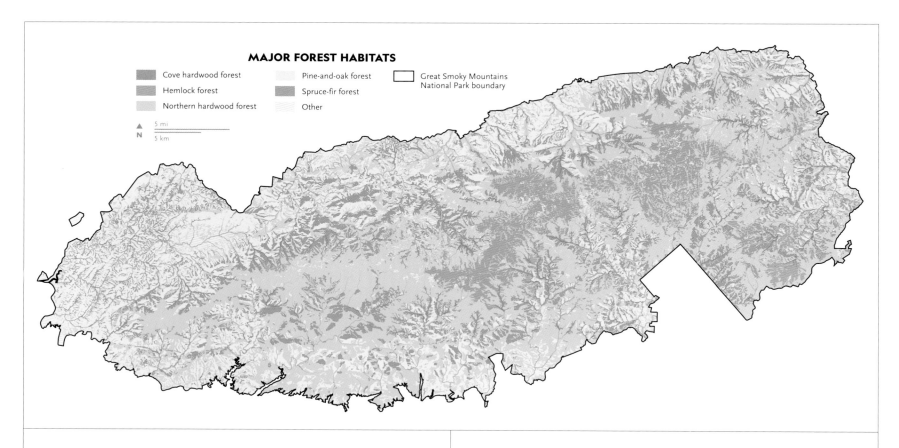

COVE HARDWOOD FOREST

PINE-AND-OAK FOREST

HEMLOCK FOREST

SPRUCE-FIR FOREST

NORTHERN HARDWOOD FOREST

Known for its lush vegetation, the park protects more than 100 native tree species and 100 native shrubs that form five major forest types: The most botanically diverse, cove hardwood forests cover enclosed valleys where abundant soil supports dogwoods, magnolias, and basswoods among its 40 to 60 tree and shrub species. Hemlock forests edge streams and swathe slopes up to 4,000 feet in elevation with pyramidal evergreens. Northern hardwood forests seen at elevations from 3,500 to 5,000 feet are home to American beech, maple trees, and more species. Pine-and-oak forests are found mostly on the park's west side, on exposed slopes and ridges, where drainage leads to drier conditions. Spruce-fir forests crown ridges and elevations above 4,500 feet with Fraser fir, red spruce, yellow birch, and mountain ash, among other species.

GREAT SMOKY MOUNTAINS NATIONAL PARK IS HOME TO 100 SPECIES OF NATIVE TREES, WHILE MOST NATIONAL PARKS HAVE FEWER THAN 20.

Nine species of rhododendron grow across thousands of acres in the park. In 1791, the flame azalea's appearance led pioneer botanist William Bartram to call it "certainly the most gay and brilliant flowering shrub yet known."

Viewed at night, the ground wriggles with nocturnal salamanders on the hunt. From the 29-inch hellbender to the two-inch pygmy salamander, these carnivores flourish colorfully, with multiple shapes and in most habitats as per their names: spotted dusky, cave, blackchin red, marbled, shovelnose, black-bellied, red-spotted, longtail, four-toed, slimy, southern gray-cheeked, southern redback, and mudpuppy. Most of these salamanders lack lungs and breathe through porous skin.

These ancient creatures tell a tale that predates the purchases and evictions surrounding the creation of this national park. Their migration began 10,000 years ago as the Pleistocene epoch glaciated much of the eastern seaboard. Salamanders, their invertebrate and insect prey, and many mammals fled and took refuge in the ice-free Great Smoky Mountains, unique for its east-west alignment, proffering cool, rainforest conditions suited to amphibians, including 10 species of frogs and four species of toads. Although other worldwide locations show declining salamander populations, Great Smoky salamanders are thriving. The greater ecosystem is dependent upon healthy populations of the amphibians, as a keystone species.

In 1976, due to creatures large but mostly small in this wild terrarium, as well as ubiquitous plant life, the park became an international biosphere reserve. In 1983, the United Nations named Great Smoky Mountains National Park a World Heritage site. After these designations, the National Park Service began a detailed record called the All-Taxa Biodiversity Inventory (ATBI). Unique to the National Park System and containing an animal database larger than any in the United States, ATBI researchers discovered another 10,000 species in the park, including 1,000 that were new to science, previously unseen elsewhere in the world.

The "Species Mapper" found on the park website shows the incredible diversity of life, along with the species locations within the Great Smoky Mountains. This tool is a shining example of the awareness and education needed—in the language of the 1916 National Park Service charter—to help keep this refuge "unimpaired for the enjoyment of future generations." ∎

The pileated woodpecker, among the largest of all forest birds, can drill holes so large that trees are often weakened. The park's elevation range creates myriad habitats for bird species.

- ▷ LOCATION **93 MILES S OF LOUISVILLE, KENTUCKY**

- ▷ SIZE **843 SQUARE MILES**

- ▷ HIGHEST POINT **PENNYROYAL PLATEAU, 925 FEET**

- ▷ VISITORS **533,206 IN 2018**

- ▷ ESTABLISHED **1941**

MAMMOTH CAVE NATIONAL PARK

At surface level, this is a small, pastoral national park, densely wooded and surrounded by verdant farmlands. Belowground, however, Mammoth has the longest known cave system in the world. Crisscrossed with more than 400 miles of labyrinthine passageways embedded with fossilized sea creatures, the cave is unusually dry, despite its subterranean river and ceilings dripping with ancient, otherworldly limestone formations. Contrary to popular opinion, the park was named for its underground size, rather than the woolly mammoth fossils commonly found elsewhere in the region.

The south-central Kentucky park's boundaries open like a tulip to the northern part of the state. Bisected east to west by 25 miles of the 384-mile-long Green River, Mammoth draws canoeists, kayakers, and anglers; visitors also come to hike its 80-plus miles of trails.

The United Nations Educational, Scientific, and Cultural Organization (UNESCO) chose Mammoth as a World Heritage site in 1981 for 130 species of cave-specific wildlife, counting 14 creatures found nowhere else in the world. This includes troglobites like the eyeless fish that live only in caves, and troglophiles like the sculpin that spend part of their lives in caves. UNESCO calls Mammoth's flora

Ancient seas and rivers carved these passageways in the world's largest known cave system, leaving fossilized creatures behind and creating fantastic limestone formations.

and fauna the richest known to caves. Three endangered species make their home there: the gray bat, the Indiana bat, and the Kentucky cave shrimp.

Of some of Mammoth's many qualifications as a specially protected site, UNESCO states:

The park illustrates a number of stages of the Earth's evolutionary history and contains ongoing geological processes . . . with huge chambers, vertical shafts, stalagmites and stalactites, splendid forms of beautiful gypsum flowers, delicate gypsum needles, rare mirabilite flowers and other natural features [that] are all superlative examples of their type.

More than 330 million years ago, when North America had shifted south and a shallow sea covered the lower continent, warm water supported a proliferation of tiny organisms. As these creatures died over 70 million years, their calcium carbonate (limestone) shells accumulated on the seafloor. Rivers flowing into the sea around this region then deposited shale and sandstone atop limestone as thick as 600 feet.

As the sea level fell 280 million years ago, the shale and sandstone became terra firma. Meanwhile, the movement of vast tectonic plates formed the supercontinent Pangaea, with forces that cracked like a nut the surface of what would one day be Kentucky. Continued uplift of the earth over two hundred million more years developed rivers that would deposit more sandstone.

Ten million years ago, the first passageways formed in Mammoth Cave when rain and river water combined with carbon dioxide in the air and soil to form carbonic acid. As this corrosive water seeped

Strange creatures found only in the park region live in Mammoth Cave's waters, including the inch-long, eyeless Kentucky cave shrimp that grazes on the surface of sediments.

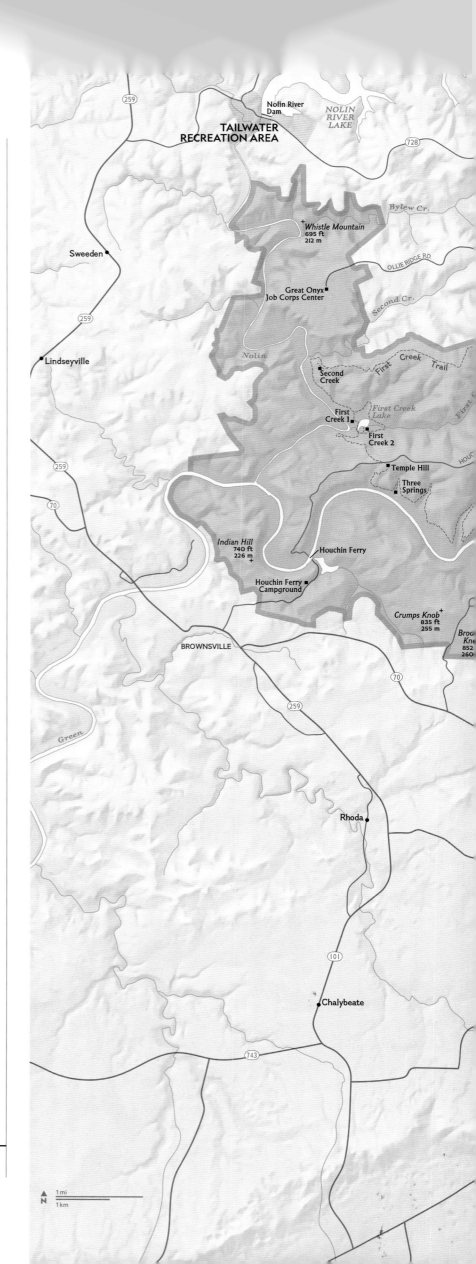

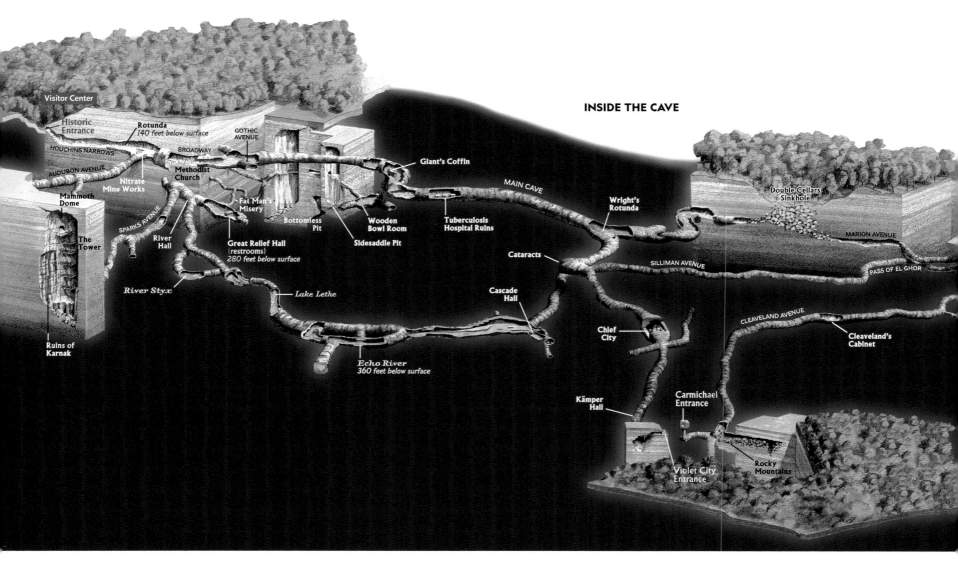

Labels on image: Visitor Center; Historic Entrance; Rotunda *140 feet below surface*; HOUCHINS NARROWS; BROADWAY; GOTHIC AVENUE; AUDUBON AVENUE; Methodist Church; Nitrate Mine Works; Mammoth Dome; SPARKS AVENUE; River Hall; The Tower; Ruins of Karnak; River Styx; Fat Man's Misery; Great Relief Hall (restrooms) *280 feet below surface*; Bottomless Pit; Wooden Bowl Room; Sidesaddle Pit; Lake Lethe; *Echo River 360 feet below surface*; Giant's Coffin; Tuberculosis Hospital Ruins; MAIN CAVE; Wright's Rotunda; Cataracts; Cascade Hall; Chief City; Kämper Hall; Carmichael Entrance; Violet City Entrance; Rocky Mountains; SILLIMAN AVENUE; Double Cellars Sinkhole; MARION AVENUE; PASS OF EL GHOR; CLEAVELAND AVENUE; Cleaveland's Cabinet

More than 405 miles of explored passages wind through Mammoth Cave, the world's longest known cave system—and by some estimates, there could be 600 miles yet to be discovered. The primary tour routes and passages shown above are only a fraction of the labyrinth.

through cracks in the sandstone that lay like a protective umbrella above the limestone, the first subterranean passages were dissolved in the limestone below. These tubular passageways are now found at approximately 600 feet above sea level.

The lower levels in Mammoth Cave were formed from river runoff in the more recent Pleistocene era, 2.5 million to 11,000 years ago. Streams also carved valleys into the caprock, leaving flat-topped ridges above. In places the caprock has completely eroded away, and exposed limestone like that found on the surface of the flat Pennyroyal Plateau. Above this are the ridge crests of the Chester Upland, overlaying the explored passages in the cave system.

Caprock—insoluble sandstone or shale topping the cave ceilings—protected the cave from being dissolved from above. Still, thousands of ground-level sinkholes on the Chester Upland show where streams and rivers penetrated the caprock into the cave and became underground rivers. The Green River also carved out passageways, along with water that drains out of the cave and into the river.

The Mammoth Cave National Park topography is called karst (after the renowned limestone Karst Plateau between Italy and Slovenia), describing the region's creation through springs, sinking streams, caves, and sinkholes.

Native Americans began exploring the cave 5,000 years ago. From the archaic hunter-gatherers to the Woodland period pottery makers and farmers, these antediluvian spelunkers (predecessors to the Shawnee and Cherokee) mined gypsum, mirabilite, Epsom, and other minerals for ceremonial or medicinal purposes for more than two millennia. Their cane torches, clothing, pottery, and charcoal petroglyphs are still being uncovered in cave passageways.

Most famously, latter-day workers pieced together an unnerving tragedy from 2,400 years ago. Pinned under a six-ton boulder that had been accidentally dislodged by an ancient digging stick, they found a body—which they nicknamed Lost John—wearing a shell necklace. Several other remains were also found, perfectly preserved by the cave's constant humidity and mid-50° to 60°F (10° to 16°C) temperatures. Outside the cave, average temperatures range from 27° to 89°F (−3° to 32°C) with varying humidity.

Kentucky folklore holds that a bear hunter in the late 1700s rediscovered the cave. Sometime between 1798 and 1802, the entrance had been surveyed and landowners began mining the cave's saltpeter with up to 70 African-American slaves. As a principal component of gunpowder, saltpeter proved invaluable during the War of 1812.

For half a century after the war, these slaves became guides for a burgeoning, internationally renowned tourist industry that showcased Native American "mummies" along with what one guide famously called a "grand, gloomy, and peculiar place." Another owner briefly set up a tuberculosis hospital within the cave, taking advantage of the soothing cave air as a potential cure. The cave's reputation grew and transformed into American legend, appearing

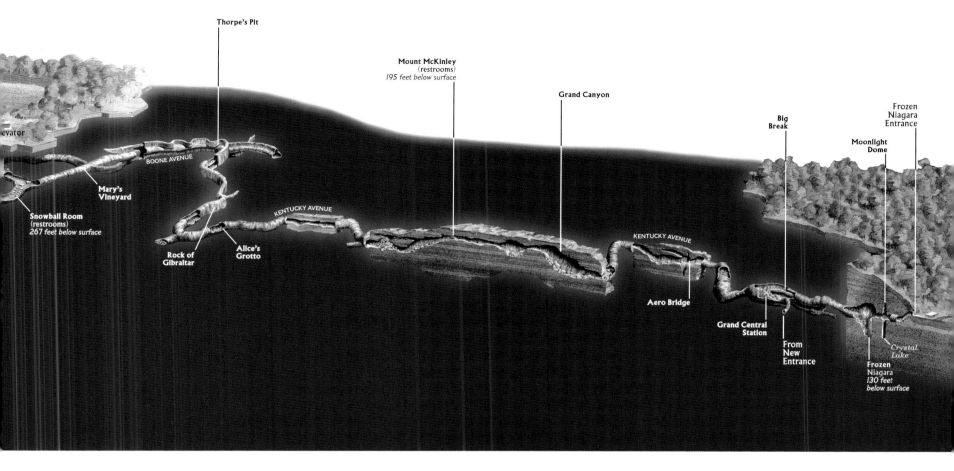

evator

Thorpe's Pit

Mount McKinley
(restrooms)
195 feet below surface

Grand Canyon

Frozen
Niagara
Entrance

Big
Break

Moonlight
Dome

BOONE AVENUE

Mary's
Vineyard

Snowball Room
(restrooms)
267 feet below surface

Rock of
Gibraltar

Alice's
Grotto

KENTUCKY AVENUE

KENTUCKY AVENUE

Aero Bridge

Grand Central
Station

From
New
Entrance

Frozen
Niagara
130 feet
below surface

Crystal
Lake

in poetry and literature, including a sperm whale analogy in Herman Melville's *Moby-Dick* in 1851: "With a lantern we might descend into the great Kentucky Mammoth Cave of his stomach."

The park's actual creation was inspired by the dramatic and true-life tragedy of Floyd Collins—an eerie remake of the ancient Lost John epic. On January 30, 1925, the accomplished spelunker Collins had opened up a new cave and managed to squeeze through a tight passageway into an undiscovered chamber. While shimmying back out, he broke his lamplight and dislodged a rock that pinned his leg, 150 feet from the entrance into Sand Cave. He spent the night trapped in this stone straightjacket, plunged into total darkness, screaming and terrified, clawing his fingers bloody while trying to escape.

The next day friends found Collins, fed him, and eventually rigged an electric light that helped keep him warm. But short of amputating his leg—which would've caused fatal blood loss—they couldn't extricate him. They tried crowbars, harness rope pulls, and a jack. He spent days immobilized and wet, as the rescue efforts intensified. Six days after being trapped, constant rains on the surface caused cave collapses around Collins. He survived, but aside from sobbing voice communications, he was now cut off from his rescuers. On

A path winds down and through the historic natural entrance to Mammoth Cave, leading to a viewing platform and the beginning of the park's more than 400 miles of explored caves.

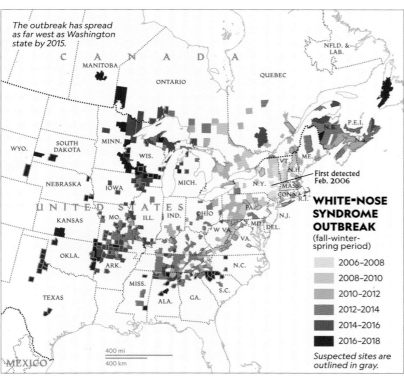

The outbreak has spread as far west as Washington state by 2015.

WHITE-NOSE SYNDROME OUTBREAK
(fall-winter-spring period)

- 2006–2008
- 2008–2010
- 2010–2012
- 2012–2014
- 2014–2016
- 2016–2018

First detected Feb. 2006

Suspected sites are outlined in gray.

400 mi
400 km

the surface, hundreds had assembled, while Collins's father capitalized on the calamity by selling pictures of his son.

As local newspapers turned the rescue into a frenzied crowd scene outside the cave, the state of Kentucky closed the dangerous passageway and engineers began digging a vertical shaft into the passage behind Collins. National Guard troops arrived to keep law and order among crowds now drawn by dramatic, nationwide radio broadcasts and newspaper reportage. As Collins prayed below, it had turned into a Prohibition-era carnival above, replete with hawkers selling moonshine and trinkets to thousands of rubberneckers.

After more than 10 days of agonizingly slow progress, they completed the shaft, but when they reached Collins, they found that he'd died two days earlier—on Friday, February 13—from exposure. In these tight, hazardous confines, they had no choice but to leave his body, still pinned by a rock.

The tragedy grew into an international media sensation, and continued with a funeral service held above the cave. Twenty thousand worshippers attended as Collins's body remained trapped below.

Two months later, the Collins family recovered the body and buried it above Crystal Cave—which Floyd had discovered on their farm in 1917—with a stalagmite as a tombstone.

When "Floyd Collins' Crystal Cave" (later recognized as part of the Mammoth Cave system) proved an unprofitable tourist operation, Floyd's father sold the farm. But the owner paid $10,000 under one condition: that he could disinter the body, do extensive cosmetic work to make Floyd presentable, and display the corpse in a glass-covered, bronze-metaled coffin inside the cave. Two years later, in 1929, the remains were stolen along the main tourist trail, then recovered the next day in a field above Green River. The corpse was missing a leg. Thereafter, Collins's glass coffin was covered and chained up inside the cave.

In 1989, surviving family convinced the Park Service to give "the Greatest Cave Explorer Ever Known"—as per his tombstone epitaph—his final burial in a nearby church cemetery. Lost John and the other mummies had also been reburied in 1976, after federal law prohibited displaying Native American remains. A steel grate now blocks the cave entrance that doomed Floyd Collins.

Compared to the essential publicity that Congress needed to establish other national parks, the Collins tragedy provided more than enough recognition for national park authorization in 1926. Lacking federal funds, like most parks in populous areas east of the Mississippi, Kentucky used eminent domain to purchase the private land above the cave system. In many cases farmers sold for pennies on the dollar. Fifteen years later, the park had acquired 600 parcels of land and its 72 square miles (later expanded by another 12 square miles) were established as Mammoth Cave National Park on July 1, 1941.

According to the "foundation document" for the park, its purpose "is to preserve, protect, interpret and study the internationally recognized biological and geologic features and processes associated with the longest known cave system in the world, the park's diverse

BATS HAVE LIVED IN THE DARKNESS OF THESE CAVES FOR MILLIONS OF YEARS, SUPPORTING THE NUTRIENT-POOR ECOSYSTEM.

forested, karst landscape, the Green and Nolin Rivers, and extensive evidence of human history; and to provide and promote public enjoyment, recreation and understanding."

Of 45 different mammals in the park, 13 are bats. Less than two centuries ago, millions of Indiana bats and gray bats were found in Mammoth Cave, but both were listed as endangered—in 1967 and 1976, respectively—due to human disturbances during hibernation. Also, unlike other bat species, Indiana and gray bats were found in relatively few caves outside the park.

An occasional cave visitor, the red bat, mostly lives in the park forests. Of the millions of bats that once lived in Mammoth, there were also big and little brown bats, tricolored bats, and the rarer, small-footed bat. Today, scarcely 3,000 bats remain.

In addition to eating insects, bats spread seeds and provide vital plant pollination outside the cave, so declining bat populations are likely to affect surrounding soybean and tobacco farms. And guano—now diminishing along with the bats—provides essential nutrients for the cave ecosystems.

The bats are now further compromised because of white-nose syndrome caused by fungus. First discovered in North America in 2006 among New York cave bats, white-nose syndrome arrived in Kentucky several years later. The fungus thrives in cool cave habitats, where it colonizes on the muzzles and delicate wings of hibernating bats. Though not directly toxic, the white, crusty fungus is a caloric drain on bats that depend upon limited fat stores during hibernation, causing them to die of starvation. Researchers are now experimenting with ultraviolet light to kill the fungus, as well as closing hibernation areas and decontaminating visitors that might carry in the fungus before they enter the cave.

Other troglophiles that make their way in and out of Mammoth include the cave crayfish, sculpin, springfish, salamanders, and various spiders. As for troglobites, the cave shrimp, the cave fly, the cave cricket, and the eyeless cave fish are translucent, blind, and adapted to navigating the perpetual dark with rows of sensory papillae. These extraordinarily well-evolved creatures exemplify the wonders of America's most capacious subterranean park, where humankind can survive only as visitors. ∎

Cave visitors in 1912 pose outside Consumptive's Room, once part of an experimental hospital testing the curative powers of cave air for tuberculosis patients.

CENTRAL PLAINS, LAKES & MOUNTAINS PARKS

CONTENTS

Water winds toward the Snake River at the Blacktail Ponds Overlook in Wyoming's Grand Teton National Park.

Map labels:
200 mi
200 km
N

CANADA
U.S.
GLACIER NATIONAL PARK
VOYAGEURS N.P.
ISLE ROYALE N.P.
Missouri
Lake Superior
MONTANA
NORTH DAKOTA
MINNESOTA
WISCONSIN
YELLOWSTONE NATIONAL PARK
SOUTH DAKOTA
Lake Michigan
IDAHO
GRAND TETON NATIONAL PARK
BADLANDS NATIONAL PARK
Mississippi
IOWA
WYOMING
NEBRASKA
ILLINOIS
UTAH
ROCKY MOUNTAIN NATIONAL PARK
Missouri
MISSOURI
COLORADO
KANSAS

▷ LOCATION **73 MILES N OF HOUGHTON, MICHIGAN**

▷ SIZE **850 SQUARE MILES**

▷ HIGHEST POINT **MOUNT DESOR, 1,394 FEET**

▷ VISITORS **25,798 IN 2018**

▷ ESTABLISHED **1940**

ISLE ROYALE NATIONAL PARK

Closer to Canada than the U.S. mainland, the archipelago of Isle Royale is more than 45 miles long and a dozen miles wide. Michigan's only national park encompasses more than 450 surrounding islets and submerged lands in northwest Lake Superior, with a boundary extending several miles north to Canadian waters. Three-quarters of the park is underwater. Easily the state's largest wilderness preserve—99 percent of its land area is federally designated wilderness—it is also the biggest island in the most expansive freshwater lake in the world. Seen from the air, the verdurous and thickly forested Isle Royale—ideal for moose—appears as a series of striated, rocky-shored peninsulas cut by water that is the color of cloudless sky. At first glance the park's myriad small, glacial-carved tarns are almost indistinguishable from the surrounding Lake Superior.

Isle Royale has only 19 different mammals—less than half of the number found on the nearby mainland. Most were carried to the island by boat, or walked across in winter on ice bridges as recently as several decades ago. The most famous residents are wolves that first migrated to the isolated Isle Royale more than 65 years ago, following the moose that had come several decades earlier. The

Snug Harbor Point is subjected to the outsize surf of Lake Superior in Isle Royale National Park, Michigan's only national park.

subsequent predator-prey study is the world's longest and most continuous work of its kind in field biology.

To reach Isle Royale, most backpackers or kayakers travel several hours by boat from Michigan or Minnesota's nearest shores. Scuba diving aficionados know this water world for a plethora of shipwrecks.

In 1671 French trappers named Isle Royale in honor of King Louis XIV, but the island had long been hunted and mined by Native Americans who paddled out from the mainland in birchbark canoes. A Jesuit missionary who visited the previous year wrote that the Ojibwe people had already named the island Minong (meaning "good place to live") and a place that was "celebrated for its copper." A rare, pure form of copper had been mined there for more than 4,500 years.

During a 19th-century copper mining boom, the island reopened to a more industrialized harvest, which was ultimately doomed by small quantities of the ore and the challenges of shipping it off such a remote island. Freight and passenger ship traffic had increased in the lake by 1881. While "threading the needle" through the narrow strait between Isle Royale and the Passage Island lighthouse to and from Canada's Thunder Bay, ships were beset by gales, blinding snowstorms, and oceanic waves. At least two dozen crashed and sunk amid the complex island archipelago.

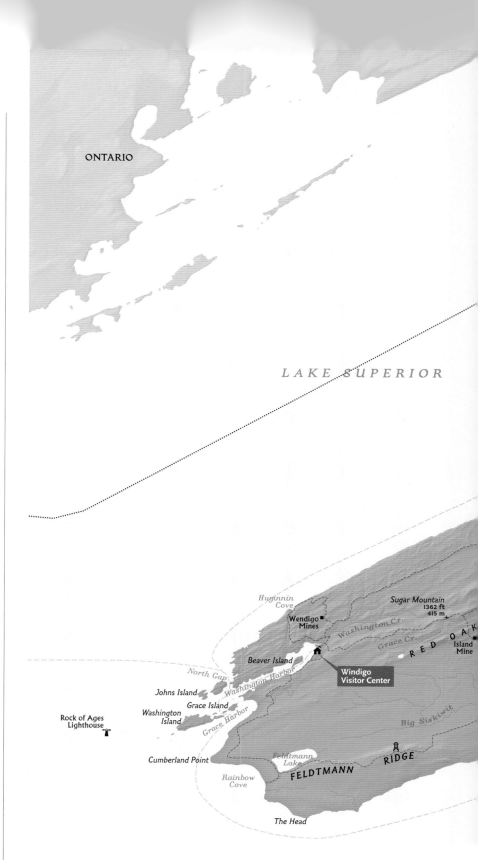

A hiker explores an open shaft at the Minong Mine on the Minong Ridge Trail. The Minong Mine was one of the island's most productive mines during the 19th-century copper boom.

Relative to its size, Lake Superior has caused more shipwrecks than any body of water in the world. Freshwater has a lower density than saltwater, making the waves on Superior steeper and closer together, and resulting in violent seas more dangerous than those of the great oceans. Waves routinely crest over 20 feet high. Combined with Isle Royale's many shoals and primitive 19th-century navigation equipment, the park waters became the Bermuda Triangle of Lake Superior, incurring nearly half of the 66 shipwrecks recorded across the giant lake.

The worst disaster occurred on the northeast side of the island, in November 1885. While loaded down with 400 tons of iron and brass, the 264-foot ship *Algoma* steamed into what experienced lake men called the greatest hurricane in years. Fortunately, only 15 passengers were on board despite accommodations for hundreds of passengers.

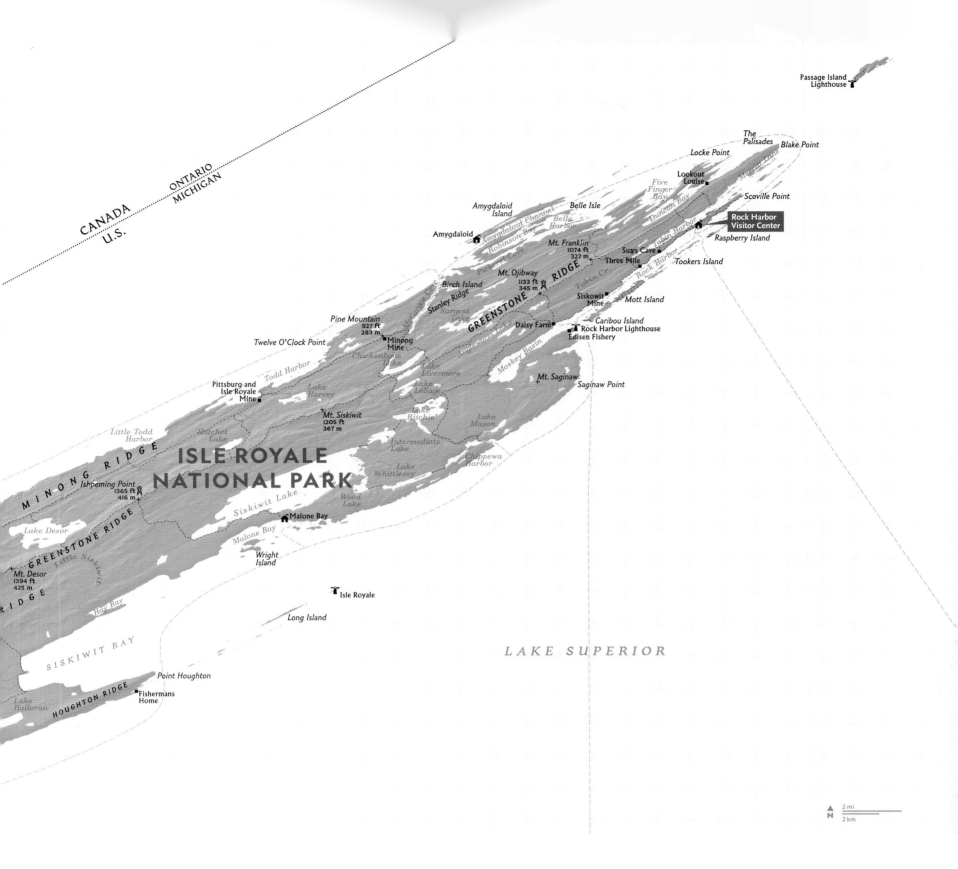

While the ship weathered the mounting waves, sails were set for stabilization. But *Algoma* lost its course in the driving snowstorm. In the last hours before dawn, just as the sails had been struck and the engines turned back on, the ship repeatedly crashed into rocks alongside Isle Royale's Mott Island, next to the present-day park headquarters. Knowing that the hull had been penetrated, the captain then tried to drive the ship onshore to prevent it from sinking.

Two of the 15 passengers and 14 crew members made it out alive. Forty-six drowned. Despite the captain and first mate's heroism during the accident, their ship certificates were suspended—if they had been using a sounding line or keeping an accurate log, they could have averted the wreck. To date, it is the greatest loss of life amid the many maritime disasters on Lake Superior. But it wouldn't be the last.

In 1918, the 532-foot-long *Chester A. Congdon* went aground on the opposite side of Isle Royale in heavy seas, blinded by fog. Although no lives were lost, the $1.5 million loss of the ship and its wheat cargo proved to be the costliest shipwreck on Lake Superior.

A few decades later, in 1947, a 525-foot-long ship, the S.S. *Emperor,* hit the same Canoe Rocks shoal in the predawn and sunk within half an hour. Although most of the crew had safely launched two lifeboats, one was pulled under from the suction of the enormous *Emperor*'s vortex as it sank beneath the calm lake surface. Twenty-one men survived but 12, including the captain, lost their lives. It had been a tranquil summer evening on the lake; accident investigators believed that the drowned first mate had fallen asleep at the wheel.

Today, buoys mark the well-preserved *Emperor* and *Congdon,* lying 25 to 100 feet deep as popular scuba diving sites. *Algoma*—badly

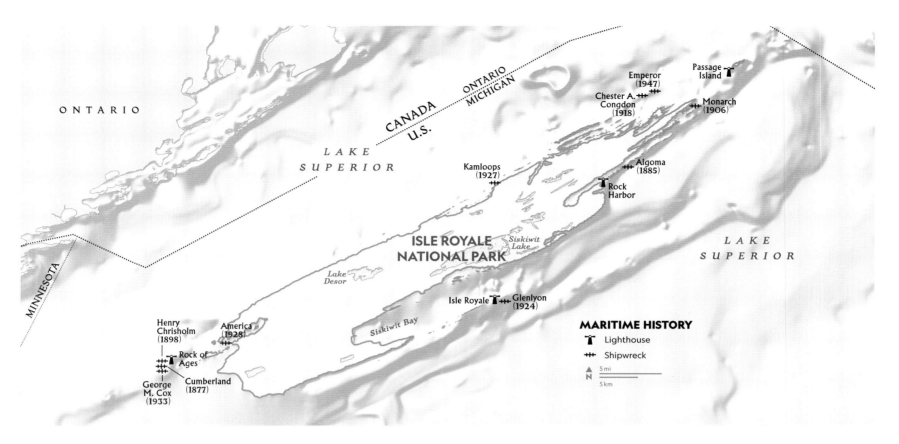

Emperor
(1947)

Passage
Island

Chester A.
Congdon
(1918)

Monarch
(1906)

ONTARIO

CANADA
U.S.

ONTARIO
MICHIGAN

LAKE
SUPERIOR

Kamloops
(1927)

Algoma
(1885)

Rock
Harbor

ISLE ROYALE
NATIONAL PARK

Siskiwit
Lake

LAKE
SUPERIOR

Lake
Desor

Isle Royale

Glenlyon
(1924)

MINNESOTA

Henry
Chrisholm
(1898)

America
(1928)

Siskiwit Bay

MARITIME HISTORY

Lighthouse

Shipwreck

Rock of
Ages

5 mi

5 km

George
M. Cox
(1933)

Cumberland
(1877)

ABOVE: **Deep below** Isle Royale's icy waters lies a maze of sunken vessels. Ten major shipwrecks dating from the 1870s to the 1940s are listed on the National Register, including *America*, a passenger vessel that is now the park's most popular dive, and *Emperor*, a bulk freighter that remains basically intact.

OPPOSITE: **The waters** around Isle Royale conceal a graveyard of shipwrecks. Remnants of the steamer *Algoma*, which sank after crashing against Mott Island in 1885, are scattered in Lake Superior.

BECAUSE OF ISLE ROYALE'S ISOLATION, VISITORS SPEND AN AVERAGE OF NEARLY FOUR DAYS THERE, WHEREAS AVERAGE VISITS TO MOST PARKS LAST ABOUT FOUR HOURS.

crushed during the wreck and scattered by wave action—is rarely visited. These and other sunken ships are protected by the Park Service as cultural treasures and are visited by over a thousand divers a year.

Despite its underwater attractions, Isle Royale is the least visited national park in the contiguous United States, the most difficult to access, and the only one that completely shuts down in winter. It has no paved roads; instead, the small island park has 165 miles of hiking trails and many paddling routes.

One of the pleasures of Isle Royale to botanists and casual visitors alike is observing more than 600 flowering plants found in the uplands, wetlands, and aquatic areas. The island is thick with blueberries and is heavily forested, but only those tree species with horizontally splayed roots—such as spruce and fir—thrive in the thin layer of soil. Plants range in size from the tall white pine crowning the island ridges to the dots of duckweed rafting on ponds. Along the surf-beaten shorelines and inside cracks in the rocks are plants such as the tiny pearlwort.

More than 60 rare plants can be found on the island. Many of these species—the low-growing black crowberry, eastern paintbrush, and the carnivorous butterwort—are otherwise found much farther north in the Arctic. These relics from the Pleistocene have managed to survive because of the cold microclimate created by the surrounding Lake Superior.

One of the most stunning of these rare plants is the prickly or three-toothed saxifrage—its five white flower petals with red dots and its translucent green stamens invite photography. Camera-carrying visitors are also drawn to more common beauties such as blooming calypso orchids, the fragrant twinflowers, the delicate lady slipper orchids, the reddened bunchberries, the purplish gay-wings, or the bell-shaped harebells.

Even more common are the big-toothed aster, sarsaparilla, asters, goldenrod, and grasses. There are more than 100 species of grasses and sedges on Isle Royale trails, along with marsh marigolds and skunk cabbages growing alongside the swamp boardwalks.

Closed to hunting and human traffic for most of the year, the park has become a rare outdoor laboratory and a pristine refuge for wildlife. Lynx and caribou existed on the island for several thousand years before hunting, trapping, mining, and other human activities eliminated the animals. While lynx were gone by the 1930s, one was briefly sighted in 1980 after crossing an ice bridge. The last caribou seen on Isle Royale was in 1925. Today the diminishing populations of resident wolf and moose have become the focus of researchers, who have continuously studied these animals since 1958.

RIGHT: **A moose** browses on vegetation in Isle Royale's forests. As moose numbers increase, so do concerns about their survival in a closed ecosystem with limited resources.

BELOW: **With annual observations** beginning in 1958, Isle Royale's wolf-moose project is the longest continuous predator-prey study of its kind. The isolated environment makes a unique case study for predator-prey interactions. Moose arrived on Isle Royale in the early 1900s and lived in a predator-free environment until the late 1940s, when wolves crossed an ice bridge to the island. After years of fluctuating populations, the number of wolves dwindled to two by 2016. During the annual winter study in 2017, the remaining wolf pair roamed territory at the island's east end and fed from five moose carcasses. In the absence of predation, researchers predict that the isle's moose population could double in the next five years. In 2018, the Park Service initiated a multiyear plan to reintroduce 20 to 30 wolves to restore predation to the island ecosystem. They released four translocated wolves in September and October 2018.

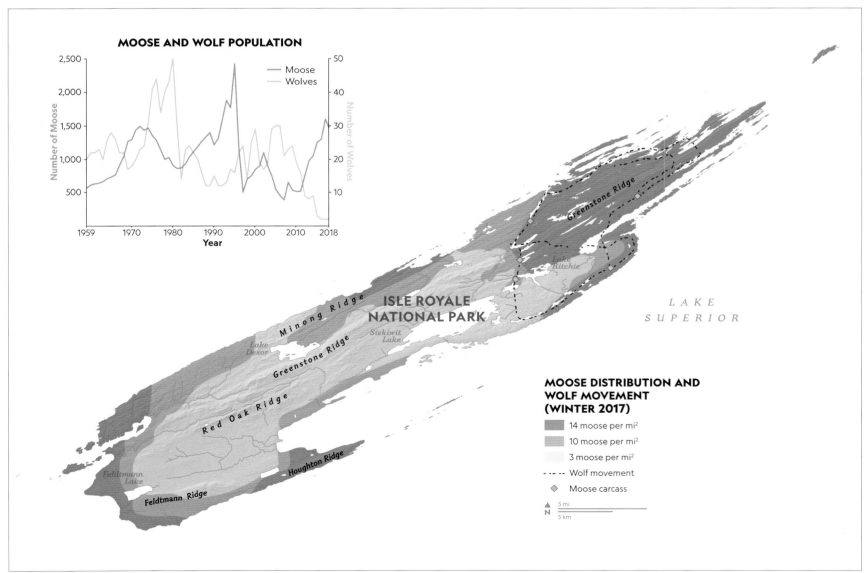

The presence and health of animals in the park—from mammals to fish to mussels—is tied to a changing climate. Without cold winters that build ice bridges for wildlife to cross from the mainland, the island lacks a method for new genes to enter an otherwise closed ecosystem. Although ice bridges were never common, they are becoming increasingly rare.

Since 1980, the lake's surface temperature has increased about 2°F (1.1°C) each decade. Meanwhile, the ice cover on the lake has decreased from 23 to 12 percent over the last century, or about 0.5 percent a year. According to a study of 235 lakes around the world conducted by the National Aeronautics and Space Administration (NASA) and the National Science Foundation, Lake Superior is one of the fastest warming lakes on the planet.

Warming temperatures on the island's many inland lakes is driving a cold-water fish called the cisco toward extinction. It is also likely that diminishing ice and warming lake temperatures have allowed invasive species like the zebra mussel, spiny water flea, and the lamprey to enter Lake Superior. If zebra mussels were to access the park lakes, it's estimated that they would cover most every habitable surface on an inland lake floor within four years; likewise, the spiny fleas would disrupt zooplankton food sources for native fish. In response, Isle Royale instructs boaters, backpackers, and divers to clean their gear and empty boat bilges outside of the park.

The celebrated wolves and moose of Isle Royale are also in jeopardy. The Isle Royale wolf-moose project has found that the decline in the wolf population is due to a genetic malformation among the isolated island family. Researchers believe this was caused when a new alpha male crossed to the island in 1997; his prolific breeding with all of the fertile females eventually resulted in inbred wolves.

Most recently, as the wolf population plummeted from a high of 50 to a single female, the moose numbers exploded to an estimated 1,600 in 2017—increasing more than 20 percent per year since 2011. Without intervention, their voracious appetites threaten the health of the island's forests and expose the growing herd to mass starvation and extinction.

For years, the Park Service's approach to wilderness preservation on the island was generally defined as "letting nature take its own course," but biologists pressed for stocking the island with more wolves. In 2018, the Park Service agreed to take action, developing strategies for the capture, relocation, and introduction of wolves from the Great Lakes region back to Isle Royale. That fall, four wolves were released on the island. One wolf died, and on January 31, 2019, an unusually cold winter formed an ice bridge that allowed one wolf to return to the mainland. The success of the new program will ultimately be measured by the music of wolves once again baying their primeval vaunts into the lake sky. ∎

A hiker explores boreal forest along the Greenstone Ridge Trail near Chickenbone Lake. Spanning nearly the length of the island, the trail traces higher elevations with stellar views.

▷ LOCATION **12 MILES E OF INTERNATIONAL FALLS, MINNESOTA**

▷ SIZE **341 SQUARE MILES**

▷ HIGHEST POINT **NEAR MEAD WOOD ROAD, 1,410 FEET**

▷ VISITORS **239,656 IN 2018**

▷ ESTABLISHED **1975**

VOYAGEURS NATIONAL PARK

n the northwoods of Minnesota, several miles shy of the Canadian border, exposed primordial rock holds glacial carved lakes. Kabetogama, Namakan, and Rainy Lakes surround the boggy Kabetogama Peninsula and hundreds more islands.

Voyageurs National Park flanks the Boundary Waters Canoe Area Wilderness, Canada's Quetico Provincial Park, and other state and national forests. The park and these other 10,000 square miles of protected aqua-wilderness are collectively known as "the Boundary Waters." Voyageurs' distance from urbanity and artificial light make it the best national park in the contiguous United States for viewing the northern lights.

Free of intrusive roadways, Voyageurs' campsites are accessible only by boats and are thus popular with anglers, paddlers, and motorboaters. The inner lakes are closed to private watercraft to prevent the spread of invasive species, but the Park Service provides boat tours and rental boats. Fishermen—like the ospreys, bald eagles, merlins, great blue herons, loons, cormorants, pelicans, and otters found in the park—chase abundant fish.

Guided by skillful Ojibwe, the park's namesake French Canadian voyageurs traveled through the interconnected border lakes more

Sunset paints the sky in Voyageurs National Park, as seen from Kabetogama Lake Overlook. As night comes, a panorama of stars appears above the secluded islands.

than a century before the nation's founding. These hearty mountain men—famous for their wilderness chorales—paddled oversize birchbark canoes, trading and freighting furs from the far reaches of North America back to Montreal.

At the southern edge of the Canadian Shield stretching to the Arctic Ocean and forming the geologic core of the continent, Voyageurs National Park contains some of the most ancient rock in North America. From a canoe, you can caress compacted bedrock nearly three billion years old—more than half the age of the withered Earth itself.

The park's central peninsula is mostly schist and gneiss created through a combination of heat, pressure, and folding and uplifting of the crust. Today it's heavily furred with new-growth forest. On the mainland, granite forged within age-old volcanoes pokes above lakes in polished ledges.

During the Pleistocene epoch 190,000 years ago, the Canadian Shield endured several glaciation events that scoured out the lakes and rounded the hills. Rocks frozen into these glaciers scratched out striations and furrows on the underlying bedrock that allow geologists and visitors alike to track the long-departed ice as it dropped erratic boulders—from the size of Volkswagens to toy cars—throughout the park.

Frances Anne Hopkins's "Shooting the Rapids," painted in 1879, depicts French Canadian fur trappers—*voyageurs*—navigating the area's wild rivers to ply their trade.

As the glaciers and their meltwaters receded more than 10,000 years ago, Paleo-Indians passed through the region. By 8000 B.C., a plant-gathering and hunting culture used more permanent shelters—two of these Archaic period sites have been found in the park and contained evidence of stone tools. The more recent Woodland period, from 100 to 900, showed the first use of ceramics, sophisticated tools, and a dependence upon wild rice.

The first European, a Frenchman, arrived in 1688, and spent the winter interacting with Ojibwe inhabitants, who had migrated from the East Coast around 1600. The ingenious Ojibwe—who thrived on fish, berries, rice, and sugar maple trees—would serve as vital guides and canoe makers for the coming wave of Frenchmen called voyageurs. Although these burly Europeans could hold their own, they depended upon these local Native Americans for herbal medicine and spiritual advice. The Ojibwe trapped fur animals and traded the pelts to the voyageurs for ammunition, flintlock rifles, blankets, and axes.

As fur-bearing animals were trapped out, the voyageurs—traveling in brigades of four to eight canoes—pushed farther west in their quest for pelts. Beaver hats in particular had become fashionable in

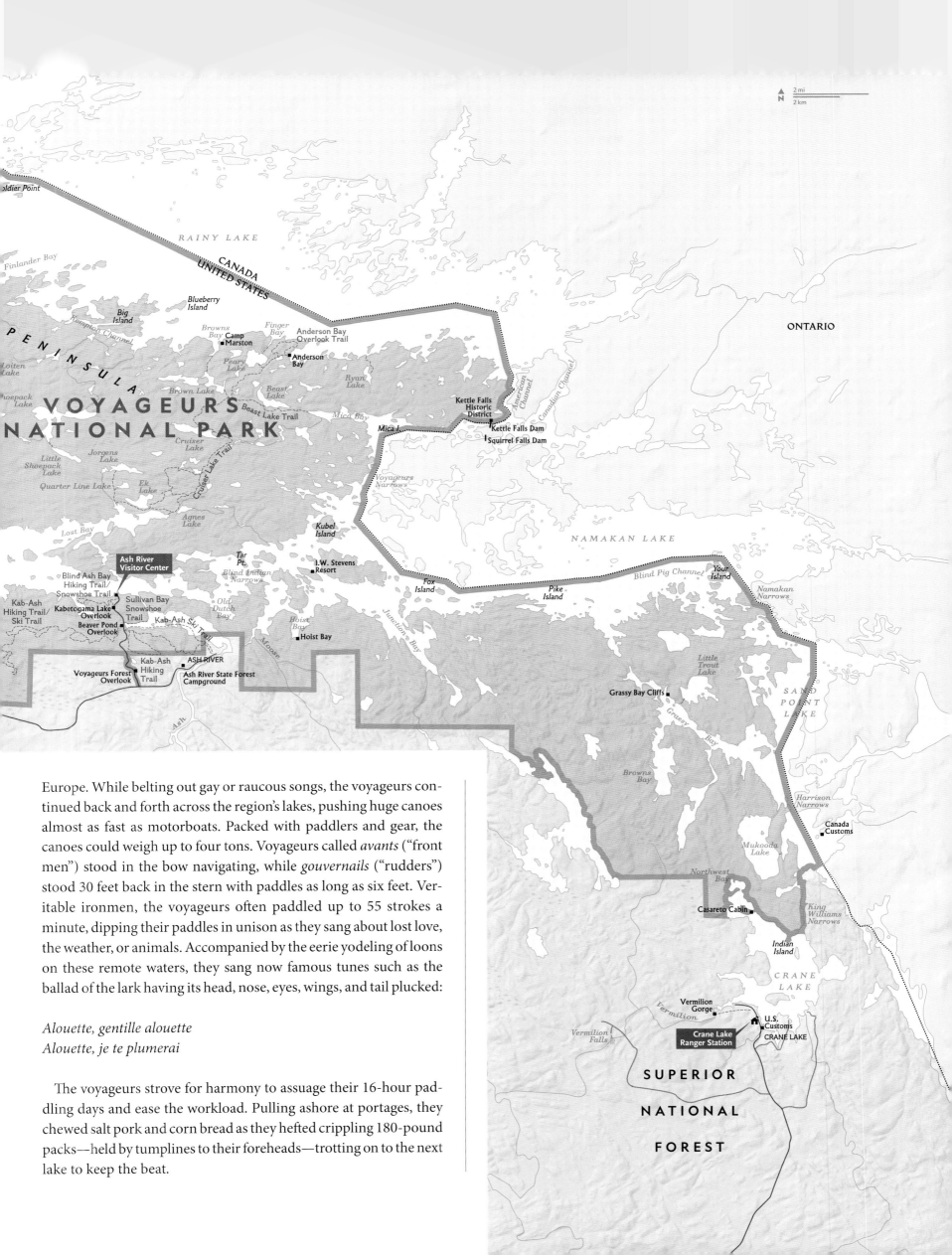

RAINY LAKE

CANADA
UNITED STATES

Soldier Point

Finlander Bay

Blueberry Island

Big Island

Kempton Channel

Browns Bay

Camp Marston

Finger Bay

Anderson Bay Overlook Trail

ONTARIO

Loiten Lake

Peary Lake

Anderson Bay

Shoepack Lake

P E N I N S U L A

Brown Lake

Beast Lake

Ryan Lake

VOYAGEURS
NATIONAL PARK

Beast Lake Trail

Mica Bay

Mica I.

Kettle Falls Historic District

Kettle Falls Dam

Squirrel Falls Dam

American Channel

Canadian Channel

Little Shoepack Lake

Jorgens Lake

Cruiser Lake

Cruiser Lake Trail

Quarter Line Lake

Ek Lake

Agnes Lake

Voyageurs Narrows

Lost Bay

Kubel Island

NAMAKAN LAKE

Ash River Visitor Center

Tar Pt.

I.W. Stevens Resort

Blind Ash Bay Hiking Trail/ Snowshoe Trail

Blind Indian Narrows

Your Island

Blind Pig Channel

Kab-Ash Hiking Trail/ Ski Trail

Sullivan Bay Snowshoe Trail

Kabetogama Lake Overlook

Beaver Pond Overlook

Kab-Ash Ski Trail

Old Dutch Bay

Fox Island

Pike Island

Namakan Narrows

Junction Bay

Hoist Bay

Moose

Hoist Bay

Little Trout Lake

Voyageurs Forest Overlook

Kab-Ash Hiking Trail

ASH RIVER

Ash River State Forest Campground

Ash

S A N D   P O I N T   L A K E

Grassy Bay Cliffs

Grassy Bay

Browns Bay

Harrison Narrows

Canada Customs

Mukooda Lake

Northwest Bay

Casareto Cabin

King Williams Narrows

Indian Island

CRANE LAKE

Vermilion Gorge

Vermilion

U.S. Customs

Vermilion Falls

Crane Lake Ranger Station

CRANE LAKE

SUPERIOR

NATIONAL

FOREST

Europe. While belting out gay or raucous songs, the voyageurs continued back and forth across the region's lakes, pushing huge canoes almost as fast as motorboats. Packed with paddlers and gear, the canoes could weigh up to four tons. Voyageurs called *avants* ("front men") stood in the bow navigating, while *gouvernails* ("rudders") stood 30 feet back in the stern with paddles as long as six feet. Veritable ironmen, the voyageurs often paddled up to 55 strokes a minute, dipping their paddles in unison as they sang about lost love, the weather, or animals. Accompanied by the eerie yodeling of loons on these remote waters, they sang now famous tunes such as the ballad of the lark having its head, nose, eyes, wings, and tail plucked:

Alouette, gentille alouette
Alouette, je te plumerai

The voyageurs strove for harmony to assuage their 16-hour paddling days and ease the workload. Pulling ashore at portages, they chewed salt pork and corn bread as they hefted crippling 180-pound packs—held by tumplines to their foreheads—trotting on to the next lake to keep the beat.

2 mi
2 km
N

A range of species including ducks, cormorants, owls, and eagles make this shifting waterscape home. Below the surface, walleye, northern pike, and lake trout make the park a sought-after fishing destination.

Until the mid 1800s, their songs reverberated through the northwoods. These voyageurs would never have imagined that, a century later, they would be immortalized by an iconic national park. Their Ojibwe mentors—savvy astronomical observers and innovators of the dream catcher hung above sleeping children's heads—continue to harvest rice around the Boundary Waters and pass on spiritual lessons to modern-day Anglos.

By 1900, the Ojibwe were moved onto reservations, and loggers and gold miners had succeeded the long-gone voyageurs. When the short-lived mining boom ended, resident miners, prospectors, saloonkeepers and shopkeepers, and other gold rushers abandoned Rainy Lake City only years after the city had been established in the northwoods. Nearly 200 people had once lived in this wet-weather place but years later, tourists would continue to visit the silent, once bustling ghost town.

Meanwhile, logging companies flourished. Trees fell and dams were built to provide a constant water supply for the sawmills taking down the dense pine forest. Logging ended in 1940 as the trees were all cut down, but longtime resorts and commercial fishing operations (mostly caviar harvested from sturgeon) continued their operations amid a barren landscape of pine stumps, slowly growing over with new forests.

Decades later, the park bought out most properties; still, over a thousand private acres remain within the park boundaries. The Park Service now maintains the dams and more than 50 fishing camps and historic buildings, including the Rainy Lake City saloon. Despite the thin soil cover remaining atop bedrock once scraped by ancient glaciers, many diverse tree species have finally taken root after forest fires and the extensive logging of a century ago. This includes basswood, pine, maples, and oak from the south—mingling with northern boreal trees such as birch, aspen, fir, and spruce. Throughout the summer, berries and wildflowers can be found in abundance.

Most visitors come to Voyageurs for the world-class fishing. Among the park's 58 fish species is the sought-after walleye, which can weigh over 20 pounds and is known for its excellent vision; the northern pike, a serpentine and sharp-toothed aggressor; the elusive muskie, which demands hundreds of casts; the non-native smallmouth bass; and the diminutive yet tasty crappie. Once caught, most of these fish are destined for the fry pan.

Still, the health of the wildlife and those who dine on it remain at risk because of mercury. In the water, deposited mercury turns to toxic methylmercury as tiny plankton consume it. Then small fish are in turn eaten by larger predators, including humans.

The whole circle of life is affected: Birds contaminated with mercury lay fewer or smaller eggs. Salamanders become sluggish. In all vertebrates, higher contaminations of mercury affect kidney function as well as neurological and hormonal systems.

Scientists linked most of the Boundary Waters pollution to coal plant smokestacks, which emit mercury as vapor that then drops earthward in rain. As the 1990 Clean Air Act amendments mandated "scrubbers" and other techniques to reduce emissions from U.S. power plants, researchers studying the Boundary Waters documented a 20 percent decline in mercury deposition between 1985 and 2011.

Still, efforts to reduce mercury in Voyageurs National Park are ongoing. Pollution is long lasting; global emissions are increasing. In 2003, researchers learned that the dams cause fluctuating water levels that increase bacteria—enhancing mercury methylation in the lakes. But as the park stabilized water levels, some of the mercury contamination declined.

By 2012, mercury in both the lake water and in yellow perch tissues decreased in two of the four lakes sampled in Voyageurs. Still, all park lakes sampled for mercury by the Environmental Protection Agency remain listed as "impaired." The Minnesota Department of Health regularly posts specific warnings about what fish and lakes to avoid in Voyageurs National Park.

Although fallout from the skies appears manageable, albeit daunting, it's not the only environmental issue confronting Voyageurs. Proposed sulfide mining projects in northern Minnesota—much like the surrounding power plants spewing mercury into the air—could further jeopardize the waters of the park. As mining corporations exploit sulfide ore deposits to extract copper, gold, and nickel, sulfuric acid and other contaminants are produced, which can leak into the surrounding waters. As pollution flows downstream and is eventually absorbed by all waters,

Four major lakes and 26 medium-size lakes compose Voyageurs National Park. With nearly 40 percent of its area covered by water, many of the park's best sights are accessible only by boat. A labyrinth of interconnected waterways provides ample opportunities for canoeing, kayaking, swimming, and fishing.

THE VOYAGEURS WHO NAVIGATED THESE WATERS BY CANOE WERE FAMOUS FOR THEIR STAMINA, PADDLING UP TO 16 HOURS A DAY.

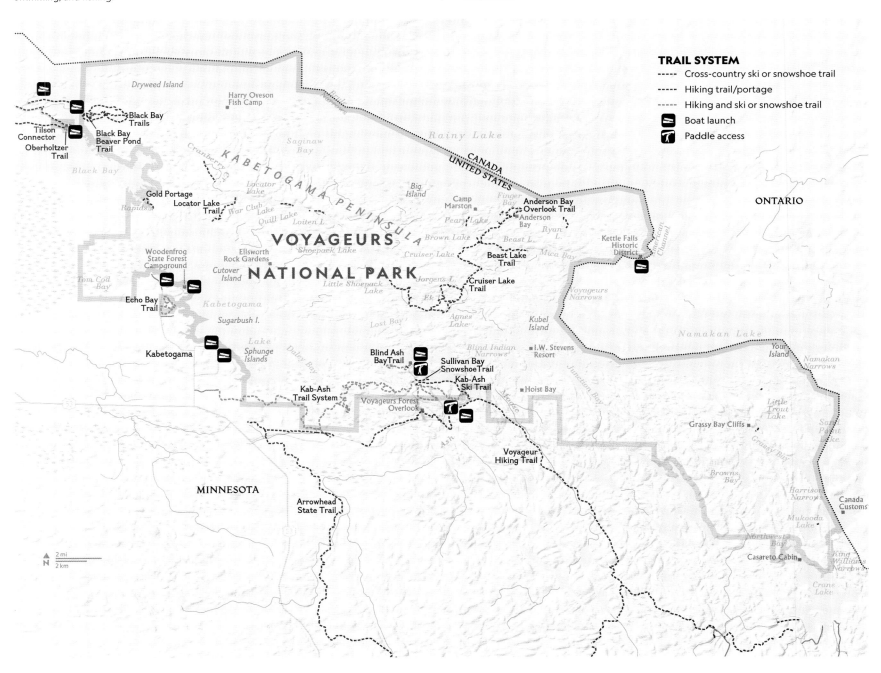

TRAIL SYSTEM
- - - - Cross-country ski or snowshoe trail
- - - - Hiking trail/portage
- - - - Hiking and ski or snowshoe trail
- Boat launch
- Paddle access

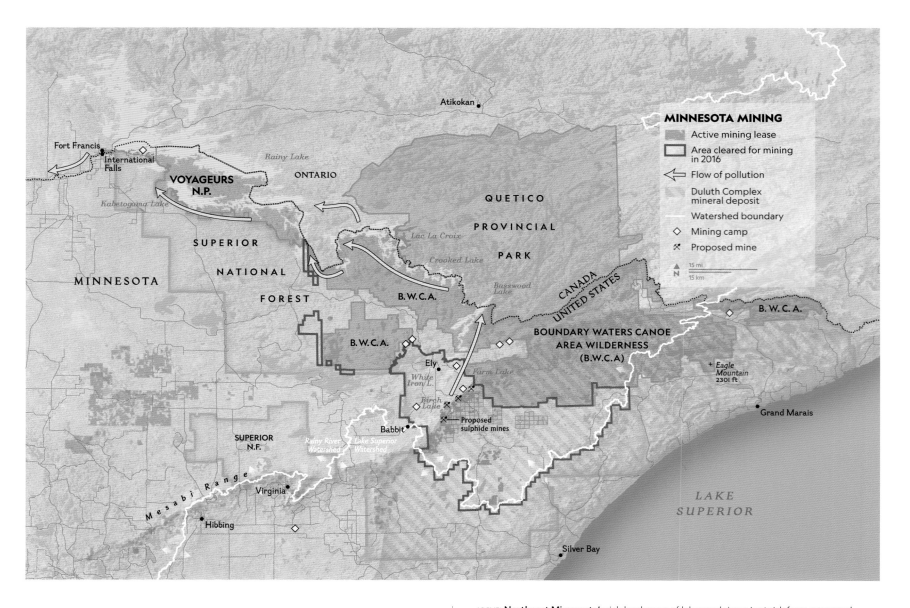

it exemplifies how park boundaries sometimes offer only an illusory safety.

ABOVE: **Northeast Minnesota's** rich landscape of lakes and rivers is at risk from proposed sulfide-ore copper mining. Extraction could seep hazardous runoff into waters that flow into protected areas such as Voyageurs National Park, Boundary Waters Canoe Area Wilderness, and Canada's Quetico Provincial Park.

OPPOSITE: **Majestic skies** over Voyageurs glow with the northern lights, created by the interplay of the sun's particles and atoms in Earth's atmosphere. These collisions create colors dependent on altitude and the atoms involved: green and red for oxygen, blue and purple for nitrogen.

High over the mines and the mercury fallout from the stratosphere—atop the ionosphere, as high as 400 miles above the Earth—the magnetosphere is being bombarded by debris and radiation streaming from the sun. Serving as a planetary-wide scrubber, the Earth's magnetic field deflects these detrimental rays and particles. Without this formidable magnetic shield, the planet would be cooked. Properly positioned in the darkest places below, Earthlings can bear witness to the bombardment called the northern lights.

Also known as the aurora borealis—as coined by Galileo in 1619, for the Roman goddess of the dawn and the Greek north wind—the lights can be seen when the sun produces the ideal radiation during clear nights from the higher latitudes of the planet where the magnetosphere weakens. At Voyageurs National Park, this spectacle happens as often as 200 nights a year.

Picture green or pink or blue shimmering bands or curtains. Sometimes they're ribbon shapes, strobing into searchlight beams, or flaring up into what appears to be an interstellar explosion. The lights snake across the night sky, morphing into heav-

enly versions of a delicate cedar frond or stream water diverting off rocks.

Until 2012, the idea that these spectacular space fireworks could also be heard hissing and crackling was derided as folklore. Yet because these particle streams from the sun often cause geomagnetic storms—interfering with electrical grids or satellite transmissions—scientists concluded that intense geomagnetic storms break open the electrical charges held by inversion layers close to the Earth's surface. As the charges are released, they escape with a stream of crackling noises.

Consequently, modern-day skywatchers in the northwoods now can turn off their flashlights to listen, look, and imagine how past Voyageurs inhabitants perceived the night sky. The Ojibwe—masters of their own universe—called the northern lights *Wawatay*. To this day, the people believe that Wataway are the spirits of ancestors dancing in the sky to celebrate life and remind onlookers below that we are all part of the celestial wonder of creation. ■

▷ LOCATION **75 MILES SE OF RAPID CITY, SOUTH DAKOTA**

▷ SIZE **379 SQUARE MILES**

▷ HIGHEST POINT **RED SHIRT TABLE, 3,340 FEET**

▷ VISITORS **1,008,942 IN 2018**

▷ ESTABLISHED **1978**

BADLANDS NATIONAL PARK

n western South Dakota, Badlands contains the largest expanse of protected prairie in the National Park System, with boundaries curling into the massive Pine Ridge Indian Reservation. The park is furred by grasslands that once blanketed nearly half of the continent, and plants and trees dot the terrain. Both ankle- and knee-high grass species support a host of animal life, from bounding pronghorn, common mule deer, and barking prairie dogs to bison that stand up to six feet tall at the shoulder.

Visitors are likely to see the megafauna grazing below bizarrely eroded, weatherworn walls and red-striped sedimentation of the surrounding buttes and mesas that dominate the horizon.

"Viewed at a distance," Jesuit Father Pierre-Jean de Smet wrote in 1848, "these lands exhibit the appearance of extensive villages and ancient castles, but under forms so extraordinary, and so capricious a style of architecture, that we might consider them as appertaining to some new world, or ages far remote."

De Smet was describing the rugged gullies, ridges, and spires that still give travelers fits while trying to traverse over and around dangerously steep terrain that shifts underfoot—as per the Lakota name Mako Sica ("land bad"). Today the Oglala Lakota Nation co-manages

Grasses fringe the Badlands' stunning rock formations, vestiges of seas covering the landscape millions of years ago. Colored striations in the rock appear from different sediments and age.

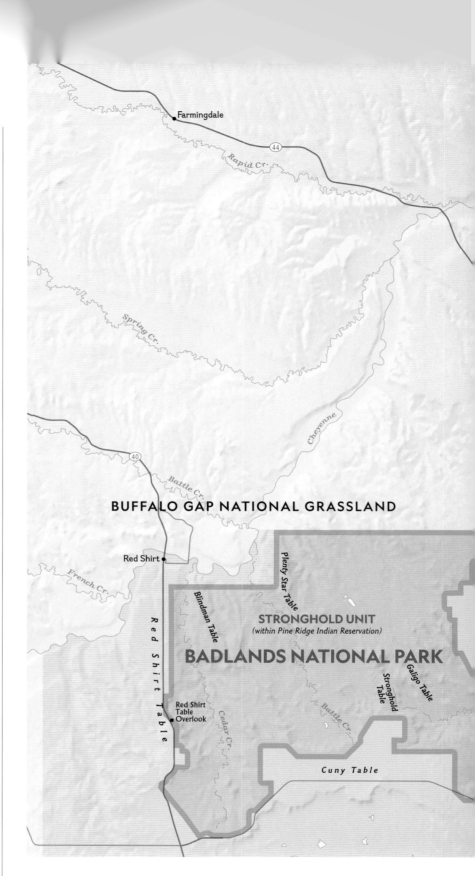

the southern Stronghold District of the park within the reservation. Centuries before paleontologists discovered the multitude of fossils there, the Lakota people referred to these former creatures as *Unktegila* ("water monsters"). Badlands holds one of the world's richest concentrations of prehistoric fossils, containing the remains of marine organisms, large mammals, and innumerable reptiles.

Unlike many other national parks, Badlands is a basic geologic landform despite its complex and angular landscape. It was initially twisted and tilted by Black Hills volcanic activity to the east, then fully shaped through deposits and erosion. The underlying fossils

The Badlands are rife with ancient fossils like this saber-toothed cat skull. The park has more late Eocene and Oligocene epoch mammal fossils than anywhere else on Earth.

are found in a depositional, six-layer cake that started more than 65 million years ago when shallow ocean buried the land. This black, mud-intensive Pierre shale level—a division of Upper Cretaceous rocks formed from shale, sandstone, and volcanic ash that looks and feels like soapy clays—contained the long-jawed sea creatures of Lakota myths, along with turtles, fish, ammonites, nautiloids, and other marine reptiles.

Up to 34 million years ago, during the late Eocene epoch, the region became a subtropical river floodplain, seen in the Chadron formation. A layer of bare and mounded gray sediments conceals sharks' teeth, shards of alligators, and fossilized wood. Remnants of the Oligocene epoch, from 34 to 23 million years ago, point to rabbit-like rodents, burrowing creatures that resembled sheep, fork-horned rhinos and hippopotamuses, giant pigs, saber-toothed cats, deer,

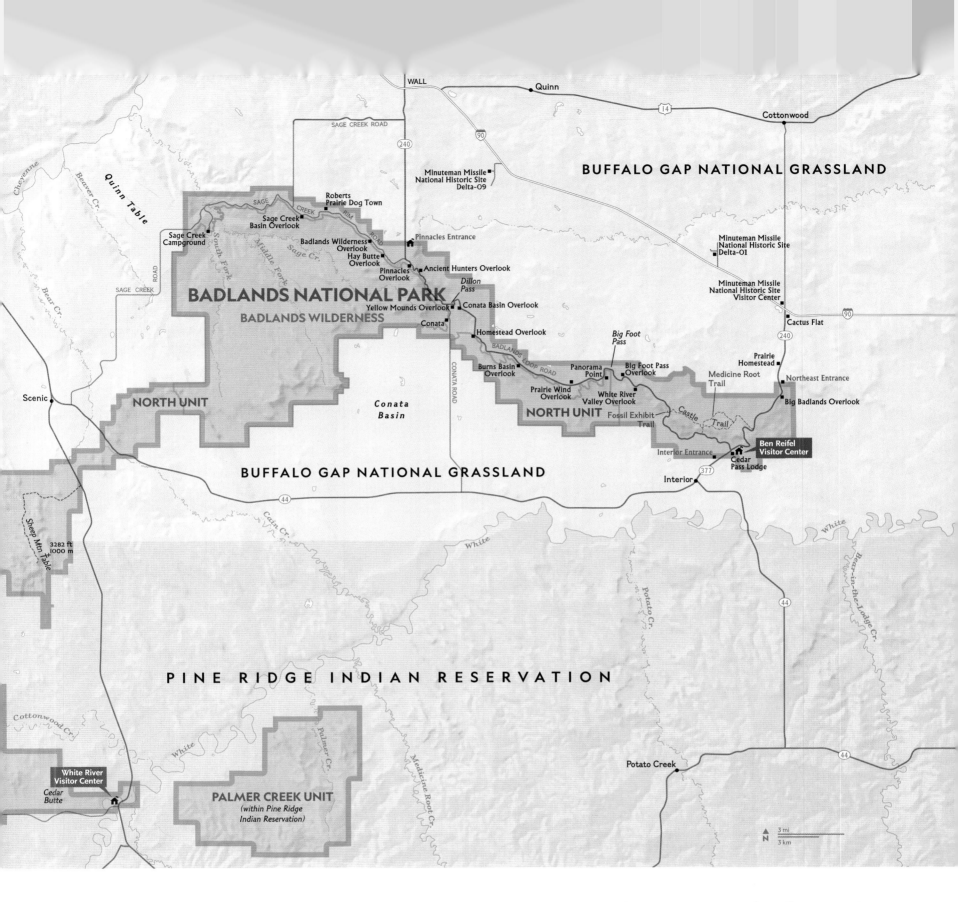

camels, and three-toed horses. The other hidden fossil treasures from this time period—found in the higher layers of the Brule formation, the Rockyford Ash, and the Sharps foundation—include fish, various reptiles, and birds—all creatures that give clues to the evolutionary process. These fossils represent a well-preserved window into the past, showing both the diversity of creatures and an accurate snapshot of the prehistoric environment.

After millions of years of deposition, erosion began tucking into the park's intricately structured layer cake. The erosion began a half million years ago as water cut through the different rocks and carved abstract shapes into the former floodplain, exposing ancient fossil soils.

So it continues. Each year, up to 16 inches of rain rakes the dissected landscape, often in fierce, midsummer thunderstorms. Then

another inch or two of sediment washes away. Gullies are cut deeper. Pinnacles crash to the ground. And more fossils poke out of the sediment like ancient sea creatures surfacing for air.

Nineteenth-century paleontologists repeatedly came and removed fossils—or bison and wolf carcasses—for display in distant museums. In 1874, Dr. O. C. Marsh of Yale University snuck into the dinosaur grounds at night because of increasing tensions with local Oglala Lakota. At the center of the conflict, an estimated 10,000 hunters poured onto the plains to collect bounties on valuable bison (also incorrectly called buffalo) hides. An average of 5,000 bison—an animal that symbolized the Plains Indians' survival—were being killed each day. The Lakota felt violated, and in their eyes, white men collecting dinosaur bones committed the same transgression as those slaughtering bison. A war party scouting for Dr. Marsh, "the Big Bone Chief," narrowly missed capturing him. Nonetheless, he relayed an Oglala Lakota complaint to Washington, D.C., officials about how the Bureau of Indian Affairs (BIA) had been denying the tribe their rations. Congress began investigating the BIA, which would undergo many needed reforms over the years.

The area's fraught cultural history is remembered in the park's Oglala Lakota Heritage Center. A treaty in 1868 had assigned the tribe to live on one of many reservations—such as the Pine Ridge Agency (later renamed Reservation); a half dozen years later the discovery of gold in the region intensified conflict over the land. Then a flood of homesteaders illegally staked their claims in violation of the 1868 treaty, and to make things worse, these settlers unknowingly referred to the Oglala Lakota as Sioux or "snake." Because the word came from their enemies, the Ojibwe, it was considered a slur. Angry at the seizure of their lands, the tribe migrated north to Canada during the summers in hopes of finding more bison—the Lakota's primary source of sustenance had been hunted out from the Dakotas. In winter, they returned to squalid camps on reservation land, where they were met with meager food and blanket handouts from the U.S. government.

BELOW LEFT: **Circa 1910,** Oglala Lakota Indians (called Sioux by white settlers) gather for a photo near Pine Ridge—what would become the South Unit of the park and reservation land called the Stronghold District.

BELOW RIGHT: **The park's namesake land features** formed slowly, starting as grains of sand, silt, clay, and other sediments first deposited during the Cretaceous period. As the parkland evolved from sea to river-cut woodland, the deposits varied, creating strata that would be ordered into groups called formations: The oldest is black Pierre Shale deposited 69 to 75 million years ago. The lighter, younger Sharps formation deposited 28 to 30 million years ago is at the top. About 500,000 years ago, erosion began sculpting the rock layers into the fantastic shapes seen today.

OPPOSITE: **Clouds brood** over otherworldly rock formations in the park—a jagged maze of canyons, gullies, ridges, and mesas accessible by foot trails and a scenic byway. The number of visitors to this land of extremes annually exceeds the population of South Dakota.

In despair and desperation—and often hungry—the people became followers of the Ghost Dance religion. Like many Plains Indians, the Oglala Lakota believed that their pacifistic, marathon dance sessions would restore their hunting grounds and make the white men go away. In early December 1890, nearly a thousand members of the tribe walked through prairie dog colonies and rattlesnake terrain, then climbed a mesa and crossed a knife-edge ridge. On the grassy, windswept promontory protected by cliffs, they called their sacred place Oonakizin or "Stronghold" (now in the southern district of the modern park boundaries).

On Oonakizin, they wore Ghost Shirts—carefully stitched with deer hide, wool, porcupine quills, and human hair and dyed red and yellow like the local sedimentary striping—that were purported to repel rifle bullets. So clad, they performed their Ghost Dance, chanting and swaying all night until they dropped from exhaustion, finishing a ceremony that they believed would manifest the vision of having their lands returned. But frightened homesteaders misinterpreted these gatherings as cultish uprisings and contacted the military.

Although the band of December 1890 safely returned to the reservation, it was the last Lakota Ghost Dance. At the end of that month, a trigger-happy and anxious military detachment of 500 heavily armed men intercepted 350 thinly clad and hungry Lakota who were 30 miles south of Oonakizin at a creek called Wounded Knee, on their way to food and safety at the reservation. After an argument between an officer and a deaf brave who didn't hear or understand the command to put down his valuable rifle, the soldiers

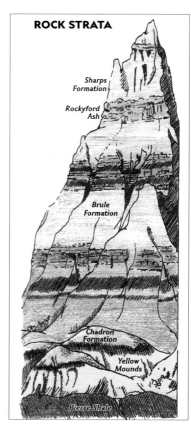

ROCK STRATA

Sharps Formation

Rockyford Ash

Brule Formation

Chadron Formation

Yellow Mounds

Pierre Shale

opened fire with huge Thompson guns. Approximately 200 Lakota were massacred, many of them unarmed and many killed while running away. Half were women and children. Thirty-one soldiers died, mostly from "friendly fire" as the Thompson guns rattled off their bullets indiscriminately into the crowd. Troops then stripped the dead of their Ghost Shirts while corpses were posed for photographs later to be sold as souvenirs. Twenty soldiers were awarded Medals of Honor.

"Although over a century has passed," reads a Badlands National Park bulletin, "neither the accusations nor the evidence has changed. Wounded Knee has become a confrontation of Good and Evil, rather than a complex misunderstanding and series of errors." Wounded Knee became an 870-acre historic landmark in 1965.

Badlands was established as a national monument in 1939, but within three years, the U.S. government needed a military bomb-testing range and appropriated 534 square miles from the Indian reservation and a small piece of the monument. Over a hundred families—including a Wounded Knee survivor, white homesteaders,

THE AMERICAN BISON IS THE COUNTRY'S LARGEST LAND ANIMAL, WEIGHING AS MUCH AS A TON, BUT IT CAN MOVE QUICKLY, REACHING SPEEDS OF UP TO 40 MILES AN HOUR.

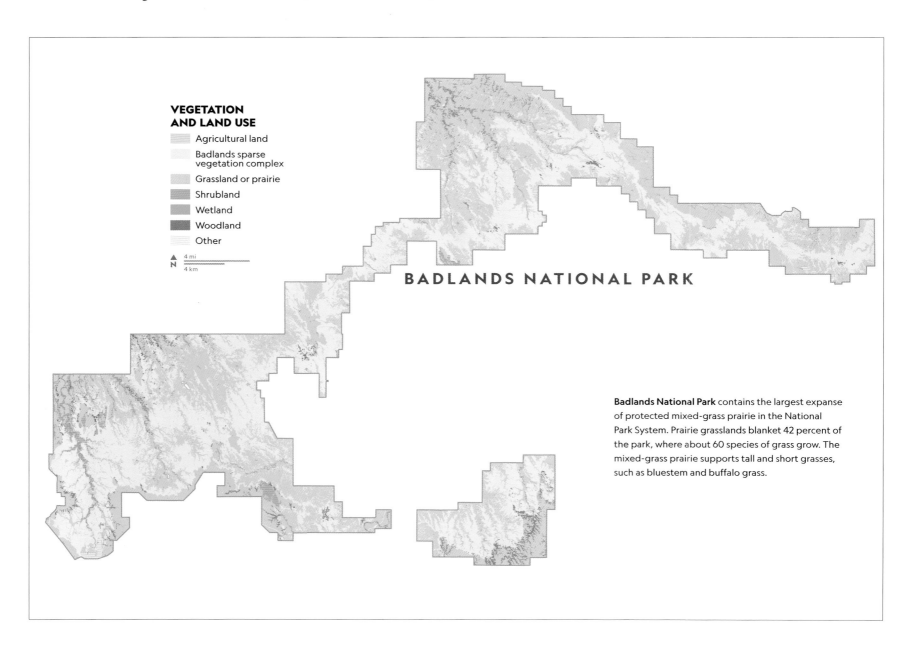

VEGETATION AND LAND USE

- Agricultural land
- Badlands sparse vegetation complex
- Grassland or prairie
- Shrubland
- Wetland
- Woodland
- Other

4 mi
4 km
N

BADLANDS NATIONAL PARK

Badlands National Park contains the largest expanse of protected mixed-grass prairie in the National Park System. Prairie grasslands blanket 42 percent of the park, where about 60 species of grass grow. The mixed-grass prairie supports tall and short grasses, such as bluestem and buffalo grass.

The American bison once inundated the Great Plains, and hunters almost wiped out the one-ton animals. Beginning in 1963, the National Park Service and the Oglala Lakota tribe reintroduced the species to the Badlands.

and active-duty WWII soldiers (both Lakota and white) were forcibly evicted from their homes and ranches on the reservation. Although residents were paid, the reimbursements weren't enough to replace their land. For several decades, the Air Force and Dakota National Guard used the southern part of the Badlands for aerial gunnery and bombing practice. There were many close calls, and although no homesteaders or Lakota were killed, more than a dozen airmen lost their lives in crashes.

Congress eventually returned most of the land to the tribe with yet another treaty revision in 1976 that added 208 square miles of monument land from the reservation that would be called the south Stronghold Unit. The Park Service then began co-managing the monument, and it became a national park two years later. But despite repeated attempts to clean up and remove decades worth of small bullets, chemical munitions, antitank rockets, magnesium-filled explosives, and several-hundred-pound bombs—park visitors and reservation residents alike still discover unexploded munitions poking out of the Badlands like insidious, toothed fossils. No one has come to any harm from these discoveries, which serve as reminders of the troubled history of Badlands National Park.

North of the reservation, paved roads lead to maintained trails, fossil exhibits, and campgrounds. In the southern, Stronghold park unit within the reservation, the only access is on private dirt and grass two-tracks owned by white ranchers or tribal members. More than 30,000 Oglala Lakota—among the poorest and most unemployed demographic of all Americans—reside there. Those hoping to explore the southern park must obtain permission from individual landowners prior to crossing their property. Less than one percent of total Badlands visitors make the effort, but for those who do, it's an extraordinary opportunity to connect with the past. Much

like the age-old hula performances in Hawai'i Volcanoes National Park, the Ghost Dances on the Stronghold evoke a forgotten piece of Americana, deeply rooted in Oglala tradition and tied to an unshakable, modern-day reverence for the land and its wildlife.

Through its otherworldly scenic wonders and fossil riches, Badlands tourist visitation annually exceeds the population of South Dakota. Nearby Mount Rushmore National Memorial, which carvers completed by knocking out the granite faces of four presidents in 1941, attracts over two million tourists a year. Visitors exploring the area often come to view yet another vestige of national fascination: the American bison. Once at 60 million strong, the bison were reduced to an estimated 325 animals remaining across the continent by 1884. The species was reintroduced to Badlands in 1963, beginning with 50 bison from Theodore Roosevelt National Park. In the 1980s, 20 more bison were brought in from Colorado National Monument. As of 2018, over a thousand bison—a threshold of stable genetic integrity—thrive in the Badlands.

Making the park a protected sanctuary for the official mammal of the United States is not only a means of conservation, but also a gesture of respect to the Oglala Lakota for whom the bison serves as an integral part of culture. In June 2017, the park held a ceremony celebrating the bison with the Oglala Lakota from the Pine Ridge Reservation. During the blessing, an eagle feather was held up as a

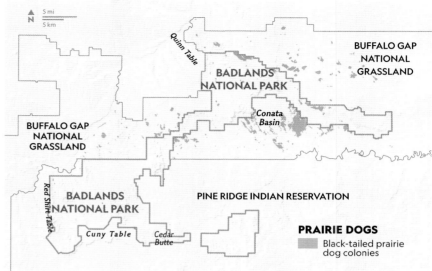

ABOVE: **A prairie dog** watches for predators, of which there are many: birds of prey, coyotes, foxes, and even black-footed ferrets keep these social, cat-size carnivores on alert.

RIGHT: **Prairie dogs'** extensive burrows create a maze of "towns" where they take shelter, along with many other species. These colonies are prime locations to observe wildlife such as burrowing owls, ferruginous hawks, and black-footed ferrets.

symbol of bringing *tatanka* (the bison) home again. "For thousands of years we have had a relationship with this animal and we still do today," said a tribe representative.

While grazing on up to 60 pounds of grasses daily, the bison play an important ecological role as natural planters in the park. Their fur catches seeds blown across the grasslands, and as they

move across the prairie, disturbing the soil with their hooves, seeds drop. In turn, prairie dogs stir up the soil and seeds that enable the grass to grow.

The mixed-grass prairie—revived when the monument closed its borders to cattle and plows—holds both tall and short grasses, including blue grama, needle-and-thread, buffalo grass, and western wheatgrass. Over 60 different grasses that serve as the vital foundation for the entire park entwine with over 400 plant species, including scores of flowers. Among the fauna this vegetation supports are predators attracted to prairie dogs: birds of prey, coyotes, foxes, and more recently, black-footed ferrets.

With its black "mask," tail, and feet, the ferret looks like a slimmed-down raccoon. Still, this member of the weasel family nearly went extinct in the 1990s, due to disease and habitat loss. Its reintroduction to the Badlands is yet another success story, like that of the bison, that shows how national parks provide crucial sanctuary for endangered wildlife, culture, and history across America. ■

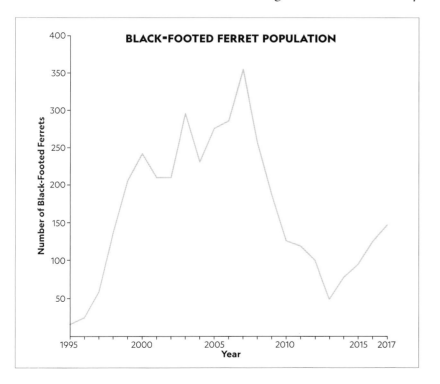

ABOVE: **On the brink** of extinction, black-footed ferrets were reintroduced into the park in 1994. Additional ferrets were released in 1999, and the population thrived for more than a decade. Then disease struck in 2008, causing a rapid decline. Thanks to mitigation efforts, the ferrets are again on the rebound.

OPPOSITE: **The sun** sets over the prairie grasslands that once covered almost half of the continent. Today, they support mammals from the tiny shrew to bobcats to bighorn sheep.

RIGHT: **Black-footed ferrets** peer above ground in a rare daytime sighting; the slender mammals usually sleep 21 hours a day and sneak into prairie dog burrows to hunt at night.

▶ LOCATION **76 MILES NW OF DENVER, COLORADO**

▶ SIZE **415 SQUARE MILES**

▶ HIGHEST POINT **LONGS PEAK, 14,259 FEET**

▶ VISITORS **4,590,493 IN 2018**

▶ ESTABLISHED **1915**

ROCKY MOUNTAIN NATIONAL PARK

n north-central Colorado, "Rocky" and its iconic Longs Peak protrudes in purple majesty above the plains that it waters below. While its east-flowing streams—including the designated Wild and Scenic Cache la Poudre River—run to the Atlantic, the mountains' west side harbors the Colorado River's Pacific-bound headwaters. Backcountry users cannot help being awed by the gemlike lakes below pocket glaciers and sought-after granite walls, such as the Diamond on Longs Peak. But the park also came into being at a time in America when automobile road trips were all the rage. So park planners set their sights high in designing and building the Trail Ridge Road. Buried under snow for half the year, it climbs continuously higher than any paved road in the country, topping out at 12,183 feet on the Continental Divide.

The spectacular mountain scenery, well-engineered roads, and proximity to Denver make Rocky one of the most visited national parks. Due to dramatic elevation changes, Rocky holds a wide variety of wildlife and diverse ecosystems. Ninety-five percent of the park is wilderness.

Rocky is one of several parks selected by NASA for a study begun in 2011. In collaboration with the National Park Service, the project

A glassy Bear Lake reflects Longs Peak, the park's tallest mountain. Trail Ridge Road and 350 miles of hiking paths beckon visitors to this popular park.

will develop and apply tools that will "assess vulnerability of ecosystems and species to climate and land use change and evaluate management options." Given overcrowding and radical ecological changes—including warming temperatures and forest fires—the future integrity of Rocky and other western parks now hangs in the balance.

The Trail Ridge Road over Rocky Mountain National Park was originally traveled more than 10,000 years ago by Paleo-Indian hunters who left projectile points while chasing mammoth and megabison. Ute and Arapaho camped in the region into the 1900s, until settlers forced them out mid-century. Arapaho elders have shared their original names for landmarks—Never Summer Mountains, Lumpy Ridge, or They Are Two Mountains (for Longs Peak) among others. In fact, Rocky boasts one of the greatest

Explorers find their way through the interior of the Hallett Glacier, now known as Rowe Glacier—one of several small glaciers found in the park.

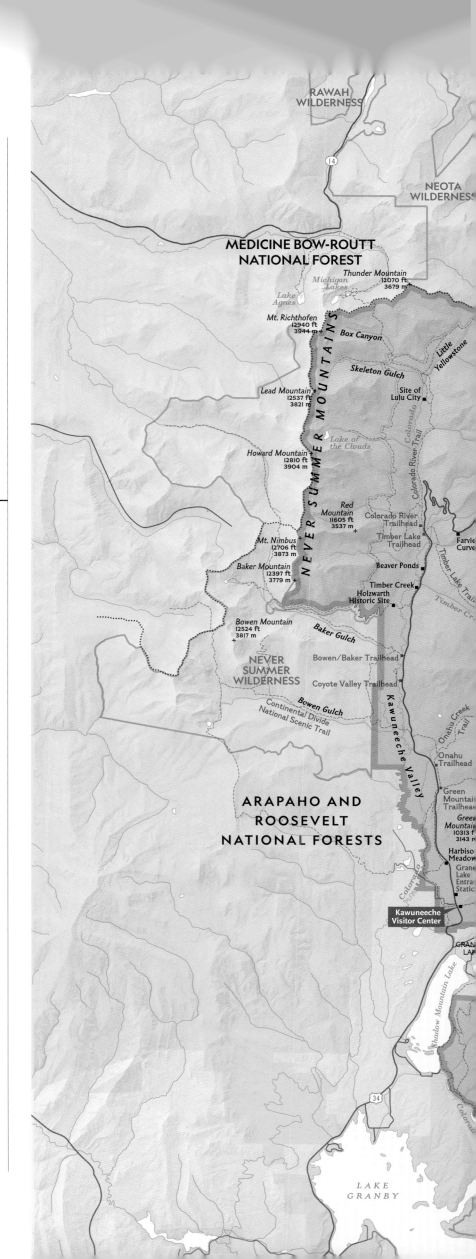

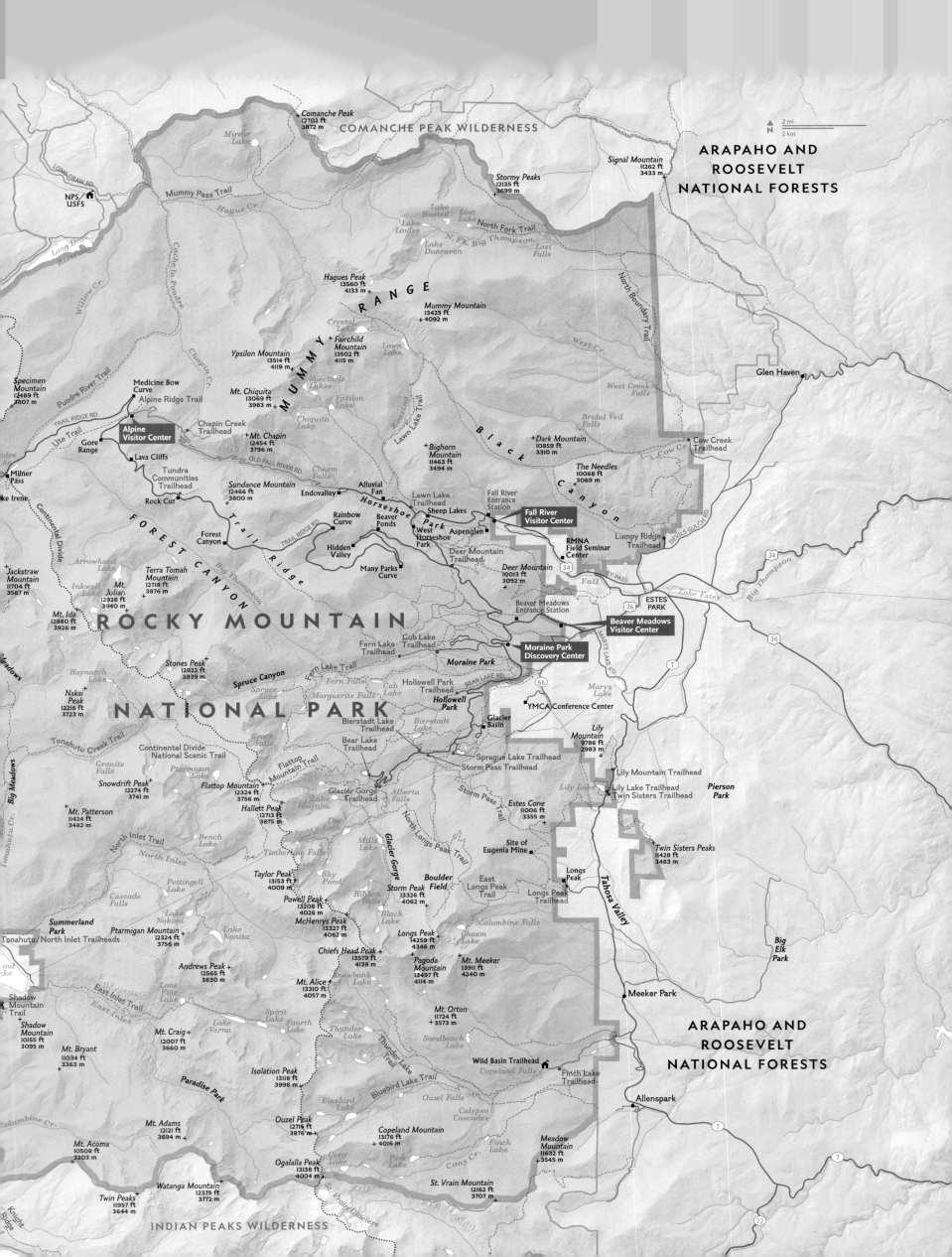

ROCKY MOUNTAIN NATIONAL PARK IS ONE OF THE COUNTRY'S HIGHEST PARKS IN TERMS OF ELEVATION. WITH A MINIMUM ELEVATION OF 7,860 FEET, IT CONTAINS 77 PEAKS OVER 12,000 FEET TALL.

concentrations of Native American names in a small area throughout the United States.

The first ascent of Longs Peak occurred in 1868 when Maj. John Wesley Powell and party spent three days bushwhacking up its west side. Their route, seldom repeated today, "required great caution, coolness, and infinite labor to make headway, life often depending upon a grasp of the fingers in a crevice that would hardly admit them," team member William Byers wrote.

On top, the major announced that they had accomplished a physical undertaking previously deemed impossible, but predicted that their accomplishment would foretell "greater achievements in such other fields." A half year later, the major would complete one of the greatest achievements in American exploration, by rowing down the headwaters of the Grand (later renamed Colorado) River through the uncharted Grand Canyon. His advice about conserving water in the arid West later proved prophetic as he served as the director of the U.S. Geological Survey.

BELOW: **Visitors soak in** sunset near the Alpine Visitor Center; at 11,796 feet above sea level, it is the highest visitor center in the National Park System.

OPPOSITE: **The Colorado River** begins its 1,450-mile path in Rocky Mountain National Park. Before reaching the valley, much of these headwaters are canaled over the Continental Divide to the eastern slope of Colorado.

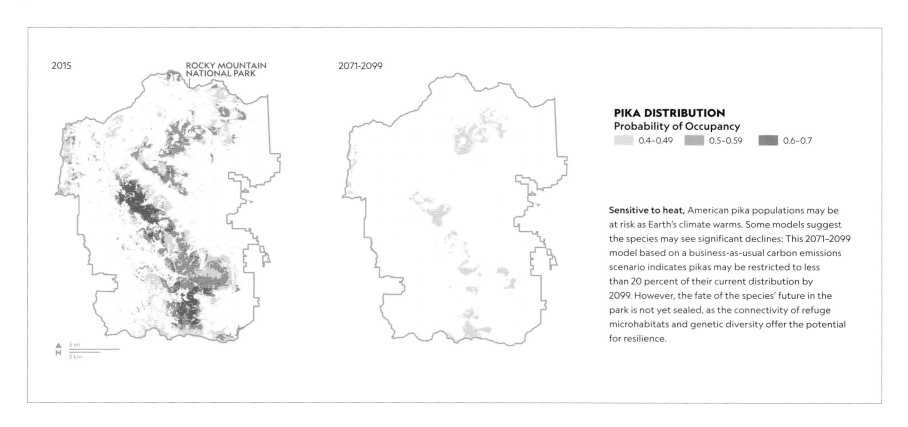

PIKA DISTRIBUTION
Probability of Occupancy

0.4–0.49   0.5–0.59   0.6–0.7

Sensitive to heat, American pika populations may be at risk as Earth's climate warms. Some models suggest the species may see significant declines: This 2071–2099 model based on a business-as-usual carbon emissions scenario indicates pikas may be restricted to less than 20 percent of their current distribution by 2099. However, the fate of the species' future in the park is not yet sealed, as the connectivity of refuge microhabitats and genetic diversity offer the potential for resilience.

5 mi
5 km
N

Pikas are highly expressive, using calls and songs to communicate with each other. Their calls are loud, but their camouflaged coat often blends in with their surroundings.

One of the earliest water projects in the Southwest began in Rocky in 1881, at 10,175 feet on La Poudre Pass. At a one percent grade, teams of laborers dug out a 20-foot-wide, six-foot-deep canal along the contours of the Never Summer Mountains. This "Grand Ditch" caught snowmelt water before it hit the Colorado River and rechanneled it eastward and over the pass, down into the Cache la Poudre River. By 1936, this scar across the park mountainside extended 16 miles, diverting over six million gallons of farm water a year to the distant eastern plains.

Thus began a series of diversion projects moving water over or under the Continental Divide. In the coming years, nature would be repeatedly reengineered to get water for agriculture and municipalities in the West. Despite park administrators' fierce objections, the Rockies' watershed became the exemplar for massive river manipulations. This trans-basin diversion, the Colorado-Big Thompson Project, tunneled 13 miles underneath Longs Peak. Completed in 1947 after nine years of labor, the Alva B. Adams Tunnel began dis-

gorging over 65 billion gallons of water a year off the western slope and out the eastern side of the park into a ganglion of dams and reservoirs that would supply 35 distant towns and cities.

Throughout these years of growth and development around the Continental Divide, several advocates—such as Enos Mills, who would make over 250 ascents of Longs Peak—argued for park preservation rather than the rapacious harvesting of water, timber, or minerals found in national forests. As a popular public speaker and author, Mills gained a national audience, and in 1908 began proposing a game refuge of over a thousand square miles. Colorado representatives introduced a park bill to Congress, but because of water usage, grazing rights, private land restrictions, and other resource extraction activities, the legislation required five major revisions.

Finally, on January 26, 1915, after nearly a decade of debate, President Woodrow Wilson signed the bill into law. Although the park had been reduced to one-third the size of Mills's original vision, the *Denver Post* declared victory. Mills—who had written more than 2,000 letters, penned 64 articles, and lectured 42 times to promote his game refuge—became known as the "Father of Rocky Mountain National Park."

By 1917, the park superintendent reported 120,000 visitors in the park, more than doubling the previous year's popularity. Because of its accessibility, Rocky drew more people than the combined visitation of Yellowstone, Yosemite, Glacier, and Crater Lake.

While visitation at other western national parks dwindled by 25 percent or more in the 1930s during the Depression, Rocky became more popular. In 1929, 256,000 people entered the park; 1,600 climbers had signed the register atop Longs Peak by that same year, completing an

WILDLIFE-WATCHERS WILL SPOT NOT JUST MEGAFAUNA IN ROCKY: MORE THAN 280 BIRD SPECIES HAVE BEEN RECORDED IN THE PARK.

arduous 5,000-foot, 7.5-mile ascent. When the Trail Ridge Road opened in 1933, nearly 300,000 people came in 83,000 automobiles. In five years, this visitation doubled. The park's popularity would help open congressional purse strings for Rocky and other national parks throughout the country, as well as serve as a guiding template for more than 30 yet-to-be-established national parks and their thoughtfully engineered roads. Eventually, shuttle buses were implemented to ease the crush of traffic jams.

Although automobile tourism would come to characterize Rocky, a smaller population of hikers, anglers, and climbers were drawn to 350 miles of hiking trails—pathways leading to scores of alpine tarns filled with fish and granite crags and 60 peaks reaching over 12,000 feet.

The park is a rock climbers' mecca. In addition to simple day climbs at Lumpy Ridge, there is an abundance of high-altitude, psychologically and physically demanding, yet desirable rock routes on the Petit Grepon, Sharkstooth, Spearhead, Hallett Peak, and Mount Meeker. Then there's the unrelenting steepness of the Diamond: more than 900 feet of vertical climbing all above 13,000 feet. Many of these world-class routes involve overnight bivouacs and long approach hikes.

In addition to five front-country campgrounds, there are many backcountry camping opportunities throughout the park. Two stables are available for horseback riders.

Amid all of the modern recreation, more than a century later, Mills's vision for a game refuge prospered, too, despite the traffic. Much of the wildlife—mule deer, lynx, bighorn sheep, foxes, bobcat, cougar, black bears, and coyotes—became habituated to the sight of cars bristling with camera lenses and binoculars.

By the early 20th century, hunting pressures and population growth killed off wolves, grizzly bears, bison, elk, and moose throughout the Rockies. But at least three of these megafauna species—elk, bighorn sheep, and moose—would eventually be reintroduced to prosper in the park and throughout the West.

Even before the park was established, Mills and other supporters recognized the potential benefits of renewing the elk population,

RIGHT: **About 7,000** Rocky Mountain bighorn sheep live within Colorado's state boundaries, but their range in North America spans from the Canadian Rockies into northern Mexico. After spending winter in high-mountain habitat, they descend to lower elevations to graze and eat soil during the spring and summer. Colorado's official state animal, these bighorn can weigh more than 300 pounds.

BELOW: **A park icon,** bighorn sheep almost disappeared in the 1950s. Today hundreds of sheep roam the park's high elevations, descending in winter to lower elevations for natural mineral-licks, rich soil, and shrubs.

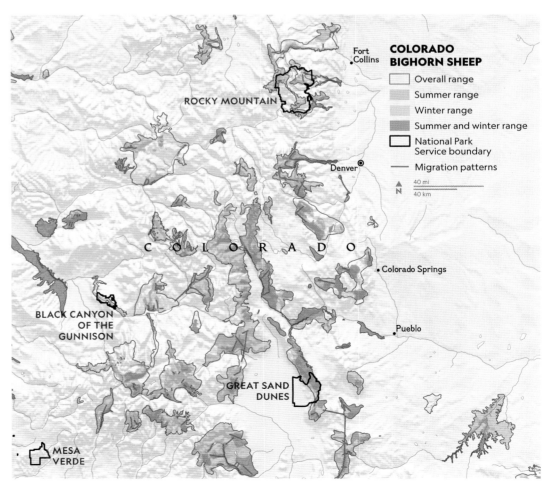

COLORADO BIGHORN SHEEP

- Overall range
- Summer range
- Winter range
- Summer and winter range
- National Park Service boundary
- Migration patterns

which was decreasing across the country. In 1914, the U.S. Forest Service reintroduced 49 elk from Yellowstone National Park to what is now Rocky. Within a year, the majestic mammals were thriving. But lacking predators, the herd exploded to an unsustainable size. The elk grazed plant life to stubble, which deprived habitat vital to birds and beavers and reduced the park's biodiversity. Park managers had no choice but to cull more than a thousand elk. By 2009, their popu-

lation density again surpassed that of any wild herd—they even stopped migrating. Despite the controversy and after rejecting a plan to reintroduce wolves to maintain the balance, the herd was culled yet again.

Bighorn sheep were nearly eradicated throughout the West by domestic sheep diseases and hunting. Rocky's low-country herds were gone in the 1950s, yet nearly 150 bighorn remained in the higher and isolated areas of the park. Unhindered by wolves and grizzly bears, bighorn populations rebounded in the 1970s; then state wildlife managers started bringing in more of them. Now as many as 400 sheep—lofting curled horns that weigh up to 30 pounds—are found at high altitudes in Rocky.

Moose, too, had all but disappeared from Colorado when two dozen were reintroduced in the northern part of the state in 1978–79. The first moose took up residence in Rocky in 1985, and by 2017, more than 50 moose had moved into the park—mostly inhabiting the wetter western side. The largest member of the deer family, these stunning creatures stand over six feet tall and weigh up to 1,600 pounds.

Although wildlife management and a proper balance of species have long proved a challenge to the park, biologists now grapple with the even trickier issue of changing climate. In the last century, the average annual temperature in Rocky has risen 3.4°F (1.9°C).

As winters continue to warm and summers get hotter, the tiny pika—essentially a mouse-bunny, sensitive to summer heat and reliant on winter snowpack for insulation against the extreme cold—may be one of the more vulnerable species.

The white-tailed ptarmigan—a high-altitude, chicken-size bird—is diminishing throughout the park for reasons yet to be established. Consequently, scientists continue to monitor wildlife populations and conditions throughout the park in hopes of identifying ways to protect the resource.

While careful to avoid controversy in its coverage of climate change, the park still strives to show both the science and the delicacy of maintaining nature's balance. This includes how an earlier spring snowmelt could affect plants and animals, or the

For centuries the relationship was mutually beneficial: Pine beetles culled older, weaker trees, producing new beetles and a healthier forest. Climate change, with its warmer, drier conditions, has upset that balance, leaving even healthy trees vulnerable to attack.

DEATH BY A THOUSAND BITES

 PINE BEETLE, ACTUAL SIZE

The tree tries to suffocate the insects by secreting resin into the beetles' boreholes.

FIRST WEEK
Selection and Invasion
The cycle begins in summer, when a lone female beetle bores into a tree's bark and releases a pheromone that attracts hundreds of other beetles.

Sixty to eighty eggs are laid in each gallery.

Phyloem layer

SECOND WEEK
Burrowing and Egg Laying
Beetles dig galleries under the bark, depositing eggs and blue fungi to feed the next generation. The galleries block nutrient flow in the tree's phloem layer.

The larvae develop cold resistance in time for winter.

THIRD WEEK TO 4 MONTHS
Hatching and Feeding
Larvae hatch and chew side galleries, feeding on the phloem and the fungi.

◀ The tree remains green for months after beetles have fatally mauled it.

Pupal stage

Fungi-carrying new adult

5 TO 12 MONTHS
Overwintering and Dispersal
The beetle larvae lie dormant until spring, when they'll turn into pupae, then adults. The new brood feeds on fungal spores before dispersing to another tree.

◀ Needles turn yellow in the dry heat of summer.

13 TO 24 MONTHS
Red Means Dead
The beetles are long gone, and the drying tree turns red. Finally it loses most of its needles and becomes gray.

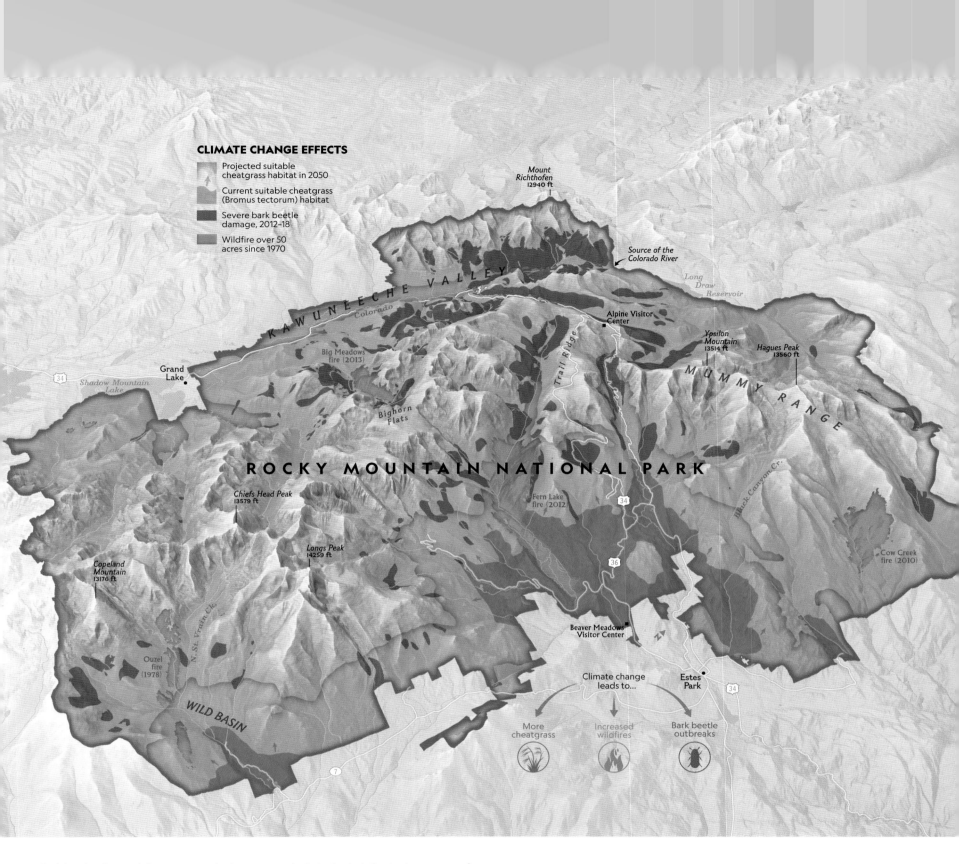

CLIMATE CHANGE EFFECTS

- Projected suitable cheatgrass habitat in 2050
- Current suitable cheatgrass (Bromus tectorum) habitat
- Severe bark beetle damage, 2012–18
- Wildfire over 50 acres since 1970

Mount Richthofen 12940 ft

Source of the Colorado River

Long Draw Reservoir

K A W U N E E C H E   V A L L E Y

Colorado

Alpine Visitor Center

Ypsilon Mountain 13514 ft

Hagues Peak 13560 ft

Big Meadows fire (2013)

Grand Lake

Shadow Mountain Lake

Bighorn Flats

Trail Ridge

M U M M Y   R A N G E

R O C K Y   M O U N T A I N   N A T I O N A L   P A R K

Chiefs Head Peak 13579 ft

Fern Lake fire (2012)

Black Canyon Cr.

Longs Peak 14259 ft

Cow Creek fire (2010)

Copeland Mountain 13176 ft

N. St. Vrain Cr.

Beaver Meadows Visitor Center

Climate change leads to...

Estes Park

Ouzel fire (1978)

WILD BASIN

More cheatgrass

Increased wildfires

Bark beetle outbreaks

Bark beetles, fires, and cheatgrass can play important ecological roles, but climate change exacerbates their effects on one another. For example, cheatgrass thrives when temperatures rise, adding kindling to wildfires that are already more intense due to drier conditions, and fires can spread faster where bark beetles have killed trees.

delivery of water to distant cities and farmlands. Or how this "new climate" has allowed invasive species such as cheatgrass to proliferate and compete with other native park plant species.

Throughout Rocky, as winter temperatures continue to warm, the rice grain–size mountain pine beetle has affected or killed about 90 percent of the park's forests. A sea of once green trees has turned dead as a red tide. Spruce beetles too have begun taking a toll.

Dead, reddened needles remain hanging on spruce and pine for several years and have 10 times less moisture than live, green boughs. So these forests stand like matches awaiting a spark. Although fires are a natural and essential part of forest ecosystem regeneration, Rocky is now caught in a cycle of unprecedented wildfires that are

burning bigger and hotter than presettlement forest fires and choking the western United States in smoke.

In 2012, the unparalleled Fern Lake winter forest fire—burning from late October into January—started from an illegal campfire and burned 3,500 acres of beetle-killed trees in the eastern park. In summer of 2013, a lightning strike blew up into the Big Meadows fire that burned over 600 acres of beetle-killed forest on the west of the Continental Divide.

The Union of Concerned Scientists believes that "climate change is producing hotter, drier conditions in the American West, which contribute to more large wildfires and longer wildfire seasons." In alignment with NASA's and the national parks' collaborative studies on this issue, the union, refuting calls to increase logging, has proposed using the latest science to improve wildfire mapping and prediction, along with implementing forest and fire management practices to reflect changes in climate. ■

▷ LOCATION **60 MILES N OF JACKSON, WYOMING**

▷ SIZE **3,468 SQUARE MILES**

▷ HIGHEST POINT **EAGLE PEAK, 11,358 FEET**

▷ VISITORS **4,115,000 IN 2018**

▷ ESTABLISHED **1872**

YELLOWSTONE NATIONAL PARK

Yellowstone is the first and most iconic national park in the world. It blankets the northwest corner of Wyoming, with another 3 percent of park falling into Montana, and the remaining one percent in Idaho. Established and signed into law by President Ulysses S. Grant, Yellowstone sets the gold standard for parks.

Its renowned geothermal features, including the legendary Old Faithful, overlie one of the Earth's largest supervolcanoes. Beginning 2.1 million years ago, this underlying hot spot coated the park with volcanic debris and lava flows. One of many later eruptions created the Yellowstone Caldera—a massive crater—surrounding and fueling the world's largest concentration of hydrothermal features and geysers. The vast steaming and waterfall-cooled landscape—with its grizzlies, succoring cubs, and wolves once more running free—is a protean miracle of nature. No visitor leaves unaffected.

Designated an international biosphere reserve in 1976, then a UNESCO World Heritage site two years later, the popular Yellowstone has faced overcrowding issues. Starting in 1995 it was briefly on the List of World Heritage in Danger because of wildlife and invasive species issues.

From Lookout Point, the Lower Falls on the Yellowstone River glistens in the morning sun. Yellowstone is the world's oldest and most famous national park.

At 34,375 square miles, the Greater Yellowstone Ecosystem is nearly 10 times larger than the park. Beyond Yellowstone and the adjoining Grand Teton National Park boundaries are several surrounding wildlife refuges, five national forests, Bureau of Land Management lands, huge private ranches, and a piece of the Wind River Reservation.

Native Americans frequented the region for more than 11,000 years, arriving after the melt-back of the Pleistocene ice sheets. These prehistoric people left behind projectile points and stone tools for hunting mammals.

As the larger ice age animals became extinct in the drying, warming climate 9,500 years ago, humans began hunting smaller animals with atlatls (spear-thrower tools) amid lodgepole and aspen forests covering the ice-scraped volcanic landscape. Still, the 8,000-foot-high, inhospitable Yellowstone Plateau and its strange, geothermal gushings prevented passing Paleo-Indians from settling. Amid more than 1,800 archaeological sites in the park are campsites, evidence of hunts and stone tools.

Three thousand years ago, as the land continued warming, human use increased and hunters developed sheep traps and bison corrals,

Advertisements like this 1924 poster encouraged people to ride the railroad and journey to Yellowstone for its vast and awe-inspiring beauty.

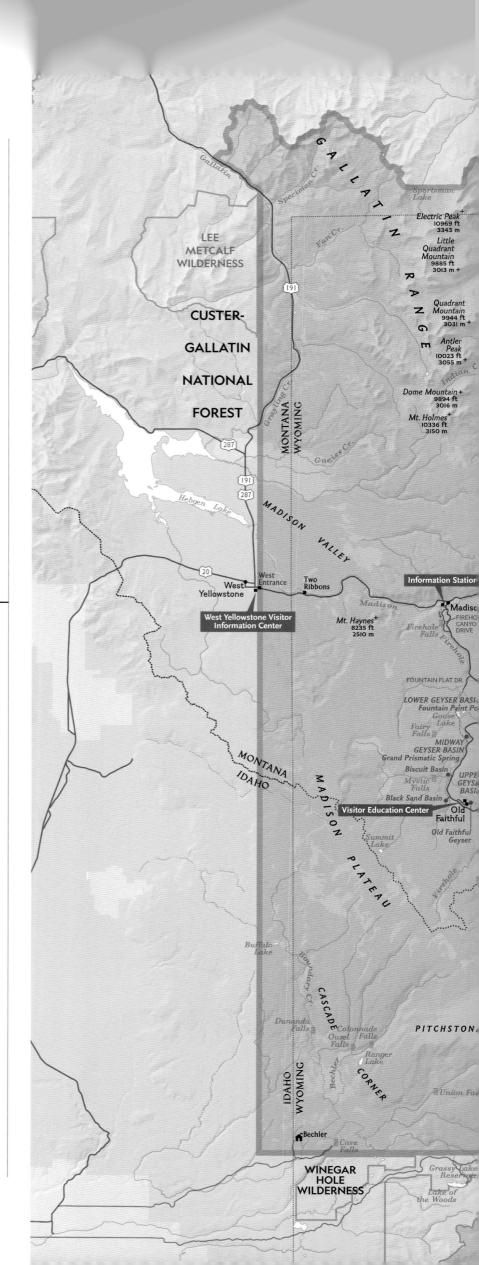

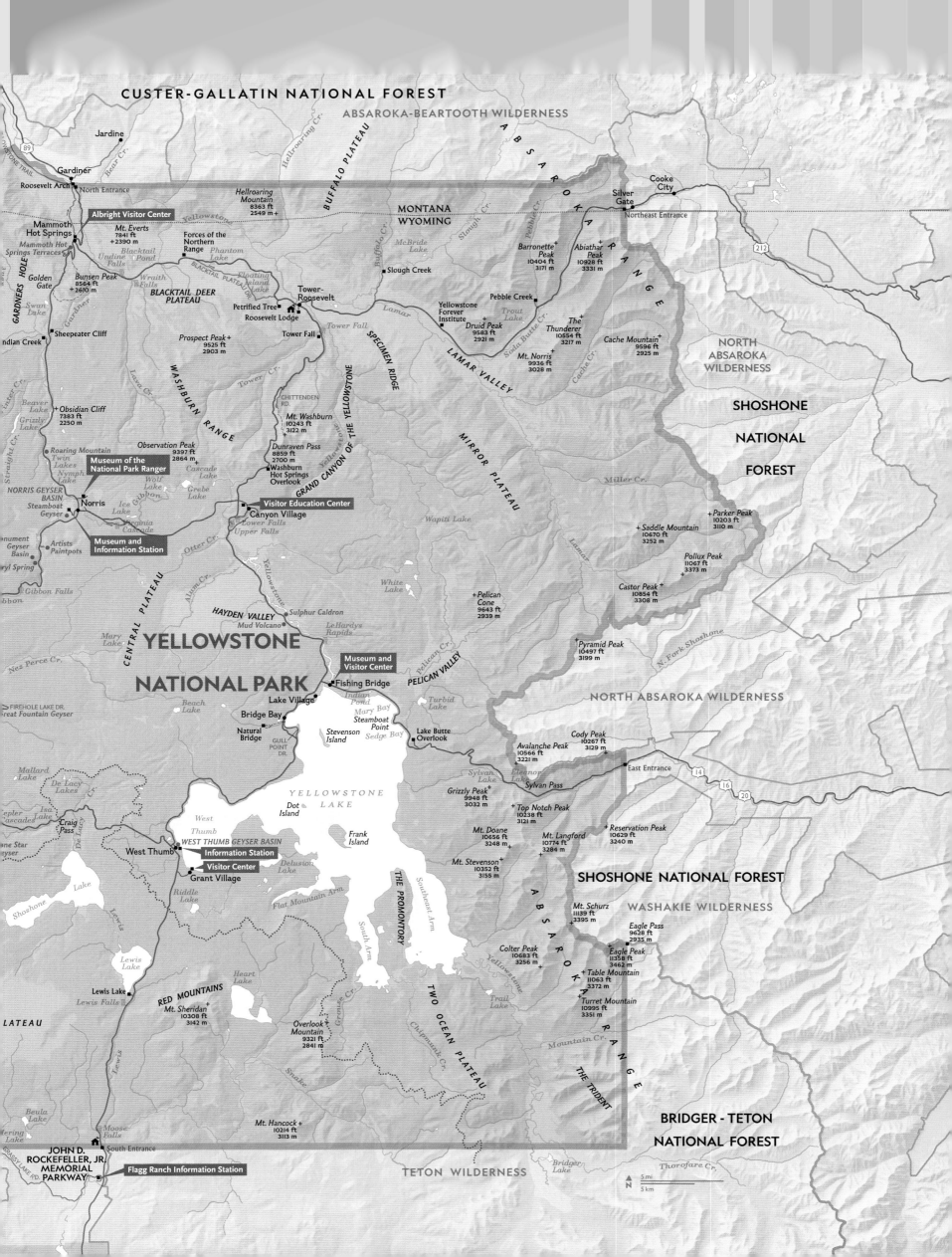

along with the more efficient bow and arrow. Early visitors' pots show that the Shoshone may have lived in the park nearly 700 years ago. The Crow people passed through sometime during the 1500s and later, around 1700, the Lakota (or Sioux). Aside from hunting trips, Native Americans avoided Yellowstone because of its extreme weather, short summers, and eerie geysers, believed to harbor evil spirits.

During the winter of 1807–1808, a renowned western trapper trekked through and described a place of fire and brimstone, which came to be known as [John] Colter's Hell. Hyperbolic reports from other mountain men described a similar, albeit half-believed, mythical landscape. Jim Bridger visited Yellowstone in 1830, and for many decades thereafter accurately described hissing geysers and great

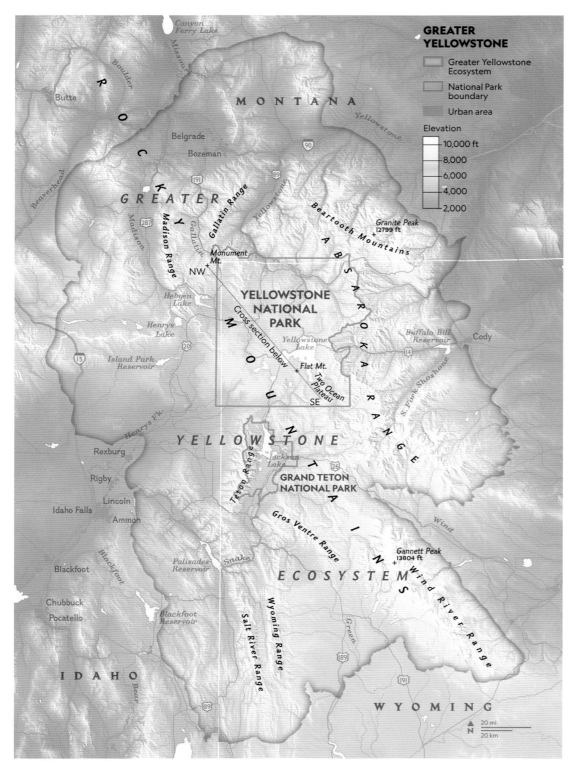

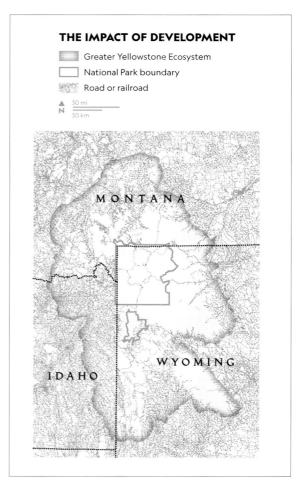

ABOVE: **Since the 1970s,** the human population in the Greater Yellowstone Ecosystem has boomed, bringing residential and commercial development and new roads. On private land, more than 50 percent of natural habitat has been lost.

LEFT: **Encompassing 22.6 million acres,** Greater Yellowstone is the largest patch of contiguous public wildlands in the lower 48 states. Drawn from the map, the cross section (below) highlights a segment of Greater Yellowstone's diverse topography. The 72-mile stretch is bound by Monument Mountain to the northwest and the Two Ocean Plateau to the southeast. The idea of a Greater Yellowstone Ecosystem, which gained traction in the 1980s, marked a giant leap forward in ecological thinking. Natural resource managers came to recognize that biological processes within Yellowstone National Park extend far beyond its borders and that activities in one place can have huge implications for the surrounding areas.

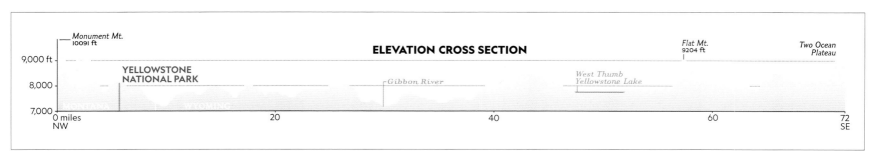

ELEVATION CROSS SECTION

springs that were hot enough to cook his meat, with other pools warm enough for delightful baths.

Organized explorations began in 1860. But it would take years for recognition that this extraordinary place of fire and ice needed protection to materialize. It fell to the great American landscape artist Thomas Moran and the photographer William Henry Jackson to inspire the Yellowstone park idea. In 1871, Moran wrote in his journal about the "magnificent forest of pines & firs all growing straight as a ships mast . . . and a beautiful lake" where they cooked and ate the finest trout he had ever seen. Along with Jackson's black-and-white scenic shots, Moran's watercolors—particularly the celestial light and sparkling waterfall within "The Grand Canyon of the Yellowstone"—carried the wonders of the landscape home to the American public, and eventually, transported them. As if cast in a spell, transformed by his time there, Moran began signing his paintings "TYM" for Thomas Yellowstone Moran.

Together with Jackson and Ferdinand V. Hayden, whose 1871 expedition galvanized scientific interest in the park, Moran persuaded Congress to create America's first national park. On March 1, 1872, during a time of fundamental political, social, and economic change that defined American Reconstruction, President Grant fittingly signed the Yellowstone National Park Protection Act. It would become the boilerplate grail for the scores of parks that would follow. The act reads: "The headwaters of the Yellowstone River . . . is hereby reserved and withdrawn

from settlement, occupancy, or sale . . . and dedicated and set apart as a public park or pleasuring-ground for the benefit and enjoyment of the people."

Still, several years later, the lack of congressional funding to protect the park resulted in chaos. The leader of a scientific expedition to Yellowstone complained about visitors gunning down the animals and fishing out the streams. Squatters were even digging or prying up colorful minerals from the hot springs, then selling them; several appointed Yellowstone superintendents couldn't stop the vandalism.

In 1877, a large band of Nez Perce (Nimíipuu) from Oregon was fleeing the Army, which had killed some of their women and children while trying to move them onto a reservation. On the run, the Nez Perce spent 13 days in Yellowstone, where they attacked several tourists, killing two, and traded their worn-out horses for the tourists' fresher steeds. So in 1886, the secretary of the interior asked that the U.S. Army take over—for more than 30 years the First Cavalry would manage Yellowstone and three other national parks as they were created in California.

Poaching, meanwhile, continued. By 1886, hunters—and disease—had decimated wild bison throughout America; only several

North American
plate movement

UTAH

Great Salt Lake

NEVADA

Volcanic feature name
Age in years — Owyhee-Humboldt
13.8 million

McDermitt
15.6–16.1 million

McDermitt
15.4–15.5
million

OREGON

Owyhee-
Humboldt
13.8 million

Bruneau-Jarbidge
12.5 million

Boise

RIVER   PLAIN

Twin Falls
8.6–10 million

Pocatello

Picabo
10.3 million

SNAKE

IDAHO

YELLOWSTONE
NATIONAL PARK

Big Bend Ridge
Caldera
2.1 million

YELLOWSTONE PLATEAU

Heise
4.3–6 million

Yellowstone
Lake

Yellowstone Caldera
0.64 million

Mallard Lake
Dome

MONTANA

Sour Creek
Dome

MADISON RANGE

WYOMING

GALLATIN RANGE

ABSAROKA RANGE

Rising
gases

Upper crustal
magma
reservoir
1400°F

N

Bozeman

BRIDGER RANGE

Lower crustal
magma
reservoir
1800°F

CRUST

Mantle
plume
2200°F

25
miles

MANTLE

The massive, superheated plume of rock under Yellowstone National Park has caused dozens of volcanic blasts, and fuels the Earth's largest collection of hydrothermal features. Eruptions of this supervolcano—so named for the violence and size of its explosions—expel so much material that the crust caves in, creating craterlike depressions called calderas. Evidence of past eruptions shifts with the Earth's crust, a migrating testament to the still active forces below.

hundred remained, mostly taking refuge in Yellowstone. Eventually this herd dwindled to less than two dozen.

Despite a previous policy of keeping domesticated animals out of the park to avoid disease and grazing competition, the military introduced ranchers' bison into the park, and started an isolated ranch within the park where the well-fed wild bison could breed with tamer bison. The herd grew.

And fortunately, the 1894 Lacey Act, which mandated jail time for poachers, allowed officials to stop the slaughter of the park's bison and other animals. After a period of interim control by the U.S. Cavalry, the National Park Service, established in 1916, instituted new programs, beginning in part with nascent interpretive talks and more farsighted game management techniques.

A century later, modern Park Service dress still resembles Yellowstone's First Cavalry hats and uniforms.

As the park was protected and developed, scientists probed to understand the caldera within. Even casual observers can see that the center of the park is flattened, with the Red Mountains, and the Gallatin, Washburn, and Absaroka Ranges surrounding it. Any mountains within the heart of Yellowstone had been blown right off the face of the Earth.

Sixty-six million years ago, volcanism first began to cook the Yellowstone region. Then, 17 million years ago, Basin and Range mountain building started stretching the land. As the North American plate pulled southwest 16.5 million years ago, a subterranean hot spot blew out more than 100 calderas, eventually stretching 500 miles, from present-day Oregon and Nevada into Idaho.

A little over two million years ago, the friction and heat of the continental plate moving over Yellowstone would trigger a gigantic explosion. The fireworks began as escaping magma released pressure and explosive volcanic gases in an eruption so massive it almost

Heat-resistant microbes create the many colors in Grand Prismatic Spring. Each ring represents a temperature zone, each supporting different types of microbes.

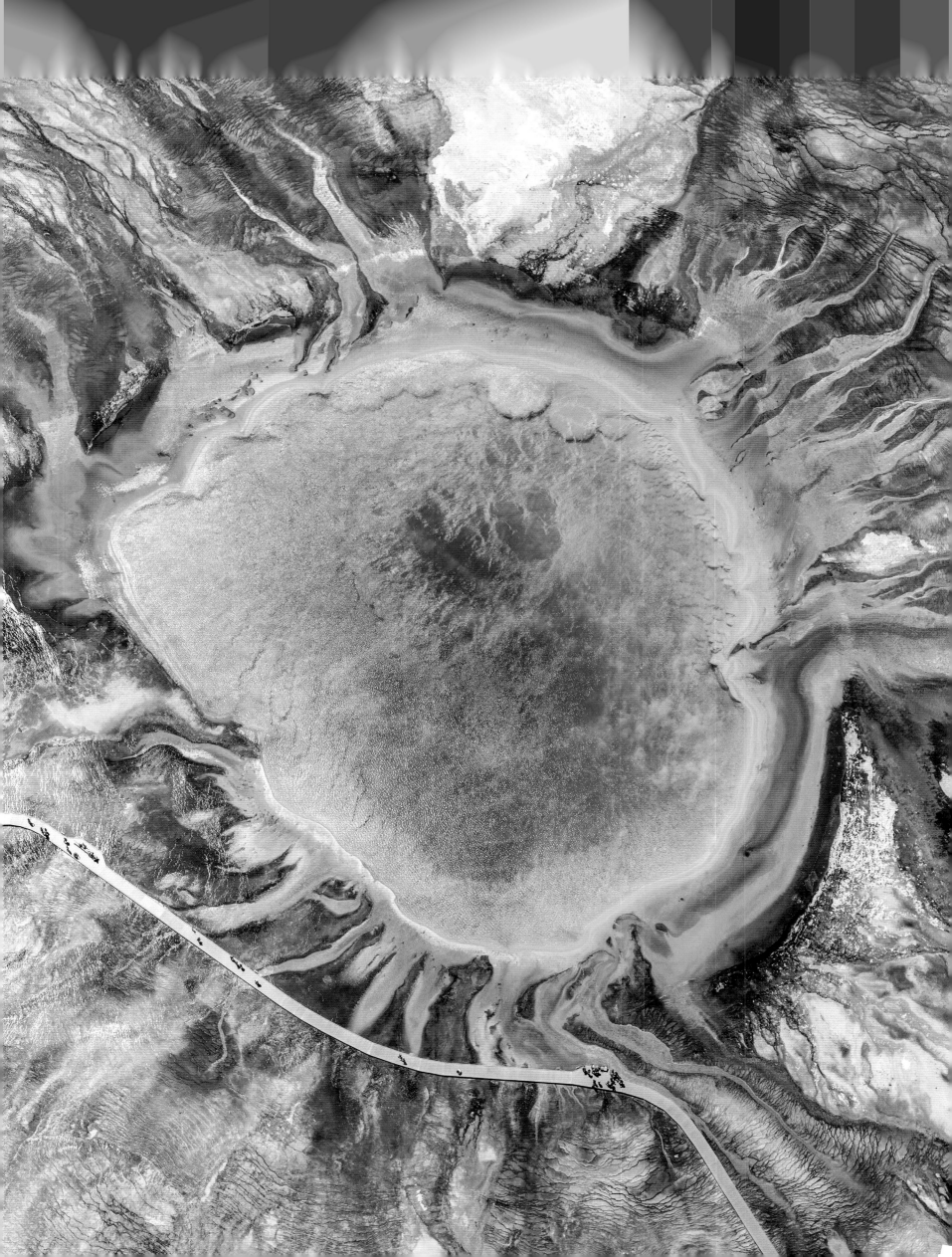

YELLOWSTONE IS HOME TO 67 MAMMAL SPECIES, THE LARGEST CONCENTRATION AMONG PARKS IN THE LOWER 48.

defies visualization. Volcanic ash and gas spewed into the atmosphere while pyroclastic flows plowed across the region like thousands of speeding locomotives. Six hundred cubic miles of debris—thousands of times greater than Mount St. Helens's 1980 eruption—showered the West. Ash covered the ground up to several feet deep for 5,790 square miles, as far away as Missouri. Wind carried sulfur clouds around the world and cooled temperatures for years. It was among one of the largest eruptions known to humankind.

So much magma exploded from the underground reservoir that the ground above collapsed and left a caldera hole larger than Rhode Island. This gaping crater, hundreds of feet deep, stretched 50 miles long and 40 miles wide across the park.

Nearly a million years later, it happened again along the edge of the first caldera. Then 640,000 years ago, the third and most recent major eruption created the 30-by-45-mile-wide Yellowstone Caldera. These three eruptions threw enough debris to fill the Grand Canyon. Subsequently, 80 smaller eruptions began spilling over Yellowstone and its caldera floors. And most recently, 70,000 years ago, magma arose and flowed across the southwest corner of the park.

Today, the reservoirs of magma are stacked on top of one another, 25 to 600 miles deep. From the top down, temperatures range from 1400°F (760°C) to 2200°F (1204°C).

These earthen ovens have created two burgeoning domes three to 12 miles below the Yellowstone Caldera rim. Depending upon magma volumes and changing temperatures, the caldera floor "breathes"

up and down along with the movements of the domes. Each year the domes rise or fall, averaging an inch of upward movement a year. Between the 20-by-14-mile Yellowstone Lake and the caldera below, the land has begun tilting and making the lake flood over trees on its southern shores, while exposing beaches on its northern shores.

In 1985, surveys showed that the entire caldera had risen more than three feet. Then it started sinking. In 2004, the caldera began another period of uplift for several years. These movements have also been correlated with increased earthquake activity. While thousands of temblors occur in the park each year, most are undetectable to passersby.

The park has myriad natural lakes and water features. The famous Old Faithful—spouting up to 184 feet high every 35 to 120 minutes—is one of 500 active geysers, amid more than 10,000 hot pools

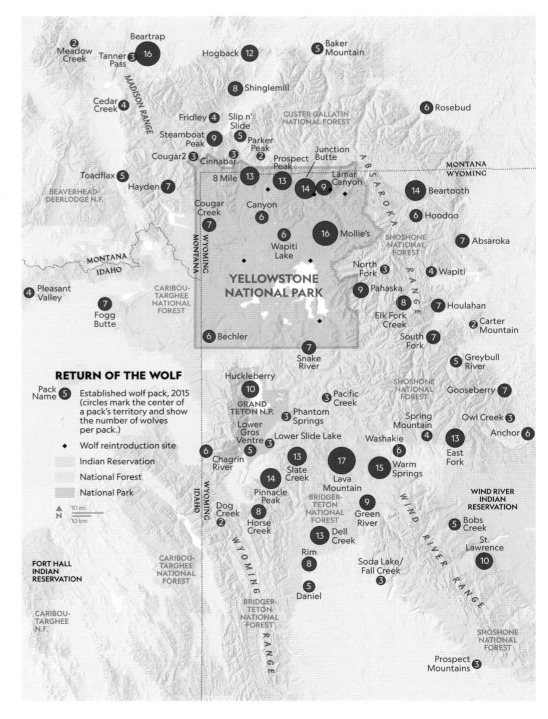

RETURN OF THE WOLF

Pack Name (5)   Established wolf pack, 2015 (circles mark the center of a pack's territory and show the number of wolves per pack.)

♦   Wolf reintroduction site

Indian Reservation

National Forest

National Park

Exterminated as vermin, gray wolves vanished from most of the lower 48 by the 1930s. In 1995 and '96, the U.S. Fish and Wildlife Service airlifted wolves from Canada in an effort to repopulate the area, and the reintroduced wolves quickly spread across the region. By 2015, the Yellowstone population reached an estimated 97 wolves.

and vents. As a measure of Yellowstone's concentration of heat, its 25 square miles of geysers contain more than half of the total geysers spread throughout the remaining 57.3 million square miles of land area on Earth. More than 14 miles of boardwalk are constantly moved, rebuilt, or readjusted to protect fragile microorganisms in warm geyser pools or to keep visitors from being scalded by hotter water. One square mile section within the Upper Geyser Basin has more than 150 different hot-water features—including geysers, fumaroles, mud pots, and hot springs. Yet only five of the major geysers (including Old Faithful) erupt with any regularity.

The gargantuan, geyser-spawning hot spot below the Earth's surface has shaken the park for hundreds of thousands of years without a new eruption. Yet over the last decade, the media have repeatedly focused on the likelihood of another violent eruption in the park. In 2015, the Yellowstone Volcano Observatory issued a response: "Although it is possible, scientists are not convinced that there will ever be another catastrophic eruption at Yellowstone."

Still, it's not hard to do some math. The three major eruptions in Yellowstone, beginning 2.1 million years ago, all occurred within a time span of 600,000 to 800,000 years—and 640,000 years have now elapsed since the Yellowstone Caldera blew. In the meantime, scientists at the observatory religiously monitor for earthquake activity with over two dozen seismograph stations, while checking for ground or stream movements with vertical motion surveys.

The Greater Yellowstone Ecosystem—with the fully protected park at its core—is one of the largest and mostly nondeveloped, temperate-zone ecosystems in the world. Along with its hydrothermal features, lakes, geologic wonders, high mountains, and diverse flora, the region is renowned for its wildlife—Greater Yellowstone's most defining component. It is the most prolific megafauna wildlife habitat in the contiguous United States.

Found throughout the seasons and roaming for hundreds of miles within Greater Yellowstone are the most genetically pure herds of bison on the continent; a few hundred of the frequently hunted moose; tens of thousands of elk, mule deer, and white-tailed deer; over 700 grizzly bears; hundreds more of the common black bears; over 200 mountain goats; up to 400 bighorn sheep in the park and outside its northern boundaries; and several hundred pronghorn. More than 30 other smaller animal species are also found in abundance, including the threatened wolverine and lynx—both in the midst of making a comeback. The large expanse of wild country and connected habitats in the Greater Yellowstone Ecosystem protect these animals from reductions and disease.

There are more than 500 wolves in the Greater Yellowstone Ecosystem. Their reentry into the wilds—after the Park Service blunder of eliminating the species from Yellowstone in the 1920s to protect the elk—is one of the great success stories of modern park management.

By the 1990s, it was obvious that the absence of wolf predation on the larger megafauna increased the numbers of unhealthy and lame animals. Reversing its policy on wolves, the U.S. Fish and Wildlife Service captured 31 wolves in Canada and released them in Yellowstone in 1995 and 1996. Because of the controversy and concern that wolves would prey upon outside ranchers' livestock, a U.S. District Court judge ordered that the wolves be removed, but this decision was appealed and overturned in 2000. After six years, the predation on livestock proved to be lighter than expected, and some of the thriving wolves from Yellowstone were transferred to Montana and Idaho. The wolves were subsequently removed from the endangered species list in those two states, but they remain on the list in Wyoming.

In the drought year of 1988, more than a third of Yellowstone—approximately 1,240 square miles—went up in smoke.

Dozens of small fires started by lightning each summer are considered normal—and hundreds of naturally caused fires had often been allowed to burn out on their own in the park. But by July 1988, the oppressive heat and dryness put the park in extreme danger. Several fires grew despite firefighting efforts. Within a week, the fires spread from 13 square miles to 155 square miles in the park. By the end of July, the fires were out of control and the park was closed. Eventually, strong winds amplified by the heat expanded the flames, and more than 230 square miles were burning among nearly a dozen different fires.

By the time that snow extinguished the last flames in September, the fires had burned down 67 buildings and caused several million dollars in damage. Including military troops, 25,000 firefighters were involved. Along with two firefighters who perished, park biologists reported that 345 elk, 36 deer, 12 moose, six black bears, and nine bison were killed.

Yellowstone reevaluated its fire management policy based on knowledge gained from the disaster and established stricter guidelines that would be adopted in national parks nationwide.

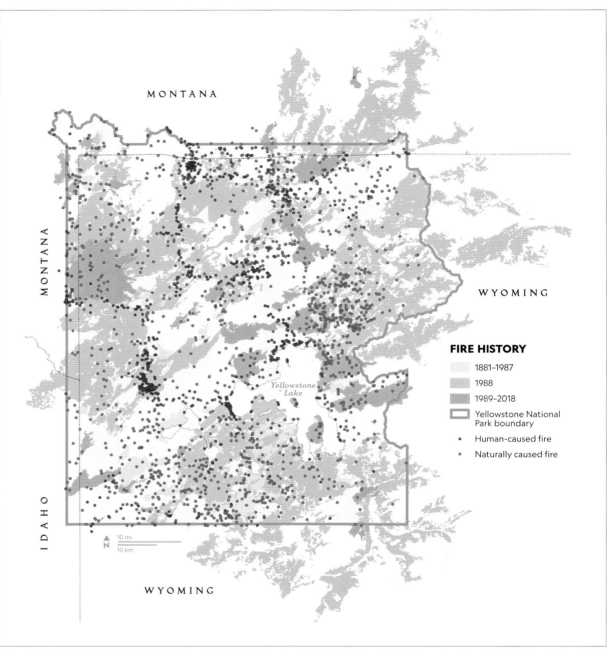

FIRE HISTORY

- 1881–1987
- 1988
- 1989–2018
- Yellowstone National Park boundary
- · Human-caused fire
- · Naturally caused fire

ABOVE: **Fires are key** to Yellowstone's ecosystem, influencing vegetation patterns and diversity. Amid severe drought in 1988, multiple fires scorched more than a third of the park, drawing attention to the necessity of fire management policies. The most active fire year since the historic 1988 fires occurred in 2016, when 70,284 acres went up in flames.

OPPOSITE: **The Yellowstone River** plunges over Upper Yellowstone Falls in Yellowstone's Grand Canyon. The park has dozens of named waterfalls and hundreds of unnamed ones, plunging from tens to hundreds of feet.

As a wildlife sanctuary, Yellowstone is still managed with the knowledge that fires regenerate parklands, and provide valuable animal grazing and habitat. Based on a 2016 survey of more than 1,200 groups, 83 percent replied that wildlife was one of the most important reasons for their visit (96 percent chose viewing natural scenery as one of the most important reasons).

Still, as one of the most popular parks, Yellowstone has a multitude of attractions, drawing wildlife or geyser or waterfall-watchers, photographers, bicyclists, winter snowmobilers, hikers (on more than a thousand miles of trails), anglers, boaters, and skiers. Not counting backcountry camping options, there are 12 campgrounds. The incredible depth and breadth of Yellowstone offers something for everyone—and over four million visitors a year prove it. ■

▷ LOCATION **5 MILES N OF JACKSON, WYOMING**

▷ SIZE **485 SQUARE MILES**

▷ HIGHEST POINT **GRAND TETON, 13,770 FEET**

▷ VISITORS **3,491,151 IN 2018**

▷ ESTABLISHED **1929**

GRAND TETON NATIONAL PARK

Stretching 45 miles over the Teton Range in northwestern Wyoming, the jagged alps of this popular park have become the emblematic American skyline. Grand Teton National Park is 10 miles south of Yellowstone and connected by the John D. Rockefeller, Jr. Memorial Parkway. Named after its highest and most photogenic mountain—thrusting 7,000 feet above the valley—the park's peaks and deep canyons are popular with climbers and hikers who hit over 200 miles of trails.

Paddlers and anglers are drawn to bodies of water like the 15-mile-long Jackson Lake, meanders of the Upper Snake River, or other streams fed by mountain snowmelt. The Tetons are relatively new mountains, yet erosion has also revealed underlying, 2.7-billion-year-old rocks. Holding some of the oldest rock in the national parks, the Teton gneiss was formed during the collision of tectonic plates, smashing together ocean floor sediment and volcanic debris. Magma then broke through the gneiss and formed intrusions that cooled over time into granite, which now caps many of the summits.

The ecosystem of Grand Teton National Park showcases prehistoric flora, including more than 1,000 plants. There are also 300 bird types, over 60 mammal species—including grizzlies protecting their

Grand Teton and the surrounding range rise as much as 7,000 feet above the 50-mile-long Jackson Hole valley at Snake River Overlook in early morning.

cubs, recently reintroduced wolves, and bison grazing the road-sides—and several different reptiles and amphibians in the park.

The Tetons are built from a broken piece of the Earth's crust forced up along the Teton Fault immediately below the range. Characteristic of these fault lines, the range has straight, steep faces without foothills.

The Tetons rose less than nine million years ago, making them juvenile and relatively unwrinkled mountains compared to the rest of the eroded, 80-million-year-old Rockies, or the elderly and rounded 300-million-year-old Appalachians. Lacking many millions of years of erosion, these young mountains stand straighter and taller than other more time-weathered peaks in the contiguous United States. Steep on the east side, and dropping off more gradually to the west, the mountains were also shaped over the last two million years by earthquakes along the Teton Fault. Seismic activity slowly pushed the western block up and the eastern block down several feet every thousand years. The incredible height difference between the tops of these two blocks dwarfs most American mountain ranges. The top of the western block of sandstone on Mount Moran is 6,000 feet above Jackson Hole, while the top of the eastern block with the same sandstone layer lies 24,000 feet beneath the valley.

Two hundred thousand years ago, Jackson Hole bore the weight of Pleistocene Ice Age glaciers. It all began as ice sheets flowed south from the Yellowstone Plateau and down along the Tetons, burying the valley with 2,000 feet of ice. Lakes were carved out. V-shaped river canyons were sculpted into U-shaped glacial valleys, while the wider Jackson Hole valley floor filled with glacial debris.

As the ice began melting 12,000 years ago, it left behind glacial polished ledges of bedrock and huge piles of rock debris, now mostly covered in forests. These fine-grained moraines can today be seen as ridges surrounding lakes in the park.

Receding ice opened the way to hunter-gatherers drawn to the abundant wildlife and plants below the mountains. The trail of their

Mormon homesteaders arrived in Jackson Hole near the turn of the 19th century, establishing a community of farmhouses—such as the barn with gable and shed below—called Mormon Row.

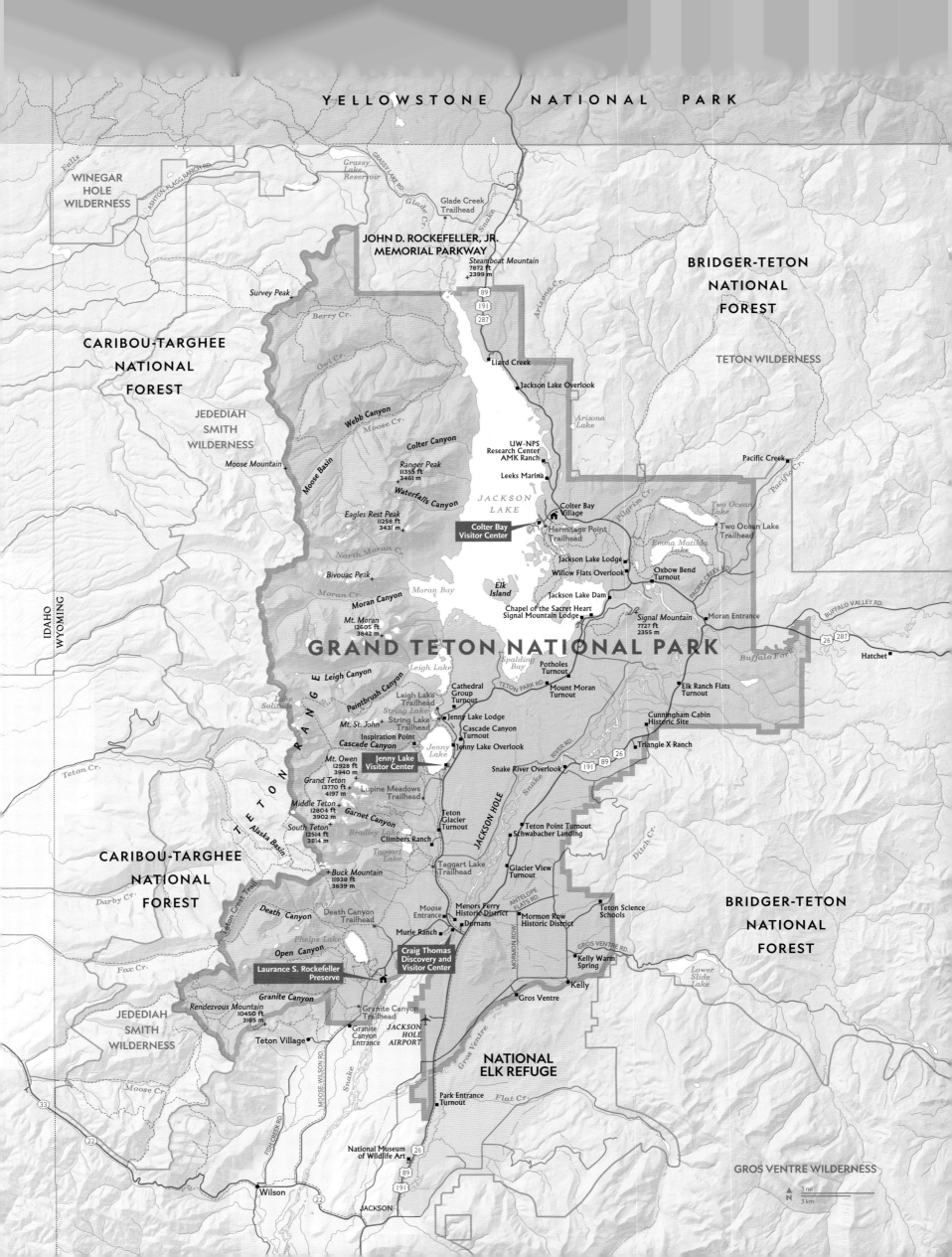

YELLOWSTONE NATIONAL PARK

WINEGAR
HOLE
WILDERNESS

Falls

Grassy Lake Reservoir

GRASSY LAKE RD.

ASHTON-FLAGG RANCH RD.

Glade Cr.

Glade Creek
Trailhead

JOHN D. ROCKEFELLER, JR.
MEMORIAL PARKWAY

Steamboat Mountain
7872 ft
2399 m

BRIDGER-TETON
NATIONAL
FOREST

CARIBOU-TARGHEE
NATIONAL
FOREST

Survey Peak

89
191
287

Berry Cr.

Owl Cr.

Snake R.

Arizona Cr.

TETON WILDERNESS

JEDEDIAH
SMITH
WILDERNESS

Liard Creek

Jackson Lake Overlook

Moose Mountain

Webb Canyon

Moose Cr.

Moose Basin

Colter Canyon

Arizona Lake

Pacific Creek

Pacific Cr.

Ranger Peak
11355 ft
3461 m

UW-NPS
Research Center
AMK Ranch

Waterfalls Canyon

Leeks Marina

JACKSON LAKE

Two Ocean Lake

Eagles Rest Peak
11258 ft
3431 m

Colter Bay
Village

Colter Bay
Visitor Center

Hermitage Point
Trailhead

Emma Matilda Lake

Two Ocean Lake
Trailhead

North Moran Cr.

Jackson Lake Lodge

Willow Flats Overlook

Oxbow Bend
Turnout

Pilgrim Cr.

Bivouac Peak

Moran Canyon

Moran Cr.

Moran Bay

Elk Island

Jackson Lake Dam

Mt. Moran
12605 ft
3842 m

Chapel of the Sacred Heart
Signal Mountain Lodge

PACIFIC CREEK RD.

Moran Entrance

BUFFALO VALLEY RD.

Signal Mountain
7727 ft
2355 m

Buffalo Fork

26
287

Hatchet

GRAND TETON NATIONAL PARK

Leigh Canyon

Leigh Lake

Spalding Bay

Potholes
Turnout

IDAHO
WYOMING

Paintbrush Canyon

Lake Solitude

TETON PARK RD.

Mount Moran
Turnout

Elk Ranch Flats
Turnout

Leigh Lake

Cathedral
Group Turnout

Teton Cr.

Mt. St. John

String Lake

Leigh Lake
Trailhead

Cunningham Cabin
Historic Site

TETON RANGE

String Lake
Trailhead

Jenny Lake Lodge

Cascade Canyon
Turnout

Inspiration Point

Cascade Canyon

Jenny Lake Overlook

Triangle X Ranch

Jenny Lake

Mt. Owen
12928 ft
3940 m

Jenny Lake
Visitor Center

SNAKE RIVER RD.

191
89
26

Grand Teton
13770 ft
4197 m

Lupine Meadows
Trailhead

Snake River Overlook

Middle Teton
12804 ft
3902 m

Garnet Canyon

South Teton
12514 ft
3814 m

Bradley Lake

Teton Glacier
Turnout

Teton Point Turnout
Schwabacher Landing

Alaska Basin

Climbers Ranch

JACKSON HOLE

Snake R.

Ditch Cr.

Taggart Lake

CARIBOU-TARGHEE
NATIONAL
FOREST

Buck Mountain
11938 ft
3639 m

Taggart Lake
Trailhead

Glacier View
Turnout

BRIDGER-TETON
NATIONAL
FOREST

Darby Cr.

Teton Crest Trail

Death Canyon

Death Canyon
Trailhead

Moose
Entrance

Menors Ferry
Historic District

ANTELOPE FLATS RD.

Teton Science
Schools

Phelps Lake

Murie Ranch

Dornans

Mormon Row
Historic District

Fox Cr.

Open Canyon

Laurance S. Rockefeller
Preserve

Craig Thomas
Discovery and
Visitor Center

MORMON ROW

GROS VENTRE RD.

Kelly Warm
Spring

Lower Slide Lake

JEDEDIAH
SMITH
WILDERNESS

Granite Canyon

Rendezvous Mountain
10450 ft
3185 m

Granite Canyon
Trailhead

Kelly

Granite
Canyon
Entrance

JACKSON
HOLE
AIRPORT

Gros Ventre

Gros Ventre

Teton Village

NATIONAL
ELK REFUGE

Moose Cr.

FISH CREEK RD.

MOOSE-WILSON RD.

Snake R.

Park Entrance
Turnout

Flat Cr.

33

National Museum
of Wildlife Art

26

89
191

GROS VENTRE WILDERNESS

22

Wilson

22

JACKSON

3 mi
N
3 km

fire pits, obsidian-stone tools, and tipi rings shows that these nomads followed the migratory elk south each winter. The Paleo-Indian culture enacted this pattern for thousands of years.

Several hundred years ago, the Shoshone arrived and continued to follow the southern migratory paths of their predecessors until they were moved onto a reservation in 1868. The Shoshone, however, became the first known people to climb the mountains and hunt the prolific bighorn sheep. Evidence of Shoshone vision quests and rock shelters can be found as high as 13,280 feet on a subpeak of the Grand Teton called the Enclosure.

Spiritually connected to the peaks, the Shoshone referred to the three highest—the Grand, South Teton, and Middle Teton—as "the

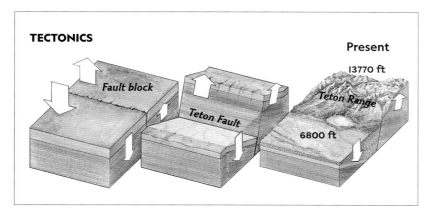

TECTONICS

Present

13770 ft

Fault block

Teton Range

Teton Fault

6800 ft

Less than 10 million years ago, two blocks of the Earth's crust collided—one lifting upward to form mountains and the other dropping downward to create the valley, resulting in the striking landscape now seen in Grand Teton National Park. Today, the active fault extends more than 40 miles along the eastern base of the Teton Range.

GLACIATION

Grand Teton

Teton Fault

Cascade Canyon Glacier

Teton Fault

Jenny Lake

Glacial moraine

N▶

As glaciers flowed south from Yellowstone two million years ago, ice sheets filled the valley, eroding mountains along the way. While carving peaks and canyons, the glaciers deposited moraines—masses of rocks and sediment—which today dam lakes along the base of the range.

THERE ARE 10 NAMED GLACIERS IN GRAND TETON NATIONAL PARK, BUT NOT ALL OF THEM ARE CONSIDERED ACTIVE, AND SOME ARE THINNING RAPIDLY.

Hoary-headed Fathers." But lonely French-Canadian trappers in the early 19th century named the peaks *Le Trois Tétons,* or the three breasts, later shortened to the Grand Teton. Later American surveyors, baffled by the Gallic comparison to female anatomy, thought the peaks looked more like shark teeth. Jackson Hole was named after the American David Jackson, who spent two decades trapping in the valley below the peaks.

The Homestead Act of 1862 had already brought settlers west, but they avoided the difficult climate of the Tetons, which averages 38 feet of snowfall each winter. It took another two decades for the valley's first settlers to eke out a living in rocky soils amid the long, cold winters and hot, dry summers. Still, ranchers toughed it out and grazed their cattle alongside elk and bison.

The controversial battle to protect the Grand Tetons and Jackson Hole started in 1882 as part of a park proposal to protect more than 25,000 migrating elk. Each winter, the herd moved out of Yellowstone and into Jackson, but even as the herd began starving and dying with diseases each winter, Teton park proposals foundered in Congress.

In the early 20th century, dude ranching boomed, ushering in herds of tourists rather than cattle. Visitors came from all over the country. This fueled development and building throughout Jackson Hole. Although the independent-minded community resisted government intrusion or parks in their valley, they acquiesced to a 39-square-mile Elk Reserve (later named the National Elk Refuge) just east of the Tetons in 1912. Without ranchers feeding the elk hay each winter, the herd would have perished. Still, the valley immediately below the Tetons was turning into a commercialized shantytown.

Enter John D. Rockefeller, Jr., who first visited in 1924. The son of America's first billionaire, Rockefeller had already helped fund and build other national parks. The man who drove him and his family beneath the awe-inspiring Tetons was the Yellowstone superintendent (and later director of the National Park Service) Horace Albright. Albright had already developed an agenda for park expansion and wanted to prevent further exploitation and acquire surrounding ranches along with the "shabby"-looking development, in addition to dude ranches, he described as "littering the roadway" and desecrating the scenery.

In short time, Rockefeller fell in love with the majestic Tetons. Taking Albright's advice, and chastened by how landowners had charged outrageous prices after he helped fund land acquisitions for Great Smoky Mountains National Park, Rockefeller used an assumed name. Then, with his buyers representing his shell outfit—the Snake River Land Company—he discreetly began purchasing land. Eventually, he amassed 35,000 acres.

In 1929, to protect the mountains and a half dozen lakes outside of Rockefeller lands, Congress created a smaller 150-square-mile version of the present-day Grand Teton National Park. The next year, when residents discovered Rockefeller's furtive land acquisitions, all hell broke loose. Disgruntled ranchers—who would have priced their land more dearly if they had known they were selling to a millionaire—said they had been swindled. The Wyoming congressional delegation claimed that citizens were going to be driven out by a Rockefeller monopoly, and blocked any future expansion of the park.

Rockefeller grew increasingly vexed—the government wouldn't take the land. Wyoming congressional representatives stood behind the local cattlemen, sheep farmers, and dude ranchers, who believed that their grazing rights and business opportunities would disappear

1929

1943

Jackson Hole
National
Monument

Current
park

1950 to
present

1972 to
present

John D. Rockefeller, Jr.
Memorial Parkway

National
Elk Refuge

with an enlarged park. Thirteen years after the park's creation, in a historic letter to President Franklin D. Roosevelt, Rockefeller threatened to sell elsewhere if his land wouldn't be accepted as a contribution to a park expansion. In 1943, Roosevelt overrode Congress and used the Antiquities Act to create the Jackson Hole National Monument alongside Grand Teton National Park.

Amid the cacophony of World War II, locals erupted in a protest that received national attention. A Wyoming senator called the president's move a "foul, sneaking Pearl Harbor blow."

Congress in turn abolished the monument by passing a new law. Roosevelt vetoed it. Then the state of Wyoming sued the National Park Service, claiming that the president had misused the Antiquities Act. Fortunately, the lawsuit was dismissed. Congressmen proposed two more laws to abolish the monument, but neither passed.

It took until 1950 for a compromise to be reached. Jackson Hole National Monument (alongside the Elk Refuge) would be added to Grand Teton National Park, but Wyoming would be exempted from the Antiquities Act—unless Congress approved the creation of another monument.

Congress finally recognized Rockefeller's philanthropy in 1972, by creating the John D. Rockefeller, Jr. Memorial Parkway connecting Yellowstone and Grand Teton National Parks. As a fitting tribute to the greatest philanthropist in national park history, the scenic road runs north where the Teton Range gently ramps down amid volcanic rocks that flowed out of Yellowstone and along the Snake River. Driving the highway today, visitors can imagine

Grand Teton National Park offers many miles of breathtaking hiking trails that range from a level meander around Jenny Lake to more rugged treks up and around the peaks.

To protect the Teton Range and its surrounding lakes, Congress established Grand Teton National Park in 1929. Fourteen years later, Franklin D. Roosevelt created Jackson Hole National Monument. Congress combined the park and monument in 1950, and dedicated the John D. Rockefeller, Jr. Memorial Parkway in 1972 in honor of the philanthropist's land contributions.

Albright behind the wheel with Rockefeller rapturously gazing up at the mountains.

Climbers have long been drawn to the unforgettable Tetons to lock their fingers on compact and solid granite, but like the park's creation, yet another storm of controversy clings to the storied peak. William Owen, Franklin Spalding, Frank Petersen, and John Shive made the first photo-documented ascent of "the Grand" in 1898, but an alleged ascent a quarter century earlier remains in dispute.

In 1872, the Yellowstone Park superintendent Nathaniel Langford and surveyor James Stevenson claimed to have reached the summit, taking advantage, they said, of melted-out divot-footholds caused by the bodies of grasshoppers stuck into the steep snowfields. Still, many experts remain suspicious that Langford's 1873 *Scribner's Monthly* account doesn't mention the technical rock climbing just below the top of the Grand Teton, nor does his description accurately match that of the true summit. Finally, Stevenson—from the government-funded Hayden Geological Survey that also explored Yellowstone that year—normally left rocks piled atop his summits. But the 1898 team found no such cairn in place.

Most climbers believe that the former team climbed the Shoshone's easier Enclosure subpeak, 500 feet below the summit of the

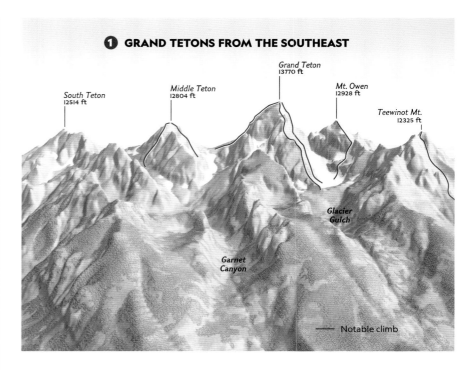

South Teton
12514 ft

Middle Teton
12804 ft

Grand Teton
13770 ft

Mt. Owen
12928 ft

Teewinot Mt.
12325 ft

Glacier
Gulch

Garnet
Canyon

— Notable climb

Grand. Even their leader, the famed geologist Ferdinand Hayden, unknowingly wrote about his men's accomplishment as if they had climbed the Enclosure rather than the Grand Teton: "So far as we can ascertain they are the only white men that ever reached its summit."

Modern technical climbing didn't take off in the Tetons for a few more decades, until the 1920s brought repeated climbs on "the Grand." Other difficult routes were established on the nine highest peaks—separated by canyons and rising over 12,000 feet—including on Mount Owen, Middle Teton, and Mount Moran. In 1929, two climbers returned from ascents in the French Alps and successfully applied European climbing techniques on a difficult new route up the East Ridge of the Grand. Then in 1931, two of the country's most classic new climbs were also established on the highest peak: the North Ridge—seen from Jackson Hole as the right-hand skyline of the Grand—averages over 63 degrees for 1,200 feet and was the hardest and most isolated climb in North America for its day. The other climb, a daring solo, was performed by and named after the teenager Glenn Exum and remains one of the most popular routes on the mountain. Exum teamed up with fellow Teton climbing pioneer Paul Petzoldt to start one of the first guide services, now called Exum Mountain Guides.

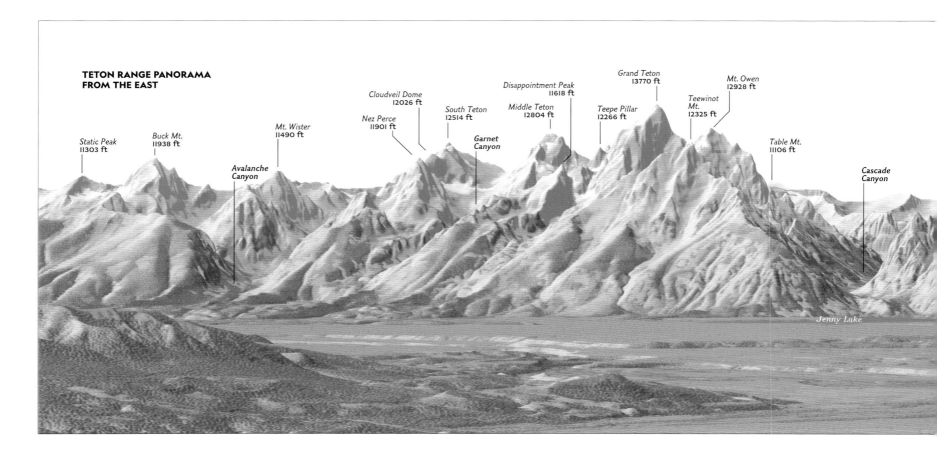

**TETON RANGE PANORAMA
FROM THE EAST**

Static Peak
11303 ft

Buck Mt.
11938 ft

Avalanche
Canyon

Mt. Wister
11490 ft

Nez Perce
11901 ft

Cloudveil Dome
12026 ft

South Teton
12514 ft

Garnet
Canyon

Middle Teton
12804 ft

Disappointment Peak
11618 ft

Teepe Pillar
12266 ft

Grand Teton
13770 ft

Teewinot
Mt.
12325 ft

Mt. Owen
12928 ft

Table Mt.
11106 ft

Cascade
Canyon

Jenny Lake

② GRAND TETON FROM THE NORTHWEST

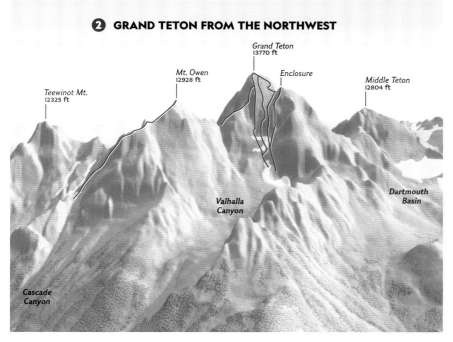

Teewinot Mt.
12325 ft

Mt. Owen
12928 ft

Grand Teton
13770 ft

Enclosure

Middle Teton
12804 ft

Valhalla
Canyon

Dartmouth
Basin

Cascade
Canyon

③ MT. MORAN FROM THE SOUTHEAST

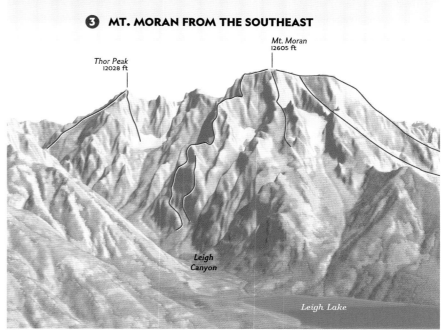

Thor Peak
12028 ft

Mt. Moran
12605 ft

Leigh
Canyon

Leigh Lake

During the latter 20th century, climbers explored more difficult cliffs in the canyons below the peaks, and by the new millennium, over 800 different climbing routes were established in the range. Today, over 90 different routes and variations lead to the summit of the Grand alone.

Most visitors—whether devoted fishermen, expert boaters, car campers, or hardcore climbers—come to this popular national park simply to stand in awe of America's majestic peak catching the last sunlight, to photograph the range in a lake reflection, or to listen to the echo of bugling elk in a Teton mountain canyon. "The peaks," Rockefeller wrote, capturing what most tourists feel, were "quite the grandest and most spectacular mountains I have ever seen . . . they present a picture of ever-changing beauty which is to me beyond compare." ▪

ABOVE: **Climbing the jagged Teton Range** has been a mainstay for mountaineers since the late 1800s. The first confirmed ascent of a major Teton peak occurred in 1898 when William Owen, Franklin Spalding, Frank Petersen, and John Shive reached the top of Grand Teton. Albert Ellingwood completed the first ascents of both the Middle and South Tetons in 1923. Following a boom of experienced climbers in the 1920s, mountaineers reached the summits of all major Teton peaks. Climbers have continued to establish a plethora of new routes across the range; today, more than 90 routes and variations lead to the summit of Grand Teton.

BELOW: **The magnificent range**—one of the most iconic sights in the National Park System—towers some 7,000 feet above Jackson Hole valley. The stunning mountain chain was formed by geologic forces less than nine million years ago. The park's namesake, Grand Teton, is the highest in the national park at 13,770 feet. Nine of the range's mountains reach more than 12,000 feet in elevation, with Mount Owen (12,928 feet), Middle Teton (12,804 feet), and Mount Moran (12,605 feet) among the tallest peaks.

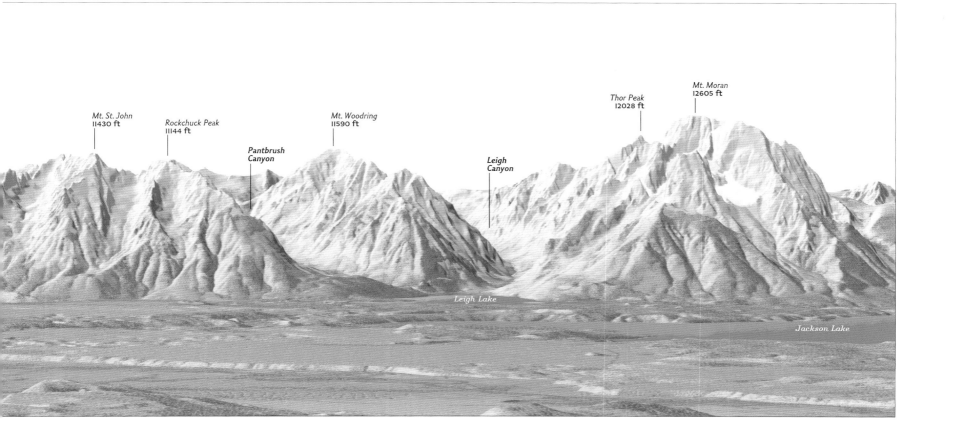

Mt. St. John
11430 ft

Rockchuck Peak
11144 ft

Pantbrush
Canyon

Mt. Woodring
11590 ft

Leigh
Canyon

Thor Peak
12028 ft

Mt. Moran
12605 ft

Leigh Lake

Jackson Lake

▷ LOCATION **30 MILES E OF KALISPELL, MONTANA**

▷ SIZE **1,583 SQUARE MILES**

▷ HIGHEST POINT **MOUNT CLEVELAND, 10,448 FEET**

▷ VISITORS **2,965,309 IN 2018**

▷ ESTABLISHED **1910**

GLACIER NATIONAL PARK

Glacier National Park straddles the Continental Divide in northwest Montana and is surrounded by Canada, the Blackfeet Indian Reservation, and national forest lands. The Livingston and Lewis Mountain Ranges' distinctive, horizontal rock-banded faces and knife-edge arêtes shelter more than two dozen shrinking glaciers.

Its wide mountain amphitheaters were carved by the relentless tonnage of long-ago ice fields after which the park was named. The ice sheets scooped out broad, U-shaped valleys with more than 700 lakes; streams drain northeast and southwest off the Continental Divide. As the hydrological apex of North America, the triangle-shaped summits of Triple Divide Peak (8,020 feet) direct rainwater to Hudson Bay, the Atlantic, or the Pacific.

Referred to as the centerpiece of the Crown of the Continent Ecosystem, the wilderness of Glacier National Park contains a wealthy biodiversity. Nearly 2,000 plant species have been identified in its prairie, montane, and alpine plant communities. Blanketed by coniferous forests up high, and cottonwood and aspen in the valleys, the park is also home to 71 mammal species, more than 260 different birds, and nearly two dozen fish species.

Seen from a trail that starts at Logan Pass Visitor Center just off scenic Going-to-the-Sun Road, Bearhat Mountain rises above Hidden Lake, one of more than 700 ice-melt lakes in Glacier National Park.

In 1932, Glacier and the adjoining Waterton Lakes National Park in Canada became the world's first International Peace Park, and the only one designated in the United States (six other U.S. national parks adjoin international borders). In 1976 the United Nations Educational, Scientific, and Cultural Organization (UNESCO) designated Glacier National Park an international biosphere reserve. And in 1995, UNESCO designated Waterton-Glacier International Peace Park a World Heritage site for its natural values.

The first humans came to the present-day park 10,500 years ago. Two thousand years later, these Paleo-Indians began venturing up into the high country to gather plants and hunt.

Based on hundreds of early archaeological sites within the park, these early Native Americans were ancestors of Shoshone, Cheyenne, Flathead (or Salish), and Kootenai residents that later lived around the park. In the early 1800s, Blackfeet took over the eastern side of the park and substituted mountain elk for bison that they normally hunted out on the plains. They referred to the high country of Glacier as "the Backbone of the World" and in an 1855 treaty, they were awarded these lands as part of their reservation.

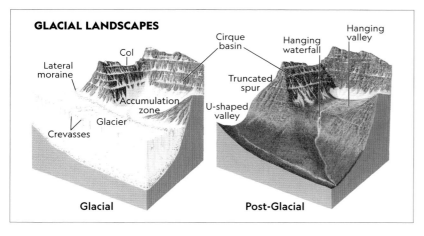

TOP: **People have lived** in this region of Montana for thousands of years. Blackfeet Indians—a nomadic group that hunted bison on the plains—look toward Mount Wilbur circa 1915.

ABOVE: **Glaciation shaped** much of the breathtaking landscape at Glacier National Park. The illustration at left depicts a typical glaciated terrain. On the right it shows the transformed landscape after the glaciers receded. Glaciation can create U-shaped valleys and hanging valleys, which can be seen at Lake McDonald Valley or above Bird Woman Falls, respectively.

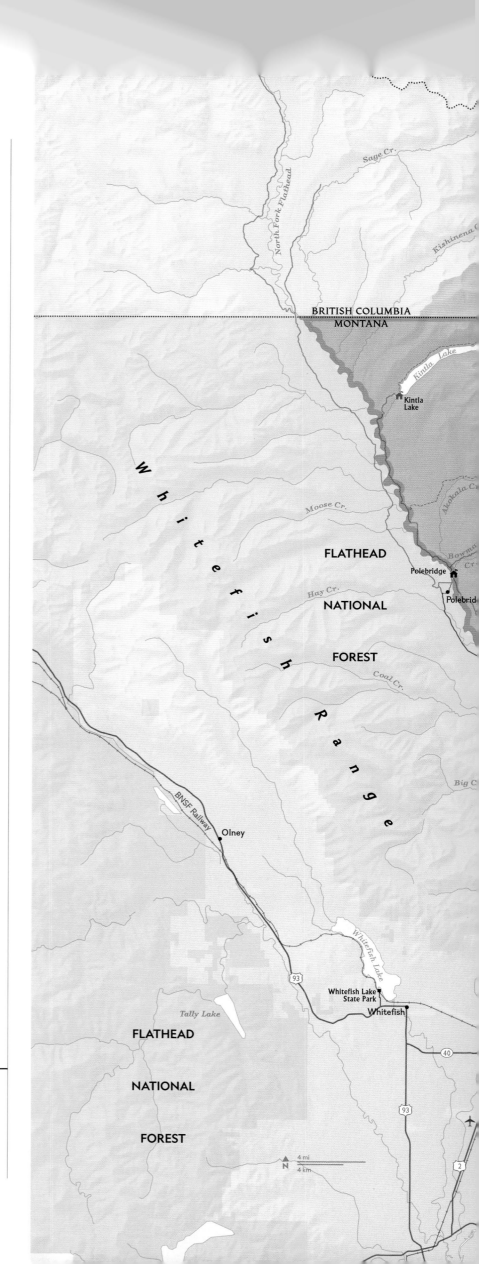

Forty years later, in another agreement negotiated by the conservationist George Bird Grinnell, Chief White Calf sold 1,250 square miles of the western half of the Blackfeet Reservation for $1.5 million. (When it later became a national park, the Blackfeet could no longer hunt, gather, and camp there as they always had—setting in motion an ongoing conflict with the U.S. government.) Grinnell and the politico Henry L. Stimson had already begun writing and speaking out to protect Glacier, which was made into a forest reserve in 1897.

More than Stimson and Grinnell, the Great Northern Railway's political influence and financial interest in hauling tourists to a new park finally convinced Congress to pass a bill in 1908. Two years later, President William Howard Taft signed Glacier National Park into law, and the next year, appointed Stimson as secretary of war (he took this post again during World War II); he also served as secretary of state.

Central to this park's allure are its glaciers. They cling like fissured gowns to the peaks, and spawn frothy waterfalls while coloring hundreds of lakes with the opaque turquoise of suspended glacial flour.

The Garden Wall is an arête showing the Ice Age as architect: Ice sheets thousands of feet thick carved this narrow rock spine, just one park feature from valleys to mountaintops marked by moving ice.

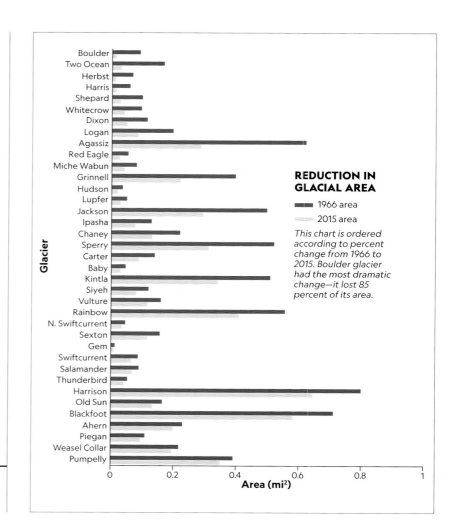

REDUCTION IN GLACIAL AREA

- 1966 area
- 2015 area

This chart is ordered according to percent change from 1966 to 2015. Boulder glacier had the most dramatic change—it lost 85 percent of its area.

Glacier (y-axis, from top to bottom): Boulder, Two Ocean, Herbst, Harris, Shepard, Whitecrow, Dixon, Logan, Agassiz, Red Eagle, Miche Wabun, Grinnell, Hudson, Lupfer, Jackson, Ipasha, Chaney, Sperry, Carter, Baby, Kintla, Siyeh, Vulture, Rainbow, N. Swiftcurrent, Sexton, Gem, Swiftcurrent, Salamander, Thunderbird, Harrison, Old Sun, Blackfoot, Ahern, Piegan, Weasel Collar, Pumpelly

Area (mi²): 0, 0.2, 0.4, 0.6, 0.8, 1

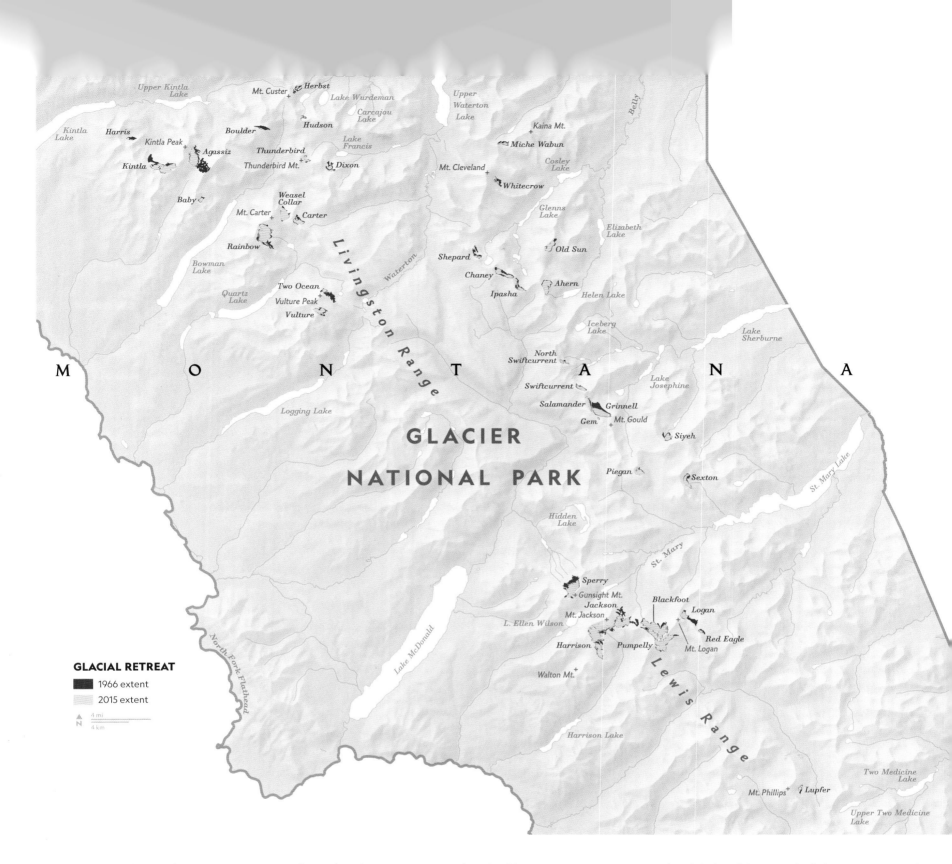

GLACIAL RETREAT

- 1966 extent
- 2015 extent

4 mi
4 km

These small, alpine glaciers are remnants from the Pleistocene ice sheets of 7,000 years ago. Until the end of the Little Ice Age in 1850, 150 of these glaciers were growing and creeping down into the valleys. But today, only 26 of these active glaciers (larger than 25 acres) remain.

As early as 1914, visitors could see that the glaciers had begun shrinking. Their retreat accelerated in direct response to the warming climate—as carbon dioxide (a greenhouse gas) increased in the atmosphere, the glaciers melted back as much as 330 feet a year.

From 1900 to 2010, the average annual temperature increase for the park was 2.4° F (1.3°C). Spring and summer minimum temperatures also increased, which may cause earlier summer glacial melt. In 2017, the U.S. Geological Survey (USGS) published an analysis of these glaciers. The results show that all the park glaciers have diminished in size—as much as 85 percent in some areas, and averaging 39 percent overall—from 1966 to 2015.

Sensitive to variations in temperature and precipitation, alpine mountain glaciers are shrinking rapidly due to climate change. A 2017 USGS report of Glacier National Park's 37 named glaciers (listed opposite and shown on the map above) revealed that the park lost more than a third of its glacial ice between 1966 and 2015. The average area reduction was 39 percent in just 50 years, and 10 glaciers lost more than half of their total area. Loss of ice is a significant loss of freshwater resources, which can have compounding ecologic effects on aquatic life, vegetation, and even drinking water in some communities. Glaciers may disappear from the park entirely between 2030 and 2080.

The park's most visited glacier, Grinnell (named after George Bird), lost 45 percent of its ice. One scientist recalled how he had to climb 20 to 30 feet up over Grinnell Glacier's edge to get onto the ice in 1991. A quarter century later, he told the *New York Times,* it was no higher than his shins. USGS climate models show if the current warming patterns continue, the active glaciers in the park will disappear as early as 2030.

Because glaciers perform as frozen reservoirs—releasing cold water in midsummer as streams begin to lose their flow—the loss of glaciers would drive out cold-water fish and kill off aquatic insects

Adapted to some of the toughest conditions on the planet, lichens thrive in Glacier National Park. These hardy species can live for thousands of years, but are sensitive to environmental changes, making them accurate gauges for clean air conditions in the park.

THE PARK STRADDLES THE CONTINENTAL DIVIDE AND A REGION KNOWN FOR EXTREME WEATHER. IN LESS THAN A DAY LOCAL TEMPERATURES CAN DROP 100°F (56°C).

upon which fish depend. Dry or warming streams will also alter surrounding vegetation.

Of nearly 2,000 plant species in the park, 46 are rare throughout Montana. One unusual plant, the slender moonwort, is a fern that grows from a single, tiny stalk, splitting into a single leaf opposite an alien-looking, fertile spike. Unlike the other 61 ferns in Glacier, moonwort spores are dispersed through the soil instead of the air and water; the plant is believed to exist as a new hybrid within the park. These Lilliputian four-inch moonworts, along with four-foot bracken ferns, prosper in the lush valleys several thousand feet below the melting glaciers.

Close to a third of the alpine and mountainous park appears to be simply covered in piles of broken-up, sedimentary rock formerly buried in ice. Yet closer examination will reveal hundreds of lichen species, spatter-colonized in neon greens or orange or yellow across the rocks. Looking about the slopes above tree line, it's also apparent that the lichen grows in soil bereft of other plants beneath the rocks. Down in the valleys, lichen has colonized the tree trunks.

Lichen is made up of fungus and algae living together in symbiosis. While the fungus gathers minerals and provides structure, the algae fulfill the light-gathering process of photosynthesis that manufactures food.

Because some lichens can live longer than 8,000 years, glaciologists can age the lichens as a means of determining when individual glaciers retreated from each rock. Just like glaciers that melt at a corresponding rate to changing climate, sensitive lichens are barometers of air pollution: Their disappearance from the rocks means that the air quality has degenerated. Blocked from necessary sunlight that allows photosynthesis, the plant dies when it can no longer produce food. Fortunately, the huge collections of lichen throughout the high country of Glacier National Park show how clean the air is, removed from urban smog.

In the Crown of the Continent Ecosystem, the forest on the wetter western side of the Continental Divide is nearly a thousand feet higher than tree line on the colder eastern side, exposed to the scouring winds and weather of the Great Plains.

Glacier's rich biodiversity is shown in the three major climatic zones within the park: Southwest of the Continental Divide are thick stands of hemlock and red cedar. The densely forested northwest and west sides contain fir and spruce. And on the eastern and more sparsely wooded prairie side are spruce, fir, and pine forests.

As in many western forests suffering from drought and warming temperatures, it's not uncommon to see swaths of orange-red or red-tipped trees being weakened and killed by spruce budworm and pine beetle. Insecticides are no longer used in Glacier due to the detrimental effects on other plants and animals, and infected trees are only cut down if they present a hazard to people or buildings. Instead, the park has successfully treated healthy Douglas fir and whitebark pine trees with pheromones that stop further insect invasions and preserve the trees.

More than any tree, the whitebark pine is a carefully watched, keystone species in Glacier, promoting biodiversity through the many plants and animals that depend upon it. The rough, flaky-skinned tree can grow up to 100 feet tall, but it's also found at the edge of tree line in fairy-tale forests of krummholz (German for "twisted wood"), with its branches intertwined and growing together to create tunnels.

Throughout the northern Rockies, whitebark pine has been invaded with a fungus from Eurasia called blister rust. First documented in

Glacier in 1939, the blister rust fungus has since infected over 75 percent of the park's whitebark pines. Blister rust starts on the branches, subsuming the plant tissue with cankers, and eventually—usually—killing the entire tree. Although there is no known cure, not all infected whitebark pines die; some are mysteriously resistant to the fungus. By harvesting the seeds of these survivor trees, and conducting a whitebark pine breeding program, the park is hopeful for the future.

A dozen different birds, eight small mammals, and two large mammals depend upon the whitebark pine for its pinecone nuts. Red

RIGHT: **The gray,** gnarled branches of a whitebark pine twist above sloping terrain. A keystone yet diminishing species, this tree's large seeds are a valuable food source for grizzly and black bears, among other animals.

BELOW: **Stretching from** Montana into the southern Canadian Rockies in British Columbia and Alberta, the 28,000-square-mile Crown of the Continent Ecosystem encompasses many ecological zones and the headwaters for three of North America's major rivers. The country's largest intact ecosystem, it harbors a diverse assemblage of wildlife, and the list of species living there has stayed the same since westward exploration in the 1800s.

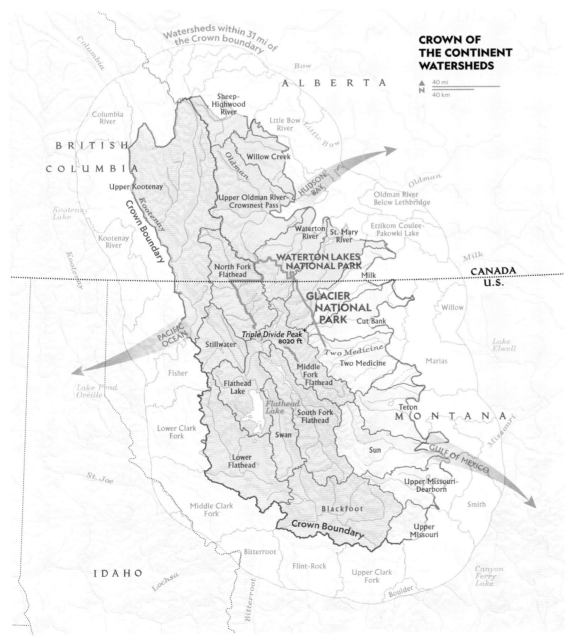

CROWN OF THE CONTINENT WATERSHEDS

squirrels cache and bury these nuts beneath piles of cone flakes on the ground, while bears then raid these hoarded, midden caches. Rich in fats, carbohydrates, and proteins, this high-energy food sustains beleaguered grizzlies more than any other animal, according to scientists. Long-listed as an endangered species due to habitat loss, grizzlies are recently being hit and killed on highways in record numbers in and around the park.

As omnivores, grizzlies consume nuts, grass, berries, roots, mushrooms, insects, and larvae for 90 percent of their diet. For the most part, grizzlies avoid humans in the park and only prey on larger animals in unique or hungry circumstances. Glacier averages one or two nonlethal, bear-human incidents a year. Since 1967, amid more than 90 million park visitors, there have been 10 bear-related fatalities in the park. Three of those fatalities involved hikers (two of them were alone). Still, more visitors—56 since 1910—have died in the park by drowning. The park recommends hiking in groups of four or more people to deter human-bear encounters. Resource managers keep tabs on nearly 300 different grizzlies and 600 black bears living in Glacier through DNA fur monitoring—with samples collected from established bear rubbing trees throughout the park.

Park researchers have also documented 50 wolverines—the densest population of this rare mammal in the United States. As for other endangered species, wolves were killed off shortly after the park was created. But in the 1980s, a wild pair crossed over from Canada, then denned and raised five pups. Ranging throughout the park, oblivious to the boundaries while chasing the elk migration, these wolves remain seldom seen and elusive—almost as if aware that their ancestors in Glacier had been extirpated. Much more commonly encountered are their prey species: deer, elk, and moose.

Among the many species of waterfowl drawn to this park of lakes is the highest density of breeding harlequin ducks in the contiguous

BELOW: **Glacier National Park** supports the highest density of breeding harlequin ducks in the lower 48. Overall, harlequin populations are declining across the West, with one known exception: a stable population along Glacier's upper McDonald Creek. Since annual surveys began in 1991, an average of nine duck pairs and 10 chicks have been observed in the park each year.

BOTTOM: **Unlike most** duck species, harlequins favor fast-flowing water and migrate east-west, leaving Glacier's cold lake system in small flocks in the late fall to spend winter along the Pacific coast.

HARLEQUIN DUCK DISTRIBUTION
Breeding
Non-breeding

GLACIER'S REMOTE, LONG-PROTECTED LANDSCAPE HAS HELPED ITS ECOSYSTEM THRIVE ALMOST UNDISTURBED FOR CENTURIES, SUPPORTING CREATURES FROM THE TWO-GRAM PYGMY SHREW TO THE 500-POUND ELK.

United States. Although populations are declining everywhere else, the park's protected lake habitat—isolated from humans—has continuously allowed a small population of the nesting pairs to return.

Wolves, wolverines, and harlequin ducks unseen, tourists are still happy to drive or even bicycle the 50-mile-long Going-to-the-Sun Road—accessing picnic areas, campgrounds, and visitor centers on either side of the Continental Divide. This engineering marvel of a highway—not built for acrophobic drivers—shares stunning views with mountain goats (the park symbol) and bighorn sheep. Down below, classic wooden boats traverse the big lakes amid historic buildings and lodges built by the Great Northern Railway more than a century ago. Advertised as "Switzerland in America," the park drew hundreds of thousands of tourists who rode the train across Montana to visit elegant and still extant, century-old buildings and inns such as the Lake McDonald Lodge, Sperry Chalet, Many Glacier Hotel, Two Medicine Store, and Granite Park Chalet.

Glacier's 700 miles of hiker-friendly trails—including the Continental Divide Trail from Mexico to Canada and the Pacific Northwest National Scenic Trail—rival that of any park trail system. In winter, ice climbers seek the abundance of frozen waterfalls. Still, the huge snowpack makes backcountry travel difficult until June. Once the streams are free of snow, Glacier National Park also offers some of the finest fly-fishing on the continent. ■

Hemmed in by mountains, forests, and meadows at the eastern edge of the park, the nearly 10-mile-long St. Mary Lake is the second biggest body of water in Glacier.

DESERT SOUTHWEST PARKS

CONTENTS

Morning light highlights the sand dunes' sinuous ripples and smooth expanses at Death Valley National Park.

▷ LOCATION **235 MILES S OF MIDLAND, TEXAS**

▷ SIZE **1,252 SQUARE MILES**

▷ HIGHEST POINT **EMORY PEAK, 7,832 FEET**

▷ VISITORS **440,091 IN 2018**

▷ ESTABLISHED **1944**

BIG BEND NATIONAL PARK

S outhwest Texas' Big Bend National Park has its own mountain range, the Chisos, of volcanic origin. It also contains canyons cutting through ancient limestone, all heated by the huge Chihuahuan Desert, and demarcated by 118 miles of the Rio Grande, the fourth longest river in the United States. The park's name comes from the river's abrupt turn: flowing southeast then northeast in a U-shaped bend along the international border. Larger than the state of Rhode Island, Big Bend has more species of cactus, bats, tropical butterflies, and birds than any other national park.

At altitudes ranging from 1,800 feet along the Rio Grande to nearly 8,000 feet in the Chisos Mountains, the park varies in moisture and temperature extremes. The heat regularly exceeds 105°F (40.5°C) in the lower elevations in late spring and early summer, and winters are mild, with occasional subfreezing temperatures.

Seen on the map as a faraway borderland, hundreds of miles from major cities, Big Bend has nonetheless become popular. Visitation has steadily increased by tens of thousands over the last half dozen years. The rugged landscape—accessed by five paved roads through the park—has become a destination for Texans (most American

Sunlight skates across the surface of the Rio Grande as it flows through Big Bend National Park, which gets its name from a sharp bend the river takes as it winds between the United States and Mexico.

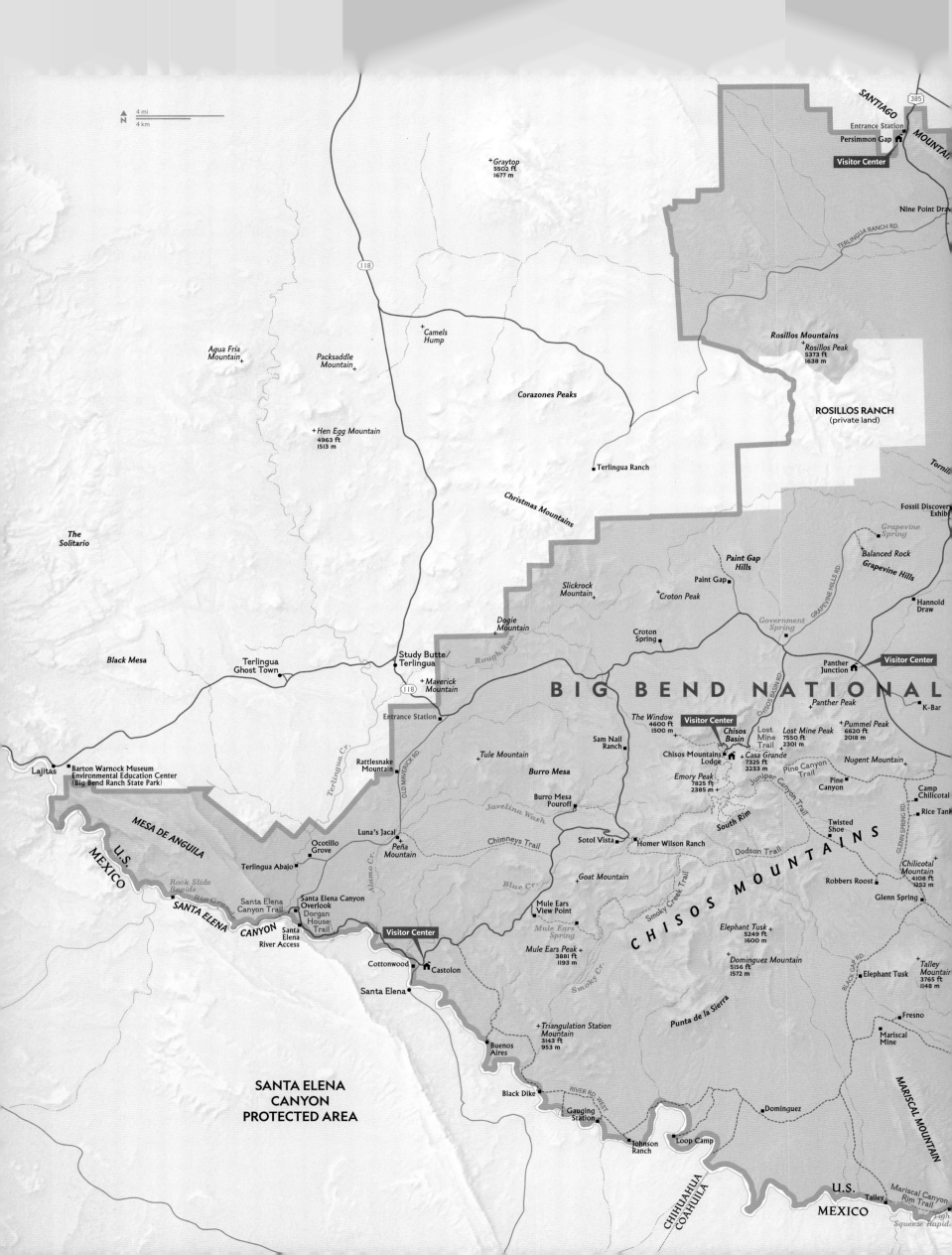

N
4 mi
4 km

+Graytop
5502 ft
1677 m

+Camels
Hump

*Agua Fria
Mountain*+

*Packsaddle
Mountain*+

Corazones Peaks

Rosillos Mountains
+*Rosillos Peak*
5373 ft
1638 m

SANTIAGO MOUNTAINS

385

Entrance Station
Persimmon Gap

Visitor Center

Nine Point Draw

TERLINGUA RANCH RD.

118

+*Hen Egg Mountain*
4963 ft
1513 m

■ Terlingua Ranch

ROSILLOS RANCH
(private land)

Christmas Mountains

*The
Solitario*

*Paint Gap
Hills*

Paint Gap

Slickrock
Mountain+

+*Croton Peak*

Balanced Rock

Grapevine Hills

Fossil Discovery
Exhibit

*Grapevine
Spring*

GRAPEVINE HILLS RD.

Hannold
Draw

*Dogie
Mountain*

Croton
Spring

*Government
Spring*

Panther
Junction

Visitor Center

Black Mesa

Terlingua
Ghost Town

Study Butte/
Terlingua

Rough Run

BIG BEND NATIONAL

118

+*Maverick
Mountain*

+*Panther Peak*

K-Bar

CHISOS BASIN RD.

Entrance Station

Terlingua Cr.

Rattlesnake
Mountain

Tule Mountain

Sam Nail
Ranch

The Window
4600 ft
1500 m

Visitor Center

*Chisos
Basin*

Lost
Mine
Trail

+*Lost Mine Peak*
7550 ft
2301 m

+*Pummel Peak*
6620 ft
2018 m

OLD MAVERICK RD.

Chisos Mountains
Lodge

+*Casa Grande*
7325 ft
2233 m

Nugent Mountain

Lajitas

Barton Warnock Museum
Environmental Education Center
(Big Bend Ranch State Park)

Burro Mesa

Burro Mesa
Pouroff

Javelina Wash

Emory Peak
7825 ft
2385 m +

Pine Canyon
Trail

*Pine
Canyon*

Camp
Chilicotal

Rice Tank

MESA DE ANGUILA

Luna's Jacal

Ocotillo
Grove

*Peña
Mountain*

Chimneys Trail

Sotol Vista

Homer Wilson Ranch

South Rim

Juniper Canyon Trail

Dodson Trail

Twisted
Shoe

GLENN SPRING RD.

MEXICO

U.S.

Terlingua Abajo

Alamo Cr.

Goat Mountain

Blue Cr.

Smoky Creek Trail

+*Chilicotal
Mountain*
4108 ft
1252 m

Robbers Roost

Glenn Spring

*Rock Slide
Rapids*

SANTA ELENA

Santa Elena
Canyon Trail

Santa Elena Canyon
Overlook

Dorgan
House
Trail

Santa
Elena
River Access

Visitor Center

CANYON

Rio Grande

Mule Ears
View Point

*Mule Ears
Spring*

Smoky Cr.

Mule Ears Peak +
3881 ft
1193 m

+*Elephant Tusk*
5249 ft
1600 m

+*Dominguez Mountain*
5156 ft
1572 m

CHISOS MOUNTAINS

BLACK GAP RD.

Elephant Tusk

+*Talley
Mountain*
3765 ft
1148 m

Cottonwood ▲ Castolon

Santa Elena

Punta de la Sierra

Fresno

Mariscal
Mine

SANTA ELENA
CANYON
PROTECTED AREA

Buenos
Aires

+*Triangulation Station
Mountain*
3143 ft
953 m

Black Dike

RIVER RD WEST

Gauging
Station

Dominguez

Johnson
Ranch

Loop Camp

U.S.

MEXICO

MARISCAL MOUNTAIN

Talley

*Mariscal
Canyon
Rim Trail*

CHIHUAHUA
COAHUILA

Squeeze Rapids

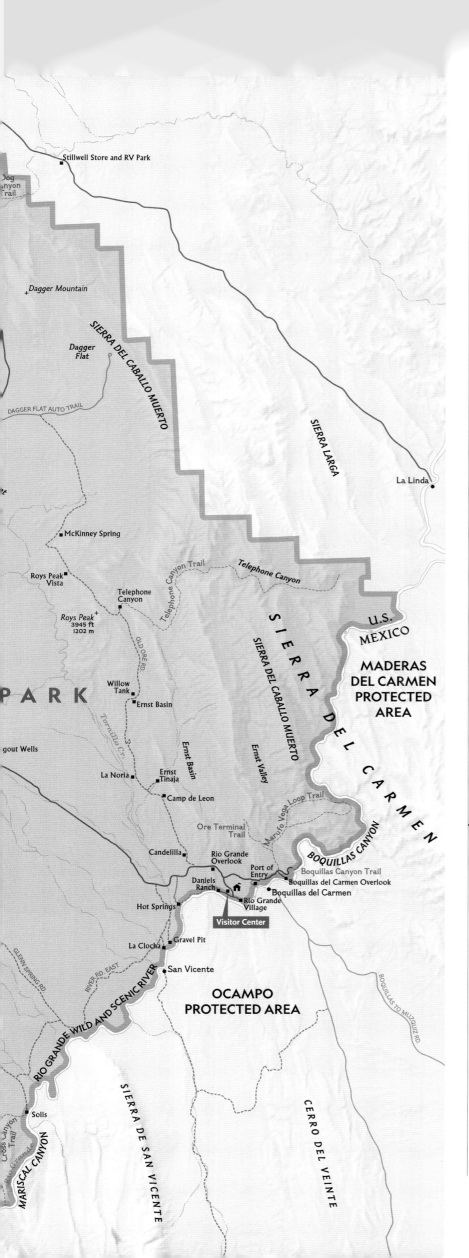

visitors are from in state). Still, "We're not a place that you drive by and visit," as one park ranger tells tourists, "You either really want to be here or are really lost."

Among many attractions, Big Bend is world renowned for its rich fossil record, documenting 130 million years from ancient sea life to dinosaurs and mammals that once roamed the land. It has drawn paleontologists for decades, as well as would-be astronomers: Big Bend is one of the darkest parks on the continent for studying the constellations. The International Dark-Sky Association awarded it a Gold Tier certification in 2012, partly due to the lack of obscuring water vapor in the high desert, as well as the elimination or dimming of lights throughout the park, removed from the glow of major urban centers.

For amateur or big-year birders alike, Big Bend has a surplus of international species to check off the list; hikers have more than 200 miles of trails for exploring and camping at backcountry locations, which more than 20,000 people take advantage of annually; and boaters have a famous—albeit drying—river to run. The Rio Grande even has its own laid-back border crossing, where tourists with passports can ferry across to the Mexican village of Boquillas.

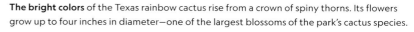

As one of six national parks sharing an international border, Big Bend is in good company. Directly across the border are the Mexican protected natural areas Maderas del Carmen and Cañon de Santa Elena. If managed cohesively, these neighboring sanctuaries more than double the protected habitat in Big Bend National Park.

The Texas Legislature first discussed a jointly managed binational park in the 1930s after the fledgling Big Bend became a state park, but it took a decade—despite Congress passing legislation that would enable national park land acquisition in 1935—and the interruption of World War II for it to actually become an established

The bright colors of the Texas rainbow cactus rise from a crown of spiny thorns. Its flowers grow up to four inches in diameter—one of the largest blossoms of the park's cactus species.

national park. Eventually, President Franklin D. Roosevelt wrote to Mexican president Manuel Ávila Camacho: "I do not believe that this undertaking in the Big Bend will be complete until the entire park area in this region on both sides of the Rio Grande forms one great international park."

One week after D-Day, as if FDR wasn't preoccupied with a global conflict, he signed the act creating Big Bend National Park on June 12, 1944. It was more than just a piece of conservation legislation: Setting aside this landscape and river for protection during the world's greatest international upheaval showed farsighted optimism. While creating an important sanctuary for America, FDR, confident that the war would end, also felt the need to reach out to other countries in the interests of peace and cooperation.

A month later, the *Houston Chronicle* featured a cartoon showing a giant magnet literally drawing crowds of people to the canyon park, with the caption: "post war tourist attraction." Still, the war hadn't ended, and only 1,400 people visited that year. Big Bend remained the only national park created amid World War II.

In addition to creating other national parks during his unmatched four terms in office, FDR—inspired by his fifth cousin, the great conservationist Theodore Roosevelt—signed the sweeping 1933 reorganization that added nearly a hundred more protected units to the National Park System. Following his death in 1945, discus-

LOWER-WATT LED LIGHTS AND SHIELDED LIGHTING INSTALLED IN THE PARK HELP MAINTAIN THE DARK SKIES FOR PRIME STARGAZING.

sions for a jointly managed, cross-border Tex-Mex park lapsed. Yet they resumed three decades later, and Mexico finally created Cañon de Santa Elena Flora and Fauna Protection Area a half century after Big Bend was established. The two park systems now work cooperatively together on multiple projects.

The September 11, 2001, attacks closed down the park's border crossing. Then in 2016, the potential for binational park cooperation faltered yet again with the proposal for a wall blocking 2,000 miles of the international border. Still, full-time residents of the park—including a small population of mountain lions and black bear—routinely cross the Rio Grande.

In the bigger picture of history, Big Bend is a paleontological paradise that showcases one of the most complete views of a prehistoric ecosystem on Earth. Its fossil record begins 130 million years ago and gives clues to what life might have been like when today's Midwest region was submerged in a huge sea. Early Cretaceous marine fossils show the presence of the oceanic predator lizard *Mosasaurus* and a fierce bony fish—*Xiphactinus*—with a powerful tail and a jaw that could open several feet wide to swallow fish whole. More docile life-forms like ammonites, sea turtles, sea urchins, oysters, and snails shared the temperate shallow waters.

During the late Cretaceous period, fossil evidence from 83 to 72 million years ago suggests that Big Bend emerged from the water as humid coastal swamp. Fearsome alligatoroids up to 40 feet long—

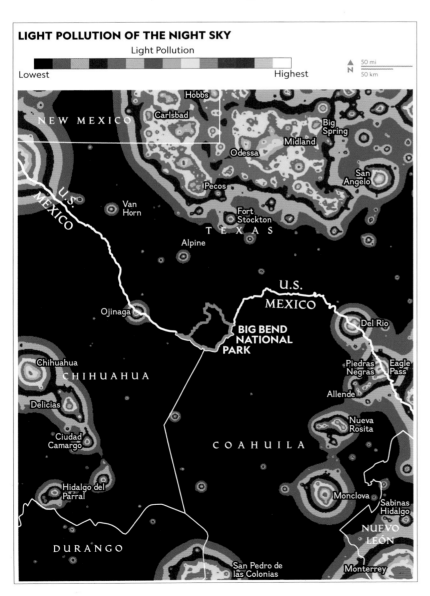

LIGHT POLLUTION OF THE NIGHT SKY

Light Pollution

Lowest   Highest

50 mi
50 km

OPPOSITE: **Big Bend's dark skies** provide a perfect canvas: Although most city dwellers can only spot a few hundred stars at night, here some 2,000 are visible, as shown right, with the Milky Way stretched over Balanced Rock.

LEFT: **Man-made lights** pollute the night sky, as shown on this map depicting artificial night sky brightness. The darker colors, such as those surrounding Big Bend National Park, indicate the most pristine skies. Skies in the blue category and higher (to the right on the scale) are considered polluted. In the summer, the Milky Way cannot be seen in skies starting in the orange category.

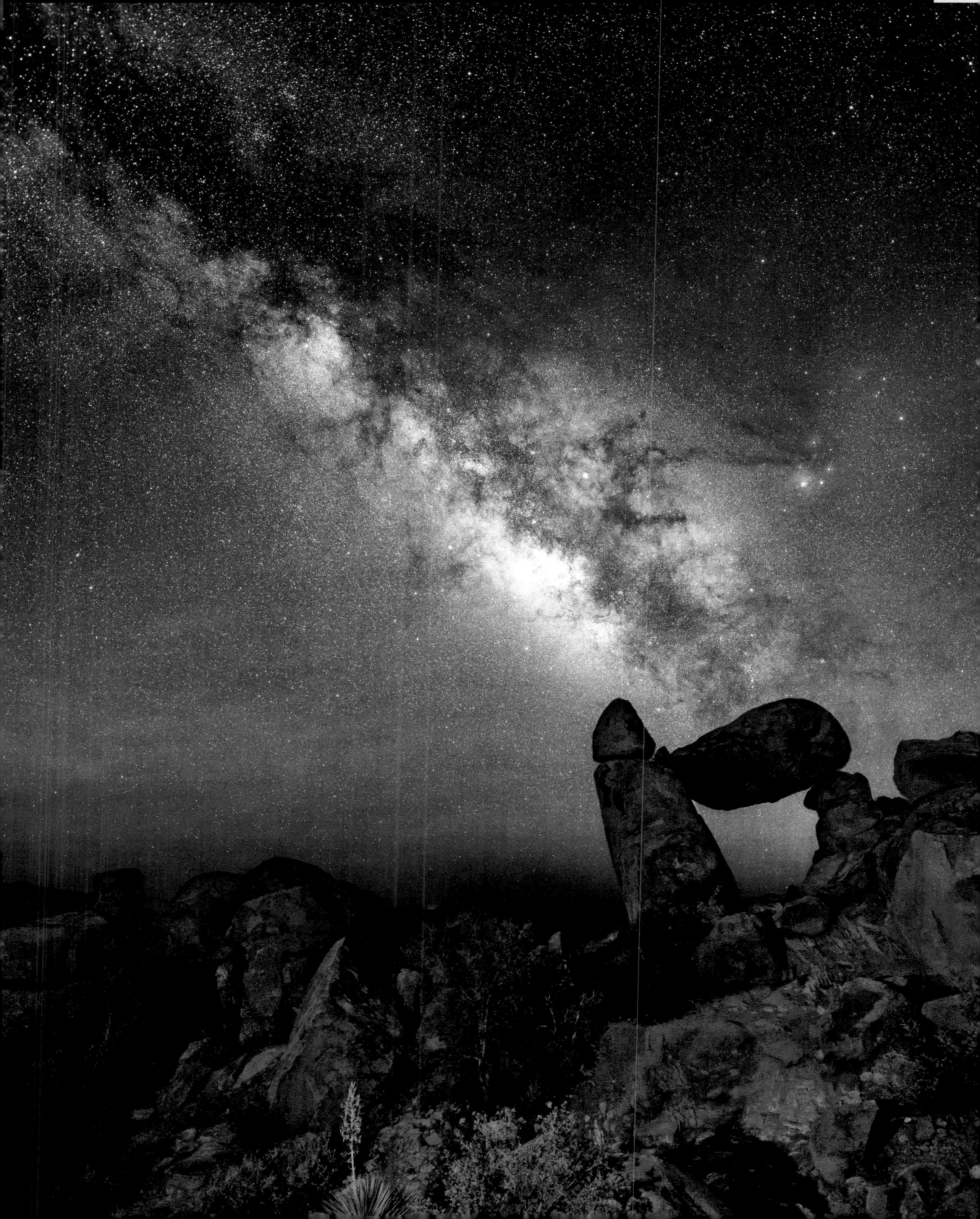

dubbed *Deinosuchus*—and tyrannosaurs preyed on horned and armored dinosaurs. Portions of the giant skull of a new species of horned dinosaur later named *Bravoceratops* (or "wild horn-face") were found in the park in 2013. Estimates put the complete skull's length up to seven feet, with brow horns over three feet long.

As the seaway began receding and the coastline moved eastward, dinosaurs like sauropods with long necks and tails and duck-billed hadrosaurs ruled the inland floodplain.

Sediments from the end of the Cretaceous (70 to 66 million years ago) point to a drier environment: Species of cypress, laurel, conifers, and mangroves appear in a fossil record that includes more than 80 species of plants.

The park's most famous fossil is a pterosaur with a 35-foot wingspan, making it the largest known flying creature of all time. The first remains were discovered in 1971, sticking out of a park arroyo and named *Quetzalcoatlus northropi* after a Mexican deity (Quetzalcóatl) and aerospace engineer John Northrop. The aircraft-size soaring pterosaur may have controlled its flight direction by turning its head and warping a wing tip—until 66 million years ago when it disappeared in the Cretaceous extinction episode.

The volcanic highland environment of the following Cenozoic era brought the diversification of mammals: Saber-toothed cats, prim-

itive dogs, early lemurlike primates, and mammoths are represented in the fossil record.

Altogether, tens of thousands of fossils have been discovered in Big Bend National Park. Among the mind-boggling insights this treasury has yielded are at least eight trees new to science. Two flowering tree species that may have been up to four feet in diameter and 160 feet high, according to scientists' estimates, were found amid 18 fossilized stumps from a small paleoforest. Because ancient tree remains are normally recovered as fallen logs or as small pieces in streambeds, this discovery was exceptional.

Wildlife in the park continues to astound today. Big Bend has more bird species than any national park. This affluence of avian life is due to the array of mountain, desert, and river habitats, accompanied by a variety of plant zones. Birds from south of the border—such as the black-capped and gray vireos, Mexican mallard, Mexican jay, Lucifer hummingbird, and varied bunting—often mingle in the park with northern birds.

Many bird-watchers are drawn to see the Colima warbler, which winters in Mexico, but breeds and nests in Big Bend for several months before hightailing it back south. Each spring's concurrent pilgrimage of binocular-toting birders—often hotfooting up the Colima Trail—have to work hard to lay eyes on this particular species, hiking miles up into the Chisos Mountains to try and get a glimpse of its red-flecked crown and yellow rump, or catch its rapid, melodic trilling.

Other rare and unusual birds found in the higher arid lands of the park include the hepatic tanager; painted redstart; common black hawk, seldom seen outside the Southwest; pyrrhuloxia with its lovely

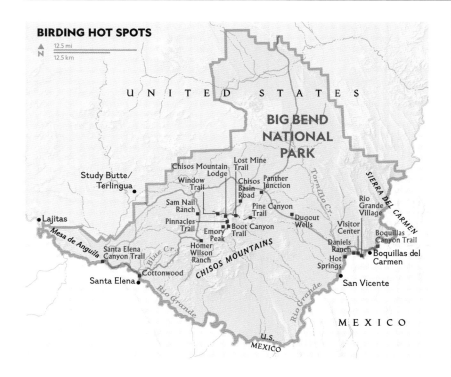

BIRDING HOT SPOTS

red mask; and high-strung, black-tailed gnatcatcher. Down along the Rio Grande, the more spectacular birds include ruddy ducks, painted buntings, black-chinned hummingbirds, elf owls, long-billed curlews, tricolored herons, tiny green kingfishers, and striking vermilion flycatchers.

In addition to birds, the Rio Grande supports 40 species of mostly tiny fish, beaver, and turtles living alongside stands of sycamore, ash, and the ubiquitous cottonwood—all crowded by invasive tamarisk and cane. Although the river valley is only one essential part of the ecosystem, the future of Big Bend National Park rides upon the larger Rio Grande—often diverted into irrigation ditches or held back behind dams. As an international river washing both U.S. and Mexican parks—it's known south of the border as Río Bravo del Norte—Big Bend faces unusual constraints in its management. Although it shares ecosystems and natural resources with Mexico, the international boundary makes conservation challenging.

Unfortunately, since the 1950s—because of agriculture, industry, and climate change—the Rio Grande has often been reduced to stilled pools throughout its 1,759-mile length. Even in the rainy season, it is routinely reduced to less than a third of its historic flows. Although 191 miles in Texas (69 within the park) were declared a Wild and Scenic River in 1978, its protection is super-seded by long-standing agricultural water rights. Instead of an essential artery connecting international ecosystems and nations, it is reclaimed and sucked dry on its path from the Colorado moun-

tain headwaters through New Mexican reservoirs and across its Tex-Mex park borderlands.

"Without many dramatic changes," reads the *Big Bend Paisano* (the park newspaper), "it seems unlikely that the 'big river in a stone box' will ever fully regain its former, natural role in the story of America's Southwest." So, in an unusual and even dramatic collab-oration with other federal agencies, the park has begun a program to keep the river flowing while monitoring agricultural pollutants.

The park and its wildlife continue to flourish. The park's newspaper name *Paisano* means "roadrunner" in Spanish. In the Big Bend region, however, it also means "fellow countryman," because this emblematic bird is like a companion, and will sometimes follow park visitors on hiking trails.

Meanwhile, the Roosevelt dream of binational or sister parks lives on, according to Big Bend administrators, who look forward to eventual joint management. The Chihuahuan Desert ecosystem remains whole and connected to the river and border, rather than split, while both countries share the common end of protecting the unique habitat and all of its creatures. ■

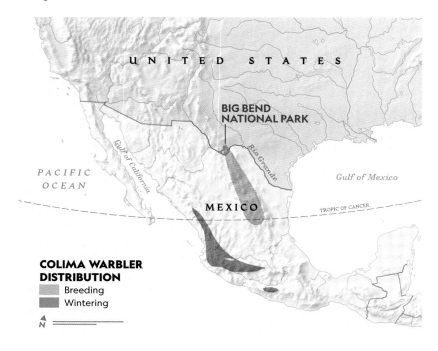

COLIMA WARBLER DISTRIBUTION
Breeding
Wintering

▷ LOCATION **6 MILES E AND W OF TUCSON, ARIZONA**

▷ SIZE **143 SQUARE MILES**

▷ HIGHEST POINT **MICA MOUNTAIN, 8,666 FEET**

▷ VISITORS **957,405 IN 2018**

▷ ESTABLISHED **1994**

SAGUARO NATIONAL PARK

n the Santa Cruz Valley of southern Arizona, flanking the city of Tucson, Saguaro National Park is 60 miles north of the Mexican border. The park is peppered with volcanic rock and bristling with its namesake cacti below the chocolate-colored Tucson and Rincon Mountains. The park protects nearly two million of its namesake saguaro, symbol of the Southwest and the country's largest cactus, reaching up to 50 feet, as well as oak, pine, mesquite, and another two dozen cacti species. Saguaro National Park is in the heart of the Sonoran Desert, which stretches over 100,000 square miles into California and Mexico.

The park's two districts are split by Tucson, one of the oldest and longest occupied cities in the country. Sites in the park span more than 8,000 years of occupation. In 2100 B.C., the Sonoran Desert People settled below what is today the western section of the park, called the Tucson Mountain District (TMD), which drains into the intermittent Santa Cruz River along Interstate 10. These ancient farmers built the earliest canal irrigation system in the contiguous United States. Later descendants are also called Hohokam, from *huhugam,* the modern-day Tohono O'odham's ("desert people") word for "ancestors."

The columnar saguaro cactus is the country's largest cactus, standing between 40 and 60 feet tall. It develops arms, as shown here—as many as 25 during its lifetime.

Thirty miles away, the cooler Rincon Mountain District (RMD) is known for its "sky island" plateau with more ruin sites that are now mostly inhabited by the seldom seen coati, black bears, and cougars. The sky islands are isolated pockets of habitat that support plant and animal species normally seen at higher latitudes. These mountaintop environments are critical as temperatures are expected to rise.

Despite its urban encroachments, Saguaro remains an intact desert of extended drought and wind, booming with fierce thunderstorms. The park can be visited most comfortably from October through April, as winter temperatures often hit 70°F (21°C) and sometimes drop slightly below freezing at night. Summer temperatures routinely exceed 100°F (38°C).

During much wetter times 10,000 years ago in southern Arizona, the first Sonoran Desert People were hunter-gatherers. As large mammals began to diminish, these hunters turned to irrigated farming. Fossilized corn—dated at 2100 B.C.—has been found below the TMD boundary at Las Capas.

Sometime before 1200 B.C.—more than a millennium before the celebrated Hohokam canal builders arrived in Phoenix, 100 miles north—the Sonoran Desert People began to channel the Santa Cruz River into at least 10 canals. The Tucson Las Capas canals watered an orderly system of 250-square-foot fields where ancient dwellers harvested 100 acres of corn and amaranth, and ate the rabbits they found pilfering their crops. Up in the mountains of the park, they hunted deer and bighorn sheep. The village supported up to 150 people, but a flood in 800 B.C. silted over their canal system and pit houses.

As the climate grew hotter and drier, the Sonoran Desert irrigation techniques for beans, squash, cotton, and tobacco spread throughout Arizona. By the year 300 in the Tucson area, the local inhabitants began painting distinctive red on sand-colored pots. As the ancient Sonoran Desert villages expanded from A.D. 600 to 900, the people there imported food and goods from neighboring tribes, on a trade route that stretched from Mexico to Casa Grande (National Monument) in southern Arizona, to northern Arizona and California. In 750, they began building oval-shaped, earthen-rimmed ball courts with centerlines and public viewing platforms. For four centuries, Sonoran Desert People from the Saguaro National Park area to northern Arizona might have kicked or whacked rubber balls with stone paddles along more than 200 courts that archaeologists would later unearth.

The Sonoran Desert People also drew or pecked art on the darker patina of rocks throughout the park. Abstract spirals, squiggly lines, astrological objects, animals, humans, and other indecipherable drawings may have denoted boundaries or solstice-related calendar dates—or even important ball game events.

In the RMD section of the park, archaeologists have excavated pit houses along with buried human remains, pots, and tools. Eventually the pit frame homes with poles evolved into aboveground, adobe structures with flat roofs and solid, rectangular walls. These harbingers of modern Santa Fe–style homes were grouped into compounds surrounding public plazas.

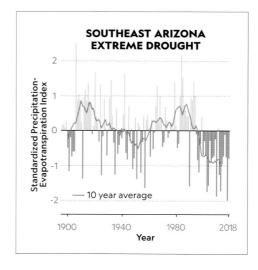

SOUTHEAST ARIZONA EXTREME DROUGHT

Standardized Precipitation-Evapotranspiration Index

—— 10 year average

Year

Drought is devastating Southwest regions more often. Saguaro has seen a significant drying trend in the last 30 years; from September 2017 to August 2018, the region had one of the most severe drought periods on record. A drought-stressed landscape may strain the park's water resources, leave the park more vulnerable to invasive species, and allow wildfires to ignite more easily. Conservation efforts like rainwater harvesting are being encouraged locally.

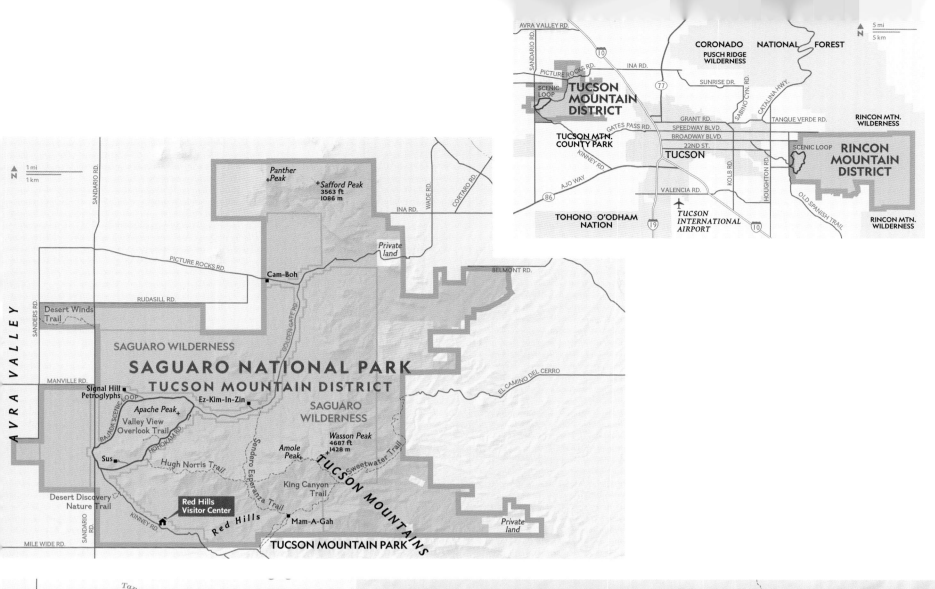

SAGUARO NATIONAL PARK
TUCSON MOUNTAIN DISTRICT

SAGUARO WILDERNESS

SAGUARO WILDERNESS

Panther Peak

Safford Peak
3563 ft
1086 m

Private land

Cam-Boh

PICTURE ROCKS RD.

RUDASILL RD.

INA RD.

WADE RD.

CORTARO RD.

BELMONT RD.

AVRA VALLEY

SANDERS RD.

SANDARIO RD.

Desert Winds Trail

MANVILLE RD.

Signal Hill Petroglyphs

Apache Peak

Valley View Overlook Trail

Sus

Ez-Kim-In-Zin

Wasson Peak
4687 ft
1428 m

Amole Peak

Hugh Norris Trail

Sendero Esperanza Trail

King Canyon Trail

Sweetwater Trail

EL CAMINO DEL CERRO

TUCSON MOUNTAINS

Desert Discovery Nature Trail

BAJADA SCENIC LOOP

HOHOKAM RD.

KINNEY RD.

Red Hills Visitor Center

Red Hills

Mam-A-Gah

Private land

SANDARIO RD.

MILE WIDE RD.

TUCSON MOUNTAIN PARK

CORONADO NATIONAL FOREST
PUSCH RIDGE WILDERNESS

AVRA VALLEY RD.

SANDARIO RD.

PICTURE ROCKS RD.

INA RD.

SUNRISE DR.

SABINO CYN. RD.

CATALINA HWY.

TUCSON MOUNTAIN DISTRICT

SCENIC LOOP

GATES PASS RD.

GRANT RD.

TANQUE VERDE RD.

RINCON MTN. WILDERNESS

TUCSON MTN. COUNTY PARK

KINNEY RD.

SPEEDWAY BLVD.

BROADWAY BLVD.

22ND ST.

TUCSON

KOLB RD.

HOUGHTON RD.

SCENIC LOOP

RINCON MOUNTAIN DISTRICT

AJO WAY

86

VALENCIA RD.

OLD SPANISH TRAIL

TOHONO O'ODHAM NATION

19

TUCSON INTERNATIONAL AIRPORT

10

RINCON MTN. WILDERNESS

5 mi
5 km

N

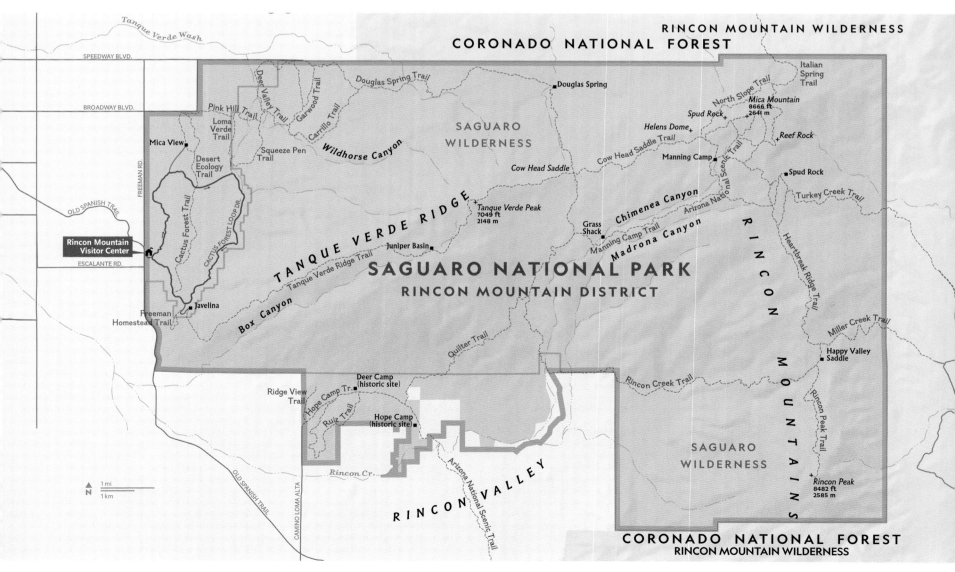

RINCON MOUNTAIN WILDERNESS

CORONADO NATIONAL FOREST

TANQUE VERDE WASH

SPEEDWAY BLVD.

BROADWAY BLVD.

OLD SPANISH TRAIL

FREEMAN RD.

ESCALANTE RD.

Douglas Spring Trail

Deer Valley Trail

Garwood Trail

Pink Hill Trail

Loma Verde Trail

Carrillo Trail

Mica View

Squeeze Pen Trail

Desert Ecology Trail

Cactus Forest Trail

CACTUS FOREST LOOP DR.

Rincon Mountain Visitor Center

Wildhorse Canyon

SAGUARO WILDERNESS

Douglas Spring

North Slope Trail

Italian Spring Trail

Mica Mountain
8666 ft
2641 m

Spud Rock

Helens Dome

Reef Rock

Cow Head Saddle Trail

Manning Camp

Spud Rock

Arizona National Scenic Trail

Cow Head Saddle

Turkey Creek Trail

TANQUE VERDE RIDGE

Tanque Verde Peak
7049 ft
2148 m

Chimenea Canyon

Grass Shack

Manning Camp Trail

Madrona Canyon

Heartbreak Ridge Trail

RINCON MOUNTAINS

Tanque Verde Ridge Trail

Juniper Basin

SAGUARO NATIONAL PARK
RINCON MOUNTAIN DISTRICT

Javelina

Freeman Homestead Trail

Box Canyon

Quilter Trail

Miller Creek Trail

Happy Valley Saddle

Ridge View Trail

Hope Camp Tr.

Deer Camp (historic site)

Ruiz Trail

Hope Camp (historic site)

Rincon Creek Trail

Rincon Peak Trail

Rincon Cr.

CAMINO LOMA ALTA

OLD SPANISH TRAIL

Arizona National Scenic Trail

RINCON VALLEY

SAGUARO WILDERNESS

Rincon Peak
8482 ft
2585 m

1 mi
1 km

N

CORONADO NATIONAL FOREST
RINCON MOUNTAIN WILDERNESS

By the early 1400s, the ancient Sonoran Desert People all but vanished along with the ancestral Puebloans (formerly called Anasazi) in other southwestern parks. Whether through disease, drought, or salinization of their crops, the farming culture crashed to an end. The Sonoran Desert People's pottery shards and stone tools can still be found among the more than 500 archaeological sites in the park, washed up in Saguaro's rocky, volcanic dirt, under a mesquite tree, or alongside stone art, resembling fragments from the still mysterious Atlantis.

By the late 19th century, prospectors settled both the Tucson and Rincon Mountains. Although 137 abandoned mine sites exist in the TMD, the only real profits—despite small copper and gold lodes—came from the sale of claims.

In 1933 Saguaro National Monument was established by President Herbert Hoover to protect the archaeological remains along with the impressive cactus forest below the Rincon Mountains. Although the act went largely unnoticed to the outside world, locals in the small city of Tucson were delighted to see one of the greatest and last remaining saguaro stands receive protection. In 1961, President John F. Kennedy increased the size of the monument by protecting and adding 25 square miles of cactus forests in the TMD. By then, landscaper thefts of the sought-after cactus were flourishing.

SAGUARO DISTRIBUTION

▨ Extant (resident)

100 mi
100 km

MOST OF A SAGUARO'S ROOTS STAY SHALLOW, GROWING OUTWARD TO ABSORB AS MUCH WATER AS POSSIBLE. IT HAS ONLY ONE TAPROOT, EXTENDING DOWN MORE THAN TWO FEET.

Because of poaching and other unknown causes, saguaros were disappearing in the monument. For a while it looked as if the saguaro would go extinct—a romantic symbol of a bygone era in the West, to be seen only as backdrop in cowboy advertising and Hollywood westerns. Local concern over the saguaro eventually led to the park's creation in 1994.

To survive in this harsh frontier, the young, waxy-skinned saguaro is weaned under "nurse plants" that provide both water and shade. In the spring, the saguaro's large, bell-shaped white and yellow, fragrant blossoms (that are the Arizona state flower) attract insects, birds, and bats to its nectar. Harvested over the millennia by Native Americans wielding long poles, its crowning fig-size fruit contains hundreds of nutty-tasting seeds surrounded by a juicy pulp. To a discriminating palate, it's sweeter than a strawberry.

Between 50 and 70 years old, the cactus can grow up to two feet wide and begin to sprout its iconic arms. After rains, a water-absorbent saguaro can weigh over two tons; one famous Arizona saguaro specimen stretched 78 feet into the desert sky before being pushed over by the wind. Nesting woodpeckers often burrow cavities that are reclaimed by cactus wrens, finches, sparrows, owls, or purple martins. In times of drought, or in dryer sections of the park, thirsty bighorn sheep, mule deer, rabbits, and pack rats eat the saguaro, which stores rainwater like a camel. Although the cactus can live up to 200 years and disperse 40 million seeds, few make it into the world as a stately saguaro.

One of 25 species of cactus found within the park, Saguaro cacti grow in the Sonoran Desert in Arizona, California, and Sonora, Mexico. Saguaros are typically found growing below 4,000 feet in elevation, and their range is limited by freezing temperatures. Since 2000, establishment of new saguaros has nearly ceased in the park.

Reproduction   Young plant   Established plant   Immature plant   Maturity   Old age   Decline

Saguaro cacti grow from seedling size to just 0.75 to 1.5 inches in their first eight years, developing under the cover of rocks or another tree. Growth rates vary by location, climate, and rainfall: In the park, saguaros usually start to display flowers at about 35 years old; branches typically emerge from 50 to 70 years of age. After that, the saguaro enters its prime reproductive years. Between 150 and 175 years—or in rare cases, possibly up to 200 years—the cactus's inevitable decline begins.

In the RMD side of the park, adult cacti establishment declined from the 1930s to the 1960s, with few surviving young saguaros. Researchers predicted that the "desert monarch" would disappear from the eastern section of the park by 2000. Then, by 1990, new cacti outnumbered mature cacti for the first time in a half century. These late-century species are now taller than many park visitors.

Still, since the early 1990s, scientists have found that despite the healthy population of adult saguaros, more than two decades of drought driven by extreme temperatures has prevented the establishment of young saguaro throughout the park. Scientists believe that the final results of the study will reveal new insights into the park's signature plant and climate change.

In Saguaro National Park, saguaro have repeatedly been dug up and sold for more than $1,000 to homeowners who cannot wait up to 70 years for legally obtained cacti to top a few feet and become decorative lawn giants. So, beginning in 2011, the park implanted thousands of young saguaro with microchips—which rangers can now scan for at nurseries or in suspiciously adorned front yards—in hopes of catching poachers and preventing further thefts.

Although the statuesque saguaros may be signature attractions for out-of-town visitors, locals revere the mesquite trees as "senior citizens of the desert." Sporting resplendent pink blossoms, the mesquite lives four times as long as the desert monarch. With its undentable dense wood that dulls saw blades, mesquite trees are stalwart nurse plants for the saguaro and another 24 species of cacti found in the park.

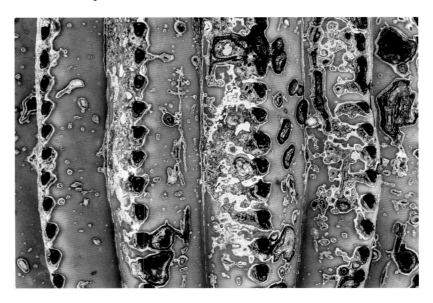

Saguaros provide food and shelter for the life among them. Small birds dig holes out of their pulpy flesh to nest in, and native people once used these "saguaro boots" as canteens.

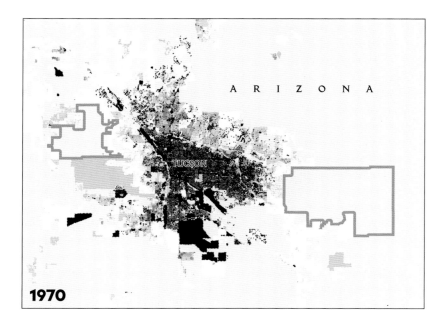

1970

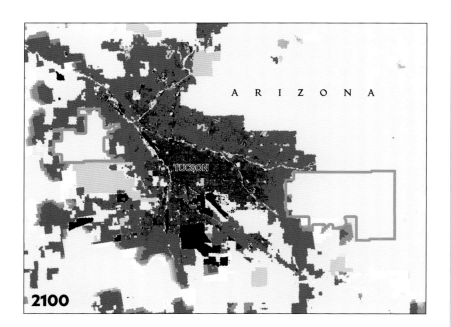

2010

2100

HOUSING DENSITY OF TUCSON, ARIZONA

Low — High

☐ Present-day Saguaro N.P. boundary

■ Commercial or industrial land
Urban or regional park
Other land

N
5 mi
5 km

Most common are the prickly pear and barrel cactus, the exotic night-blooming cereus, or the slightly rarer Bisbee beehive cactus. Those who saunter to higher altitudes in the springtime park can find claret cup cacti with bright red blossoms. Throughout the park are scores of crested saguaros that have grown into strangely mutated shapes. In this unusual, eye-catching form, the cactus spreads into a fan, resembling the head of a cauliflower. Scarcest of them all is the multipronged organ pipe cactus: Only one exists in the park (more are protected at Organ Pipe Cactus National Monument). Like the volunteers who watch over park archaeological sites, the cacti guardians—ever wary of *cactiphiles*—keep their lips sealed about the locations of these treasures. Yet national parks are designed for visitors to explore and make discoveries. Seek and ye shall find.

Urban growth, with its roads and subdivisions impinging on Saguaro National Park, shows no sign of slowing. Since 1933, the greater Tucson metro area has expanded from 60,000 to nearly a million people. Another million tourists visit the park each year, prompting managers to evaluate human impact to mount an educational program that will protect the national park. Surrounded by private land and residences, the TMD side is encumbered by traffic noise, nighttime lights, and the general hustle and bustle of city life that disrupts wildlife and other park resources. (RMD is buffered on the north and east by uninhabited national forest.)

Although early residents and park planners did not foresee the city sprawl, Saguaro has the opportunity to meet the future as a model urban park of the West—much like the parks that the great landscape architect Frederick Law Olmsted, Sr., designed more than a century ago on the built-up East Coast.

"It is one great purpose of the Park[s] to supply to the hundreds of thousands of tired workers," Olmsted wrote, "who have no opportunity to spend their summers in the country, a specimen of God's handiwork that shall be to them, inexpensively, what a month or two in the [remote wilderness parks] is, at great cost, to those in easier circumstances."

This desert national park likewise has a legacy of "supplying" the people surrounding it. This applies to both tourists and Tucson's population of white and Hispanic residents, or Tohono O'odham from the reservations south and west of the park (Native Americans comprise 3 percent of the local population). Just as the Tohono O'odham continue to harvest the saguaro fruit in TMD prized by their *huhugam* ancestors, Saguaro National Park is committed to engaging all of the public with the thorny issues of modern urban park conservation. ■

▷ LOCATION **230 MILES S OF SALT LAKE CITY, UTAH**

▷ SIZE **120 SQUARE MILES**

▷ HIGHEST POINT **ELEPHANT BUTTE, 5,653 FEET**

▷ VISITORS **1,663,557 IN 2018**

▷ ESTABLISHED **1971**

ARCHES NATIONAL PARK

I n eastern Utah alongside the Colorado River, this high-altitude desert park contains more than 2,000 natural sandstone arches rising above slickrock domes amid windows, balanced rocks, spires, and fins. As part of the Colorado Plateau, immediately north of the burgeoning resort town of Moab, this red, geologic wonderland lies against a backdrop of the often snow-covered La Sal Mountains. It holds the greatest concentration of arches in the world.

The conservationist Edward Abbey immortalizes the draw and value of this unusual park in his book *Desert Solitaire*:

A weird, lovely, fantastic object out of nature like Delicate Arch has the curious ability to remind us—like rock and sunlight and wind and wilderness—that out there is a different world, older and greater and deeper by far than ours, a world which sustains the little world of men as sea and sky surround and sustain a ship . . .

More specifically, these sandstone rock walls arose from an ancient sea and were carved over the eons by rain and wind into fins, windows, and arches. Decades after the region was discovered and set

Standing 46 feet high and 32 feet wide, Delicate Arch is the largest freestanding arch amid the more than 2,000 natural rock formations that inspired the park's name.

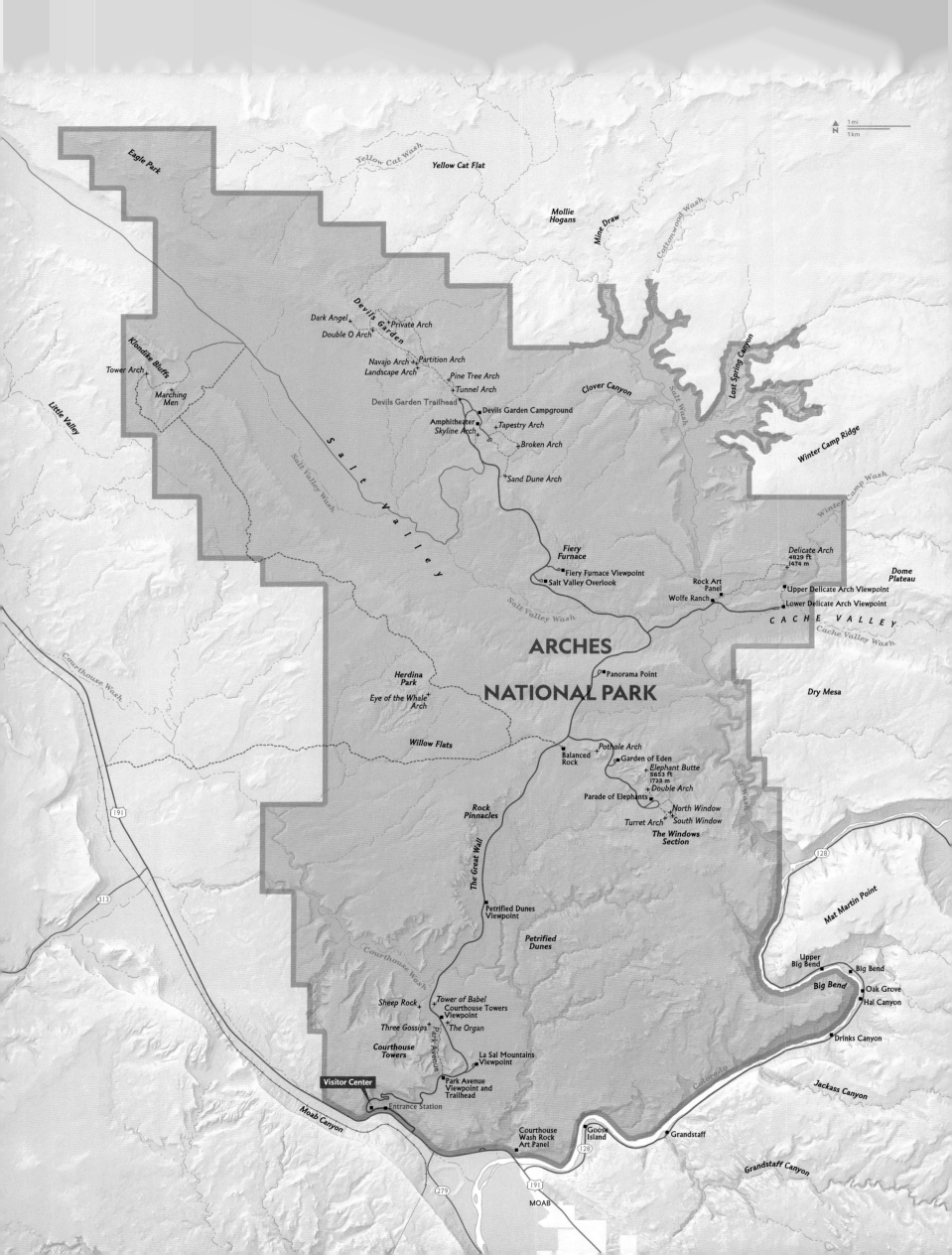

Eagle Park

Yellow Cat Wash

Yellow Cat Flat

Mollie Hogans

Mine Draw

Cottonwood Wash

Klondike Bluffs

Tower Arch

Marching Men

Little Valley

Devils Garden

Dark Angel • + Private Arch
Double O Arch +

Navajo Arch + + Partition Arch
Landscape Arch + + Pine Tree Arch
+ Tunnel Arch
Devils Garden Trailhead
■ Devils Garden Campground
Amphitheater + + Tapestry Arch
Skyline Arch +
+ Broken Arch

+ Sand Dune Arch

Salt Valley Wash

Salt Valley

Clover Canyon

Salt Wash

Lost Spring Canyon

Winter Camp Ridge

Winter Camp Wash

Fiery Furnace
■ Fiery Furnace Viewpoint
■ Salt Valley Overlook

Delicate Arch
4829 ft
1474 m

Dome Plateau

Rock Art Panel
Wolfe Ranch

■ Upper Delicate Arch Viewpoint
■ Lower Delicate Arch Viewpoint

CACHE VALLEY

Cache Valley Wash

ARCHES

NATIONAL PARK

Herdina Park

Eye of the Whale + Arch

Willow Flats

■ Panorama Point

Dry Mesa

Pothole Arch
Balanced Rock ■ ■ Garden of Eden
Elephant Butte
5653 ft
1723 m
+ + Double Arch
Parade of Elephants
North Window
Turret Arch + + South Window
The Windows Section

Rock Pinnacles

The Great Wall

■ Petrified Dunes Viewpoint

Petrified Dunes

Mat Martin Point

Upper Big Bend
Big Bend
Big Bend
Oak Grove
Hal Canyon

Sheep Rock + + Tower of Babel
Courthouse Towers Viewpoint
Three Gossips + + The Organ

Drinks Canyon

Courthouse Towers

Park Avenue

La Sal Mountains Viewpoint

Colorado

Jackass Canyon

Visitor Center

Park Avenue Viewpoint and Trailhead

■ Entrance Station

Moab Canyon

Courthouse Wash Rock Art Panel

Goose Island

128

Grandstaff

279

191

MOAB

Grandstaff Canyon

191

313

Courthouse Wash

128

1 mi
1 km
N

aside by President Hoover as a monument in 1929, erosional forces continue to whittle the soft sandstone landscape.

***

Several hundred million years ago, the repeated evaporation of inland seas left behind a magnificent bed of salt 200 miles long and 115 miles wide called the Paradox formation. Sea salt was deposited nearly a half-mile thick in some places; in others—where the salt bed liquefied and flowed under the weight of sandstone and other deposited sediment—the salt layer is more than two miles thick.

As the Colorado Plateau lifted upward, the underlying salt continued to flow under the massive weight of deposits that spilled off the Uncompahgre Plateau. Eventually, these Morrison, Entrada, and Navajo sandstone layers shifted and buckled up and down. Because salt is less dense than the rock layers, it flowed up into domes, forcing the rock above it to split and crack like loaves of rising bread. In places, the salt caught in these vertical cracks, and began to fracture and deform the sandstone. Over the millennia, this aboveground salt washed away and disappeared.

The erosion continued, mostly as rainwater, seeping into and deepening and widening the vertical cracks into the sandstone. As winter ice formed, it expanded against these fins of sandstone, breaking open caves. Many fins simply collapsed into rubble piles. Wind carried abrasive, cutting grains of sand into partially formed holes on the rock and scoured the holes deeper. This water and wind action eventually created freestanding fins (throughout today's park there are hundreds of these vertical rock slabs, veritable building blocks for more arches.) Those holey fins that remained—chipped by more frost action, scoured by the wind, and beaten over the ages by rain— became the arches of this internationally renowned national park.

By definition, the openings on arches must be bigger than three feet in any dimension; otherwise, the formation is known as a window. Unlike natural bridges that span canyon walls (found elsewhere in Utah), arches are an altogether effective and almost perfect load-bearing shape: distributing the stresses of weight evenly and abiding by natural laws of physics in providing stability with incredible efficiency.

It would take weeks to hike to and investigate each of the 2,000 arches, many of which are named. Broken Arch, although it looks ready to fall, is still intact and surrounded by wildflowers in the spring. Landscape Arch is 306 feet wide and has the longest span of any arch in North America. Sand Dune Arch is next to a parking lot and surrounded by soft sand. Double O Arch is two arches mounted on top of each other on a hill where you can search for more arches.

The snow beneath Landscape Arch hints at how important water is to this terrain's continual evolution. Rain and snow continue to erode the sandstone and create fantastic shapes.

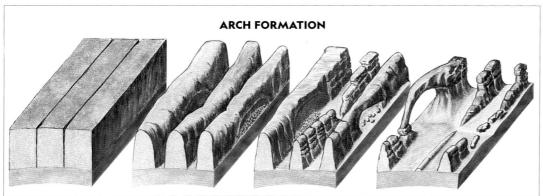

ARCH FORMATION

ABOVE: **Framed by the North Window,** Turret Arch is in the park's Windows Section, home to a rich concentration of arches. These sandstone formations do fall, but not often—the last to topple was Wall Arch in 2008.

LEFT: **The park's iconic arches** began as sand and sediments deposited on the salt bed of an evaporated sea millions of years ago. As the heavier sediments compressed into rock, the salt bed destabilized and began shifting; rock layers rose into domes, and cavities opened. Groundwater later started dissolving the salt base, and the sandstone domes collapsed and cracked. Ice appeared in the fissures, expanding and pressuring the rock. Then erosion slowly sculpted the broken structures into rock slabs called fins; further weathering wore through fins to create arches.

ABOVE: **Sandstone arches** aren't the park's only draw: More than 700 species of plants bloom here, including the rare Canyonlands biscuitroot and this San Juan onion plant.
RIGHT: **Arches National Park** boasts the world's largest density of arches—more than 2,000 arches have been documented within park boundaries. This map shows the general location of about half of the park's arches. In the legend, "featured" arches are those recommended by the National Park Service, and "large" arches are those that span 15 feet or more.

Double Arch, 112 feet high, is the tallest in the park. Turret Arch sports a pillar on its side.

All of the park's arches are Entrada sandstone—colored reddish brown or pale orange—that was originally deposited in the sea as sand 235 million years ago. The Navajo sandstone seen in the lower elevations of the park is an arresting pink, white, or pale orange. It was deposited in the sea more than 250 million years ago. The most renowned Entrada sandstone formation, Delicate Arch, rises 60 feet high and is topped off with a younger Curtis formation sandstone that came from ancient sand dunes. Featured on Utah license plates and on a postage stamp, Delicate Arch has become the symbol of the park. Like all giant arches, this fragile-looking arch is a monument to the precision of nature, a form first imitated by humans in 2100 B.C., as builders scrapped a rectangular lintel for a stronger, arched doorway leading into the Edublalmahr Temple in Iraq. As visitors stand dwarfed beneath Delicate Arch, it evokes a sense of impermanence. How

can this multiton monolith of ancient sea sand be suspended so high into the desert air?

Half a dozen miles from Delicate Arch, sometime during the black of the night on August 4, 2008, Wall Arch—the park's 12th largest formation at 33 feet tall with a 55-foot span—cracked, exploded, and collapsed into a heap of sandstone boulders. The trail was closed and rerouted.

In 1947, Arches National Park managers started discussing Delicate Arch's eastern leg, which looked ready to collapse. For years, suggestions (contained in a Park Service file entitled "Delicate Arch Stabilization Project") and memos recommended plastering up or gluing the eastern pillar to help prevent the narrow-legged beauty from its inevitable collapse. Instead, recognizing that hundreds of thousands of visitors each year hike in 1.5 miles, then remain beneath the arch while picnicking and photographing the wonder of nature above, the Park Service installed warning signs: "Keep Off Arch."

Natural arches aren't the only allure. A few hundred yards off the park road, the most frequently viewed formation is Balanced Rock, a 128-foot-high, 3,600-ton Entrada sandstone boulder perched atop an eroding pedestal of mudstone. In February 1976, Chip Off the Old Block—a smaller version of Balanced Rock resting atop the same foundation—collapsed. No one saw it happen.

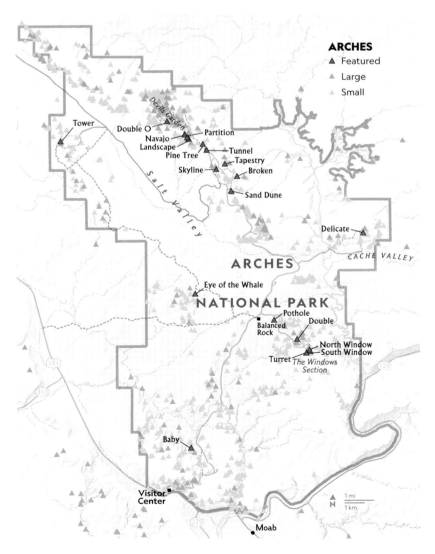

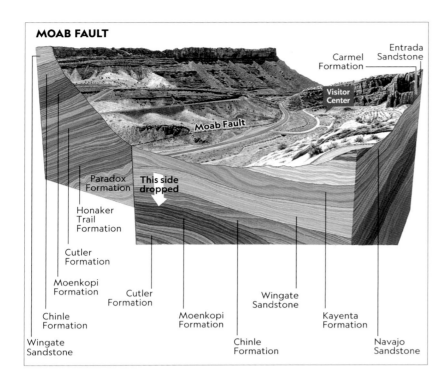

MOAB FAULT

Entrada Sandstone

Carmel Formation

Visitor Center

Moab Fault

Paradox Formation

This side dropped

Honaker Trail Formation

Cutler Formation

Moenkopi Formation

Cutler Formation

Chinle Formation

Moenkopi Formation

Wingate Sandstone

Kayenta Formation

Wingate Sandstone

Chinle Formation

Navajo Sandstone

Roughly six million years ago, extreme pressure cracked and shifted the Earth's crust, causing the east wall of the Moab Canyon to drop more than 2,600 feet below the west side. The movement from the faulting caused horizontal misalignment of the rock layers (shown above). Located just south of the visitor center, the Moab Fault has layers up to hundreds of millions of years old, spanning from the Honaker Trail formation (Pennsylvanian era) to Navajo sandstone (Jurassic era).

Today Balanced Rock is popular with stargazers and photographers. At sunset the Entrada sandstone often turns red-orange, as if on fire, with the La Sal peaks lit by alpenglow on the horizon.

Water continues to be the dominant sculptor of the desert as rain washes over soft rock and carries off balanced rocks and arches and pillars and domes grain by grain, down the canyons and into the already silt-laden Colorado River that forms the southern park boundary. Amid the steep, thousand-foot-high Navajo sandstone of this huge bend on the river, the rainwater has painted huge blackened murals of desert varnish on the red walls. Those who sit long enough amid the swirl of a river rushing past the reconstructed bottom of a long-forgotten sea will be rewarded with a raven's reverberating, raucous cry—echoing back and forth off the canyon walls.

Many thousands of years ago, Paleo-Indians gazed upon the distant arches with a sense of wonder, but avoided the eerie formations amid the hot desert. Their spear points and camps were found at lower elevations, near water and game. A later archaic culture of nomadic hunters also avoided the park. Two thousand years ago (and perhaps even earlier) the ancestral Puebloans (formerly called Anasazi) and Fremont cultures arrived. Since these people saw the Arches area as a frontier, mostly bereft of game and lacking water, the modern-day park was not continuously occupied.

Although no building sites remain, the ancestral Puebloans and Fremont people left behind compelling rock art, mostly in the valleys surrounding the park. Etched into the walls as petroglyphs or

A GROUP OF DEDICATED RESEARCHERS, NOW KNOWN AS THE ARCH HUNTERS, STARTED DEVELOPING SCIENTIFIC STANDARDS FOR MEASURING AND RECORDING ALL OF THE PARK'S ARCHES IN THE 1970S.

painted with dyes as pictographs, their panels—often placed on darker varnished sandstone for better visibility—evoke astonishment. Scholars speculate that these drawings of anthropomorphs with broad shoulders and elaborate headdresses represent shamanistic visions produced during trancelike states, though it's also not hard to imagine the otherworldly figures as visiting aliens.

ABOVE: **Balanced Rock** teeters 128 feet in the air, though it's not actually performing a balancing act—the rock is attached to its Dewey Bridge mudstone base.

OPPOSITE: **Ute Indians** carved hunting petroglyphs near Wolfe Ranch that show figures on horseback, suggesting that this particular rock art was created after the mid-1600s when they acquired horses.

A visitor rappels along one of the park's 10 official canyoneering routes. Of the many layers of rock found in Arches, the most dominant is the reddish brown Navajo sandstone that started forming more than 200 million years ago.

After leaving their imprint on rock, these ancient artists vanished into thin air as Utes moved into the region about 700 years ago. The Utes replaced their predecessors' animist abstractions with straight-forward wall peckings of riders on horseback amid bighorn sheep.

In the mid-1800s, trappers arrived and settlers slowly moved into nearby Moab. The first known European visitor inside Arches left his name and date etched onto a rock fin: Denis Julien, June 9, 1844.

The 1929 creation of Arches National Monument left out Delicate Arch, and set aside two small, disconnected sections of desert. Still, by using the Antiquities Act, the monument would protect hundreds more sandstone formations for scientific and educational value. In 1938, the boundaries were expanded to include Delicate Arch, and in 1960 the monument was enlarged to allow a new road and other tourist facilities to be built.

The creation of the monument and the park preserved more than sandstone. Amid the juniper, slickrock (smooth floors of sandstone), and sand dunes are gardens of blackened, lumpy-looking crusts called cryptogamic soils. These little-known crusts—sometimes thousands of years old—are often overlooked as visitors stare up toward stunning sandstone arches, oblivious to the mostly invisible yet equally phenomenal plants crunching to death beneath their feet. Cryptogamic soils are found around the world, in deserts or in the Arctic, often composing up to 70 percent of the ground cover.

These complexes of fungus, moss, lichens, and algae are dominated by cyanobacteria, or blue-green algae, which is the oldest life-form—predating the creation of arches by three billion years. In our once carbon dioxide–saturated world, vast mats of cyanobacteria used photosynthesis to convert the planet into an oxygen-rich atmosphere that would sustain the Earth's myriad life-forms. Fast-forward to the 21st century and the cyanobacteria within cryptogamic soils have become an essential foundation of desert ecology.

Seen through a microscope, the sticky fibers of cyanobacteria throughout Arches tie minuscule pieces of soil and sand together. When wet, this mat becomes a sponge, swelling with water, allowing the cryptogamic soil to bind the desert floor into a plant community that blocks wind and water erosion. Eventually, these mats provide a stable growing platform for grasses, cacti, shrubs, and trees.

Outside protected parks, grazing livestock and development have destroyed cryptogamic soils throughout the Desert Southwest. Cyanobacteria can take decades to recover, and it can take centuries for the mosses and lichens within the soil to regrow after a single hoof, boot, or tire destroys the delicate plants.

Botanists have concluded that the destruction of these crypto-gamic soils has created another problem throughout the Southwest. Without the protective rug of microorganisms holding onto rain-water, desert soils lose their wind resistance, turn into sand dunes, or blow away. Without protected parks such as Arches, the desert dust is carried into the atmosphere and blown around the world—as shown through isotope tracings.

As Utah's national parks become increasingly over-crowded, Arches uses educational signage to keep people from straying off designated trails or roads and destroying the fragile cryptogam. More than a million visitors come to this tiny park each year; 4,000 people constitutes a slow day, but the average visit—touring by automobile—lasts only two hours. The park recommends walking only on slickrock or in sandy washes when off established hiking trails to avoid stepping on the cryptogam.

Arches National Park also has biking, rock climbing, and hiking on more than two dozen miles of trails. Backcountry use is limited. With summer temperatures more than 100°F (38°C), hiking can be challenging and even dangerous in the debilitating heat. Spring and fall are ideal seasons, with daytime highs averaging from 60 to 80°F (16 to 27°C), and temperature fluctuations of over 40°F (22.2°C) in a day. Winters are cold but offer the best opportunity to beat the crowds and gaze upon Entrada sandstone in soft light: defying gravity while blanketed in snow. ■

RIGHT: **Captivated by** the spectacular display of arches, visitors are often unaware of the intricacies of the soil below. A living soil made of cyanobacteria, mosses, lichen, and fungi called biological or crypto-grammic soil crust covers 70 percent of the park. Once damaged, it can take years to grow back, which is why the Park Service urges visitors to stay on designated trails.

BELOW: **Snow blankets** the rocks at North Window in winter, a peaceful time in Arches National Park. The crowds are gone, with cool temperatures ranging from a high of 50°F (10°C) to a chilly low of 0°F (−18°C).

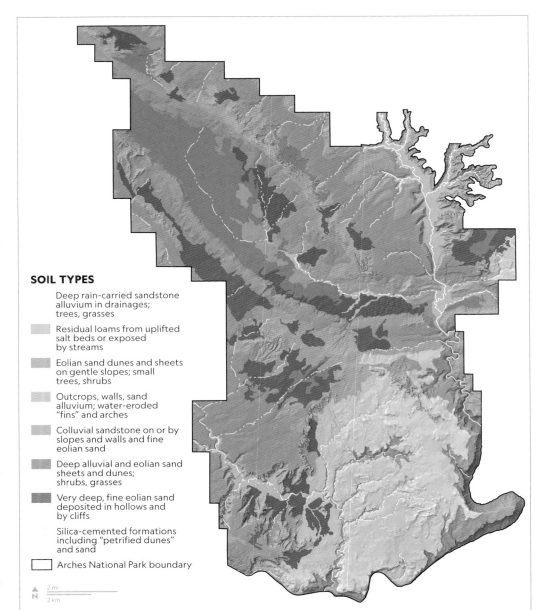

SOIL TYPES

Deep rain-carried sandstone alluvium in drainages; trees, grasses

Residual loams from uplifted salt beds or exposed by streams

Eolian sand dunes and sheets on gentle slopes; small trees, shrubs

Outcrops, walls, sand alluvium; water-eroded "fins" and arches

Colluvial sandstone on or by slopes and walls and fine eolian sand

Deep alluvial and eolian sand sheets and dunes; shrubs, grasses

Very deep, fine eolian sand deposited in hollows and by cliffs

Silica-cemented formations including "petrified dunes" and sand

Arches National Park boundary

N   2 mi
    2 km

- LOCATION **244 MILES SE OF SALT LAKE CITY, UTAH**
- SIZE **527 SQUARE MILES**
- HIGHEST POINT **CATHEDRAL POINT, 7,120 FEET**
- VISITORS **739,449 IN 2018**
- ESTABLISHED **1964**

CANYONLANDS NATIONAL PARK

Dramatic red-rock canyons, buttes, mesas, and two great rivers define this southeastern Utah park. The confluence of the Green and Colorado Rivers divides the park into its aptly named Island in the Sky, the Needles, and the Maze districts. Glen Canyon National Recreation Area borders the west side of Canyonlands, which is otherwise surrounded by public Bureau of Land Management (BLM) lands.

Canyonlands National Park is in the heart of the Southwest on the Colorado Plateau, isolated from cities in a desert devoid of forests other than sparse piñon and juniper up high, or cottonwoods clinging to canyon bottoms. Traveled by nomads as early as 9,000 years ago, then briefly farmed by ancestral Puebloans (formerly called Anasazi) whose rock art is still visible today, the parklands were mostly preserved by rugged and hard-to-access geography until the 19th century. Then an army of uranium prospectors built hundreds of miles of roads throughout the area. Although the miners eventually departed, their roads remain.

Today visitors can expect to see soaring big birds, healthy herds of desert bighorn sheep, grazing mule deer, bank beavers in the rivers, lizards and snakes sunning on rocks, and rodents scurrying

The Loop, a double oxbow in Canyonlands, highlights water's power to carve its own path. The walls of this dramatic "entrenched meander" are 500 feet high—about as high as a 50-story building.

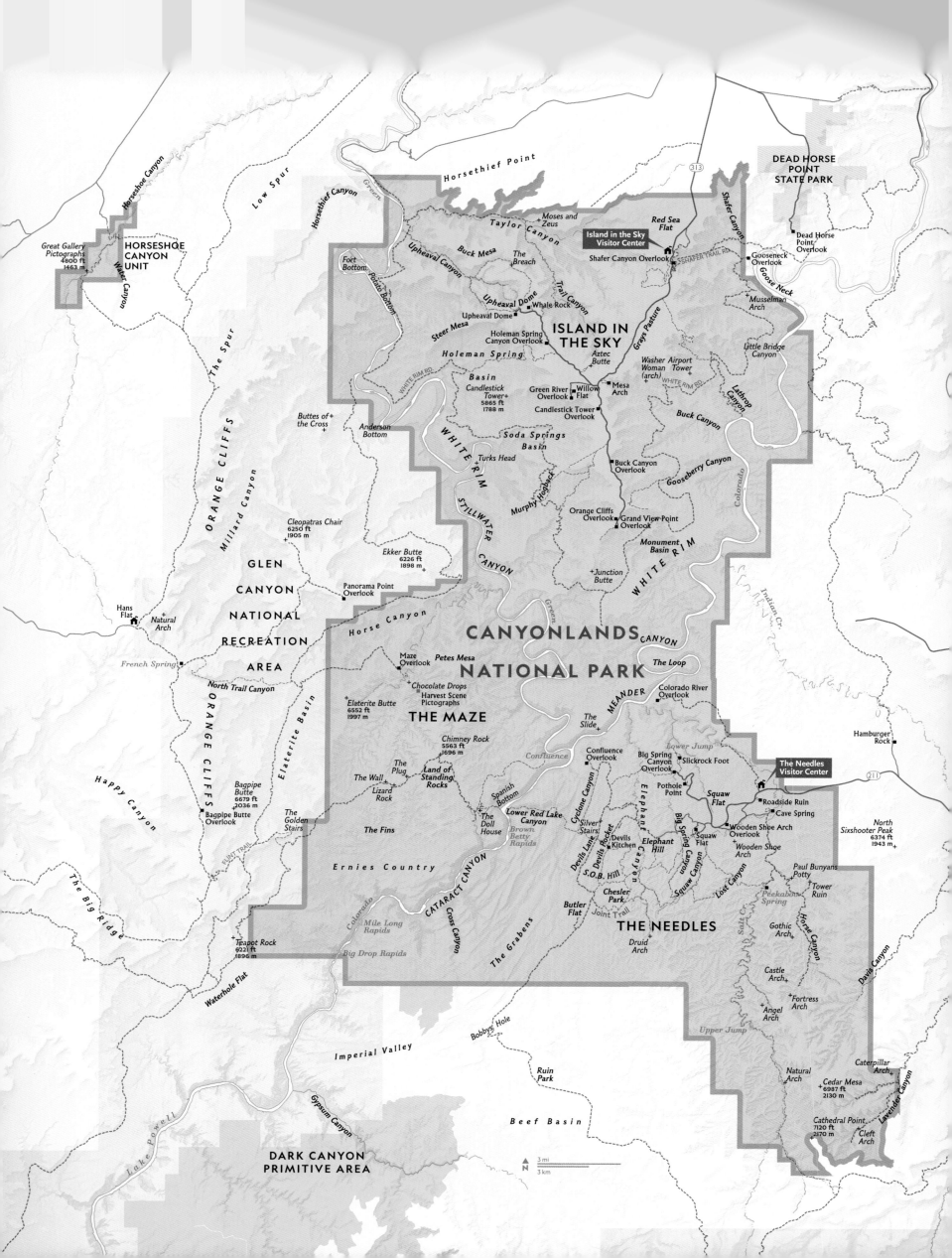

HORSESHOE CANYON UNIT

Great Gallery Pictographs
4800 ft
1463 m

DEAD HORSE POINT STATE PARK

Horseshoe Canyon

Water Canyon

Low Spur

Horsethief Point

313

Horsethief Canyon

Green

Taylor Canyon

Moses and Zeus

Red Sea Flat

Shafer Canyon

Dead Horse Point Overlook

Buck Mesa

The Breach

Island in the Sky Visitor Center

Gooseneck Overlook

Fort Bottom

Upheaval Canyon

Trail Canyon

Shafer Canyon Overlook

SHAFER TRAIL RD

Goose Neck

THE SPUR

Potato Bottom

Upheaval Dome

Whale Rock

Musselman Arch

Steer Mesa

Holeman Spring Canyon Overlook

ISLAND IN THE SKY

Grays Pasture

Little Bridge Canyon

ORANGE CLIFFS

Holeman Spring

Aztec Butte

Washer Woman Tower (arch)

WHITE RIM RD

Airport Tower

Lathrop Canyon

Basin

Candlestick Tower+ 5865 ft 1788 m

Green River Overlook

Willow Flat

Mesa Arch

Buttes of the Cross

Anderson Bottom

Candlestick Tower Overlook

Buck Canyon

Soda Springs Basin

Gooseberry Canyon

WHITE RIM

Colorado

Turks Head

Murphy Hogback

Buck Canyon Overlook

Orange Cliffs Overlook

Grand View Point Overlook

Cleopatras Chair 6250 ft 1905 m

Monument Basin

WHITE RIM

GLEN

Ekker Butte 6226 ft 1898 m

Panorama Point Overlook

Junction Butte

CANYON

Hans Flat

Natural Arch

NATIONAL

Horse Canyon

CANYONLANDS

Green

Indian Cr.

French Spring

RECREATION

North Trail Canyon

NATIONAL PARK

The Loop

Colorado River Overlook

AREA

Maze Overlook

Petes Mesa

Chocolate Drops

Harvest Scene Pictographs

The Slide

MEANDER

Hamburger Rock

ORANGE CLIFFS

Elaterite Basin

Elaterite Butte 6552 ft 1997 m

THE MAZE

Chimney Rock 5563 ft 1696 m

Confluence

Confluence Overlook

Big Spring Canyon Overlook

Slickrock Foot

The Needles Visitor Center

211

Happy Canyon

The Wall

The Plug

Land of Standing Rocks

Pothole Point

Squaw Flat

Roadside Ruin

Cave Spring

Bagpipe Butte 6679 ft 2036 m

Lizard Rock

Spanish Bottom

Cyclone Canyon

Silver Stairs

Elephant Canyon

Squaw Flat

Wooden Shoe Overlook

North Sixshooter Peak 6374 ft 1943 m

Bagpipe Butte Overlook

The Golden Stairs

The Fins

The Doll House

Lower Red Lake Canyon

Brown Betty Rapids

Devils Lane

Devils Pocket

Devils Kitchen

Elephant Hill

Big Spring Canyon

Wooden Shoe Arch

Paul Bunyans Potty

FLINT TRAIL

Ernies Country

CATARACT CANYON

S.O.B. Hill

Squaw Canyon

Lost Canyon

Peekaboo Spring

Tower Ruin

Cross Canyon

Chesler Park

Butler Flat

Joint Trail

THE NEEDLES

Gothic Arch

Horse Canyon

The Big Ridge

Mile Long Rapids

The Grabens

Druid Arch

Salt Cr.

Castle Arch

Davis Canyon

Teapot Rock 6221 ft 1896 m

Big Drop Rapids

Colorado

Fortress Arch

Angel Arch

Waterhole Flat

Bobbys Hole

Upper Jump

Lake Powell

Gypsum Canyon

Imperial Valley

Ruin Park

Natural Arch

Cedar Mesa 6987 ft 2130 m

Caterpillar Arch

Lavender Canyon

DARK CANYON PRIMITIVE AREA

Beef Basin

Cathedral Point 7120 ft 2170 m

Cleft Arch

3 mi
N
3 km

Geologist and ethnologist John Wesley Powell led the first successful expedition in wooden dories down the Green and Colorado Rivers. Above, Powell (third from the left in the center boat) begins his second expedition at Green River Station, Wyoming, in 1871.

through the cacti. More than four times the size of nearby Arches National Park, with less than half the visitation, Canyonlands abounds with backcountry opportunities: mountain biking, backpacking, canyoneering, four-wheeling, and boating, to name a few. More than any other desert park, visitors come to Canyonlands for solitude and adventure.

During the dawn of the modern environmental movement, Canyonlands National Park's creation evoked the same preservation versus resource development storm that exists in Utah today. In 1961, Senator Frank Moss introduced the first park legislation, with support from Secretary of the Interior Stewart Udall. But Utah Governor George Clyde and Senator Wallace Bennett fought the proposal as one that would "lock up" Utah lands. Heated controversy ensued.

Bennett criticized Udall for his "grandiose pie-in-the-sky scheme" that could only be used for viewing the scenery. "All commercial use and business activity would be forever banned," Bennett said, referring to potential mineral extraction, "and nearly all of Southern Utah's growth would be forever stunted."

It came down to reconciling the differences between what Udall called the "scenery purists" versus the "resource hogs." By 1963, Moss and Udall had compromised and reduced the size of the proposed park, cutting out sections prized for hunting, grazing, or minerals. More debate and more compromise followed, along with

a delay that allowed the Defense Department to fire rockets over the proposed park. Conservationists suffered another blow in 1963, with the damming of the exquisite Glen Canyon on the Colorado River immediately downstream of the proposed national park. (This came after they had prevented a dam from being built upstream of the proposed national park, in Echo Park—now Dinosaur National Monument.)

As water began to fill Glen Canyon and pool upstream toward Canyonlands, President Lyndon B. Johnson finally signed the new park into law on September 12, 1964 (nine days after he signed the Wilderness Act). Canyonlands would be the first national park created in seven years—since Virgin Islands—and stands as the finest moment in Udall's environmental legacy. Moss deserved much of the credit for the creation of the park, one of the most satisfying moments in his career.

Seen from a high-flying plane, the confluence of the Green—running 700 miles from Wyoming's Wind River Range—and the 1,450-mile Colorado forms a northwest-tilting anchor, hooking into the three unique landforms made into park districts. To the north looms the Island in the Sky, a broad mesa with a bird's-eye view of the river

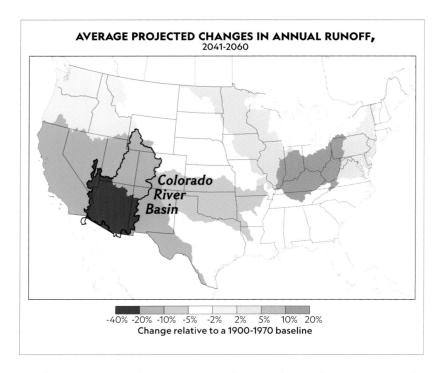

AVERAGE PROJECTED CHANGES IN ANNUAL RUNOFF,
2041-2060

Colorado River Basin

-40% -20% -10% -5% -2% 2% 5% 10% 20%
Change relative to a 1900-1970 baseline

Runoff—precipitation that flows into rivers and lakes rather than seeping into the ground—is projected to change in the United States. Estimates indicate that in the Colorado River Basin's 243,000-square-mile drainage area, runoff may decrease between 10 and 40 percent by 2060, compared with 20th-century levels.

2,000 feet below. To the south, the Needles district bristles with red- and white-banded pinnacles, grabens, and arches. And west of the confluence are the hinterlands of the Maze, a great place to lose oneself in the study of ancient rock art panels.

In July 1869, after two months of rowing from the headwaters of the Green River, John Wesley Powell reached the confluence during his legendary first river descent. After climbing up the

walls, he wrote about the view in his book *The Exploration of the Colorado River and Its Canyons:* "From the northwest comes the Green in a narrow winding gorge. From the northeast comes the Grand [Colorado], through a canyon that seems bottomless from where we stand. Away to the west are lines of cliffs and ledges of rock—not such ledges as the reader may have seen where the quarryman splits his blocks, but ledges from which the gods might quarry mountains."

The blocks are huge reddened and frost-shattered Wingate sandstone that line either side of the essential irrigation artery of the Southwest. In the 1922 agreement known as the Colorado River Compact, delegates surrounding the Colorado River parceled out its water to seven states and Mexico. Unknowingly making their calculations during the wettest period in history, they estimated the river's flow at 20.6 million acre-feet (maf)—more than six quadrillion gallons—a year. That's enough water to support 35 million modern households, even though 80 percent of the river is used for agriculture. By 2018, following much drier years, the river's volume had dropped to 12.5 maf—4 maf less than the delegates had split up and allocated to the seven member states and Mexico. Amid climate change and population growth, the deficit underscores what most experts believe will be a water crisis for the Southwest.

Still, during early summer in the heart of Canyonlands National Park, where these two great rivers join and boaters test themselves on incredibly challenging rapids—it's hard to see the shortage. After all, the two major Colorado River dams are downstream.

Rainbows arc over Pothole Point in the Needles area, where rainwater collects in indentations in the sandstone whenever a storm sweeps through.

CANYONLANDS' MAZE OF ROCK WALLS SHELTERED OUTLAWS SUCH AS BUTCH CASSIDY, WHOSE GANG HAD A HIDEOUT HERE CALLED ROBBERS ROOST.

Several miles below the confluence, the river slows and backs up, until suddenly plunging into the hair-raising Cataract Canyon rapids. For 16 miles, the river drops 30 feet a mile, channeling more water than any rapid found on the entire river. During heavy snow years, meltwater feeds the river from hundreds of miles upstream and eventually explodes through Cataract Canyon, thunderously pushing boulders downstream and creating eddy whirlpools big enough to hold airplanes (in 1985, during an illegal ice cream drop to boaters, a Cessna with a 36-foot wingspan crashed into one of these eddies and never reemerged).

Throughout the narrow, steep-walled Cataract Canyon, an Asian-looking, delicate-fronded plant with fetching pink flowers greens the riverbanks amid the rubble of sandstone and cryptogamic soils. Imported to the American Southwest in the 1800s as an ornamental shrub, the tamarisk plant began flourishing faster than water engineers could plant them along canals for erosion control, where the long, iron-legged plant stabilized shifting sandbanks. Although it took decades, the drought-resistant Chinese emigrant spread its collective roots toward an unforeseen plant succession. Millions of tamarisks crowded upstream and held up the riverbanks from Mexico to Colorado. Bushwhack-challenged boaters began carrying saws for what they called "the cockroach tree" that blocked campsites and access to the river. Classified as a noxious weed, the tree can grow up to a foot a month, eventually stretching up to 30 feet.

In an already water-compromised region, the trees hoard water, restrict stream flow, dry up desert springs, and further reduce essential Colorado River water for agriculture, municipalities, native plants, and wildlife. Seeking relief, land managers loosed hungry goats, bulldozed riverbanks, and used herbicide, but tamarisk still seemed to be winning the battle.

So, in 2001, the U.S. Department of Agriculture released a foreign beetle into select tamarisk groves. The olive-backed and striped beetle—the size of a long, fat rice grain—hails from the same region of Asia as the tamarisk and eats its leaves. Thus, in the Old World, the plant has not reached the same plague proportions that it has in Canyonlands and throughout the Colorado River Basin.

Although the beetle was never released in the park, it spread throughout the Southwest. And recently, the tide began turning. The goal isn't to eradicate the tamarisk so much as to restore a balance. So in Canyonlands, park managers are starting to replant species to fill the void of dying tamarisk lost to the beetles.

Most park visitors frequent Island in the Sky, close to Moab, Utah. The Needles area, also accessible by road, draws a smaller percentage of park visitors, while the remote Maze and its pinnacled labyrinth of canyons called the Doll House remain one of the most isolated and seldom traveled corners of the contiguous United States. Horseshoe (formerly Barrier) Canyon, a detached section of park northwest of the main park, is known for nomadic artifacts dating back 9,000 years. The rock art there, unlike most of the panels in the park, was created by archaic-period nomads, and could be up to 7,000 years old. Horseshoe in particular is famous for its Great Gallery, which shows more than 80 ocher-painted anthropomorphic figures up to eight feet tall.

In 2004, the National Park Service released these tamarisk beetles in Canyonlands to control the spread of the non-native tamarisk tree, first brought to the Southwest in the 1800s.

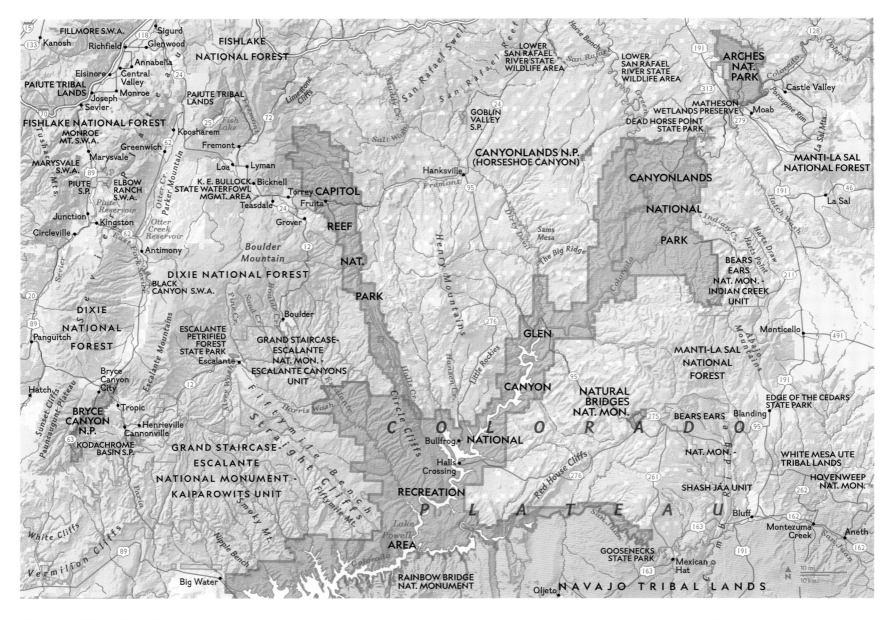

LAND OWNERSHIP IN SOUTHERN UTAH

- Bureau of Land Management
- National Forest Service
- National Park Service
- Private land
- State Parks and Wildlife Management Areas
- Tribal lands
- BLM National Monument boundary

The ancestral Puebloans (formerly called Anasazi, which meant "ancient enemies" in Navajo) first migrated into the Needles district of the park around the year 1200. Believed to have left Mesa Verde 100 miles to the southeast when it became overpopulated, the ancestral Puebloans built dwellings and granaries—used to store squash, maize, and beans—that are still scattered throughout the park.

Tree rings show that these people lived briefly in Canyonlands, during a wetter time that supported farming. They wore fur or feather robes; plant-fiber sandals; and shell, bone, or stone jewelry. In addition to planting, they gathered piñon nuts, wild rice, and sunflower and mustard seeds to be ground into flour. They kept dogs and turkeys.

In the 12th century it stopped raining and warlike Utes arrived. According to some archaeologists, the combination of drought and newcomers forced the ancestral Puebloans to head farther south

ABOVE: **An intricate patchwork** of federal, state, and tribal lands surrounds Canyonlands National Park. The region is steeped in cultural history, archaeological sites, and resources: Coal and uranium fuel debate over resource extraction at two nearby monuments that the Bureau of Land Management administers—Bears Ears and Grand Staircase-Escalante.

OPPOSITE: **Around A.D. 1200**, the ancestral Puebloans (formerly Anasazi) migrated from Colorado's Mesa Verde to the Needles, building permanent settlements. They purportedly used False Kiva, a stone circle on the lip of a cave, as a site for religious ceremonies.

and abandon Canyonlands. Today, with perseverance, potsherds can be found poking out of the sand near their surviving granaries; visitors now know to leave these artifacts untouched.

It's not hard to picture the lives of the ancestral Puebloans amid the ruin sites, where drawings of bighorn sheep or hunters with spears along with crescent moons, lightning bolts, and snakes endure. In addition to carefully pecked or painted anthropomorphs guarding the walls, the artists often left "negative" handprints throughout the park. By spitting out mixtures of gypsum, urine, and yarrow from their mouths against their hands held against the wall, the former inhabitants effectively left their signatures along with a hint of flesh and blood. Being careful not to touch or smudge their artwork, you can caress Wingate walls and feel the same heat of sandstone felt by the ancient artist—they could've passed through just yesterday. ■

▷ LOCATION **220 MILES S OF SALT LAKE CITY, UTAH**

▷ SIZE **378 SQUARE MILES**

▷ HIGHEST POINT **BILLINGS PASS, 8,960 FEET**

▷ VISITORS **1,227,627 IN 2018**

▷ ESTABLISHED **1971**

CAPITOL REEF NATIONAL PARK

G rand Staircase-Escalante National Monument, Glen Canyon National Recreation Area, and Forest Service land surround this 70-mile-long, 10-mile-wide park of south-central Utah. The northern head of Capitol Reef is bisected by Highway 24 and the Fremont River, while the southern, narrowing tail of the park can only be reached in a four-wheel-drive vehicle, on horseback, by mountain bike, or by foot.

Seen from the air as a colorful collage of zigzagging canyons—with a lightning bolt pattern echoed by ancient Fremont potters—Capitol Reef is defined by its geology. Most striking is the 100-mile-long wrinkling of the Earth's crust called the Waterpocket Fold—seen from a distance as a pronounced step in the rock layers. Among geologists, it is the axis for all the strata within the park.

Early settlers named Capitol Reef after the rotunda domes they'd seen atop capitol buildings. They encountered these rock obstacles alongside cliffs as if they were sailors at sea confronting reefs. This section of the park also preserves a 19th-century settlement with active fruit orchards. The abandoned town of Fruita—and other green, pastoral valleys and canyon bottoms of the park—provide a

The Fremont River meanders through Capitol Reef National Park, a land of geologic wonders and dramatic beauty in south-central Utah.

striking contrast to the austere shale layers and the dizzyingly steep, vibrantly toned red and white sandstone precipices.

The creation of the region dates back to a period of sedimentary deposits 270 million to 80 million years ago. Nearly 10,000 feet of earth was washed or blown in and then tilted into a geologic layer cake with the older rocks molding the western park, and the younger rocks frosting the east. This layering holds ancient rivers and swamps from the Chinle formation, dunes of the Navajo sandstone, and shallow oceans represented by the Mancos shale—showing how this region started at sea level.

The Navajo sandstone layer was laid down roughly 200 million years ago. This sandstone layer came from the Navajo *erg,* a massive invasion of fine-grained sand analogized to the Sahara. For 15 million years, it spanned 200,000 square miles surrounding ancient Utah. In Capitol Reef, the erg reached depths of 1,100 feet, and today it can be seen in cutaways along the Waterpocket Fold as massive white or tan Navajo sandstone cliffs. It also created the rotunda-like domes.

Originally, the giant erg was considered waterless and devoid of life. But in the early 2000s, a geologist made a startling discovery: a giant stromatolite fossil—a chalky mound that looked like an onion in the process of being peeled—embedded in the Navajo sandstone backcountry. Found in ancient marine environments elsewhere in the world and normally less than a couple feet high, the gigantic 16-foot-high stromatolites in Capitol Reef had somehow grown alongside the sand dunes of the Navajo erg.

Formed by cyanobacteria more than three billion years ago, stromatolites are among the Earth's oldest organisms that allowed later life to flourish through oxygenation of the atmosphere. But cyanobacteria needed water. Thus, the discovery redefined the Navajo erg: Rather than a sterile sea of sand, the stromatolites proved that for thousands of years the dunes had stopped blowing and shifting to stabilize around a region of lakes.

More than 150 million years later, tectonic plate activity lifted the region up thousands of feet. Along with the rest of the Colorado Plateau, the uplift occurred evenly and kept the distinctive layers of the park roughly horizontal, which created the layer cake appearance seen in strata throughout southwestern parks. Capitol Reef's Waterpocket Fold, however, provided a "wrinkle" on the usual geologic formation.

Multihued rock layers define Capitol Reef's sandstone walls. White dome formations in Navajo sandstone—evoking domed roofs of capitol buildings—inspired the park's name.

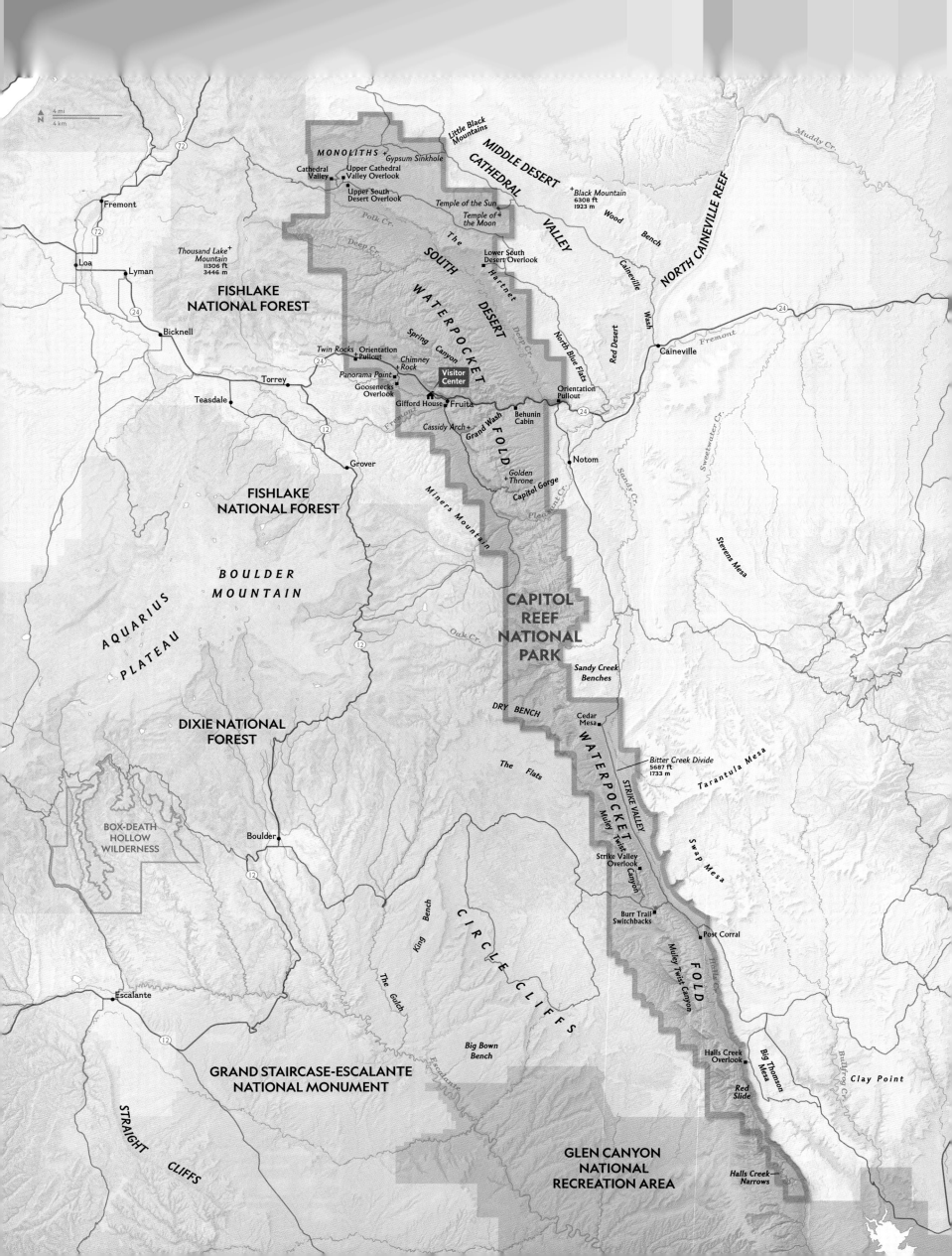

CREATING THE WATERPOCKET FOLD

Deposition   Uplift   Erosion

A crease in Capitol Reef's rock layers, the Waterpocket Fold began as roughly 10,000 feet of sedimentary rock deposited in the Capitol Reef area—once a different environment with oceans, rivers, swamps, and deserts. Between 50 and 70 million years ago, plate tectonics lifted the west side 7,000 feet higher than the eastern layers, creating a fault line over which the rock layers folded. Erosive forces continue to sculpt the tilted strata.

The Waterpocket Fold was created by a "step-up" in the layers that formed 50 to 70 million years ago during a major mountain-building event in the American West. As an ancient and buried fault shifted upward on its west side, overlying rock layers draped above and formed a bend in the rock strata—or monocline—that is 7,000 feet higher than the eastern layers. Capitol Reef's monocline is a steep and cliffed hill that runs 100 miles through the park.

Over the last 15 to 20 million years, continued Colorado Plateau uplift caused erosion. Water exposed the fold surface—hence the name Waterpocket Fold—and formed graceful arches, rich-colored cliffs, huge domes, sky-high spires, unadulterated monoliths, and twisty canyons. Even in this desert climate, water is the chief sculptor, followed by its assistant, gravity (in rock falls or rock creep), and wind, which provides the final light, polishing touch in shaping the cliffs.

The hardness of different rock layers also determines the land's susceptibility to erosion. Soft shale layers seen in the Chinle formation form slopes and low hills. Harder strata—such as the white Navajo sandstones, the dark red Entrada, or the pinkish Wingate—form steep cliffs.

But yet another anomaly can be seen scattered on the hillsides above the canyon bottoms: pockmarked and angular black boulders

as big as nine feet in diameter. These chunks of basalt and andesite—originally created in lava flows 20 million years ago—look patently out of place amid the more colorful sandstone and shale contours of the Waterpocket Fold. After the last ice age, landslides and debris flows pushed these boulders off the surrounding mountains and down onto broad valley floors. Then at the rate of approximately 30 inches every thousand years, the Fremont River and other streams cut canyons up to 600 feet deep into the prehistoric valleys and down into the tilted sandstone of the Waterpocket Fold.

Today, those timeworn valleys have their own mesas eroded into—called strath terraces—within mid-elevations of the park. In places, the canyon-carving streams have rounded the ancient and once angular volcanic boulders as if hard, black tools were turned on a lathe.

As the black boulders were still being transported in semiliquid debris flows, bands of archaic nomadic hunter-gatherers in 7000 B.C. became the first humans to live in the park, making their homes in caves, and leaving behind rock art. "A one-of-a-kind tapestry of thoughts and actions spans the rock canvas before you," reads a Park Service sign in Capitol Reef. "Anthropomorphs (human figures), zoomorphs (animal figures), geometric and astronomic designs weave their way across the rock . . . Pecked and painted by a succession of American Indian artists, the composition took over 7,000 years to create—from the Archaic Period to historic times."

Most of the art in Capitol Reef is petroglyphs, pecked into the darker patina of the rock by the

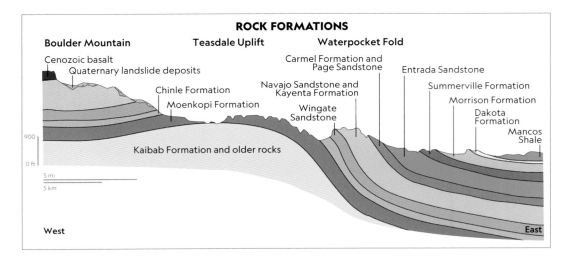

ROCK FORMATIONS

Boulder Mountain   Teasdale Uplift   Waterpocket Fold

Cenozoic basalt
Quaternary landslide deposits
Chinle Formation
Moenkopi Formation
Carmel Formation and Page Sandstone
Navajo Sandstone and Kayenta Formation
Wingate Sandstone
Entrada Sandstone
Summerville Formation
Morrison Formation
Dakota Formation
Mancos Shale
Kaibab Formation and older rocks

900
0 ft
5 mi
5 km

West   East

LEFT: **Capitol Reef** protects more than 200 million years of visible rock record, chronicling changes on the Earth's surface. As the region transitioned from beaches and tidal flats to tropical jungle to dry desert, sediments were deposited into what would eventually be 19 rock layers, grouped into formations, with the oldest at the bottom. Creation of the Waterpocket Fold exposed the spectacle of rock strata that park visitors see today. From the visitor center, the Moenkopi is the oldest visible layer, and the high Navajo sandstone is the youngest.

OPPOSITE: **Formed some 20 million years ago,** these dark volcanic basalt boulders stand out against the red spires of the Castle beyond them—all shaped by ancient rivers, wind, and time.

PIONEERS WHO SETTLED IN THE FREMONT RIVER AREA LABORED TO SURVIVE IN THE FLOODPLAIN, WHICH COULD SUSTAIN NO MORE THAN 10 FAMILIES AT A TIME.

Fremont people to expose the lighter surface underneath. These rock artists, named after the park river, lived from A.D. 300 to 1300 in Capitol Reef.

Although the Fremont culture is often confused with the ancestral Puebloans who lived south of Capitol Reef, there are several unique differences: Fremont people made distinctive rod-and-bundle–style baskets, sewed their moccasins with heels made from the dewclaws of deer or bighorn sheep, constructed trapezoidal human clay figures decorated with necklaces and blunt hairstyles, and made thin-walled gray pottery.

In Capitol Reef, the Fremont grew beans, squash, and corn. Like their ancestors, they hunted rabbits, wood rats, deer, and bighorn sheep, and they gathered berries, nuts, bulbs, yucca, rice grass, and prickly pear cactus—all still found in the park. Their farmsteads were small with up to three pit houses, and they stored their food in granaries. Although the Fremont River looked little more than a large brook to settlers unacquainted with the desert, the Fremont people made due for centuries with irrigation ditches for their crops.

Sometime in the 14th century, as the Ute migrated in and the climate dried, the Fremont culture vanished—just like the ancestral Puebloans.

While reconnoitering a northern railroad route to the Pacific Ocean, the explorer John Charles Fremont passed through in the winter of 1853. In subzero cold, the expedition daguerreotypist, a Jewish American named Solomon Nunes Carvalho, resolutely painted the distinctive "Mom and Pop" spires in the northern park and photographed Cathedral Valley.

"I succeeded beyond my utmost expectations," Carvalho wrote of the expedition in his journal, "often standing up to my waist in snow, buffing, coating and mercurializing plates in the open air." Many of the men on the journey had worn out their moccasins and walked in stocking feet. As their gaunt horses and mules dropped from exhaustion, 26 of them were butchered and eaten. One man, horribly frostbitten, died from exposure the day before they reached Parowan, Utah, 100 miles west of the Waterpocket Fold.

In the 1880s, Mormon pioneers arrived in the park's most fertile valley and began to settle the town they called Junction—renamed Fruita in 1906. Eventually, taking advantage of the long growing season in the warm microclimate, they planted hundreds of fruit trees, alfalfa, and vegetables. The isolated hamlet—a refuge for bandits and polygamists—flourished, with its consistent small river flows immune from those floods that wiped out most big river desert towns.

Although President Franklin D. Roosevelt had created the tiny 59-square-mile Capitol Reef National Monument by proclamation in 1937, the park received no funding. For six years in the 1940s, no visitors came to the monument. Everything changed in 1952, when a road into Fruita was paved and the Park Service began purchasing the small private orchards. After a campground and a visitor center

In the 1990s, researchers used Carvalho's daguerreotypes to determine that the 1853 Fremont expedition passed through the modern-day park rather than San Luis Valley, as was previously believed.

were built in the 1960s, the monument would begin receiving more than a hundred thousand visitors a year. Eventually Capitol Reef National Monument would be expanded to six times its previous size.

Capitol Reef's conversion to a national park proved controversial in Utah. As the legislation was being crafted, cattle grazing was expected to be phased out within 25 years. Later congressional action extended the phase-out to the lifetimes of children in families that had previously grazed cattle in the monument area who were born before President Richard Nixon signed park legislation on December 18, 1971.

Today, overnight campers can wake in the Capitol Reef backcountry to the sound of bighorn sheep, mule deer, or cows chomping on grass (three other western national parks honor historic grazing usage). During the day, visitors can hunt for fossils from a forgotten millennium or pick fruit in the Fruita Historic District. Within two miles of the visitor center, cherries, apricots, peaches, pears, apples, plums, mulberries, almonds, and walnuts still flourish on over 3,000 trees. Although the fruit varieties are common, these are heirloom trees, more than 100 years old. So the fruit is generally sweeter, meatier, and packed with more taste than mass-produced fruit found in grocery stores.

Settlers in what is now the Fruita Historic District relied on the Fremont River as a lifeline, setting up vegetable farms and fruit orchards at the junction of the river and Sulphur Creek. Once known as a local Eden, the area still maintains historic orchards, boasting nearly 3,000 trees.

Mormons settled and planted fruit trees in Junction (later renamed Fruita) in the 1880s—trying, as religious leader Brigham Young put it, to "... render the earth so pleasant that when you look upon your labors you may do so with pleasure, and that angels may delight to come and visit your beautiful locations."

Summer temperatures can hit 100°F (38°C), with evenings cooling to 50 or 60°F (10 to 16°C). Fall and spring are most ideal for hiking, backpacking, canyoneering, or horseback riding. November through February, temperatures range from 30 to 45°F (−1.1 to 7°C) and below freezing at night. No matter the season, seeing new-fallen snow mantling the ancient Navajo sandstone dunes, or watching a thunderstorm over the Waterpocket Fold can be contemplative journeys through time itself. ■

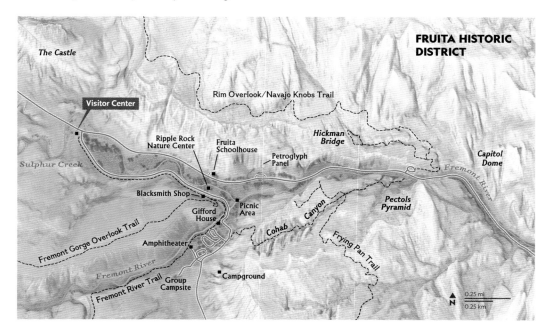

FRUITA HISTORIC DISTRICT

The Castle

Visitor Center

Rim Overlook/Navajo Knobs Trail

Ripple Rock Nature Center

Fruita Schoolhouse

Hickman Bridge

Petroglyph Panel

Sulphur Creek

Fremont River

Capitol Dome

Blacksmith Shop

Gifford House

Picnic Area

Pectols Pyramid

Cohab Canyon

Amphitheater

Frying Pan Trail

Fremont Gorge Overlook Trail

Fremont River

Fremont River Trail

Group Campsite

Campground

0.25 mi
0.25 km

N

▷ LOCATION **80 MILES NW OF FLAGSTAFF, ARIZONA**

▷ SIZE **1,904 SQUARE MILES**

▷ HIGHEST POINT **NORTH RIM LOOKOUT TOWER, 9,165 FEET**

▷ VISITORS **6,380,495 IN 2018**

▷ ESTABLISHED **1919**

GRAND CANYON NATIONAL PARK

I n northwest Arizona, the second most visited national park is the only one to encompass one of the seven natural wonders of the world: the Grand Canyon. Celebrated for its stunning depths and surrounded by public lands and three Indian reservations, the venerable 277-mile-long park would appear to be protected from development. But because of mineral riches and the popularity of the canyon, developers have sought to profit from it for more than a century.

"I want to ask you to keep this great wonder of nature as it now is," said President Theodore Roosevelt, who made "the Grand" a national monument in 1908. "I hope you will not have a building of any kind, not a summer cottage, a hotel or anything else . . . to mar the wonderful grandeur, the sublimity, the great loneliness and beauty of the canyon. Leave it as it is. You cannot improve on it. The ages have been at work on it, and man can only mar it."

Roosevelt was also creating refuge for over 500 animal species, including a wealth of birds. Recently the California condor was reintroduced to the park region. Six other animal species are federally endangered (at risk of extinction), and three more are listed as threatened (severely depleted). Grand Canyon's array of wildlife

Fresh snow fringes the Grand Canyon's South Rim. For six million years, the Colorado River has been carving out this sprawling canyon up to 6,000 feet deep.

includes many types of arachnids and insects, 22 different snakes, 18 lizards, and one tortoise species.

Along with the extensive tributary canyons, the Grand—viewed by most awestruck visitors while clutching a guardrail—is prized for the exposed layers of ancient and colorful rocks. Seen from the more popular South Rim, the seldom visited North Rim is only 18 miles across the gorge, but it's a circuitous, 220-mile drive by car.

The diversity in climates is also breathtaking: Visitors can break trail through snow on the rims while boaters on the Colorado River's world-class white water below are often clad in bathing suits. The park is visited like an inverse mountain, with vertical drops of up to 6,000 feet. The descent can be a stroll, but it's the return trip back up in the heat of day that's a killer. Only river runners, conditioned hikers, or mule riders pass below the rims through the nearly two

billion years of geologic history en route to the canyon bottom. It's like a journey through time.

The mnemonic *Know The Canyon's History, Study Rocks Made By Time* serves as a guide for descending through the main rock layers in the Grand:

Know stands for the cream to grayish white colored Kaibab limestone (250 million years old). *The* represents the gray and sometimes yellow Toroweap formation (255 million years old), which contains similar sea fossils to those seen in the Kaibab layer. *Canyon's* is the white to cream-colored Coconino sandstone (260 million years old), holding fossilized reptile tracks from petrified

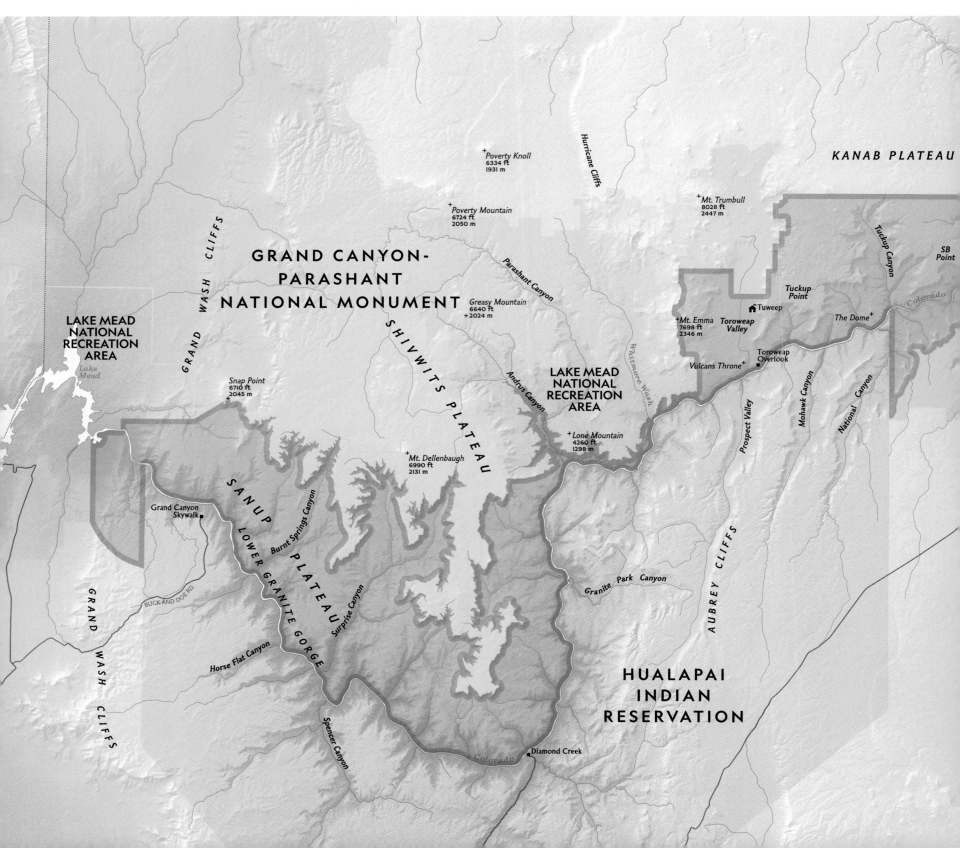

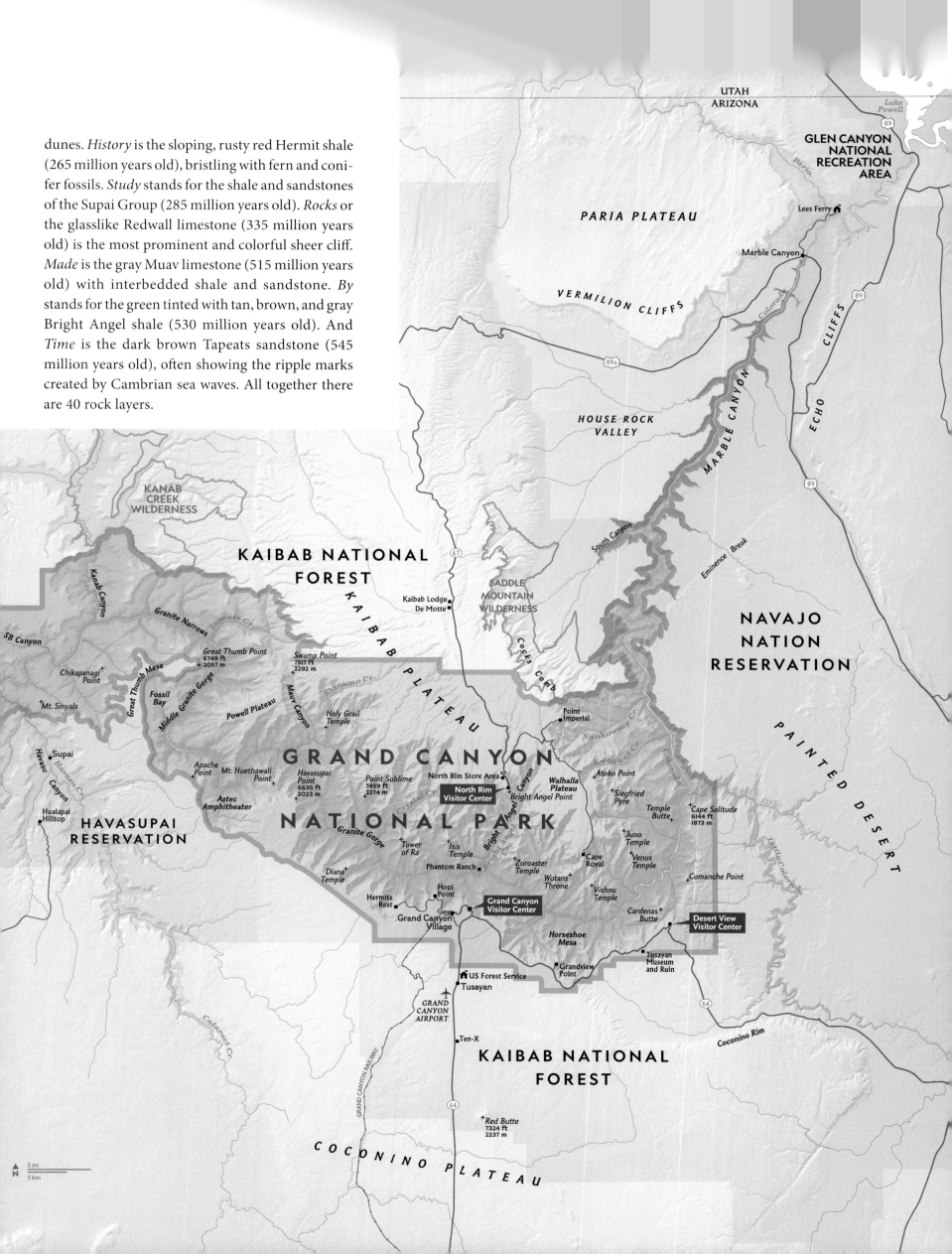

dunes. *History* is the sloping, rusty red Hermit shale (265 million years old), bristling with fern and conifer fossils. *Study* stands for the shale and sandstones of the Supai Group (285 million years old). *Rocks* or the glasslike Redwall limestone (335 million years old) is the most prominent and colorful sheer cliff. *Made* is the gray Muav limestone (515 million years old) with interbedded shale and sandstone. *By* stands for the green tinted with tan, brown, and gray Bright Angel shale (530 million years old). And *Time* is the dark brown Tapeats sandstone (545 million years old), often showing the ripple marks created by Cambrian sea waves. All together there are 40 rock layers.

THE CANYON'S EXPOSED ROCK SEQUENCE

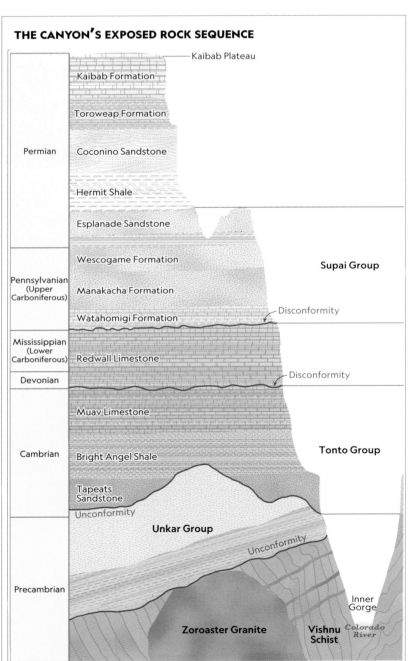

Kaibab Plateau

Kaibab Formation

Toroweap Formation

Permian

Coconino Sandstone

Hermit Shale

Esplanade Sandstone

Wescogame Formation

Supai Group

Pennsylvanian (Upper Carboniferous)

Manakacha Formation

Watahomigi Formation

Disconformity

Mississippian (Lower Carboniferous)

Redwall Limestone

Devonian

Disconformity

Muav Limestone

Cambrian

Bright Angel Shale

Tonto Group

Tapeats Sandstone

Unconformity

Unkar Group

Unconformity

Precambrian

Inner Gorge

Zoroaster Granite

Vishnu Schist

Colorado River

There are mystery layers as well. The Great Unconformity shows up to 1,200-million-year gaps in time where no rocks are preserved. Any prehistoric remnants that might have been fossilized in these layers were likely eroded away by seas or simply never deposited more than 550 million years ago.

A journey to the bottom of the Grand will bring visitors to the final, unforgettable Vishnu schist, injected with beautiful dikes and sills of pink Zoroaster granite. Those lucky—or brave—enough to descend this far cannot help but palm these extremely dense and shiny dark gray or black basement rocks, revered as the volcanic and metamorphic elders of the canyon. Cooked and smoothed down from the roots of an early mountain range, they date from 825 million to 1.8 billion years ago.

These layers wouldn't be visible without the upheaval of the Colorado Plateau. It began 75 million years ago as a gargantuan and grinding collision of tectonic plates slowly yet inexorably lifted the West from sea level, until the Rockies eventually reached nearly three miles into the sky. To the west of the mountains, 18 million years ago, the stretching of the Earth's crust created a Basin and Range drainage for a river system that flowed off the Colorado Plateau and roared through the eastern Grand Canyon. Eight million years later, a river began to cut north from the Gulf of California, eventually connecting to the Basin and Range drainage system. This produced the Colorado River 5.5 million years ago. In fits and starts, the river began to exca-

The walls of the Grand Canyon reveal a cross section of the Earth's crust that dates back to 1.8 billion years ago. The stratigraphic column shows the layers of rock formed over time: The oldest rocks are at the bottom of the sequence; the youngest rocks at the top. The layers run horizontally; any tilting or warping reflects a major geologic event. This breathtaking rock record sprawls for miles through the park.

vate the Grand, as ice age melting hurled a torrent that dwarfed the modern river.

Beginning 1.8 million years ago, volcanic activity in the Grand Canyon blocked the river with over a dozen huge lava dams in the lower canyon, which formed lakes up to a half-mile deep. Over the millennia, all of these dams burst free as the river built up behind them; one caused a flood unlike any cataclysm in the West. Man-made dams were eventually put in to support a water storage system—before western representatives fully understood the repercussions to downstream ecosystems or how changing climate in the 21st century might begin drying up the reservoir. Today, environmentalists dream of a new cataclysm for the Glen Canyon Dam, built in 1963, so that the Colorado River might once again be set free a dozen miles upstream of the park.

Canyon aficionados and boatmen archly refer to a period of time long before concrete dams blocked the river upstream as the "Pre-dam-brian." Way back then, when the river thunderously carried boulders downstream, and many brown pelicans stalked the eddies, millions upon millions of fish thrived in the warm water cutting the canyon.

These Grand Canyon fish developed unique survival strategies, such as fin adaptations that allowed them to flutter or drop like submarines. Their bodies are barracuda shaped for speed, but they use this form to cope with the speed of the water rather than speeding through it. Before their disappearance, catching most of the eight native fish species—bluehead, flannelmouth sucker, or the endangered razorback suckers; speckled dace; bonytails; roundtail or humpback chubs; and the huge Colorado pikeminnows—would feel like reeling in a sea mammal with a fishing rod.

The once abundant humpback chub, listed in 1967 as an endangered species, may be the most remarkable of all the canyon fish. These old, native minnows have thick skin, embedded scales, and small eyes to cope with turbulence and silt characteristic of the muddy Colorado River waters. Unlike the keen eyes of trout, chub eyes are underdeveloped because of neuromast

THE HEART OF THE
GRAND CANYON
Grand Canyon National Park, Arizona
Produced by the Cartographic Division
National Geographic Society
ROBERT E. DOYLE, PRESIDENT
NATIONAL GEOGRAPHIC MAGAZINE
GILBERT M. GROSVENOR, EDITOR
in collaboration with the
Museum of Science, Boston, Massachusetts
BRADFORD WASHBURN, DIRECTOR

Disappointed by the lack of detailed maps available for hikers and scientists, cartographer Bradford Washburn decided to take the matter into his own hands: In 1970, he led a multiyear effort to create this striking map of the Grand Canyon, which was published in the July 1978 issue of *National Geographic* magazine.

TEMPERATURES HERE RISE 5.5°F (3°C) WITH EVERY 1,000 FEET OF ELEVATION LOSS, SO THE HOT CANYON FLOOR OFTEN EXCEEDS 100°F (38°C).

ABOVE: **This trilobite**—a prehistoric marine animal—found in the Bright Angel shale is one of many fossils preserved in the Grand Canyon; some finds date back 1.2 billion years.

OPPOSITE: **Afternoon sun** brightens the canyon cliffs at Nankoweap. Wind and water have slowly carved out these walls over many millennia, revealing some 40 identified rock layers.

chemoreceptors on their heads that allow them to smell faraway food. They sense sound through a lateral line of tuning-fork sensors that send vibrations to their air bladders and inner ears, enabling them to home in on an otherwise invisible struggling insect as it passes by in the turbid floodwaters.

The chub's humped back allows it to hold flat on the bottom and remain upright in raging floods—so beauty can be found in form, even though it's a strange, ancient-looking creature. For spawning, the chub needs warm backwater eddies and thick sand beaches. Hatcheries, or well-designed aquariums, can simulate these conditions, but tank fish prove inferior slugs next to those hardy survivors reared in the flash-flooding currents at the bottom of the Grand.

Yet since Glen Canyon Dam was built, the first 60 miles of the Grand Canyon river bottom has been denied those floods of six million metric tons of sand a year. In the 1960s, the reservoir climbed to full behind the dam. When released into the Grand Canyon, this reservoir bottom water—clear as gin, instead of red like the rest of the Colorado River—proved perfect for the newly introduced and

The Grand Canyon was home to eight species of native fish, six of which are endemic—found only in the Colorado River Basin. The ratio of distinctive regional species may be due to the river's isolation, as well as its varying environments, water flow, and temperatures. The humpback chub, far left, a large silver minnow with a thick bulge behind its head, and the razorback sucker, an elongated fish of up to 36 inches with a bony protrusion on its back, are both endangered. The speckled dace is the only native fish species now commonly seen in the area.

non-native trout. But the dwarf-headed, cartilaginous-backed chub, along with the other native fish species, could no longer migrate past the dam or succeed below it in the Big Chill. Scientists found that the 46°F (8°C) water cooling the habitat below the dam limited chub growth to a millimeter a month: ideal snacking size for the hungry trout newcomers. In warmer water common to the Grand Pre-Dambrian epoch, the chub grew up to seven millimeters a month. To spawn, the fish requires waters of 61°F (16°C) or warmer.

Today, researchers are carefully monitoring the chub populations, along with their vital pooled backwaters. The confluence of the Colorado and Little Colorado Rivers in Grand Canyon supports the largest of the six remaining populations of humpback chub in the world (a 2009 survey estimated at least 6,000 chub remaining throughout eight river locations in the park—a mere fraction of their pre-dam populations). In case of extinction, the chubs are reared at a fish hatchery in New Mexico. Otherwise, the pikeminnow, roundtail chub, and bonytail no longer exist in the Grand Canyon.

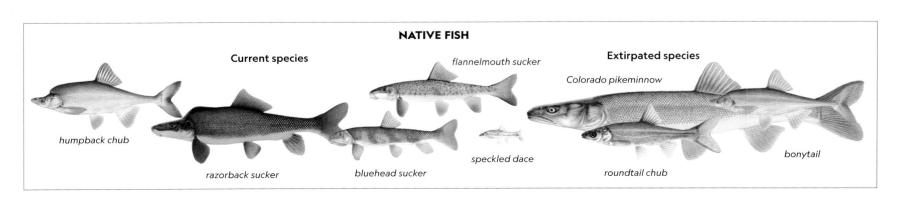

NATIVE FISH

Current species — flannelmouth sucker — **Extirpated species** — Colorado pikeminnow

humpback chub — razorback sucker — bluehead sucker — speckled dace — roundtail chub — bonytail

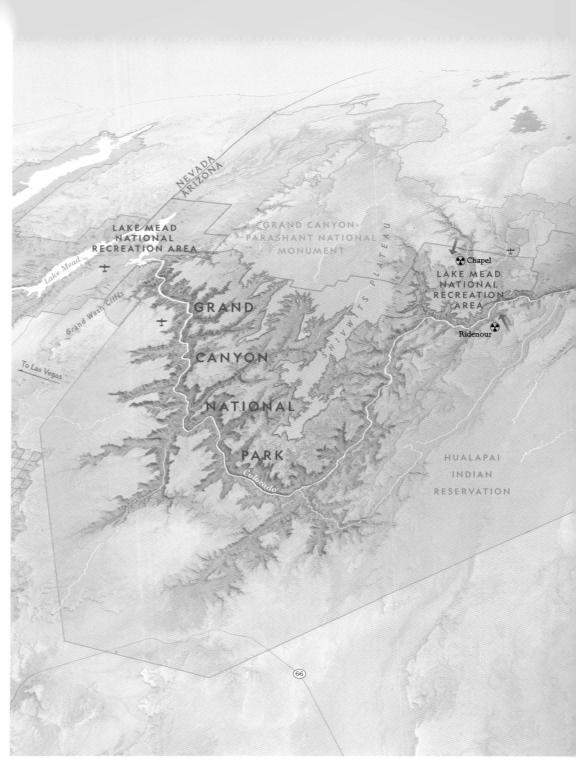

ABOVE: **The 710-foot-high** Glen Canyon Dam was mostly completed in 1963, built to harness the Colorado River. It created Lake Powell, the second largest reservoir in the country—large enough to capture all the snowmelt and prevent Lake Mead from overflowing.

RIGHT: **Human activities** may seem dwarfed by the 1,904 square miles of the Grand Canyon, but their impact could be wide-reaching. Rising tourist numbers, air traffic, mining, and development have increasingly encroached on the parklands. Meanwhile, the patchwork of federal, state, and tribal landownership complicates conservation efforts.

During a time when ground sloths still walked the Earth, nomadic Paleo-Indians hunted large mammals around what would one day be a national park. Although Paleo-Indian sites are extremely rare in the Southwest, two relics have been discovered in Grand Canyon National Park: The oldest, a piece of chert used for a spear tip 13,000 years ago, was carried by a hunter from 200 miles away in New Mexico and dropped or thrown on the South Rim. Archaeologists unearthed another chert stone tip, dated 2,500 years later, down inside the canyon and along the river.

During the Archaic period, beginning 9,800 years ago, canyon dwellers left rock art, fire pits, and stone hunting tools throughout the park. Most startling are more than 500 stick figurines—carbon-dated from 2,000 to 4,000 years ago. Ranging from one to 11 inches long, these single willow twigs were split and bent to depict game animals and occasionally stuffed with animal dung. (They remain archived at the National Park Museum Collection on the South

Rim). For two millennia, without variation, the shamanistic makers held to this specific and deliberate figurine form.

At two other ancient sites in the Southwest, stick figures depicted different animals. Children may have used some of the figures before being discarded. Yet in the Grand Canyon, the split-stick figurines

EXPLORER JOHN WESLEY POWELL CALLED THE CANYON THE "MOST SUBLIME SPECTACLE ON THE EARTH."

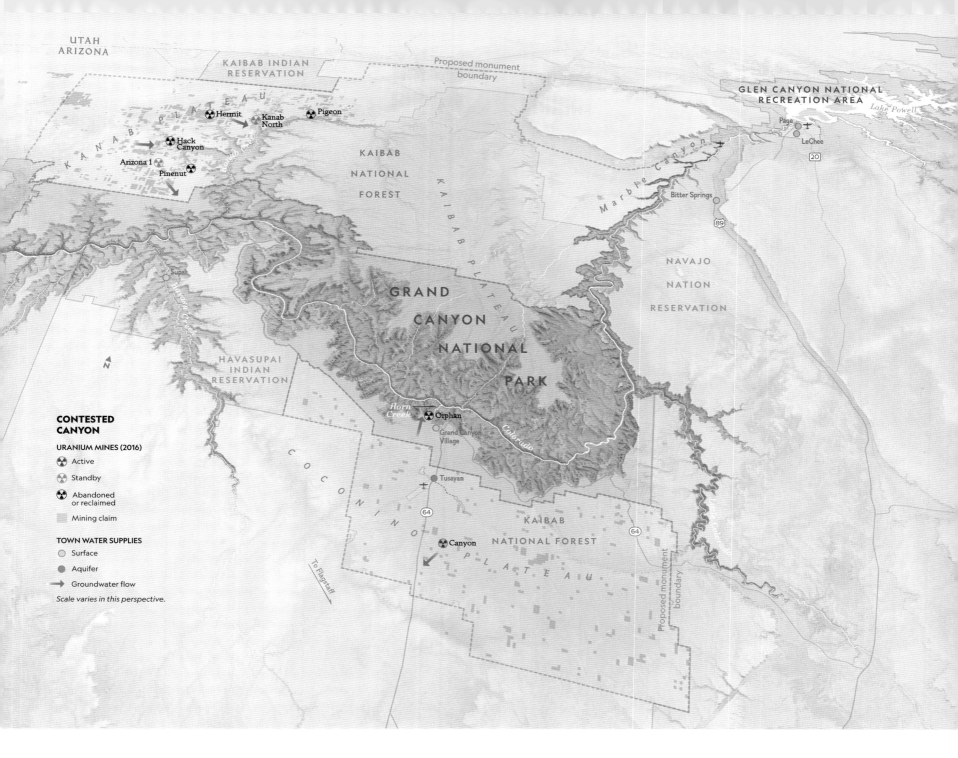

CONTESTED
CANYON

URANIUM MINES (2016)
⬢ Active
⬢ Standby
⬢ Abandoned
 or reclaimed
▦ Mining claim

TOWN WATER SUPPLIES
◯ Surface
● Aquifer
→ Groundwater flow
Scale varies in this perspective.

were not toys or mere pieces of art. They were found in deep, unin-habited caves in the Redwall limestone layer, carefully placed under rock cairns. Many were found inside high, steep cliffs that can only be accessed today with ropes and climbing gear. The stick figures—occasionally pierced with separate twigs resembling darts through the animals' bodies—may have served as a magic spell for hunters to capture their totem animals.

The canyon is rife with thousands more relics, dwelling sites, and the prehistoric trails of the Archaic people and their ancestral Puebloan descendants. As they learned how to grow corn 3,000 years ago, they began building villages on terraces within the canyon. Cultivation of beans and squash followed, then the building of granaries to store their food. By the Formative period 1,500 years ago, the ancestral Puebloans began a more sedentary lifestyle, weaving baskets from thin yucca fibers, then firing gray ceramic pots with blackened designs.

At first the ancestral Puebloans built circular pit houses beneath overhangs or in caves. Then their construction progressed into aboveground masonry block homes incorporating outdoor living

The discovery of uranium in the 1940s led to decades of mining in the Grand Canyon area. One mine on Forest Service land is still active. Contamination has occurred near older sites, including Hack Canyon and Orphan Mines, where erosion and problems with containment have allowed uranium to seep into waterways such as Horn Creek.

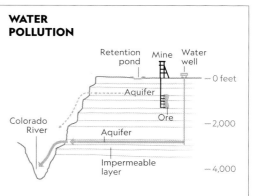

WATER POLLUTION

space. The structures were grouped into tiny villages. Eventually the throwing atlatl spear was replaced with the bow and arrow; more art decorated the surrounding sandstone walls.

After 1100, living structures were integrated with fire pits and storage rooms. By 1300, Paiute hunter-gatherers moved into the river canyon and the ancestral Puebloans vanished. By the time of European contact, Hualapai, Havasupai, and Navajo people were

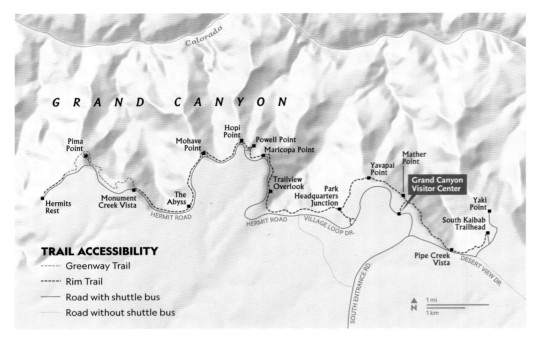

The well-defined Rim Trail makes one of Earth's most magnificent sights easily accessible. Spanning about 13 miles from the South Kaibab trailhead west to Hermits Rest, the trail is mostly paved and shaded with minimal elevation change and multiple points suited for wheelchair users.

found living in and around the Grand. Their reservations now surround the park.

In 2013, the National Park Service began working with 11 tribes and bands historically associated with the Grand Canyon to convert the Desert View Visitor Area at the southeast edge of the park into an intertribal cultural heritage center that will orient visitors to the Native American legacy of the park.

Since western settlement, there have been attempts to exploit the Grand Canyon's riches: a proposed railroad line along the river, guano mining of bat caves, and tourists being shuttled into the canyon by helicopters and boats.

Most egregious is the uranium mining that began in 1949 and then petered out several decades later. In the early 21st century, a market spike briefly renewed interest in the radioactive "yellow dirt," and the hundreds of claims staked around the park swelled into the thousands. According to a U.S. Geological Survey report from 2010, groundwater that drains into the Grand Canyon from the mines has levels of uranium unsafe for drinking.

In 2012, the Department of the Interior put a 20-year ban on uranium mining activity on 1,500 square miles surrounding the park so that scientists can evaluate the risks on plants, animals, and groundwater. Yet some uranium mines established before the ban are unaffected. For example, the Canyon Mine, located five miles from the South Rim, could contaminate the park and beautiful turquoise waterfalls within the Havasupai Reservation down inside the Grand alongside the Colorado River. Adding to the challenge are more recent efforts by the uranium industry to overturn the 2012 ban.

Other riches are inherent in the creation of a protected national park, and few recreational destinations are as dramatic and revered as those within the Grand. Activities run the gamut from fishing, horseback riding, stargazing, and studying rock art to rowing for three weeks down the Colorado River or trekking rim to rim.

Hiking, in particular, offers everything from flat-paved rim trails to strenuous overnight backpacking down thousands of feet of switchbacked trails to the river. Trails that drop deep into the Grand are often underestimated because of the lack of water, scorching sun, and huge temperature differences between the rim and canyon bottom. Rangers routinely perform rescues for ambitious hikers, often struck with heat exhaustion, who lack the energy to climb back up to the rim.

Spanning elevations from 9,000 to 2,000 feet, the park experiences a variety of weather conditions. During summer on the river, temperatures rise over 100°F (38°C); 5,000 feet above on the South Rim, high temperatures climb above 80°F (27°C). Still, snow can fall even in June above 7,000 feet. The higher North Rim closes by late October, but the South Rim is open year-round. Fall is an ideal time throughout most of the park with temperatures 20 to 30°F (11.1° to 16.7°C) cooler than summer. Winter brings snow to most of the Grand, while spring usually breaks in mid-April, matching fall temperatures and offering ideal conditions for the several million visitors who explore the park each year. ◼

LEFT: **A group** explores the North Rim by mule. Rides such as this one along the North Kaibab Trail are offered on select routes in limited numbers to minimize impacts.

OPPOSITE: **Visitors follow** the Bright Angel Trail toward Indian Garden. Hiking is a favored pastime at the Grand Canyon, but knowledge of conditions is key: Rangers rescue over 250 dehydrated and heat-exhausted hikers a year.

▷ LOCATION **163 MILES NE OF LAS VEGAS, NEVADA**

▷ SIZE **230 SQUARE MILES**

▷ HIGHEST POINT **HORSE RANCH MOUNTAIN, 8,726 FEET**

▷ VISITORS **4,320,033 IN 2018**

▷ ESTABLISHED **1919**

ZION NATIONAL PARK

n southwest Utah, the state's oldest park is also one of the nation's most popular parks. Often accessed by Interstate 15 from Las Vegas as part of the well-traveled "Grand Circle" of Southwest parks, Zion's annual visitation now outnumbers Yellowstone, 15 times its size.

The half-mile-deep, 15-mile-long gorge of Zion Canyon is the park's dominant feature, created over millennia as the North Fork of the Virgin River steadily sliced into a tilting fault block of the Markagunt Plateau. This down-cutting of water exposed a majestic display of Triassic and Jurassic sediments, including the 2,000-foot cliffs of red Navajo sandstone that have become emblematic of the park.

In 2009, 153 miles of the North Fork and its tributaries were designated a Wild and Scenic River—the only one in Utah. The North Fork's canyon widens out into a gentler valley of great palisade walls and slickrock peaks, fringed with hanging valleys and culminating at the town of Springdale, outside the southern park boundary. Other Zion drainages have also carved out scores of deep slot canyons beneath the characteristic buttes, mesas, and natural arches.

The expansive view from the popular hiking destination Angels Landing reveals a landscape cut with the Zion Canyon and the Virgin River flowing through it.

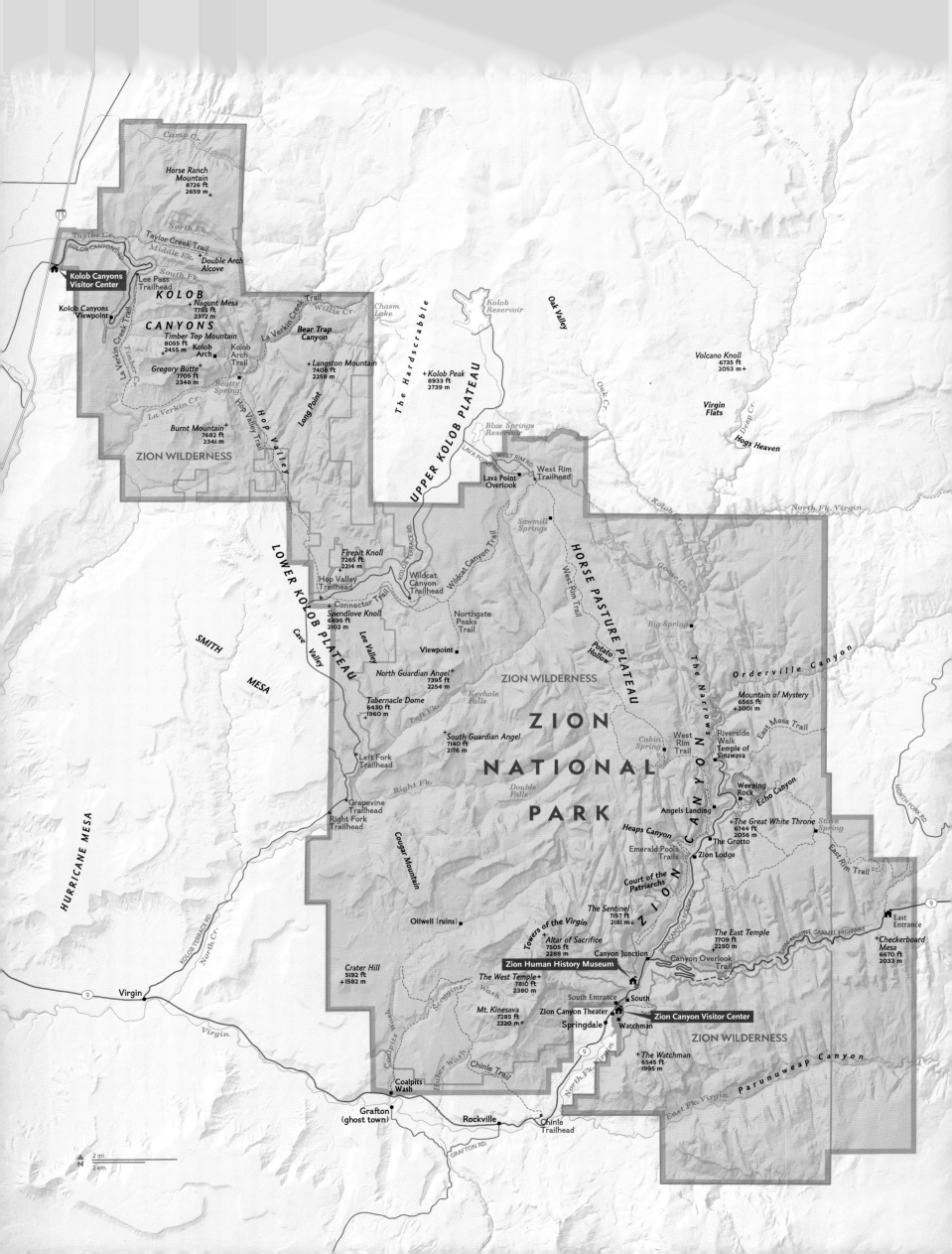

Horse Ranch
Mountain
8726 ft
2659 m

KOLOB

Taylor Creek Trail
Double Arch
Alcove

**Kolob Canyons
Visitor Center**

Kolob Canyons
Viewpoint

Lee Pass
Trailhead

Nagunt Mesa
7785 ft
2372 m

Bear Trap
Canyon

Timber Top Mountain
8055 ft
2455 m

Kolob
Arch

Kolob
Arch Trail

Gregory Butte
7705 ft
2348 m

CANYONS

Beatty
Spring

Langston Mountain
7408 ft
2258 m

+Kolob Peak
8933 ft
2739 m

Volcano Knoll
6735 ft
2053 m

Chasm
Lake

Oak Valley

Kolob
Reservoir

UPPER KOLOB PLATEAU

Virgin
Flats

Hogs Heaven

Burnt Mountain
7682 ft
2341 m

ZION WILDERNESS

Blue Springs
Reservoir

Lava Point
Overlook

WEST RIM RD.

West Rim
Trailhead

LOWER KOLOB PLATEAU

Firepit Knoll
7265 ft
2214 m

Hop Valley
Trailhead

Connector Trail

Spendlove Knoll
6895 ft
2102 m

Lee Valley

Cave Valley

Wildcat
Canyon
Trailhead

Wildcat Canyon Trail

Northgate
Peaks
Trail

Viewpoint

Sawmill
Springs

HORSE PASTURE PLATEAU

Big Spring

Potato
Hollow

SMITH

MESA

North Guardian Angel
7395 ft
2254 m

Tabernacle Dome
6430 ft
1960 m

South Guardian Angel
7140 ft
2176 m

ZION WILDERNESS

Keyhole
Falls

Left Fk.

ZION

NATIONAL

PARK

Double
Falls

Cabin
Spring

West
Rim
Trail

The Narrows

Orderville Canyon

Mountain of Mystery
6565 ft
2001 m

East Mesa Trail

Riverside
Walk
Temple of
Sinawava

Weeping
Rock

Echo Canyon

Left Fork
Trailhead

Right Fk.

Cougar Mountain

Grapevine
Trailhead

Right Fork
Trailhead

Angels Landing

Heaps Canyon

Emerald Pools
Trails

Zion Lodge

Court of the
Patriarchs

+The Great White Throne
6744 ft
2056 m

The Grotto

State
Spring

NORTH FORK RD.

East Rim Trail

HURRICANE MESA

KOLOB TERRACE RD.

NORTH CR.

Oilwell (ruins)

The Sentinel
7157 ft
2181 m

Towers of the Virgin

Altar of Sacrifice
7505 ft
2288 m

Canyon Junction

Zion Human History Museum

The West Temple
7810 ft
2380 m

The East Temple
7709 ft
2250 m

ZION-MOUNT CARMEL HIGHWAY

Canyon Overlook
Trail

East
Entrance

+Checkerboard
Mesa
6670 ft
2033 m

Crater Hill
5192 ft
1582 m

Mt. Kinesava
7285 ft
2220 m

Scoggins Wash

South Entrance

Zion Canyon Theater

Springdale

South

Watchman

Zion Canyon Visitor Center

ZION WILDERNESS

Virgin

Virgin

Coalpits Wash

Chinle Trail

Huber Wash

+The Watchman
6545 ft
1995 m

Parunuweap Canyon

Coalpits
Wash

Grafton
(ghost town)

Rockville

Chinle
Trailhead

East Fk. Virgin

North Fk. Virgin

GRAFTON RD.

2 mi
2 km

N

At a crossroads of the Colorado Plateau, Mojave Desert, and Basin and Range vegetation zones, the park unites various microhabitats in its rugged landscape. A robust range of flora and fauna thrive, including upward of 900 vascular plant species and 400 animal species.

Today the park maintains three campgrounds, a dozen miles of paved trails, and more than 100 miles of wilderness trails—plus innumerable canyoneering routes that run the gamut. A popular hike in the Narrows—the tightest stretch of the Zion Canyon at just 20 to 30 feet wide—requires wading through knee-deep water in the Virgin River. Another more technical journey along the Left Fork of the North Creek, known as the Subway, is a feat of route finding, rappelling, and swimming for permit-carrying adventurers.

As part of the Grand Staircase geologic formation—representing 110 to 270 million years of history—the land that is now Zion was uplifted, tilted, and eroded into a series of colorful cliffs that stretch contiguously across the Southwest, stepping up progressively higher in elevation from south to north. The bottom Kaibab formation layer at Zion, for instance, is the top layer at the Grand Canyon (south of the park). Zion's top Cedar Mountain formation—formerly called Dakota formation—forms Bryce Canyon's basement (north of the park).

The sedimentary rocks of Zion were initially deposited as gravel, sand, mud, and limy ooze in and around tropical, equatorial seas, and eventually consolidated into layers. The oldest Kaibab formation—laid down in a shallow sea 270 million years ago—is seen only in the western part of the park today.

Rising from the river basin, Zion's following rock layers are a record of Mesozoic (middle) geologic history: The reddish brown Moenkopi formation was deposited 240 to 250 million years ago on slick tidal flats, rivers, and floodplains surrounding the sea. The Chinle formation was then deposited in the channels and floodplains of a large river system 210 to 225 million years ago. Its bottom portion, the Shinarump Conglomerate Member, is made of gravel and cobble once deposited by gushing rivers. The upper portion, known as the Petrified Forest Member, is mostly mudstone that lower-energy rivers left behind. Above the Chinle formation are the steep Kayenta formation and Moenave formation layers that began as deposits in rivers 185 to 210 million years ago.

The entrance to the Narrows, the tightest section of Zion Canyon, shows how water—among other natural forces—has shaped the area over millions of years.

COMPLETED IN 1930, THE PARK'S 25-MILE ZION-MOUNT CARMEL HIGHWAY WAS AN ENGINEERING FEAT THAT REQUIRED BLASTING THROUGH OVER 5,000 FEET OF ROCK.

The most prominent layer in the park, of course, is the Navajo sandstone, a remnant of the giant, sand desert that inundated Utah and part of Arizona for millions of years. The dunes in Zion reached their deepest point—2,100 feet—throughout the entire 200,000-square-mile expanse of sand. Today, landmarks like the Great White Throne, Angels Landing, and the Sentinel show ancient dunes stretching toward the sky as petrified monoliths. Closer examination on some formations can even reveal cross-bedding lines that show the prevailing direction of ancient winds blowing across the sand.

The more visible yet harder-to-access Temple Cap formation "caps" the dramatic east and west Temple cliffs above the south park entrance. Formed by tidal flats and coastal sand dunes 170 to 175 million years ago, the high-elevation Temple Cap is a combination of sandstone and mudstone.

Still higher, the Carmel formation layer was deposited in the shallow, warm Sundance Sea 165 to 170 million years ago. Hikers can find its mudstone, sandstone, and gypsum mixed with marine fossils on top of the rim trails on the east side of the park.

The relatively young 120-million-year-old Cedar Mountain formation—seen atop Zion's highest point—is a brown, pebbly sediment deposited by rivers flowing out of mountains. Although thousands of feet of additional rock layers once existed above, erosion has removed these long-ago deposits from Zion's mountaintops.

Over the ensuing hundreds of millennia, mineral-laden waters filtered through Zion's compact sediments. Eventually, pressure and cementing agents like colorful iron oxide, calcium carbonate, or silica slowly turned the layers to stone: Great dunes became sandstone, mud and clay became shale or mudstone, and seabeds became limestone.

STRATIGRAPHY

Temple Cap Formation

Navajo Sandstone

Navajo Sandstone

Kayenta Formation

Kayenta Formation

Petrified Forest
Member of the
Chinle Formation

Mojave Formation

Chinle Formation

Shinarump Conglomerate

Moenkopi Formation

Shinarump Conglomerate

Moenkopi Formation

Virgin
River

Then, like the rest of the Southwest, the sea bottom lifted with the Colorado Plateau, ever so slowly, over thousands of years, for two vertical miles. This relentless yet mostly unseen rise continues today, evidenced by small earthquakes and landslides in Zion.

The final sculpting occurred as water rushed off stone, scouring, polishing, and cutting into the landscape. Because Zion lies on the tilted, western edge of the Colorado Plateau, the streams have a steep gradient and huge erosive force. Eventually, the North Fork of the Virgin River slashed through the highest layers and down several thousand feet to form Zion Canyon. The process of water as the ultimate landscape polisher over the ages can be seen, in its microcosmic power, in frequent and sometimes dangerous Zion flash floods that swell rivers into raging giants. Each year the river moves 2.7 million metric tons of sediment and rock.

Twelve thousand years ago, people passed by this area while stalking megafauna. Zion Canyon was not as deep then as it is today. Eight thousand years ago, mammal life changed and humans adapted to different food sources—this Archaic culture left behind stone tools, baskets, and sandals in Zion caves.

The many rock layers found in Zion were deposited between 110 and 270 million years ago. The oldest layer, the Kaibab formation, is made up of marine limestone and siltstone from a tropical sea, while the iconic Navajo sandstone visible throughout the park was formed by sand dunes in an ancient desert when dinosaurs roamed the Earth.

Two thousand years ago, the area's benevolent climate allowed Fremont and ancestral Puebloans (formerly known as Anasazi) to supplement hunting and gathering with planted corn until a combination of drought and flooding forced them out 800 years ago. Shortly thereafter, Paiute people came and thrived for half a millennium.

In the 1860s, Mormon pioneers homesteaded around the Virgin River and planted fruit trees, tobacco, and sugarcane. To these people of faith, the concept of being "gathered to Zion"—as they came to call settling any new lands in Utah—embodied their sense of home as a God-given refuge. Around this time, most of the Paiute died from European diseases or were moved south onto reservations. For nearly a decade, the canyon's physical and aesthetic bounties were solely a place of deliverance for Mormons.

When the ethnographer and explorer John Wesley Powell visited in 1872, he called the narrow canyon floor Mukuntuweap (Paiute for "straight canyon," referring to the near-vertical sandstone walls). Painters and photographers also came and captured the scenery for a wider American audience. The artist Frederick Dellenbaugh displayed his paintings of the paradisiacal canyon at the 1904 World's Fair and published "A New Valley of Wonders" in the influential *Scribner's Magazine,* in which he mused:

One hardly knows just how to think of [the Great Temple monolith]. Never before has such a naked mountain of rock entered our minds. Without a shred of disguise its transcendent form rises pre-eminent. There

Home to more than 153 miles of meandering designated Wild and Scenic Rivers, nearly 84 percent of the land in Zion National Park is protected wilderness. Another 9 percent of Zion's land is managed as recommended or proposed wilderness—these areas may be considered for future wilderness designation by Congress.

WILDERNESS AND WILD AND SCENIC RIVERS

National Park Service Wilderness
Potential Wilderness
Recommended Wilderness
Wild River
Recreational River
Scenic River
Intermittent river

is almost nothing to compare to it. Niagara has the beauty of energy; the Grand Canyon of immensity; the Yellowstone of singularity; the Yosemite of altitude; the ocean of power; this Great Temple of eternity.

President William Howard Taft proclaimed it Mukuntuweap National Monument in 1909—shocking and insulting locals as well as the Church of Jesus Christ of Latter-day Saints, who preferred their "Zion" to the Indian name. Over the next decade, locals complained loudly enough to be heard in Washington, D.C. In 1919, in an era not known for celebrating Native Americans, Congress enlarged the area and renamed it Zion National Park on the advice of the acting director of the newly created U.S. National Park Service, Horace Albright, who had become enchanted with the land after visiting a few years earlier.

In 1937, a separate section of Zion National Monument was added to the northwest part of the park, which became the Kolob Canyons area in 1956. Today, this more remote expanse of Navajo sandstone peaks—punctuated by canyon streams, waterfalls, and high-elevation juniper and ponderosa pine forests—is a cooler, quieter retreat from the ever growing crowds of Zion. A scenic drive along with trails and backcountry routes access views of the crimson formations, including one of the world's largest freestanding arches.

The road to Zion's popularity had been paved in 1930, with the completion of the 25-mile Zion–Mount Carmel Highway—nearly doubling traffic to over 55,000 visitors. This road connects Zion to Grand Canyon and Bryce National Parks via a man-made, mile-long tunnel cut through the Navajo sandstone walls, with large windows revealing spectacular views of Zion Canyon below.

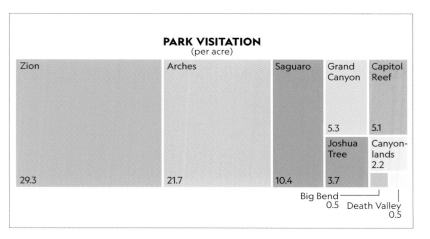

PARK VISITATION
(per acre)

Zion	Arches	Saguaro	Grand Canyon	Capitol Reef
			5.3	5.1
			Joshua Tree	Canyon-lands 2.2
29.3	21.7	10.4	3.7	

Big Bend — 0.5   Death Valley 0.5

LEFT: **Zion's visitation** soared over the past five years, with numbers climbing to 4.3 million visitors in 2018. This averages to 29.3 visitors per acre in 2018, which surpasses rates seen at other parks in the region. Most visitors spend the majority of their visit in Zion Canyon, a narrow six-mile corridor, further compounding crowding.

BELOW LEFT: **Though highly trafficked,** the trek to the renowned Angels Landing isn't for the fainthearted: Reaching the top lookout involves a rocky scramble that requires extreme caution.

As trails and more roads were built, even more visitors came. Facing mounting congestion, managers closed the park to private vehicles for several months in 2000, and implemented a propane- and electric-powered shuttle bus system. But within a dozen years, the shuttle system became swamped as visitation doubled.

Today, as annual visitation tops four million, even trails have continuous lines. Well-intentioned tourists flock to the park ready to walk, bike, climb, or simply stand in awe of the surreal sandstone. The route to one of the park's best known overlooks, Angels Landing, is heavily trafficked despite its heart-pumping switchbacks and a demanding final ascent up a narrow ridge, where chain cables have been installed for safety. Most hikers agree that the summit affords a magnificent panorama.

Gentler trails and scenic drives provide more moderate—albeit equally congested—ways to take in the views. From the Weeping Rock alcove with its hanging wildflowers to the misty Emerald Pools along the North Fork to the sun-scorched Canyon Overlook high above, the park's splendors attract travelers for quick half-day treks and weeklong excursions alike.

The Park Service is attentive to how these masses crowd the rest of Zion's population: over 78 mammal species, including coyotes, elk, mule deer, bighorn sheep, porcupines, bats, elusive mountain lions, and the rare black bear; 291 species of birds including rare peregrine falcons, bald eagles, and California condors; 37 different reptiles and amphibians; and eight species of fish (compromised by the hundreds of people who wade up the Narrows most days). The desert ecology—cryptogamic soils and other fragile plants—is

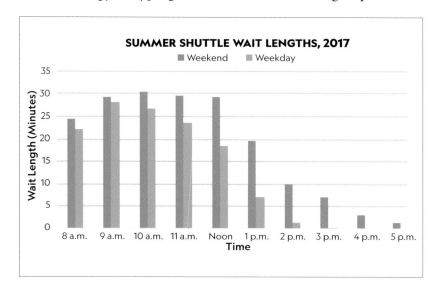

SUMMER SHUTTLE WAIT LENGTHS, 2017
■ Weekend ■ Weekday

Wait Length (Minutes) / Time

The park established a free shuttle system in 2000 to combat impacts of growing visitation and traffic congestion. By 2017, the shuttle system saw more than 6.3 million riders, many of whom experienced long lines and wait times. During the summer, the park's most popular season, morning shuttle waits averaged between 25 and 30 minutes.

also at risk from human impact, including waste along the trails and trash.

Proposed new solutions include raising park entrance fees and requiring reservations to enter the park and its high-demand hiking trails—both of which epitomize a management paradox: Congress created national parks to accommodate people while simultaneously preserving the environment.

Today, all eyes remain on Zion for solutions above and beyond shuttle buses. Zion, after all, is an innovative place, renowned for a food sustainability program and a visitor center that conserves energy with evaporative cooling towers instead of conventional energy-intensive air-conditioning.

For now, those averse to crowds visit during the November through February off-season. Although mild winters bring light snow and rain to lower elevations, temperatures can still reach 60°F (16°C). Spring has unpredictable, often wet weather, particularly in March. And summer reaches an insufferable 95 to 110°F (35 to 43°C) down low. Fall conditions—particularly during the breathtaking late-October foliage—are warm, clear, and—like visiting the Sistine Chapel—spectacularly crowded.

Even so, solitude can be found in the backcountry. Amid fewer people, chances are better for spotting the more elusive and federally threatened and endangered species, such as the Mexican spotted owl, the southwestern willow flycatcher, or the desert tortoise. And whether alone or in a crowd, most visitors leave haunted with the beauties of Zion and its canyons. ■

AMONG ZION'S MANY GEOLOGIC WONDERS ARE DOZENS OF FREESTANDING ARCHES, INCLUDING THE MASSIVE KOLOB ARCH, SEEN BY FEW VISITORS DUE TO ITS REMOTE LOCATION IN THE PARK'S BACKCOUNTRY.

OPPOSITE: **Cooling temperatures** and autumn foliage make fall the best time to visit Zion, while the Virgin River—the park's lifeblood and primary erosion agent—continues to shape the land around it.

BELOW: **Listed as** federally threatened since 1993, Mexican spotted owls find sanctuary in the park's shaded canyons and old-growth forests, where they hunt rodents and beetles.

▶   LOCATION **49 MILES E OF PALM SPRINGS, CALIFORNIA**

▶   SIZE **1,238 SQUARE MILES**

▶   HIGHEST POINT **QUAIL MOUNTAIN, 5,814 FEET**

▶   VISITORS **2,942,382 IN 2018**

▶   ESTABLISHED **1994**

JOSHUA TREE NATIONAL PARK

n Southern California, just north of Interstate 10, Joshua Tree National Park is at the intersection of the Mojave and Colorado Deserts, uniting two distinct ecosystems. The park's austere mountains and hundreds of house-size granite boulders rise above sparse stands of otherworldly Joshua trees. Popular lore has it that passing Mormons named the outspread branches of these trees after the biblical Joshua, arms raised in supplication to the sky.

The park's higher and wetter western side contains most of the Joshua trees, as well as rock outcroppings that protect oak, pine, and juniper. The drier, more thinly vegetated eastern side of the park tilts upward out of the parched Pinto Basin into the rock-studded Eagle and Cox-comb Mountains. The lower Coachella Valley in the southeastern park holds dunes, grasslands, and palm trees surrounding wildlife-rich oases. Throughout this plant paradise are 813 higher plant species, 240 bird species, 41 mammal species, and 40 reptile species.

Summer daytime temperatures, particularly in the Colorado Desert section of the park, routinely exceed 100°F (38°C). In winter, the higher mountains are often frosted with snow and the lower levels of the park average 60°F (16°C). Nights chill below 32°F (0°C)—but that doesn't keep stargazers away from the phenomenal dark-sky views.

Traces of winter snow dot the ground around the signature plants of Joshua Tree National Park, an unexpected sight in this desert land known for sizzling summer temperatures.

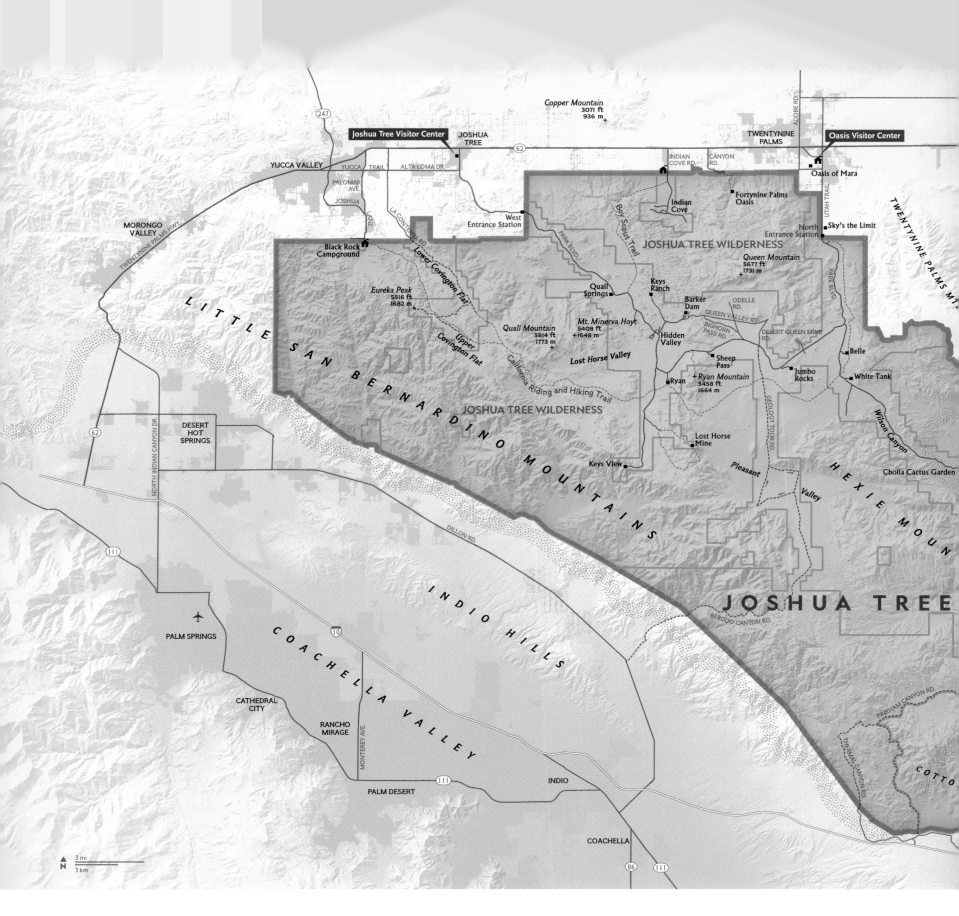

Ten percent of Joshua Tree's annual visitors come for the world-class rock climbing. In 1949, the first recorded climbs took place on the rough-textured monzogranite—pushed out of the ground as magma plutons more than 100 million years ago and slowly eroded into the jigsaw pieces of rock seen today. Studding the park as tan or gray earth jewelry, and ranging in size from breadbaskets to small buildings, the proliferation of stone awakens the imagination. This geologic showcase of boulders, steep cliffs, domes, and outcrops has been popularized by thousands of climbing routes where adventurous athletes climb, boulder, highline, and slackline, or just take in spectacular views. Thanks to the balmy park air, even winter is open season for these sports.

But the breathtaking displays of granite can just as easily be enjoyed on the ground. Hikers can explore nearly 200 miles of trails, shared with horseback riders and mountain bikers. These routes bend past boulder fields like Wonderland of Rocks in the northern park, where strikingly shaped stones obscure groves of Joshua trees. Farther east, Jumbo Rocks Campground is nested against a panorama of towering boulders. And looming nearby is the massive granite dome of Skull Rock, with its "eye sockets" hollowed out by rain.

Botanical trails showcase the vegetation in its surprising variety. Closer to standing water along Barker Dam Loop, broadleaf cattail and willow appear. Moving into the Colorado Desert in the park's midsection, the 10-acre Cholla Cactus Garden is one of the park's

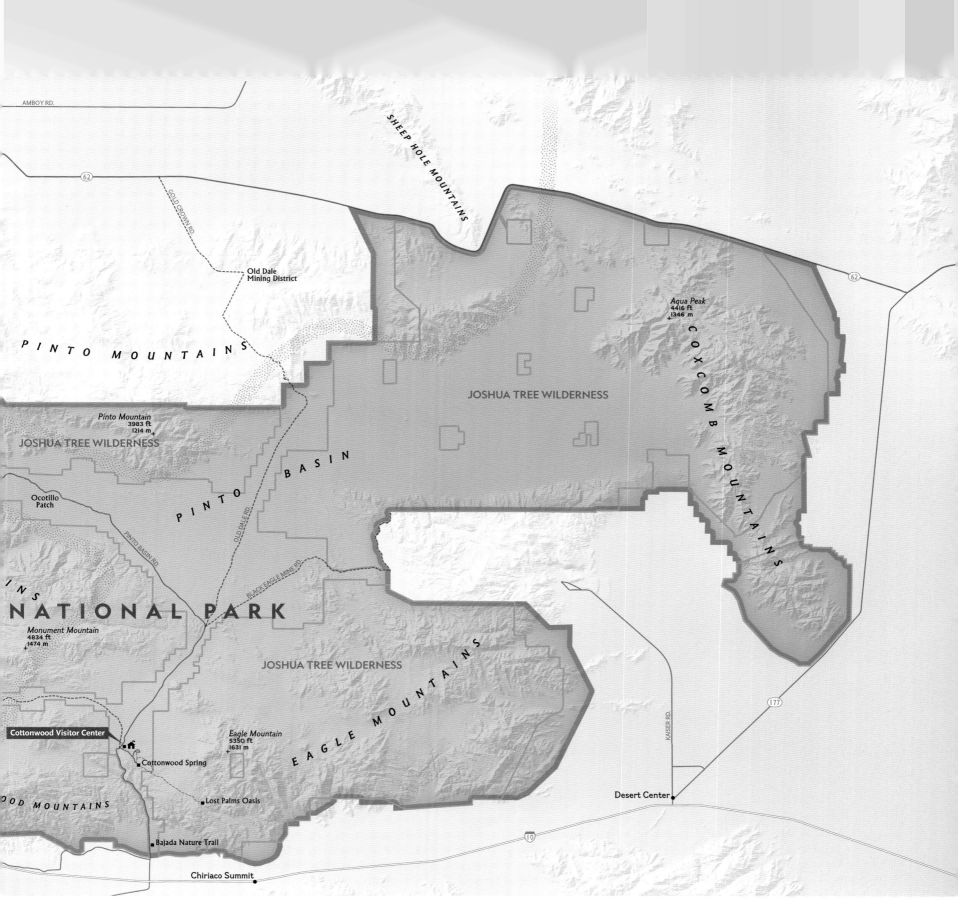

few teddy bear cholla stands, set in the Pinto Basin amid a flat stretch of creosote and burrobush. The aptly named cacti look furry enough to hug but will bite with a thousand small thorns. The lower-elevation climate also hosts patches of the unusual-looking ocotillo plant, with its spindly, thorned stems fanning toward the sky. After sufficient rains, the usually dormant plant will leaf out for one or two days, and its famously beautiful blooms appear in a burst of fiery red-orange.

In the park during cooler months, careful wildlife observers might also spot desert inhabitants such as lizards, rattlesnakes, hawks,

Even with relentless sun, scant water, and temperatures that can soar over 100°F (38°C), hundreds of species like this blooming ocotillo have evolved with fascinating adaptations for enduring the desert heat.

The high Mojave Desert habitat hosts a variety of flora and fauna, all of which are adapted to what would seem a harsh landscape. The Joshua tree can grow over 40 feet tall—at rates of just one-half inch to three inches a year—and shelters the loggerhead shrike, which impales its prey on the tree's spiny leaves. Rather than drink water, the pinacate beetle absorbs what it needs from fungus and decaying plants. The black-tailed jackrabbit's large ears help regulate its body temperature, with blood vessels that dilate to vent heat as temperatures soar.

ravens, rabbits, or squirrels—though many resident critters remain elusive. The desert tortoise, for one, spends 95 percent of its time underground and is a federally threatened species. Still, a lucky spring visitor might discover one of these ancient reptiles ambling at its average 0.2-mile-an-hour pace.

Joshua Tree is larger than the state of Rhode Island, with nine campgrounds and 500 tent sites accessible from 93 miles of paved roads. Another 106 miles of backcountry dirt roads, many of which date from the 19th-century homestead and gold mining era—lead deeper into the park.

The Joshua Tree area has been inhabited by humans for at least 5,000 years, beginning with the mysterious and nomadic Pinto culture, whose hunters attached stone spear points to small, wooden-shafted

ABOVE: **Reptiles** tend to be better adapted to arid places like Joshua Tree. The ancient, slow-moving Mojave desert tortoise spends most of the day in cooler underground dens.

BELOW: **The formation of Jumbo Rocks** began over 100 million years ago, as magma cooled into stone and eventually cracked under pressure. Water and erosion eventually finished shaping the stone.

spears, propelled from atlatl throwers. Like the Fremont and ancestral Puebloans of other southwestern areas, the Pinto culture may have been driven off by drought.

In wetter times several millennia later, Cahuilla, Chemehuevi, and Serrano hunter-gatherers lived in and around the park. The nomadic Mojave Indians also passed back and forth through the present-day park on trails linking the Colorado River to the California coast. Native Americans made use of more than 120 plant species and hunted reptiles, amphibians, rabbits, deer, and bighorn sheep. Today the park protects over 700 archaeological sites and 88 historic structures. Descendants from all four Native American cultures continue to live in the area surrounding the park; outside the northern boundary, the Chemehuevi (aka Luiseño) have a reservation in Twentynine Palms, California.

From 1870 to 1945, cattlemen took advantage of what used to be tall and abundant grasslands. They dug a system of watering tanks and roads still used in the park today. The ranch of William F. Keys and his family is also on the National Register of Historic Places and offers a glimpse of how early settlers lived in the remote desert environment. The ranch house, schoolhouse, store, and workshop remain, as well as cars, trucks, mining equipment, and other spare

JOSHUA TREE'S HERBARIUM, A BOTANICAL INVENTORY DOCUMENTING SOILS, HABITAT, AND OTHER KEY DATA ABOUT PLANT LIFE, CONTAINS MORE THAN 3,500 SPECIMENS.

parts that show the commercial side of land use. Gold miners and homesteaders tunneled out more than five million dollars of nuggets from hundreds of small pit mines in the area, burning Joshua trees for fuel while they were at it.

As development burgeoned in 1920s California, an unlikely civic activist stepped forth. Minerva Hamilton Hoyt had been cut from a different cloth than more swashbuckling preservationists like John Muir and Teddy Roosevelt; the former southern belle didn't need to clamber on ice or stalk big game to effect change. An avid gardener, Hoyt had lost an infant son, and later, her husband. She subsequently found comfort in the stark and aesthetic desert landscapes outside her home in Pasadena. Hoyt grew inspired by the uncanny resilience of plants that survived—and even thrived—in the harsh climate.

At the same time, she witnessed widespread destruction of her cherished Joshua trees and other plants through poaching and road building. Cactus gardens had become all the rage in Los Angeles, and Hoyt was horrified that they were being uprooted from Southern California wilds. "The desert with its elusive beauty possessed me," Hoyt wrote, "and I constantly wished that I might find some way to preserve its natural beauty."

Though she was influential in recommending that Death Valley be set aside as a monument, her efforts to set aside Joshua Tree—which she wanted to call the Desert Plants National Park—were repeatedly rebuffed by President Hoover.

Packing passion and ferocity behind her genteel upbringing, the "apostle of the desert" arranged a personal meeting with incoming President Franklin D. Roosevelt, then found a friend in Secretary of the Interior Harold Ickes. When the Park Service pitched a 138,000-acre park, Hoyt complained to Ickes, pushing for a million acres. She succeeded in having Interior officials agree to a larger park and finally convinced the Roosevelt administration to set aside

OPPOSITE: **The Cholla Cactus Garden** has almost 10 acres of teddy bear cholla, whose stem joints are prone to hook themselves to anything in contact, hence their nickname "jumping cholla."

BELOW: **Keys Ranch** stands testament to the grit of cattle ranchers, miners, and homesteaders like William F. Keys and his family who made their living in the Mojave.

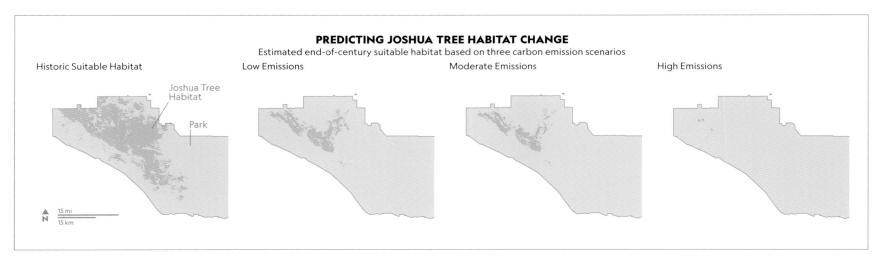

PREDICTING JOSHUA TREE HABITAT CHANGE
Estimated end-of-century suitable habitat based on three carbon emission scenarios

Historic Suitable Habitat

Joshua Tree
Habitat

Park

15 mi
15 km

Low Emissions

Moderate Emissions

High Emissions

ABOVE: **Climate change** may greatly reduce areas in the park that have livable habitat for the park's namesake species, the Joshua tree. These maps predict end-of-century distribution under three emission pathway scenarios; all show significant reductions in suitable habitat for the species by 2100.

RIGHT: **Ground-level ozone** can be detrimental to human health and the environment. Although ozone concentrations improved since the 1990s, concentrations at Joshua Tree National Park still frequently exceed recommended levels.

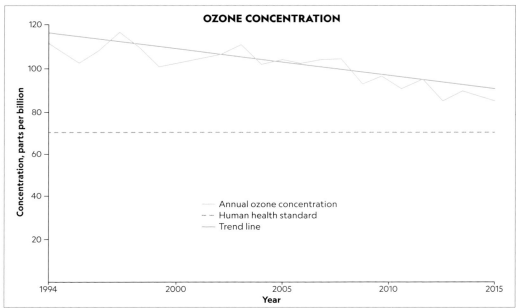

Joshua Tree National Monument in 1936. (She was also influential in creating the largest state park in California, Anza-Borrego Desert State Park, south of Joshua Tree.)

In 2013, despite a policy not to bequeath people's names in wilderness areas, the U.S. Board on Geographic Names dubbed a black-varnished, 5,405-foot peak in the west-central park Mount Minerva Hoyt. A species of Mexican cactus (*Mammillaria hamiltonhoytea*) was also named in her honor.

Until 11,000 years ago, Joshua trees—growing up to 40 feet high and 150 years old—thrived throughout the U.S. Southwest. As Earth grew warmer and drier, their range contracted to the park and small parts of Utah, Nevada, and Arizona.

Native Americans used the trees' tough leaves for sandals and baskets, while flower buds and seeds supplemented their diet. Its outspread arms end in new growth fanning out in quilled tufts of green, while the shaggy trunks often bear the dead foliage of previous seasons. Below, the roots cling to the ground like human toes.

From a distance, the Joshua tree might look more like a twisted version of park evergreens. But the "tree" actually belongs to the Agave family, in a subgroup of flowering plants that includes grasses and orchids. It does not have annual tree rings, but rather grows as a vertical stem without branches for the first few decades of its life. Up close, it resembles its neighboring relative in the park, the Mojave yucca, which has longer, wider leaves with fibrous threads.

The pollination of Joshua tree flowers—growing off the branch tips—is a 40-million-year-old marvel of coevolution: a marriage between yucca plants and a tiny white-winged, black-goggled moth. These moths mate on Joshua tree branches, then the female lays her eggs in a recently opened flower and collects pollen. As the moth eggs hatch, the larvae eat the Joshua tree seeds, leaving just enough behind for new plant growth. Each Joshua tree can only be pollinated by this single species of yucca moth. Neither can exist without the other.

New Joshua tree life begins with the seed germinating in the ground, which only happens during increasingly uncommon rainstorms. Like its statuesque cousin, the saguaro cactus, Joshua tree sprouts often depend upon the protective branches of a nearby nurse plant for shade and water collection. The problem is that seedlings lack the extensive root network of mature trees and need regular rain—now in short supply with extended droughts—to survive.

Today, the eponymous tree of Hoyt's desert plants park is at risk. An ongoing University of California study found few or no young Joshua trees in about 30 percent of its range within the park, contributing to a push to list the tree as a federally threatened species. Weather records from the northern end of the park show that the mean temperature has increased 2°F (1.1°C) over the last 40 years. But the real danger to park plants is that nighttime lows are nearly

SUMMER TEMPERATURES IN JOSHUA TREE HAVE SPIKED UP TO A SWELTERING 118°F (48°C) IN JULY, THE WARMEST MONTH ON AVERAGE, AND DIPPED AS LOW AS 10°F (-12°C) IN DECEMBER.

8°F (4.4°C) above average, meaning that even without a change in precipitation, the evaporation rate is higher and less water is available to the plants. Based on climate projections with a 5.4°F (3°C) increase, the Joshua tree's range could be reduced up to 90 percent by the end of this century.

In this garden haven, there are more than 800 species of plants to consider: creosote bushes with a sweet post-rain redolence; desert willows that grow into thick woodlands; six-foot-tall chuparosa that flower red throughout the year; 10-foot-tall desert lavender emitting a minty fragrance; mostly leafless smoke trees with pealike flowers; showy blue palo verde trees, armored with spines and brightened with yellow blooms; Muller oaks that grow at higher elevations in the park and feed wildlife with their acorns; and piñon pines that can grow up to 1,000 years old—if not attacked by invasive pine beetles previously held in check by lower winter temperatures.

All of these plants are threatened by air pollution more common to eastern national parks. Most of this pollution—thick with nitrogen and sulfur particulates—is blown out of the Los Angeles Basin by predominant westerly winds. Joshua Tree has exceeded its critical load—the term scientists use to describe the amount of pollution above which harmful changes in sensitive ecosystems occur. Desert plants adapted in formerly low-nitrogen soils must now compete with non-native grasses—such as red brome—and other exotic plant species that thrive with the added nitrogen fertilizer.

Compounding it all, nitrogen levels in the Joshua Tree soil react with sunlight and create some of the highest ground-level ozone levels throughout the National Park System—exceeding Environmental Protection Agency air quality standards. At times the park posts health warnings as ozone hits elevated levels that affect both humans and highly sensitive ozone species like Goodding's willow and skunkbush sumac. The Park Service and other researchers are monitoring these levels and studying such impacts so that they can focus protective efforts where most needed to keep this special ecosystem healthy and enjoyable.

After all, in this wonderland of shaggy trees and fantastic monzonite formations, climbers, hikers, bikers, bird-watchers, astronomers, and plant lovers alike need only pause, smell the cactus flowers, and gaze out over the surreal desert landscape to appreciate its significance. ■

Parts of Joshua Tree offer some of the darkest nights in Southern California. Stargazing conditions are best on clear, moonless nights, when visitors can often spot constellations.

▷ LOCATION **118 MILES W OF LAS VEGAS, NEVADA**

▷ SIZE **5,270 SQUARE MILES**

▷ HIGHEST POINT **TELESCOPE PEAK, 11,049 FEET**

▷ VISITORS **1,678,660 IN 2018**

▷ ESTABLISHED **1994**

DEATH VALLEY NATIONAL PARK

n southeast California's Mojave Desert along the Nevada border, Death Valley is a park of extremes. It is the hottest, driest, lowest place on the continent and the largest park in the lower 48. Ninety-one percent of the park is designated wilderness. Visitors come to experience the stark, infinite-looking panoramas, lush oases, and bright sand dunes. Its dry crystalline air and separation from urbanity make it one of the best parks for stargazing on the continent.

Death Valley stretches 156 miles northwest to southeast, encompassing all of its namesake valley with its floor of rocks, sand, and salt flats. A half dozen cream- to brown-colored desert mountain ranges with huge elevation gains tower above the valley. The park was named by lost and starving emigrants—one of whom succumbed to the heat—while taking an ill-advised shortcut through blistering dry lake beds—or playas—to the California gold fields in 1849.

For preceding millennia, the Timbisha Shoshone residents had called their valley Tumpisa, or "rock paint," referring to the red ocher color they applied to their bodies from local clay. Today, a small population of the Timbisha Shoshone lives in a 300-acre village in

Although snow shines on the Panamint Mountains in the distance, Death Valley below is known for its scorching temperatures and arid conditions, seen here from Zabriskie Point.

the heart of Death Valley. The national park is one of only several to allow Native Americans to continue living within park boundaries.

More than 1,000 species of thirsty native plants endure in the park. Tough native creosote bushes that provide shade and sustenance to amphibians and reptiles surround medicinal mesquite trees. Non-native species like tamarisk and palm trees—first planted by pioneers—compete for water and soil.

Over 400 species of animals live in the surprisingly rich desert biome. Majestic desert bighorn browse desert globemallow, catclaw, and fourwing saltbush. Soaring birds catch thermals in parched skies bereft of clouds, while innumerable small birds nest among yucca plants and spare stands of pine, juniper, and Joshua trees.

In the summer of 1913, Death Valley hit a scorching 134°F (57°C), the hottest temperature ever recorded on Earth. During that heat wave, the thermometer climbed above 129°F (54°C) for five days in a row. That same year, in February, the park mercury fell to a record low of 15°F (−9.4°C). Usually December is the coldest month, averaging lows of 39°F (4°C) and highs of 65°F (18°C).

Although the century-old extremes have not yet been broken, in July 2018, the average monthly temperature reached 108.1°F (42.2°C), which broke the world monthly heat record of 107.4°F (41.8°C) set the previous July in Death Valley. During these heat waves, temperatures often remain in the triple digits all night long.

These records are measured at the lowest point on the continent, 282 feet below sea level: Badwater Basin. The depth and shape of Death Valley—a long, narrow basin insulated by high, steep mountain walls—influences heat. As the sun bakes the bare ground through clear, dry air, heat radiates from the rocks. At nighttime, as the hot air rises, it remains trapped by the high, slightly cooler valley walls, which push the air back down two vertical miles. At low altitudes, it is warmed once again and circulated through the valley.

Death Valley is also the driest place in North America, due in part to its rain shadow geography. Winter storms rolling eastward from the Pacific Ocean are blocked by four different mountain ranges that capture incoming rain or snow. By the time clouds reach the park, most of the moisture is gone.

The drying climate (compared with the wetter prehistoric times) no longer provides the precipitation to recharge the underlying aquifer. Although the higher mountains of the park can receive over 15 inches of rainfall a year, the average annual precipitation at sea level is 1.92 inches. In 1929 and 1953, no rain was recorded; in the driest stretch of time recorded (1931 to 1934), a mere 0.64 inches of rain fell in 40 months.

During rare rainstorms in the sparsely vegetated park, flash floods often reshape the land and leave behind shallow lakes. In 2005, an exceptionally wet winter flooded the expansive salt flat of Badwater and spurred the park's greatest wildflower season. Death Valley is known for its spring superblooms that occur only with well-timed

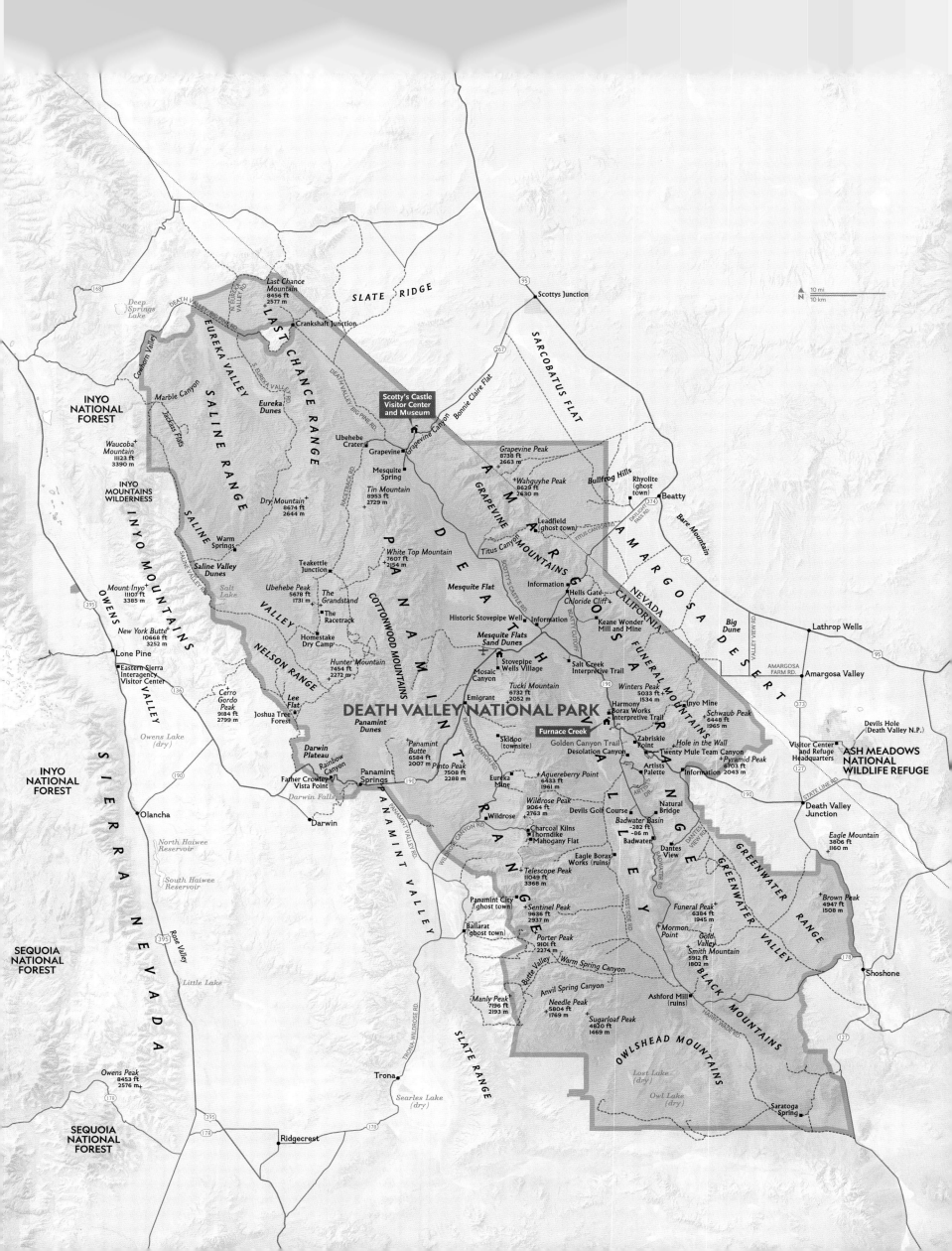

A **well-timed** burst of rain in Death Valley can create a rare spring superbloom like this one seen in 2016: Millions of seeds sprouted in a spectacular albeit fleeting display.

winter and spring rainfall, ample sunlight, and minimal drying winds. When those precise conditions are met, the desert erupts with color: Purple, pink, yellow, and white blooms enliven flats and foothills, then blossom in the upper valleys and mountain slopes later in the spring and early summer.

Color can be found year-round elsewhere in the park: In the Furnace Creek area, weather and oxidation have turned volcanic ashfalls into a geologic panorama drenched in blues, greens, and reds along a twisting, nine-mile stretch of road known as Artist's Drive. Nearby Golden Canyon, named for its flaxen hues, is a maze of canyons and arresting contoured hills that can be explored on foot. To the north are the steep, ruddy cliffs of Red Cathedral.

Death Valley National Park set the record for the highest air temperature on Earth on July 10, 1913, when the temperature soared to 134°F (57°C). The graph (right) shows the average annual and average 10-year temperature at Death Valley. The 10-year interval smooths fluctuations, making it useful to identify long-term trends. Here it shows that temperatures are on the rise.

THE RARE DEVILS HOLE PUPFISH MAY HAVE RESIDED IN THE DEEP, WATER-FILLED CHASM CALLED DEVILS HOLE FOR UP TO 20,000 YEARS.

Perhaps the most popular place for viewing the park's exceptional topography and unexpected colors is Zabriskie Point. The curvature of eroded mudstone is all the more striking set against the flat expanse of valley below and mountains reaching skyward in the distance. At dawn and sunset, it's a photographer's paradise. Manly Beacon, famously photographed by Ansel Adams in the 1950s, can be seen jutting above the foothills as light paints the terrain in pinks and oranges.

The sunrise vista is rivaled at Dante's View. West of this lookout, the Panamint Mountains and Telescope Peak loom over the Badwater Basin below. Beyond the Panamint Range tower the barely

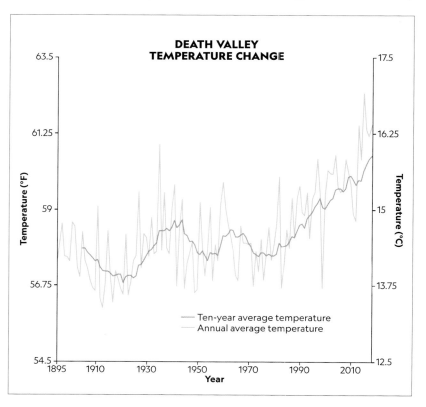

DEATH VALLEY TEMPERATURE CHANGE

Temperature (°F) / Temperature (°C)

— Ten-year average temperature
— Annual average temperature

Year

Coyote

Creosote bush

Sidewinder

Pallid bat

Notch-leaf
phacelia

Kit fox

White-lined
sphinx moth

Desert hairy
scorpion

Brown-eyed
evening primrose

Desert
kangaroo rat

visible Sierra Nevada. To the northwest is Devil's Golf Course, where wind and rain have shaped rock salt into crooked spires. (The warped terrain once prompted a writer to remark that only the devil could golf there.) The tiny salt crystals that compose it make a chorus of pops as they burst in the heat.

Death Valley's otherworldly wonders span from the Mesquite Flat Sand Dunes—the largest dune field in the park, with its gorgeous smooth and rippled sand mounds rising from the clay floor of an ancient lake bed—to the Ubehebe crater, a 600-foot-deep maar volcano in the northern park.

Death Valley comes to life after the sun sets and the sky becomes a starry tapestry. As temperatures dip, nocturnal species emerge: The evening primrose's white flowers blossom, joining spring blooms of notch-leaf phacelia. The desert kangaroo rat, which can survive without drinking water, scurries about mesquite with its hearing sensitive to approaching owls. Small kit foxes—known for their sizable ears—forage near Furnace Creek, where desert hairy scorpions lurk.

December day, when pond ice began breaking up beneath the rocks with popping and cracking sounds. He learned that when the playa floods just enough to form floating ice during winter nights—but not enough to cover the rocks—the ice melts during the day. This causes floating ice floes to be driven across the playa water by wind, which shoves the rocks along the soft mud. Following these ideal conditions, lucky visitors can glimpse the zigzagging pathways of these impressive moving stones.

Elsewhere in the park, visitors revel in the magic of crystalline night skies, solitude, and adventure. Although there are few maintained trails, backpackers and hikers walk the wide-open desert washes and canyon bottoms of the park, in quietude reminiscent of another era.

Nine thousand years ago, the Nevares Spring People lived amid the park and its former lakes during a wetter time with many large game animals. The culture was displaced by the Mesquite Flat People 5,000 years ago, followed by the Saratoga Springs People, both of whom left behind mysterious, circular petroglyphs on the rocks of the park 2,000 years ago.

The Timbisha Shoshone came to the valley to hunt and gather plants 1,000 years ago. Adapting to the intense heat, they moved up into the cooler mountains to escape the oven of summer and harvest pine nuts while hunting rabbits and other small game. In winter they descended to their homes in Panamint or Death Valley. The people are renowned for revering all life-forms, including both animals and plants. Because their culture prohibited killing mesquite trees and other plant food sources, the tribe only burned trimmed wood for

Among the park's most intriguing natural anomalies are the "sailing stones" at the three-mile-long, two-mile-wide Racetrack playa in the Scotty's Castle area. After tumbling off adjoining mountainsides onto the desert floor, rocks as large as 700 pounds appeared to be moving while no one was watching, etching an eerie and inexplicable trail in the dirt in their wake. Some boulders "sailed" as far as 1,500 feet, fueling a mystery that perplexed scientists for decades. Years would pass without any movement, then fresh tracks would appear.

In 2011, a paleobiologist placed GPS tracking devices on rocks brought in from outside the park (so that the native rocks wouldn't be disturbed). Two years later, he struck Racetrack pay dirt on a thawing

The Park System contains the highest and lowest points in North America: Denali in Denali National Park, which reaches 20,310 feet, and Death Valley's Badwater Basin, which plunges 282 feet below sea level. Often referred to as a land of extremes, Death Valley also holds records for being the hottest and driest place on Earth.

ELEVATION EXTREMES

▲ Highest continent elevation
▼ Lowest continent elevation
— Europe-Asia boundary

THE AREA'S NAME ORIGINATED IN THE WINTER OF 1849–50. AS A GROUP OF PIONEERS FINALLY EMERGED FROM THE VALLEY AFTER BEING LOST, ONE SUPPOSEDLY SALUTED: "GOODBYE, DEATH VALLEY."

By the 1880s, the desert-dwelling Shoshone were crowded out of and nearly evicted from their homelands by miners. Best known was the Harmony Borax Works, which harvested the cotton-ball–like crystals of the mineral sodium borate—used for cleansers and glazing—from evaporated lake bottoms. The company, whose one mill site remains on the National Register of Historic Places, would become famous for its huge mule wagon teams, later replaced with a railroad. Other large-scale mines—including gold, copper, and lead operations—surrounded boomtowns, but most were abandoned in the early 20th century. Only the borax business prevailed: In 1920, the evaporated lakes and mines of the region still provided the world's largest source of borax; in four years, Harmony had hauled 20 million tons of the mineral from Death Valley.

The Pacific Coast Borax Company took over Harmony's operation, but kept the area as part of its reserves. In 1927, they built the luxury Furnace Creek Inn (still in operation today under a different name) and hauled tourists in on the railroad, even though visitors preferred using their own cars. Despite the golf course, swimming pool, and tennis courts that followed, the company sought national park branding to keep their tourism business alive.

fuel. Then, as the trees flourished from their care, they harvested the bean pods and pounded the seeds into a flour. By living among and pruning these mesquite groves, they promoted the health of the species and practiced a form of sustainable landscaping that the park would eventually emulate.

A water tank car at Harmony Borax Works preserves the memory of the mineral sodium borate being harvested from evaporated lake bottoms. This once booming operation began in the 1880s and was renowned for using large mule teams to transport its product.

Enter Stephen Mather, who visited Death Valley 10 years after becoming the first director of the Park Service. Though impressed with the scenic, wild landscape, Mather declined the company's request to help make Death Valley a national park. He feared accusations of favoritism: Until 1904 Mather had worked for Pacific Coast Borax—devising its successful 20 Mule Team Borax (pulling a wagon filled with the mineral) trademark. Then he had started his own borax business, which made him a wealthy man. His fortune allowed him to pursue other passions, including his leadership role in the fledgling National Park Service, where he took no salary and paid employees out of his pocket.

Still, Mather suggested that Pacific Coast Borax use a grassroots media campaign to build support for the area's protection. After Mather's death in 1930, the new director Horace Albright lit the Death Valley torch, but Congress didn't understand why an arid desert landscape deserved park designation. Plus, the remaining active mining claims couldn't easily be amalgamated into a national park.

With considerable public support, Albright urged President Hoover to bypass Congress. In February 1933, Hoover created Death Valley National Monument through presidential proclamation, which temporarily banned the filing of new mining claims and prospecting. Four months later, Congress reopened mining and by then, huge ore

The sun accentuates ripples in the expansive Mesquite Flat Sand Dunes, which encompass dune types: crescent dunes with wide sand mounds; linear dunes with straighter, longer ridges; and pyramidal star dunes that often form in places with multidirectional wind patterns.

trucks and bulldozers had replaced mules. As strip and open-pit mines began to scar the landscape, a public outcry ensued.

In 1976, Congress passed the act that banned open-pit mines, new claims, and required the National Park Service (in Death Valley and other national parks) to examine the validity of thousands of earlier mining claims. Four years later, stricter environmental standards were put in place that allowed limited mining to resume.

Finally, in 1994, Congress saw the light in the desert. The monument was abolished and Death Valley National Park was established through the California Desert Protection Act (simultaneously creating Joshua Tree National Park and Mojave National Preserve). The park took over unpatented mining claims and enlarged its boundaries by over 2,000 square miles. Congress also required the Park Service to study the suitability of lands inside of and surrounding the park for a tribal reservation. Six years later the Timbisha Shoshone Homeland Act transferred over 7,000 acres to the tribe, including 300 acres in the park. In 2005, the last borax operation shut down, and the park can now be appreciated for both its historical mines and the desert tranquility of the ages. ■

PACIFIC NORTHWEST PARKS

CONTENTS

A pine forest surrounds America's deepest lake, Crater Lake in Oregon, which fills a six-mile-wide caldera created by a volcanic eruption some 7,000 years ago.

Map labels:

150 mi
150 km

CANADA
U.S.

MONTANA

OLYMPIC NATIONAL PARK

WASHINGTON

MOUNT RAINIER NATIONAL PARK

Columbia

IDAHO

OREGON

CRATER LAKE NATIONAL PARK

Snake

PACIFIC OCEAN

NEVADA

UTAH

CALIFORNIA

YOSEMITE NATIONAL PARK

KINGS CANYON NATIONAL PARK

SEQUOIA NATIONAL PARK

Colorado

ARIZONA

- ▶ LOCATION **60 MILES E OF FRESNO, CALIFORNIA**

- ▶ SIZE **1,353 SQUARE MILES**

- ▶ HIGHEST POINT **MOUNT WHITNEY, 14,494 FEET**

- ▶ VISITORS **1,928,617 IN 2018**

- ▶ ESTABLISHED **1890**

SEQUOIA & KINGS CANYON NATIONAL PARKS

Rising high above the Central Valley of California and guarding the western slope of the southern Sierra Nevada is an alpine wonderland of colossal trees. Whether gasping at high altitude or running the white water, visitors access the backcountry park mostly by foot or on horseback. Sequoia Canyon, the second oldest national park in the system, and Kings Canyon (established 1940) are connected and jointly managed as one park.

Directly north of Sequoia, Kings Canyon is a mile-deep, glacier-carved valley amid flowered mountain meadows. The land is topped by numerous 14,000-foot peaks surrounding Mount Whitney, the highest peak in the lower 48. The park also protects groves of the world's largest tree by volume—its namesake sequoia.

Ninety-seven percent of Sequoia and Kings is designated wilderness. The park is buffered by the 907-square-mile John Muir Wilderness on the north, the Monarch Wilderness (70 square miles) in between, and three national forests.

The huge Sierra Nevada snowfalls ultimately drain down the Kern and Kaweah Rivers, and two forks of the Kings River—originally named the River of the Holy Kings by an 1805 Spanish expedition.

Sequoia trees can live a long time—more than 3,000 years. As nature lover John Muir once put it, "barring accidents they seem to be immortal . . . unless destroyed by man, they live on indefinitely."

The park's huge elevation gradient and wealth of eco-zones hold over 20 percent of the plant species found in California. At lower altitudes, the wooded foothills are broken by willow, sycamore, and hardwood drainages. The mid-range elevations hold the rich forests of sequoia and other evergreens. Up high, adjoining several thousand feet of tundra, are mountain hemlock, along with lodgepole, foxtail, and whitebark pine trees. Half of the park is old-growth forest, and in 1976 the entire park was designated by UNESCO as part of the Sequoia–Kings Canyon Biosphere Reserve. Mountaineering and rock climbing are popular on the compact granite found on peaks and spires throughout the park. There are also over 800 miles of footpaths, including the famous 215-mile John Muir Trail, routing from Mount Whitney to Yosemite Valley. One trail leads a half mile into the marble formations of Crystal Cave, one of more than 275 caves that highlight the incredible yet little-known backcountry diversity of the park.

Archaeologists from Sequoia and Kings Canyon have found obsidian-flake spear points, rock-ring dwelling foundations, and stone bowl fragments—dated from 8,000 to 10,000 years ago. Obsidian spear points from the surrounding Sierras have routinely been dated to 13,000 years old.

More recently, the descendants of these ancient people include the Foothills Yokuts, Monache, and the Tübatulabal. Several languages and subtribes existed within these groups, whom 19th-century settlers collectively referred to as Paiute.

As the 1849 gold rush brought in tens of thousands of emigrants, they poked up most every drainage in the Sierras, carrying with them diseases that devastated Native Americans. The Great Flood of 1862, brought on by a month of continuous rain and snow in Southern California, caused local indigenes on both sides of the Sierra to starve. At the same time, on the eastern side of the Sierras, the Owens Valley Indian War—fought between the Paiute and ranchers with military support—eventually forced nearly a thousand Native Americans onto a reservation southwest of today's park. Today, the descendants of these former Sequoia–Kings Canyon people can be found scattered throughout the San Joaquin Valley. The park has preserved more than 500 Native American historical and archaeological sites.

Following these conflicts, mania with the big trees took hold. They were cut down for lumber or made into cane and candlestick souvenirs. The conservationist John Muir, who had first come to the area in the early 1870s, tried to protect what he called "a magnificent

Crowds gather around a mighty sequoia that loggers worked hard to fell. Early park proponents sought the protection of these trees from the lumber trade and other commercial interests.

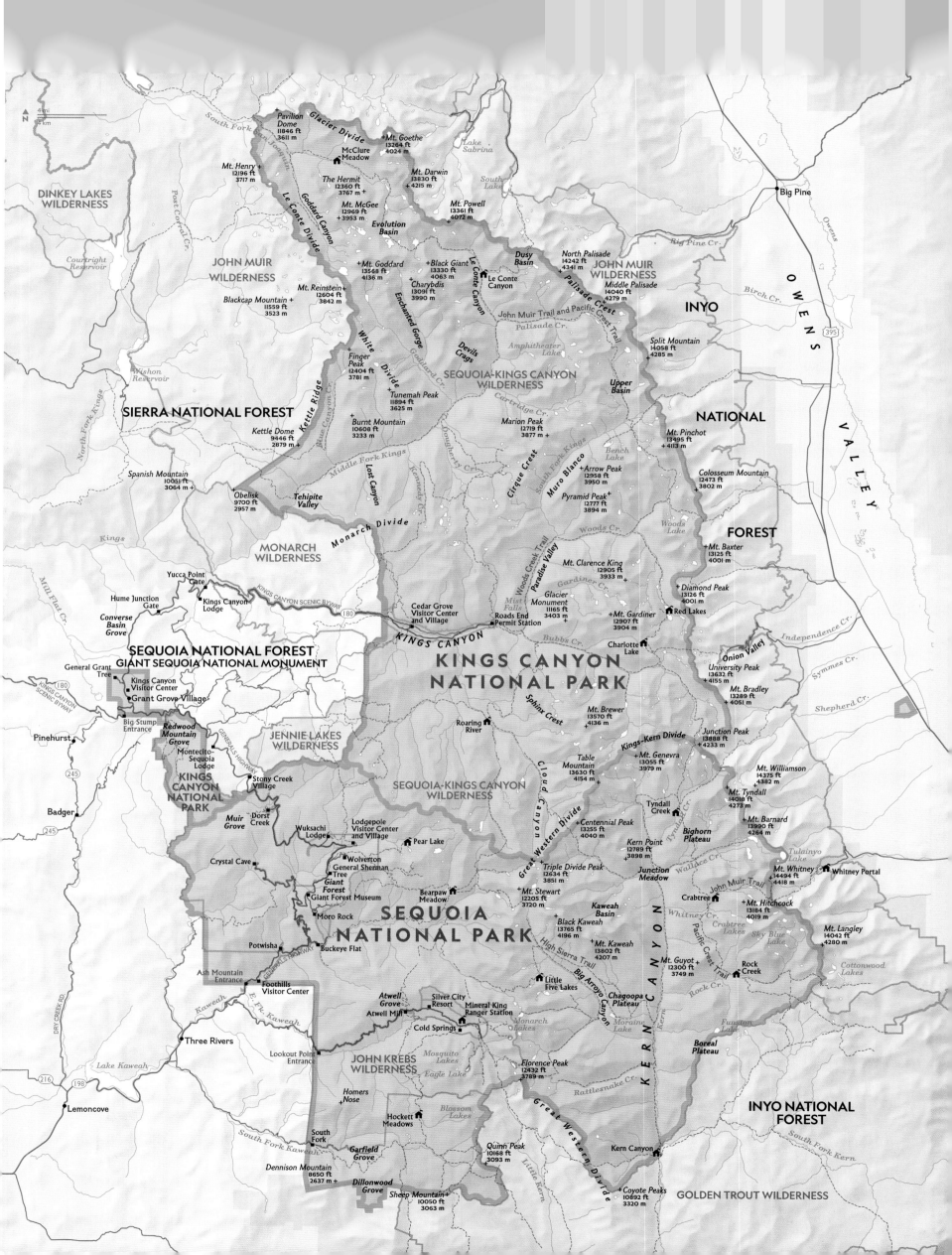

N 4 mi / 2 km

DINKEY LAKES
WILDERNESS

South Fork San Joaquin

Pavilion
Dome
11846 ft
3611 m

Glacier Divide

McClure
Meadow

+ Mt. Goethe
13264 ft
4024 m

Lake
Sabrina

Mt. Henry +
12196 ft
3717 m

Le Conte Divide

Goddard Canyon

The Hermit
12360 ft
3767 m

Mt. Darwin
13830 ft
+ 4215 m

South
Lake

Mt. McGee
12969 ft
+3953 m

Evolution
Basin

Mt. Powell
13361 ft
4072 m

Big Pine

JOHN MUIR
WILDERNESS

+ Mt. Goddard
13568 ft
4136 m

+ Black Giant
13330 ft
4063 m

Le Conte Canyon

Dusy
Basin

North Palisade
14242 ft
4341 m

JOHN MUIR
WILDERNESS

Le Conte Canyon

Middle Palisade
14040 ft
4279 m

INYO

Big Pine Cr.

Mt. Reinstein +
12604 ft
3842 m

Charybdis
13091 ft
3990 m

Le Conte
Canyon

Palisade Crest Trail

Blackcap Mountain +
11559 ft
3523 m

Enchanted Gorge

John Muir Trail and Pacific Crest Trail

Split Mountain
14058 ft
+ 4285 m

NATIONAL

Wishon
Reservoir

White
Divide

Finger
Peak
12404 ft
3781 m

Devils
Crags

Palisade Cr.

Amphitheater
Lake

SIERRA NATIONAL FOREST

Courtright
Reservoir

Post Corral Cr.

SEQUOIA-KINGS CANYON
WILDERNESS

Upper
Basin

Mt. Pinchot
13495 ft
+ 4113 m

Kettle Ridge

Kettle Dome
9446 ft
2879 m +

Tunemah Peak
11894 ft
3625 m

Cartridge Cr.

Marion Peak
12719 ft
3877 m +

Bench
Lake

Colosseum Mountain
12473 ft
3802 m

Blue Canyon Cr.

Burnt Mountain
10608 ft
3233 m

Goddard Cr.

Dougherty Cr.

South Fork Kings

Cirque Crest

Muro Blanco

+ Arrow Peak
12958 ft
3950 m

Spanish Mountain
10051 ft
3064 m +

Middle Fork Kings

Lost Canyon

Kennedy Cr.

Pyramid Peak +
12777 ft
3894 m

+ Obelisk
9700 ft
2957 m

Tehipite
Valley

Monarch Divide

Woods Cr.

Woods
Lake

FOREST

Kings

MONARCH
WILDERNESS

Paradise Valley

Mt. Clarence King
12905 ft
3933 m +

+ Mt. Baxter
13125 ft
4001 m

North Fork Kings

Woods Creek Trail

Gardiner Cr.

+ Diamond Peak
13126 ft
4001 m

Mill Flat Cr.

Yucca Point
Gate

Hume Junction
Gate

Kings Canyon
Lodge

KINGS CANYON SCENIC BYWAY

Cedar Grove
Visitor Center
and Village

180

Glacier
Monument
11165 ft
3403 m

Mist
Falls

Roads End
Permit Station

+ Mt. Gardiner
12907 ft
3904 m

Red Lakes

Independence Cr.

Converse
Basin
Grove

180
KINGS CANYON
SCENIC BYWAY

Roads End
Permit Station

Bubbs Cr.

Charlotte
Lake

Onion Valley

Symmes Cr.

SEQUOIA NATIONAL FOREST
GIANT SEQUOIA NATIONAL MONUMENT

KINGS CANYON

KINGS CANYON
NATIONAL
PARK

University Peak
13632 ft
+ 4155 m

Mt. Bradley
13289 ft
+ 4051 m

Shepherd Cr.

General Grant
Tree

Kings Canyon
Visitor Center

Grant Grove Village

Sphinx Crest

Mt. Brewer
13570 ft
4136 m

Junction Peak
13888 ft
+ 4233 m

Pinehurst

Big Stump
Entrance

Redwood
Mountain
Grove

JENNIE LAKES
WILDERNESS

GENERALS HIGHWAY

Roaring
River

Kings-Kern Divide

+ Mt. Genevra
13055 ft
3979 m

Mt. Williamson
14375 ft
4382 m

245

KINGS
CANYON
NATIONAL
PARK

Montecito-
Sequoia Lodge

Stony Creek
Village

Table
Mountain
13630 ft
4154 m

+ Mt. Tyndall
14018 ft
4273 m

Badger

245

Muir
Grove

Dorst
Creek

Wuksachi
Lodge

Lodgepole
Visitor Center
and Village

Pear Lake

SEQUOIA-KINGS CANYON
WILDERNESS

Cloud Canyon

+ Centennial Peak
13255 ft
4040 m

Tyndall
Creek

Bighorn
Plateau

+ Mt. Barnard
13990 ft
4264 m

Crystal Cave

Wolverton
General Sherman
Tree

Giant
Forest

Giant Forest Museum

Bearpaw
Meadow

Great Western Divide

Triple Divide Peak
12634 ft
3851 m

Kern Point
12789 ft
+ 3898 m

Junction
Meadow

Wallace Cr.

Tulainyo
Lake

Mt. Whitney
+ 14494 ft
4418 m

Whitney Portal

Moro Rock

+ Mt. Stewart
12205 ft
3720 m

Kaweah
Basin

Junction
Meadow

John Muir Trail

Crabtree

+ Mt. Hitchcock
13184 ft
4019 m

Crabtree
Lakes

SEQUOIA
NATIONAL PARK

Kaweah

+ Black Kaweah
13765 ft
4196 m

+ Mt. Kaweah
13802 ft
4207 m

Whitney Cr.

Pacific Crest Trail

Sky Blue
Lake

Mt. Langley
14042 ft
4280 m

Potwisha

GENERALS HIGHWAY

Buckeye Flat

High Sierra Trail

Big Arroyo Canyon

Mt. Guyot +
12300 ft
3749 m

Rock
Creek

Cottonwood
Lakes

Ash Mountain
Entrance

Foothills
Visitor Center

Little
Five Lakes

KERN CANYON

Rock Cr.

Atwell
Grove

Silver City
Resort

Mineral King
Ranger Station

Chagoopa
Plateau

Kaweah

Atwell Mill

Cold Springs

Monarch
Lakes

Moraine
Lake

Funston
Lakes

Three Rivers

Lookout Point
Entrance

JOHN KREBS
WILDERNESS

Mosquito
Lakes

Eagle Lake

Florence Peak
12432 ft
3789 m

Boreal
Plateau

E. Fk. Kaweah

Homers
Nose

Blossom
Lakes

Rattlesnake Cr.

Great Western Divide

INYO NATIONAL
FOREST

Lake Kaweah

216

198

DRY CREEK RD.

Hockett
Meadows

Quinn Peak
10168 ft
3093 m

Lemoncove

South Fork Kaweah

South
Fork

Garfield
Grove

Kern Canyon

Little Kern

South Fork Kern

Dennison Mountain
8650 ft
2637 m +

Dillonwood
Grove

Sheep Mountain +
10050 ft
3063 m

Great Western Divide

Coyote Peaks
10892 ft
3320 m

GOLDEN TROUT WILDERNESS

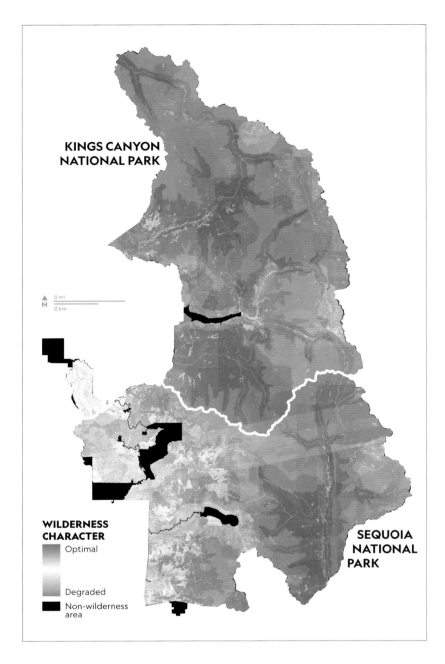

Wilderness makes up nearly 97 percent of Sequoia and Kings Canyon National Parks. This natural sanctuary borders wilderness in the Inyo, Sierra, and Sequoia National Forests—combined, these areas create the largest expanse of continuous wilderness in the state. On the map at left, blue indicates optimal wilderness quality and red depicts degraded quality.

sequoias and tripling the original size of Sequoia National Park (this act also created Yosemite National Park).

In this era preceding the National Park Service, the U.S. Army Cavalry was dispatched from San Francisco to manage these parks for the next two decades. In 1903, they built a wagon trail, which quickly drew huge crowds into the massive trees. In 1926, Sequoia was expanded yet again to include the western side of Mount Whitney and Kern Canyon.

In 1940, after decades of contentious debate between environmentalists, miners, and hydroelectric interests seeking to build dams in the river gorges, Congress created Kings Canyon National Park, signed into law by President Franklin D. Roosevelt. The new park

growth of giants grouped in pure temple groves" from the sawmills, and the lower-altitude plant life from "woolly lawnmowers" (as he nicknamed cattle and sheep). Despite his and California Senator John F. Miller's 1881 proposal to create a park, the bill failed to clear the committee. As Muir turned his energy to preserving Yosemite, loggers sharpened their saws and continued toppling sequoias by the grove.

A local newspaper editor, George Stewart, continued the preservation drumbeat, with the support of San Joaquin farmers who were concerned about how increased logging would affect their essential watershed. Fortunately, the brittle sequoia wood made poor lumber.

On September 25, 1890, Stewart and other proponents finally met with success: President William Henry Harrison signed the bill for Sequoia National Park. It was the first park to protect a living organism. A week later, Harrison signed another act that created the adjoining General Grant National Park, protecting another grove of

The General Sherman tree is one of the world's oldest trees and the largest measured by volume. Its base stretches 37 feet across, and its widest branch is a whopping 6.8 feet in diameter.

included the former acreage of General Grant National Park and protected more sequoias. During World War II, to save expenses, Sequoia and Kings Canyon National Parks were managed as one.

For many visitors, the beating heart of the park is the General Sherman tree—named, like leviathans in neighboring groves, for Civil War heroes. A half-mile walk on a paved trail in the Giant Forest puts viewers before this humbling tree. At 275 feet high, the

A slender, 250-mile-long corridor on the western slope of the Sierra Nevada is the giant sequoia's only natural habitat. All but eight of the 67 identified sequoia groves lie south of the Kings River. These southern groves usually hold more—and larger—trees. As shown in the elevation cross section, conditions that suit the tree's growth and reproduction exist in a narrow elevation range. The Sierra's eastern slope is too dry for sequoias, which need rain and the deep moisture of heavy snowmelt. The Giant Forest (bottom left map), a grove in Sequoia National Park, protects 41 named sequoias and sequoia groups, including the President (bottom right graphic) and, measuring only slightly bigger, Earth's most massive tree, the General Sherman.

sun-blocking crown spreads out over 100 feet. With its volume of over 52,000 cubic feet, it is the largest tree now living on Earth. It's also among the oldest trees on the planet, germinated over 2,700 years ago, and the widest, at 37 feet across.

Farther west, the General Grant tree falls just behind General Sherman in size. President Calvin Coolidge designated this enchanting giant the nation's Christmas tree in 1926, at the urging of local officials who held the first holiday program under the tree on Christmas day the year before. The tradition continues today with an annual holiday "Trek to the Tree," which is decorated with a wreath placed by park rangers.

Sequoias grow naturally only at elevations of 5,000 to 8,000 feet on the western slope of the California Sierras, within a 250-mile-long, nine-mile-wide corridor that stretches out of the park and into Yosemite. Sequoia–Kings Canyon has 40 groves, each holding a range of one to tens of thousands of sequoia trees, as well as a wealth of other tree species. The uniquely American tree has been

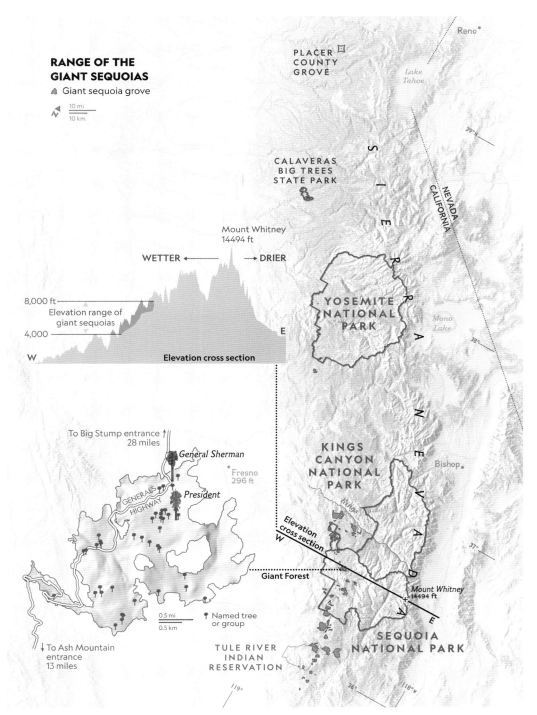

RANGE OF THE GIANT SEQUOIAS

🌲 Giant sequoia grove

10 mi / 10 km

WETTER ← → DRIER

Mount Whitney 14494 ft

8,000 ft — Elevation range of giant sequoias
4,000
W — Elevation cross section

PLACER COUNTY GROVE

Reno

Lake Tahoe

CALAVERAS BIG TREES STATE PARK

SIERRA NEVADA

NEVADA / CALIFORNIA

YOSEMITE NATIONAL PARK

Mono Lake

To Big Stump entrance 28 miles

General Sherman
Fresno 296 ft

GENERAL HIGHWAY
President

KINGS CANYON NATIONAL PARK

Bishop

Elevation cross section
W

Giant Forest

0.5 mi / 0.5 km

Named tree or group

To Ash Mountain entrance 13 miles

TULE RIVER INDIAN RESERVATION

Mount Whitney 14494 ft

SEQUOIA NATIONAL PARK

THE PRESIDENT
Sequoiadendron giganteum
HEIGHT: 247 ft
AGE: at least 3,200 years
DIAMETER AT BASE: 27 ft
TOTAL VOLUME: 54,000 cubic feet

Dead spire

Foliage removed on right to show limb structure

— 200 ft —

— 100 ft —

California white fir up to 247 ft

Ponderosa pine up to 267 ft

Pacific dogwood up to 75 ft

successfully transplanted to Australia and parts of Europe, though they will not naturally reseed outside of their native range.

Dependent on aquifers that are replenished by the deep Sierra winter snowpack, the giant trees need mild temperatures to thrive and attain bulks like the icons General Sherman or General Grant. Forest fires are essential to sequoia propagation. Scars in other Sequoia tree rings dating back 2,000 years show that fires have occurred every three to 35 years amid the groves. With fibrous bark up to three feet thick, the bigger trees are insulated and protected from intermediate-scale forest fires. Even burns that penetrate the bark and scar the inner tree can heal, scabbing over with new bark that insulates the trees from future fires.

Although fires burn away other competing undergrowth, sequoia seeds depend on mineral-rich soil for germination. About a hundred feet upward, more than 10,000, two-inch cones bear the seeds. After a half dozen years, the cones—which prosper in sunlight found near the treetops—will release 300,000 to 400,000 seeds. But if the forest hasn't burned and the seeds fall on duff rather than mineral soil, they won't germinate. Forest fires allow the cones to dry out and rain down their seeds onto a properly prepared, burned-duff forest floor below. Sequoia and Kings Canyon were the first western national parks to use prescribed burning to protect and ensure the rejuvenation and long-term survival of trees. This practice started in the 1960s and continues today to reduce hazardous fuel loads and to maintain a healthy forest.

Douglas squirrels also play an important role in sequoia reproduction: opening up the seed-bearing cones, chewing on the cone scales, and releasing the oat-size seeds to the ground. For the sequoia species to persist, one tree—over its couple-thousand-year life—has to produce just one mature offspring.

It's hard to gauge let alone appreciate the size of a sequoia, with its trunk wider than most city streets. Each year they expand their mass by approximately 40 cubic feet—the equivalent of a one-foot-wide, 50-foot-high tree—making them one of the faster-growing organisms in the world.

To date, aside from briefly shedding their needles during prolonged droughts, the trees have not been affected by changing climate or catastrophic fires sweeping the state. Still, the aged sequoias depend on groundwater from the snows to survive California's increasingly dry summers. If this comes in the form of rain rather than snow, the rapid runoff—as opposed to slow snowmelt releasing water throughout the summer—would be deleterious to younger trees. Consequently, university researchers have installed 16 research stations throughout the giant sequoia and redwood forest ranges to keep tabs on the precious giants as temperatures are expected to warm.

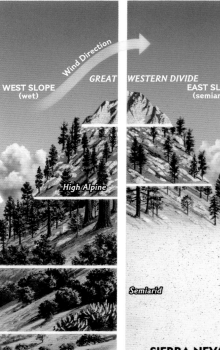

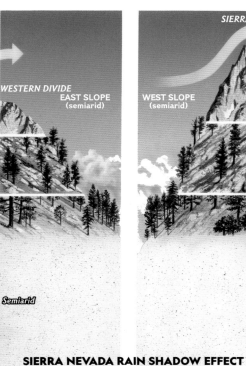

SIERRA NEVADA RAIN SHADOW EFFECT

LEFT: **This diagram,** which exaggerates mountain steepness for comparison purposes, shows the rain shadow effect on the Great Western Divide (left) and the Sierra Crest (right). As air moves from low to high elevations, it cools and expands, releasing moisture as precipitation. This precipitation feeds abundant vegetation west of the mountain, but little moisture remains when it reaches the east side. Once over the crest of the mountain, air warms and clouds disperse, leading to less rainfall.

OPPOSITE: **Sequoia National Park** may be known for its trees, but it also protects impressive geologic features like the granite dome known as Moro Rock, whose summit provides sweeping views.

A web of lush ecosystems covers the greatest vertical relief of any protected area in the contiguous United States. These varied ecosystems span from the Sierra Nevada foothills, which abound with oak woodlands and chaparral shrublands, to the alpine zone, which is home to approximately 600 vascular plant species.

SIERRA NEVADA ECOSYSTEMS

High Elevation ▢ Alpine
▢ Subalpine
Low Elevation ▢ Coniferous forest
▢ Canyons and foothills

5 mi
5 km
Approximate foreground scale

Kings National Wild and Scenic River

Kings

6589 ft
Grant Grove
Village

OWENS
395

SIERRA
NEVADA
CREST

OWENS VALLEY

KINGS CANYON NATIONAL PARK

John Muir Trail and Pacific Crest Trail

Kings Canyon

Cedar Grove Village
4635 ft

Kings–Kern Divide

Kings–Kaweah Divide

Lodgepole Village
6720 ft

Giant Forest Museum
6409 ft

SEQUOIA NATIONAL PARK

Foothills Visitor Center
1700 ft

Three Rivers

Kaweah

Lake Kaweah

GREAT WESTERN DIVIDE

Kern Canyon

Kern

Mt. Whitney
14494 ft

John Muir Trail

Pacific Crest Trail

Kern National Wild and Scenic River

High above the trees, in glaring high-altitude light, is a landscape of hanging valleys, waterfalls, cirques, glacial rock, and hundreds of small lakes all carved by ancient and departed glaciers. Snowfields and relatively new glaciers (created in the last millennium) cling to many of the loftiest peaks—though they are thinning from year to year. Scientists expect that continued warming conditions will melt most of this ice within several decades.

For now, the summer park is festooned with snowmelt streams—cold enough to make thirsty backpackers' teeth ache—as they roar down into canyons and gorges on either side of the Sierra Crest. In a 1910 *Out West* article, the historian Ernestine Winchell described the waters on a shimmering summer day in the northern park:

Across the river and below the dome Crown Creek races in sparkling cascades to grind a score of horrible pot-holes big enough to swallow a horse and rider; leaves that ferocious task to foam lightly down a cliff as Silver Spray Fall, whirls lazily in a pool at its foot, and then hurries to join Kings River in its journey to the desert.

Most of this water now runs into the agricultural San Joaquin River, and during increasingly rare wet years, joins the Sacramento River and empties into the Pacific.

The Sierra snowpack irrigates over 1,550 species of vascular plants in the park, along with over 350 different animal species, found in an amazing, 13,000-foot-plus elevation range. It begins at 1,300 feet with oak woodlands and chaparral-slicked foothills. These lower elevations slither with snakes and knock with the sound of acorn woodpeckers. Add to that the musky smells of both gray fox and skunks, plus the silence of elusive bobcats, and wandering black bears (the last grizzly amid the burgeoning populace of California was seen in the wilds of Sequoia and Kings National Parks a century ago).

In the more densely wooded montane forest—scented with both pine and cedar—are stealthy mountain lions and dozens of resident bird species, including the huge pileated woodpecker, the colorful western tanager, and flitting violet-green swallows and white-throated swifts.

Above 9,000 feet, the subalpine forest stretches to the 12,000-foot tree line, then up into the alpine zone with more than 600 different

---

Black bears range from the foothills to the high country, digging up roots and ripping apart logs foraging for food. Despite their name, they vary in color, from dark brown to blonde.

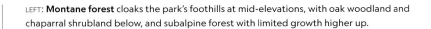

LEFT: **Montane forest** cloaks the park's foothills at mid-elevations, with oak woodland and chaparral shrubland below, and subalpine forest with limited growth higher up.

tering against scree and clambering into the safety of the crags.

Most of this terrain is seldom visited wilderness. Although the Giant Forest is easily accessible from the Generals Highway, no east-west road crosses either park. Beyond the sequoia groves, several days are needed to reach and then take in the vast, rugged splendor—from deep canyons to windswept peaks and all the quiet grandeur that lies between. ■

species of plants. Many of the smaller cushion plants—such as the oval-leaved buckwheat or the showy sky pilot plant—nestle close to the ground to avoid drying winds. Here the scream of the marmot might be heard along with the whistle of the pika. And thanks to recovery efforts, the bighorn sheep, endangered in the High Sierra but reintroduced to the park in 2014, can sometimes be heard clat-

RIGHT: **A scenic link** between Sequoia and Yosemite National Parks, the John Muir Trail was named after the legendary naturalist. Often referred to as the "Father of our National Parks," John Muir was instrumental in the creation of both parks.

BELOW: **The 211-mile John Muir Trail** winds through Yosemite Valley in Yosemite National Park, along the ridge of the Sierra Nevada, and to the summit of Mount Whitney in Sequoia National Park. Towering at 14,494 feet, Mount Whitney is the highest point in the conterminous United States.

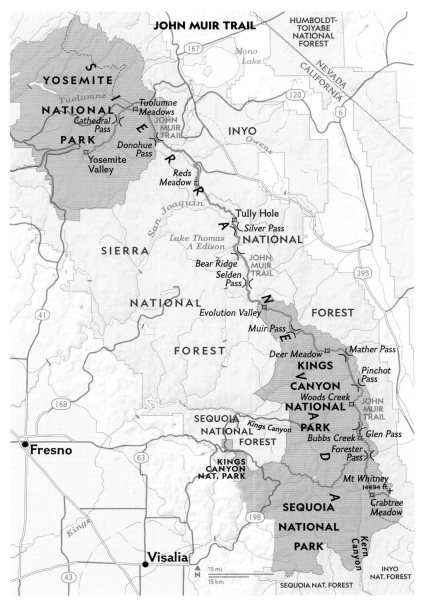

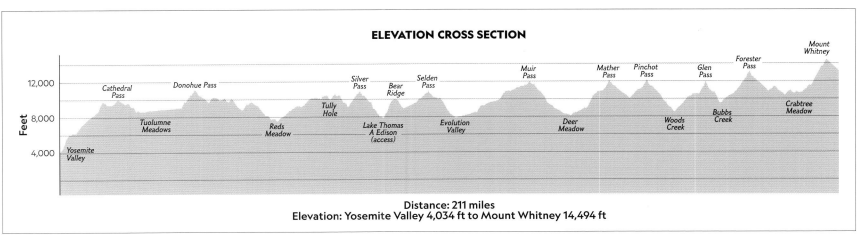

ELEVATION CROSS SECTION

Distance: 211 miles
Elevation: Yosemite Valley 4,034 ft to Mount Whitney 14,494 ft

▷ LOCATION **176 MILES SE OF SACRAMENTO, CALIFORNIA**

▷ SIZE **1,169 SQUARE MILES**

▷ HIGHEST POINT **MOUNT LYELL, 13,114 FEET**

▷ VISITORS **4,009,436 IN 2018**

▷ ESTABLISHED **1890**

YOSEMITE NATIONAL PARK

Amid the central Sierra Nevada, California harbors a park as big as the state of Rhode Island, but with 10 times the elevation range and a fraction of the pavement. Yosemite (yoh-SEM-i-tee) is one of the oldest and most popular national parks in America, but most of its annual four-million-plus visitors remain in the one-mile-wide, seven-mile-long Yosemite Valley, spanning less than one percent of the total park. Its Merced River—one of two designated Wild and Scenic Rivers, including the Tuolumne—winds lazily through meadows and pine forests dwarfed by the tallest and most challenging granite monolith in the world, El Capitan.

Yosemite has 1,600 miles of streams, thousands of ponds and lakes, 800 miles of hiking trails, and 214 miles of paved roadway. The 2,425-foot Yosemite Falls—a frothing white ribbon of snowmelt—is the tallest waterfall in California, but only one of many huge cascades concentrated in the valley.

Surrounding Yosemite, the Emigrant Wilderness, the Hoover Wilderness, the Ansel Adams Wilderness, and two national forests supplement nearly 95 percent of wilderness acreage designated within the park. Made a World Heritage site in 1984, Yosemite is

Seen from Yosemite's Tunnel View, this iconic shot of El Capitan, Bridalveil Fall, and Half Dome in the Yosemite Valley captures the park's indescribable grandeur.

internationally known for its dramatic topography, and more recently, it's gaining recognition for its biological diversity. Amid its glacial polished granite cliffs, sequoia groves, high mountains, flowered meadows, and expansive forests are a variety of rich habits supporting over 400 species of vertebrates.

Before white settlers arrived, resident Indians called their valley Ahwahnee ("big mouth"). Ahwahnee was inhabited for several thousand years, though humans may have visited the area as early as 10,000 years ago. More recently, tribes such as the peaceful Miwok visited the area to trade, but they were careful not to intrude on territory of the Ahwahneechee Paiute inhabiting the Central Valley, whom they referred to as Yo Semities, loosely translated to "grizzly bear"—possibly referring to the band's fierce warriors, or for other social reasons not known.

When miners began settling near the valley during the mid-19th-century California gold rush, food and resource competition—and tensions—escalated. "Motivated by plunder," according to Dr. Lafayette Bunnell's book *Discovery of the Yosemite,* the Ahwahneechee Paiute began killing white settlers. In 1851, Bunnell ventured into the valley with a volunteer army on a mission to end the murderous raids on settlers. The Mariposa Battalion became the first white men to record their impressions of the huge granite cliffs and waterfalls—though their discoveries were tarnished by brutality. Although both sides committed atrocities, the militia killed 23 Yo Semities and burned their food caches and teepee-shaped cedar-bark *umacha* houses. The captured Paiute Yo Semities, with their Chief Tenaya, were forced onto a reservation near Fresno.

Tenaya and some of his warriors fled the reservation the next year to return to their Yosemite home. But after robbing and killing several miners, Tenaya fled the valley with the military in pursuit. While hiding out with the Mono Paiute east of Yosemite, Tenaya and his men stole horses from their hosts and returned to Yosemite. The Mono Paiute gave chase. In the ensuing battle, depicted through conflicting reports, the Mono Paiute ran out of arrows and subdued the chief by throwing a rock at him, and then stoned him to death—as befitting Paiute custom. (The chief's name was later given to Tenaya Peak and Tenaya Lake below it, the jewel of the Yosemite National Park high country.)

After these conflicts, some Ahwahneechee eventually returned to the valley and settled in close communities, but by 1910, after the

A young Miwok girl and woman mind the fire by an *umacha* (cedar bark teepee) in the park. Life changed drastically for Yosemite's native people during the California gold rush in the 1840s.

BUFFALO SOLDIERS– AFRICAN-AMERICAN CAVALRY REGIMENTS CREATED BY CONGRESS IN 1866– WERE SOME OF THE PARK'S FIRST RANGERS.

park was created, most of the original Ahwahneechee population was dead or missing. Survivors from other neighboring tribes—including the Miwok—came to the area, where a better living could be made laboring, selling baskets, or performing dances. In 1920, the Indian village of Ahwahnee was built for tourists in Yosemite Valley. Its bark houses and other structures representing 19th-century Sierra Nevada Miwok culture remain, found today behind the Yosemite Museum. Seven years later, the rustic Ahwahnee Hotel was built on another original village site. (The

popular inn, now a national historic landmark, was renamed the Majestic Yosemite Hotel in 2016.)

The last Native American village in Yosemite was leveled in 1969; but more than half a century later, Wahhoga was revitalized with the construction of cedar-sided umachas and a roundhouse as the village's spiritual center. The American Indian Council of Mariposa County/ Southern Sierra Miwuk Nation elders have an agreement with the Park Service allowing the native community to use the site at will.

In the 1860s, the Mariposa Grove of Giant Sequoias in Wawona, another Native American encampment south of Yosemite Valley, began attracting tourists. A hotel was built, and eventually a carriage road was chopped through a 26-foot-wide, 234-foot-tall sequoia in what is today the southern portion of the park. For nearly a century, vehicles would continue traveling into the park by driving through the more the 2,100-year-old tree, which collapsed from a snow load in 1969.

As this extraordinary stretch of Earth gained attention, President Abraham Lincoln signed the Yosemite Grant Act that set aside 44

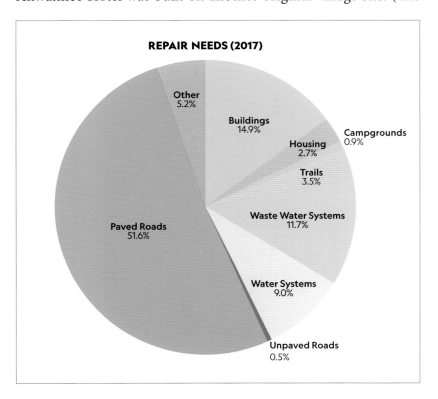

Budget constraints postponed more than $11 billion of critical repairs to roads, buildings, trails, water systems, and other facilities in the National Park System in 2017. Yosemite National Park has the highest deferred maintenance costs of any national park at $582,000,000, with paved roads making up half its repair needs.

Monarch butterflies alight on milkweed. John Muir described Yosemite's meadows as "so brightly enameled with flowers and butterflies that it may well be called a garden-meadow . . ."

square miles as federal land for public use and preservation. Although not a national park, the two protected areas—Yosemite Valley and the Mariposa Grove—laid the bureaucratic groundwork for creating the first national park, Yellowstone, eight years later. Three months after Lincoln signed the Grant Act, in September 1864, the California governor Frederick Low accepted the management of Yosemite from the federal government. That year, 147 tourists came to the state park. As California built and improved stagecoach roads, visitation steadily increased; by 1888, 4,000 tourists came to the park.

During this time, the naturalist John Muir fell under the spell of the Sierra Nevada's big trees and budding meadows. But while employed as a sheepherder and building a sawmill, Muir began to see how these activities—along with mining, logging, and tourism—impacted the land. So Muir used his gifts as a writer and an outspoken orator to help create a national park.

His first published story from California, however, had more to do with science than preservation. As conventional geologists of the day espoused the theory that cataclysmic events shaped Yosemite

In 1881, two brothers were paid $75 to widen a gap in the massive Wawona Tree in Mariposa Grove, creating a tunnel seven feet across, nine feet high, and 26 feet long that tourists could drive through. Eventually the tree fell during a winter storm in 1969.

Valley, Muir found glacial deposits and striations etched into the granite that showed how glaciation had slowly sculpted the valley. In 1871 he published "Yosemite Glaciers" in one of the nation's leading newspapers, the *New-York Tribune*. In his book *My First Summer in the Sierra,* he described the valley's "noble walls—sculptured into endless variety of domes and gables, spires and battlements and plain mural precipices—all a-tremble with the thunder tones of the falling water."

With the support of congressmen and the all-powerful Southern Pacific Railroad, on October 1, 1890, President Harrison signed a bill to create a park of 1,512 square miles (several hundred miles bigger than the modern park), not including the land already set aside in the Yosemite Valley and the Mariposa Grove Grant. The fine print referred to the land as a "reservation," which appeased development

ABOVE: **President Theodore Roosevelt** and park advocate John Muir admire the view from Glacier Point in Yosemite Valley in 1903, during a camping trip that would influence future conservation actions.

BELOW: **Yosemite boasts** myriad cascading waterfalls such as Bridalveil Fall, Horsetail Fall, Sentinel Falls, Ribbon Fall, and Yosemite Falls, one of the world's tallest waterfalls at 2,425 feet. The best time to view the falls is in the spring, with runoff peaking in May or June.

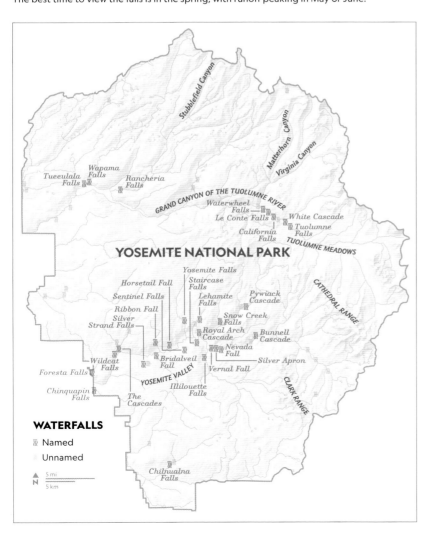

interests opposed to the creation of a national park and left wiggle room to readjust the boundaries by hundreds of square miles for mining, timber, and farm lands. Yosemite became America's third national park; the U.S. Army managed it.

But Muir—who began convincing officials to eliminate grazing from the park and continued his public campaigning by writing for such prestigious publications as *The Century Magazine*—still had work to do. In 1903, the future father of the national parks spent

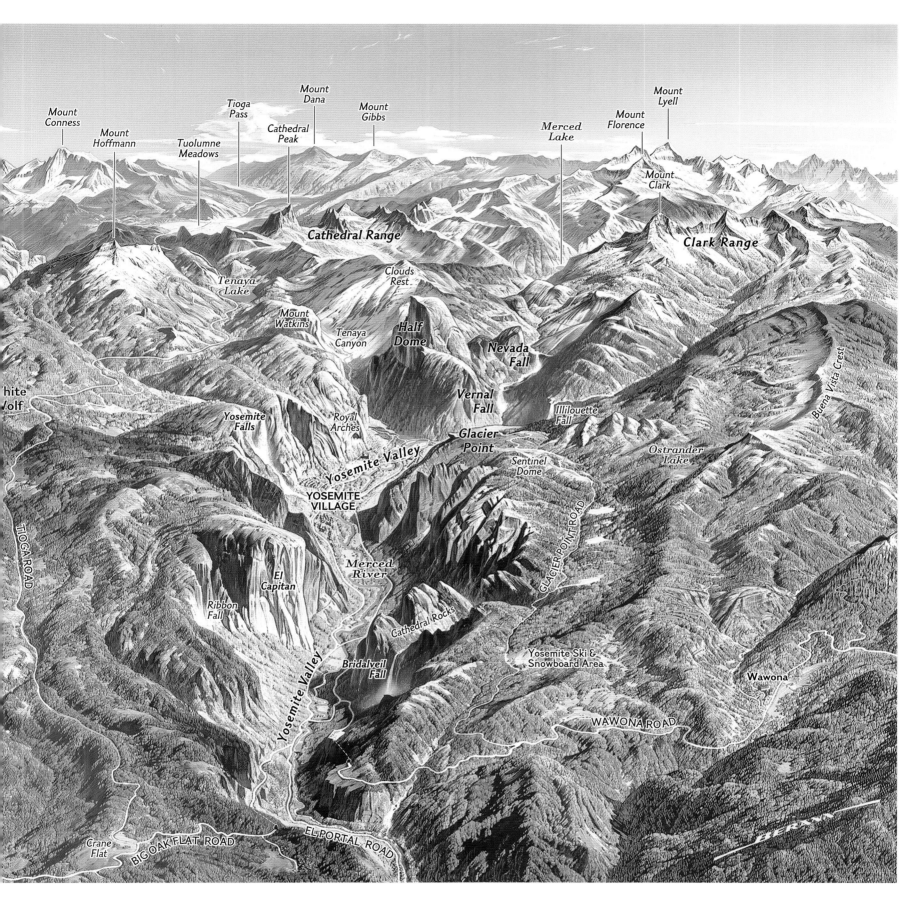

Mount Conness · Mount Hoffmann · Tioga Pass · Tuolumne Meadows · Mount Dana · Cathedral Peak · Mount Gibbs · Merced Lake · Mount Florence · Mount Lyell · Mount Clark

Cathedral Range · Clark Range

Tenaya Lake · Clouds Rest · Mount Watkins · Tenaya Canyon · Half Dome · Nevada Fall · Buena Vista Crest

hite Wolf · Yosemite Falls · Royal Arches · Vernal Fall · Illilouette Fall · Ostrander Lake

Glacier Point · Yosemite Valley · Sentinel Dome

YOSEMITE VILLAGE

TIOGA ROAD · El Capitan · Merced River · GLACIER POINT ROAD

Ribbon Fall · Cathedral Rocks · Yosemite Ski & Snowboard Area · Wawona

Yosemite Valley · Bridalveil Fall · WAWONA ROAD

Crane Flat · BIG OAK FLAT ROAD · EL PORTAL ROAD

BERANN

three days in Yosemite with the "conservation" president, Theodore Roosevelt—one of the most significant camping trips in conservation history. By trip's end, Muir had bent his younger and more impressionable companion's ear about the wonders of glaciers and mountains that the president had never been exposed to, convincing him to return the neglected Yosemite Valley and Mariposa Grove to federal protection. Three years later, under the authority of the newly created American Antiquities Act, Roosevelt signed a bill that

Renowned Austrian panoramist Heinrich Berann painted this vibrant illustration using artistic distortions to highlight Yosemite's awe-inspiring scenery. Berann widened Yosemite Valley and exaggerated iconic natural features, including Half Dome and El Capitan.

took back the grant lands from California and created a whole and relatively contiguous ecosystem.

THE PARK SERVICE ESTIMATES THAT THOUSANDS OF CLIMBERS COME TO THE PARK ANNUALLY, AND OF THOSE, UP TO 25 PARTIES REQUIRE EMERGENCY RESCUE.

From May through September, during the most comfortable months in Yosemite, it scarcely rains. High temperatures can reach 95°F (35°C), but it generally remains 20 degrees cooler. At night the temperatures stay above freezing. In winter, volatile storms often approach rapidly and stay for days, blanketing the higher elevations of the park with snow. Most of the rain—averaging 36.78 inches a year—comes in spring, when the waterfalls gush and the lower elevations turn lush and verdant.

With five major vegetation zones ranging through 11,000 feet of elevation, Yosemite has one of the largest intact habitat systems in California (by contrast, Sequoia and Kings Canyon National Parks' boundaries stop along the crest of the Sierra Nevada). The park has more than 160 rare plants and holds 20 percent of the state's total plant species. Along with three sequoia groves, Yosemite still holds over 300 square miles of old-growth forest surrounded by meadows.

The variety of habitats supports approximately 90 different mammals; 17 have special state or federal status due to declining populations or concern about their distribution. The most celebrated and photographed of all park mammals is the opportunistic and always hungry black bear—grizzlies haven't existed in California for more than a century, despite their prominence on the state flag. Like the grizzly, the black bear usually sports brown or even blonde fur. More than 300 roam the park, as well as more frequently seen mule deer, fox, and squirrels. Up high in northeastern Yosemite, lucky visitors might spot the endangered Sierra Nevada bighorn sheep, once again standing as white sentinels against the tawny precipice after more than a 100-year absence from the Cathedral Range.

Most visitors drive into Yosemite Valley from the west. The breathtaking Tunnel View shows the 3,000-foot sweep of El Capitan granite on the left, directly across the valley from the surging, 620-foot Bridalveil Fall, and the aptly named Half Dome in the distance. First climbed in 1875 by a barefoot local who slathered his feet in sticky pine pitch, Half Dome now has a cable-assisted route up its backside, hiked up by as many as 3,000 visitors a day. For most tourists, walking to and photographing the many waterfalls, bulging with spring runoff, is a principal draw in itself.

For a smaller subset of visitors, the smooth granite of Yosemite provides an irresistible call. Dr. Bunnell couldn't conceive of climbing El Capitan in 1851, but while passing it he wrote, "I felt like saluting, as I would some dignified acquaintance." Other men of his generation had to go sink their fingers into granite cracks, beginning in 1869 when Muir brazenly soloed up a technically difficult chimney to reach the top of Cathedral Peak.

CLIMBING MILESTONES

Pioneer era

1952	Climbers go to 400 feet to identify a ponderosa pine for the Park Service.
1958	First major ascent: Warren Harding and team climb the Nose in 47 days over a 12-month period.
1961	Second major ascent: The Salathé Wall is climbed in nine days by Royal Robbins, Tom Frost, and Chuck Pratt.
1964	First route on the Southeast Face: Royal Robbins, Yvon Chouinard, Tom Frost, and Chuck Pratt scale the North America Wall.
1968	First single-climber ascent: Royal Robbins spends nine days on the Muir Wall.

Clean climbing era (minimal permanent hardware)

1972	Five routes are created in one season, including Cosmos, the first established by a single climber.
1975	The Nose is climbed in less than 24 hours by Jim Bridwell, John Long, and Billy Westbay.

Free-climbing and speed-climbing era

1988	First free climb of a major route: Todd Skinner and Paul Piana scale the Salathé Wall.
1990	First climbing of two El Cap routes in one day: Dave Schultz and Peter Croft do the Nose and Salathé Wall.
1993	Lynn Hill becomes first to free climb the Nose. A year later she free climbs the route in 23 hours.
2010	A new route, the Prophet, is free climbed by Leo Houlding and Jason Pickles.
2015	Tommy Caldwell and Kevin Jorgeson become first to free climb the Dawn Wall.
2017	First free solo of a major route: Alex Honnold scales Freerider without safety gear or ropes in 3 hours, 56 minutes.

EL CAPITAN CLIMBING ROUTES

— Route named in timeline
— Other route

Thanksgiving Ledge

Alex Honnold became the first person to free solo El Capitan on June 3, 2017. He completed the Freerider route, with slight modifications, after spending a year choreographing thousands of precise moves.

Big wall climbing began in 1958 when a pioneering team led by Warren Harding spent 47 days over 16 months climbing the prominent prow up the middle of El Capitan. Before this date, an ascent of "the Nose" had been deemed impossible. Any means of making upward progress was acceptable: pulling on pitons driven into the cracks, or drilling bolts into the rock to take direct aid, rather than free-climbing with only the use of hands and feet while belayed by ropes. As Yosemite climbers upped worldwide standards, the new challenge lay in eliminating the time-consuming direct-aid techniques with rapid, free-climbing. "The valley" became renowned for its plethora of crack climbs, the polished domes of the Tolumne area, and many, long difficult free climbs.

El Capitan's 2,916 vertical feet of granite have made Yosemite an international proving ground for climbers for decades. Climbers spend months—even years—creating new routes up in order to top out. As gear and climbing styles have evolved, speed and the elimination of artificial aid have become the new frontier. On a peak-season day, 60 climbers might dot El Cap, many on the world-famous route, the Nose.

Among hundreds of other valley classic routes, the Nose remains a sought-after "tick" for rock climbers. In 1993, the American climber Lynn Hill became the first person to free-climb the route; the next year she came back and repeated it in a fast day. In 2017, the wunderkind American climber Alex Honnold performed the unthinkable on another difficult El Capitan route: a mind-blowing ropeless solo.

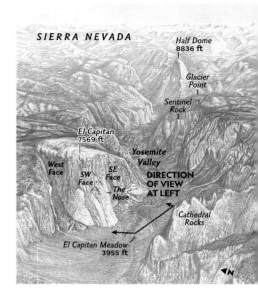

In summer 2018, during record-breaking fires throughout California, Yosemite National

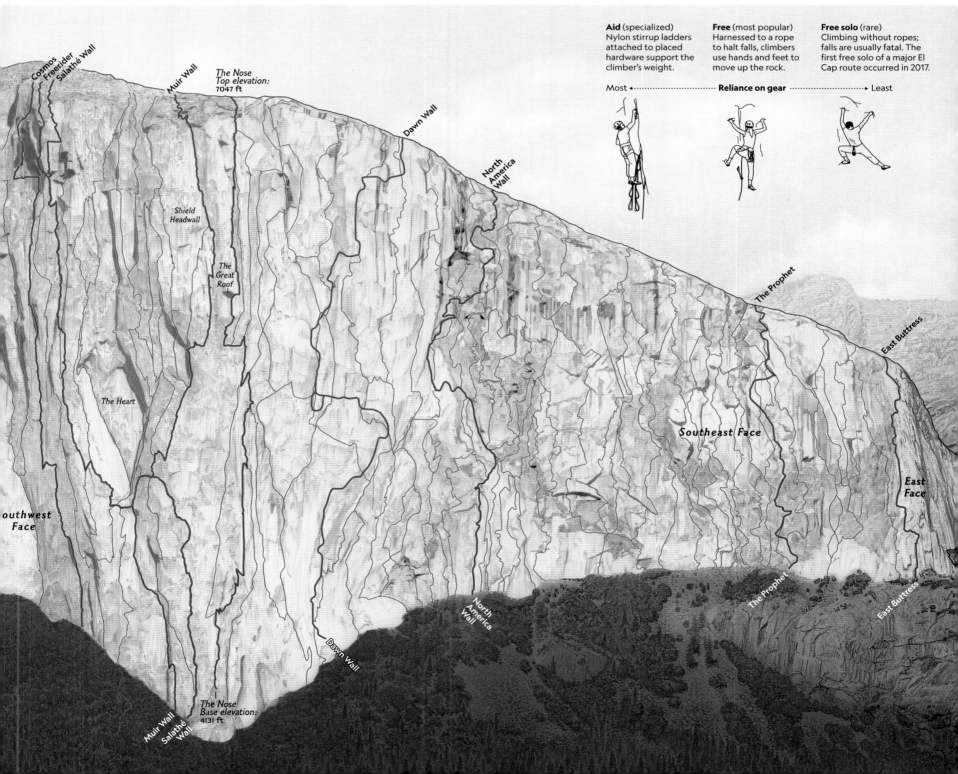

Aid (specialized)
Nylon stirrup ladders attached to placed hardware support the climber's weight.

Free (most popular)
Harnessed to a rope to halt falls, climbers use hands and feet to move up the rock.

Free solo (rare)
Climbing without ropes; falls are usually fatal. The first free solo of a major El Cap route occurred in 2017.

Most ←--------------- **Reliance on gear** ---------------→ Least

Park closed down from the 150-square-mile Ferguson Fire. To save the ancient sequoias, firefighters wrapped the bigger tree bases with reflective fireproof blankets, then dug away burnable duff and cut brush. The 200 trees of the Mariposa Grove and 20 giants of the Merced Grove escaped unscathed. During the 2013 Rim Fire that burned over 400 square miles in the northwestern park, crews saved the 25 trees of the Tuolumne Grove by setting backfires to ward off the main fire.

Before western settlement, lightning strikes regularly burned through at low intensities and cleared out undergrowth, or Native Americans deliberately lit fires—all of which kept more open space between the trees and limited flammable fuel, holding forest fires in check. Prior to the park's creation, an average of 16,000 of Yosemite's 748,000 acres may have burned under natural wildfires each year.

Today, almost a century of fighting and suppressing fires has altered the natural balance and led to overgrown and unhealthy, dense forests that are more vulnerable to catastrophic crown fires now seen throughout the west.

In 1970, with limited resources, the Park Service began lighting prescribed fires in Yosemite. Scheduling these fires depends on weather, air quality, and fuel conditions—let alone minimizing smoke in populated areas of the park. These fires are intentionally set to meet certain objectives, such as protecting sequoias or burning a section of forest that has become overgrown. In two of the three sequoia groves, the park's thinning of trees alongside the sequoias seems to have helped their reproduction. Although the prescribed burn program has not addressed the vast acreage of the whole park, it is but one way that the Park Service aims to protect Yosemite's natural order.

The spirit of environmental stewardship and reverence runs deep in Yosemite, cradle of the conservationist Sierra Club, founded in 1892. The original reading room and information center for Yosemite Valley survives today as the Yosemite Conservation Heritage Center, on the south side of the valley in old Yosemite Village. With front-porch views of Half Dome and Yosemite Falls, the building remains an educational center and focal point for Sierra Club members and park visitors.

Even eloquent park advocates like Muir knew that for the land's majesty to be understood, it just needed to be seen. As a charter member and first president of the Sierra Club, he imagined: "If people in general could be got into the woods, even for once, to hear the trees speak for themselves, all difficulties in the way of forest preservation would vanish." ■

BELOW, LEFT: **Fires were** a regular component of Yosemite's ecosystem for centuries. Yet in the 1850s, fire suppression became common, leading to overgrown, unhealthy forests. Aiming to rekindle the natural balance, the Park Service began restoring fires to Yosemite in the 1970s.

BELOW, RIGHT: **Several record-breaking fires** raged through California in 2018, including the Ferguson Fire. Started by a sparking vehicle on July 13, the fire spread southwest of Yosemite, burning nearly 100,000 acres. The smoke prompted park closures during peak tourism season.

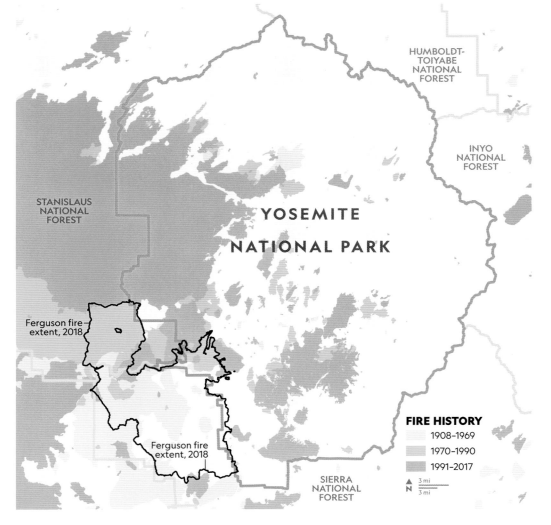

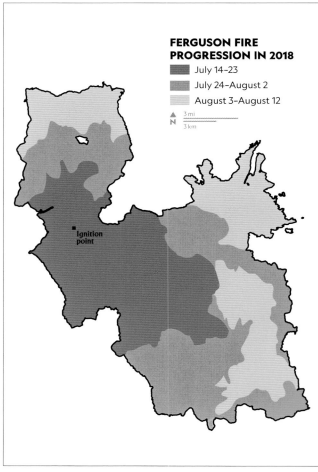

▷ LOCATION **85 MILES SE OF SEATTLE, WASHINGTON**

▷ SIZE **369 SQUARE MILES**

▷ HIGHEST POINT **MOUNT RAINIER, 14,410 FEET**

▷ VISITORS **1,518,491 IN 2018**

▷ ESTABLISHED **1899**

MOUNT RAINIER NATIONAL PARK

Neighboring Seattle and Tacoma share views—and debate ownership—of "the mountain" that looms on their horizon. Although the park lies more than 60 miles away from either city in western Washington State, the dazzlingly bright, icy volcano rises abruptly from the surrounding landscape as a reminder of wild beauty awaiting in the backyard.

Rainier has three major peaks—Liberty Cap, Point Success, and Columbia Crest, the summit. The highest mountain in Washington and the pinnacle of the Cascade Range, Rainier is subjected to Pacific Ocean storms that dump prodigious loads of snow and rain. Despite the inference of being *rain-ier,* the mountain was named in 1792 by explorer and captain George Vancouver, for his friend, Rear Adm. Peter Rainier. Still, 35 square miles of permanent snowfields and 25 glaciers make it the largest glaciated mountain in the contiguous United States. Mount Rainier is also the third most topographically prominent mountain in the United States, measuring 13,210 feet from its highest elevation to the lowest terrain surrounding it (only Denali and Mauna Kea exceed it by that measure). It served as a training ground for the first American ascent of Mount Everest in 1963.

Sunset on the Wilson and Nisqually Glaciers, two of 25 Mount Rainier glaciers seen during autumn above the Paradise area. The namesake mountain is the most topographically prominent peak in the lower 48.

The mountain is surrounded by meadows rife with wildflowers, innumerable streams, and 142 square miles of old-growth forest. In 1988, 97 percent of the park was designated as wilderness. The park's southern boundary abuts another 25 square miles of the Tatoosh Wilderness along with other national forests.

Mount Rainier was the first park built with a master architectural design plan. Eventually, the entire park was named a national historic landmark for its rustic-style buildings—a design approach that the Park Service adopted in the early 1900s. Colloquially called Parkitecture, the look would become a template throughout the national parks for simple designs utilizing pergola entrance gates, native stone, and artfully placed logs. As intended, the buildings of Rainier became accessories to the surrounding environment, reviving pioneer construction techniques that blended in with timeless nature.

As the ice age released its grip on the mid-elevations of the mountain 9,000 years ago, animals and plants began to flourish, and may have attracted the first hunter-gatherers. The earliest surefire evidence of humans in the park is a 4,000- to 5,800-year-old projectile point found below the mountain. In 1963, park archaeologists discovered a 1,200-year-old, seasonal rock shelter with stone tools and a fire pit containing charred deer, beaver, and goat.

The park did not support permanent dwelling sites. But until the 19th century, ancestors of the modern-day Puyallup, Nisqually, Squaxin Island, Cowlitz (Taidnapam), Yakama, and Muckleshoot tribes surrounding the area climbed to lower and mid-elevations on the mountain they called Takhoma ("mother of waters") to procure food or take spiritual journeys. To date, over 75 prehistoric sites have been identified with stone tool quarries, food-storage pits, short-term hunting camps, long-term base camps, kill areas, and butchering sites. All six local tribes maintain their spiritual connection to the mountain.

Opened in 1917, the Paradise Inn is an emblem of the rustic Parkitecture that Mount Rainier popularized within the National Park System, sparking debate about development in wilderness areas.

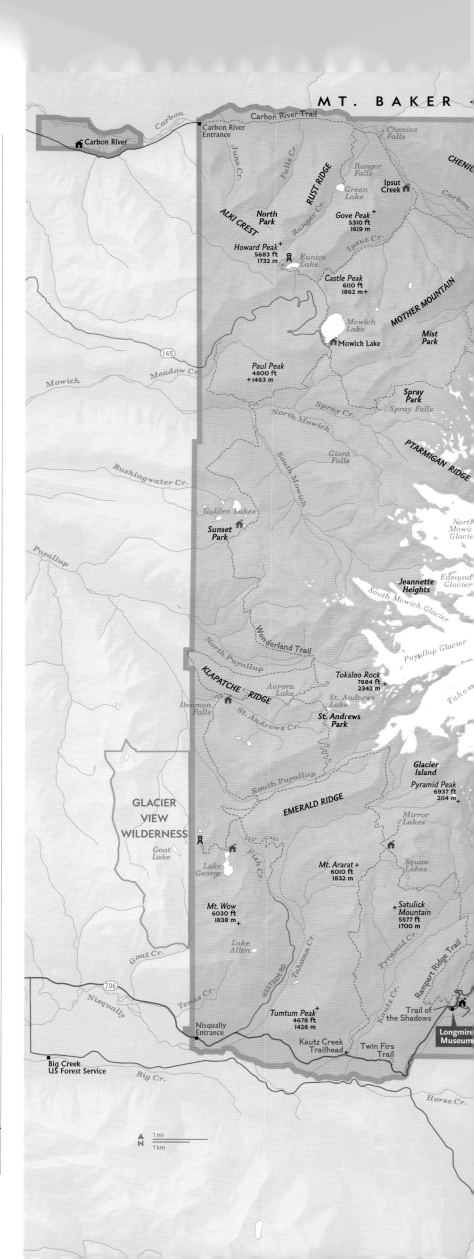

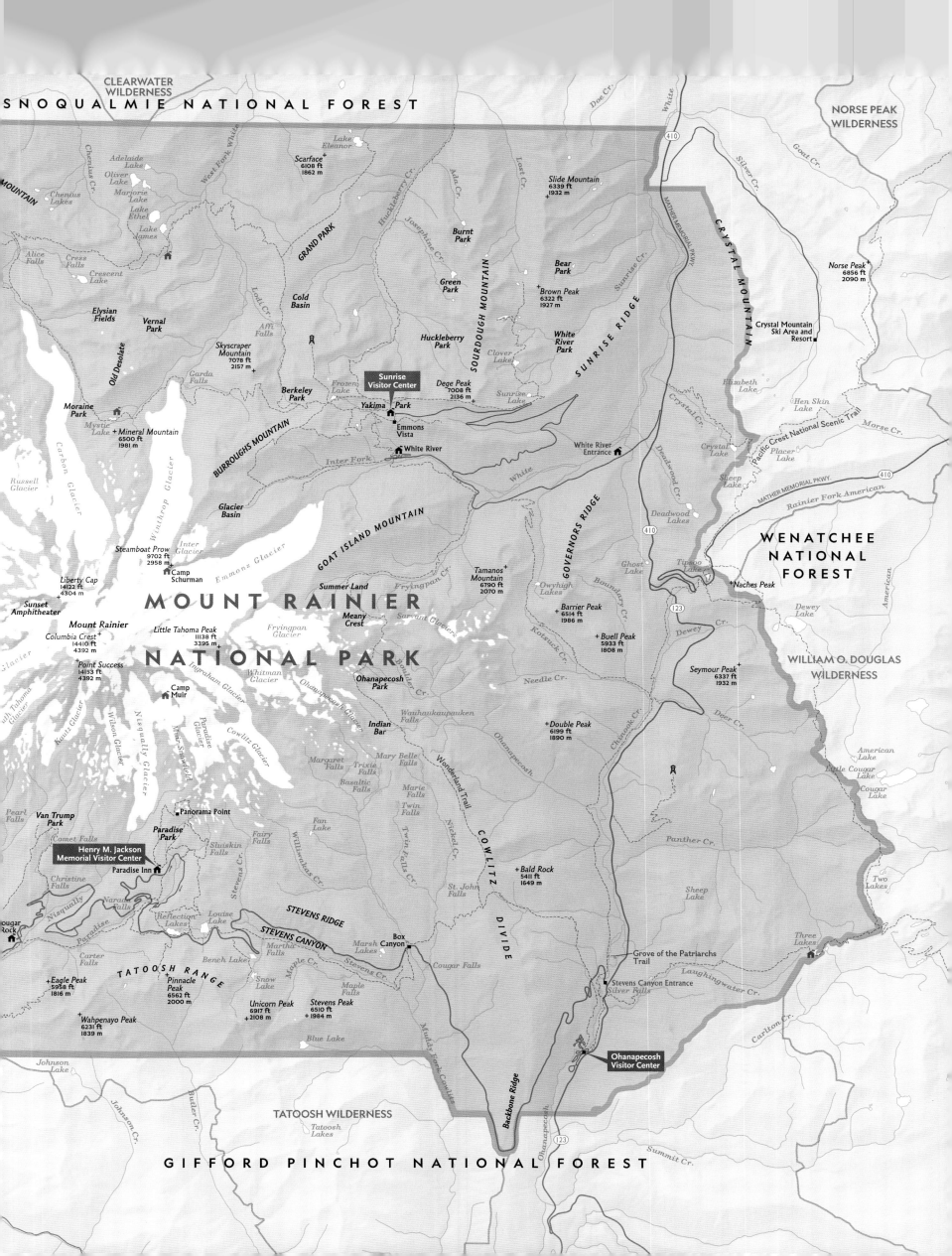

The Pacific Forest Reserve set up in 1893 covered most of Mount Rainier (omitting the western portion), but visionary conservationists like John Muir believed the mountain needed further protection. (The forest reserves, later renamed national forests, had a more utilitarian, multiple-use philosophy that allowed logging and grazing.) Muir began proposing the area be made into a national park after his 1888 climb that inspired his essay "An Ascent of Mount Rainier."

In 1897, the area was expanded and renamed the Mount Rainier Forest Reserve. Muir joined a local grassroots movement, involving the fledgling Sierra Club (of which he was the first president), to campaign for national park designation. In the half dozen bills floated to D.C. over the years, the onus was convincing Congress that the park wouldn't cost the taxpayers money. Then the boundaries had to show a park that wouldn't withhold mineral or timber resources from the national purse strings.

Also crucial to the park's creation was a statement of scientific value from the U.S. Geological Survey (USGS) and the influential scientists of the nascent National Geographic Society. So, in 1896, the renowned USGS scientist Israel Russell traversed the mountain; finding no minerals or potential for stock raising or agriculture, he wrote in *Scribner's Magazine* that natural parks allowed one to renew their health, breathe free air, and cultivate "the aesthetic sense that is awakened in every heart by an intimate acquaintance with nature in her finer moods." Equally important, Russell described Mount

In 1888, John Muir and most of his climbing party (attorney Daniel W. Bass, mountaineers P. B. Van Trump and Edward S. Ingraham, and teenager N. O. Booth) reached the summit of Mount Rainier.

TWENTY-FIVE MAJOR GLACIERS STRETCH ACROSS MOUNT RAINIER, COVERING APPROXIMATELY 35 SQUARE MILES OF THE VOLCANO.

Rainier as a place that would empower scientists by creating a laboratory for those studying geology, and volcanism in particular.

More support followed. Vermont senator George Edmunds said that the mountains he had visited in Switzerland couldn't compare to "this grand isolated mountain." Many mountaineers wrote articles or testified before Congress on the recreational values of a park that surrounded Mount Rainier.

By March 2, 1899—when President William McKinley signed the bill—Mount Rainier was a fait accompli, the nation's fifth national park and the last established in the 19th century. Its creation from a national forest (reserve) set a precedent for the new century: numer-

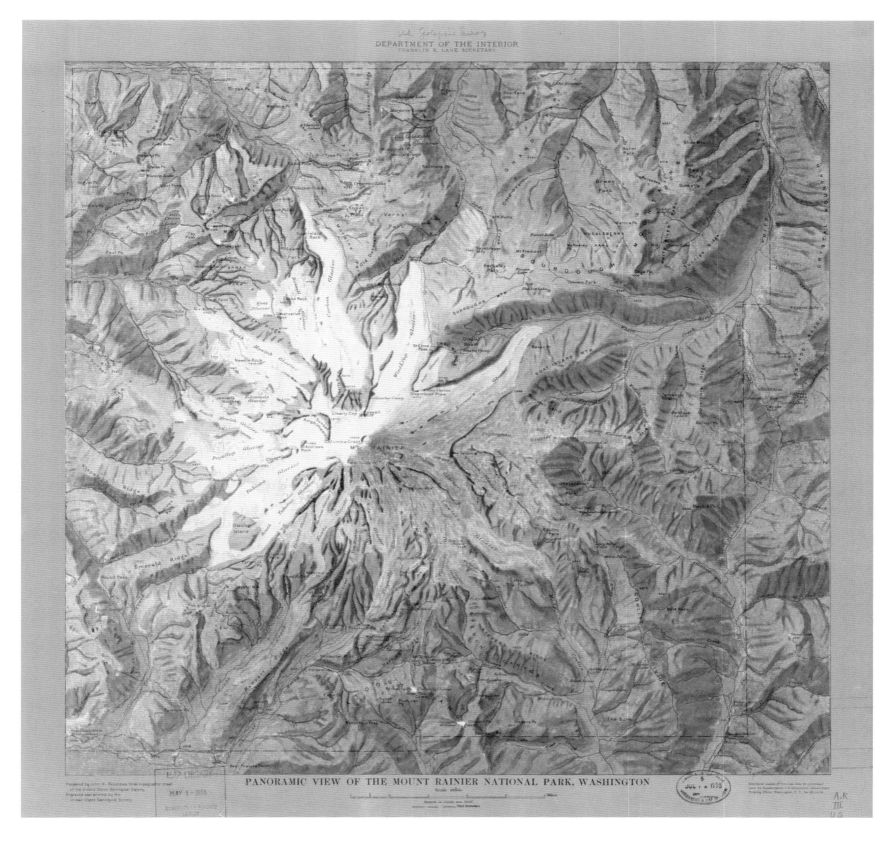

PANORAMIC VIEW OF THE MOUNT RAINIER NATIONAL PARK, WASHINGTON

Cartographer John H. Renshawe created this map of Mount Rainier around 1914, using spot heights to show relief and put the mountain's topography into perspective within the surrounding land.

ous national parks hewn from multiuse forest conservation lands and preserved, rather than managed for resource extraction. As popular as the Forest Service concept had become, Rainier bolstered the budding national park ideal of setting aside national treasures, without exploiting the resources, for present and future generations.

As with all Cascade Range volcanoes, subduction produced Mount Rainier when the dense Juan de Fuca plate first dove beneath North America 36 million years ago. But Rainier, along with its strato-

volcano neighbors, rose up like a sleeping giant in the last million years and repeatedly blew its top. The most pronounced eruption cycle ended only a thousand years ago. These explosive events accumulated enough lava to form the tall cone seen glowing roseate during sunsets from as far away as Vancouver, Canada, to the north and Corvallis, Oregon, to the south—both more than 170 miles away.

Although lava had built the mountain more than a thousand feet

higher than today's Columbia Crest, the summit cone blew apart during an eruption 5,600 years ago. In its wake, Rainier sported two large summit craters, seen by circling astronauts as dimples on the mountain's face. Over many millennia, volcanic mudflows, or lahars that were several hundred feet deep, reached as far as 60 miles away, to what is now Puget Sound.

In 1985, Colombia's Nevado del Ruiz, a similar stratovolcano, had a moderate eruption that generated little lava or poisonous gases. But its pyroclastic flows melted the glaciers and sent lahars rushing down riverbeds to the sleeping town of Armero 30 miles way, killing 20,000 people there, and another 3,000 in its path. Finally, it stopped in its tracks and congealed, 60 miles from the melted volcano.

In part because of the lack of disaster preparedness in Colombia, volcanoes hit the United Nations' map of awareness. In collaboration with other agencies, the USGS—vigilant since Russell's first survey in 1896—continues to monitor and study the dormant Rainier. They've learned that below the summit ice cap, an active thermal system has melted out a two-mile-long labyrinth of steam tunnels and caves, heated by magma beneath the volcano. Volcanic heat and gas combined with frozen soil and icy water to make the summit caves a compelling laboratory for extreme conditions that might have been seen on a much younger planet Earth.

The chemistry of the harsh caves also gives clues to the future of the volcano, which continues to signal that it's alive, if snoozing. Since the

last ice age, several dozen explosive eruptions have spread Rainier's pumice and ash across the state. Seattle residents last reported seeing small explosions on the summit in 1894. After Mount St. Helens, Mount Rainier is also the second most seismically active volcano in the region. Today, as the Juan de Fuca plate continues submarining beneath North America, the park experiences a score of small earthquakes each year.

Given the mountain's proximity to nearly four million residents, Mount Rainier is the country's most dangerous volcano—more for the threat of non-eruption debris flow than an eruption. Rainier's cubic mile of glaciers—equivalent to an ice cube with mile-wide sides—has all the ingredients to send a viscous locomotive of mud and debris toward Seattle.

Preparations—both visible and behind the scenes—are ongoing. Most of the surrounding towns along river valleys—such as Auburn, Washington, 40 miles away from Mount Rainier—are demarcated with blue Volcano Evacuation Route signs. And the mountain is now one of 16 UN-appointed Decade Volcanoes being closely watched, with teams analytically applying science and emergency management tactics to mitigate potential catastrophe.

For mountaineers paying attention to seismic and weather information and proper glacial travel techniques, summiting Mount Rainier

Picturesque Mount Rainier is one of the most hazardous volcanoes in North America. Below, the map shows areas that could be affected by debris flows, lahars (volcanic mudflows), lava flows, and pyroclastic flows (avalanches of hot rock and volcanic gases) in a future eruption. Approximately 80,000 people live in zones that lahars are capable of reaching.

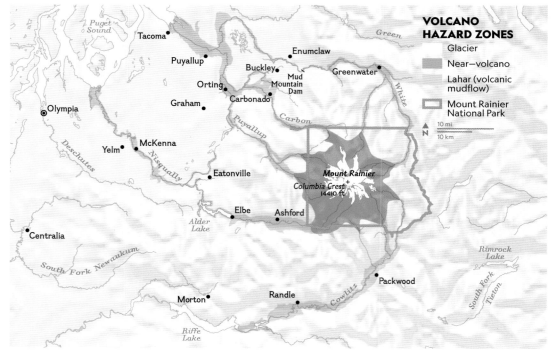

VOLCANO HAZARD ZONES

- Glacier
- Near–volcano
- Lahar (volcanic mudflow)
- Mount Rainier National Park

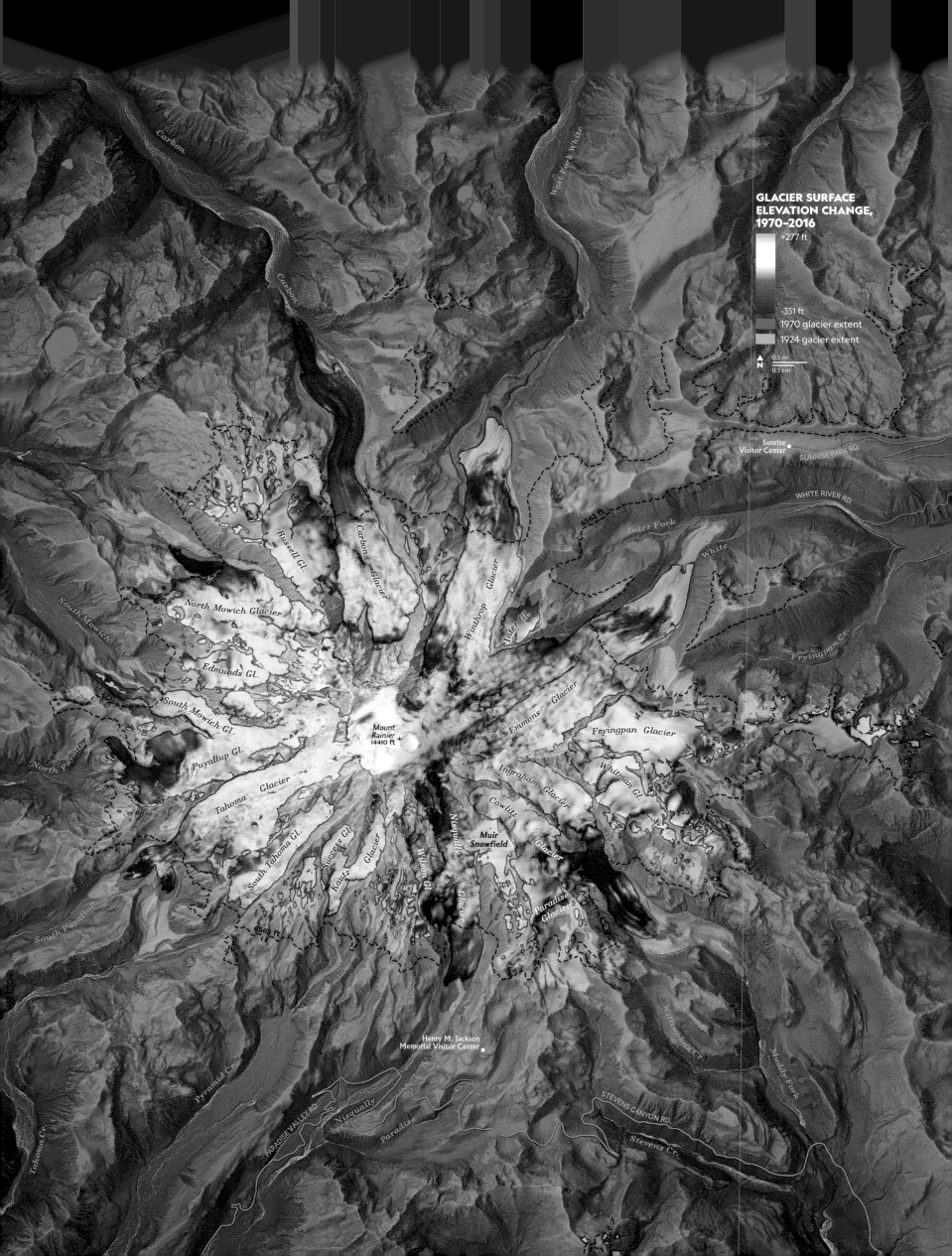

GLACIER SURFACE
ELEVATION CHANGE,
1970–2016

+277 ft

-351 ft
1970 glacier extent
1924 gacier extent

0.5 mi
N   0.5 km

Carbon

West Fork White

Carbon

Russell Gl.

Carbon Glacier

Winthrop Glacier

Inter Fork

6562 ft

White

Sunrise
Visitor Center

SUNRISE PARK RD

WHITE RIVER RD

North Mowich Glacier

Inter Gl.

South Mowich

Edmunds Gl.

Emmons Glacier

Fryingpan Cr.

South Mowich Gl.

Puyallup Gl.

Fryingpan Glacier

North Puyallup

Mount
Rainier
14410 ft

Ingraham Glacier

Whitman Gl.

Tahoma Glacier

Cowlitz

South Tahoma Gl.

Success Gl.

Kautz Glacier

Wilson Gl.

Nisqually Glacier

Muir
Snowfield

Glacier

Paradise
Glacier

South Puyallup

6562 ft

Pyramid Cr.

Henry M. Jackson
Memorial Visitor Center

Wellesakas Cr.

Muddy Fork

Tahoma Cr.

PARADISE VALLEY RD

Nisqually

Paradise

STEVENS CANYON RD

Stevens Cr.

is a reasonable objective. As the Pacific Northwest's dominant landmark, the mountain holds a magnetic attraction for beginners and experts alike. As many as 13,000 climbers—almost half of whom are guided—attempt the mountain each year, averaging a 50 percent success rate. Those who retreat are typically turned back by lack of conditioning, high winds, or approaching storms. An oft observed phenomenon on Rainier is the spectacular lenticular cloud cap. It hovers like a UFO over the summit, usually on fair days, foretelling a change in winds or weather.

The normal climbing route, Disappointment Cleaver, takes most mountaineers two or three days, including a 10,188-foot bivouac at Camp Muir. All the routes up Mount Rainier require technical skills for clambering up moderately steep and crevassed glaciers. On a good day, climbers need lots of sun lotion, UV glacier glasses, high-altitude acclimatization, patience, and the ability to put one foot in front of the other for hours on end.

The most popular destination in the park, as well as the common start to a Rainier climb, is at 5,400-foot-high Paradise—18 miles up to road's end on the southern side of the mountain. Winters there average 700 inches of snowfall a year; spring snowbanks can reach 20 feet high. Summer temperatures at the edge of tree line range from 70°F (21.1°C) to 30°F (−1.1°C), while summit temperatures rarely drop below 0°F (−17.7°C). In winter, when Paradise is popular with cross-country skiers and snowshoers—temperatures range from 30°F (1.1°C) to 0°F (−17.7°C). The summit can be as cold as minus 30°F (−34°C), not counting significantly colder windchill factors.

Whether returning from a climb, setting out on a trail, dining, or spending the night at the stately Paradise Inn (listed on the National Register of Historic Places), there are stunning panoramic views up and down the mountain at this hub—one of five developed areas in the park. Opened for business in 1917, the Paradise Inn was designed by a Tacoma architect utilizing seasoned logs cut from cedars killed by fire in the Silver Forest below; today it is still outfitted with forest-made furniture, stone fireplaces, a grand piano, and hundreds of dining guests nightly.

In 1931, the Park Service approved a strange and short-lived experiment next to the inn. Amid the rarefied air and scenic topography, a nine-hole golf course was built and advertised "to make profane golfers contemplative, and the contemplative golfers better men." But as the Great Depression caused a precipitous decline in visitors and falling snow quickly blanketed the greens, it closed down after only two months. (Today, Death Valley and Yosemite—among other parks—have 18-hole golf courses within their borders.) At Mount Rainier, pristine alpine meadows were deemed appropriate landscape.

The wildflower-bedecked meadows at Paradise and throughout the park are as sought after by botanists and photographers as the

summit is pursued by mountaineers. Late-summer snowmelts cause sudden, dramatic blooms of anemones, lilies, saxifrages, valerians, penstemons, harebells, hawkweeds, Indian paintbrushes, lupines, arnicas, monkey flowers, cinquefoils, larkspurs, shooting stars, and many others across a rainbow of colors. Even after frosts in late August, the meadows remain vivid thanks to seedpods and autumn foliage.

Three dozen trails wander more than 260 miles through the park, leading over streams milky with glacial till. Hiking trails through both forest and meadow are as advanced as the 93-mile-long Wonderland Trail circling the entire mountain—comprising a portion of the 2,650-mile-long Pacific Crest Trail from Mexico to Canada—or as simple day hikes.

Surprisingly, amid all of the glaciation above 7,000 feet, nearly three-fifths of the park is forested. Lower-elevation forests include fragrant stands of western red cedar, Douglas fir, and western hemlock. Higher up are noble and Pacific silver firs, Alaskan yellow cedar, and white pine.

Wandering the park, hikers, campers, and even drivers along the 147 miles of roads commonly encounter megafauna—reclusive elk, frequent black-tailed deer, foraging black bear, high-alpine mountain goats, and opportunistic coyotes—as well as innumerable smaller rodents. Even a short visit reveals that the wonders of Mount Rainier National Park extend for many miles below the icy volcano. ■

At lower elevations, the meadows that ring the icy mountain burst to life in spring and summer, producing stands of bright lupines among hundreds of other wildflower species.

▷ LOCATION **250 MILES SE OF PORTLAND, OREGON**

▷ SIZE **286 SQUARE MILES**

▷ HIGHEST POINT **MOUNT SCOTT, 8,929 FEET**

▷ VISITORS **720,659 IN 2018**

▷ ESTABLISHED **1902**

CRATER LAKE NATIONAL PARK

O n a crest of the Cascade Range in remote southwest Oregon, amid hills and forests, is a six-mile-wide, profoundly blue lake atop a dormant volcano. Crater Lake is the deepest lake in the United States, and among the deepest lakes in the world.

Unlike most lakes, its source water comes from only snow or rain, without sediments or minerals, making it one of the cleanest and clearest lakes in the world.

The lake lies in the caldera of Mount Mazama, once a 12,000-foot-tall volcano that erupted and collapsed—blowing nearly a mile off its top—more than 7,000 years ago. Since Native Americans witnessed the cataclysm that flung ash hundreds of miles, the event remains a revered myth among indigenous people and locals alike. It took centuries for the crater to fill with rain and snowmelt, surrounding two strangely shaped cinder cone islands jutting above the water.

Boat tours venture out on the lake, while a 33-mile road and 30 overlooks circle the rim of the caldera, 900 to 1,900 feet above the water. The scenic overlooks are welcome respite for summer cyclists who huff up and down Rim Drive's steep inclines, acclimating to thinner high-altitude air. Hikers favor the Rim Trail tracing the road

Rabbitbrush blooms above Crater Lake. Its waters are home to the rare Mazama newt, or water dog, found nowhere else in the world.

from Rim Village to Merriam Point along the western arc of the lake. During long winters, the annual snowfall average of 43 feet draws cross-country skiers and snowshoers to the lakeside—so long as the remaining open entrance roads are plowed. Snowmobiling is allowed only on the unplowed road from the North Entrance park boundary to the North Junction.

The lake itself occupies only 10 percent of the park, which is otherwise coated with volcanic debris and draped in old-growth forest—including 15 species of conifers—and etched with streams. The park's diverse vegetation and undisturbed habitat supports 50 mammal species, including significant populations of Roosevelt elk, pronghorn, black-tailed deer, coyotes, squirrels, chipmunks, and porcupines. Visitors in summer months occasionally see mountain lions, pine martens, weasels, and black bears. There are eight species of amphibians, including a rare newt found only in Crater Lake, and four species of reptiles. Crater Lake is Oregon's sole national park, 60 miles north of the California border and surrounded by national forests.

BOTTOM: **In the 1930s,** artist Paul Rockwood painted this north-facing perspective of Mount Mazama. Its eruption left a bowl-shaped depression that would later become Crater Lake.

BELOW: **The 12,000-foot Mount Mazama** formed from recurrent small volcanic eruptions occurring over 400,000 years (1). An eruption 7,700 years ago—the most violent in the mountain's history—blasted pumice and ash into the sky (2). When its magma chamber emptied, Mount Mazama couldn't support its weight, and the mountain collapsed on itself, forming a caldera (3). Over centuries, rain and snowfall filled the deep basin with water, forming Crater Lake as we know it today (4). It's likely that at some point in the future, Mount Mazama will erupt again (5).

Crater Lake's maximum depth—first measured using piano wire and a lead weight during a geologic survey in 1886—was 1,996 feet. The initial measure was later corrected to 1,943 feet during a 2000 geologic survey using a high-resolution acoustic mapping system.

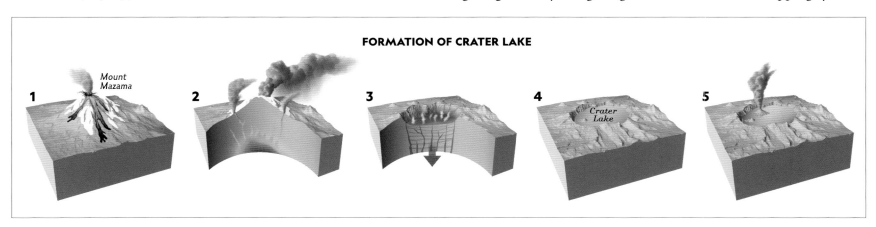

FORMATION OF CRATER LAKE

1 Mount Mazama 2 3 4 Crater Lake 5

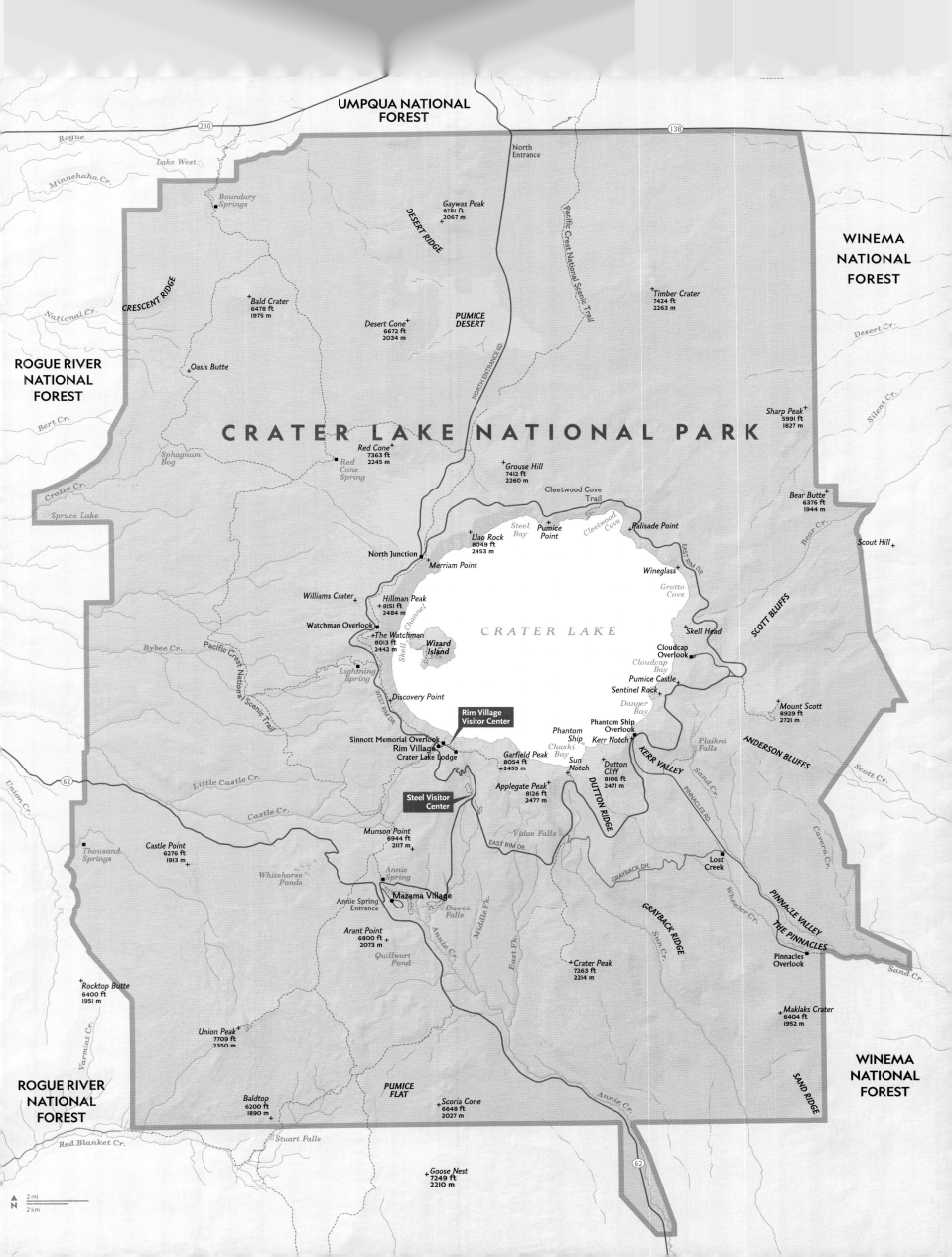

UMPQUA NATIONAL
FOREST

230   138

North
Entrance

WINEMA
NATIONAL
FOREST

*Boundary
Springs*

Gaywas Peak
6781 ft
2067 m

DESERT RIDGE

Timber Crater
7424 ft
2263 m

ROGUE RIVER
NATIONAL
FOREST

CRESCENT RIDGE

Bald Crater
6478 ft
1975 m

Desert Cone
6672 ft
2034 m

PUMICE
DESERT

Pacific Crest National Scenic Trail

NORTH ENTRANCE RD

Oasis Butte

Rogue

Minnehaha Cr.

Lake West

National Cr.

Desert Cr.

Sharp Peak
5991 ft
1827 m

CRATER LAKE NATIONAL PARK

Bert Cr.

*Sphagnum
Bog*

Red Cone
7363 ft
2245 m

*Red
Cone
Spring*

Grouse Hill
7412 ft
2260 m

Cleetwood Cove
Trail

Bear Butte
6376 ft
1944 m

Scout Hill

Crater Cr.

Spruce Lake

Llao Rock
8049 ft
2453 m

*Steel
Bay*

*Pumice
Point*

*Cleetwood
Cove*

Palisade Point

EAST RIM DR

Bear Cr.

SCOTT BLUFFS

Silent Cr.

North Junction

Merriam Point

Williams Crater

Hillman Peak
+8151 ft
2484 m

Wineglass

*Grotto
Cove*

Watchman Overlook

Bybee Cr.

The Watchman
8013 ft
2442 m

Pacific Crest National Scenic Trail

*Lightning
Spring*

Skell Channel

Discovery Point

*Wizard
Island*

CRATER LAKE

Skell Head

Cloudcap
Overlook

*Cloudcap
Bay*

Pumice Castle

Sentinel Rock

*Danger
Bay*

Mount Scott
8929 ft
2721 m

ANDERSON BLUFFS

Scott Cr.

WEST RIM DR

**Rim Village
Visitor Center**

Sinnott Memorial Overlook
Rim Village
Crater Lake Lodge

*Phantom
Ship*

Phantom Ship
Overlook

Kerr Notch

*Chaski
Bay*

*Sun
Notch*

Garfield Peak
8054 ft
+2455 m

*Dutton
Cliff*
8106 ft
2471 m

KERR VALLEY

*Plaikni
Falls*

PINNACLES RD

Cavern Cr.

62

**Steel Visitor
Center**

Little Castle Cr.

Applegate Peak
8126 ft
2477 m

DUTTON RIDGE

Castle Cr.

Castle Point
6276 ft
1913 m

*Thousand
Springs*

Munson Point
6944 ft
2117 m

Vidae Falls

EAST RIM DR

GRAYBACK DR

*Lost
Creek*

Sun Cr.

GRAYBACK RIDGE

Wheeler Cr.

PINNACLE VALLEY

THE PINNACLES

Union Cr.

*Whitehorse
Ponds*

*Annie
Spring*

Mazama Village

*Duwee
Falls*

Annie Spring
Entrance

Arant Point
6800 ft
2073 m

*Quillwort
Pond*

Annie Cr.

Middle Fk.

East Fk.

Crater Peak
7263 ft
2214 m

*Pinnacles
Overlook*

Sand Cr.

Maklaks Crater
6404 ft
1952 m

Rocktop Butte
6400 ft
1951 m

Varmint Cr.

Union Peak
7709 ft
2350 m

Baldtop
6200 ft
1890 m

PUMICE
FLAT

Scoria Cone
6648 ft
2027 m

Annie Cr.

SAND RIDGE

WINEMA
NATIONAL
FOREST

ROGUE RIVER
NATIONAL
FOREST

Red Blanket Cr.

Stuart Falls

Goose Nest
7249 ft
2210 m

62

2 mi

N

2 km

Referencing that depth against the surface elevation of 6,170 feet, the lake level is monitored daily. Isolated from rivers and streams, the freshwater rises and falls with changes in precipitation, seepage, and evaporation.

The near-symmetrical 4,000-foot-deep caldera cupping the lake water formed during the violent eruption and collapse of Mount Mazama, part of the chain of volcanoes that includes Mount St. Helens. Today the park grounds are still littered with two-inch bits of pumice, expelled into the sky from the top of the exploding volcano around 5700 B.C. The volcano's most destructive eruption fired pumice stones up to 30 miles away and leveled the landscape by filling in the valleys with debris. East of the volcano in the rain shadow of the Cascade Range, visitors' feet still kick through gray bits of granular and ashy guts of a mountain blown apart. Sparse forests, under 150 feet tall, show that low-nutrient volcanic soils cannot sustain large trees.

Crater Lake has four major forest zones inhabited by black bears, mountain lions, elk, and spotted owls. Entering the park, visitors see the scraggly ponderosa pine forest beginning at about 4,500 feet. At 5,000 feet, a vast lodgepole pine section spreads out with dense, scraggly stands of thin-trunked trees, sometimes referred to as a

NO STREAMS OR RIVERS FLOW IN OR OUT OF CRATER LAKE, REPLENISHED ONLY BY RAIN AND SNOW AS ONE OF THE WORLD'S CLEANEST BODIES OF WATER.

"dog's hair forest." The last tall trees, mountain hemlocks dominate above 6,000 feet with limited underbrush. At 7,500 feet, near the summits, more open groves of whitebark pine appear, through which one can view the park below.

Looking over the landscape, it's obvious, despite a volcanic past, that glaciers also groomed the region—moraine ridges where ice pushed up piles of solidified lava (igneous rock) bear evidence. Hikers commonly find glassy pieces of rock where cooling lava had been transfigured by glaciers, now long departed. On Mount Mazama's southern slopes, lava filled three large canyons.

After the caldera had been formed, the volcano continued to unleash smaller eruptions. These "burps" of magma created cinder cone formations that sealed up the caldera floor. Eventually, meltwater and precipitation surrounded or subsumed the cones. The largest one—named Wizard Island for its sorcerer's hat shape—extends about 750 feet above the surface at the western end of the lake. A hiking trail now leads from a dock up the forested slope to a crater summit, known as the Witch's Cauldron.

Although much of the surrounding landscape had been laid to waste during the eruption and nearby humans wouldn't have survived the blast, archaeologists have found sandals and other artifacts buried under volcanic detritus from 7,700 years ago. Subsequently, the mountain may have been used as a place for prayer or vision quests for the

LEFT: **Snowmelt feeds** approximately 120 miles of perennial streams and 70 miles of intermittent streams flowing from the sides of Mount Mazama, forming waterfalls like Vidae Falls.

OPPOSITE: **Trees up to** 800 years old inhabit Wizard Island, the cinder cone that rises some 750 feet out of Crater Lake and the volcanic equivalent of an iceberg only partially seen above the water.

ancient Makalak people and their modern-day Klamath descendants, who lived south of the volcano. Still, no evidence of dwellings existed where the park is today, before or after the eruption.

White prospectors climbed onto the caldera and laid eyes on the bluest water they had ever seen in 1853. Their writings about encounters with the indigenous people emphasize a common "fear" of the lake as a sacred "High Place" not for human eyes;

some locals didn't even acknowledge to the white men that the lake existed. One prospector wrote: "We learned from a medicine man that this place was looked upon as sacred, and death came to any Indian who gazed upon the lake." But such accounts fail to consider how the Native Americans' respect for the natural wonder might compel their reluctance to discuss it with outsiders. Or, a more pragmatic reason for their distance from the lake: the lack of fish and game, as well as the physical inconveniences of reaching it.

Volcanologists of the mid-19th century had not yet resolved how the caldera was formed, but the mythology the Native Americans

This bathymetric map reveals Crater Lake's depths, with darker blues showing deeper areas and lighter blues indicating shallower places. The lake's deepest point is 1,943 feet, making it among the deepest lakes in the world. Because its water comes from precipitation, it has had record-breaking clarity and is known for its pristine blueness.

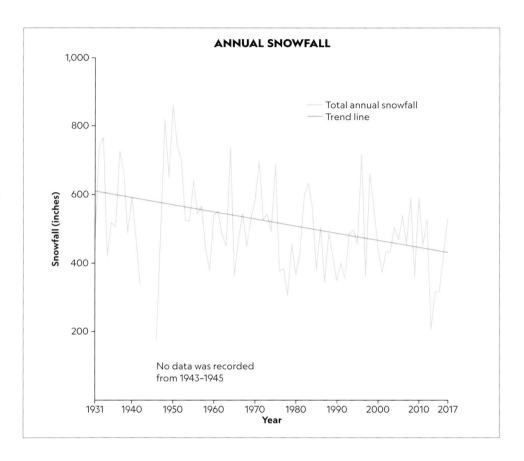

perpetuated would later be shown to have parallels with scientific theories of geologic occurrences. The creation story, variations of which had been passed down for generations, was recorded in 1865, when the Klamath Chief Lalek related it to William Colvig, a volunteer in the First Oregon Cavalry serving at Fort Klamath south of the lake. Decades before science showed how such volcanoes collapsed and formed craters, Lalek predicted that there would be later scientific discoveries that would confirm the ancient Native American explanation for Crater Lake's creation.

Meanwhile, tales of the enigmatic landmark had begun to circulate and stir interests farther afield. Crater Lake National Park's founding father, William Gladstone Steel read a newspaper article about its discovery as a Kansas schoolboy and became determined to see the lake. Fifteen years later, in 1885, he finally did. Its simple grandeur so inspired him that Steel dedicated himself to preserving it. "While standing on the rim of the lake . . . the thought occurred to me that at no point around this wonderful cauldron had the hand of man yet desecrated it with peanut stands or other marks of desolation and something should be done to forever save it for the people of this great country," he later reminisced in a speech at a National Parks Conference.

Salvation meant making the area a national park, which took Steel two decades to accomplish. He worked doggedly to spark public interest, get newspaper coverage, and lobby Congress until a bill finally made it to the House in 1902, and President Theodore Roosevelt personally intervened to pass the legislation. That same year, the president finally signed Crater Lake National Park into being.

Another fruit of Steel's campaigning for the Cascades is the name Mount Mazama. In 1896, he suggested that the U.S. Geological Survey (USGS) name the volcano after his climbing club the Mazamas. But the Klamath had long called Crater Lake and the surrounding mountain Giiwas ("sacred place"; Steel used the Aztec word *mazamas,* thinking that it meant mountain goats, but it actually translates as the plural of "small deer"). Today the Park Service respectfully asks its visitors to honor the sanctity of the volcano. The Crater Lake Visitor Center shares a Klamath origin story of Giiwas:

The spirit of the mountain was called Chief of the Below World (Llao). The spirit of the sky was called Chief of the Above World (Skell). Sometimes Llao came up from his home inside the earth and stood on top of [Giiwas], one of the highest mountains in the region. During one of these visits, he saw the Makalak chief's beautiful daughter and fell in love with her. He promised her eternal life if she would return with him to his lodge below the mountain. When she refused, he became angry and declared that he would destroy her people with fire. In his rage, he rushed up through the opening of his mountain and stood on top of it and began to hurl fire down upon them.

A Klamath man gazes over the lake while posing for a photo in the early 1920s. The Klamath revered the sacred Mount Mazama as Giiwas, which remains a powerful spiritual place.

BEFORE A NEWSPAPER EDITOR POPULARIZED THE CRATER LAKE NAME IN 1869, EARLY ONLOOKERS HAD ALSO SUGGESTED BLUE LAKE AND LAKE MAJESTY, AMONG OTHER APPELLATIONS.

The mighty Skell took pity on the people and stood atop Mount Shasta [120 miles south] to defend them. From their mountaintops, the two chiefs waged a furious battle. They hurled red-hot rocks as large as hills. They made the earth tremble and caused great landslides of fire. The people fled in terror to the waters of Klamath Lake [30 miles south].

Two holy men offered to sacrifice themselves by jumping into the pit of fire on top of Llao's mountain. Skell was moved by their bravery and drove Llao back into Giiwas. When the sun rose next, the great mountain was gone. It had fallen in on Llao. All that remained was a large hole. Rain fell in torrents, filling the hole with water.

A single trail down the steep-sided caldera into Cleetwood Cove allows visitors to investigate the jewel blue lake more closely. Although swimming is allowed from the cove, most people are content to dip in a toe and realize that, for most of the year, Crater Lake is shockingly cold. (Except it's not as cold or snowy as it used to be—the lake's width has not frozen since 1949.)

Measured by decades since the 1930s, average snowfalls have steadily dropped from 614 inches to 455 inches (during the 2000s). As for the lake, the Park Service has monitored its temperatures since 1965. In the ensuing half century, the average summer surface water temperature has increased by 5°F (2.8°C). Swimmers can now take advantage of the lake during the heat of summer when it gets as warm as 65°F (18°C), but warm surface water doesn't mix as readily with the cold water below it; few stay in for more than a few strokes. By late October, periods of rain and snow begin, and with the exception of boat tours, most visitors avoid time on the lake.

The water's phenomenal blueness has nonetheless dazzled visitors for generations. The blueness comes from the water clarity—due partly to the lack of suspended particles coming in from source streams—and its great depth. In 1972, Crater Lake's Secchi disk measurement (a technique of lowering a black-and-white disk in the water until it is no longer visible) set a North American lake record for clarity of 144 feet—doubling the clarity of most lakes.

Its clearness also comes from a dynamic mixing of water caused by temperature and density differentials between the surface and lower depths, as well as days-long storms that bring winds. Most winters, the resultant mixing of water brings nutrients off the bottom of the lake. But researchers from the USGS, the Park Service, and the University of Trento speculate, based on different climate change scenarios, that continued warming temperatures could stop the mixing for several years. This would lead to a buildup of organic nutrients on the lake bottom, potentially causing algae blooms when the nutrients are finally brought to the surface—dulling the lake's incredible blueness and its record clarity.

OPPOSITE: **The hundreds of pinnacles** rising from Sand Creek Canyon started as ancient volcanic vents, where rising heat hardened ash into spires later revealed by erosion.

RIGHT: **A swimmer** braves Crater Lake's chilly waters, leaping from Cleetwood Cove, the only water access, open as weather allows—usually from late June to September.

Kerr Valley

Dutton Cliff

Applegate
Peak

Garfield Peak

Sun
Notch

Phantom Ship

Crater Lake

Crater Lake
Lodge

Starting near the Crater Lake Lodge, the 1.8-mile hike to Garfield Peak (one way) winds up a ridgeline with an elevation gain of just over 1,000 feet, providing spectacular views of Crater Lake below. To reach the summit, hikers ascend through hemlocks and red fir trees into whitebark pines and subalpine firs.

researchers tied it to shore but severe storms stopped their work until they let "him" float free again. The tree, according to park naturalists, "swims" over three miles a day across the lake. Rangers believe that Crater Lake's cold and nearly sterile water have preserved the tree, while the higher density of the submerged roots keeps it balanced and upright.

Crater Lake—long a mythical place for the Klamath—has other apparitions that can make even skeptical visitors sit upright. Best known are the repeated reports of ghostly fires or lights seen at night on the uninhabited Wizard Island. At least one ranger has sought to put out what she thought, from a distance, was an illegal campfire, which disappeared upon her arrival. The Klamath attribute such sightings to Llao, the spirit from the underworld, who briefly arises to hurl fire from Giiwas.

Over several months in 1945, credible witnesses, including the park superintendent, repeatedly saw clouds rise from the lake and disappear, despite the lack of any apparent volcanic activity. An unusual number of bigfoot and UFO sightings—along with a report of a monster swimming beneath a visitor's boat—have also been reported in the park.

It is fact that the lake has no native fish, but from 1888 to 1941, it was stocked with trout and salmon. Unlike most parks, there are no limits or licenses required to catch and remove the plentiful rainbow trout and kokanee salmon (using artificial lures only). Elsewhere in the many streams of the park, are four species of trout, including the only native non-introduced Dolly Vardens, rainbows, brooks (the most abundant fish), and browns. Reptiles include different subspecies of garter snake and the commonly found lizard of the West, the three-inch-long sagebrush lizard. Among the eight different amphibians are the abundant Cascade frogs, the Pacific tree frog, the tailed frog, the long-toed salamander, and the western toad.

Rarest of the amphibians, the park is also home to the Mazama (or Crater Lake) newt, or waterdog, found nowhere else in the world. The newt used to cluster by the hundreds near the Crater Lake shorelines, but beginning in 2008, the masses were reduced by a predatory crayfish that began thriving in the warming lake. Researchers

Over past decades, researchers have been stumped about exactly where Crater Lake water flows. Because precipitation more than doubles the lake's evaporation, approximately two million gallons of water an hour seep through the lower caldera walls. No other outside water sources have yet been found that carry the water, so it's presumed that the lake resurfaces in nearby rivers through aquifers.

Yet another phenomenon is a 450-year-old hemlock tree called the Old Man, which can be seen bobbing unanchored and always upright in Crater Lake, seemingly defying the laws of physics since it was first seen floating about the lake in 1896. Legend holds that the Old Man can even control the weather: At one point lake

call the crayfish the perfect invaders because of their appetite for small fish and newts. The park has begun removing them by the thousands, but thus far, their numbers remain unchecked, the intruders still darting in the shallows along the shoreline.

Along with the steep 1.1-mile climb from the lake up to the rim on the Cleetwood Cove Trail, there are 90 miles of hiking trails. Treks up Mount Scott, the park's highest peak, or Garfield Peak offer bird's-eye views of the round lake and its crater. Otherwise, the park's short-length trails are easy or moderate, with the exception of the Pacific Crest National Scenic Trail. In its 2,650-mile length, the trail builders deliberately routed up to the Crater Lake rim so that thru-hikers would not miss this park—one of the most memorable splendors between Canada and Mexico. ◼

CRATER LAKE IS FAMOUS FOR ITS STORIES OF FLOATING TREES THAT AFFECT THE WEATHER, EERIE CAMPFIRE SIGHTINGS, UFO REPORTS, AND MISSING PERSONS.

Sunlight spills into clouds hanging over Mount Scott, the park's highest peak. At the summit, hikers can find astounding views of the lake—though it too is often covered by clouds.

▷ LOCATION **92 MILES W OF SEATTLE, WASHINGTON**

▷ SIZE **1,441 SQUARE MILES**

▷ HIGHEST POINT **MOUNT OLYMPUS, 7,980 FEET**

▷ VISITORS **3,104,455 IN 2018**

▷ ESTABLISHED **1938**

OLYMPIC NATIONAL PARK

dging the Pacific Ocean, 20 miles from Canada on western Washington's Olympic Peninsula, Olympic National Park is a landscape of startling contrasts: surf-beaten beaches, lush rainforests, glaciated peaks, and a drier eastern slope all united in its boundaries. The wild park is 100 square miles larger than the urbanized peninsula of Cape Cod but encircled by a national forest, with many ocean-side valleys that are wetter than any park in the continental United States.

Due to its pristine nature, including animal and plant species found nowhere else on the planet and the largest remaining temperate rainforest in the Pacific Northwest, UNESCO designated the park an international biosphere reserve in 1976. Deeming it unmatched in the world and the best natural area in the entire Pacific Northwest, UNESCO also chose it as a World Heritage site in 1981—for "outstanding examples of ongoing evolution and superlative natural phenomena."

Navigating the park's rich ecosystems are over 600 miles of trails. These footpaths climb alongside a dozen boisterous rivers raging off snowy peaks and roaring toward the ocean, through breathtaking terrain and abundant wildlife. One of the champions of the park and

Tidal pools blush with color at sunset on Shi Shi Beach. Accessible by a day hike, it's a popular spot for summer beachgoers and campers along the 70-plus-mile Wilderness Coast.

Stretching between towering Mount Olympus and the Pacific Ocean, the Olympic Mountains are an impressive string of icy peaks, most of which are protected within the park.

its backcountry, the Supreme Court Justice William O. Douglas, staged a media-intensive beach hike in 1958, during a protest that prevented new road construction from defiling the wild coast. "To be whole and harmonious, man must also know the music of the beaches and the woods," he wrote. "He must find the thing of which he is only an infinitesimal part and nurture it and love it, if he is to live."

The Olympic Mountains are an Atlantis raised from the sea, with marine fossils embedded into summit rocks. These rocks, born in the depths of the Pacific 55 million years ago, accumulated from sand and mud into thick, almost horizontal layers of sandstone and shale. Then volcanic action spewed lava out of the sea bottom and topped off the layers.

Thirty million years ago, as the ocean floor collided with the North American plate, most of the basalt, sandstones, and shales subducted under the continent. But when the ocean plate periodically stopped moving, the lighter ocean rocks rose above the heavier parts of the oceanic crust and bobbed up above the continental plate like a cork, until the layers crumbled up into the nascent Olympic Mountains.

Eventually, 30,000 years ago, continental ice sheets as thick as 3,500 feet flowed out of the north and collided against the unbending Olympic Mountains, just as a frozen river flows around an immovable boulder. The ice trenched out the Strait of Juan de Fuca to the north and Puget Sound to the east—separating the Olympic Peninsula from the mainland. These ice sheets sat as gargantuan masses, compressing the earth; then they drew back, and then bulldozed

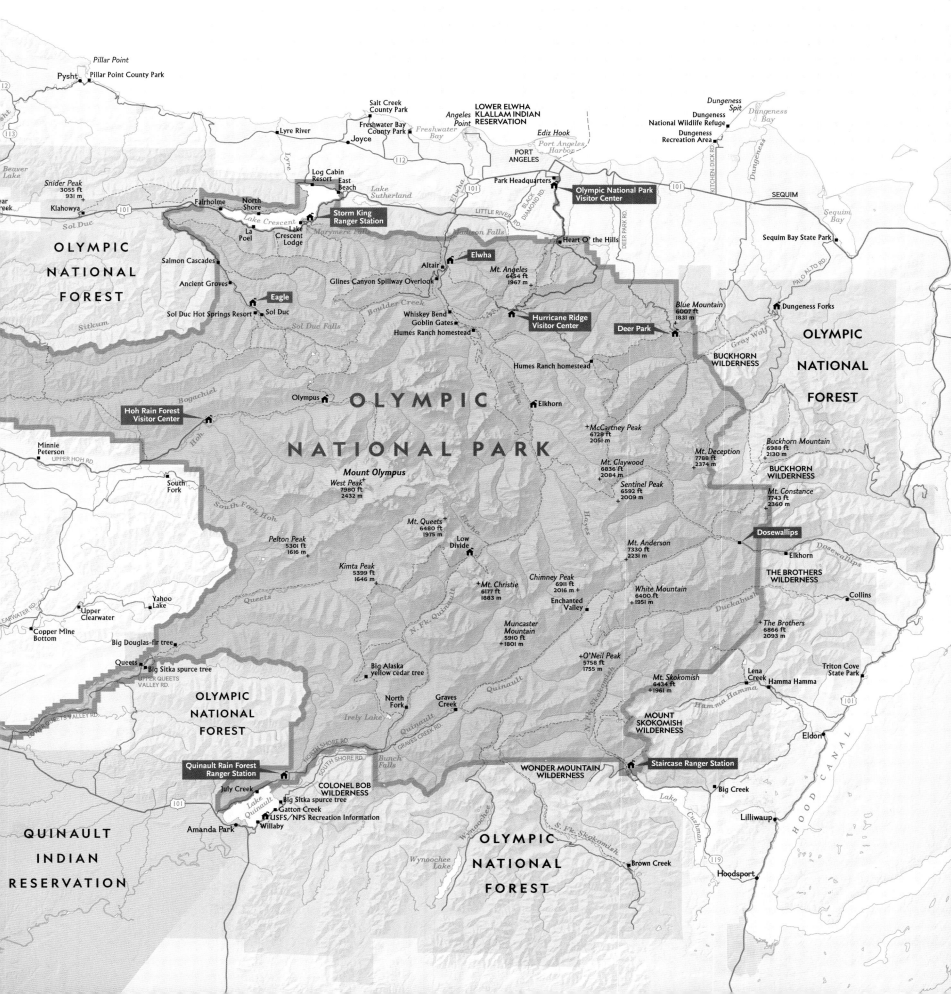

STRAIT OF JUAN DE FUCA

Pillar Point
Pysht
Pillar Point County Park

12

113

Beaver
Lake

Snider Peak
3055 ft
931 m
Klahowya

Sol Duc
101
Fairholme

OLYMPIC

NATIONAL

FOREST

Sitkum

Minnie
Peterson
UPPER HOH RD.

South
Fork

Salmon Cascades

Ancient Groves

Sol Duc Hot Springs Resort   Sol Duc

Eagle

North
Shore
La Poel

Lake
Crescent
Lodge

Lyre River

Lyre

Joyce

Salt Creek
County Park
Freshwater Bay
County Park

Log Cabin
Resort   East
Beach

Lake
Sutherland

Storm King
Ranger Station

Marymere Falls

Lake Crescent

LOWER ELWHA
KLALLAM INDIAN
RESERVATION

Angeles
Point

Freshwater
Bay

Ediz Hook

PORT
ANGELES

112

Madison Falls

Altair

Glines Canyon Spillway Overlook

Boulder Creek

Whiskey Bend
Goblin Gates
Humes Ranch homestead

Hoh Rain Forest
Visitor Center

Bogachiel

Hoh

South Fork Hoh

Olympus

OLYMPIC

NATIONAL PARK

Mount Olympus
West Peak
7980 ft
2432 m

Mt. Queets
6480 ft
1975 m

Elwha

Low
Divide

Hayes

Mt. Angeles
6454 ft
1967 m

Elwha

Humes Ranch homestead

Elkhorn

Hurricane Ridge
Visitor Center

Deer Park

McCartney Peak
6729 ft
2051 m

Mt. Claywood
6836 ft
2084 m

Sentinel Peak
6592 ft
2009 m

Port Angeles Harbor

Park Headquarters

LITTLE RIVER RD.

BLACK DIAMOND RD.

Heart O' the Hills

101

Olympic National Park
Visitor Center

DEER PARK RD.

Blue Mountain
6007 ft
1831 m

BUCKHORN
WILDERNESS

Mt. Deception
7788 ft
2374 m

Dungeness
Spit

Dungeness
National Wildlife Refuge
Dungeness
Recreation Area

SEQUIM

Sequim
Bay

Sequim Bay State Park

Dungeness Forks

OLYMPIC

NATIONAL

FOREST

Buckhorn Mountain
6988 ft
2130 m

BUCKHORN
WILDERNESS

Mt. Constance
7743 ft
2360 m

Dosewallips

KITCHEN-DICK RD.

PALO ALTO RD.

Dungeness
Bay

Gray Wolf

Pelton Peak
5301 ft
1616 m

Kimta Peak
5399 ft
1646 m

Queets

Mt. Christie
6177 ft
1883 m

Mt. Anderson
7330 ft
223l m

Chimney Peak
6911 ft
2016 m

White Mountain
6400 ft
1951 m

Elkhorn

Dosewallips

THE BROTHERS
WILDERNESS

Collins

Duckabush

Copper Mine
Bottom

Upper
Clearwater

Yahoo
Lake

CLEARWATER RD.

Big Douglas-fir tree

Queets
Big Sitka spurce tree
UPPER QUEETS
VALLEY RD.

N. Fk. Quinault

Enchanted
Valley

Muncaster
Mountain
5910 ft
1801 m

Big Alaska
yellow cedar tree

O'Neil Peak
5758 ft
1755 m

Mt. Skokomish
6434 ft
1961 m

The Brothers
6866 ft
2093 m

N. Fk. Skokomish

Lena
Creek

MOUNT
SKOKOMISH
WILDERNESS

Hamma Hamma

Triton Cove
State Park

Hamma Hamma

Hood Canal

Eldon

UPPER QUEETS VALLEY RD.

OLYMPIC

NATIONAL

FOREST

North
Fork

Graves
Creek

Irely Lake

Quinault

Quinault

GRAVES CREEK RD.

NORTH SHORE RD.

SOUTH SHORE RD.

Bunch
Falls

Quinault Rain Forest
Ranger Station

July Creek

Lake
Quinault

COLONEL BOB
WILDERNESS

Big Sitka spurce tree
Gatton Creek
USFS/NPS Recreation Information
Willaby

Amanda Park

101

QUINAULT

INDIAN

RESERVATION

Wynoochee
Lake

WONDER MOUNTAIN
WILDERNESS

Staircase Ranger Station

Big Creek

Lake
Cushman

S. Fk. Skokomish

OLYMPIC

NATIONAL

FOREST

Brown Creek

Lilliwaup

Hoodsport

119

101

MORE THAN A DOZEN PARK ANIMALS ARE FOUND NOWHERE ELSE, INCLUDING THE OLYMPIC MARMOT, THE SECOND RAREST OF NORTH AMERICAN MARMOTS.

anew throughout the retreats and surges of the Ice Age, until wasting away 20,000 years later.

By 10,000 years ago, the bulk of the ice had melted or retreated, revealing a barren landscape of rounded hills and flattened meadows. For a time, huge megafauna crossed these barren, alpine-glaciered mountains, trailed by human hunters. (In 1977, a prehistoric mastodon was found buried just outside the park with a spear point in its ribs.) For the next 9,000 years, as forests took root, cushioning and shading the ice-scraped peninsula, human hunters continued to chase large mammals across some of the most rugged terrain in the modern-day park. As these ancient people disappeared, their stone tools melded into the moss and dirt, or under the glaciers—the only traces of their passage.

The Ice Age had isolated the peninsula as a veritable island, removed from normal life-forms on the mainland. Today, eight plants and 14 animals in the park have evolved into species found only on the peninsula. All evoke a sense of wonder, from the hairy Olympic mountain milk vetch plant, to the slender Olympic mudminnow, the gregarious Olympic marmot, or the waterfall-loving Olympic torrent salamander.

As the human population increased 3,000 years ago, the hunter-gatherers of the peninsula shifted their tactics toward animal-rich waters for sustenance. They hunted the gray whales and other sea mammals, gathered shellfish, and netted salmon. Profiting from the same red cedar they carved into giant canoes, these people sheltered themselves from the heavy rains in their elaborately built longhouses.

Out at sea in 1788, beyond the canoes, the English sea captain John Meares confronted the peninsula's tallest mountain, appearing

Olympic National Park's mosaic of ecosystems, shown together here, yields a rich web of life. The coast is habitat for intertidal and marine species ranging from sea moss to giant kelp, around which otters play. Connecting ocean and land are rivers and lakes supporting abundant vegetation: salmonberry, western horsetail, salal, and more. These waterways wind inland through forests that differ by elevation zone, populated by Sitka spruce and western red cedar, among other species. At higher elevations, subalpine forest finally gives way to rocky slopes and glaciers.

Himalayan as it rose dramatically in the distance (yet only half the height of Mount Rainier, farther inland). Meares named the peak Mount Olympus after the home of the Greek gods.

Over the 19th century, many of the original coastal dwellers living beneath Mount Olympus perished from foreign diseases. Adding to

In 1897, following public outcry about timber or railroad companies consuming public lands, President Grover Cleveland created 13 forest reserves throughout America as he left office. The 3,000-square-mile Olympic Forest Reserve (surrounding the modern-day park) was easily the largest and most valuable, but logging companies complained that it was too large for the public good. By 1901, the powerful logging companies succeeded in taking back most of the reserve's lower forests for timber harvesting and homesteading. But public protests about the vanishing rainforest again alerted lawmakers.

Although forest preservation would factor into the region's salvation, the Roosevelt elk would ultimately create the park. Found mostly west of the Cascades in the Pacific Northwest, the unique creature is the largest of four elk subspecies. These statuesque animals wandered the Olympic Peninsula for thousands of years, their bugling becoming the music of the temperate rainforest.

One of the few animals in North America with ivory teeth, the elk—called *wapiti* by Plains Indians—were being cut down as quickly as old-growth forests for sport, meat, and money. Amid pleas for the creation of an elk refuge, the big game hunter turned conservationist President Theodore Roosevelt stepped into the fray in 1909. Wielding the Antiquities Act like a club, he waved it, single-handedly creating Mount Olympus National Monument. The designation was intended to protect the summer range and calving grounds of the Roosevelt elk—named, of course, for its advocate in office. But the understaffed and underpowered National Forest Service managed the monument, and logging continued, even with boundaries closed to timber companies.

Elk hunting, as well as poaching, also continued. By 1937, nearly a thousand elk that Roosevelt had intended to protect were slaughtered. Without the monument, the entire elk population of the area might have been wiped out.

the strain, white settlers increased competition for what had once seemed plentiful food resources on land and sea for local tribes—the Hoh, Jamestown S'Klallam, Elwha Klallam, Makah, Port Gamble S'Klallam, Quileute, Quinault, and Skokomish. But by the latter part of the century, as forests fell before the loggers and fish and elk populations diminished, many of the old ways were suspended.

Despite this upheaval, the indigenous people held onto certain traditions: carving, basket making, hunting whales (a right given back to the Makah tribe), and fishing—so long as these resources can be preserved according to local laws. Most of these tribes now have reservations on the Olympic Peninsula.

So in 1938, Theodore's fifth cousin President Franklin D. Roosevelt signed a bill creating a national park. Over the next two years, the boundaries were repeatedly expanded, and on the cusp of World War II, Olympic National Park, now a wide-ranging ecosystem, had become the third biggest park in America. Today's General Management Plan for the park reflects the original purpose of both Roosevelts to preserve the largest population of Roosevelt elk in its natural environment in the world.

The park is diverse because of myriad parts: the interior glaciered mountains; the lush, west-side rainforest; and the rugged coastline. Although the park has numerous entry points, none of these roads penetrate the park, which has helped to preserve the wild and natural landscapes throughout (in 1988, Congress designated 95 percent of the park as wilderness).

The western coastal sliver of the park—60 miles long and several miles wide—is wild, sandy, and rocky beach alongside forest. The Hoh and Quillayute Rivers (among many other smaller streams) drain the park highlands into the surf. Although more accessible than the deep rainforest, the coast can be challenging for foot travel with changing tides and huge driftwood trees and undergrowth fringing the beaches. Midway along the park's coast is the sleepy resort town of La Push, home to 800 Quileute tribe members and the westernmost Zip Code in the lower 48.

One of the most popular walks is the Ozette Loop, a nine-mile loop down a boardwalk through a coastal cedar swamp thence several miles along the beach. Sediment layers called turbidites striate parts of the shore, punctuated with mélange outcrops that locals refer to as "smell rocks" for the petroleum odors wrested from the depths of the Earth. These house-size formations are embedded with mixed rock and fragments that hint at past geologic events.

A dozen miles inland, the Hoh and Quinault Rain Forests often receive 150 inches of annual precipitation, making Olympic the wettest national park in the lower 48. Moss-draped conifers—red cedar, western hemlock, Sitka spruce, and Douglas fir—dominate the temperate rainforests. On the drier eastern side of the park, under the Olympic Mountains' rain shadow, the trees are smaller with sparser undergrowth, but still part of the park's old-growth forest totaling 572 square miles.

Snowy Mount Olympus is the park landmark. Home to the largest ice fields on the peninsula, the peak is cloaked by the three-mile-long Hoh Glacier and the similar-size Blue Glacier. Like thick white jackets on the mountain, the nearly 900-foot-thick glaciers plow downward several feet a day. Runoff from these glaciers provides an essential lifeline for aquatic life, particularly during less rainy summers when streams would otherwise run dry. Old-growth forests rely on meltwater for cooling, too. But a 2009 glacier inventory showed sobering results for the wettest park in America: Over 27

OPPOSITE: **Olympic National Park** holds some of America's last remaining temperate rainforest like the Quinault Rain Forest, called "Valley of the Rain Forest Giants" for its huge trees.

BELOW: **Young beachcombers** explore the Ozette Loop Trail, which winds through coastal forest and miles of rocky beach, showcasing the park's beauty and diversity.

OVER 95 PERCENT OF OLYMPIC NATIONAL PARK IS DESIGNATED WILDERNESS. RENAMED THE DANIEL J. EVANS WILDERNESS IN 2016, IT'S AMONG THE LARGEST WILDERNESS AREAS IN THE LOWER 48.

DAM REMOVAL, 2011–2014
⊠ Dam removed (year of removal)

STRAIT OF JUAN DE FUCA

NEARSHORE AREA

Port Angeles

ELWHA DAM (2012)

GLINES CANYON DAM (2014)

Elwha
Watershed

OLYMPIC

NATIONAL

PARK

N
5 mi
5 km

ABOVE: **The removal** of the Elwha and Glines Canyon Dams, completed in August 2014, marked the successful conclusion of the largest dam removal project in United States history. This landmark project helped restore and revive fish and wildlife habitats in the Elwha Watershed.

LEFT: **At the end** of the 17.4-mile Hoh River Trail, hikers glimpse Mount Mathias, the East Peak of Mount Olympus, Glacier Pass, and the 2.6-mile-long Blue Glacier—all after traversing multiple ecosystems from temperate rainforest to subalpine meadow.

years, 82 glaciers disappeared. Fewer than 184 glaciers remain in the park, and among those, their diminishing ice mass is of grave concern. The lack of meltwater has caused the Quinault River to reach record lows.

Meanwhile, a dam removal project on another river has made it a laboratory for studying ecosystem recovery. Between 2011 and 2014, the two large dams on the Elwha River were taken out, renewing access to over 70 miles of habitat for salmon, and releasing millions of cubic yards of sand and silt to the coast where freshwater

meets the Strait of Juan de Fuca. Researchers are monitoring the impact of these changes on hydrology as well as wildlife.

One of many wildlife success stories for Olympic National Park is the reintroduction of the fisher—a small member of the weasel family—trapped out by the early 1900s. Beginning in 2008, the park released 90 fishers into the forests. Researchers have since located several breeding dens of the elusive mammal.

Along the park's coast, the year-round harbor seal residents are commonly viewed while hauled out on rock outcrops or feeding in intertidal zones. Porpoises, sea lions, and sea otters frolic in the surf.

Farther out in the ocean, gray whales blow misty jets of vapor a dozen feet into the air; on occasion, they come in closer to feed on bottom sediments at the mouths of the Quillayute and Hoh Rivers. On a more microcosmic level, exploring Kalaloch's Beach 4 and Mora's Hole-in-the-Wall tide pools at low tide can yield bright sea stars, anemones, and sea urchins.

Park rivers support runs of five species of Pacific salmon. Looking skyward, over 300 species of birds are found through the park, including at-risk marbled murrelets and northern spotted owls.

In addition to several hundred remaining Roosevelt elk, black-tailed deer and large populations of black bears and cougars provide balance among more than 60 terrestrial mammals.

July through September is often dry in the Olympics, particularly on the park's east side. Although it rains from early winter through the month of June, spring is the best time to revel in the incredible lushness of the western park, all but dripping green on moss-armored trees, lichen-festooned stumps, and giant ferns. Along with innumerable backcountry camping opportunities, 14 front-country campgrounds have hundreds of sites, from which rain jacket–wearing visitors can take in the unprecedented riot of life. ∎

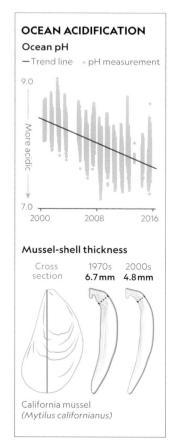

OCEAN ACIDIFICATION
Ocean pH
— Trend line · pH measurement

9.0

More acidic ←

7.0

2000   2008   2016

Mussel-shell thickness

| Cross section | 1970s 6.7mm | 2000s 4.8mm |

California mussel
(*Mytilus californianus*)

ALASKA & HAWAI'I PARKS

CONTENTS

GATES OF THE ARCTIC
N.P. &
PRESERVE

RUSSIA

ALASKA

*Bering
Sea*

DENALI
NATIONAL PARK
& PRESERVE

CANADA

UNITED STATES

KATMAI
N.P. & PRESERVE

*Gulf of
Alaska*

GLACIER BAY
N.P. &
PRESERVE

PACIFIC OCEAN

200 mi
200 km
N

PACIFIC OCEAN

HAWAI'I

200 mi
200 km
N

HAWAI'I VOLCANOES
NATIONAL PARK

Sun shines on the craggy, snow-laden heights of Denali in Alaska—at 20,310 feet, it is North America's tallest mountain.

▷ LOCATION **50 MILES NW OF JUNEAU, ALASKA**

▷ SIZE **5,128 SQUARE MILES**

▷ HIGHEST POINT **MOUNT FAIRWEATHER, 15,325 FEET**

▷ VISITORS **597,915 IN 2018**

▷ ESTABLISHED **1980**

GLACIER BAY NATIONAL PARK AND PRESERVE

Buried in the roadless panhandle of Southeast Alaska and accessed by boat through the Inside Passage is an expanse of glaciers flowing out of the Fairweather Range. The park is bisected by its namesake Glacier Bay, bordering Icy Strait to the south and the tempestuous Gulf of Alaska to the west. Unlike other Alaskan national parks that extend only to the mean high tide line, the 949 square miles of ocean within the bay—comprising 19 percent of the park—is entirely managed by the Department of the Interior.

Glacier Bay National Park and Preserve is known for its 1,045 glaciers, covering 27 percent of the park. This includes seven active tidewater glaciers—frequently viewed from boats, at safe distances—calving into ocean waters. Cruise ship passengers comprise more than 95 percent of the park's visitors. Up to a thousand backcountry campers come each year, mostly in sea kayaks or small boats because there are no backcountry trail systems. Ten seldom climbed, high-altitude peaks rear above the bay, while the northern park protects a section of the Alsek River's world-class white water.

UNESCO designated Glacier Bay—along with the adjacent U.S. and Canadian national parks of Wrangell–St. Elias, Kluane, and

Snow and ice define the high, frozen regions of Glacier Bay National Park. These icebergs on a gravel bar in Muir Inlet are from McBride Glacier, the only tidewater glacier in the East Arm.

Yakutat Glacier

TONGASS
NATIONAL
FOREST

Novatak Glacier

BRABAZON RANGE

Alsek

TATSHENSHINI-ALSEK
PROVINCIAL PARK

Alsek

Tatshenshini

Mt. McDonnell
5481 ft
1671 m

Towagh Glacier

Tsiatka Glacier

Thope Glacier

Buckwell Glacier

Tsirku Glacier

BRITISH COLUMBIA
ALASKA

3

SAINT ELIAS MOUNTAINS

Alsek

BRITISH COLUMBIA
ALASKA

Konamoxt Glacier

ALSEK RANGE

Mt. Harris
5177 ft
1578 m

TAKHINSHA

Alsek Glacier

Alsek
Lake
Gateway
Knob

Mt. Hay
8870 ft
2704 m

Melburn Glacier

Hay Glacier

Tikke Glacier

GRAND PACIFIC GLACIER

CANADA
UNITED STATES

Morse Glacier

Muir Glacier

Cushing Glacier

Mt. Brock
4990 ft
1521 m

Dry Bay
Ranger
Station

GLACIER BAY
NATIONAL PRESERVE

Public use cabin

Mt. Lodge
10530 ft
3210 m

Mt. Barnard
8214 ft
2504 m

CARROLL GLACIER

Dry
Bay

E. Alsek

Doame

DECEPTION HILLS

GRAND PLATEAU GLACIER

Ferris Glacier

Rendu Glacier

Mt. Abdallah
5964 ft
1818 m

Tarr Inlet

Rendu Inlet

Russell Island

Queen Inlet

White
Thunder
Ridge

Wachusett
Inlet

GULF OF
ALASKA

Mt. Root
12860 ft
3920 m

Margerie Glacier

Mt. Merriam
5083 ft
1549 m

Mt. Fairweather
15300 ft
4669 m

Mt. Quincy Adams
13650 ft
4161 m

Jaw
Point

Johns Hopkins Inlet

Lamplugh Glacier

Reid
Inlet

Cape
Fairweather

FAIRWEATHER GLACIER

Mt. Salisbury
12000 ft
3658 m

Johns Hopkins Glacier

Reid Glacier

Gilbert
Peninsula

Lituya Mountain
11750 ft
3582 m

FAIRWEATHER RANGE

Mt. Abbe
8750 ft
2667 m

Tlingit
Point

Mt. Orville
10495 ft
3199 m

GLACIER BAY
NATIONAL PARK

GLACIER BAY

Lituya Glacier

Mt. Bertha
10204 ft
3110 m

Drake
Island

Mt. Crillon
12726 ft
3879 m

Geikie Inlet

Interglacial
stumps

Lituya
Bay

North Crillon Glacier

BRADY
ICEFIELD

Crillon
Lake

Mt. La Perouse
10728 ft
3270 m

Wood
Lake

Lake
Seclusion

La Perouse Glacier

BRADY GLACIER

Abyss
Lake

Dundas

PACIFIC
OCEAN

Palma
Bay

Icy Point

Astrolabe
Point

Dixon Harbor

Torch Bay

Graves Harbor

Graves
Rocks

Taylor
Bay

Dundas
Bay

CROSS SOUND

Inian
Islands

Cape
Spencer

Port Althorp

Elfin Cove

Idaho Inlet

Cape
Bingham

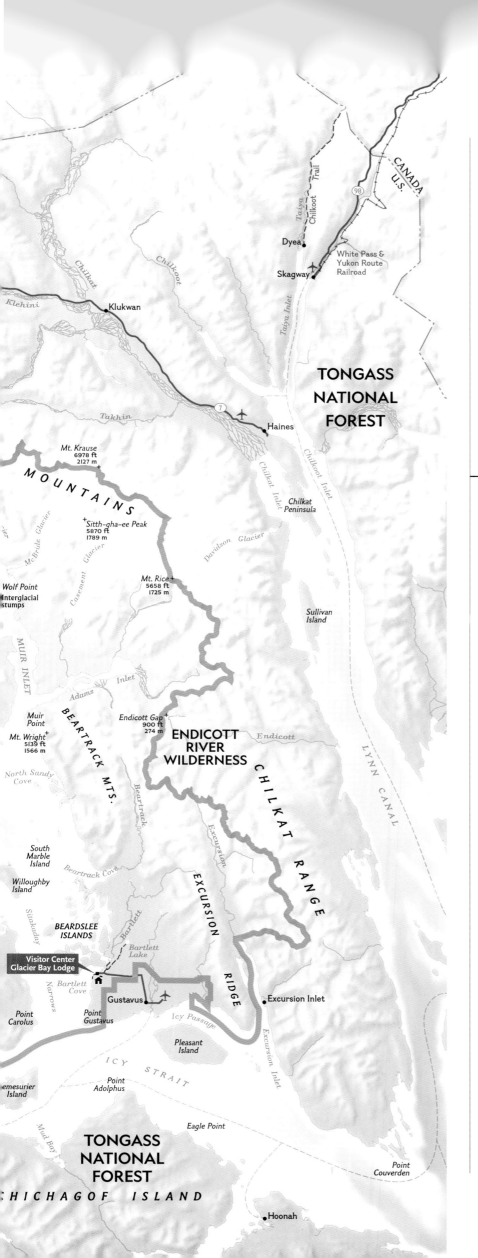

Tatshenshini-Alsek—as a 38,000-square-mile World Heritage site that is one of the largest protected land-based ecosystems on the planet. The park is rich with about 270 bird species and 40 mammal species. Its ample waters have also helped prevent the extinction of formerly endangered steller sea lions and humpback whales within the park. But the planetary-scale forces at work in Glacier—including earthquakes, megatsunamis, and surging or collapsing glaciers—have exacted a heavy toll on humans.

When the major continental glaciers retreated 13,000 years ago, the land—relieved from the tremendous mass of ice—sprung up. Soils developed, and forests returned. Rivers ran from remnant glaciers and wildlife flourished. Within several thousand years, the climate stabilized into a cool, coastal-temperate rainforest. Although it rains

The marine waters in Glacier Bay stretch across 607,100 acres, making it one of the country's largest protected marine areas. A vast array of sea creatures make these waters home.

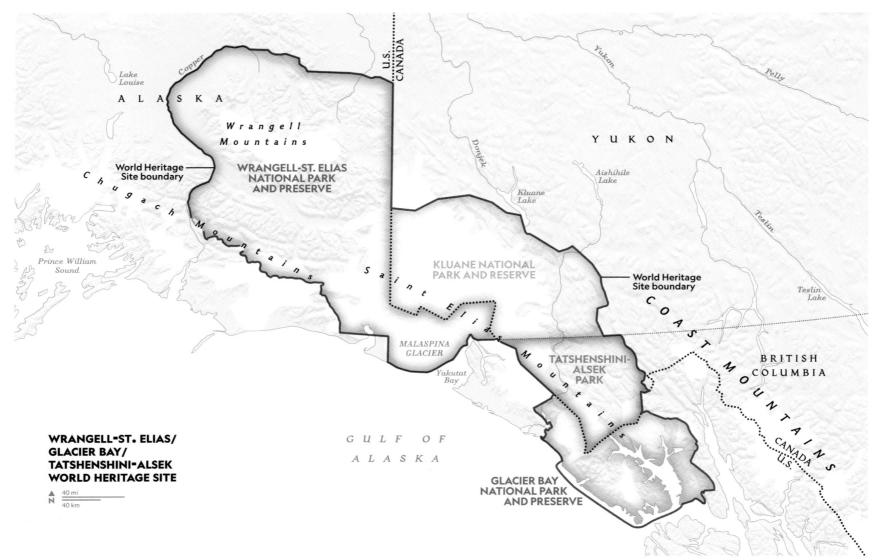

WRANGELL-ST. ELIAS/
GLACIER BAY/
TATSHENSHINI-ALSEK
WORLD HERITAGE SITE

▲ 40 mi
N
40 km

most of the year at sea level, as much as 100 feet of snow falls each year in the Fairweather Range. Winter temperatures can drop to minus 10°F (-23°C), while summers below the glaciers average 50 to 60°F (10 to 16°C).

Seven hundred years ago, the Arctic, northern Europe, and the high latitudes of North America began cooling again. This Little Ice Age lasted for nearly 500 years, until the mid-19th century. Local Huna Tlingit (pronounced *Klinkit*) oral history remembers the land below today's huge bay as a broad, river valley in 1680, with villages below a truncated glacier. This is all verified by radiocarbon dating.

Over the next few decades of Little Ice Age cooling, the enormous accumulation of snow in the mountains flowed down and filled the valley as a huge new glacier, jutting into the waters of Icy Strait. The Tlingit were forced to abandon their homeland. In 1794, as the glacier began to recede, the British sailor Joseph Whidbey—under the command of Captain George Vancouver—became first to document the several-thousand-foot-high sheet of ice that reached back

GLACIER BAY'S ONLY ROAD, FROM THE AIRPORT TO THE PARK'S VISITOR CENTER, IS JUST 10 MILES LONG.

"as far as the eye could distinguish." Its enormous weight carved out today's Glacier Bay, as deep as 1,410 feet below sea level.

Eventually, after the glacier had receded more than 30 miles up into the newly created bay, the American naturalist John Muir arrived in 1879. Over the next two decades, "the professor" repeatedly returned to this land of ice, which would allow him to understand the long-vanished glaciers that had carved Yosemite Valley. Trapped on Brady Glacier in bad weather, with crevasses all around, Muir was forced to cross a flimsy snow bridge in front of his tiny canine companion Stickeen. But the dog hesitated. On opposite sides of the dangerous crevasse, their eyes met in a riveting moment of communication that showed Muir's respect for animals—Stickeen then scooted across safely.

More than anyone else's, Muir's writings about such adventures inspired the creation of the park. He recounted one climb, a thousand feet above the bay, in his book *Travels in Alaska*:

While sunshine streamed through the luminous fringes of the clouds and fell on the green waters of the fiord, the glittering bergs, the crystal bluffs of the vast glacier, the intensely white, far-spreading fields of ice, and the ineffably chaste and spiritual heights of the Fairweather Range, which were now hidden, now partly revealed, the whole making a picture of icy wildness unspeakably pure and sublime.

Muir also encouraged late 19th-century steamship tourism. Following Muir's lead, the American ecologist William Cooper made repeated scientific surveys and proposed federal protection for the bay in 1922. By 1925, President Calvin Coolidge proclaimed it Glacier Bay National Monument, citing the "unique opportunity for the scientific study of glacial behavior and resulting movements and developments of flora and fauna and of certain valuable relics of interglacial forests." Then President Franklin D. Roosevelt more

In 1680, Glacier Bay was an ice-filled valley. Over decades, the glacier slid down the valley, reaching its maximum extent around 1750, during the Little Ice Age. But shrinking followed: By 1880, the glacier had retreated 45 miles, gouging out the valley. The melting continued, and today tidewater glaciers can be found 65 miles up Glacier Bay.

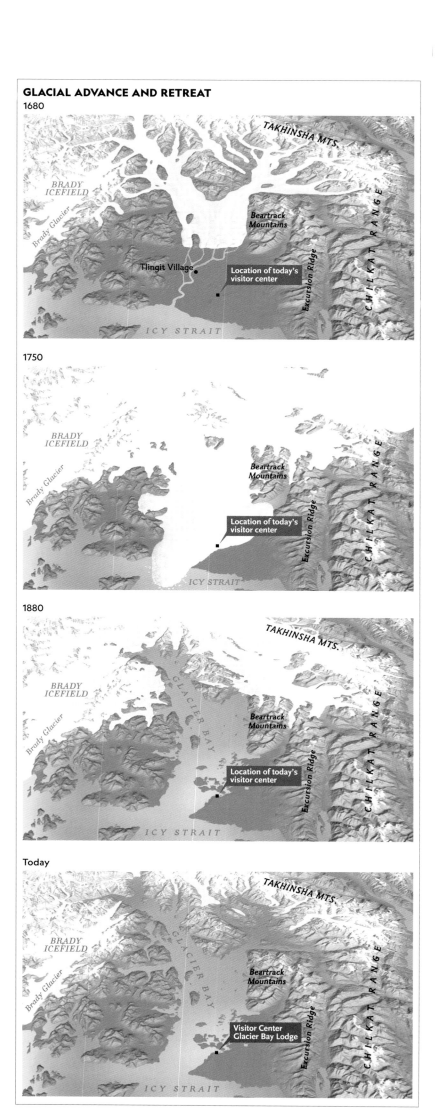

GLACIAL ADVANCE AND RETREAT
1680
1750
1880
Today

TIDEWATER GLACIERS

FAIRWEATHER RANGE

JOHNS HOPKINS GLACIER

Johns Hopkins Inlet

Tidewater glaciers like Johns Hopkins Glacier move ice like a slow-motion conveyor belt, in this case shifting it toward the sea. There it forms a protective shoal by taking material from the upper slope and depositing it farther down. Tidewater glaciers advance and retreat according to local conditions, but many of the ice sheets that feed them are thinning.

than doubled the monument in 1939 to protect its brown bears and other wildlife.

The first seasonal ranger didn't arrive until 1949, and more employee facilities were built in the late 1950s. By 1969, following the wake of early steamships, cruise ships began plying the bay.

Ten years later, President Jimmy Carter added 817 square miles of protected lands to Glacier Bay. In 1980, under the park-creating heyday of the Alaska National Interest Lands Conservation Act, another 89 square miles were protected as a hunting preserve, and the whole monument became Glacier Bay National Park and Preserve. Most of the park remains completely protected wilderness.

Today the tidewater glaciers have retreated more than 65 miles from Icy Strait. All but a few of the park's myriad glaciers are receding, and in many cases, rapidly thinning due to climate change.

Between 1949 and 2016, anthropogenic greenhouse gas emissions have increased average summer temperatures in nearby Juneau by 2.2°F (1.2°C); winter temperatures have increased by 7°F (3.9°C). A temperature spike in Alaska that began in the mid-1970s corresponds to a tripling of glacial thinning throughout the state in that period.

Over the last half of the 20th century, Alaska glaciers have contributed the largest single measured glaciological contribution to sea level, with an annual volume increase of 12.3 cubic miles of water, which equates to a sea level rise of 0.006 inch a year. This surge of ice water melting into the sea comes from natural glacial receding or retreating in length, and increasingly, from the thinning height of these glaciers. Alaska's addition of even less than an inch to sea level rise over the next century, combined with runoff from a much larger volume of ice rapidly melting in Antarctica and Greenland,

Tidewater glaciers are active in summer, when they occasionally "calve" into saltwater, bringing ice blocks of up to 200 feet crashing into the sea.

could be cataclysmic. Then, among other changes, ocean acidification increases as more meltwater escalates carbon dioxide levels.

Billions of tons of melted glacial ice in the park allowed the land to rise, through what scientists call isostatic rebound. Although this phenomenon promotes landslides and instability, movements between the Pacific and North American tectonic plates are the principal cause of earthquakes, breaking the lightened landscape above like crust on rising bread.

Ground zero is the 124-mile-long Fairweather Fault—directly above the colliding tectonic plates—running parallel to the coast and cleaving the western edge of the park. Consequently, over the past 150 years, there have been four major tremors and one severe earthquake that registered 8.8 on the Richter scale north of Glacier Bay, and one that shook the entire southeast Alaskan coast in 1899. Glacier Bay's tidewater Muir Glacier was so badly shattered that steamships couldn't penetrate the maze of icebergs for a decade.

Inside Lituya Bay's sheltered waters, alongside the Fairweather Fault, geologists have found evidence of earthquakes repeatedly causing giant waves. Most recently, on July 9, 1958, a 7.9 Richter scale quake lifted the earth along the Fairweather Fault 21 feet horizontally and 3.5 feet vertically. Nine hundred miles south in Seattle, 20 musicians in a floating orchestra pit mounted on an inland stage bounced up and down for five minutes. One hundred miles away, in a bay outside Yakutat, Alaska, three berry pickers were lost when Khantaak Island dropped 100 feet into the sea.

Thirteen miles from the epicenter, the earthquake shook loose a landslide alongside Lituya Glacier. As 90 million tons of rock splashed into Lituya Bay, the 1,200-foot front of the glacier also collapsed and exploded down into the water, causing the world's largest recorded wave. Its unprecedented size—expanded through the sloshing, bathtub effect inside the steep-walled bay—made it a heretofore unknown "megatsunami."

On July 9, 1958, an earthquake triggered an avalanche along the Fairweather Fault and created the largest known tsunami in history, destroying this swath of forest, below.

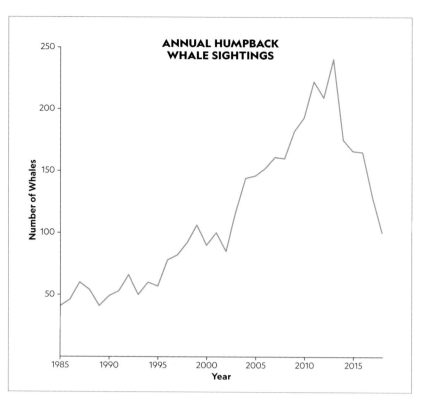

ANNUAL HUMPBACK WHALE SIGHTINGS

ABOVE: **Biologists count** humpback whales in Glacier Bay and Icy Strait between June 1 and August 31 each year, while they feed on schooling fish after fasting through winter. From 1985 to 2013, the population grew about 5 percent annually, reflecting the species' recovery from commercial whaling. In 2014, the count declined suddenly, likely due to the combined effects of a marine heat wave, a strong El Niño in 2015–16, and climate change on the whales' food supply.

LEFT: **An adult humpback whale** breaches in Alaskan waters. They aren't the world's biggest whales, but they are imposing, with flippers that can grow up to 16 feet long. Their name comes from the arched-back hump that forms before they make deep dives.

The wave detonated 1,740 feet up the opposite mountainside and ripped through a forest, scouring away every piece of vegetation—along with roots and soil—down to bedrock. Mature four-foot-diameter trees were snapped off at their bases, stripped of their bark by water particle velocities exceeding 100 feet a second, and hurled into the bay. Barnacles were stripped from rocks underwater.

Seven miles away, the earthquake woke crews on three 40-foot boats, anchored in the mouth of the bay. "The noise was deafening," one survivor, Howard Ulrich wrote. The Fairweather Range above the bay looked like it was smoking with avalanches. As he watched the unbelievable wave engulf the 246-foot-high Cenotaph Island from two miles away, Ulrich threw a life jacket on his 8-year-old son. Because Ulrich couldn't pull up the anchor, he let out all 200 feet of chain and steered into what he estimated to be a 75-foot-high wave: The chain broke "like it was a string." The boat shot skyward, crested the wave, and threw them shoreward up over the trees. In the backwash, the boat returned to the bay, still upright, as Ulrich steered around trees and roots and bushes rushing past in the white water.

The second boat's crew tried to motor out into the Gulf of Alaska, but caught by the wave while exiting through the narrow channel out of Lituya Bay, the boat was flung out into the deep waters of the ocean, immediately sinking and drowning the couple on board. Only an oil slick remained on the surface.

At the same time, a husband and wife anchored in the third boat were swept up by the wave and thrown toward the ocean, 80 feet above a rocky, forested spit of land alongside the bay's channel entrance (from where eight mountain climbers had been flown off two hours earlier). "We went way over the trees and I looked down on rocks as big as an ordinary house as we crossed the spit," Bill Swanson said. "It felt like we were in a tin can and somebody was shaking it."

As spectacular as collapsing glaciers, watching the acrobatic, humpback whales of Glacier Bay leap out of the sea is unforgettable. These school bus–size cetaceans weigh over 30 tons, but still manage to vertically "spy hop" their bodies straight up above surface for up to a half minute as if to spy on the tour boats watching them, until sliding deftly back into the water. While breaching sideways out of the sea, they often belly flop back in with a thunderous splash.

Humpbacks "bubble-net feed" to capture fish. Diving deep into the bay beneath schools of small fish, they swim in a shrinking circle and herd their prey by releasing bubbles, as if turning on Jacuzzi jets and trapping the fish inside them. Then the whales collectively rise to the surface with mouths agape, sieving the fish yet releasing the water through baleen plates (humpbacks lack teeth). In one gulp, a whale will swallow hundreds of fingerlings and then continue gorging on up to a half ton of prey per day.

The Park Service has monitored whale populations in Glacier Bay since 1985. Biologists have learned how to identify each whale

cruise ships (each holding up to 4,000 passengers). Whether in kayak or cruise ship, visitors are prohibited from approaching within a half mile of whales.

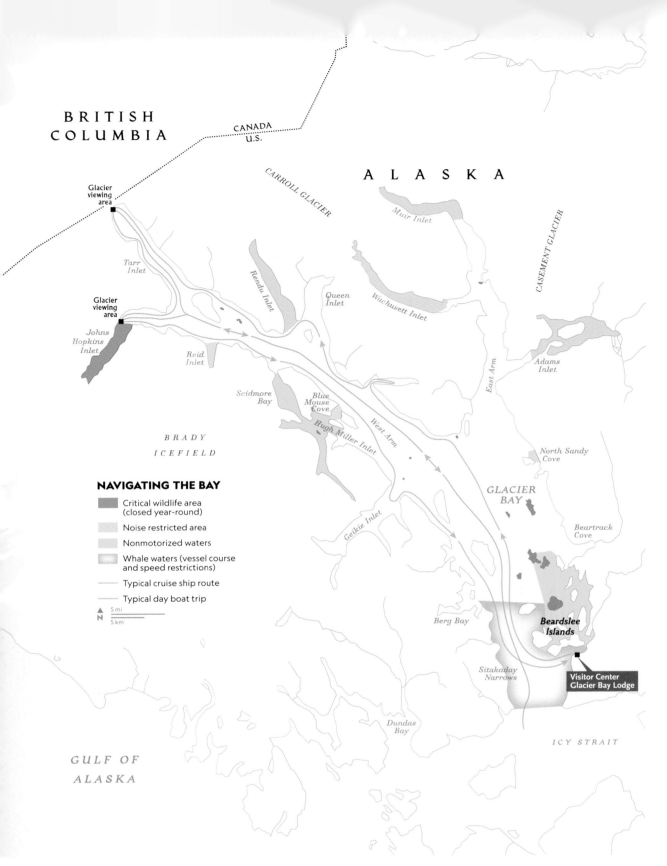

NAVIGATING THE BAY

- Critical wildlife area (closed year-round)
- Noise restricted area
- Nonmotorized waters
- Whale waters (vessel course and speed restrictions)
- Typical cruise ship route
- Typical day boat trip

5 mi
5 km

Touring Glacier Bay by cruise ship is one of the best ways to view the park's spectacular sights. Typical ship routes are shown above, but courses often vary with weather conditions. Most cruises spend about 10 hours on the bay and cover more than 120 miles. Restrictions along sections of the bay protect wildlife and help keep the waters pristine.

among the dozens that enter the park each spring, after spending the winter in Hawaiian or Mexican waters to mate or give birth. Some individuals have been returning for more than 40 years.

Alaskan humpback populations have steadily increased since whale hunting was outlawed in 1966 in the North Pacific. After cruise ships collided with and killed two humpback whales in 2001 and 2004, speed limits are enforced in whale zones. The entrance to Glacier Bay is capped at a maximum of two cruise ships each day. During summer peak season, entrance is limited to a total of 153

Long before whales sang in these waters, when ice prevailed, four clans—extended family and social groups—inhabited Glacier Bay. According to the Chookaenedí clan, when the Grand Pacific Glacier advanced down the main valley in the early 1700s, it came with the speed of a running dog and destroyed everything in its path. These clans dispersed to different settlements, but today most northern Tlingit can trace their origins to the valley before the glacier came. They eventually returned for seasonal harvests, but once the area became a monument in 1925, tribal activities changed.

Many national parks with large protected sections of wilderness have re-created scenic and wildlife-rich landscapes bereft of people. In most of today's uninhabited parklands, the vision derived from the 1964 Wilderness Act often overlooks those cultures that were at home hunting and gathering in these places long before the parks were established. To a large extent, these indigenous and original inhabitants of the parks even viewed themselves as part of nature. Such was the case with the Tlingit.

In their minds, subsistence—which fulfilled a moral and religious duty—transcended mere economic activity. Before the hunt, Tlingit purified themselves through abstinence from sex, fasting, bathing, and never speaking of the animal to be killed. They only killed for food, without wasting the flesh or mocking the animal. Fish were treated respectfully by returning their offal to streams or burning it for proper reincarnation. Even berries held an inner spirit (*yeik*) that had to be treated with respect.

By the late 1930s, despite their transition to cash-oriented commercial fishing, trapping, seal hunting, and prospecting, the people remained deeply connected to Glacier Bay through their smokehouses below salmon streams and frequent harvests of berries and gull eggs. When these activities were prohibited in the 1960s, relations became strained between the Huna Tlingits and the Park Service.

But times are changing in Glacier Bay National Park and Preserve. In 2014, President Barack Obama signed a law to allow Tlingit to continue sustainable harvests of gull eggs in the park. These harvests had always traditionally heralded the arrival of good traveling weather and relief from hunger. The Tlingit name for the islands studding Glacier Bay is K'wát' Aaní ("Land of the Seagull Eggs"), and the gulls there are thought to produce richer and more abundant eggs than anywhere in Southeast Alaska. To the Huna Tlingit, K'wát' Aaní is considered an essential part of the sacred landscape.

The park then began to celebrate its cultural heritage. On August 25, 2016—the 100-year anniversary of the National Park Service—tribal members dedicated a 2,500-square-foot clan house, built by the Park Service and featuring the craftsmanship of Tlingit on the south shore of Bartlett Cove inside Glacier Bay. Flanked by two Tlingit-carved, 20-foot-high totem poles, the house draws visitors from around the world to learn about Huna Tlingit culture and history, 250 years after the Little Ice Age inundated their ancestral homeland. ■

The grand unveiling of the Xunaa Shuká Hít on August 25, 2016, marked an important milestone for Glacier Bay's tribal members: a homecoming after a glacier destroyed their villages 250 years ago.

THE ANCESTORS OF THE HUNA TLINGIT PEOPLE LIVED AT GLACIER BAY LONG BEFORE THE LAST GLACIER ADVANCE. THEY CALLED IT S'E SHUYEE, MEANING "EDGE OF THE GLACIAL SILT."

▷ LOCATION **122 MILES SW OF FAIRBANKS, ALASKA**

▷ SIZE **9,492 SQUARE MILES**

▷ HIGHEST POINT **DENALI SUMMIT, 20,310 FEET**

▷ VISITORS **594,660 IN 2018**

▷ ESTABLISHED **1917**

DENALI NATIONAL PARK AND PRESERVE

Just below the geographic midpoint of Alaska is an awe-inspiring sanctuary of mountains, forests, tundra, glaciers, and ice-cold rivers. This Massachusetts-size park spans a third of the entire Alaska Range, topped off by Denali high up in thin air and plunging four vertical miles to the Yentna River.

Although mountain climbers come from all over the world to attempt the continent's highest peak, Denali, most visitors are drawn to the north side of the park to view the spectacular landscape and its wildlife. Dall sheep, bears, caribou, moose, foxes, wolves, and dozens of other mammals wander the park, which is bisected by a 92-mile dirt road that leads from headquarters to Wonder Lake, two dozen miles from the base of Denali. The wildlife viewing opportunities along that road—seen from Park Service visitor buses and enhanced by a vast tundra plain, backlit by towering mountains—show why the park was created more than a century ago.

One hundred and sixty-six bird species pass through the park in summer months. Through a "Critical Connections" program developed in Denali, miniaturized tracking devices placed on numerous avian species, including nesting golden eagles—now threatened by

Wonder Lake is the largest kettle lake beneath Mount Brooks, Denali (formerly called Mount McKinley), and the Alaska Range in the wild landscape of Denali National Park.

human activity outside the park—allow the birds to be accurately trailed throughout North America. Biologists have found evidence to show that Alaska's national parks may provide more critical nesting habitat for migratory birds than nearly all the other national parks in the lower 48.

Birds in particular show how the preservation ideals of our national parks have essential, international consequences. Close to 80 percent of the species nesting in Alaska's national parks are migratory, with incredible, wide-ranging flights. Witness Denali's arctic terns: Each year they fly up to 50,000 miles to Antarctica and back, performing the longest migration of any animal on Earth. More than a dozen park bird species—from chickadees to ravens—remain for the winter.

As for other residents, recent wildlife estimates show that the park contains about 2,000 moose, more than 4,000 Dall sheep, up to 350 grizzlies on the north side of the Alaska Range (with even more grizzlies subsisting on plentiful salmon habitats on the south side), roughly 2,000 caribou, and about 50 wolves. These megafauna suffer minimal hunting, highway, or railroad losses within protective park boundaries, and give researchers and visitors a unique opportunity to study the uninterrupted processes of nature that support the integrity of wildlife populations.

More than any other prey, the wide-ranging caribou herd supports predators throughout the northern park. Research has shown that caribou mortality each year is directly linked to heavy winters, as

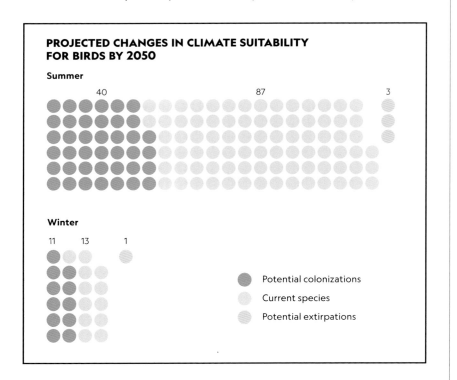

PROJECTED CHANGES IN CLIMATE SUITABILITY FOR BIRDS BY 2050

Summer

40   87   3

Winter

11   13   1

● Potential colonizations
○ Current species
◍ Potential extirpations

Climate suitability—the range of temperatures and precipitation necessary to survive—for a quarter of bird species in U.S. national parks may change significantly if carbon emissions continue at current rates. Scientists have predicted the number of bird species that may have new suitable climate (potential colonizations) and the number of species that may be left with no suitable climate (potential extirpations) in the park system. In Denali National Park, an influx of 40 new bird species may move in during the summer by 2050.

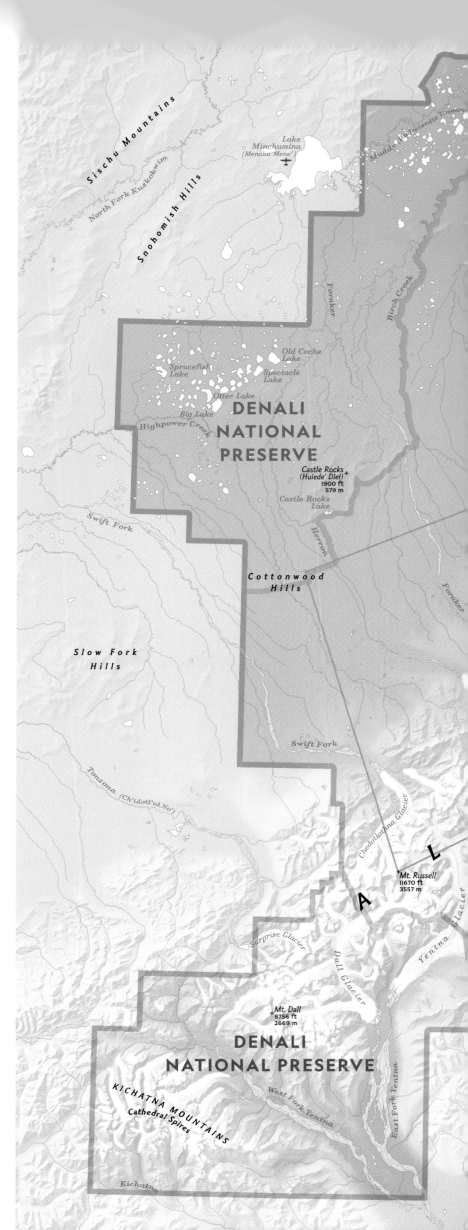

DENALI
NATIONAL PARK

Chilchukabena
Lake

Starr
Lake

Chitsia Mountain
3862 ft
1117 m

Healy
Medical Clinic

Stampede Trail

Kantishna Hills

Private vehicles
prohibited
beyond
mile 15

Mt. Healy
5700 ft
1737 m

Wilderness
Access Center

Savage River
Loop Trail
Primrose Ridge

Savage Alpine
Trail

Park
Headquarters

Riley Creek

Denali
Visitor Center

Kankone Peak
4987 ft
1520 m

Wyoming
Hills

Sanctuary
River

Savage River

Teklanika River

Triple Lakes
Trail

Triple Lakes

Sable Mt.
6002 ft
1830 m

Igloo Creek

Double Mt.
5899 ft
1798 m

Fang Mt.
6736 ft
2053 m

Kantishna

Polychrome Mt.
5790 ft
1765 m

Toklat River

DENALI WILDERNESS

Wonder
Lake

Eielson
Alpine
Trail

Wonder Lake

McKinley
Bar Trail

PARK ROAD

Gorge Creek Trail

Eielson
Visitor Center

Mt. Pendleton
7840 ft
2389 m

Cantwell

DENALI HIGHWAY

Scott Peak
8828 ft
2691 m

Summit

Summit Lake

West Fork Glacier

Broad Pass

DENALI WILDERNESS

Muldrow Glacier

West Fork

Mt. Mather
12123 ft
3695 m

Peters Dome
10600 ft
3231 m

Mt. Koven
12210 ft
3722 m

Mt. Deception
11768 ft
3587 m

Mt. Eldridge
10433 ft
3180 m

North Peak
19470 ft
5934 m

Denali
(Mt. McKinley)
South Peak
20310 ft
6190 m

Mt. Silverthrone
13220 ft
4029 m

Ohio Creek

Mt. Crosson
12800 ft
3901 m

Don Sheldon
Amphitheater

Buckskin Glacier

Eldridge Glacier

Mt. Foraker
(Ts'udots'in
Denaze)
17400 ft
5303 m

Mt. Hunter
14573 ft
4427 m

Mooses Tooth
10335 ft
3150 m

Mt. Stevens
13895 ft
4235 m

DENALI
NATIONAL PARK

The Great Gorge

Denali View North

Little Coal
Creek Trailhead

Ermine Hill
Trailhead

Kesugi Ridge

Devils Canyon

Susitna

Avalanche Spire
10105 ft
3080 m

Tokositna Glacier

Ruth Glacier

Tokosha
Mountains

Visitor Information
Alaska Veterans Memorial
Byers Lake Campground

DENALI
STATE
PARK

Dutch Hills

Peters Hills
(K'enuqak'itnetant)

Lower Troublesome Creek

Upper Troublesome
Creek Trailhead

K'esugi Ken

Denali
Viewpoint
South

Walter Harper
Talkeetna
Ranger Station

Trapper
Creek

Talkeetna

PETERSVILLE ROAD

10 mi
10 km

N

Wolves band together for survival during the harsh Denali winters. Over 10 wolf packs call the park home, and studies suggest the number of individual wolves there is climbing after a record low in 2016.

deep snow allows bears and wolves and other predators to catch young calves that cannot escape through the drifts. The more solitary moose suffer similar losses, but what they lack in protective herd strength, they make up for in aggressive behavior. During the fall rut, even a grizzly bear—up to 900 pounds—will avoid a six-foot-tall, 1,400-pound, bloodshot-eyed, snorting bull moose with flaps of bloodied skin hanging from its palmated antlers. Although the cows aren't as large, one well-aimed kick while guarding a calf can shatter a wolf's skull.

Denali National Park also offers one of the world's best natural research laboratories for observation of wild wolves. Since 1986, wildlife managers have radio-collared over 400 wolves, then regularly tracked them by airplane. From the ground, researchers have inspected hundreds of kill sites to learn that wolves mostly eat very young or older prey. Subsisting largely on caribou, Dall sheep, and moose, wolves also stalk beavers and snowshoe hares.

Surprisingly, a study conducted on the northwest edge of the park, mostly with the Bearpaw (River) wolf pack, shows that up to 34 percent of these wolves' diets consist of salmon. Wildlife biologists suspected that salmon sustained the wolves, often seen along the salmon-rich rivers without moose or caribou present. The moment of truth came in scanning 73 dead wolf bones from all over the park; researchers discovered much higher, salmon-related isotopes in the bones from the Bearpaw pack. Although wolves had been known to eat fish in coastal Alaska and Canada, this unprecedented Denali study was first to show inland wolves eating salmon.

Still, even this ultimate predator struggles to survive in a land of extremes. From 1986 to 2013, causes of death among 238 wolves that researchers had collared showed that 100 were killed by natural causes (including avalanche, starvation, drowning, old age, and disease); 79 were killed by other wolves; and 59 were killed by humans, usually after these wolves left park boundaries. As in most parks, the ultimate goal is to maintain healthy populations of wild animals through proper management—for instance, closing down and protecting areas that contain wolf denning sites. Unfortunately, little can be done to protect wolves leaving the park boundaries.

The loss of such a signature predator, once vigorously hunted here, could topple the relationships with prey, like the Dall sheep that make this park so unique. Protecting the Dall sheep—in fact, more

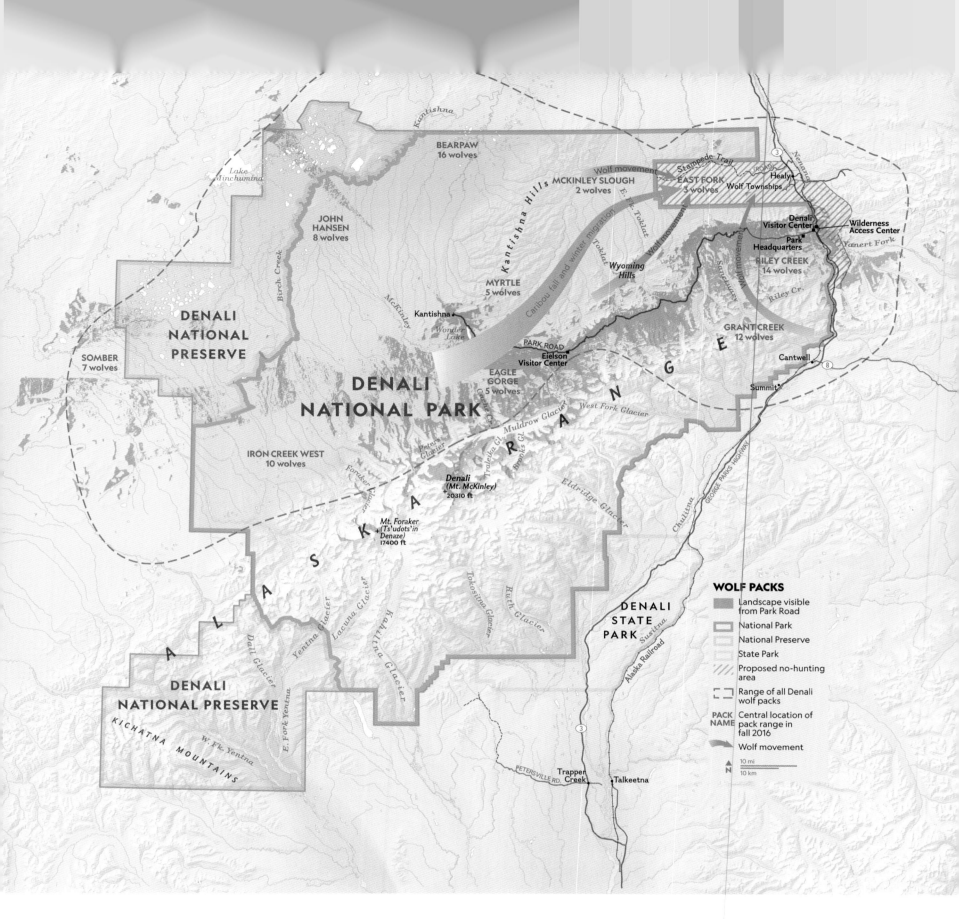

WOLF PACKS

- Landscape visible from Park Road
- National Park
- National Preserve
- State Park
- Proposed no-hunting area
- Range of all Denali wolf packs
- PACK NAME Central location of pack range in fall 2016
- Wolf movement

Denali National Park is one of the few places where people can see gray wolves in their natural habitat. Visitors can try to spot them from the shuttle buses along the 92-mile Park Road.

than protecting the wolves or any other wild game, let alone the preservation of North America's highest peak—led to the creation of the original park.

Beginning in summer of 1907, before the park existed, the naturalist-hunter and retired mine investor Charles Sheldon spent a year in residence amid this wilderness Shangri-la studying the sheep. His concern about hunters selling the sought-after sheep meat to miners led him to envision the creation of a game refuge, referred to in his journal as Denali National Park. But it would take years of lobbying Congress—along with the support of Teddy Roosevelt, the mountain climber Belmore Browne, and the Boone and Crockett and Campfire Clubs—to get Congress on board in Washington.

In January 1917, *National Geographic* magazine released an influential article about the potential park and how 2,000 Dall sheep had been killed in the previous year's hunts to feed workers on the burgeoning construction of the Alaska Railroad. Congress finally passed the legislation, but approved a political name honoring former U.S. president William McKinley, who had been assassinated in 1901, rather than the historical "Denali" for both the park and the mountain. On February 26, 1917, President Woodrow Wilson

GLACIERS DOMINATE SOME 1,500 SQUARE MILES OF DENALI NATIONAL PARK, COVERING ABOUT ONE-SIXTH OF THE ENTIRE PARK.

signed the bill into law for Mount McKinley National Park, then gave the pen to Sheldon.

McKinley would join a dozen older parks to be administered by the National Park Service that had been created in 1916. Yet Congress neglected to fund the park for five years; in 1921, lawmakers appropriated $8,000. And the boundaries of this original, parallelogram-shaped park would undergo a controversial series of shape-shifting moves and expansions over the next six decades.

In 1922, because the area east of the boundary contained unprotected populations of Dall sheep and caribou, the boundary was

ABOVE LEFT: **A bull caribou** pauses amid the willows in autumn—prime mating season in the park. The bulls fight for breeding rights, charging and clashing their antlers against those of their competitors.

LEFT: **In this subarctic wilderness,** only the hardiest plants survive—like Alaska jasmine, one of more than 1,500 species of vascular plants, mosses, and lichens found in Denali.

BELOW: **Congress created** Mount McKinley National Park in 1917, and expanded its area in 1922 and 1932. Congress tripled the park's size in 1980 and changed its name to Denali National Park and Preserve, honoring the Athabaskan name for the continent's tallest mountain.

PARK BOUNDARY EVOLUTION

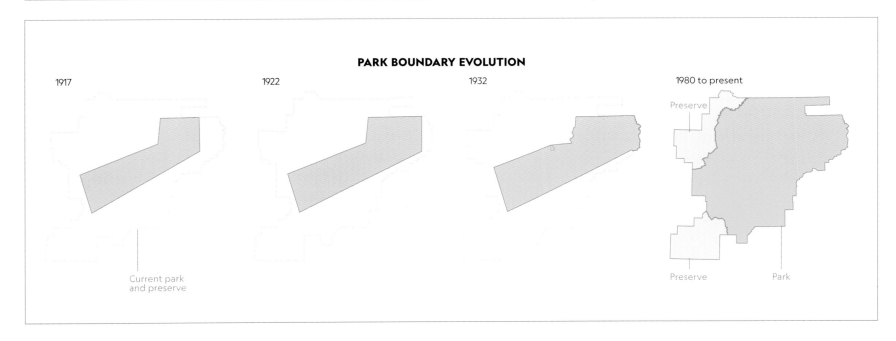

1917

1922

1932

1980 to present

Preserve

Current park and preserve

Preserve   Park

expanded toward the Nenana River and up to the crest of the Alaska Range. Ten years later, a landscape architect stimulated another executive order to stretch the boundary even farther to include the western banks of the Nenana River—a natural boundary for wildlife. Local miners and the expanding population of the nearby coal town of Healy were outraged to lose prime hunting grounds and potential mining opportunities. On the other side of the park in 1932, the boundaries were expanded northward to take in the alluring mirror-perfect haven of Wonder Lake, along with game-rich and heavily hunted hills outside the mining region of Kantishna.

By the late 1960s, many game biologists believed that the old boundaries did not serve the ecologic integrity and protection of wildlife. Numerous proposals stretched the borders in three different directions. But for decades, Alaskan hunting and mining interests, supported by state government, fought the federal expansion. World-wide recognition, if not expansion, came in 1976, when the United Nations named the park an international biosphere reserve. McKin-ley was honored for being one of the largest protected ecosystems, as well as encompassing the highest mountain on the continent.

In 1980, with wilderness vanishing throughout the United States, the newly minted Alaska National Interest Lands Conservation Act tripled the size of the park, making it the third largest sanctuary in the National Park System. Although Mount McKinley kept its name under the federal government for another 35 years (until 2015), the State Board on Geographic Names honored the original Athabaskan name. Living in 11 tribal groups throughout Interior Alaska, the Athabaskan or Dene people called the mountain Denali ("the high one"). To honor the original inhabitants, the federal government renamed the enlarged park Denali National Park and Preserve. The latter "preserve" zones remained open to hunting and local subsis-tence use, whereas the original park boundary was reclassified as "wilderness," prohibiting motorized access. These new boundaries swept over the Alaska Range to canvas the entire mountain massif, down to its southern glacial toes.

Long before the first passage of ice age glaciers, during the Creta-ceous period 70 million years ago, dinosaurs roamed over a nascent Denali. But it took until 2005 to find their tracks cast in the stone alongside the prints of modern-day grizzlies in the mud. That sum-mer, two dozen miles from park headquarters, a University of Alaska professor pointed toward the surrounding sedimentary rock and explained to his students how it often preserves dinosaur tracks in other regions. At that moment, a student spotted a print—nine by six inches—of a three-toed therapod and asked, "Like this one?" The professor couldn't have been more surprised. Until then, the discov-ery of dinosaur tracks was rare amid Interior Alaska.

On the lower Ruth Glacier, beneath the granite walls of the Ruth Gorge, the ice begins to break up, crush, and drop its payload of pulverized rock, while flowing slowly over time down to lower elevations, carving out the land.

THE WOOD FROG IS THE PARK'S ONLY AMPHIBIAN. IT FREEZES SOLID IN WINTER BUT SURVIVES BECAUSE OF GLUCOSE CIRCULATING THROUGH ITS BODY, WHICH KEEPS ITS CELLS ALIVE UNTIL SPRING.

To date, hundreds more sites have been uncovered with thousands of fossils that show evidence of ancient birds, flying reptiles, clams, worms, and various invertebrates. In 2016, four pieces of fossilized duck-billed hadrosaur bones—up to three inches long—were uncovered. Paleontologists believe that dinosaurs crossed the Bering Land Bridge and adapted to living in the polar forest that covered prehistoric Alaska and the Arctic. Several million years later, a more catastrophic, volcanic era began. Eventually, the dinosaurs vanished.

About 57 million years ago, magma cooled below the surface of the Earth and formed the granitic, Denali pluton beneath the sea that surrounded the region. Two to five million years ago, tectonics—created by the Pacific plate subducting beneath the North American plate—pushed up the mountain's harder pluton rocks through the softer seabed rocks, creating Denali and its erosion-resistant granite. Today, surrounding the summit, the conspicuous fractured black shale from the ancient seabed can still be seen surrounding the compact pink granite.

Hands down, among all mountains of the world, Denali wins the greatest vertical rise from dry land, stretching 18,000 feet from its northern tundra base to the summit. By comparison, Everest rises only 12,000 feet. Denali's 14,000-foot northern aspect, called the

Waterways like this meandering stream are a vital part of the ecosystem in Denali; they provide habitat for river plants, bugs, and fish, and a rest stop and hunting ground for caribou, wolves, and more.

South Peak
20310 ft

North Peak
19470 ft

DENALI

SOUTH BUTTRESS

EAST BUTTRESS

Mt. Foraker
17400 ft

Mt. Hunter
14573 ft

Mt. Stevens
13895 ft

Mt. Huntington
12240 ft

Mt. Dan Beard
10260 ft

RUTH
AMPHITHEATER

Mt. Dickey
9545 ft

Mt. Barrille
7650 ft

Avalanche Spire
10105 ft

KAHILTNA GLACIER

THE GREAT GORGE

RUTH GLACIER

Mt. Goldie
6315 ft

TOKOSITNA GLACIER

Tokosha
Mountains

Wickersham Wall, arguably forms the biggest mountain face in the world.

Given Denali's subarctic location and sudden storms, the mountain is colder and higher—for human physiology—than similar 20,000-foot mountains closer to the Equator. A thermometer left on the mountain for 19 years and later tested by the U.S. Weather Bureau (renamed the National Weather Service) registered minus 100°F (−73°C). Also, because the atmosphere thins closer to the poles of the Earth and reduces barometric pressure, Denali *feels* like a 24,000-foot peak near the Equator—all of which explain why it is so difficult to climb.

From 1903 to 1912, eight different teams attempted to reach the summit. Finally, in 1913, former prospector Harry Karstens—called the Seventymile Kid—spearheaded the first successful ascent. With years of winter survival experiences under his belt, including as Sheldon's guide in 1907–08 during the prolonged sheep study, Karstens (age 33) proved the ideal leader. Though he was not actually paid to guide the titular leader Archdeacon Hudson Stuck (49), Walter Harper (20), and Robert Tatum (21), few Alaskan pioneers could have filled Karstens's shoes on Denali's Muldrow Glacier in 1913.

Of historical significance, Karstens later became first superintendent of the park surrounding the mountain; Harper, half Athabaskan, became the first of his party to stand on the South Summit. Along with his step-chopping skills and ability to keep up with Karstens and carry the archdeacon's load, the eagle-eyed Harper also spotted a flagpole planted two miles away on the North Summit ridge. For most climbers, this flagpole sighting would settle the controversy over two miners—called "Sourdoughs" after their bread—who made the claim, doubted by many, in 1910 that they had reached that lower summit in a superhuman 18-hour round-trip sprint from 11,000 to 19,470 feet. In contrast, Karstens and company spent weeks above 11,000 feet and suffered dearly from altitude sickness, cold, and fumes from their cooking stove.

Nineteen years elapsed before anyone would attempt the mountain again. A four-man Park Service expedition climbed both Denali summits, but they saw no sign of the 1910 flagpole. On their descent, though, they discovered another team of climbers, but one lay dead and frosted with new snow on the Muldrow Glacier. It appeared that he had fallen into a crevasse and died from his injuries after climbing out. He had been trying to rescue yet another teammate, irrecover-

able and buried in one of many bottomless-looking crevasses. Of three more teammates waiting below, one was debilitated by illness, another got lost—all needed a rescue.

These first two deaths by crevasse fall would stand as historical testament to the mountain's many hazards: climbing falls, deadly storms, altitude illness, avalanches, and frostbite. Park Service rangers have now rescued hundreds of climbers; 126 have died.

In 1951, the virtuoso Bostonian climber and scientist, Dr. Bradford Washburn, made Denali a more accessible, if not easier, mountain to climb. By utilizing ski airplane support and eschewing the more difficult overland approach up the Muldrow Glacier, Washburn and his team landed high on the south side of the Alaska Range. After walking up the sinuous Kahiltna Glacier, they climbed onto the crest of the West Buttress and reached the summit in less than two weeks round-trip.

Climbers from all over the world would continue to follow Washburn's footsteps. Half succeeded in reaching the summit. The mountain would be soloed, skied, hang glided, and climbed in winter; by dog team, by 11- and 78-year-olds, by amputees, and by the blind. In 2014, a Catalonian ran from 7,000 feet to the summit and back in under 12 hours.

Although these feats were completed on the moderate West Buttress route, climbers made breathtaking ascents on three dozen other routes—many more technically difficult—encircling the mountain. In 1976, an American soloed the steep granite Cassin Ridge (normally a two-week climb) in 36 hours, and in 2018, another American reduced it to an eight-hour climb; in 1998, a lone Romanian skied the Wickersham Wall in seven hours. Although only a few unskied and unclimbed routes remain, most modern mountaineers stick to the well-traveled trail up the West Buttress. By end of the 2018 season, out of 45,389 attempts since 1903, 23,573 climbers succeeded in reaching the summit. Pioneering on the mountain is now a thing of the past, but the work of wildlife researchers throughout this massive national park below is only beginning. ■

ABOVE LEFT: **Created by** cartographer Brooke E. Marston using satellite images and digital elevation data, this oblique bird's-eye view map emphasizes the majesty of Denali. Although a handful of nearby mountains exceed 13,000 feet—including Mount Foraker, Mount Hunter, and Mount Silverthorne—none tops Denali, which at 20,310 feet is not only the highest point in the Alaska Range, but also the highest point in North America. It's one of the world's coldest mountains, too, with winds that rage over 150 miles an hour and temperatures that can reach minus 100°F (−73 °C).

ABOVE: **A climber** looks out toward Mount Foraker from the high slopes of Denali. More than a thousand climbers attempt Denali each year, with about a 50 percent success rate.

▷ LOCATION **250 MILES NW OF FAIRBANKS, ALASKA**

▷ SIZE **13,238 SQUARE MILES**

▷ HIGHEST POINT **MOUNT IGIKPAK, 8,510 FEET**

▷ VISITORS **9,591 IN 2018**

▷ ESTABLISHED **1980**

GATES OF THE ARCTIC NATIONAL PARK AND PRESERVE

This giant park straddles the central Brooks Range and encompasses the Endicott and Schwatka Mountains, which are separated by broad, U-shaped valleys, carved by long-departed glaciers. Gates of the Arctic is entirely above the Arctic Circle, unlike any other national park. In the northern park during winter, the sun doesn't rise for nearly a month; in summer the sun doesn't set for nearly two months. By August, autumn cooling and snow turn the lush carpet of tundra plants a brilliant scarlet and gold.

Looking across the park's vast tundra can be disorienting. There are few trees or other visual cues. Distant grizzlies look like nearby ground squirrels. Rich with wildlife, Gates approximates the wide-open wonders of the Great Plains before settlement: Wolves chase moose through the dwarf willow, grayling flit through pellucid waters, sandhill cranes strut along the river banks, and huge herds of caribou migrate through—their leg ligaments clicking like casta-nets—in an uncountable blur of tawny color and movement.

Beneath thousands of caribou paths, melting permafrost soaks the tundra throughout the park in summer, watering a wealth of Lilli-putian plant life from underground. Still, the region's climate is

Wildflowers bloom in Aquarius Valley below the Arrigetch Peaks. As the continent's northernmost park, Gates of the Arctic is known for its rugged and remote tundra landscapes.

TOP: **There are no roads** or trails through this vast wilderness; most locals and visitors fly on bush planes to get to the Nunamiut mountain village of Anaktuvuk Pass, shown above.

ABOVE: **Caribou are vital** to Nunamiut Eskimo culture—not only as a food source but as a spiritual kinship with animal souls, as seen in this Nunamiut boy's artistic mask made from caribou hide.

considered to be an Arctic desert. Summer backpackers escape the wet ground on the higher tundra and in the stony mountains. Most spectacular are the granite Arrigetch Peaks—meaning "fingers of the outstretched hand" in Inupiat—towering above aquamarine tarns with some of the best adventure rock climbing in Alaska. Paddlers circumvent the wet, lower-elevation spongy tussocks, thick willows, or boreal forest furring the southern boundaries on a multitude of twisting waterways. In 1980, reflecting the rare, pristine character of the park, six of these huge streams were designated Wild and Scenic Rivers.

The park has no established trails, roads, visitor centers, or modern infrastructure. Concealed in the tundra or buried in riverbanks, however, are thousands of archaeological sites—with animal remains, engraved bone artifacts, and stone tools—revealing nomadic hunting cultures from more than 12,000 years ago. These hunters moved in small bands following the caribou and other animals, while also relying on berries.

As the nomadic hunting life came to an end by the 1930s, Nunamiut descendants of Inupiat Inuit settled in Anaktuvuk Pass (population 325), the park's sole village, strategically placed along a migratory route of the caribou. Like other indigenous people of the north, the Nunamiut regard caribou—or *tuktu*—as a symbolic lifeline.

Few lower 48 national parks allow hunting within their boundaries, but Gates of the Arctic is one of a dozen recently established northern sanctuaries that have factored in indigenous peoples' rights through the 1980 Alaska National Interest Lands Conservation Act (ANILCA). The act included a "Subsistence Management and Use" provision for national parks stating that "Alaska Natives and other rural residents were granted hunting and fishing rights when fish and game are not under outside threat."

In addition to Anaktuvuk Pass, 10 villages surround Gates of the Arctic National Park and Preserve that qualify as "resident zone communities" where other indigenous people or local residents are allowed to continue traditional subsistence hunting, trapping, and fishing within both park and preserve boundaries. Otherwise, sport or guided hunting and trapping for nonlocals is allowed by permit only in the southern preserve boundaries. The preserve comprises nearly a million of the park's 8.4 million acres; another 164,000 acres within the park boundaries are owned by native corporations or the state.

Gates of the Arctic is a migratory stomping ground for the largest band of caribou in Alaska: the western Arctic herd. After its peak population of nearly a half million in 2003, the herd numbers plummeted by half, and then—as typical among fluctuating caribou populations—began to grow again in 2017.

The western Arctic herd has a 140,000-square-mile range, throughout northwestern Alaska, from the Arctic Ocean, to the Yukon River. In the spring, pregnant females lead the migration to calving grounds north of the Brooks Range. As a predator-avoidance technique, the caribou briefly form huge aggregations akin to the massing of migratory animals in the Serengeti. In the fall, as temperatures cool and the days shorten, they break into

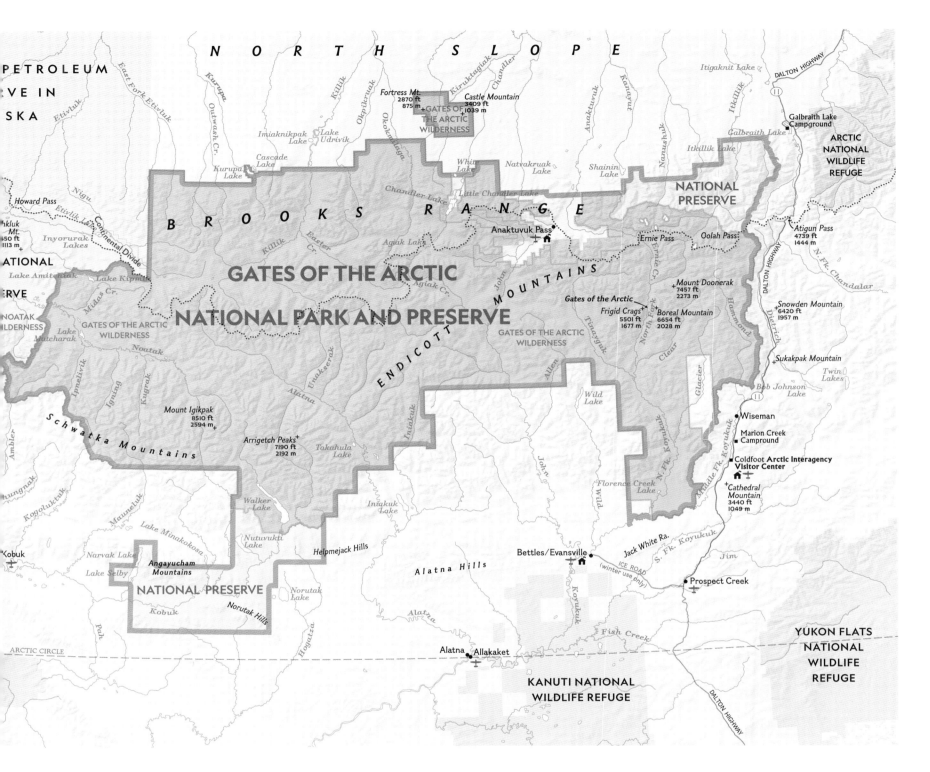

bands and migrate back over the Brooks Range, galloping across the tundra and swimming the park rivers. Poetically referred to as "gray shepherds of the tundra," caribou have uniquely splayed hooves that act as snowshoes, scoops for digging up food, or flippers in the water. Their hollow strands of fur give them buoyancy. Unlike other members of the deer family, both male and female caribou grow antlers.

Despite land protections, the broad movements of this special herd have been challenged by the last half century of development and warm winters that bring rain and coat their grazing areas with an impenetrable armor of ice. Combined with the adjacent Noatak Wilderness Area west of the park, the caribou utilize 12.9 million acres of this contiguous protected land. It's larger than any wilderness area in the United States, yet it's still not enough to contain the wide-ranging herd.

Whether visitors paddle for a week in the headwaters, or continue for more than a month out of the park and over 400 miles to the Chukchi Sea, with repeated caribou encounters, Gates is famous for innumerable lakes and rivers. Its six designated Wild and Scenic Rivers are undammed and selected for remarkable scenic, recreational, wildlife, or cultural values. This includes most of the Noatak, the longest protected watershed in all the National Wild and Scenic Rivers System; 102 miles of the North Fork of the Koyukuk River flowing through the mountain "Gates" of the park's name; half of the 125 miles of the popular John River flowing out of Anaktuvuk Pass; the entire 83 miles of the Alatna River, cascading out of the Arrigetch Peaks; half of the 280 miles of the large Kobuk River; and all 44 miles of the seldom paddled

ABOVE: **Female caribou** migrate across the tundra in herds that can tally about half a million animals. Their grazing significantly impacts plant and lichen communities in the park.

LEFT: **Hundreds of thousands of caribou**—or reindeer—form the Western Arctic herd that roams across 140,000 square miles in northwestern Alaska. The state's largest herd often migrates south across the Kobuk River during fall and journeys north to calving grounds during spring, though these patterns can shift.

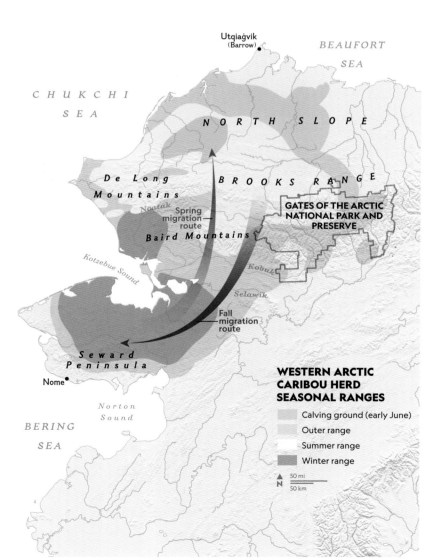

Utqiaġvik (Barrow)

BEAUFORT SEA

CHUKCHI SEA

NORTH SLOPE

De Long Mountains

BROOKS RANGE

Noatak

Spring migration route

GATES OF THE ARCTIC NATIONAL PARK AND PRESERVE

Baird Mountains

Kobuk

Kotzebue Sound

Selawik

Fall migration route

Seward Peninsula

Nome

Norton Sound

BERING SEA

WESTERN ARCTIC CARIBOU HERD SEASONAL RANGES

Calving ground (early June)
Outer range
Summer range
Winter range

50 mi
50 km

Tinayguk River. The national park manages all of these waterways.

The creation of Gates hinged on its principal explorer, Bob Marshall. Following a few hardy prospectors and a group of government surveyors cowed by premature winter, Marshall made his second trip to the Arctic in 1930, looking for blank spaces on the map rather than gold or oil. As an early visionary with the U.S. Forest Service, he already had a reputation for speaking out for the protection of wild places. "There is just one hope for repulsing the tyrannical ambition of civilization to conquer every inch on the whole earth," Marshall wrote that year in *Scientific Monthly*. "That hope is the organization of spirited people who will fight for the freedom and preservation of the wilderness."

While exploring the Koyukuk drainage, Marshall dubbed the region Gates of the Arctic for the distinctive portal between Boreal Mountain and Frigid Crags—peaks that he also named. He continued with his epic peak-climbing quest, rambling throughout the range while surveying plants and mapping; in 1935, he founded the Wilderness Society with a like-minded team of conservationists dedicated to saving wild places. Marshall died young, at age 38, but his posthumously published book *Alaska Wilderness: Exploring the Central Brooks Range* would lead to the park's creation. The Wilder-

BOTH MALE AND FEMALE CARIBOU GROW ANTLERS. MALES SHED THEIRS IN AUTUMN, WHILE PREGNANT FEMALES DON'T USUALLY SHED UNTIL AFTER GIVING BIRTH IN LATE SPRING. MALE ANTLERS CAN WEIGH UP TO 29 POUNDS A PAIR.

ness Society's enduring philosophies would also forge the 1964 Wilderness Act—the principal legislation protecting 90 percent of the northernmost park acreage.

Within two decades of Marshall's death, oil and precious minerals were discovered in Arctic Alaska. In 1956, the Wilderness Society

members Olaus and Mardy Murie followed Marshall's lead by advocating for and eventually creating the Arctic National Wildlife Range—immediately east of Marshall's portal. America's foremost caribou scientist, Olaus Murie backed Marshall's wilderness and plant science advocacy with a strategy that would set aside areas large enough to protect both the Arctic ecosystem and its peripatetic caribou herds.

The conservation movement ramped up in the 1960s, and the range (renamed a refuge and enlarged to a massive 19.5 million acres) brought more attention to the neglected northern wilderness. Subsequently, National Park Service planners took a page from Marshall's books and identified the central Brooks Range as a potential park. At the same time, the state of Alaska began bulldozing a road several hundred miles across the fragile tundra, exposing the permafrost below, in a misguided effort to provide access to oil fields north of the Brooks Range. This laceration through the wilderness, named the Hickel Highway after the Alaskan governor who funded it, still scars the northern park today.

In the late 1960s, proposals to render Gates of the Arctic a national monument fell on deaf ears. The ensuing decade saw the incomplete Hickel Highway scrapped in favor of the 414-mile Dalton Highway, intended to service the Trans-Alaska Pipeline and Prudhoe Bay oil fields. Throughout the 1970s in D.C., lawmakers squabbled with oil and mineral lobbyists who argued against large parks during the preparation of the sweeping ANILCA legislation, which would create Gates along with 43,585,000 acres of new parklands.

The Ambler Access project aims to construct a 211-mile road for industrial use, connecting Dalton Highway to the Ambler Mining District. If built, the two-lane gravel road would cross state and federal lands, including approximately 20 miles through Gates of the Arctic National Park and a span over the Kobuk Wild River.

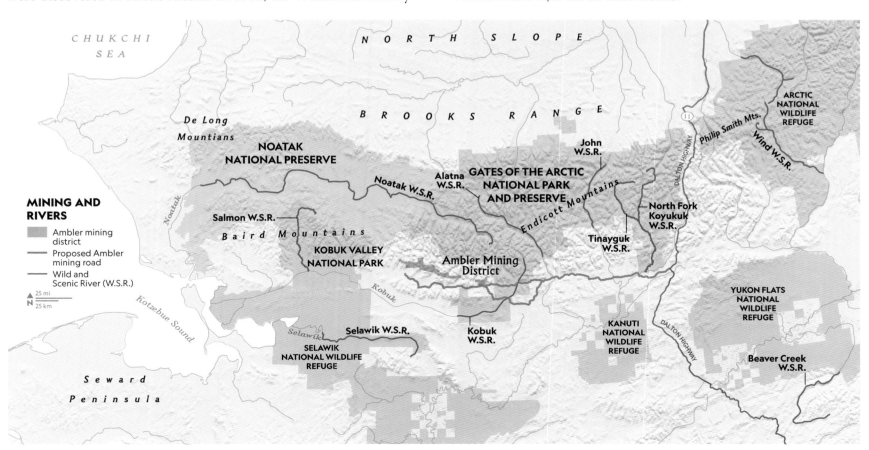

MINING AND RIVERS

- Ambler mining district
- Proposed Ambler mining road
- Wild and Scenic River (W.S.R.)

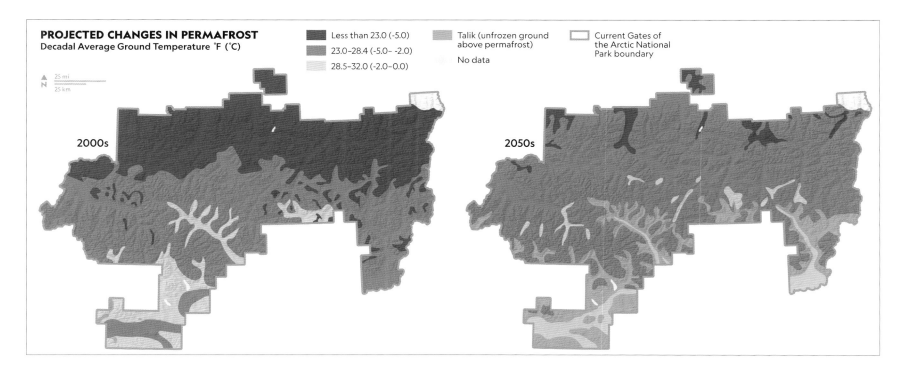

PROJECTED CHANGES IN PERMAFROST
Decadal Average Ground Temperature °F (°C)

- Less than 23.0 (-5.0)
- 23.0–28.4 (-5.0– -2.0)
- 28.5–32.0 (-2.0–0.0)
- Talik (unfrozen ground above permafrost)
- No data
- Current Gates of the Arctic National Park boundary

25 mi
N
25 km

2000s

2050s

Finally, in 1978, President Carter designated these areas, including Gates, as national monuments. And in 1980, Congress passed the ANILCA park legislation. Gates of the Arctic National Park and Preserve stretched 200 miles west of the pipeline, closed to all mineral extraction, as part of an 800-mile band of protected Arctic (including the Arctic Refuge and Noatak Wilderness) and became the second largest national park in the system. The only exception: a provision allowing a road to be built across the southern preserve and the Kobuk River to access the Ambler mining district.

In an era of climate change and population growth, protection can be a relative term even in this remote national park. Among the evolving complexities of the dynamic landscape, concerned scientists have documented a phenomenon known as "greening of the Arctic" caused by shorter, warmer winters. Because the length of the growing season controls plant life—the energy supply and habitat for wildlife—these greening changes can disturb the entire ecosystem.

As annual temperature averages rise, the permafrost that underlays nearly 40 million acres of Alaskan Park Service lands is beginning to thaw. Permafrost directly beneath the tundra stabilized plant growth, animal habitat, and water flow in Gates of the Arctic until now. But thawing below the active "frosting" layer and down into the frozen "cake" has caused lakes to disappear, trees to slump over in a phenomenon Alaskans call "drunken forests," streams to fill with sediment, and myriad vegetation changes. Thermokarsts—where the active layer of tundra and plants has slumped into large sinkholes

Permafrost—ground that stays frozen year-round—supports grasses, flowers, and berries of the Arctic tundra. Ground temperature modeling predicts the impact that climate change may have on near-surface permafrost temperature in Gates of the Arctic National Park; such variations could affect ecosystems, in addition to infrastructure like buildings and roads.

or landslides created by permafrost melt—are increasingly common in the park.

As scientists continue to monitor thawing permafrost, the fragile landscape remains a magnetic escape for those who seek true wilderness, whether they arrive by aircraft or on foot. The park's remoteness and total lack of visitor services are an inherent defense from crowding, so that those willing to make the journey might experience something akin to what Marshall once described as dropping back in time into an unspoiled, primordial world. ∎

OPPOSITE: **A hiker pauses** near the granite spires of the Arrigetch Peaks—a dream destination for rock climbers around the world—in the remote Endicott Mountains.

RIGHT: **Though the** shallow and rocky tundra over permafrost can't support trees, many alpine plants like this purple mountain saxifrage thrive off the ice thawing under the ground in summer.

▷ LOCATION **250 MILES SW OF ANCHORAGE, ALASKA**

▷ SIZE **6,396 SQUARE MILES**

▷ HIGHEST POINT **MOUNT DENNISON, 7,606 FEET**

▷ VISITORS **37,818 IN 2018**

▷ ESTABLISHED **1980**

KATMAI NATIONAL PARK AND PRESERVE

At the head of the Alaska Peninsula is a landscape of glaciated volcanoes and cerulean lakes alongside the Pacific Ocean. The fourth largest national park in the system, Katmai is wider, taller, and deeper than the state of Connecticut. But the seldom visited park—accessible to the outside world only by aircraft or boat—has only one nearby town, King Salmon (population 374), outside its western boundary.

Eighty percent of Katmai's four million acres are permanently protected wilderness; sport and subsistence hunting are permitted in less than a half million acres of the northern preserve. Bordering Katmai are another 1.5 million protected acres in the Becharof National Wildlife Refuge and the bear-rich McNeil River State Game Sanctuary and Refuge.

The park attracts visitors from all over the world to watch its 2,000 brown bears diving, splashing, and swimming after salmon, but it is also known for being the locus of the greatest volcanic eruption of the 20th century. A dozen miles from its coast, a string of equally impressive and unpredictable volcanoes still smolder. In 1912, an eruption spawned a superheated river of lava and hurled ash around

The summer sun sets on mountain peaks at Geographic Harbor in Amalik Bay, a historic landmark and an Archeological District with sites more than 7,000 years old.

the world—cooling the Northern Hemisphere by 2°F (1.1°C) for months. Six years later, President Wilson established Katmai National Monument, believing that the 40 square miles of still steaming pumice and red-hot fumaroles rivaled Yellowstone.

Katmai's volcanoes conceal a rich cultural history. Mostly buried in volcanic ash—along with projectile points, ceramic vessels, carvings, and subterranean homes—is the legacy of a half dozen, forgotten hunting cultures that preceded the national park.

As early as 25,000 years ago Ancient Beringians became the first humans to occupy Alaska. The first evidence of people—known as the Northern Archaic tradition—living in the park occurred 5,000 years ago. These nomads of the forest made simple campsites in pursuit of caribou and seasonal salmon runs. Their notched arrowheads are now valued relics, but any traces of these hunters' nets or fishing gear have long since disappeared.

Next on the scene were the Arctic small tool tradition people, whose settlement has been dated by radiocarbon techniques to 3,850 years ago. Rather than the impermanent campsites of their predecessors, they built and lived in dugout houses. Remains of more than a dozen of these rough square homes—originally reaching 12 feet high and surrounding a central rock fireplace built with remains of fish teeth—were found adjoining the Brooks River in Katmai. Tools were also uncovered: These early dwellers used scrapers for removing animal hides, small adze blades with polished bits, and flint burins.

Three thousand years ago the people of the small tools tradition disappeared or were absorbed by other cultures. Then, 2,250 to 900 years ago, the people of the Norton tradition, migrating from

---

Katmai's extensive coastline is a refuge, nesting place, and hunting ground for an abundance of birds like this horned puffin, who will spend most of winter at sea.

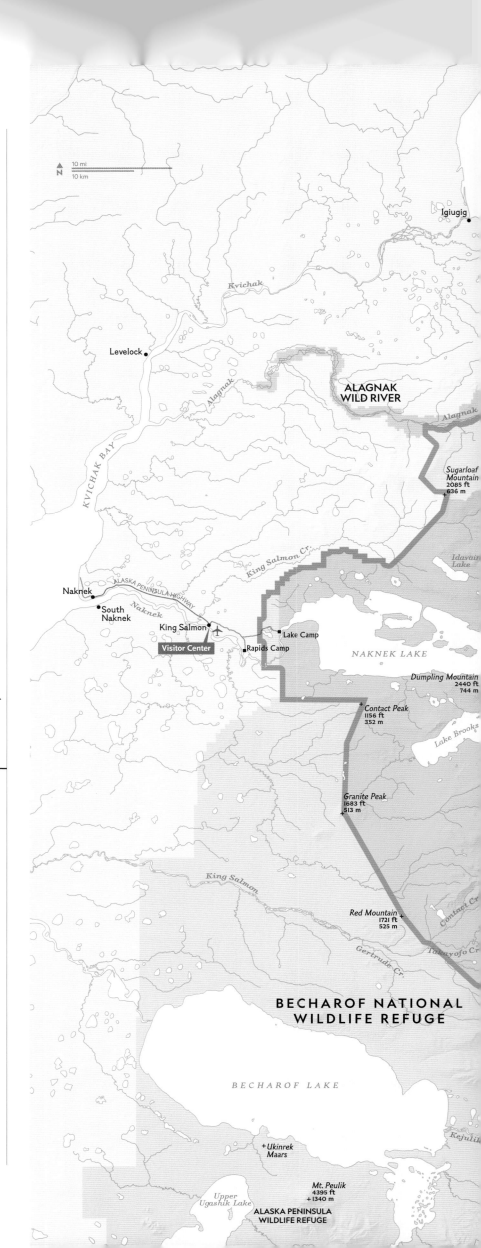

ILIAMNA LAKE

AUGUSTINE ISLAND

Gibraltar Lake

KAMISHAK BAY

COOK INLET

Funnel Cr.

Mirror Lake

Spectacle Lake

Moraine Cr.

Crosswind Lake

KUKAKLEK LAKE

Battle River
Wilderness Retreat

McNeil Falls

McNeil Cove

Akumwarvik Bay

KATMAI
NATIONAL
PRESERVE

Royal Wolf Lodge

McNeil Lake

McNEIL RIVER
STATE GAME
SANCTUARY

KAMISHAK SPECIAL
USE AREA

Nonvianuk Patrol Cabin

Battle Lake

Pirate Lake

Nonvianuk

NONVIANUK LAKE

Kulik
Lodge

Kulik Lake

Little Kamishak

McNeil

Enchanted
Lake Lodge

Oakley Peak
4625 ft
1410 m +

American Cr.

Hammersley Lake

Strike Cr.

Spotted Glacier

Mt. Douglas
7063 ft
2153 m +

Sukoi Bay

Cape Douglas

Murray Lake

Kamishak

Douglas

Fourpeaked Glacier

Grosvenor
Lodge

Fourpeaked Mountain
6903 ft
2104 m +

Lake Coville

Free Use
Public Cabin

Portage Trail

Lake Grosvenor

KATMAI
NATIONAL PARK

Big

North Arm

Bay of Islands

Hardscrabble Cr.

Kaguyak Crater +

Swishak
Patrol Cabin

Swishak Bay

Brooks
Camp

Visitor Center

Savonoski

Mt. La Gorce
3183 ft
+ 970 m

Wolverine Falls

Hallo Bay
Wilderness Camps

Cultural Site

Brooks Falls

Iliuk Arm

Savonoski
(abandoned village)

Devils Desk
6411 ft
+ 1954 m

Hook Glacier

+ Kukak Volcano
6700 ft
2042 m

Ninagiak Island

Hallo Bay

+ Mt. Kelez
3250 ft
991 m

Mt. Katolinat
4730 ft
+ 1442 m

Margot Falls

Rainbow

Mt. Denison
7606 ft
2318 m + Mt. Steller
7300 ft
2225 m

Hallo Glacier

Three Forks
Overlook

Mt. Griggs
7600 ft
+ 2316 m

Katmai
Wilderness Lodge

Ukak

Serpent Tongue Glacier

Valley of Ten Thousand Smokes

Snowy Mountain
7090 ft
2161 m +

Devils Cove

Knife Cr.

Buttress Range

Windy Cr.

Mt. Katmai
6715 ft
2047 m

Kukak Bay

Novarupta
2760 ft
+ 841 m

Crater Lake

Kaflia Bay

+ Trident Volcano
6010 ft
1832 m

Angle Cr.

Mt. Mageik
7259 ft
2210 m +

Martin Cr.

Katmai

Hidden Harbor

Kinak Bay

Kuliak Bay

Kejulik Mountains

Alagogshak Cr.

Kejulik

Geographic
Harbor

Amalik Bay
Patrol Cabin

Missak Bay

AFOGNAK
ISLAND

Amalik Bay

Takli Island

SHELIKOF STRAIT

Katmai Village
(abandoned)

Dakavak Bay

Katmai Bay

Kashvik Bay

Cape Kubugakli

KUPREANOF STRAIT

Alinchak Bay

KODIAK ISLAND

Puale Bay

BEFORE THE DESTRUCTIVE ERUPTION FORCED OUT VILLAGERS IN 1912, SEVERAL YEAR-ROUND VILLAGES AND SEASONAL CAMPSITES WERE USED FOR FISHING, HUNTING, AND GATHERING INSIDE TODAY'S PARK.

Canada, arrived in southern Alaska. They were the first fishermen to intensively harvest the salmon runs on the Alagnak River—now a 48-square-mile, federally protected section of Wild and Scenic River outside the western park boundary, which Katmai manages. In dozens of pit homes once lit by seal lamps in a four-acre village site along the riverbanks, archaeologists have uncovered scores of tools, including *ulus* (knives), hammer stones, adzes, whetstones, and harpoon points. Evidence shows that they fired ceramic pots strengthened with plant fibers.

Nine hundred years ago, the Thule ancestors of modern Inuit came to the region. In several small villages amid the present-day park, they too built semisubterranean houses and introduced marine hunting techniques for harvesting sea mammals and fish. Like their

predecessors, the Thule people thrived amid Katmai's bounty of wildlife. In the flatter part of the park, among the many huge lakes, are snowshoe hares, wolves, coyotes, beavers, lynx, wolverines, otters, caribou, moose, and many small mammals. Along the jagged and rainy coast, seals, sea lions, and orca prey on salmon, while humpback whales devour small fish and krill. More than a hundred species of birds also inhabit the region.

By the late 1700s, Russian fur hunters arrived in the Aleutian Islands ready to expand their trade. They pressed the Thule inhabitants, whom they referred to as Alutiiq, into service for their skill at hunting fox, otters, and birds. American traders resumed these practices after Alaska was purchased in 1867. Although relations had been strained between Russians and natives, the Russian Orthodox religion and its uniquely onion-domed churches—with long false windows and scalloped trim—remained throughout southern Alaska after the U.S. government took over. Many natives gave up long-held traditional beliefs and became followers of Christ.

Throughout the millennia of human history—from the Paleo-Arctic tradition to the Thule—natural phenomena repeatedly forced these cultures from the Katmai region. Violent eruptions shook the Earth and flung ash and lava flows across homes and hunting grounds. The volcanoes that caused this can be traced back to 180 to 190 million years ago, as the supercontinent Pangaea broke apart and the Pacific plate was created, floating atop the Earth's mantle.

Over millions of years, the northern boundary of the 140-million-square-mile Pacific plate began subducting under the North American plate and pushing up against the Alaska Peninsula. As the

OPPOSITE: **The most voluminous** volcanic eruption of the 20th century, the 1912 Katmai-Novarupta spewed ash high into the stratosphere, dusting Europe two weeks later.

BELOW: **This cutaway** of a pit house shows what life was like for an indigenous family in Katmai. The home includes several features to help protect its inhabitants from severe weather conditions: an entry tunnel, a central fire ring, and layers of moss on the roof and walls to serve as insulation. Animal skins are used for bedding, and a seal oil lamp illuminates the space.

Mount Griggs, formerly Knife Peak, is a stratovolcano and one of the park's tallest peaks, rising 7,600 feet at the edge of the Valley of Ten Thousand Smokes.

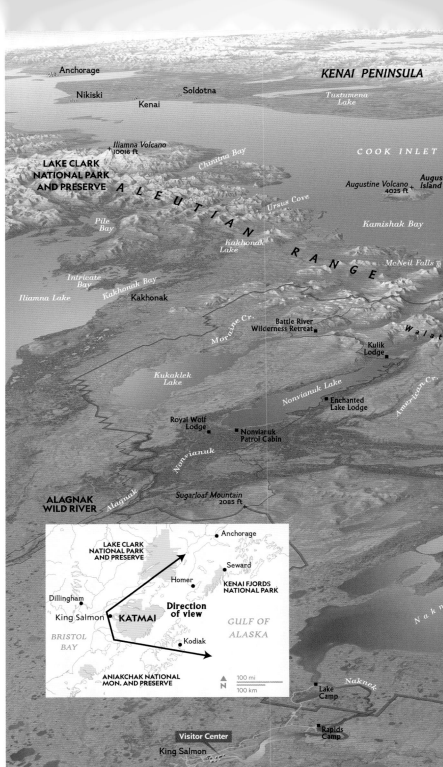

Pacific plate submarined at a 45-degree angle under the lighter North American plate, it tore out the Aleutian Trench, 2,200 miles across the ocean floor. West of Katmai, the 50- to 100-mile-wide Aleutian Trench drops more than five miles deep into the ocean floor, showing the unfathomable forces generated by a head-on collision of the planet's crustal plates.

Eventually, moving at the rate of 2.5 inches a year, the saturated rocks of the Pacific plate continued bulldozing under the North American plate. Water was released, and it rose toward the Earth's surface. Like adding chemical flux to solder, the melting point of surrounding rocks was lowered, and more liquid magma—as hot as 2372°F (1300° C)—boiled up as rocks continued dissolving into this subterranean cauldron, collecting in massive underground reservoirs beneath the Alaska Peninsula. As explosive gases and steam force the magma to the surface, it erupts through vents. Over the millennia, the cooling magma—which becomes lava (and eventually, igneous rock) aboveground—combines with ash to pile up into volcanoes. The

northern boundary of these colliding plates would force up magma that created the 1,600-mile-long Aleutian Range of volcanoes.

Violent earthquakes are common around colliding tectonic plates in subduction zones. Subduction zones also tend to build the tall and steep-sided, classic cones called stratovolcanoes. Due to Katmai's proximity to the underlying subduction, the park contains an incredibly dense cluster of 14 active volcanoes, including: Mount Griggs, Mount Kaguyak, Mount Mageik, Mount Trident, and Mount Katmai.

From 2.6 million to 11,700 years ago, the volcanic eruptions combined with other forces to shape the land. Pleistocene glaciers carved out the lakes and alternately scoured away volcanic ash, then were reburied by it. Moraines formed across the 600-mile-long Alaska Peninsula and the Aleutian Islands stretching another 1,000 miles west.

Three major landforms define Katmai National Park and Preserve. The Shelikof Strait coast curves into bays and coves, with rugged cliffs and canyons rising from the beaches. Inland, the Aleutian Range sweeps upward into glacier-covered slopes and volcanoes that rise to elevations over 7,000 feet. The northwestern park is considered the lake region, with the vast Naknek Lake at the heart.

Then, in early June 1912, the Katmai subduction zone's magma reservoirs began overloading. For nearly a week, residents as far as 160 miles away felt severe earthquakes.

On the morning of June 6, villagers in the coastal village of Katmai, 19 miles away from the eruption zone, fled in their kayaks as the earthquakes grew stronger. At 1 p.m., an explosion was heard 750 miles away in Juneau. At the same time, 55 miles away from the eruption, the crew of the steamship *Dora* in Shelikof Strait saw an ash cloud towering up into the atmosphere. They motored full speed toward the open ocean. Within two hours, a thick ash cloud abruptly enveloped *Dora* and day turned to night as lightning bolts flashed all around them. *Dora* remained under the ash cloud until they reached the gulf the next day.

On June 9, in Kaflia Bay, 30 miles away from the eruption, a fisherman wrote to his wife under lantern light about the mountain that had burst. In places, the ash piled 10 feet deep. "In a word it is terrible and we are expecting death at any moment, and we have no water," wrote the survivor Ivan Orloff, a half Russian, half Aleut chief. "Here are darkness and hell, thunder and noise . . . Perhaps we shall see each other again."

The eruption cloud had risen 20 miles into the stratosphere. Ash shrouded most of southern Alaska and the Yukon Territory, leaving a haze over British Columbia. A day after the eruption, the ash cloud passed over Virginia; two weeks later, ash fell across Europe. Stronger and larger than any other recorded eruption in North America—30 times that of Mount St. Helens in 1980—the Katmai eruption was the first large volcano that erupted on land, its pyroclastic flow (a high-density mix of lava blocks, pumice, ash, and volcanic gas) rushing north at 100 miles an hour, rather than being lost to the ocean.

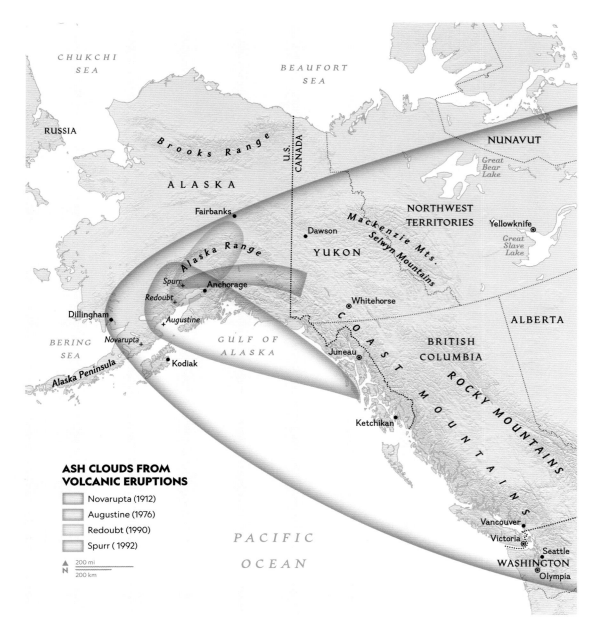

ASH CLOUDS FROM
VOLCANIC ERUPTIONS

- Novarupta (1912)
- Augustine (1976)
- Redoubt (1990)
- Spurr (1992)

200 mi
200 km

The historic 60-hour-long eruption at Novarupta on June 6, 1912, was the most voluminous volcanic event of the 20th century: Over the course of three days, 3.1 cubic miles of magma exploded. Ash spread across the region, far surpassing the range of ashfall seen during the eruptions of nearby Augustine, Spurr, and Redoubt.

The still burning cataclysm quickly became a giant outdoor laboratory. Seven different National Geographic Expeditions came to investigate and witnessed tens of thousands of fumaroles, whooshing up in gaseous columns, making a discordant, thousand-feet-high, steam-whistle concert. Investigators named it "The Valley of Ten Thousand Smokes."

At first, scientists believed that the previously active Mount Katmai had erupted again, if only because its twin summits collapsed into a 1.9-mile-wide, 2,000-foot-deep crater (now filled by a lake). Elsewhere, snowfields and glacial streams had flashed away in steam. Glaciers would remain covered with ash for decades. A once verdant V-shaped river course had been transformed into a smoldering mass of pumice and ash hundreds of feet deep that stretched as far as the eye could see.

After the monument was established in 1918, *National Geographic* publications prompted more visitations to the incredible, smoking valley. Because the science of volcanology was in its infancy, it took

decades to nail down the eruption's source. Eventually, scientists discovered that the magma reservoir underneath Mount Katmai, 6,716 feet, had been released six miles away through a 200-foot-high vent earlier named Novarupta. As Novarupta (Latin for "new eruption") finished disgorging its payload of inner-earthen hell, Mount Katmai collapsed into the emptied magma reservoir below. Most of the ash and pumice that darkened the Earth's skies and blanketed the land had been expelled from the Novarupta vent. By the 1930s, the fumaroles finally cooled as the residual heat dissipated and the Valley of Ten Thousand Smokes, at least for a time, fell silent.

Over the decades, the monument boundaries repeatedly expanded. In 1960 the Park Service built a road 23 miles from the popular fishing at Brooks River to the Valley of Ten Thousand Smokes (today buses service that road). By 1980, the Alaska National Interest Lands Conservation Act (ANILCA) had added a million acres, and Katmai National Park and Preserve became a reality.

When the smoking calderas and geysers of steam had relented, fishing became the main draw—until park promoters figured out that Katmai still evoked Yellowstone, and then some. Thanks to wild salmon, Alaskan brown bears easily outnumber and outweigh Yellowstone's bears.

The 2.5-mile-long Brooks River, although short, typifies the many streams that draw the brown bears' favorite meal: sockeye (or red) salmon. In terms of caloric expenditure measured against caloric gain, no other available park food—moose, grubs, pea vine, or ground squirrels—is so easily obtained. Brooks Falls, in particular, creates a temporary barrier to migrating salmon, making them ready prey. Up to 70 bears come to eat daily while visitors—numbering in the tens of thousands each year—watch from the safety of a nearby viewing platform.

Since time immemorial, millions of spawning salmon have made an annual return from the Pacific to their exact spawning grounds in the streams around the park. Consequently, there are easily more coastal brown bears (the smaller grizzlies live inland, but are the same species) than people living on the Alaska Peninsula. Katmai may shelter the largest population of protected bears in the world.

The park preserves the living laboratory left by the Katmai-Novarupta eruption, including at least 14 active volcanoes—some of which are still steaming—and this Mount Katmai caldera.

PARK BOUNDARY EVOLUTION

1918

Current park and preserve

National Monument

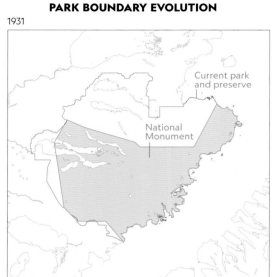

1931

Current park and preserve

National Monument

1980 to present

Current park and preserve

President Woodrow Wilson established Katmai National Monument in 1918 to protect the Valley of Ten Thousand Smokes, and in 1931 President Herbert Hoover enlarged it by 1.6 million acres. The 1980 Alaska National Interest Lands Conservation Act (ANILCA) expanded the monument to its present size and redesignated it Katmai National Park and Preserve.

Three to five feet wide at the shoulder, the biggest male bears stand nearly eight feet tall. Their distinctive shoulder humps—unlike the lean-shouldered polar or black bears found outside Katmai—are prodigious muscles used for digging clams, roots, or insects. The sight of a ground squirrel being unearthed is unforgettable: The bear throws dirt and rocks 10 feet backward until the prey is grabbed and then swallowed in a single gulp.

In part because of the electric fences surrounding Brooks Camp, and in part because of visitors' practicing good camping

techniques, there has been only one bear encounter with human fatalities in all the decades with visitors in close proximity to bears. Ninety-one years after Chief Orloff wrote goodbye to his wife from Kaflia Bay as the Novarupta explosion buried his fishing camp in ash, the amateur naturalist Timothy Treadwell and his girlfriend Amie Huguenard arrived and set up camp on this overgrown shoreline on the park's southern shore. Treadwell had defied, evaded, and even been ticketed by Park Service rangers for 13 years while illegally camping next to the bears of Katmai and brazenly storing food in his tent. He had embarked on a

Katmai isn't all ice and snow: In the warmer summer months, wildflowers burst to life in meadows like this one on Nukshak Island and Hallo Bay.

noble mission: to protect bears from hunting, poaching, and loss of habitat—even though brown bears are not endangered in Alaska and were protected here inside park boundaries (bear hunting is allowed in the preserve only). Yet Treadwell ignored all precautions, touching and even swimming with the bears as if they were domestic pets instead of wild animals. Late on October 5, 2003, a 28-year-old bruin tragically killed Treadwell and Huguenard.

Since then, the park has continued to provide advice for proper bear etiquette and safety. This includes avoiding camping on bear trails or near moving water, using electric fences for camps, carrying bear spray, and using bear-proof food containers.

Although most visitors come to see the bears, the park's coasts have offered refuge for the sea otter among the other 42 mammal species there. Sought after for its luxuriant fur, the sea otter was nearly wiped out by fur traders; by 1850 less than a few hundred remained in isolated pockets of Alaska. Initially listed as threatened, the population of this keystone species has slowly rebounded. Monitoring in the park has shown that their numbers increased substantially since the early 1990s, and have remained at high and stable densities in recent years. The sight of a sea otter floating on its back in the mists offshore, breaking open a mussel with a rock, is just one of the park's many unsung pleasures. ■

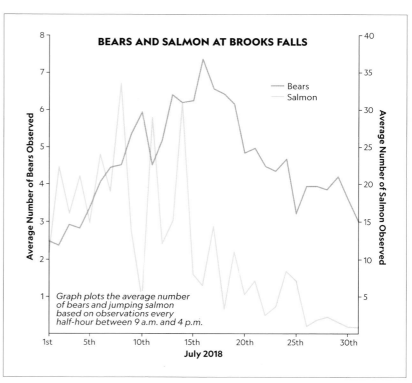

BEARS AND SALMON AT BROOKS FALLS

Average Number of Bears Observed

Average Number of Salmon Observed

— Bears
— Salmon

Graph plots the average number of bears and jumping salmon based on observations every half-hour between 9 a.m. and 4 p.m.

1st   5th   10th   15th   20th   25th   30th

July 2018

TOP: **Coastal brown bears** wait for sockeye salmon, one of five species of Pacific salmon that spawn every year in the nearly pristine rivers and lakes of Alaska.

ABOVE: **One of the** world's greatest seasonal concentrations of brown bears gathers at Brooks River—where hungry bears can find migrating salmon starting in late June. The bear count along the river peaks in mid-July after most salmon have migrated through the stream.

- ▷ LOCATION **30 MILES SW OF HILO, HAWAI'I**

- ▷ SIZE **520 SQUARE MILES**

- ▷ HIGHEST POINT **MAUNA LOA, 13,677 FEET**

- ▷ VISITORS **1,116,891 IN 2018**

- ▷ ESTABLISHED **1916**

HAWAI'I VOLCANOES NATIONAL PARK

Rising from sea to summit on the Big Island of Hawai'i, this park is farther south than any point within the continental United States, and is part of the most remote island chain in the world: Hawai'i Volcanoes National Park is 2,400 miles from California and 3,850 miles from Japan.

Its isolation in the Pacific makes for an unusually high proportion of species found nowhere else in the world. Like a veritable Galápagos, the park serves as a 333,000-acre endemic laboratory for studying evolution. Most animals hitched rides, floated, or flew to the island, including bats, the only native mammal in the park, and a colorful assemblage of birds including six endangered species. More than Darwin's celebrated yet low-lying South American atolls, Hawai'i Volcanoes National Park has an incredible diversity of wildlife habitats, stretching nearly three miles above sea level. The different ecosystems include alpine, subalpine, and upland forests; rainforest; mid-elevation woodland, lowland, and coast. All are plagued with troublesome invasive species, even in the lunar landscape of the Ka'ü Desert, immediately below the Kīlauea crater.

Most visitors go to the park to see Kīlauea and Mauna Loa eruptions. These and the other three volcanoes that built the

Seen from the top of Mauna Kea, Mauna Loa is the planet's most massive single mountain, largest active volcano, and the highest point in the park.

KONA INTERNATIONAL
AIRPORT AT KEAHOLE

8271 ft
2521 m

HUALĀLAI

Kaloko-Honokōhau
National Historical Park
Kailua-Kona

13677 ft
4169 m

Moku'āweoweo
Caldera

Mauna Loa
Weather
Observatory

Mauna
Loa Cabin

Pu'uhonua o Hōnaunau
National Historical Park

MAUNA LOA

MAUNA LOA
WILDERNESS

HAWAI'I VOLCANOES
NATIONAL PARK
KAHUKU UNIT

'Ainapō Trail

Halewai Cabin

Trailhead gate

Kapāpala
Gate

'AINAPŌ RD.

Ocean
View

KAHUKU

Ka'ū Desert
Trailhead

KAHUKU RD.

KA'Ū FOREST RESERVE

Maunaiki

Ka'ū Desert Trail

SOUTH POINT RD.

Great Crack

Southwest Rift Zone

Hilina Pali
Overlook

Pāhala

Ka'ū Desert Trail

Pepeiao
Cabin

Hilina

Nā'ālehu

KA'Ū DESERT WILDERNESS

Punalu'u

Ka'aha Trail

Ka'aha

PACIFIC OCEAN

island of Hawai'i drop another 16,408 feet below sea level. At 30,085 feet from base to summit, Mauna Loa is a thousand feet greater than Mount Everest (Mauna Kea, just outside the park, has 33,474 feet of vertical relief). As part of the Hawaiian-Emperor seamount chain of volcanoes extending from the ocean floor, the range is twice as long and several thousand feet higher than the Himalaya. And the park's mountains are still building: The 4,091-foot-high Kīlauea (meaning "spreading, much spewing") has been erupting significantly since 1983, according to the U.S. Geological Survey, and is one of the world's few drive-up calderas—though access was limited following a May 2018 eruption. Although the 60-mile-long, 30-mile-wide Mauna Loa is the largest active volcano on Earth, Kīlauea is the most productive.

In the minuscule span of geologic time—275,000 years ago—since Kīlauea began blowing its top, the island has expanded by thousands of acres. The volcano's daily lava output could resurface a 20-mile-long, double-lane highway.

This island-building activity shows how the Hawaiian-Emperor seamount chain was created over the last 85 million years. Including at least 129 active, dormant, and extinct volcanoes, the chain stretches 3,700 miles to the Aleutian Trench. The Pacific Ocean plate's slow slide over underlying magma is known as hot spot volcanism, and is unlike the boundary volcanism of two tectonic plate edges colliding in distant Alaskan or Pacific Northwest parks. Over 300 miles wide, the hot spot drops nearly 1,200 miles deep, containing a 2730°F (1500°C) magma chamber 60 miles down. Over the coming millennia, as the Pacific plate continues sliding several inches a year to the northwest—at the rate of 32 miles each million years—more volcanoes will be created from the underlying hot spot. (A recent theory proposes that the

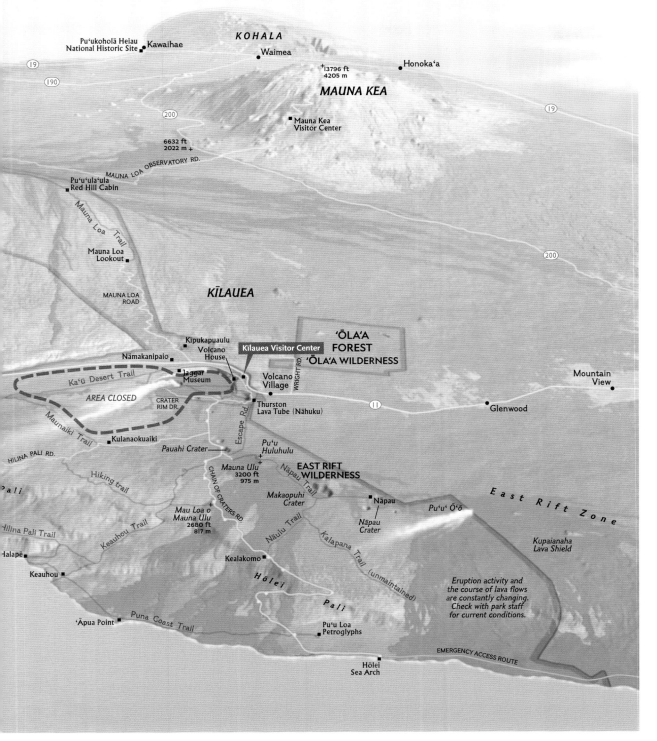

mysterious hot spot moves under the Pacific plate instead of being fixed.) Although the volcanic activity on the farthest Hawaiian island, Niihau, is six million years old, the park's newest volcanoes date back only 800,000 years as part of the most recently created island, Hawaiʻi, in the Pacific plate's slide northwest. A newer submarine volcano named Loihi has begun building as a seamount southeast of the park, plunging 3,000 feet down to the seafloor, but it isn't predicted to emerge as an island for at least 10,000 years.

Typical of hot spot volcanism, Kīlauea and Mauna Loa are massive shield volcanoes, irregular in shape, gently sloped, and lacking the classic rounded craters of the more common stratovolcanoes. During shield volcano eruptions, magma often gushes from fissured rifts and pours down the mountainsides, congealing into lava tubes that resemble waterslides. This basaltic magma is "runny" and usually releases the gases before explosively erupting—unlike more viscous magma found on mainland stratovolcanoes. All of these

factors make volcano viewing possible in Hawaiʻi Volcanoes National Park. Witnessing lava spewing downhill like a river—particularly at night in red molten, animate-looking forms—is among the singular wonders of the National Park System, and explains why the park draws more than two million visitors each year.

Still, there are volcanic hazards, routinely broadcasted along with local weather forecasts. Earthquakes are frequent. The gas streaming from Kīlauea is known as *vog* (volcanic smog), an acidic, toxic cloud that can cause respiratory distress along with flu-like symptoms. "Falling Pele's hair"—an airborne volcanic thread—will scratch car windshields and irritate eyes and lungs.

MEASURED FROM MAUNA LOA'S BASE MORE THAN THREE MILES BELOW SEA LEVEL, THE 13,679-FOOT VOLCANO EXCEEDS THE 29,035-FOOT MOUNT EVEREST IN TOTAL HEIGHT.

Then there's *laze*. As the scalding lava flows down the volcanoes into the sea, it creates more fine particles of volcanic glass suspended in the air along with a billowing hydrochloric acid steam cloud as corrosive as battery acid. These gases badly burned and then killed two onlookers along the coast in the eruption site beneath Kīlauea in 2000. Even swimming in the ocean, superheated from nearby lava flows, can prove deadly.

Aside from these well-known dangers, the slow-moving Hawai'i lava flows have caused relatively few casualties compared to explosive mainland volcanoes. Still, hundreds of homes were destroyed outside the park during Kīlauea's 2018 eruption, which resulted in a park closure lasting more than four months. The event collapsed the Halema'uma'u summit crater, which dropped more than 1,600 feet. Molten rock covered 13.7 square miles of land, reaching up to 80 feet deep in some places.

Lava flows have endangered humans for centuries. In 1790, a party of native Hawaiians—some of whom left their footprints in the lava now displayed in the Ka'ü Desert—were killed during an uncommon, explosive eruption. All were descendants of master mariners who had sailed here from the 2,000-mile-distant Marquesas in A.D. 400.

More evidence of early lives in the park can be found 16 miles below the southern rim of the volcano at Pu'u Loa (meaning "long hill")—a sacred place to the Hawaiian people. Chiseled several centuries ago into a smooth, old lava flow are more than 23,000 carvings depicting canoe sails, cryptic geometric designs, feathered capes, and anthropomorphic figures. This collection of petroglyphs is the largest in the Pacific.

The people believed that the goddess Pele lived in the Halema'uma'u crater atop the Kīlauea volcano, banished to Hawai'i by her father for seducing a sister. One of many ancient legends tells of how Pele was celebrating her new island refuge while running away from her father and the sister, Nāmaka, the goddess of the ocean. When Pele first arrived to the island of Hawai'i, escaping the waves that Nāmaka would throw at her, she danced a hula amid the island's craters to show that she had won.

Today the hula dance is considered an art. Its characteristic flowing, emotive foot, hip, or hand movements represent waves in the ocean, volcanic eruptions, swimming fish, or the swaying of trees in the wind. Hawaiians continue to leave gifts of flowers in the crater as an offering to Pele, the goddess of fire and volcanoes purportedly embodied in the lava. Poking these flows with a stick is considered disrespectful, and removing hardened basalt-magma rocks from the

OPPOSITE: **Volcanic eruptions** offer potent reminders that much of nature's machinations are beyond human control. Opposite, lava from the Kīlauea volcano flows into the ocean; the lava is so hot it boils the water even while it starts to cool, giving off a noxious haze.

BELOW: **The Hawaiian hot spot,** more than 900 miles deep, fuels magma chambers whose eruptions create a volcanic island. As the Pacific tectonic plate moves northwest, about three inches a year, it carries the island off the hot spot. Without fuel, eruptions stop and the island sinks.

ENGINE OF AN ISLAND CHAIN

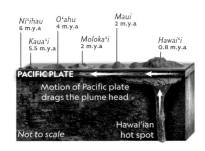

Minimum age of islands, dated to millions of years ago; Moloka'i and Maui were once connected.

RISE AND FALL OF A HAWAI'IAN VOLCANO

Undersea origins
Mauna Kea began to form over a million years ago. Magma rising through fissures in the ocean crust slowly built a volcanic cone of pillow lava and glassy fragments.

Breaking the surface
About 800,000 years ago Mauna Kea rose above sea level, and mountain building began. Eruptions became explosive and effusive. Layer upon layer of lava sculpted a shield volcano.

Winding down
Mauna Kea's shield building phase ended about 130,000 years ago. Cinder cones at the summit mark the location of subsequent eruptions, which buried a larger central caldera.

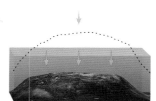

Back to the sea
Severed from the hot spot, Mauna Kea and its sister volcanoes will erode and sink due to their sheer weight, which depresses the seafloor.

HOW A LAVA TUBE IS FORMED

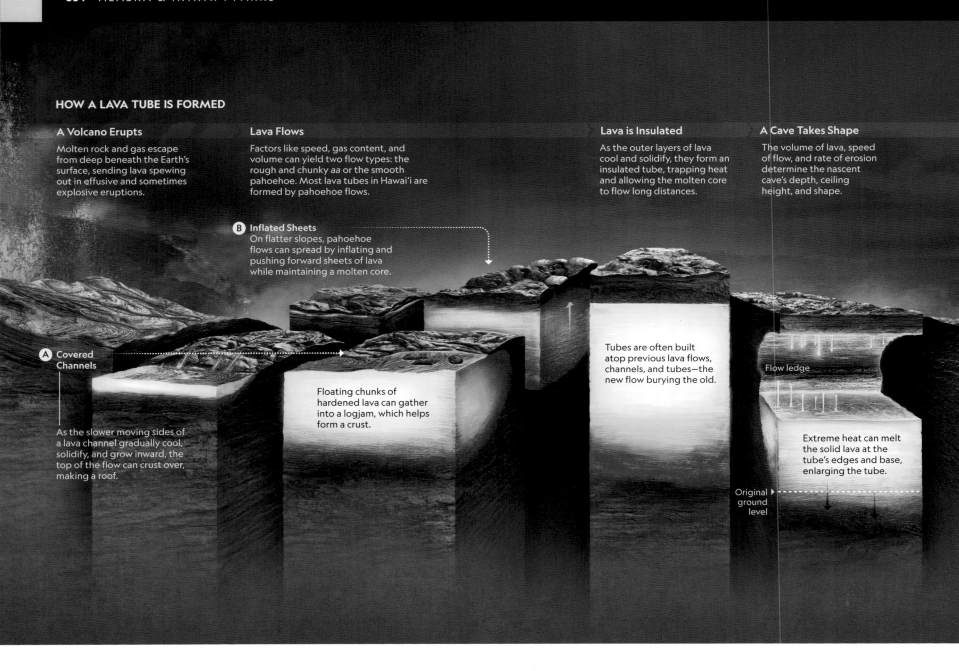

A Volcano Erupts
Molten rock and gas escape from deep beneath the Earth's surface, sending lava spewing out in effusive and sometimes explosive eruptions.

Lava Flows
Factors like speed, gas content, and volume can yield two flow types: the rough and chunky *aa* or the smooth pahoehoe. Most lava tubes in Hawai'i are formed by pahoehoe flows.

Lava is Insulated
As the outer layers of lava cool and solidify, they form an insulated tube, trapping heat and allowing the molten core to flow long distances.

A Cave Takes Shape
The volume of lava, speed of flow, and rate of erosion determine the nascent cave's depth, ceiling height, and shape.

B Inflated Sheets
On flatter slopes, pahoehoe flows can spread by inflating and pushing forward sheets of lava while maintaining a molten core.

A Covered Channels

As the slower moving sides of a lava channel gradually cool, solidify, and grow inward, the top of the flow can crust over, making a roof.

Floating chunks of hardened lava can gather into a logjam, which helps form a crust.

Tubes are often built atop previous lava flows, channels, and tubes—the new flow burying the old.

Flow ledge

Extreme heat can melt the solid lava at the tube's edges and base, enlarging the tube.

Original ▶ ground level

island is said to bring a curse from the goddess. Eruptions are attributed to her love longings; whole forests and towns have been annihilated by her unpredictable, explosive nature. Sightings of the goddess have been reported throughout the islands for centuries, moving about in lava clouds and within magma flows.

Below Pele's home, amid lush tropical fern forest, is the Thurston Lava Tube. Formed 500 years ago when hot lava cooled and crusted over, the 20-foot-high, 600-foot-long cave and its colorful minerals are now illuminated with electric lights. "Here," as Mark Twain said of Kīlauea in 1866, "was room for the imagination to work!"

Lorrin Thurston, a newspaper publisher, discovered the tube shortly after Hawai'i became a territory in 1900. Thurston began a letter- and editorial-writing campaign to make the region into a park while wining and dining visiting congressman, going so far as to barbeque food over hot magma and impressing upon them the potential merits of protecting the volcanoes as a new park. After a decade of Thurston's advocacy, President Wilson signed the legislation for the first national park to be created in a territory.

The congressional act of August 1, 1916, named the protected lands Hawai'i National Park, a "pleasure ground for the benefit and enjoy-

Visitors explore 400-foot-long Nahuku, or the Thurston Lava Tube, discovered by local newspaper publisher Lorrin Thurston in 1913. Today, amber LED lights illuminate the way.

Lava Escapes

If the lava volume increases or debris blocks the tube, lava can push up through open "skylights" or burst through cracks, making new surface flows or tubes.

New Land Is Made

Since Kīlauea's ongoing Puu Oo eruption began in 1983, hundreds of acres have been added to the southeast coast of Hawaii's Big Island.

Skylight

As the top of the tube cools, cracks can form in the ceiling, causing portions to cave in.

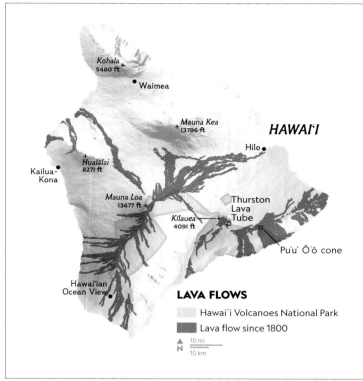

ABOVE: **Of the Big Island's** five volcanoes, only Kīlauea, Mauna Loa, and Hualalai have erupted since 1800. Kīlauea's most recent eruption occurred on May 3, 2018, and subsequent lava flows, earthquakes, ash plumes, and collapse explosions caused extensive damage: Hawai'i Volcanoes National Park had to shut down for more than four months.

LEFT: **Hawai'i's** basaltic shield volcanoes have produced some of the world's deepest and longest lava tubes—tunnels carved by rivers of molten rock. Caves etched by flowing water can take millions of years to form, while a volcanic eruption can generate miles of lava tubes in a matter of weeks or months. Thousands of these tubes twist, braid, and intersect beneath the surface of Hawai'i's Big Island.

ment of the people." In 1959, Hawai'i finally became the 50th state in the Union. Two years later, in the same act that split off and renamed Haleakalā as a separate national park on the island of Maui, the main park on the Big Island was renamed Hawai'i Volcanoes National Park.

During his campaigning for the park, Thurston had also helped raise funds for the volcanologist Thomas Jaggar to live and perform observations atop the volcano Kīlauea. Having borne witness to the aftermath of Mount Pelée eruption on Martinique in 1902 that killed 29,000 people, Jaggar was impressed with Kīlauea's frequent yet relatively benign eruptions, its accessibility, and the potential for developing new knowledge about volcanoes. His work began in 1911, amid small cabins built alongside the caldera, next to the main volcano vent. Through the years, this base expanded into the permanent Hawaiian Volcano Observatory atop Kīlauea, now protected with reinforced concrete after an earthquake cracked open a wall. Next door is the historic Volcano House hotel and restaurant.

Volcanology was in its infancy when Jaggar launched his research, but for 30 years, he monitored seismic activity, volcanic gases, and changes in the shape of the volcano after eruptions. His work atop the volcano allowed him to establish fundamental techniques, and

to pioneer many new monitoring instruments. Run alternately by the National Weather Service and the National Park Service, and then later serving as military and park headquarters during and after World War II, the observatory was finally taken over by the U.S. Geological Survey and moved closer to the main vent. Today the observatory provides daily posts and live webcam coverage of the eruptions, while modern electronics register vog and eruption conditions that mandate park closures.

In 1951, atop neighboring Mauna Loa, the Park Service built a weather station that would become one of the most important observation facilities on Earth. Several years later, it was fortified and moved to a safer location, several thousand feet down the north side of the volcano, just outside of park boundaries. While the U.S. Weather Service ran the Mauna Loa Observatory, many other institutions conducted myriad atmospheric measurements.

Weather forecasts and climate knowledge cannot get much better than that found in clean air more than 11,000 feet above the sea in this isolated island chain. Near sea level, from summer to winter, temperatures vary by only about 10°F (5.6°C). Although the coast averages a high of 83°F (28.3°C) and a low of 68°F (20°C), the

temperature on the summits can drop another 15°F (8.3°C). Record high and low temperatures in the park both occurred in 1983: 93°F (34°C) and 31°F (−0.5°C).

The park biome is categorized as a tropical and subtropical broadleaf forest. In addition to reducing temperature variations, the tropical climate is known for large amounts of rain—varying from 20 inches a year on the coast to more than 144 inches at midelevation, windward exposures. December is the rainiest month.

The moisture has created a plant paradise that has evolved over millions of years on the Hawaiian island chain. More than 90 percent of the islands' native plants are not found anywhere else in the world. Consequently, the park is an invaluable protected—albeit threatened—herbarium. There are hundreds of species of trees, fungi, orchids, mosses, and ferns, but many of these plants face threats from invasive flora and fauna introduced over the last 200 years. In particular, non-native animals—including wasps, ants, mosquitoes, rats, feral cats, mongoose, cattle, sheep, pigs, and goats—graze and nest amid these plants, or eat native animals, making Hawai'i Volcanoes one of the most vulnerable parks in the system. Hawai'i leads the United States for endangered species and even extinctions.

As for nonanimal invaders, nearly 200 plant species in the park—many introduced by ranchers for grazing animals—are classified as noxious weeds or invasive. Often resistant to fire, spread by the wind or birds, these herbaceous newcomers usually smother native vegetation.

Currently, the most insidious invasive species is a fungus, which is killing the 'ōhi'a trees. The strong 'ōhi'a wood is a keystone species and a symbol of Hawai'i's unique resilience, treasured throughout the islands for watershed protection and shade canopy and used in carvings, canoes, and totems. But in 2010 a South American fungus arrived and began choking the species to death, killing swaths of forest as quickly as Ebola. Locals call it Rapid 'Ōhi'a Death. Tens of thousands of trees have died throughout the island. Rangers have tried to limit the spread of fungus by closing sections of the park, asking visitors to clean shoes and clothing before hiking in the forest, and keeping 'ōhi'a wood (the fungus is prevalent in wood parts) out of the park. To date there is no known cure but officials have prevented the fungus from spreading to the other islands, and a seed bank is being created in case the tree becomes extinct.

As the park wrestles with saving a forest species that creates oxygen and absorbs carbon dioxide from the atmosphere, the Mauna Loa Observatory has been measuring fluctuations in carbon dioxide

THE PARK'S PLANTS HAVE EVOLVED IN ISOLATION. AT LEAST 1,000 NATIVE SPECIES OF FLOWERING PLANTS GROW IN HAWAI'I, AND 90 PERCENT OF THEM ARE FOUND NOWHERE ELSE.

levels since 1958. More than a half century ago, the principal scientist Charles David Keeling was astonished to learn that measurements showed carbon dioxide concentrations increasing during the winter and dropping in summer. Keeling's data literally showed the Earth inhaling and exhaling as forests dropped and regrew leaves through the seasons. Yet over coming decades, his observations revealed how burning fossil fuels caused a rapid increase of carbon dioxide in the atmosphere. He warned of the dangers of this upward trend long before global warming became widely publicized.

The observatory has now performed the world's longest running measurements of carbon dioxide in the atmosphere. Scientists refer to the graph of this ominous increase as the Keeling Curve. When it all began in the late 1950s, carbon dioxide measurements were about 310 parts per million in the Northern Hemisphere; today the carbon dioxide level averages 400 parts per million. Thus, much of the modern understanding of climate change—that atmospheric carbon dioxide increases are due to the actions of mankind—all began here, atop this Hawaiian volcano. It's one of the most extraordinarily lush yet fiery ecosystems within the National Park System. ∎

A fungal disease is killing swaths of 'Ōhi'a trees in Hawai'i Volcanoes National Park. Known as Rapid 'Ōhi'a Death (ROD), the fungus clogs a tree's vascular system, depriving the canopy of water and, in some cases, killing the tree. Park officials have been conducting surveys to test for the disease; red dots on the map show where ROD has been detected.

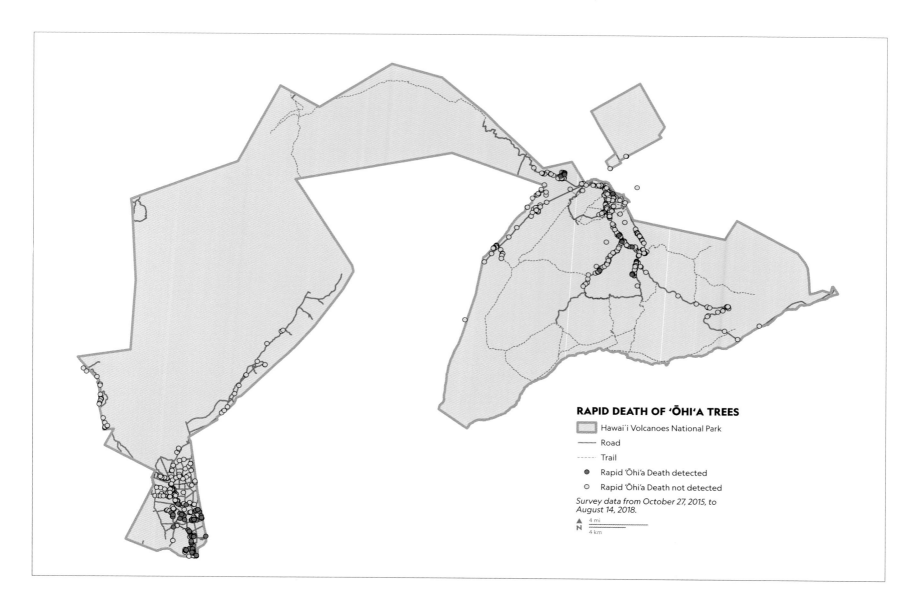

RAPID DEATH OF 'ŌHI'A TREES

- ▢ Hawai'i Volcanoes National Park
- —— Road
- - - - - Trail
- ● Rapid 'Ōhi'a Death detected
- ○ Rapid 'Ōhi'a Death not detected

Survey data from October 27, 2015, to August 14, 2018.

4 mi
4 km

MORE NATIONAL PARKS AT A GLANCE

CONTENTS

The canopy of an old-growth
floodplain forest of cypress and tupelo in
South Carolina's Congaree National Park

VIRGIN ISLANDS NATIONAL PARK

▶ LOCATION **50 MILES E OF SAN JUAN, PUERTO RICO** ▶ SIZE **20 SQUARE MILES**
▶ HIGHEST POINT **BORDEAUX MOUNTAIN, 1,277 FEET** ▶ VISITORS **112,287 IN 2018** ▶ ESTABLISHED **1956**

The 29th national park dominates St. John Island and its surrounding coral reefs, mangroves, and cays. As one of three large islands amid 50 smaller cays in the U.S. Virgin Islands, the hilly St. John is known for its blue-green waters lapping against white-sand beaches. These tropical islands are the only U.S. territory where cars are driven on the left side of the road.

In 1493, Columbus named the islands after the legendary beauties St. Ursula and her holy virgins. By the early 1700s, a Danish flag flew over most of the islands. Sugar plantations worked by West African slaves defined life on St. John for more than two centuries until Denmark abolished slavery in 1848. Eventually, tropical storms and poverty overtook the island.

In 1917, to prevent European incursions into America during World War I, the United States purchased and restored Columbus's name to the Danish West Indies. Several decades later the renowned philanthropist Laurance Rockefeller donated more than 5,000 acres of the island and Congress created the park. Today, visitors come to the park for its snorkeling, boating, and bird-watching.

The living coral inside the park, along with the adjacent Virgin Islands Coral Reef National Monument, is its most vital resource. Yet recent destructive hurricanes and bleaching caused by warming ocean temperatures have jeopardized this precious marine organ-

ABOVE: **At the turn** of the 18th century, the Annaberg Sugar Mill was one of St. John's biggest sugar works. The ruins offer a window into the mill's inner workings and the lives of slave laborers who toiled here.

OPPOSITE: **Laurance Rockefeller** donated Trunk Bay, one of the most famous beaches on St. John Island, to the National Park Service. A 225-yard snorkeling trail awaits underwater.

ism. One of many features at stake are the celebrated white-sand beaches produced by marine algae and living coral.

Inland, the park's lush forests shelter some of the many invasive species plaguing the tropics: wild donkeys, deer, mongoose, pigs, and goats. Bats are the only mammals native to the paradisiacal island. ∎

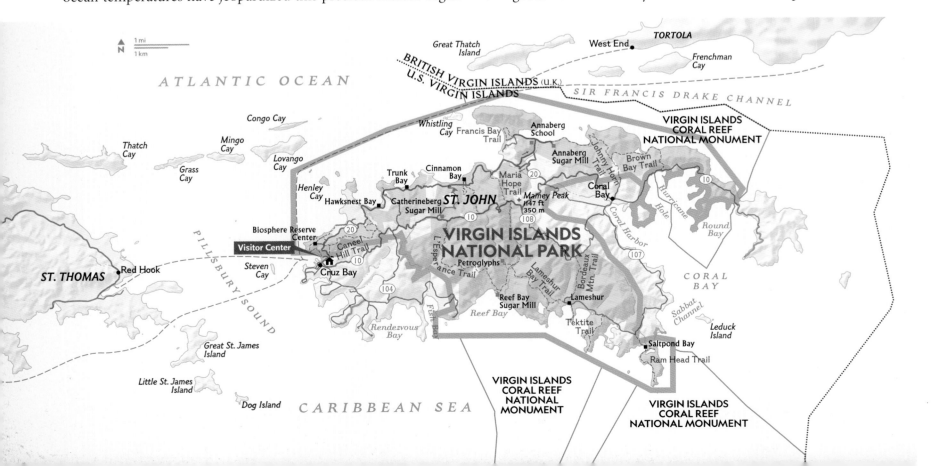

BISCAYNE NATIONAL PARK

▷ LOCATION **10 MILES S OF MIAMI, FLORIDA** ▷ SIZE **270 SQUARE MILES**
▷ HIGHEST POINT **TOTTEN KEY, 9 FEET** ▷ VISITORS **469,253 IN 2018** ▷ ESTABLISHED **1980**

Biscayne National Park is 95 percent water, with its remaining 8,649 acres of land split between fossilized coral-limestone islands and tentacle-legged mangroves. The park contains the northern end of the wide, 170-mile-long arc of the Florida Reef—the third greatest coral reef system in the world. Biscayne is renowned for its Maritime Heritage Trail, offering snorkelers and divers mooring access to six shipwrecks amid a rich archaeological legacy of 70 more boats that sunk under park waters.

Elliott Key, the largest island in the park, also forms the northernmost Florida Key. The eastern park boundary drops off into deep water, while most of the western boundary stretches across sea grass beds in shallow Biscayne Bay to encompass mangrove swamps on the mainland.

First proposed as part of Everglades National Park, Biscayne became a monument in 1968 to prevent proposed seaport development. It took another 12 years for Congress to establish the park "to preserve and protect for the education, inspiration, recreation, and enjoyment of present and future generations a rare combination of terrestrial, marine, and amphibious life in a tropical setting of great natural beauty."

The islands provide nesting grounds for sea turtles, while the adjoining waters and reefs protect over 800 species of coral, seabirds, fish, and whales—including 20 threatened and endangered species. This includes the declining numbers of the large and colorful Schaus' swallowtail butterfly and a population of extremely rare cactus—semaphore prickly pear, growing up to eight feet tall and named for its resemblance to the railway signal arm.

Aqua-park activities abound, including guided boat tours and paddling in kayaks and canoes, and world-class angling for bonefish, tarpon, grouper, snapper, and spiny lobsters. ■

Biscayne's mostly submerged 173,000 acres form part of the world's third longest coral reef tract, where a vibrant expanse of corals shelter aquatic life.

CONGAREE NATIONAL PARK

▷ LOCATION **20 MILES SE OF COLUMBIA, SOUTH CAROLINA** ▷ SIZE **41 SQUARE MILES**
▷ HIGHEST POINT **OLD BLUFF ROAD, 140 FEET** ▷ VISITORS **145,929 IN 2018** ▷ ESTABLISHED **2003**

The only national park in South Carolina lies between Lake Marion and Columbia, in the center of the state. Congaree is named after the Native American people who lived there prior to settlement. The appellation is also shared with the meandering, oxbow river that defines the park's southern boundary. Most of the park is designated wilderness.

Congaree shelters the largest old-growth, bottomland hardwood forest left in the Southeast. The park was established after more than three decades of local grassroots advocacy to prevent logging and save the biologically diverse and dynamic floodplain ecosystem. As a floodplain, without standing swamp water, the Congaree River regularly jumps its banks to disperse nutrient-rich water that sustains massive trees.

Fifteen tree species in the park are the tallest known specimens in the world, all over 130 feet tall, including a 167-foot loblolly pine and a cherrybark oak, sweet gum, American elm, swamp chestnut oak, and an overcup oak. Several bald cypress trees first took root here as the first Europeans arrived 500 years ago.

Below Spanish moss–draped branches and the stalagmite-shaped knees of cypress trees, reflections in the tea-colored water evoke Monet. Water snakes, frogs, catfish, and alligator gar slither past. Out in deeper creeks, amid the drilling staccato of woodpeckers working tupelo trees, river otters splash in the current. Although

A boardwalk snakes through the Congaree Biosphere Reserve, part of the largest intact expanse of old-growth bottomland hardwood forest in the Southeast.

water covers most of the park, bobcats, deer, and invasive feral pigs—that destructively eat native plants and animals—roam the elevated bluffs.

Spring and autumn are the optimal seasons to avoid 90°F (32°C) summer heat and humidity (and mosquitoes), or winter flooding. ■

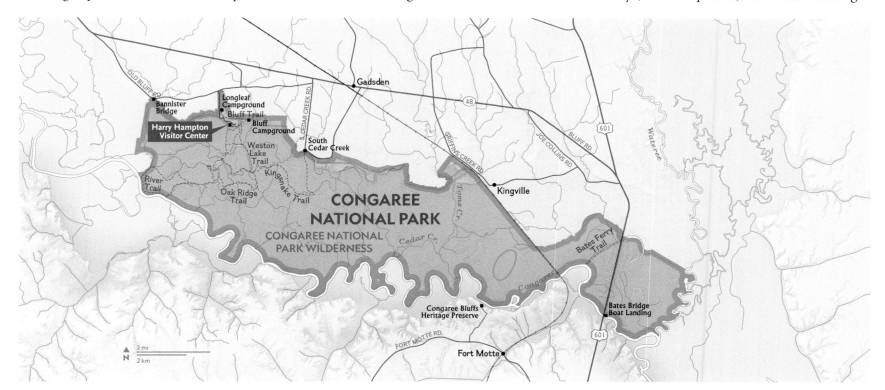

CUYAHOGA VALLEY NATIONAL PARK

▷ LOCATION **15 MILES S OF CLEVELAND, OHIO** ▷ SIZE **51 SQUARE MILES**
▷ HIGHEST POINT **BRUSH ROAD, 1,164 FEET** ▷ VISITORS **2,096,053 IN 2018** ▷ ESTABLISHED **2000**

The Cuyahoga River forms the backbone of this 22-mile-long, 5-mile-wide park. Bisected by freeways between the Akron and Cleveland skylines in northern Ohio, the park serves as an easily accessed nature sanctuary for city residents. Congress first set aside Cuyahoga as a National Recreation Area in 1974 to provide "the maintenance of needed recreational open space necessary to the urban environment."

Its proximity to industry and environmental disasters, at first, made it seem an unlikely national park. In 1985, the Park Service acquired the adjoining 47-acre Krejci Dump to be added to the recreation area. After a visitor became ill picking up waste, an Environmental Protection Agency (EPA) analysis revealed many toxic chemicals buried in the ground, so the area was closed.

After a decade-long lawsuit recovered the costs for a Superfund cleanup site, the Recreation Area became a national park. Working with the EPA, the National Park Service removed 371,000 tons of contaminated soils and debris. Today the former dump—still being monitored for residual toxicity—has been restored to a wetland, and Cuyahoga Valley has become a model for restoration of an industrial area to its native ecology.

The scenic Cuyahoga River ("crooked river" in Iroquois) surrounds tree-covered hills, golf courses, marshes, a scenic railroad, and the Ohio and Erie Canal. Used in the mid-1800s as a supply route before the railroads, the towpath along the canal runs through the park for 20 miles. Enjoyed for walking, biking, horseback riding, and cross-country skiing, the towpath is one of more than 125 miles of trails throughout the popular park. ∎

A train passes through the Peninsula Depot station on the Cuyahoga Valley Scenic Railroad, which traverses the length of the national park.

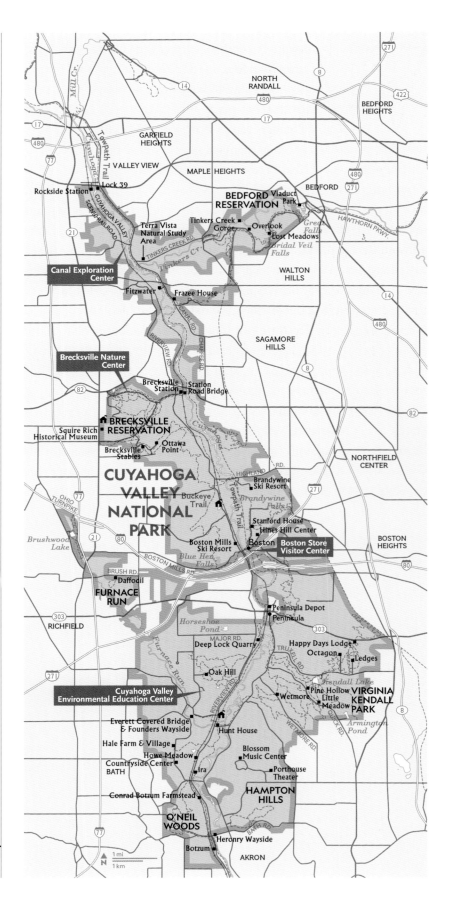

INDIANA DUNES NATIONAL PARK

▷ LOCATION **43 MILES SE OF CHICAGO, ILLINOIS** ▷ SIZE **24 SQUARE MILES**
▷ HIGHEST POINT **MOUNT BALDY, 718 FEET** ▷ VISITORS **1,756,079 IN 2018** ▷ ESTABLISHED **2019**

With its 15 miles of shore under the constant sculpting forces of Lake Michigan's wind and waves, Indiana's only national park has high sands from which visitors can see the skyline of Chicago across the lake and hear the rhythmic flurry of passing trains. Fifty miles of trails lead through the park's dunes, wetlands, prairies, rivers, and forests.

Less than an hour's drive from the Windy City, the region faced development a century ago, so advocates for the area's preservation made the dunes a state park in 1926. In a later compromise that allowed a huge port to be built for the nearby metropolis, the dunes were designated as a National Lakeshore in 1966. Then on February 15, 2019, the dunes became a newly anointed national park through a spending bill signed by President Donald Trump.

The park is heralded for its singing sands that can be heard from 30 feet away—caused by the quartz crystals, moisture, and the friction from footsteps creating a clear, ringing sound. The phenomenon may occur once a month under optimal conditions. Distinctive for its biodiverse flora, the park contains over 1,100 species of vascular plants. University of Chicago professor Henry Cowles coined the term "plant succession" (for change in flora over time) based on his studies of this ecologically rich shoreline in 1899.

The lakeshore is also an essential nesting grounds and stopover for more than 350 species of birds, funneled into the park's sands

One of America's newest national parks, Indiana Dunes has multiple swimming beaches along the southern shore of Lake Michigan, as well as extensive trails for hiking and biking.

and marshes during spring and fall migrations. Visitors come to swim and camp in the summer, while snowshoeing and cross-country skiing are popular in winter. Finally, this diminutive yet eclectic park shelters over 60 historic structures, including houses from the 1933 Chicago World's Fair. ∎

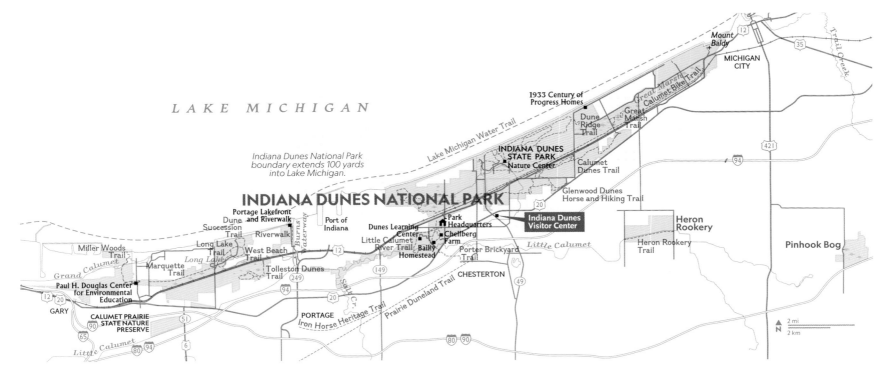

GATEWAY ARCH NATIONAL PARK

▶ LOCATION **DOWNTOWN ST. LOUIS, MISSOURI** ▶ SIZE **0.14 SQUARE MILE (91 ACRES)**
▶ HIGHEST POINT **449 FEET** ▶ VISITORS **2,016,180 IN 2018** ▶ ESTABLISHED **2018**

The tallest man-made arch in the world soars above verdant landscaping on the west bank of the Mississippi River, surrounded by the renovated historic district of downtown St. Louis, Missouri. Formerly named Jefferson National Expansion Memorial, the Gateway Arch stretches 630 feet high and wide and is at the center of one of the newest and smallest national parks.

In an architectural contest in 1947, the architect Eero Saarinen's design was chosen among 172 other entries to commemorate President Thomas Jefferson and his pivotal Louisiana Purchase. Symbolizing the opening of the West with St. Louis (formerly the French capital of Upper Louisiana) as its gateway, the architect spoke of the "monumental form" of Paris's most famous arch, so Saarinen—whose buildings would become famous for grace and glamour—strove to create a heartland version of the Arc de Triomphe.

Assembled from 142 different sections of 12-foot-long, prefabricated steel, with 38,107 tons of concrete, the hollow arch is supported by 54-foot-wide legs. As the final 17-foot-wide, 8-foot-long keystone was craned into place, if the top had been more than 0.4 millimeter out of synch laterally, the two legs would not have aligned. The arch was completed in 1965 for $13 million, two million dollars less than what France charged the United States for President Jefferson's Louisiana Purchase.

Along with a statue of Jefferson, there is a museum, theater, and visitor center at the base of the arch. The museum's gallery recalls when St. Louis was a trade center for exchanging goods

This statue memorializes Dred and Harriet Scott, whose landmark case proved a turning point in America's relationship with slavery. It's one of many notable sights in this ode to St. Louis's role in westward expansion.

with local Native Americans, and officials following the call of Manifest Destiny.

Today, trams on either side of the arch lift visitors to an observation deck at the top, where views reach 30 miles in every direction. From a vantage point higher than any St. Louis skyscraper, the Missouri River can be seen flowing to the north out of the plains, where Jefferson sent Lewis and Clark on their journey of westward discovery two centuries ago. ■

OLD COURTHOUSE
Dred and Harriet Scott statue
LUTHER ELY SMITH SQUARE
MARKET ST.
CHESTNUT ST.
PINE ST.
To MetroLink
MEMORIAL DR.
OLD CATHEDRAL
Visitor Center Entrance
GATEWAY ARCH NATIONAL PARK
To the North Gateway
North Exit
South Exit
VISITOR CENTER
Museum at the Gateway Arch (Underground)
THE GRAND STAIRCASE
Accessible Route to the Arch
To Lewis and Clark statue

HOT SPRINGS NATIONAL PARK

▷ LOCATION **60 MILES SW OF LITTLE ROCK, ARKANSAS** ▷ SIZE **9 SQUARE MILES**
▷ HIGHEST POINT **MUSIC MOUNTAIN, 1,405 FEET** ▷ VISITORS **1,506,887 IN 2018** ▷ ESTABLISHED **1921**

H ot Springs National Park is located in the city of the
same name in central Arkansas. The park's pine, oak,
and hickory forested mountains encircle the northern
edge of the city, centered over 43 thermal springs and
26 miles of hiking trails and bisected by Highway 7.
Hot Springs is the second smallest and oldest land parcel set aside
for a national park. Congress created Hot Springs Reservation in
1832, 40 years before Yellowstone, "for the future disposal of the
United States . . . to be preserved for future recreation."

The European Hernando de Soto discovered the springs in 1541,
although Paleo-Indians had frequented the area since 12,000 B.C.,
possibly bathing in the hot waters well before de Soto's finding. A
year after the 1803 Louisiana Purchase, American government
officials observed people summering there, living in huts and
"resorting to the Springs for the recovery of their health."

Even before official park designation in 1921, Hot Springs Reservation had become a destination for curing health issues such as
nervous disorders and arthritis. Recognizing the curative powers of
steam cabinets and bathing in or drinking from the potable waters,
the National Park Service hired superintendents from the Public
Health Service to oversee sanitation and various spa treatments.

Seeping through Ouachita Mountain rocks as rainwater more
than 4,000 years ago, the fossil water is heated to an average temperature of 143°F (62°C) by the natural heat of the Earth a mile
underground. Artesian pressure forces the water up through a
fault to the base of Hot Springs Mountain. Each day the reservoir
collects about 700,000 gallons of water. In addition to bathing,
visitors come to tour eight ornate, late Victorian-era bathhouses—
many styled in Spanish
colonial architecture and
restored by the National
Park Service—along Bath-
house Row. ∎

Thermal waters thought to have
healing powers prompted pioneers
to build Bathhouse Row in the late
19th century. The eight elegant
buildings seen today, now
surrounding the north end of
Hot Springs, Arkansas, were
constructed between 1892 and
1923 and are part of a national
historic landmark district.

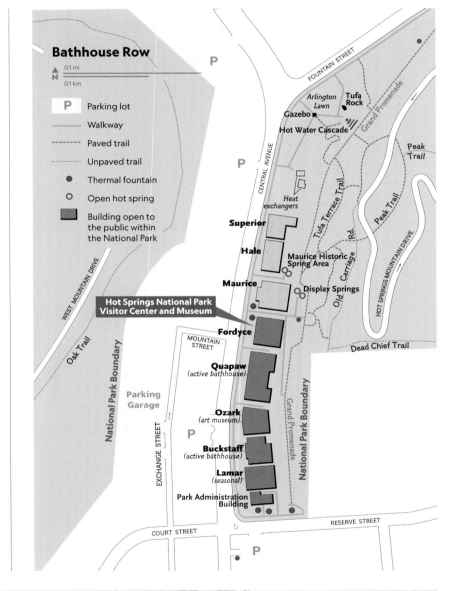

THEODORE ROOSEVELT NATIONAL PARK

▷ LOCATION **130 MILES W OF BISMARCK, NORTH DAKOTA** ▷ SIZE **110 SQUARE MILES**
▷ HIGHEST POINT **PECK HILL, 2,865 FEET** ▷ VISITORS **749,389 IN 2018** ▷ ESTABLISHED **1978**

Tucked away in southwestern North Dakota, with a South and North Unit 70 miles apart, and the tiny Elkhorn Ranch Unit in between, this park is connected by the winding Little Missouri River and the Maah Daah Hey Trail. A seldom visited badlands—defined as a highly eroded plateau lacking vegetation—the cutoff hilltops and austere, knife-blade ridges are scoured by winds and are unwelcoming in winter. Yet, at closer examination, the isolated park hosts hundreds of species of wildflowers beneath multicolored, fantastically shaped and textured sedimentary cliffs. Then there's the unexpected amount of wildlife: wild horses, deer, elk, pronghorn antelope, bighorn sheep, and most notably bison that Theodore Roosevelt—a hunter, conservationist, and co-founder of the Boone and Crockett Club—helped save from extinction.

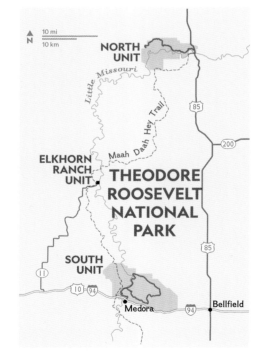

ABOVE: **When young Theodore Roosevelt** came to the Dakota Territory to hunt bison in 1883, the land's rugged and unique character inspired him to set it aside for protection.

OPPOSITE: **The sun rises** over the mist-shrouded Little Missouri River, which connects the three park units as it twists through badlands and meadows.

Appropriately, given Roosevelt's interest in protecting wildlands, this is the only national park named after a person. He acquired the 218-acre Elkhorn Ranch in 1884 and returned repeatedly to raise livestock and pursue what he famously called "the strenuous life." His experience later inspired him to protect 230 million acres of park and public lands throughout the country. "I would not have been President," he said, "had it not been for my experience in North Dakota."

After his death in 1919, the name of these protected badlands morphed from the Theodore Roosevelt Recreation Demonstration Area in 1935 to the Theodore Roosevelt National Wildlife Refuge in 1946, to the Theodore Roosevelt National Memorial Park—the only one of its kind ever established—in 1947. After boundary expansion, it became a national park on November 10, 1978, "to protect diverse *cultural* and natural resources"—another way of saying that the park is all about Roosevelt's legacy. ∎

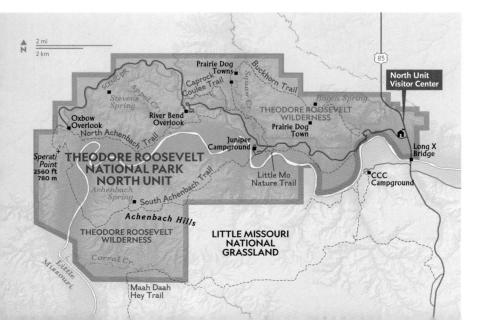

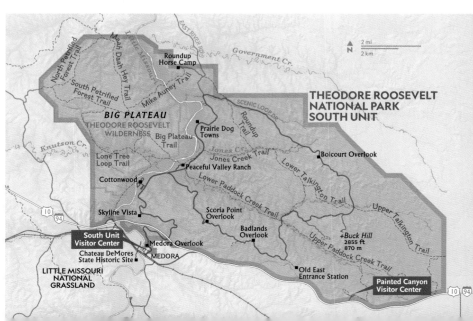

WIND CAVE NATIONAL PARK

▶ LOCATION **60 MILES S OF RAPID CITY, SOUTH DAKOTA** ▶ SIZE **53 SQUARE MILES**
▶ HIGHEST POINT **RANKIN RIDGE, 5,013 FEET** ▶ VISITORS **656,397 IN 2018** ▶ ESTABLISHED **1903**

South Dakota's Wind Cave is due south of Mount Rushmore and west of Badlands National Park, surrounded by Custer State Park and the Pine Ridge Indian Reservation. Its 140-plus miles of explored cave passageways—laced with intricate boxwork calcite formations—are the sixth longest on Earth.

The cave's windy nature was first described by two white brothers in 1881, though the Lakota of the region had known about it. The cave proved lucrative as a tourist attraction and was named after wind gusts—created by changing barometric pressure—at the entranceway. The Wonderful Wind Cave Improvement Company added lit-up stairways inside the cave, and outside, a hotel and an offering of stagecoach rides. After miners went to court against the Improvement Company to take ownership, the Department of the Interior ruled that neither party had legal claim and in 1901, closed both the cave and the rolling, ponderosa pine hills to homesteaders. Two years later, the great conservationist President Theodore Roosevelt signed the legislation creating Wind Cave National Park, making it the first park in the world created to protect underground features.

In the 1930s, the park was enlarged to include a nearby game preserve that had been created to reestablish the American bison across the Great Plains. Bison soon thrived on the largest mixed-grass prairie in the United States. Later, the park introduced elk and pronghorn antelope, followed by black-footed ferrets to cull the overpopulation of prairie dogs. Still it's a delicate balancing act to save over 50 types of native grasses from overgrazing while maintaining the health of the same megafauna that Lewis and Clark once described as "so numerous" that they "darkened the whole plains." ∎

In Wind Cave, green mixed-grass prairie meets ponderosa pine forest; plants and animals from several distinct geographical areas coexist in the park bounds.

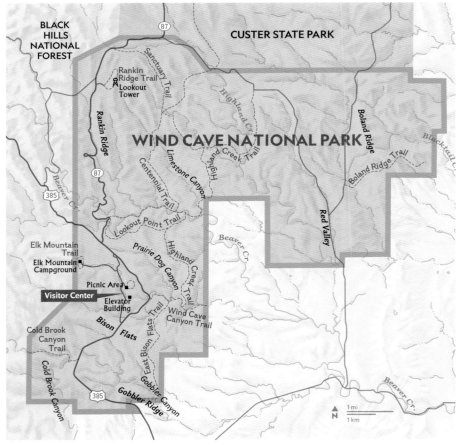

Thin, honeycomb-like calcite fins—or boxwork—decorate Wind Cave's ceiling within the sixth longest explored cave passageway in the world.

CARLSBAD CAVERNS NATIONAL PARK

▷ LOCATION **145 MILES NE OF EL PASO, TEXAS** ▷ SIZE **73 SQUARE MILES**

▷ HIGHEST POINT **GUADALUPE RIDGE, 6,535 FEET** ▷ VISITORS **465,912 IN 2018** ▷ ESTABLISHED **1930**

Surrounded by the Chihuahuan Desert and the Guadalupe Mountains, Carlsbad Caverns contains more than 120 caves stretching over 200 miles. The park's rocky canyons and piñon-juniper forests—with over 50 miles of backcountry trails—provide sanctuary for 54 species of amphibians and reptiles; 357 different birds; and 67 mammal species, including deer, mountain lions, bobcats, and coyotes. Unlike other caves carved out by streams, the caverns were formed by acidic groundwater dissolving massive limestone

A scientist admires rarely seen rimstone dams at Lake Castrovalva in Lechuguilla Cave, where access is limited.

chambers, encrusted with gypsum (a by-product of sulfuric acid and limestone).

Three miles of the main, 30-mile-long cavern are open to visitors to ogle a stalagmite 62 feet tall within the Big Room's 255-foot-high ceiling, hung with stalactites that look like chandeliers. The room's most popular feature is the 700-foot-deep "Bottomless Pit."

On summer evenings, hundreds of thousands of Mexican free-tailed bats—flying as fast as 60 miles an hour—swarm out of the cave entrance to feed along with 16 other bat species and a colony of cave swallows. The free-tailed Mexican species, known as guano bats for their prodigious droppings, prompted large-scale mining in Carlsbad Caverns from 1903 to 1957. Much of the guano was railroaded to California for fertilizing citrus fields.

President Calvin Coolidge signed a proclamation through the Antiquities Act in 1923 establishing Carlsbad Cave National Monument, lauding its "extraordinary proportions . . . unusual beauty and variety of natural decoration." Increasing crowds prompted rangers to build a stairway in 1925 (then an elevator) so visitors were no longer lowered in by a former guano bucket. Five years later, Congress passed legislation creating Carlsbad Caverns National Park. ■

The park hosts 17 bat species, including a huge colony of Brazilian free-tailed bats that venture out nightly in a spectacular flurry from spring through fall.

GUADALUPE MOUNTAINS NATIONAL PARK

▷ LOCATION **110 MILES E OF EL PASO, TEXAS** ▷ SIZE **135 SQUARE MILES**
▷ HIGHEST POINT **GUADALUPE PEAK, 8,749 FEET** ▷ VISITORS **172,347 IN 2018** ▷ ESTABLISHED **1972**

Guadalupe Mountains National Park abuts the New Mexico border in western Texas, alongside the hamlet of Pine Springs. Isolated and less visited than nearby Carlsbad Caverns (the parks are connected by the Guadalupe Ridge Trail), the Guadalupe Mountains enclosed by the park are part of a limestone reef from an ancient, shallow sea. To the west, a vertical mile below the mountains, the evaporated Pleistocene lake of Salt Basin holds the unexpected 2,000-acre wonder of shining, white gypsum and pale red quartz sand dunes up to 60 feet high. The eastern boundaries contain sage and scrublands, dotted with springs that form small oases amid the desert.

The center of the park is dominated by sharp canyons and 8,000-foot peaks rising 3,000 feet above their base. The limestone El Capitan looks like one of the Dolomites from the Italian mountain range. Unlike the cliff of the same name in Yosemite, this remote and featureless face isn't ideal for rock climbing, yet the nearby Guadalupe Peak, the highest point in Texas, is accessed by a 4.1-mile trail. Its summit artificially juts six feet higher with an unlikely, three-sided, stainless steel pyramid placed there by American Airlines in 1958 to honor an overland mail route. This southern edge of the Guadalupe Mountains range has had at least three fatal wrecks; aircraft and hikers alike are subjected to tornadic winds, caused by cold high-pressure air mixing with warm, low-pressure dust storms rolling off the Chihuahuan Desert.

Authorized by Congress in 1966, Guadalupe Mountains National Park preserves "outstanding geological values together with scenic and other natural values of great significance." ∎

ABOVE: **A hiker** follows the Guadalupe Peak Trail through the park, home to the world's most extensive Permian fossil reefs and the four highest peaks in Texas.

OPPOSITE: **Sunrise lights** up the limestone that forms the thousand-foot-high cliff of El Capitan, which can be seen from the Guadalupe Peak Trail.

This American Airlines sign at Guadalupe Peak's summit commemorates pioneer airmen who risked their lives on the dangerous mail route that passed overhead.

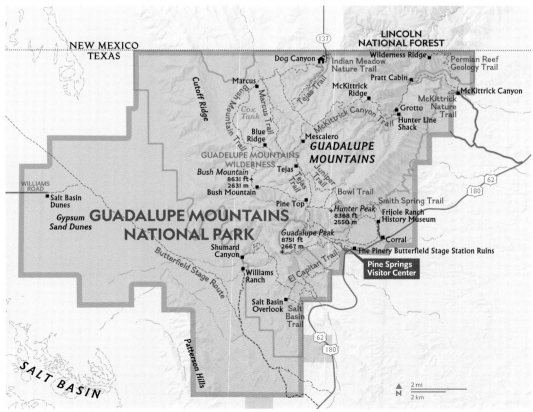

GREAT SAND DUNES NATIONAL PARK AND PRESERVE

▷ LOCATION **239 MILES S OF DENVER, COLORADO** ▷ SIZE **233 SQUARE MILES**
▷ HIGHEST POINT **TIJERAS PEAK, 13,604 FEET** ▷ VISITORS **442,905 IN 2018** ▷ ESTABLISHED **2004**

Great Sand Dunes is a phantasmagoric, ever shifting 176-billion-cubic-foot sandbox cradled beneath the jagged Sangre de Cristo Mountains in south-central Colorado. Reaching up to 750 feet above the stunning San Luis Valley, these are the tallest sand dunes in North America. Fat-tire mountain biking, sandboarding, hiking, and horseback riding are popular on and around the dunes. In 2009, the greater region was named the Sangre de Cristo National Heritage Area to honor the early inhabitants.

Bighorn sheep, bobcats, coyotes, fox, elk, mule deer, pronghorn antelope, bison, kangaroo rats, and many smaller mammals wander between the valley and the alpine tundra of the park. Great Sand Dunes is also a refuge to at least a half dozen insects found nowhere else in the world. The Great Sand Dunes tiger beetle—with its white hairy legs, metallic green head, and copper-colored violin on its back—is a wonder equal to the dunes themselves.

Grain by grain, these volcanic and ancient seabed sands washed down from either side of the valley and accumulated in lakes. As the lakes subsided over the millennia, reversing winds piled the dunes higher atop a natural pocket at the foot of the mountains. Wind and water continue to rebuild and shape the dunes like the hands of Psamathe, the Greek goddess of sand.

Precipitation in this high-altitude desert—based at 8,200 feet above sea level—averages a scant 11.3 inches a year. The sand surface can reach 150°F (66°C) in summer and drop to 20°F (−6.6°C) in winter. Air temperatures range from 80°F (27°C) to below zero, with cool summer nights. The dry air and limited light pollution make this park a sought-after stargazing destination. ■

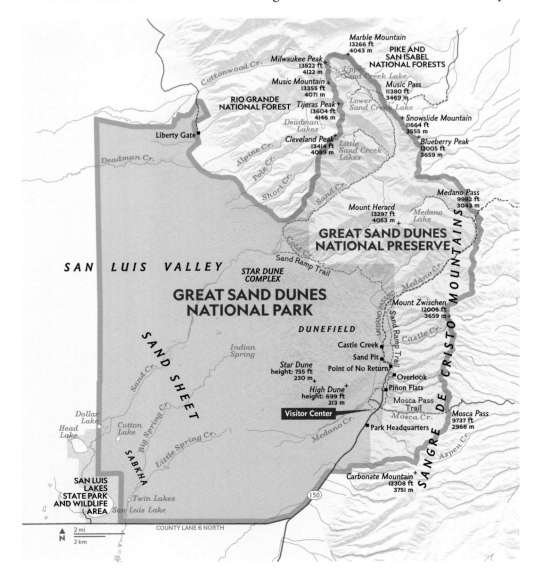

The sun casts shadows on North America's tallest dunes, with Mount Herard looming in the background. Visitors can hike or even sled down the dunes, but in summer months the sand surface can be scorching.

BLACK CANYON OF THE GUNNISON NATIONAL PARK

▷ LOCATION **12 MILES E OF MONTROSE, COLORADO** ▷ SIZE **48 SQUARE MILES**
▷ HIGHEST POINT **SIGNAL HILL, 8,775 FEET** ▷ VISITORS **308,962 IN 2018** ▷ ESTABLISHED **1999**

Colorado's 53-mile-long Black Canyon rises in dusky rock walls a half mile over the Gunnison River. Although the mighty Colorado River drops an average 7.5 feet a mile through the Grand Canyon, the "Gunny" plummets 43 feet a mile through the Black Canyon. The park encloses 14 miles of river, flowing past cold rock exposed at the bottom of the gorge that dates to 1.7 billion years ago. From river to rim, the Painted Wall—named for white-banded granitic dikes that gristle the dark Precambrian gneiss—is the highest cliff in Colorado and world-renowned among climbers. At its deepest, Warner Point, the canyon drops 2,722 feet; at the Narrows along the river, the canyon is only 40 feet wide.

Sixty million years ago, the Black Canyon region shuddered with volcanoes. When this period of uplift ended two million years ago, the Gunny followed an earthen fold, as the weight of water slowly cut through rock at the rate of one foot per thousand years. Eventually, the river exposed a sinuous crack yawning into the Earth—so deep that the narrowest stretches receive little more than half an hour of sunlight a day.

The "blackness" of the canyon repelled the local Utes, who lived on the rim but never went in deeper for fear of losing their lives. In 1853, Capt. John W. Gunnison attempted this descent, which

The Gunnison River carves through the Black Canyon of the Gunnison, a park that boasts some of the oldest rock, steepest cliffs, and most sought-after climbing in North America.

he wrote about as "the roughest, most hilly and most cut up" topography he had ever seen.

In 1933, President Herbert Hoover proclaimed Black Canyon a national monument. After four decades of study, a 2008 decree mandated flows (through the three dams above the park) that would better protect the natural integrity of the river downstream.

More than a dozen miles of roads access 18 scenic overlooks into the abyss. Most tourists heed the ancient Ute wisdom and gather behind guardrails, high above the roaring river. Fewer than one percent of park visitors—mostly expert anglers, rock climbers, or seasoned kayakers—descend to the river for its gold medal waters and challenging rapids. ∎

MESA VERDE NATIONAL PARK

▶ LOCATION **35 MILES W OF DURANGO, COLORADO** ▶ SIZE **81 SQUARE MILES**
▶ HIGHEST POINT **PARK POINT, 8,569 FEET** ▶ VISITORS **563,420 IN 2018** ▶ ESTABLISHED **1906**

Near the Four Corners region, in Southwest Colorado on a dry plateau redolent of pine sap and swept by desert winds, this park protects nearly 5,000 ancestral Puebloan (formerly Anasazi) archaeological sites—including 600 cliff dwellings—that date back to A.D. 550. Surrounding the ancient habitations, numerous park trails lead past petroglyphs, showing handprints, bighorn sheep, and anthropomorphic beings that were pecked onto rock walls centuries before Gutenberg invented the press.

Avoided by the Utes as sacred places, and only ogled by passing prospectors, the most spectacular ruin was first explored by two local ranchers in 1888. Now known as Cliff Palace, the ancient city with more than 200 stone and mud rooms built around a three-story tower was in a vast sandstone cavern. After roping down, the astonished ranchers discovered a stone ax still hafted to its wood handle, intact ceramic pots, and three unharmed skeletons buried in the rubble. It looked as if the inhabitants had just left, though the ancestral Puebloans inexplicably departed 700 years ago. The continent's largest cliff dwelling still embodies the enduring mystery of their disappearance.

Mesa Verde (Spanish for "table green") was named after the surrounding forests of juniper and piñon. One rare plant, the Cliff Palace milk vetch is endemic to the park and found nowhere else in the world.

Before the park was created, walls had been broken down and hundreds of relics were stolen for private collections or hauled off to museums around the world, President Theodore Roosevelt signed into law the Antiquities Act of 1906 to prevent looting and protect "historic and prehistoric structures, and other objects of historic or scientific interest that are situated upon the lands owned or controlled by the Government." Three weeks later, Roosevelt established Mesa Verde—the first national park created to protect a location of cultural significance and respectfully "preserve the works of man." ■

ABOVE: **This ancestral Puebloan** canteen has a small mouth, globular body, and two perforated handles for hanging from a cord.

OPPOSITE: **Cliff Palace** was home to the ancestral Puebloan people for more than 700 years, from 600 to 1300. Its rooms and kivas sheltered some 100 inhabitants.

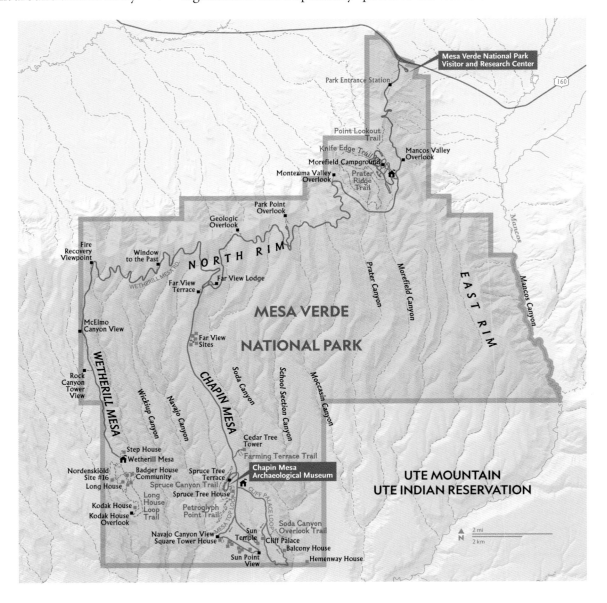

PETRIFIED FOREST NATIONAL PARK

▶ LOCATION **110 MILES E OF FLAGSTAFF, ARIZONA** ▶ SIZE **346 SQUARE MILES**
▶ HIGHEST POINT **PILOT ROCK, 6,235 FEET** ▶ VISITORS **644,922 IN 2018** ▶ ESTABLISHED **1962**

The 35th parallel—the highway of Paleo-Indians, wagon trains, a railroad, historic Route 66, and today's Interstate 40—splits this Arizona park, which overlays the eastern edge of the 7,500-square-mile Painted Desert. Chinle formation sediments brilliantly redden this expanse of sparsely vegetated hills and flat-topped mesas.

The allure of this "Triassic Park" is its fossilized, coniferous logs from the dawn of the dinosaurs. Most of the petrified wood fell from 200-foot-tall trees, with trunks up to eight feet in diameter, related to Africa's monkey puzzle trees. Buried 225 million years ago under volcanic ash that protected the wood from decay, the tree tissues slowly filled with sediments that replaced and replicated the wood, and hardened into a waxy and luminous quartz. There are also several hundred species of fossilized plants and animals: ginkgo and cycad trees, ferns, giant reptiles, and early dinosaurs. These fractured, subtropical remains are propped across the Painted Desert like incandescent tombstones memorializing primordial life.

Beginning in the 1850s, incredulous that what appeared to be wood weighed more than cement, passing surveyors, settlers, and collectors broke apart or hauled off these shimmering fossils by the truckload. Like many federal lands that were protected in the early 20th century, Petrified Forest National Monument was created in 1906 under the Antiquities Act. Legends persist about those who have stolen petrified wood from the park being cursed with bad luck.

The park has a phenomenal, lesser known collection of ancestral Puebloan (formerly Anasazi) rock art. Panels like "Newspaper Rock" surround hundreds of archaeological sites—such as the 700-year-old house ruins of Puerco Pueblo, named after the intermittent and muddy river bisecting the park. Today visitors can imagine the former villagers who once grew corn and cotton, and carved astrological petroglyphs alongside the petrified gems from ancient forests. ∎

At Rainbow Forest, the ground is covered in petrified wood, which gets its rich colors from three main minerals: pure quartz, manganese, and iron oxide.

BRYCE CANYON NATIONAL PARK

▶ LOCATION **268 MILES S OF SALT LAKE CITY, UTAH** ▶ SIZE **56 SQUARE MILES**

▶ HIGHEST POINT **RAINBOW POINT, 9,115 FEET** ▶ VISITORS **2,679,478 IN 2018** ▶ ESTABLISHED **1928**

Renowned for six square miles of colorful hoodoos that dwarf any similar earth pillars, Bryce Canyon is a series of amphitheaters in southwestern Utah. Its trails drop 2,000 feet from the 9,000-foot Paunsaugunt Plateau.

The spindly hoodoos were carved more than 40 million years ago from soft sandstone and shale deposits. Sixteen million years ago, as the Colorado Plateau uplifted, vertical cracks broke the soft, iron oxide–suffused pink or red cliffs. These eventually eroded into the freestanding hoodoos topped with harder and protective stone helmets. From the long view, purple and reddish pastel cliffs are mixed with an architecture of windows, walls, and arches. And during changing light, the multicolored house of Bryce glows as if a fire were burning within.

To the God-fearing rancher Ebenezer Bryce—a Mormon pioneer who built a road into the plateau in the late 1870s—the wilderness landscape was chaos. "Helluva place to lose a cow," Bryce would say.

The Paiute, who lived in the area for centuries, believed that in the time before humans, the hoodoos existed as live beings. "Because they were bad," a surviving elder told a park naturalist, "coyote turned them all into rocks . . . some standing in rows, some sitting down, some holding onto others. You can see their faces, with paint on them just as they were before they became rocks."

In 1891 the Paiute were relocated to a reservation, 10 years after Bryce moved to Arizona. Naming it after Ebenezer, President Warren G. Harding created Bryce National Monument in 1923. A year later, Congress renamed it Utah National Park, until changing it back to Bryce several years later and officially establishing the park. ■

Rich red rock spires called hoodoos—shaped by ice and rain—are ubiquitous in Bryce Canyon; the park holds the largest concentration of them on Earth.

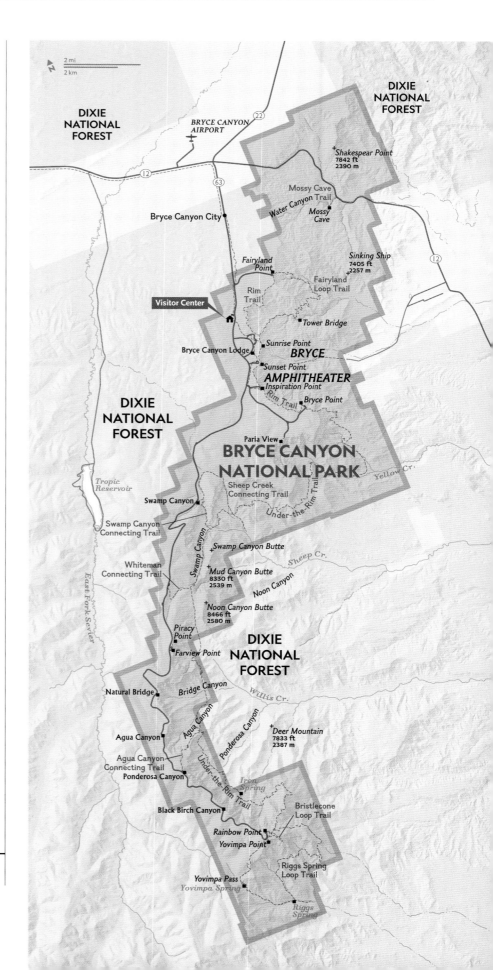

GREAT BASIN NATIONAL PARK

▷ LOCATION **234 MILES SW OF SALT LAKE CITY, UTAH** ▷ SIZE **121 SQUARE MILES**
▷ HIGHEST POINT **WHEELER PEAK, 13,060 FEET** ▷ VISITORS **153,094 IN 2018** ▷ ESTABLISHED **1986**

Several miles from the Utah border in east-central Nevada, this park is dwarfed by the vast, 209,162-square-mile Great Basin. All moisture in this arid bowl of the West evaporates, sinks underground, or flows into salty lakes without reaching the ocean.

Thriving in the park's dry conditions are groves of bristlecone pines—the oldest trees now living on Earth—growing in isolated patches at tree line. In 1964, a researcher cut down an extraordinary bristlecone named Prometheus, estimated to be 4,900 years old—the oldest tree then known. Bristlecones are now protected on federal lands.

Three thousand feet above the stump of Prometheus, Wheeler Peak is accessed by a strenuous, 8.6-mile trail—one of 13 maintained trails in Great Basin. On its north side lies the only permanent snowfield left in Nevada, the Wheeler Peak Glacier.

The park is mostly known for its cave systems; there are at least 42 caves with thin and leaflike folia formations, bulbous stalactites, and rounded shields. Discovered in the late 19th century, the underground topography was originally protected as Lehman Caves National Monument in 1922. Long Cold, the deepest

known cave in Nevada (closed and too dangerous for the public) is 436 feet down, with permanent ice at the bottom. Tens of thousands of visitors come each year for a tour of Lehman Caves, descending from the desert of ancient pines into wondrous, limestone rooms of glowing translucent crystals and alien-looking mineral formations carved by waters. Once underground, one can imagine subterranean life in the dark: the wriggle of eyeless shrimp, the crinkled flutter of bat wings, and the crawl of the Great Basin cave pseudoscorpion, a strange arachnid with its long antennae. ■

ABOVE: **Ohio miner** and rancher Absalom Lehman is believed to have discovered the Lehman Caves in the 1880s. He was known to give stalactites as gifts to his family back East.

OPPOSITE: **Among the world's** oldest living trees, bristlecone pines are the ultimate survivors, despite exposure to high winds and frigid temperatures.

NORTH CASCADES NATIONAL PARK

▷ LOCATION **120 MILES NE OF SEATTLE, WASHINGTON** ▷ SIZE **789 SQUARE MILES**

▷ HIGHEST POINT **GOODE MOUNTAIN, 9,206 FEET** ▷ VISITORS **30,085 IN 2018** ▷ ESTABLISHED **1968**

Along the border of Canada in northern Washington, the park is split into two districts bordering Lake Chelan and Ross Lake National Recreation Areas. This North Cascades National Park Complex encompasses 1,070 square miles, 93 percent of which is further protected as the Stephen Mather Wilderness. As a statement of the area's wildness, there are only six miles of roads—all unpaved—in the scantly visited complex.

Named for its abundance of waterfalls frothing out of high snows, North Cascades' stream-rich topography feeds hundreds of lakes. With 9,000 feet of relief, the alpine terrain is popular among adventurous climbers and hikers who seek lung-buster trails like Purple Creek, which switches back 57 times in 7.5 miles toward the peaks.

The park also holds 312 glaciers, making it the most glaciated national park in the lower 48. Like most other glaciated areas over the last century, the ice coverage has shrunk by half. Still, the ancient and old-growth evergreen forests, combined with prolific plant life, make the park remarkably lush. Over 1,600 plant species, with only three listed as threatened, are found in eight different life zones. To combat the creep of invasive species throughout campgrounds and along trails, the park has been replanting thousands of native plants grown from seeds and cuttings.

The wetter western side of the park receives more than 200 inches of rainfall a year, making the lower valleys temperate rainforests. Compared to the eastern slope, the western park receives an average of 76 more inches of precipitation and 407 more inches of snowfall each year. It's a skiing paradise in winter. ■

Lewis Lake—one of more than 500 lakes and ponds hidden in the park's mountain terrain—glistens amid a sea of pine trees below Black Peak.

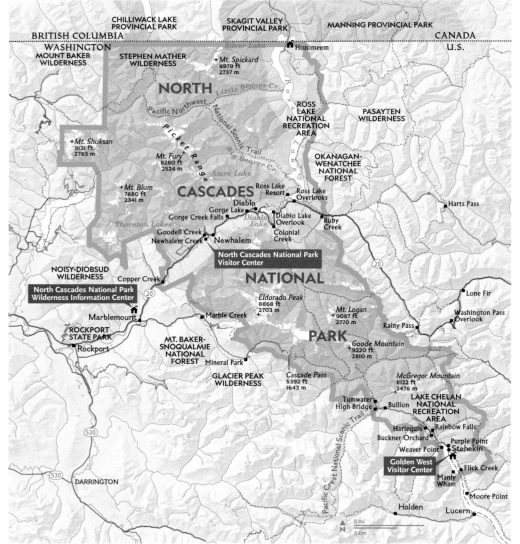

LASSEN VOLCANIC NATIONAL PARK

▷ LOCATION **180 MILES N OF SACRAMENTO, CALIFORNIA** ▷ SIZE **167 SQUARE MILES**
▷ HIGHEST POINT **LASSEN PEAK, 10,456 FEET** ▷ VISITORS **499,435 IN 2018** ▷ ESTABLISHED **1916**

Located in the Cascade Range of Northern California, Lassen is the only national park in the contiguous United States with a volcano that erupted in the 20th century. In 1914, Lassen Peak—one of the largest plug dome volcanoes, rising 2,000 feet above its base—spewed lava for several years. Now a quiescent—albeit smoking—volcano, Lassen was part of a larger volcano that built up 600,000 years ago by lava too thick to flow off the peak. The region had been volcanically active for three million years.

The park's panorama is the only one to hold all four volcano types—plug dome, strato, cinder cone, and shield—with underlying magma created by the Juan de Fuca tectonic plate plowing under North America. As massive winter snowfalls or rains from higher park elevations melt or run underground, the water is superheated by molten rock below to create a steaming, hydrothermal landscape of hot springs, fumaroles, and boiling mud pots.

Scattered throughout the park in four different plant zones are stands of old-growth red fir, the keystone and often stunted-looking whitebark pine, and several deciduous tree species. There are also innumerable streams and lakes, meadows colored by spring wildflowers, and hundreds of plant species. The minuscule Lassen copper moss, draped with strange fruit, is found in only four other high-elevation locations outside the park. Nearly 300 vertebrate species—including black bears, fox, mountain lions, and mule deer—roam the park.

Lassen Volcanic National Park has over 5,000 feet of elevation gain, and is crisscrossed with over 150 miles of trails that beckon visitors like a mountainous version of Yellowstone. ■

Lassen contains all four volcano types—shield, strato, cinder cone, and plug dome—and a wealth of steaming fumaroles like Big Boiler pool in the Bumpass Hell area.

A 1930s poster shows Lassen Peak erupting. Though the area is now dormant, it's full of active steam vents, bubbling mud pots, and boiling springs.

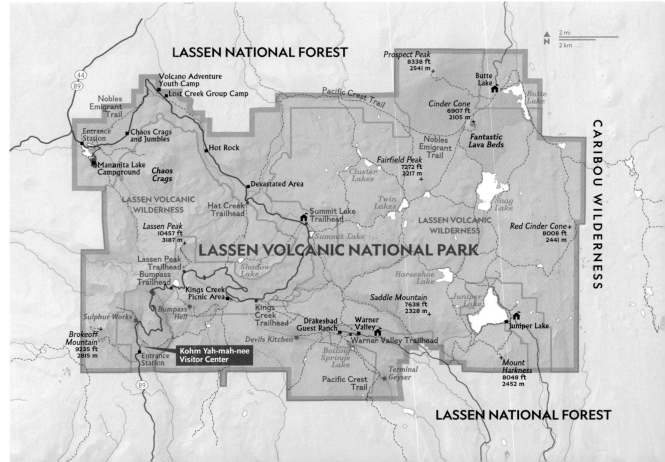

PINNACLES
NATIONAL PARK

▶ LOCATION **71 MILES S OF SAN JOSE, CALIFORNIA** ▶ SIZE **42 SQUARE MILES**
▶ HIGHEST POINT **NORTH CHALONE PEAK, 3,304 FEET** ▶ VISITORS **222,152 IN 2018** ▶ ESTABLISHED **2013**

East of California's Salinas Valley, in the Gabilan (Coastal) Range, Pinnacles—earlier known as Palisades—is known for the lava spires that rise from boulder-studded canyons and rolling chaparral hills. The pinkish brown lava rock, breccia, forms a seven-mile-long, 2.5-mile-wide slab, which rises a half mile high, covering 80 percent of the park. The rock is dappled red, green, yellow, and brown with 293 species of lichen. President Theodore Roosevelt proclaimed it a national monument in 1908, and following his lead 105 years later, President Barack Obama made it a national park.

Most of the park is wilderness and a mecca for rock climbers and lepidopterists—it's possible to net 71 different butterfly species.

Because it has been protected for more than a century, Pinnacles—supported by so many pollinating insects—is an oasis of native vegetation. The flowering plants also provide sustenance to the highest bee diversity per square mile of anyplace on Earth. Thirty-two miles of trails wind through the jumbled rock formations and talus fields.

Enlarged numerous times, it's still the sixth smallest park in the system, but the animal life in Pinnacles is remarkable: For instance, 14 species of bats live in unusual talus caves, formed by boulders in the steep canyons. The park also teems with reptiles and amphibians, while its protected aeries draw more than 160 species of birds, including California condors, prairie falcons, great horned owls, golden eagles, and peregrine falcons.

The park has large daytime temperature variations—30° to 50°F (16.7° to 27.8°C)—because the 40-mile-distant and moderating Pacific Ocean climate is blocked by a mountain range. Pinnacle's semiarid conditions are compared to the Mediterranean, with summer heat often reaching 100°F (38°C). ∎

ABOVE: **The park** may be small, but the craggy folds of its rock formations protect more than 160 bird species, including this California quail, which tends to build its nest on the ground.

OPPOSITE: **Rock spires** and ribs like these in the High Peaks area cover most of Pinnacles National Park, creating a shelter for a surprising array of species.

CHANNEL ISLANDS NATIONAL PARK

▶ LOCATION **93 MILES W OF LOS ANGELES, CALIFORNIA** ▶ SIZE **390 SQUARE MILES**
▶ HIGHEST POINT **DIABLO PEAK, 2,450 FEET** ▶ VISITORS **366,250 IN 2018** ▶ ESTABLISHED **1980**

Twenty miles offshore in the cool California current, the park includes five of the eight remarkable Channel Islands: San Miguel, Santa Rosa, Santa Cruz (the largest), Anacapa, and Santa Barbara. The park is surrounded and further protected by the Channel Islands National Marine Sanctuary.

Thousands of years of isolation created a unique island habitat. The marine life ranges from blue whales to microscopic plankton. On land, human remains of a female skeleton found on Santa Rosa Island were dated to more than 13,000 years ago—the oldest human remains found in North America. Archaeological sites show continuous occupation from this Ice Age era, when the islands were connected to land. Woolly mammoth remains have also been discovered, including a pygmy species, which underwent dwarfing as the Channel Islands were isolated from the mainland. Later the Tongva and Chumash people paddled out from the mainland on redwood plank canoes and established villages on several of the islands.

The Bureau of Lighthouses (forerunner of the U.S. Coast Guard) first drew the National Park Service's interest to the Santa Barbara and Anacapa Islands in 1932, and six years later the

A boat skims through Potato Harbor on Santa Cruz Island, one of five isolated islands protected in this park, along with 1,252 square nautical miles of surrounding sea.

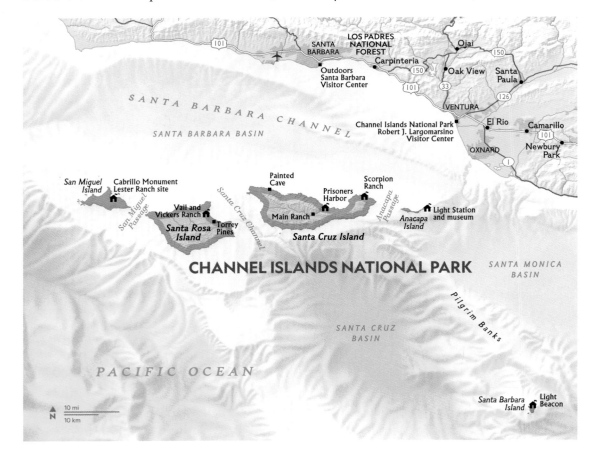

CHANNEL ISLANDS NATIONAL PARK

islands were named a national monument. Subsequent efforts by federal officials and local advocates for protecting ocean life helped designate the park.

More than 2,000 species of plants and animals live within the eight Channel Islands, which are a UNESCO biosphere reserve. Over time some vertebrate species have evolved into distinct Channel Islands subspecies, such as the deer mouse and island fox—two of 145 endemic species. Some species—like the island scrub jay and the Santa Cruz Island silver lotus—are found only on that island. The park is renowned for its sea caves; the 100-foot-wide, quarter-mile-long Painted Cave—filled with colorful rocks and lichens—is one of the deepest sea caves on Earth. Channel Islands also offers scuba diving, sea kayaking, spearfishing, trail running, camping, and hiking—all an hour and a half by boat from the mainland. ∎

REDWOOD NATIONAL PARK

▷ LOCATION **130 MILES NW OF REDDING, CALIFORNIA** ▷ SIZE **121 SQUARE MILES (FEDERAL LAND)**
▷ HIGHEST POINT **COYOTE PEAK, 3,170 FEET** ▷ VISITORS **482,536 IN 2018** ▷ ESTABLISHED **1968**

Stretched 37 miles along northern California's booming Pacific Ocean coast, Redwood National Park is a matrix of federal and state lands protecting the tallest trees on Earth. The regional climate of 60 to 140 inches of rainfall a year—combined with fog and rich soil—allows the redwoods to grow over 300 feet tall and up to 2,000 years old. A deep stillness can be found amid the old giants, towering above ferns and moss. The misty forest understory supports a fragrant spring flowering of rhododendron, azalea, and prolific berries. Bears, river otters, deer, elk, beaver, and cougars amble and feed below flying squirrels.

Two hundred miles of trails link up wild rivers, vast prairies, coastal cliffs, and beaches, where hikers can peer up toward ancient treetops or watch sea lions and harbor seals playing in the surf. The park attracts hundreds of bird species including three species of cormorants, white-tailed kites, multiple sandpipers, Vaux's swifts, acorn woodpeckers, and California brown pelicans.

California established the four adjoining state parks after clearcutting in the 1920s took its toll on over 3,000 square miles of old-growth redwood forests. More than four decades later, after 90 percent of the trees had been cut down, Congress approved a national park. In 1978 after wrangling with the timber industry, 79 more square miles of already logged forest were added to the park. Since then, seeding Douglas fir trees has created unhealthy second-growth forests, with up to 20,000 fast-growing Douglas firs an acre (that once held 20 to 30 slow-to-propagate redwoods) taking over the old-growth forest. Restoration efforts—such as selectively thinning out the Douglas firs—continue today. ■

A stand of redwoods rises through fog. Many visitors are awestruck by the experience of standing among them—author John Steinbeck described it as a "cathedral hush."

WRANGELL–ST. ELIAS
NATIONAL PARK AND PRESERVE

▷ LOCATION **200 MILES E OF ANCHORAGE, ALASKA** ▷ SIZE **20,587 SQUARE MILES**
▷ HIGHEST POINT **MOUNT ST. ELIAS, 18,009 FEET** ▷ VISITORS **79,450 IN 2018** ▷ ESTABLISHED **1980**

Bordered by Canada's huge Kluane National Park and Preserve to the east and drained by the 290-mile-long, silt-laden Copper River on the west, Wrangell–St. Elias is the largest national park. More than 30 percent glaciated, it shares with Canada the greatest nonpolar ice body—the Bagley Icefield. Along its edges, the bulbous Malaspina Glacier canvasses 1,500 square miles as the planet's ultimate piedmont glacier. The 70-mile stretch of the Hubbard Glacier makes it North America's longest tidewater glacier, explosively calving icebergs from its six-mile-wide terminus into the sea.

Seldom visited yet commonly ogled from Alaska-bound planes as an expanse of glaciers and peaks thrusting abruptly above the blue Pacific, the park encompasses or partially includes four mountain ranges: the volcanic Wrangell Mountains, the high Alaska Range, the broad Chugach Mountains, and the coastal St. Elias Mountains.

The pyramidal Mount St. Elias—second highest in both Canada and the United States, with an international boundary across its summit—was first climbed in 1897 by the Italian Duke of the Abruzzi, accompanied by his noblemen. The difficult mountain is rarely repeated. Proclaimed a national monument in 1978, the area was a year later designated a World Heritage site. Following two decades of debate, the monument was enlarged through the Alaska National Interest Lands Conservation Act, signed into law on December 2, 1980, by President Jimmy Carter. The new park and preserve were created to protect the region, from temperate rainforest to tundra; to provide continued access for recreation; to allow sport hunting use in its preserve; and to protect wildlife. ■

ABOVE: **Dwarfed by** the sweeping ice, a bush plane flies over a glacier in remote Wrangell–St. Elias, which is almost six times the size of Yellowstone National Park.

OPPOSITE: **The park** encompasses some of North America's tallest mountains. Many of them, like 9,358-foot Tanada Peak, shown here, were once volcanoes.

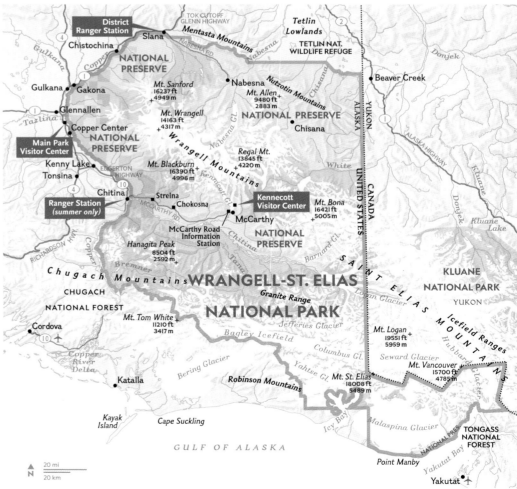

A 60-mile dirt road leads to the abandoned mill towns of the Kennecott Copper Mine, where operations peaked from 1911 to 1938. It is now a historic landmark.

KENAI FJORDS NATIONAL PARK

LOCATION 130 MILES S OF ANCHORAGE, ALASKA ▶ **SIZE 1,047 SQUARE MILES**
HIGHEST POINT UNNAMED PEAK, 6,450 FEET ▶ **VISITORS 321,596 IN 2018** ▶ **ESTABLISHED 1980**

On the eastern shore of the Kenai Peninsula above the town of Seward is a score of breathtaking fjords and inlets fringing the Gulf of Alaska. The water thrums with marine life below the splash of innumerable waterfalls draped over quartz-seamed graywacke cliffs. On land, the park's snows are hemmed in by a narrow forest of spruce rising hundreds of feet high and smaller mountain hemlock.

Because half the park envelops the Harding Icefield, stretching 700 square miles over the Kenai Mountains, the effects of climate change are startling. Despite over 400 inches of snowfall annually on the ice field, the average temperatures in Alaska have increased approximately 3°F (1.7°C) over the past 60 years. From 1986 to 2005 the Pedersen Glacier—one of 38 arms flowing off the ice field—has melted back slowly but steadily at the rate of 75 feet a year.

One of Alaska's few easily accessed glaciers—the Exit Glacier—is in Kenai Fjords, a short hike from a spur road off the Seward Highway. On the 8.2-mile round-trip up the Harding Icefield Trail, park rangers have shown two centuries of Exit Glacier melting with signs. Surrounded by ground rather than insulated by the ice field, Exit Glacier has retreated more than 300 feet in some years. Bared by melting ice, the stony ground quickly becomes furred with mosses and shrubs.

Because most of the park is easily accessed by boat, visitors come to watch whales, porpoise, sea lions, and harbor seals feeding on krill and salmon. Immediately above there are often murres, kittiwakes, murrelets, puffins, bald eagles, and peregrine falcons; on the higher peaks, mountain goats appear as white dots. Along the shorelines, startled moose, grizzlies, and black bears duck into thorny devil's club as approaching onlookers point, gasp, and aim their cameras at this sensational jut of land against sea. ▪

Icebergs bob along in Bear Glacier Lagoon, a lake set between the park's longest glacier and its moraine. Paddlers are advised to keep a safe distance from the unpredictable icebergs.

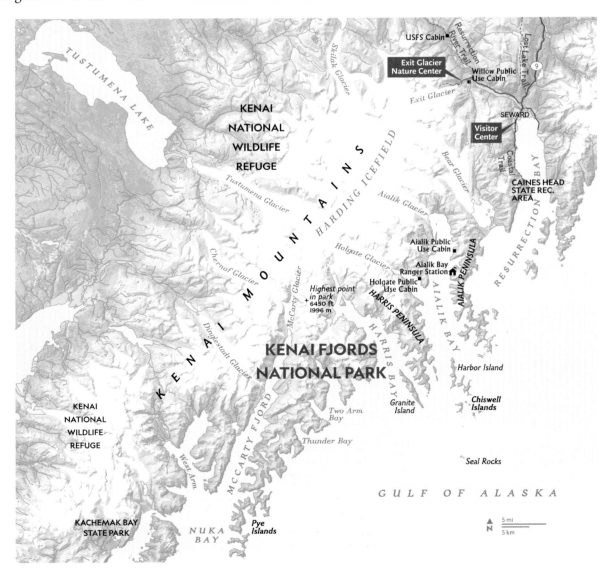

LAKE CLARK NATIONAL PARK AND PRESERVE

▷ LOCATION **120 MILES SW OF ANCHORAGE, ALASKA** ▷ SIZE **6,297 SQUARE MILES**
▷ HIGHEST POINT **MOUNT REDOUBT, 10,197 FEET** ▷ VISITORS **14,479 IN 2018** ▷ ESTABLISHED **1980**

At the glaciated junction of the Aleutian and Alaska Ranges, Lake Clark National Park and Preserve is known for its microcosmic representation of the state, replete with wilderness adventure, glaciers, salmon, bears, caribou, tundra, forests, seacoast, marshes, shimmering lakes, wild rivers, cultural heritage, and volcanoes.

Although Mount Iliamna only puffs out smoke and steam, the eruptive Mount Redoubt has spewed ash over southern Alaska four times since 1902. At approximately four million acres, the park and preserve is as large as Hawai'i, yet it has less than seven miles of trails and lacks roads, campsites, and visitor facilities. Accessible only by boat or airplane, its namesake 42-mile-long lake is the site of Port Alsworth (population 159) on private land within the park.

Up to three million salmon a year migrate through park waters, including three designated Wild and Scenic Rivers: the Tlikakila, the Chilikadrotna, and the Mulchatna. The Kvichak River is the most productive sockeye (red) salmon fishery on Earth. After hatching in upper rivers and lakes, the juvenile fish make a three-year journey out into the Pacific, traversing hundreds of miles before swimming back upriver to the precise headwaters of their birth, where they spawn and die.

Congress created the park to protect the salmon fishery along with wide-ranging ecosystems. Lake Clark provides diverse sanctuary for 800 plant species, 37 land mammals, 187 bird species, and two dozen different fish.

Dick Proenneke's log cabin, built in the 1960s with local materials and simple hand tools, was listed in 2007 on the National Register of Historic Places. Today it's a destination for anybody wanting to pay homage to Alaskan conservation and one man's can-do spirit. ∎

Reachable by plane or a daylong hike on the Tanalian Trails, Kontrashibuna Lake is a secluded destination for fishing and camping.

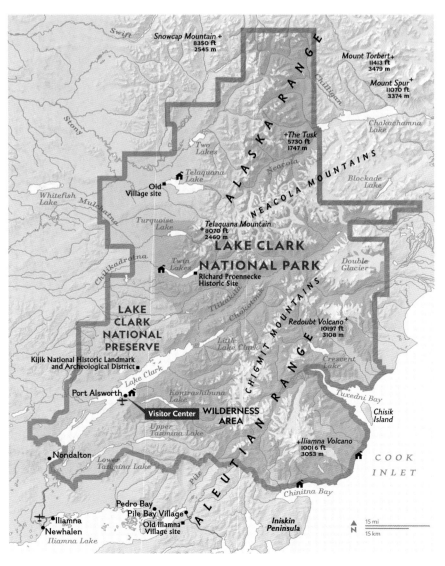

Year-old sockeye leave their freshwater birthplace in the park for the ocean. Several years later they reverse their journey up the Newhalen River.

HALEAKALĀ NATIONAL PARK

▷ LOCATION **140 MILES E OF HONOLULU, HAWAI'I** ▷ SIZE **52 SQUARE MILES**

▷ HIGHEST POINT **PU'U 'ULA'ULA (RED HILL), 10,023 FEET** ▷ VISITORS **1,044,084 IN 2018** ▷ ESTABLISHED **1916**

Thirty miles northwest of the Big Island in Hawai'i, the massive volcano Haleakalā formed most of the island of Maui. The park stands on the island's east end, encompassing the volcano.

After a 37-mile, 10,000-foot climb up the Haleakalā Highway, watching the sun rise or set across a crater a half mile deep and two and a half miles wide is breathtaking. Legend has it that the demigod Maui lassoed the sun god Lā and made her promise to move more slowly through the sky—in Polynesian culture, the summit is sacred.

Haleakalā was established as part of Hawai'i National Park—now called Hawai'i Volcanoes National Park on the Big Island—just weeks before the creation of the National Park Service on August 25, 1916. In 1961, Haleakalā was split into its own management unit to inspire visitors and protect the many species found nowhere else on Earth. Its 24,719 wilderness acres comprise 75 percent of the park.

According to a recent analysis of U.S. Fish and Wildlife Service data, Haleakalā shelters more endangered species than any national park: 81 flowering plants, six nonflowering plants, 10 birds, three insects, two mammals, and one reptile. This record 103 endangered species is nearly twice that of neighboring Hawai'i Volcanoes, with

ABOVE: **The ghostly** silvery hairs, fleshy leaves, and low-growing rosette of the Haleakalā silversword allow it to survive in a hot, dry world.

OPPOSITE: **Haleakalā crater,** seen here in the foreground, isn't actually a volcanic crater—it was formed by erosion as it chipped away at the mountain.

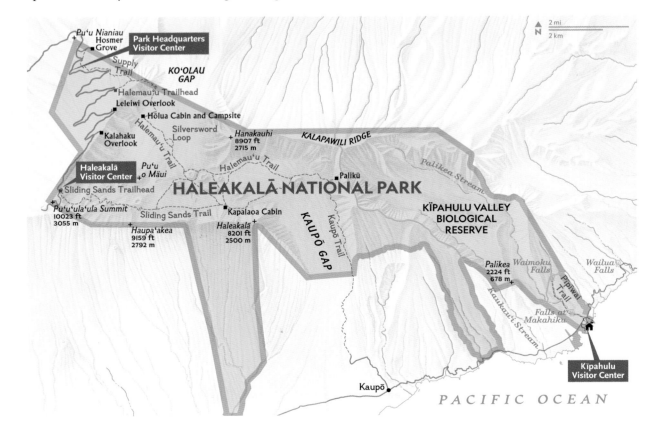

53 endangered species. Both host the exceptionally rare silversword—at one time seen thick as snow blanketing the volcanic slopes—that lives up to 90 years, flowering only once with a spectacular silver stalk, then dying, scattering its seeds to the wind.

Whether as seeds, spores, insects, spiders, birds, or small plants, the teeming abundance of life within Haleakalā evolved over the millennia and countless reproduction cycles. From lush forests rich with birdsong, and numerous park viewpoints, one can picture new life arriving as waves beat and breathe rhythmically against the volcanic shores, amid the vast expanse of ocean bluing in the distance. ■

KOBUK VALLEY NATIONAL PARK

▶ LOCATION **100 MILES E OF KOTZEBUE, ALASKA** ▶ SIZE **2,736 SQUARE MILES**
▶ HIGHEST POINT **MOUNT ANGAYUKAQSRAQ, 4,760 FEET** ▶ VISITORS **15,500 IN 2017** ▶ ESTABLISHED **1980**

Two dozen miles north of the Arctic Circle, inserted between the Selawik National Wildlife Refuge and the Noatak National Preserve in the Brooks Range, Kobuk is one of the least visited and most remote national parks. Set aside to protect 30 square miles of sand dunes and its namesake river, Kobuk is one of less than a dozen national parks without road access. No trails or facilities exist in the park.

The Baird and Waring Mountains of the Alaskan Interior enclose the Kobuk Valley to create a microclimate, that—to the surprise of many overheated visitors—has summer highs approaching 90°F (32°C). In mid-valley, outwash from the rock-crushing Ice Age has deposited three sections of otherworldly, 100-foot-high sand dunes (studied by NASA for their semblance to Martian dunes). Extensive wetlands along the Kobuk River are also famous for blizzards of mosquitoes, continuous summer sunshine, and brutal, subzero winters.

The park encompasses the transitional edges of subarctic boreal forest and shrubby Arctic tundra, which is enduring habitat for porcupines, wolves, foxes, black and grizzly bears, Dall sheep, moose, river otters, lynx, wolverines, snowshoe hares, and numerous small rodents. In spring and fall, up to a half million of the Western Arctic caribou herd migrates through the park, along with over 160 species of birds.

Humans have lived amid this wildlife cornucopia for more than 12,000 years, hunting caribou or relying on the rich stores of fish. Today, as in past millennia, native Inupiat fishermen depend upon four different species of salmon that run the river 75 miles from the sea, along with Dolly Varden, grayling, burbot, lamprey, whitefish, and smelt. Most tourists come with both fishing rods and paddles. ■

Ahnewetut Creek flows through a surprising landmark: the Great Kobuk Sand Dunes. Left behind by the last ice age, they are the Arctic's largest active sand dunes.

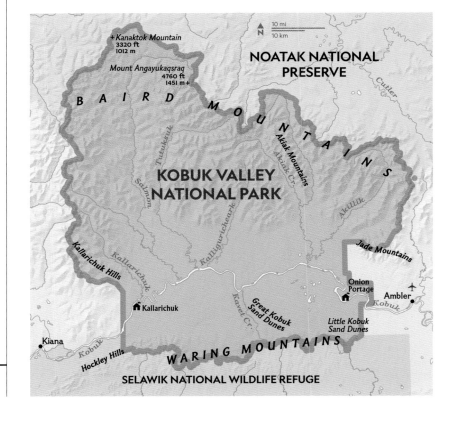

A caribou herd splashes across the Kobuk River. They make a massive migration twice a year, crossing the park to reach their wintering and calving grounds.

NATIONAL PARK OF AMERICAN SAMOA

▷ LOCATION **2,600 MILES SW OF HONOLULU, HAWAI'I** ▷ SIZE **21 SQUARE MILES**
▷ HIGHEST POINT **LATA MOUNTAIN, 3,160 FEET** ▷ VISITORS **28,626 IN 2018** ▷ ESTABLISHED **1988**

Located closer to New Zealand than the United States, American Samoa is the most far-flung and usually the least visited national park. The park units are on portions of three islands—Tutuila, Ta'ū, and Ofu—amid the five islands of American Samoa ("sacred earth"), the only U.S. territory south of the Equator. The territorial capital and park headquarters are in Pago Pago on Tutuila Island, one of the world's wetter places. Sixty miles east, the landmark Lata Mountain rises from the remote Ta'ū Island, next to Ofu Island.

Although the park was established in 1988, the Park Service could not purchase traditional communal land. So, in 1993, Congress signed a 50-year lease agreement with eight participating villages. The park protects a paleotropical rainforest and its only native mammals are bats. Over 350 species of native birds, including the endemic Samoan starling, found nowhere else in the world, live in the islands. A third of the park is marine waters, with 250 coral species and 950 species of fish.

Samoa's weather is warm and humid, without winter or summer, but a tropical wet season runs from November through April, while the drier, trade-wind season gusts cause rougher surf on the south side of the islands. The average annual temperature is 80°F (27°C).

Fishing is world-class, and the Park Service maintains a dozen trails. Ofu Island has a protected reef for snorkeling and diving, along with a famous white-sand beach. Coupled with the park's wonders, the islands are permeated with Samoan culture. Distinct customs are collectively called *fa'asamoa*—the Samoan way—and include evening prayers known as *Sa* and the sharing of 'ava, a local drink. ∎

One of the least visited national parks, American Samoa's secluded sand beaches and pristine fringing reefs offer relative solitude in addition to spectacular scenery.

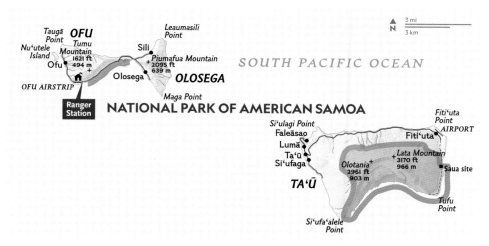

A giant fruit bat stretches a wing—with a span that can reach up to three feet—as it hangs from a limb in a rainforest on Tutuila Island.

COMPLETE LIST OF PARK UNITS

NATIONAL BATTLEFIELDS
Antietam National Battlefield, Maryland
Big Hole National Battlefield, Montana
Cowpens National Battlefield, South Carolina
Fort Donelson National Battlefield, Kentucky and Tennessee
Fort Necessity National Battlefield, Pennsylvania
Monocacy National Battlefield, Maryland
Moores Creek National Battlefield, North Carolina
Petersburg National Battlefield, Virginia
Stones River National Battlefield, Tennessee
Tupelo National Battlefield, Mississippi
Wilson's Creek National Battlefield, Missouri

NATIONAL BATTLEFIELD PARKS
Kennesaw Mountain National Battlefield Park, Georgia
Manassas National Battlefield Park, Virginia
Richmond National Battlefield Park, Virginia
River Raisin National Battlefield Park, Michigan

NATIONAL BATTLEFIELD SITE
Brices Cross Roads National Battlefield Site, Mississippi

NATIONAL MILITARY PARKS
Chickamauga and Chattanooga National Military Park,
  Georgia and Tennessee
Fredericksburg and Spotsylvania County Battlefields Memorial
  National Military Park, Virginia
Gettysburg National Military Park, Pennsylvania
Guilford Courthouse National Military Park, North Carolina
Horseshoe Bend National Military Park, Alabama
Kings Mountain National Military Park, South Carolina
Pea Ridge National Military Park, Arkansas
Shiloh National Military Park, Tennessee
Vicksburg National Military Park, Louisiana and Mississippi

NATIONAL HISTORICAL PARKS
Abraham Lincoln Birthplace National Historical Park, Kentucky
Adams National Historical Park, Massachusetts
Appomattox Court House National Historical Park, Virginia
Blackstone River Valley National Historical Park, Rhode Island
Boston National Historical Park, Massachusetts
Cane River Creole National Historical Park, Louisiana
Cedar Creek and Belle Grove National Historical Park, Virginia
Chaco Culture National Historical Park, New Mexico
Chesapeake and Ohio Canal National Historical Park,
  District of Columbia, Maryland, and West Virginia

Colonial National Historical Park, Virginia
Cumberland Gap National Historical Park, Kentucky,
  Tennessee, and Virginia
Dayton Aviation Heritage National Historical Park, Ohio
First State National Historical Park, Delaware
George Rogers Clark National Historical Park, Indiana
Harpers Ferry National Historical Park, Maryland, Virginia,
  and West Virginia
Harriet Tubman National Historical Park, New York
Harriet Tubman Underground Railroad National Historical Park,
  Maryland
Hopewell Culture National Historical Park, Ohio
Independence National Historical Park, Pennsylvania
Jean Lafitte National Historical Park and Preserve, Louisiana
Kalaupapa National Historical Park, Hawai'i
Kaloko-Honok'hau National Historical Park, Hawai'i
Keweenaw National Historical Park, Michigan
Klondike Gold Rush National Historical
  Park, Alaska and Washington
Lewis and Clark National Historical Park, Oregon
  and Washington
Lowell National Historical Park, Massachusetts
Lyndon B. Johnson National Historical Park, Texas
Manhattan Project National Historical Park, New Mexico,
  Tennessee, and Washington
Marsh-Billings-Rockefeller National Historical Park, Vermont
Martin Luther King, Jr. National Historical Park, Georgia
Minute Man National Historical Park, Massachusetts
Morristown National Historical Park, New Jersey
Natchez National Historical Park, Mississippi
New Bedford Whaling National Historical Park, Massachusetts
New Orleans Jazz National Historical Park, Louisiana
Nez Perce National Historical Park, Idaho, Montana, Oregon,
  and Washington
Palo Alto Battlefield National Historical Park, Texas
Paterson Great Falls National Historical Park, New Jersey
Pecos National Historical Park, New Mexico
Pu'uhonua o Hōnaunau National Historical Park, Hawai'i
Rosie the Riveter/World War II Home Front National Historical
  Park, California
Salt River Bay National Historical Park and Ecological Preserve,
  Virgin Islands
San Antonio Missions National Historical Park, Texas
San Francisco Maritime National Historical Park, California
San Juan Island National Historical Park, Washington
Saratoga National Historical Park, New York

Sitka National Historical Park, Alaska
Thomas Edison National Historical Park, New Jersey
Tumacácori National Historical Park, Arizona
Valley Forge National Historical Park, Pennsylvania
War in the Pacific National Historical Park, Guam
Women's Rights National Historical Park, New York

NATIONAL HISTORIC SITES

Allegheny Portage Railroad National Historic Site, Pennsylvania
Andersonville National Historic Site, Georgia
Andrew Johnson National Historic Site, Tennessee
Bent's Old Fort National Historic Site, Colorado
Boston African American National Historic Site, Massachusetts
Brown v. Board of Education National Historic Site, Kansas
Carl Sandburg Home National Historic Site, North Carolina
Carter G. Woodson Home National Historic Site,
 District of Columbia
Charles Pinckney National Historic Site, South Carolina
Christiansted National Historic Site, Virgin Islands
Clara Barton National Historic Site, Maryland
Edgar Allan Poe National Historic Site, Pennsylvania
Eisenhower National Historic Site, Pennsylvania
Eleanor Roosevelt National Historic Site, New York
Eugene O'Neill National Historic Site, California
First Ladies National Historic Site, Ohio
Ford's Theatre National Historic Site, District of Columbia
Fort Bowie National Historic Site, Arizona
Fort Davis National Historic Site, Texas
Fort Laramie National Historic Site, Wyoming
Fort Larned National Historic Site, Kansas
Fort Point National Historic Site, California
Fort Raleigh National Historic Site, North Carolina
Fort Scott National Historic Site, Kansas
Fort Smith National Historic Site, Arkansas and Oklahoma
Fort Union Trading Post National Historic Site, Montana
 and North Dakota
Fort Vancouver National Historic Site, Washington
Frederick Douglass National Historic Site, District of Columbia
Frederick Law Olmsted National Historic Site, Massachusetts
Friendship Hill National Historic Site, Pennsylvania
Golden Spike National Historic Site, Utah
Grant-Kohrs Ranch National Historic Site, Montana
Hampton National Historic Site, Maryland
Harry S. Truman National Historic Site, Missouri
Herbert Hoover National Historic Site, Iowa
Home of Franklin D. Roosevelt National Historic Site, New York
Hopewell Furnace National Historic Site, Pennsylvania
Hubbell Trading Post National Historic Site, Arizona
James A. Garfield National Historic Site, Ohio
Jimmy Carter National Historic Site, Georgia
John Fitzgerald Kennedy National Historic Site, Massachusetts
John Muir National Historic Site, California

Knife River Indian Villages National Historic Site, North Dakota
Lincoln Home National Historic Site, Illinois
Little Rock Central High School National Historic Site, Arkansas
Longfellow House–Washington's Headquarters National
 Historic Site, Massachusetts
Maggie L. Walker National Historic Site, Virginia
Manzanar National Historic Site, California
Martin Van Buren National Historic Site, New York
Mary McLeod Bethune Council House National Historic Site,
 District of Columbia
Minidoka National Historic Site, Idaho
Minuteman Missile National Historic Site, South Dakota
Nicodemus National Historic Site, Kansas
Ninety Six National Historic Site, South Carolina
Pennsylvania Avenue National Historic Site, District of Columbia
President William Jefferson Clinton Birthplace Home
 National Historic Site, Arkansas
Pu'ukoholā Heiau National Historic Site, Hawai'i
Sagamore Hill National Historic Site, New York
Saint-Gaudens National Historic Site, New Hampshire
Saint Paul's Church National Historic Site, New York
Salem Maritime National Historic Site, Massachusetts
San Juan National Historic Site, Puerto Rico
Sand Creek Massacre National Historic Site, Colorado
Saugus Iron Works National Historic Site, Massachusetts
Springfield Armory National Historic Site, Massachusetts
Steamtown National Historic Site, Pennsylvania
Theodore Roosevelt Birthplace National Historic Site, New York
Theodore Roosevelt Inaugural National Historic Site, New York
Thomas Stone National Historic Site, Maryland
Tuskegee Airmen National Historic Site, Alabama
Tuskegee Institute National Historic Site, Alabama
Ulysses S. Grant National Historic Site, Missouri
Vanderbilt Mansion National Historic Site, New York
Washita Battlefield National Historic Site, Oklahoma
Weir Farm National Historic Site, Connecticut
Whitman Mission National Historic Site, Washington
William Howard Taft National Historic Site, Ohio

INTERNATIONAL HISTORIC SITES
Saint Croix Island International Historic Site, Maine

NATIONAL LAKESHORES
Apostle Islands National Lakeshore, Wisconsin
Pictured Rocks National Lakeshore, Michigan
Sleeping Bear Dunes National Lakeshore, Michigan

NATIONAL MEMORIALS
Arkansas Post National Memorial, Arkansas
Arlington House, The Robert E. Lee Memorial, Virginia
Chamizal National Memorial, Texas
Coronado National Memorial, Arizona

De Soto National Memorial, Florida
Federal Hall National Memorial, New York
Flight 93 National Memorial, Pennsylvania
Fort Caroline National Memorial, Florida
Franklin Delano Roosevelt Memorial, District of Columbia
General Grant National Memorial, New York
Hamilton Grange National Memorial, New York
Johnstown Flood National Memorial, Pennsylvania
Korean War Veterans Memorial, District of Columbia
Lincoln Boyhood Home National Memorial, Indiana
Lincoln Memorial, District of Columbia
Lyndon Baines Johnson Memorial Grove on the Potomac, District of Columbia
Martin Luther King Jr. Memorial, District of Columbia
Mount Rushmore National Memorial, South Dakota
Perry's Victory and International Peace Memorial, Ohio
Port Chicago Naval Magazine National Memorial, California
Roger Williams National Memorial, Rhode Island
Thaddeus Kosciuszko National Memorial, Pennsylvania
Theodore Roosevelt Island, District of Columbia
Thomas Jefferson Memorial, District of Columbia
Vietnam Veterans Memorial, District of Columbia
Washington Monument, District of Columbia
World War I Memorial, District of Columbia
World War II Memorial, District of Columbia
Wright Brothers National Memorial, North Carolina

NATIONAL MONUMENTS

African Burial Ground National Monument, New York
Agate Fossil Beds National Monument, Nebraska
Alibates Flint Quarries National Monument, Texas
Aniakchak National Monument, Alaska
Aztec Ruins National Monument, New Mexico
Bandelier National Monument, New Mexico
Belmont-Paul Women's Equality National Monument, District of Columbia
Birmingham Civil Rights National Monument, Alabama
Booker T. Washington National Monument, Virginia
Buck Island Reef National Monument, Virgin Islands
Cabrillo National Monument, California
Camp Nelson National Monument, Kentucky
Canyon de Chelly National Monument, Arizona
Cape Krusenstern National Monument, Alaska
Capulin Volcano National Monument, New Mexico
Casa Grande Ruins National Monument, Arizona
Castillo de San Marcos National Monument, Florida
Castle Clinton National Monument, New York
Castle Mountains National Monument, California
Cedar Breaks National Monument, Utah
César E. Chávez National Monument, California
Charles Young Buffalo Soldiers National Monument, Ohio
Chiricahua National Monument, Arizona

Colorado National Monument, Colorado
Craters of the Moon National Monument, Idaho
Devils Postpile National Monument, California
Devils Tower National Monument, Wyoming
Dinosaur National Monument, Colorado and Utah
Effigy Mounds National Monument, Iowa
El Malpais National Monument, New Mexico
El Morro National Monument, New Mexico
Florissant Fossil Beds National Monument, Colorado
Fort Frederica National Monument, Georgia
Fort Matanzas National Monument, Florida
Fort McHenry National Monument and Historic Shrine, Maryland
Fort Monroe National Monument, Virginia
Fort Pulaski National Monument, Georgia
Fort Stanwix National Monument, New York
Fort Sumter National Monument, South Carolina
Fort Union National Monument, New Mexico
Fossil Butte National Monument, Wyoming
Freedom Riders National Monument, Alabama
George Washington Birthplace National Monument, Virginia
George Washington Carver National Monument, Missouri
Gila Cliff Dwellings National Monument, New Mexico
Governors Island National Monument, New York
Grand Portage National Monument, Minnesota
Hagerman Fossil Beds National Monument, Idaho
Hohokam Pima National Monument, Arizona
Homestead National Monument of America, Nebraska
Honouliuli National Monument, Hawai'i
Hovenweep National Monument, Colorado and Utah
Jewel Cave National Monument, South Dakota
John Day Fossil Beds National Monument, Oregon
Katahdin Woods and Waters National Monument, Maine
Lava Beds National Monument, California
Little Bighorn Battlefield National Monument, Montana
Montezuma Castle National Monument, Arizona
Muir Woods National Monument, California
Natural Bridges National Monument, Utah
Navajo National Monument, Arizona
Ocmulgee National Monument, Georgia
Oregon Caves National Monument and Preserve, Oregon
Organ Pipe Cactus National Monument, Arizona
Petroglyph National Monument, New Mexico
Pipe Spring National Monument, Arizona
Pipestone National Monument, Minnesota
Poverty Point National Monument, Louisiana
Pullman National Monument, Illinois
Rainbow Bridge National Monument, Utah
Reconstruction Era National Monument, South Carolina
Russell Cave National Monument, Alabama
Salinas Pueblo Missions National Monument, New Mexico
Scotts Bluff National Monument, Nebraska

Statue of Liberty National Monument, New Jersey and New York
Stonewall National Monument, New York
Sunset Crater Volcano National Monument, Arizona
Timpanogos Cave National Monument, Utah
Tonto National Monument, Arizona
Tule Springs Fossil Beds National Monument, Nevada
Tuzigoot National Monument, Arizona
Virgin Islands Coral Reef National Monument, Virgin Islands
Waco Mammoth National Monument, Texas
Walnut Canyon National Monument, Arizona
White Sands National Monument, New Mexico
World War II Valor in the Pacific National Monument, Alaska,
 California, and Hawai'i
Wupatki National Monument, Arizona
Yucca House National Monument, Colorado

NATIONAL PARKS

Acadia National Park, Maine
Arches National Park, Utah
Badlands National Park, South Dakota
Big Bend National Park, Texas
Biscayne National Park, Florida
Black Canyon of the Gunnison National Park, Colorado
Bryce Canyon National Park, Utah
Canyonlands National Park, Utah
Capitol Reef National Park, Utah
Carlsbad Caverns National Park, New Mexico
Channel Islands National Park, California
Congaree National Park, South Carolina
Crater Lake National Park, Oregon
Cuyahoga Valley National Park, Ohio
Death Valley National Park, California and Nevada
Denali National Park, Alaska
Dry Tortugas National Park, Florida
Everglades National Park, Florida
Gates of the Arctic National Park, Alaska
Gateway Arch National Park, Missouri and Illinois
Glacier Bay National Park, Alaska
Glacier National Park, Montana
Grand Canyon National Park, Arizona
Grand Teton National Park, Wyoming
Great Basin National Park, Nevada
Great Sand Dunes National Park, Colorado
Great Smoky Mountains National Park, North Carolina
 and Tennessee
Guadalupe Mountains National Park, Texas
Haleakalā National Park, Hawai'i
Hawai'i Volcanoes National Park, Hawai'i
Hot Springs National Park, Arkansas
Indiana Dunes National Park, Indiana
Isle Royale National Park, Michigan
Joshua Tree National Park, California

Katmai National Park, Alaska
Kenai Fjords National Park, Alaska
Kings Canyon National Park, California
Kobuk Valley National Park, Alaska
Lake Clark National Park, Alaska
Lassen Volcanic National Park, California
Mammoth Cave National Park, Kentucky
Mesa Verde National Park, Colorado
Mount Rainier National Park, Washington
National Park of American Samoa, American Samoa
North Cascades National Park, Washington
Olympic National Park, Washington
Petrified Forest National Park, Arizona
Pinnacles National Park, California
Redwood National Park, California
Rocky Mountain National Park, Colorado
Saguaro National Park, Arizona
Sequoia National Park, California
Shenandoah National Park, Virginia
Theodore Roosevelt National Park, North Dakota
Virgin Islands National Park, Virgin Islands
Voyageurs National Park, Minnesota
Wind Cave National Park, South Dakota
Wrangell–St. Elias National Park, Alaska
Yellowstone National Park, Idaho, Montana, and Wyoming
Yosemite National Park, California
Zion National Park, Utah

NATIONAL PARKWAYS

Blue Ridge Parkway, North Carolina and Virginia
George Washington Memorial Parkway, District of Columbia,
 Maryland and Virginia
John D. Rockefeller Jr. Memorial Parkway, Wyoming
Natchez Trace Parkway, Mississippi

NATIONAL PRESERVES

Aniakchak National Preserve, Alaska
Bering Land Bridge National Preserve, Alaska
Big Cypress National Preserve, Florida
Big Thicket National Preserve, Texas
Craters of the Moon National Preserve, Idaho
Denali National Preserve, Alaska
Gates of the Arctic National Preserve, Alaska
Glacier Bay National Preserve, Alaska
Great Sand Dunes National Preserve, Colorado
Katmai National Preserve, Alaska
Lake Clark National Preserve, Alaska
Little River Canyon National Preserve, Alabama
Mojave National Preserve, California
Noatak National Preserve, Alaska
Tallgrass Prairie National Preserve, Kansas
Timucuan Ecological and Historic Preserve, Florida

Valles Caldera National Preserve, New Mexico
Wrangell-St. Elias National Preserve, Alaska
Yukon-Charley Rivers National Preserve, Alaska

NATIONAL RESERVES
City of Rocks National Reserve, Idaho
Ebey's Landing National Historical Reserve, Washington

NATIONAL RECREATION AREAS
Amistad National Recreation Area, Texas
Bighorn Canyon National Recreation Area, Montana
 and Wyoming
Boston Harbor Islands National Recreation Area, Massachusetts
Chattahoochee River National Recreation Area, Georgia
Chickasaw National Recreation Area, Oklahoma
Curecanti National Recreation Area, Colorado
Delaware Water Gap National Recreation Area, New Jersey
 and Pennsylvania
Gateway National Recreation Area, New Jersey and New York
Gauley River National Recreation Area, West Virginia
Glen Canyon National Recreation Area, Arizona and Utah
Golden Gate National Recreation Area, California
Lake Chelan National Recreation Area, Washington
Lake Mead National Recreation Area, Arizona and Nevada
Lake Meredith National Recreation Area, Texas
Lake Roosevelt National Recreation Area, Washington
Ross Lake National Recreation Area, Washington
Santa Monica Mountains National Recreation Area, California
Whiskeytown-Shasta-Trinity National Recreation Area, California

NATIONAL RIVERS
Big South Fork National River and Recreation Area, Kentucky
 and Tennessee
Buffalo National River, Arkansas
Mississippi National River and Recreation Area, Minnesota
New River Gorge National River, West Virginia
Ozark National Scenic Riverways, Missouri

NATIONAL WILD AND SCENIC RIVERS AND RIVERWAYS
Alagnak Wild River, Alaska
Bluestone National Scenic River, West Virginia
Delaware National Scenic River, New Jersey, New York,
 and Pennsylvania
Great Egg Harbor National Scenic and Recreational River,
 New Jersey
Missouri National Recreational River, Nebraska
 and South Dakota
Niobrara National Scenic River, Nebraska
Obed Wild and Scenic River, Tennessee
Rio Grande Wild and Scenic River, Texas
Saint Croix National Scenic Riverway, Minnesota and Wisconsin

Upper Delaware Scenic and Recreational River, New York
 and Pennsylvania

NATIONAL SCENIC TRAILS
Appalachian National Scenic Trail, Maine to Georgia (13 states)
Natchez Trace National Scenic Trail, Alabama, Mississippi,
 and, Tennessee
Potomac Heritage National Scenic Trail, District of Columbia,
 Pennsylvania, and Virginia

NATIONAL SEASHORES
Assateague Island National Seashore, Maryland and Virginia
Canaveral National Seashore, Florida
Cape Cod National Seashore, Massachusetts
Cape Hatteras National Seashore, North Carolina
Cape Lookout National Seashore, North Carolina
Cumberland Island National Seashore, Georgia
Fire Island National Seashore, New York
Gulf Islands National Seashore, Florida and Mississippi
Padre Island National Seashore, Texas
Point Reyes National Seashore, California

OTHER DESIGNATIONS
Catoctin Mountain Park, Maryland
Constitution Gardens, District of Columbia
Fort Washington Park, Maryland
Greenbelt Park, Maryland
National Capital Parks–East, District of Columbia
National Mall and Memorial Parks, District of Columbia
Piscataway Park, Maryland
Prince William Forest Park, Virginia
Rock Creek Park, District of Columbia
White House, District of Columbia
Wolf Trap National Park for the Performing Arts, Virginia

ACKNOWLEDGMENTS

Amid the time and research and countless rewrites I couldn't have started or completed this work without my stellar literary agent, Elizabeth Kaplan. I would also like to thank those experts whom I consulted on Glacier, Grand Canyon, Yellowstone, Grand Teton, Big Bend, Everglades, and Denali National Parks and on climate change for their close reads: Blase Reardon; Jim Kirschvink; Gary Kofinas, University of Alaska, Fairbanks; Bill Kight; Denny Capps and Debbie Reiswig, Denali National Park; Don Corrick and Tom Vanden-Berg, Big Bend National Park; and Matthew A. Brown, Jackson School Museum of Earth History.

As for the super knowledgeable board of advisors—Jane Anderson, Jim Cook, and Melanie and Kim Heacox—you have all greatly enhanced this atlas, so thank you!

And to the National Geographic team: senior editor Susan Hitchcock, art director Sanaa Akkach, designer Nicole Miller, senior photo editor Meredith Wilcox, director of cartography Debbie Gibbons, research editor Irene Berman-Vaporis, cartographer Michael McNey, and project editor Anne Staub, as well as researcher Eva Dasher, caption writer Kate Armstrong, and copy editor Heather McElwain. The knowledge and skill that you bring to your work and to this book only elevates the already iconic organization you work for. And I couldn't be more appreciative of National Geographic's support of my work over the last dozen years.

These professionals and experts above all boosted this atlas with accuracy, timelessness, and reverence. On behalf of the national parks: Thank you.

ABOUT THE AUTHOR

JON WATERMAN has worked as a wilderness guide and as a National Park Service ranger, exploring—in boats, by foot, or on dogsleds—remote places around the world. He has received three grants from the National Geographic Society Expeditions Council, and his award-winning writing and photography have appeared in numerous national magazines and newspapers. He has written 14 books on adventure and the environment. He lives in Carbondale, Colorado.

BOARD OF ADVISORS

KIM HEACOX is an author and former park ranger who worked in Death Valley, Glacier Bay, Katmai, and Denali National Parks. Heacox's opinion editorials have appeared in *The Guardian* and the *Washington Post*. His novel *Jimmy Bluefeather* is the only work of fiction in 20 years to win the National Outdoor Book Award. He is the author of National Geographic's *The National Parks: An Illustrated History*, published in celebration of the Park Service's centennial anniversary.

MELANIE HEACOX decided while visiting Yellowstone at age seven that she wanted a life as a park ranger. Now retired after 35 years as a naturalist, trainer, and mentor, she has great memories of time spent at Grand Canyon, Denali, Katmai, and especially Glacier Bay National Park, where she met and married Kim Heacox.

JANE ANDERSON started her career with the National Park Service at Yellowstone in 1973. Since then Anderson has worked in many parks—Everglades, Denali, the George Washington Memorial Parkway, and Mesa Verde—in a variety of roles, including as backcountry ranger. She retired in 2015 as the deputy fee manager for the NPS, and now lives in Colorado with her hiking companions, Will Morris and dog Nutmeg.

JAMES E. COOK's career spans almost 40 years in conservation and the arts management, beginning with three summer seasons as a National Park Service ranger in Glacier National Park. As CEO for Western National Parks Association, Cook continues his love affair with national parks by supporting 71 NPS units across the West through its educational programs, products, and services.

MAP CREDITS

Federal Lands: Data Sources: Bureau of Land Management; U.S. Fish & Wildlife Service; U.S. Forest Service; National Park Service.

National Park System: Data Source: National Park Service.

INSIDE THE NATIONAL PARK SYSTEM

HISTORY OF THE PARKS

National Park System Growth: Data Source: National Park Service.

TECTONICS

West Coast Tectonics: Data Sources: USGS Earthquake Hazards Program and USGS National Earthquake Information Center (NEIC), *earthquake.usgs.gov;* Smithsonian Institution, Global Volcanism Program, *volcano.si.edu;* USGS and the International Association of Volcanology and Chemistry of the Earth's Interior, *vulcan.wr.usgs.gov.*

Hot Spots: Graphic: *National Geographic,* May 2016. Manuel Canales and Henán Cañellas. Consultants: Duncan Foley, Pacific Lutheran University; Robert Fournier, U.S. Geological Survey.

Volcanism: Graphic: National Park Service Harpers Ferry Center.

Faults: Map: National Park Service Harpers Ferry Center.

GEOLOGY

Karst Landscapes: Data Source: David J. Weary and Daniel H. Doctor, 2014, Karst in the United States: A digital map compilation and database: U.S. Geological Survey Open-File Report 2014–1156, 23 p., *doi.org/10.3133/ofr20141156.* Consultants: David J. Weary and Daniel H. Doctor.

Sedimentary Rocks: Map: National Park Service Harpers Ferry Center.

Physiography: Map: National Park Service Harpers Ferry Center.

CLIMATE CHANGE

Average Temperature Trends: Data Source: NOAA's National Centers for Environmental Information (NCEI). Consultant: Chris Fenimore, NOAA's National Centers for Environmental Information (NCEI).

Extreme Drought: Data Source: Abatzoglou, J. T., D. J. McEvoy, and K. T. Redmond, in press, "The West Wide Drought Tracker: Drought Monitoring at Fine Spatial Scales," *Bulletin of the American Meteorological Society.* Consultant: Richard R. Heim, National Centers for Environmental Information (NCEI).

Glacial Retreat: Graphic: *National Geographic,* December 2016. Data Sources: National Park Service; Dan Fagre and Mark Fahey, U.S. Geological Survey.

Sea-Level Rise: Graphic: *National Geographic,* December 2016. Data Sources: National Park Service; Everglades Foundation; Florida International University; South Florida Water Management District.

ECO-REGIONS & FLORA

Wilderness Areas: Map: *National Geographic,* September 2014. Data Sources: U.S. Geological Survey; Wilderness.net; Wilderness Society.

Eco-regions: Data Source: 2017 Ecoregions by Resolve: Eric Dinerstein, David Olson, Anup Joshi, Carly Vynne, Neil D. Burgess et al., 2017. "An Ecoregion-Based Approach to Protecting Half the Terrestrial Realm." *BioScience,* Volume 67, Issue 6, 1 June 2017, pp. 534–545. *doi.org/10.1093/biosci/bix014.*

Species Richness: Data Source: NPSpecies—The National Park Service biodiversity database. IRMA Portal version. *irma.nps.gov/npspecies.* Accessed April 4, 2019.

Non-Native Species: Data Source: EDDMapS. 2018. Early Detection & Distribution Mapping System. The University of Georgia—Center for Invasive Species and Ecosystem Health. Available online at: *www.eddmaps.org.* Accessed October 16, 2018. Consultant: Terri Hogan, National Park Service.

WILDLIFE

Migrations: Map: *National Geographic,* May 2016. Data Sources: Matthew Kauffman, Wyoming Migration Initiative, University of Wyoming; James E. Meacham and Alethea Y. Steingisser, Infographics Lab, University of Oregon; Andrew J. Hansen, Montana State University; Sarah Dewey, Ann W. Rodman, Douglas W. Smith, Daniel Stahler, Erin Stahler, and P. J. White, National Park Service; Eric Cole, National Elk Refuge; Bruce B. Ackerman and Paul Atwood, Idaho Fish and Game; Ron Aasheim, Justin Gude, Kelly Proffitt, and Neal Whitney, Montana Fish, Wildlife and Parks; Alyson Courtemanch, Renny Mackay, and Doug McWhirter, Wyoming Game and Fish Department; Paul C. Cross and Lisa Landenburger, Northern Rocky Mountain Science Center.

Endemic Species: Data Source: U.S. Fish & Wildlife Service—Upper Colorado River Endangered Fish Recovery Program.

Biodiversity: Data Sources: Great Smoky Mountains National Park, National Park Service; Discover Life in America. Consultant: Becky Nichols, Great Smoky Mountains National Park, National Park Service.

Endangered Species: Data Sources: National Park Service; The Nature Conservancy; Roemer et al., 1994. The Use of Capture-Recapture Methods for Estimating Monitoring and Conserving Island Fox Populations.

ARCHAEOLOGY & PALEONTOLOGY

Top Sites: Data Source: National Park

Service. Consultants: Stanley Bond (Archaeology) and Vincent L. Santucci (Paleontology), National Park Service.

Cenozoic Era Fossils: Map: National Park Service Harpers Ferry Center.

Ancestral Puebloan: Map: National Park Service Harpers Ferry Center.

Mound Builders: Map: National Park Service Harpers Ferry Center.

CULTURAL LANDSCAPES

Cliff Dwellings: Art: Courtesy National Park Service, Harpers Ferry Center. Commissioned Art Collection, artist Roy Andersen.

Native Americans: Map: National Park Service Harpers Ferry Center.

Underground Railroad: Map: National Park Service Harpers Ferry Center.

Immigrants: Map: National Park Service Harpers Ferry Center.

VISITOR EXPERIENCE

Park Visitation: Map: *National Geographic,* October 2016. Data Source: National Park Service Visitor Use Statistics.

Diversity: Data Sources: Yellowstone National Park Visitor Use Study (Summer 2016); Annual Estimates of the Resident Population by Sex, Single Year of Age, Race, and Hispanic Origin for the United States: April 1, 2010, to July 1, 2016. U.S. Census Bureau, Population Division. Release Date: June 2017.

Accessibility: Data Source: National Park Service.

Deferred Maintenance: National Park Service Asset Inventory Summary, Data as of September 30, 2017.

HUMAN IMPACTS

Park Proximity to Cities: Data Sources: D. J. Weiss, A. Nelson, H. S. Gibson, W. Temperley, S. Peedell, A. Lieber, M. Hancher, E. Poyart, S. Belchior, N. Fullman, B. Mappin, U. Dalrymple, J. Rozier, T. C. D. Lucas, R. E. Howes, L. S. Tusting, S. Y. Kang, E. Cameron, D. Bisanzio, K. E. Battle, S. Bhatt, and P. W. Gething. "A global map of travel time to cities to assess inequalities in accessibility in 2015." (2018). *Nature. doi:10.1038/ nature25181*; National Park Service.

Air Quality: Data Source: National Park Service Air Resources Division.

Night Sky: Data Sources: F. Falchi, P. Cinzano, D. Duriscoe, C. C. M. Kyba, C. D. Elvidge, K. Baugh, B. A. Portnov, N. A. Rybnikova, R. Furgoni (2016): Supplement to: The New World Atlas of Artificial Night Sky Brightness. GFZ Data Services. *doi.org/10.5880/GFZ.1.4.2016.001;* F. Falchi, P. Cinzano, D. Duriscoe, C. C. M. Kyba, C. D. Elvidge, K. Baugh, B. A. Portnov, N. A. Rybnikova, R. Furgoni, The new world atlas of artificial night sky brightness. *Sci. Adv.* 2, e1600377 (2016). *doi.org/10.1126/sciadv.1600377.* Consultant: Fabio Falchi, Istituto di Scienza e Tecnologia dell'Inquinamento Luminoso (Light Pollution Science and Technology Institute).

Water Quality: Data Source: Delaware River Basin Commission. Consultant: John R. Yagecic, Delaware River Basin Commission.

EXTREMES

Data Source: National Park Service.

THE GLORY OF THE NATIONAL PARKS

Park Locations: National Park Service.

EASTERN COAST & FOREST PARKS

ACADIA

Bedrock Geology: Data Source: Braun, Duane D., 2018, Bedrock geology of Mount Desert Island: Maine Geological Survey, Geologic Map 18-16, map, scale 1:30,000. Consultant: Duane D. Braun.

Jordan Pond: Map: National Park Service Harpers Ferry Center.

Park Boundary Evolution: Data Source: Acadia National Park, National Park Service.

EVERGLADES

Threatened Wetlands: Map: *National Geographic,* September 2018. Data Sources: National Park Service; Landsat 8, U.S. Geological Survey; Florida Fish and Wildlife Research Institute; NASA; U.S. Census Bureau.

Water Flow: Maps: National Park Service Harpers Ferry Center.

Burmese Python Sightings: Data Source: EDDMapS. 2018. Early Detection & Distribution Mapping System. The University of Georgia—Center for Invasive Species and Ecosystem Health. Available online at *www.eddmaps.org.* Accessed July 25, 2018.

Habitats of the Everglades: Map: National Park Service Harpers Ferry Center. Art: National Park Service/Robert Hynes.

SHENANDOAH

Bedrock Classes: Data Sources: 2009. Digital Geologic Map of Shenandoah National Park and vicinity, Virginia (NPS, GRD, GRI, SHEN, SHEN digital map). NPS Geologic Resources Inventory Program. Lakewood, CO; Gathright TM. 1976. Geology of the Shenandoah National Park, Virginia. Virginia Division of Mineral Resource Bulletin. No. 86. Commonwealth of Virginia Department of Conservation and Economic Development. Charlottesville, Virginia. Consultant: Jalyn Cummings, Shenandoah National Park, National Park Service.

Housing Density: Data Source: National Park Service. 2013. NPScape Standard Operating Procedure: Housing Measure—Current and Projected Housing Density. Version 2015-04-14. National Park Service, Natural Resource Stewardship and Science. Fort Collins, Colorado.

Traffic Count: Data Source: National Park Service Visitor Use Statistics.

DRY TORTUGAS

Coral Habitat: Data Source: Waara, R. J., and others. 2011. The 2010 Benthic Habitat Map for Dry Tortugas National Park. Natural Resource Technical Report NPS/SFCN/ NRTR—2011/474. National Park Service.

Fort Jefferson: Photo: Peter Green. Consultants: Chris Beers and Glenn Simpson, Dry Tortugas National Park, National Park Service.

GREAT SMOKY MOUNTAINS

National Park Popularity: Data Source: National Park Service Visitor Use Statistics.

The Appalachian Trail: Data Source: National Park Service.

Great Smoky Mountains Trails: Data Source: National Park Service.

Major Forest Habitats: Art: Courtesy National Park Service, Harpers Ferry Center Commissioned Art Collection, artist Robert Hynes. Data Source: Madden, M.; Welch, R.; Jordan, T.; Jackson, P.; Seavey, R.; and Seavey, J., 2004. Digital Vegetation Maps for the Great Smoky Mountains National Park, Final Report to the U.S. Dept. of Interior, National Park Service, Cooperative Agreement Number 1443-CA-5460-98-019, Center for Remote Sensing and Mapping Science, University of Georgia, Athens, Georgia. 112 pp. Consultants: Marguerite Madden and Sergio Bernardes, Center for Geospatial Research, University of Georgia.

MAMMOTH CAVE

Inside the Cave: Art: Richard Schlecht. Copyright 1984 by National Geographic Society. Consultants: Dave Wyrick and Rickard Toomey, Mammoth Cave National Park, National Park Service.

White-Nose Syndrome: Data Source: White-nose syndrome occurrence map by year (2018). Data last updated: October 1, 2018. Available online at: *whitenosesyndrome.org/resources/map.*

CENTRAL PLAINS, LAKES & MOUNTAINS PARKS

ISLE ROYALE

Maritime History: Data Sources: Isle Royale National Park, National Park Service; NOAA National Centers for Environmental Information.

Moose and Wolves: Data Source: Ecological Studies of Wolves on Isle Royale. Annual report 2016-17 by Rolf O. Peterson and John A. Vucetich. School of Forest Resources and Environmental Science, Michigan Technological University, Houghton, Michigan. 31 March 2017. Used with permission. Consultant: Rolf O. Peterson, Michigan Technological University.

VOYAGEURS

Trail System: Data Source: National Park Service.

Minnesota Mining: Data Sources: U.S. Forest Service; Minnesota Department of Natural Resources; U.S. Geological Survey; Minnesota Center for Environmental Advocacy; Esri; Ontario Ministry of Natural Resources and Forestry; Twin Metals Minnesota. Consultants: Rebecca Rom and Matt Norton, Northeastern Minnesotans for Wilderness; Tom Myers, University of Nevada, Reno; Lee Frelich, University of Minnesota.

BADLANDS

Rock Strata: Art: Badlands National Park, National Park Service.

Vegetation and Land Use: Data Source: 2005. Geospatial data for the Vegetation Mapping Inventory Project of Badlands National Park.

Prairie Dogs: Data Sources: U.S. Forest Service; National Park Service.

Black-Footed Ferret Population: Data Sources: National Park Service; U.S. Forest Service; Prairie Wildlife Research; Oglala Sioux Parks and Recreation Authority.

ROCKY MOUNTAIN

Pika Distribution: Data Sources: Donelle Schwalm, Clinton W. Epps, Thomas J. Rodhouse, William B. Monahan, Jessica A. Castillo, Chris Ray, and Mackenzie R. Jeffress, "Habitat Availability and Gene Flow Influence Diverging Local Population Trajectories Under Scenarios of Climate Change: A Place-Based Approach." *Global Change Biology* (2016) 22, 1572–1584, *doi:10.1111/gcb.13189;* Pikas in Peril Research Project: Rocky Mountain National Park. Consultant: Thomas J. Rodhouse, Rocky Mountain National Park, National Park Service.

Colorado Bighorn Sheep: Data Source: Colorado Parks and Wildlife, Colorado Department of Natural Resources.

Death by a Thousand Bites: Graphic: *National Geographic,* April 2015. Art: Samantha Welker. Data Source: Diana Six, University of Montana.

Climate Change Effects: Map: *National Geographic,* February 2019. Data Sources: Colorado State Forest Service; USDA Forest Service; National Park Service; Jason

Sibold and Amanda West, Colorado State University; GeoMAC, U.S. Geological Survey.

YELLOWSTONE

Greater Yellowstone: Map: *National Geographic,* May 2016. Data Sources: U.S. Geological Survey; Yellowstone National Park.

The Impact of Development: Map: *National Geographic,* May 2016. Data Sources: U.S. Geological Survey; Andrew Hansen, Montana State University.

The Fire Within: Map: *National Geographic,* May 2016. Manuel Canales and Hernán Cañellas. Data Sources: Robert B. Smith and Jamie Farrell, University of Utah; Duncan Foley, Pacific Lutheran University; Henry Heasler and Cheryl Jaworowski, National Park Service; Jacob Lowenstern, U.S. Geological Survey; University of Utah Seismology and Active Tectonics Research Group; Dennis Feeney, Idaho Geological Survey (Map Files, Line of Evidence, based on data by Robert B. Smith).

Return of the Wolf: Map: *National Geographic,* March 2010. Data Sources: U.S. Fish and Wildlife Service; Idaho Department of Fish and Game; Montana Fish, Wildlife & Parks; Wyoming Game and Fish Department; Nez Perce Tribe; National Park Service; Blackfeet Nation; Confederated Salish and Kootenai Tribes; Wind River Tribes; Confederated Colville Tribes; Spokane Tribe of Indians; Washington Department of Fish and Wildlife; Oregon Department of Fish and Wildlife; Utah Department of Natural Resources; and USDA Wildlife Services. 2016. Northern Rocky Mountain Wolf Recovery Program 2015 Interagency Annual Report, M. D. Jimenez and S. A. Becker, eds. USFWS, Ecological Services, 585 Shepard Way, Helena, Montana, 59601.

Fire History: Data Source: Spatial Analysis Center, Yellowstone National Park.

GRAND TETON

Tectonics: Art: © Merri Nelson.

Glaciation: Art: © Merri Nelson.

Park Boundary Evolution: Data Source:

Grand Teton National Park, National Park Service.

Teton Range: Maps: © 2012 University of Oregon. *Atlas of Yellowstone* by W. Andrew Marcus, James E. Meacham, Ann W. Rodman, and Alethea Y. Steingisser. Contributing expert Alexander M. Tait.

GLACIER

Glacial Landscapes: Art: National Park Service, Harpers Ferry Center Commissioned Art Collection, artist Robert W. Tope.

Glacial Retreat: Data Source: Fagre, D. B., McKeon, L. A., Dick, K. A., and Fountain, A. G., 2017, Glacier margin time series (1966, 1998, 2005, 2015) of the named glaciers of Glacier National Park, MT, USA: U.S. Geological Survey data release, *doi.org/10.5066/F7P26WB1.*

Reduction in Glacial Area: Fagre, D. B., McKeon, L. A., Dick, K. A., and Fountain, A. G., 2017, Glacier margin time series (1966, 1998, 2005, 2015) of the named glaciers of Glacier National Park, MT, USA: U.S. Geological Survey data release, *doi.org/10.5066/F7P26WB1.*

Crown of the Continent: Data Sources: Lehner, B., Grill G. (2013): "Global river hydrography and network routing: baseline data and new approaches to study the world's large river systems." *Hydrological Processes,* 27(15): 2171–2186. Data is available at *www.hydrosheds.org;* Crown Managers Partnership (point of contact), Erin Sexton (principal investigator), Great Northern Landscape Conservation Cooperative (administrator), LCC Network Data Steward (administrator), Watersheds in the Crown of the Continent (2016).

Harlequin Duck Distribution: Data Source: The Birds of North America, *birdsna.org,* maintained by the Cornell Lab of Ornithology.

DESERT SOUTHWEST PARKS

BIG BEND

Night Sky: Data Sources: F. Falchi, P. Cinzano, D. Duriscoe, C. C. M. Kyba, C. D. Elvidge, K. Baugh, B. A. Portnov, N. A. Rybnikova, R. Furgoni (2016): Supplement to: The New World Atlas of Artificial Night Sky Brightness. GFZ Data

Services. *doi.org/10.5880/GFZ.1.4.2016. 001;* F. Falchi, P. Cinzano, D. Duriscoe, C. C. M. Kyba, C. D. Elvidge, K. Baugh, B. A. Portnov, N. A. Rybnikova, R. Furgoni, The new world atlas of artificial night sky brightness. *Sci. Adv.* 2, e1600377 (2016). *doi.org/10.1126/sciadv.1600377.* Consultant: Fabio Falchi, Istituto di Scienza e Tecnologia dell'Inquinamento Luminoso (Light Pollution Science and Technology Institute).

Pterosaur: *National Geographic,* November 2017. Art: Fernando G. Baptista. Data Sources: Dave Martill and Mark Witton, University of Portsmouth; Nizar Ibrahim, National Geographic Explorer; Michael Habib, USC and Natural History Museum of Los Angeles County.

Birding Hot Spots: Data Source: National Park Service. Consultant: Thomas Vandenberg, Big Bend National Park, National Park Service.

Colima Warbler: Data Source: The Birds of North America, *birdsna.org,* maintained by the Cornell Lab of Ornithology.

SAGUARO

Extreme Drought: Data Source: Abatzoglou, J.T., D.J. McEvoy, and K.T. Redmond, in press, "The West Wide Drought Tracker: Drought Monitoring at Fine Spatial Scales," *Bulletin of the American Meteorological Society.* Consultant: Richard R. Heim, National Centers for Environmental Information (NCEI).

Saguaro Distribution: Data Source: Burquez Montijo, A., Butterworth, C., Baker, M., and Felger, R. S. 2017. *Carnegiea gigantea.* IUCN 2019. *The IUCN Red List of Threatened Species.* Version 2019-1. *www.iucnredlist.org.* Downloaded in April 2019.

Saguaro Cactus Life Cycle: Art: Courtesy National Park Service, Harpers Ferry Center Commissioned Art Collection, artist Robert Hynes. Consultant: Don Swann, Saguaro National Park, National Park Service.

Housing Density: Data Source: National Park Service. 2013. NPScape Standard Operating Procedure: Housing Measure—Current and Projected Housing Density. Version 2015-04-14. National Park Ser-

vice, Natural Resource Stewardship and Science. Fort Collins, Colorado.

ARCHES

Arch Formation: Art: National Park Service/Bill Von Allmen.

Arch Density: Data Source: Arch data provided by the World Arch Database, copyright 2018 Stone Canyon Media Corp. and copyright 2018 Thomas Van Bebber and Cynthia Bell. Used by permission. Consultants: Tom Van Bebber; Arches National Park.

Moab Fault: Art: Courtesy National Park Service, Harpers Ferry Center Commissioned Art Collection, artist Michael A. Hampshire.

Soil: Data Source: National Park Service—SRI (Soil Resources Inventory), Soil Survey Geographic (SSURGO) for Arches National Park, Utah. Consultant: Vic Parslow, USDA Natural Resources Conservation Service.

CANYONLANDS

Runoff: Data Source: Krista A. Dunne and Paul C. D. Milly, U.S. Geological Survey.

Landownership: Data Source: Automated Geographic Reference Center (AGRC), State of Utah, *gis.utah.gov/data/cadastre/ land-ownership.*

CAPITOL REEF

Waterpocket Fold: Graphics: National Park Service Harpers Ferry Center.

Rock Formations: Graphic: Ron Blakey © Colorado Plateau Geosystems, Inc. *cpgeosystems.com.*

Fruita Historic District: Map: National Park Service Harpers Ferry Center.

GRAND CANYON

Rock Sequence: Art: Chapel Design & Marketing and XNR Productions.

Native Fish: Art: Illustrations © Joseph R. Tomelleri.

Contested Canyon: Map: *National Geographic,* September 2016. Data Sources: Bureau of Land Management; Coconino Plateau Water Advisory Council and Watershed Partnership; Donald Bills, U.S. Geological Survey; Eric Frye and

Edward Schenk, National Park Service; Esri; Grand Canyon Escalade; Grand Canyon West; Stephanie Smith and Roger Clark, Grand Canyon Trust.

Accessibility: Data Source: National Park Service.

ZION

Stratigraphy: Photo: Jim Tarpo. Consultant: Dave Sharrow.

Wilderness and Scenic Rivers: Data Source: Zion National Park, National Park Service.

Overcrowding: Data Source: National Park Service Visitor Use Statistics.

Shuttle Wait Times: Data Source: Zion National Park, National Park Service.

JOSHUA TREE

Illustration: Art: National Park Service/Robert Hynes.

Habitat Change: Data Source: Lynn C. Sweet, Tyler Green, James G. C. Heintz, Neil Frakes, Nicolas Graver, Jeff S. Rangitsch, Jane E. Rodgers, Scott Heacox, Cameron W. Barrows. "Congruence Between Future Distribution Models and Empirical Data for an Iconic Species at Joshua Tree National Park." *Ecosphere.* In press. Consultants: Lynn C. Sweet and Cameron W. Barrows, Center for Conservation Biology, University of California, Riverside.

Ozone: Data Source: National Park Service Air Resources Division.

DEATH VALLEY

Temperature Change: Data Sources: PRISM Climate Group, Oregon State University, *http://prism.oregonstate.edu,* created 28 Nov 2018; National Park Service.

Illustration: Art: National Park Service/Liz Bradford.

PACIFIC NORTHWEST PARKS

SEQUOIA & KINGS CANYON

Wilderness Character: Data Source: Tricker, James; Landres, Peter; Fauth, Gregg; Hardwick, Paul; Eddy, Alex. 2014. Mapping wilderness character in Sequoia and Kings Canyon National Parks. Natural Resource Technical Report NPS/SEKI/

NRTR-2014/872. Fort Collins, CO: U.S. Department of the Interior, National Park Service, Natural Resource Stewardship and Science. 82 p. *www.fs.usda.gov/tree search/pubs/46623.*

Giant Sequoias: Infographic: *National Geographic,* December 2012. Art: Robert van Pelt, Humboldt State University (HSU). Data Sources: Steve Sillett, HSU; Bureau of Land Management; National Park Service; U.S. Geological Survey; Bill Kruse, Kruse Imaging; Dwight Willard; Sierra Nevada Ecosystem Project; D'arcy Trask, Cyark.

Rain Shadow Effect: Art: Courtesy National Park Service, Harpers Ferry Center Commissioned Art Collection, artist Rob Wood.

Ecosystems: Map: National Park Service Harpers Ferry Center.

John Muir Trail: Map: National Geographic John Muir Trail Topographic Map Guide (#1001).

Elevation Model: Map: National Geographic John Muir Trail Topographic Map Guide (#1001).

YOSEMITE

Repair Needs: Data Source: National Park Service Asset Inventory System. Data as of September 30, 2017.

Waterfalls: Data Sources: National Park Service; National Hydrography Dataset, U.S. Geological Survey.

Yosemite Panorama: Art: National Park Service Harpers Ferry Center.

El Capitan: Map: *National Geographic,* May 2011. Art: Martin Gamache, Clay Wadman, Aldo Chiappe, Jason Lee. Data Sources: Ken Yager; Tom Frost; Yosemite National Park.

Fire History: Data Source: Fire Perimeters Version 17_1. California Department of Forestry and Fire Protection, *frap.fire. ca.gov.* Accessed March 14, 2019.

Ferguson Fire: Data Sources: Incident Management Teams; USDA Forest Service; National Park Service.

MOUNT RAINIER

Volcano Hazards: U.S. Geological Survey. Consultant: Joseph Bard, U.S. Geological Survey.

Glacier Change: *National Geographic,* May 2019. Data Sources: David Shean, University of Washington; Scott Beason, Paul Kennard, and Jon Riedel, National Park Service; U.S. Geological Survey.

CRATER LAKE

Formation of Crater Lake: Graphics: National Park Service Harpers Ferry Center.

Bathymetry: Map: Chaney Swiney.

Snowfall: Data Source: Crater Lake National Park, National Park Service.

Garfield Peak: Map: National Park Service Harpers Ferry Center.

OLYMPIC

Wildlife Illustration: Art: National Park Service/John Dawson.

Removal of Dams: Data Sources: U.S. Geological Survey; Washington State Department of Ecology; Washington State Department of Natural Resources.

Ocean Acidification: Graphic: *National Geographic,* December 2016. Data Sources: Tim Wootton and Cathy Pfister, University of Chicago.

ALASKA & HAWAI'I PARKS

GLACIER BAY

UNESCO World Heritage Site: Data Sources: Parks Canada; National Park Service.

Glacial Advance and Retreat: Maps: National Park Service Harpers Ferry Center.

Tidewater Glaciers: Art: Courtesy National Park Service, Harpers Ferry Center Commissioned Art Collection, artist Jaime Quintero.

Humpback Whales: Data Source: Neilson, J. L., C. M. Gabriele, and L. F. Taylor-Thomas. 2018. *Humpback whale monitoring in Glacier Bay and adjacent waters 2017: Annual progress report.* Natural Resource Report NPS/GLBA/NRR—2018/1660. National Park Service, Fort Collins, Colorado. Consultants: Christine Gabriele and Janet Neilson, Glacier Bay National Park and Preserve, National Park Service.

Park Waters: Data Source: Glacier Bay National Park and Preserve, National Park Service.

DENALI

The Future of Birds: Data Source: Wu et al. (2018) "Projected avifaunal responses to climate change across the U.S. National Park System." PLOS ONE. *doi.org/10.1371 /journal.pone.0190557.*

Wolf Packs: Map: *National Geographic,* February 2016. Data Source: National Park Service.

Park Boundary: Maps: *National Geographic,* February 2016. Data Source: National Park Service.

Alaska Range: Map: © Brooke E. Marston.

GATES OF THE ARCTIC

Western Arctic Caribou Herd: Data Sources: Alaska Department of Fish and Game; National Park Service. Consultant: Lincoln S. Parrett, Alaska Department of Fish and Game.

Mining and Rivers: Data Sources: National Wild and Scenic Rivers System; Bureau of Land Management, *eplanning.blm.gov/ epl-front-office/eplanning/planAndProject Site.do?methodName=dispatchToPattern Page&currentPageId=111135,* released April 27, 2018.

Projected Changes in Permafrost: Data Source: Panda, S. K., V. E. Romanovsky, and S. S. Marchenko. 2016. *High-resolution permafrost modeling in the Arctic Network national parks, preserves and monuments.* Natural Resource Report NPS/ARCN/ NRR—2016/1366. National Park Service, Fort Collins, Colorado. Consultant: Santosh Panda, Geophysical Institute, University of Alaska Fairbanks.

KATMAI

Pit House: Art: Courtesy National Park Service, Harpers Ferry Center Commissioned Art Collection, artist Michael A. Hampshire.

Katmai Panorama: Map: National Park Service Harpers Ferry Center.

Ash Clouds From Volcanic Eruptions: Data Source: Fierstein, Judy, and Hildreth, Wes, 2000. *Preliminary Volcano-Hazard Assessment for the Katmai Volcanic Cluster*, Alaska: U.S. Geological Survey Open-File Report 00-489, 59 pp., *pubs.usgs.gov/ of/2000/0489.*

Park Boundary Evolution: Data Source: National Park Service, Alaska Region GIS Team.

Bears and Salmon at Brooks Falls: Data Source: *Bears of Brooks River 2018: A Guide to Their Identification, Lives, and Habits,* Katmai National Park and Preserve, National Park Service.

HAWAI'I VOLCANOES

Rise and Fall of a Hawaiian Volcano: Graphics: Supplement to *National Geographic,* September 2012. Alejandro Tumas and Hernán Cañellas.

How a Lava Tube Is Formed: Graphic: *National Geographic*, June 2017. Art: Tomáš Müller. Data Sources: Don Coons and Michael Warner, Cave Conservancy of Hawaii.

Lava Flows: Map: *National Geographic*, June 2017. Data Sources: U.S. Geological Survey, Hawaiian Volcano Observatory; National Park Service.

Rapid Death of 'Ōhi'a Trees: Data Source: Hawai'i Volcanoes National Park, National Park Service.

Reference maps based on National Park Service maps.

National Geographic Cartographic Staff
Irene Berman-Vaporis
Riley Champine
Debbie Gibbons
Michael McNey

Additional Contributors
Mapping Specialists, Ltd.
Ross Donihue
Scott Elder
Gus Platis
Shelley Sperry

Special thanks to Jim Eynard, Joseph Milbrath, Wade Myers, and Tom Patterson of the National Park Service.

ILLUSTRATIONS CREDITS

PLACE-NAME INDEX

TOPICAL INDEX

ATLAS OF THE
NATIONAL PARKS

Since 1888, the National Geographic Society has funded more than 13,000 research, exploration, and preservation projects around the world. National Geographic Partners distributes a portion of the funds it receives from your purchase to National Geographic Society to support programs including the conservation of animals and their habitats.

National Geographic Partners
1145 17th Street NW
Washington, DC 20036-4688 USA

Get closer to National Geographic explorers and photographers, and connect with our global community. Join us today at nationalgeographic.com/join

For information about special discounts for bulk purchases, please contact National Geographic Books Special Sales: specialsales@natgeo.com

For rights or permissions inquiries, please contact National Geographic Books Subsidiary Rights: bookrights@natgeo.com

Library of Congress Cataloging-in-Publication Data
Names: Waterman, Jonathan, author. | National Geographic Society (U.S.) issuing body.
Title: National Geographic atlas of the National Parks / Jonathan Waterman.
Description: Washington, D.C. : National Geographic, [2019] | Includes index.
Identifiers: LCCN 2019009040 | ISBN 9781426220579 (hardcover)
Subjects: LCSH: National parks and reserves--United States--Guidebooks.
Classification: LCC E158 .W38 2019 | DDC 917.304--dc23
LC record available at https://lccn.loc.gov/2019009040

Printed in China

19/PPS/2